IDI AMIN: HERO OR VILLAIN?

HIS SON JAFFAR AMIN AND OTHER PEOPLE SPEAK

Introductory Edition

Jaffar Amin and Margaret Akulia

www.idiamindada.com

IDI AMIN: HERO OR VILLAIN?

ISBN 9780986614903

A series devoted to uncovering Idi Amin's story in its entirety, layer by layer, telling all the truth and shedding light on the untruths! Compiled and co-written by Jaffar Amin and Margaret Akulia in Kakwa Adiyo narration style and format.

"This is not a conventional book series but a true story being told in book format in a "different" way. It should be viewed as such."

"This series is dedicated to our father Idi Amin Awon'go Alemi Dada and all the people who are still 'groaning' under the very same 'oppressions' that 'created' him."

About this Series

Idi Amin Dada ruled the East African country of Uganda from January 1971 to April 1979 when he was ousted from power by a combined force of the Tanzania Peoples' Defence Force and Ugandan exiles operating through Tanzania. He left a controversial and conflicted legacy, as depicted by Oscar-winning film star Forest Whitaker in the hit movie "The Last King of Scotland"; but have authors and filmmakers who have attempted to tell his story to date really told the whole truth? Have they delved deep enough to uncover everything there is to know about Idi Amin, everything there is to tell about him and what actually happened during his rule and after he was forced to live in exile, first in Libya and then in Saudi Arabia? "No" says his son Jaffar Amin and other people!

In this unprecedented series devoted to telling Idi Amin's story in its entirety and not just "selected" parts, Margaret Akulia engages his son Jaffar Amin and other people in candid "conversation" about his legacy. As the world continues to pronounce "A Guilty Verdict" on Idi Amin after "finding him guilty beyond reasonable doubt", many people are adamant in asserting that "others" and not Idi Amin committed the "mass murders" attributed to him in Uganda!

Was Idi Amin "Framed" or "Guilty as Charged"? Was something "insidious" going on during his rule in Uganda as alleged by many? What role did racism, colonialism, neocolonialism, classism, religion, tribalism and greed play in "creating" Idi Amin? What should be made of the "conspiracy theories" relating to the actual "culprits" being "at large"? Who are these "culprits" and should the "ruling" by alleged "kangaroo courts" that have presided over his case to date be accepted as final? What would the "evidence" show in a proper Court of Law in relation to allegations of "mass murder", economic unfairness towards Ugandan Asians and the "conspiracy theories" that have surfaced since Idi Amin was ousted from power? What should be made of the conflicting characterization of Idi Amin as a Hero and Villain at the same time? What are the lessons the global community can learn from his actual story?

Many Ugandans welcomed the military coup by Idi Amin in 1971 and vowed undying allegiance. Others took a more cautious "wait and see" approach. On the day of the coup, large crowds of Ugandans rejoiced deliriously. They demonstrated their support for Idi Amin by flooding the streets of Kampala, "dancing" and "singing" to their heart's content. However, 8 years later, the same Ugandans were rejoicing deliriously, "dancing" and "singing" for "someone else" after having done the same thing for Kabaka Mutesa II and Apollo Milton Obote when the Kabaka became the first President of post colonial and "Independent" Uganda and Obote its first Prime Minister.

What is wrong in Africa? Is "Western style" democracy possible or even ideal in the continent of Africa? What can be done to stop the perpetual bloodbaths that have characterized "African Politics" since "Independence" from colonial powers? Why is Africa languishing in poverty despite its wealth of resources? What about the lessons ingrained in Idi Amin's story including the time he became involved in the "age old fight" between the Arabs and Israelis? What made Idi Amin choose sides in the tussle by breaking the rock solid relationship he had with Israel until 1972 and taking up with the Ummah (Community of Muslim Believers) instead? What are the stakes for Jews, Muslims, Christians and "everyone" else in this "fight to the death" between Israelis and Arabs?

Become involved in solving a "Jigsaw Puzzle" that may well provide answers to the world's problems! Learn about Idi Amin's actual story in its entirety. Compare details in this book series and related films with details contained in the Fictional Novel and Film "The Last King of Scotland" and other books and films about Idi Amin. Opportunities will be provided through Learning Circles intended for individuals and groups to discuss issues raised, with the purpose of coming up with solution-oriented strategies.

About Jaffar Amin

Jaffar Amin is the son of Idi Amin Dada the Ugandan President who ruled Uganda from January 1971 to April 1979 and was depicted in the hit movie "The Last King of Scotland" starring Oscar-winning Film Star Forest Whitaker. During his formative years, he attended Kabale Preparatory School, a Missionary School located in Kigezi District, Uganda until 1979 when he and his family fled Uganda and lived in exile, first in Libya and then in Saudi Arabia. While in exile during the Eighties, Jaffar Amin attended school in the UK, studying for "O" and "A" Level Certificates in London and Leicester. Jaffar Amin's exile ended in 1990, when he returned to Uganda. He is the Founder and Chief Executive Officer of the Al-Amin Foundation whose objectives include promoting and protecting the positive legacy of Idi Amin Dada.

Table of Contents

A Refugee

The Canada Immigration Officer flashed a warm smile at me and welcomed me to Canada. After stamping my Landed Immigrant Papers and United Nations Travel Document and telling me that I could proceed into the Airport Terminal, I followed the other passengers to the Baggage Area to retrieve my luggage before heading to "INTERNATIONAL ARRIVALS". I had arrived in Vancouver, Canada, my final destination and new home at last!

After a horrific refugee experience that took me to the Congo, Sudan, Lesotho and finally Canada, I couldn't have asked for a better country to call home. I was looking forward to becoming a Canadian Citizen after three years and contributing fully, to my new home.

A Representative of the World University Service of Canada, the Canadian Non- Governmental Organization that sponsored me to Canada as a Student Refugee would be waiting to drive me to the University of British Columbia. As with all Refugee Students they sponsor to Canadian universities and colleges, the World University Service of Canada had worked tirelessly to ensure that I got my Landed Immigrant Status and Papers before arriving in Canada and that my transition to a new life would be as smooth as possible.

I was grateful for their tireless efforts and relieved that I didn't have to go through the "hassle" of reclaiming Refugee Status upon arriving in Canada, which can be as traumatic as the refugee experience that often involves living in dire straits in Refugee Camps itself. I had disembarked the plane and followed the other passengers into the Airport Terminal Building at Vancouver International Airport, unsure how my life was going to unfold in Canada.

After fleeing the war to overthrow Idi Amin and living as a refugee in the Congo and then the Sudan, I was awarded a United Nations scholarship to study at the National University of Lesotho. While in the process of completing my final year in an undergraduate Business Degree Program, I applied to the World University Service of Canada for sponsorship and was sponsored by the organization to Canada as a Student Refugee and Landed Immigrant.

Vancouver was going to become my home for an indefinite period and I was looking forward to settling down after applying for and acquiring my Canadian Citizenship. I had not looked forward to the "freezing winters" of Canada until the Canadian Bursar at the National University of Lesotho told me that Vancouver where I was destined was the warmest and most beautiful part of Canada. The Bursar had made a "Canadian joke" and said, "How did you get so lucky?" referring to the fact that I was coming to Vancouver and not a "freezing" part of Canada and we had both laughed at the joke.

During the flight from London to Vancouver, images of my life had flashed through my mind starting from the time I was a little girl growing up in Uganda, to the time I was forced to flee Uganda because I was from Idi Amin's Kakwa tribe. I had been deeply saddened by the fact that my only crime had been belonging to the same tribe as Idi Amin and Tribal Vigilantes and certain pockets of the forces that overthrew him were hell bent on murdering anyone associated with him by tribe, religion and region of origin. I had resented the fact that I had to flee for my life and leave the only country I had called home because I belonged to Idi Amin's Kakwa tribe. I had despised the Tribal Vigilantes and the pockets of soldiers who appointed themselves Judge, Jury and Executioner of anyone associated with Idi Amin by tribe, religion and region of origin with a passion. This is because I have utmost respect for the rule of law and believe that everyone deserves a chance to be heard and no one should be found guilty until proven so in a Court of Law. My resentment coupled with my traumatic refugee experience prompted me to tell my story of victimization years after settling in Canada - a country I have deep admiration for.

I could not help reflecting about Idi Amin and his rule in Uganda and the tribalism that forced me to flee for my life during that memorable flight from London to Vancouver. I have continued to reflect about tribalism and other forms of bigotry long after settling in Canada. I regularly dialogue in my mind about which is worse: "racism" or "tribalism?" My deep reflection has led me to conclude that "tribalism" is a form of bigotry that is as despicable as "racism". I now know that the two forms of bigotry along with the others are intended for accomplishing the very same despicable purposes - dehumanizing others! Tribalism still dies hard in Uganda and other African countries. However, to date, this form of bigotry hasn't really received the same attention racism has. Anyone who has been a victim of Tribalism will relate to the ugly and monstrous head it continues to rear in all African countries, including Uganda.

Numerous emotions flooded my mind during that flight from London to Vancouver. My mind went back to the day Idi Amin took over power from Apollo Milton Obote in a military coup on January 25, 1971 and then the day Amin was overthrown by Wakombozi (Liberators/"Saviours") from Tanzania on April 11, 1979. It had been 8 years since I fled Uganda for my life but the memories were still fresh!

The days following Idi Amin's overthrow had been filled with bloodshed and mass murder by opposing sides. Some people had been all out to avenge the murder of relatives who had been killed during Idi Amin's eight-year rule. Other people had murdered anyone even remotely suspected of "colluding" with the opposing sides. Families and friends had been divided along political lines and become arch-enemies. People had been killed for resembling suspected enemies. People had been falsely accused of spying and tribal vigilantes had judged and executed them. It had been a "terrible crime" to be associated with Idi Amin by tribe, religion and region of origin. A death sentence had been passed on everyone from Idi Amin's tribe, religion and region of origin including myself. You didn't have to have committed a crime during Idi Amin's 8-year rule in Uganda - just being associated with him by tribe, religion and region of origin was enough to "earn" you a death sentence. I had been caught up in a crossfire that was not of my making but nonetheless, I had to flee for my life which is how I ended up in Canada. I am glad I did!

A Storyteller

I had a lot of mixed emotions the day I disembarked the plane at Vancouver International Airport and first set foot on Canadian soil. I was excited about having a country I could finally call home and a passport that would allow me to travel freely. As a Canadian Citizen, I knew I would enjoy civil liberties and privileges many people around the world only dreamt about! However, the trauma of having experienced life as a Female Refugee ran very deep and I was cognizant even before arriving in Canada that I would have to resolve this trauma at some point to live a normal life, which is how I started writing and "Telling Stories".

In my role as a Storyteller, I often work with subjects of true stories to bring their stories to life, while providing Learning Opportunities for audiences. Idi Amin's story is ripe with such Learning Opportunities and his son Jaffar Amin agrees! As I do with my "Storytelling" Projects involving other subjects, in this series, I will be working with Jaffar Amin and other people to bring his father Idi Amin's story to life by uncovering the story in its entirety, layer by layer. This we will do while providing the Learning Opportunities I speak of above!

My Storytelling projects are often narrated in Kakwa Adiyo narration style and format, which is what Jaffar Amin and I use in the series Idi Amin: Hero or Villain? His Son Jaffar Amin and Other People Speak. Adiyo are oral historical narrative accounts of history and events of the past and telling Adiyo has existed for generations in the Kakwa tribe. The Narration Process includes other participants "jumping in to make any corrections or to state a forgotten issue". Consequently, as the series Idi Amin: Hero or Villain? His Son Jaffar Amin and Other People Speak unfolds, we invite all parties to "jump in" and make any corrections or share information known to them as participants would in an Adiyo Narration Process.

Repetitions are common in Kakwa Adiyo narrations, which will be the case as you read the accounts Jaffar Amin and I have compiled and co-written in the same style and format. Consequently, we thank readers and participants in advance for maintaining an open mind about the method being used to tell Idi Amin's story in this series. We also apologize in advance for inadvertent errors, misrepresentations, misappropriations, inaccuracies and infringements. However, we will endeavor to make corrections and revise information in subsequent Editions and parts of the series as the case would be in an Adiyo Narration Process. We will also add information as the Narration Process proceeds and the series unfolds.

As Idi Amin's story is being told in Kakwa Adiyo narration style and format in this series, the process of compiling information and co-writing the story involved "jumping in", poking, prying, probing and asking the same tough and annoying questions Jaffar Amin asked his father during their life in exile! Throughout the process, Jaffar stayed very objective and consistent in providing answers to questions directed to him.

I thank him wholeheartedly for allowing his voice to be used as the Primary Voice to introduce the series Idi Amin: Hero or Villain? His Son Jaffar Amin and Other People Speak. I also thank him immensely for allowing substantial information and material taken and excerpted from his book titled Rembi's Mystical Legacy to be the main information presented in this Introductory Edition of the series.

As the series unfolds, further reading and research is encouraged in order to compare and corroborate information obtained through various sources and to enhance in depth understanding of issues raised by Idi Amin's legacy.

Meeting Jaffar Amin

"Our father had his faults. I do not see the period of his rule in Uganda with "rose-tinted glasses." However, we need to counter-balance history with all the truth!" insisted Jaffar Amin to me when I asked him what he thought about the hit movie "The Last King of Scotland" and the "zillions" of books and articles that have been written about his father. It is a response he regularly provides without "flinching."

"After overthrowing Apollo Milton Obote in the military coup on the eve of January 25, 1971 and being hailed "Jogoo! Joggo!" ("Hero! Hero") by fellow soldiers, Dad embarked on a mission to liberate Uganda's underdogs and oppressed people everywhere. However, something happened to derail his noble agenda," Jaffar points out sadly.

Let's do a follow up to "The Last King of Scotland". Let's tell your father's story through you, I offered with excitement because I have always wanted to tell Idi Amin's story from a different angle than what has been told to date and I was convinced that Jaffar would provide an authentic voice for telling the story. I didn't see why this couldn't be the "perfect" time to tell the story from the angle I was going to anyway after the fictional novel and hit movie "The Last King of Scotland" resurrected the memory of Idi Amin.

At the time I had the above conversation with Jaffar Amin, the fictionalized novel and hit movie "The Last King of Scotland" was the most recent attempt at telling Idi Amin's "convoluted" and "complicated" story. It was one more addition to the "zillions" of films, books and articles about Idi Amin that had made the rounds around the globe without telling the entire story for full context. So, immediately following the release of the hit movie, most of our conversations revolved around the hoopla that was generated by both the novel and the movie. It was also where we decided to begin our exploration at the time of compiling information for the Introductory Edition of the series Idi Amin: Hero or Villain? His Son Jaffar Amin and Other People Speak.

As a child growing up in Idi Amin's Kakwa tribe and hometown of Ko'boko (Ko'buko), Uganda, I had been privy to family conversations relating to Idi Amin. I know that there is a lot more to Awon'go Alemi as the Kakwa like to refer to Idi Amin than has been written and reported to date. I wanted to facilitate the telling of the story in its entirety while providing the Learning Opportunities my "Storytelling" projects are primarily intended for.

Prior to the above conversation with Jaffar Amin about "The Last King of Scotland", we had been in communication regarding very extensive information he has gathered for his book projects through Personal Accounts, Secondary Sources, The Internet, Library and Archival Research. He too had embarked on telling his father's story from a different angle than it has been told to date!

Jaffar and I met on the Internet a couple of years ago when he "fired" me an email to introduce himself as Idi Amin's son, after "stumbling" onto my website and reading statements Ligito, a controversial character in my book projects made about his father Idi Amin Awon'go Alemi Dada. Ligito is from the Kakwa tribe and he has no qualms whatsoever about challenging injustice and telling it like it is. The statements he made about Idi Amin were not very nice and Jaffar wanted to "set the record straight!"

I was intrigued and "tickled" by Jaffar's boldness and immediately recognized the Kakwa tribal characteristic of "risk taking", "fearlessness" and often "taking the bull by the horns" so to say! Traditionally, the Kakwa don't "stab people in the back" – no, no – that is too cowardly. If they have something to say to you, they like to say it to your face; if they have a beef to settle with you, they approach you from the front so that you can see them coming and defend yourself. They will stab you in the stomach if they must and not in the back so to say.

Ligito

"The British 'created' Idi Amin. They should stop abrogating their responsibility and start pointing the fingers at their damn selves and not anyone else", mouths Ligito, the controversial character in my book projects that prompted Jaffar Amin to "fire" me the first email introducing himself as Idi Amin's son.

Ligito doesn't give a damn and he always speaks what is on his mind even if it offends people. I have included a related excerpt below for context from my book project titled Adroru's Story: A Semi-Autobiography that outlines a time Adroru boarded a flight to Johannesburg, South Africa at Jomo Kenyatta International Airport in Nairobi, Kenya, during apartheid in South Africa. We wish to advise that opinions and any "allegations" contained in Ligito's statements do not necessarily reflect the views of Jaffar Amin, me as a Facilitator, Co-compiler and Co-writer or any entity or individual associated with the series and related projects.

Ligito loves telling stories and funny jokes and he is often seen surrounded by a very large crowd that had gathered to listen to one of his stories and shots at his latest object of ridicule. No one, not even Revered Kakwa Temezi (Elders) are exempted from Ligito's mockery and ridicule. He never shies away from taking shots at anyone or any situation and always seems to know things other people don't.

Ligito has travelled and lived in distant and foreign lands, some of which have very "strange" customs and practices he often talks about, mocks and ridicules. Although some people dismiss several of Ligito's stories and jokes as ridiculous and fictitious, others often reflect on the wisdom and truth contained in them and their relevance to life. Ligito has an opinion and a story to tell, about everything under the sun! He has no qualms whatsoever about telling it like it is and challenging injustice, which he despises with a passion!

The Airhostess asked to see Adroru's ticket and Passport before she could board the flight to Johannesburg, South Africa. As Adroru handed her the ticket and the United Nations Travel Document that had been issued in lieu of a Passport by the office of the United Nations High Commissioner for Refugees in Geneva, Switzerland, her mind wondered off to an experience she had at Jomo Kenyatta International Airport. Adroru had travelled by KLM, the Royal Dutch Airlines, from Khartoum, Sudan, to Nairobi, Kenya and was en-route to Johannesburg, South Africa and then her final destination, Maseru, Lesotho.

Before boarding the flight to Johannesburg, Adroru had woken up with a startle to an announcement in English, Swahili and Afrikaans. She had fallen asleep as she waited to board her flight to Johannesburg, South Africa. Adroru had been denied entry into Nairobi by Kenyan Immigration Authorities, because she was considered "Stateless", as a Refugee. Mr. Wilson of the Windle Charitable Trust, a passionate advocate for refugees had attempted to get Adroru into Kenya so that she could rest at his home before proceeding to Johannesburg on her way to Maseru, Lesotho. However, Kenyan Immigration Officers had not relented. Mr. Wilson was a Kenyan of British ancestry, having settled in Kenya with his family as a child, during the colonial period and lived there for most of his adult life.

"Mr. Wilson is a good man. He is not like many British nationals who despised Awon'go during his rule in Uganda and unfairly labeled anyone associated with Awon'go by tribe, religion and region of origin as his "henchman"", Ligito had mouthed one time while hearing accounts of Mr. Wilson's relentless work to assist African refugees.

Mr. Wilson had vehemently opposed the ill treatment of Ugandan refugee students from the West Nile region of Uganda and devoted a lot of energy and effort into trying to secure places of higher learning for these students, in various countries. Adroru had met Mr. Wilson in the Sudan during an interview she had with him for a scholarship to study at a university in West Africa.

As Adroru was clearing Kenyan Immigration that day, she happened to be glancing around when she caught sight of Mr. Wilson talking to Kenyan Immigration Officials about an Ethiopian student refugee that had just arrived in Kenya on Windle Charitable Trust Scholarship. Adroru could not believe her eyes as she screamed, "Mr. Wilson", "Mr. Wilson".

It had been so good and exciting to see a familiar and friendly face among faces that had all seemed to say, "You are a Ugandan refugee?" Despite the continuing murders of people associated to Idi Amin by tribe, religion and region of origin, most people had become convinced that it was safe to live in Uganda after the overthrow of Idi Amin, unless you were guilty of atrocities committed during his regime. So, Adroru had received suspicious looks from the Kenyan Immigration Officers, which she had ignored while thinking "You are all so stupid and ignorant!" a characteristic mischievous smile lingering on her lips as she thought that.

Mr. Wilson had approached Adroru with the same excitement and congratulated her on attaining a United Nations scholarship to study in Lesotho. They caught up on each other's activities - Mr. Wilson's efforts to secure scholarships for student refugees in Africa and Adroru's efforts to initiate and lead projects aimed at publicizing the plight of Ugandan student refugees unfairly labelled by the international community as Idi Amin's henchmen and therefore undeserving of assistance. Then Mr. Wilson had approached the Kenyan Immigration Officials on behalf of Adroru, for a Transit Visa to Kenya. However, the Kenyan Immigration Officers had declined to give Adroru the Transit Visa because she was considered "Stateless" as a refugee. So, Adroru had stayed cooped at Jomo Kenyatta International Airport until the time came to board her flight to Johannesburg, South Africa.

Adroru had laid down on one of the couches in the Transit Lounge and drifted off to sleep due to exhaustion, after a Kenyan female Airport Security Guard asked her in Swahili because it was getting dark and late, "Je! Mama huendi nyumbani?" ("Gee! Ma'am, aren't you going home?"), meaning it was getting kind of late to be sitting at a deserted airport alone. Adroru had responded to the question by telling the security guard, "Mimi ni mkimbizi" ("I am a refugee") and continued that she didn't have a home to go to and she hadn't been allowed to get out of Jomo Kenyatta Airport.

Adroru's mind had again gone back to her traumatic refugee experience and the mass exodus of Ugandan Kakwas into neighbouring Congo and the Sudan after Idi Amin was overthrown on April 11, 1979. She had remembered the suffering and hardship her family experienced during Idi Amin's regime despite coming from Idi Amin's tribe, the suffering her family experienced during the war to overthrow Idi Amin and the suffering her family experienced in the process of fleeing the war and after the war. She had felt so lonely, so alone and so homeless that she hadn't been able to stop the tears from flooding down her cheeks. She had cried herself to sleep, waking up with the startle when she heard the announcement to board her flight to Johannesburg in fifteen minutes.

Adroru had continued to reflect on her refugee experience in the Congo and the Sudan and never understood the sad sequence of events that unfolded before and during her stay in the two countries of Asylum. She could not shake off the deep sadness that continued to engulf her because of her horrific refugee experience. In the Congo, where she first landed after Idi Amin was ousted from power, Mobutu Sese Seko's Army, commonly referred to as the Kamanyola had terrorized Ugandan refugees with unimaginable torture methods of interrogation. The soldiers would often scream, "Akangi na kamba" ("Tie with a rope") in Lingala, a Bantu language spoken in the Democratic Republic of the Congo, as Ugandan refugees faced brutal interrogation in the hands of the unruly and starved soldiers. In the Sudan, Adroru had endured such a horrific life that it took her years of counselling to forge a "normal" existence.

As on her first day at Kagote Primary School in Fort Portal, Western Uganda, her first day in Sacred Heart Senior Secondary School in Gulu, Northern Uganda and the days she landed as a refugee in the Congo and the Sudan, she felt insecure and scared. Only this time she was alone and she was headed for South Africa, where Black people were considered inferior to White people and other lighter skinned people.

Ligito had recounted stories of mistreatment of Black people in South Africa because of the colour of their skins, during the times he told stories about Nelson Mandela and the Apartheid System in South Africa. Adroru had herself studied and read several books on South Africa and her aunt who was married to Uganda's Ambassador to Lesotho during Idi Amin's government had also told her stories of encounters they had with South Africans.

During the time she attended Sacred Heart Senior Secondary School, the Catholic Boarding School for girls in Gulu, Northern Uganda, Adroru and her classmates had studied Peter Abrahams' book "Mine Boy" as a Literature Text. They had learnt about Xuma the Mine Boy and the mistreatment of Black South Africans by White South Africans. As they studied Mine Boy, Adroru had been saddened by the fact that there were still Black people in other parts of the world who were considered less than human. However, Adroru had never in a million years imagined that she would end up in a part of the world, where Black people were considered inferior because of skin colour. She had never really been prepared to have a first hand experience of some of the stories Ligito told about South Africa.

Adroru sighed and wondered what was going to become of her now as she approached the Airhostess on her way to board the flight to Johannesburg, South Africa. She wondered what Ligito would say about her impending encounter with the Apartheid System of South Africa that he despised with a passion and the suspicious look she was getting from the Airhostess.

Adroru suppressed a chuckle as she looked at the Airhostess and dialogued in her head, "You stupid, pompous, ugly, puffed up, croaking frog". Adroru had a lingering smile on her lips as she recalled the times she and Ligito made fun of people that look down upon others and referred to them as stupid, ugly, puffed up, croaking frogs. She and Ligito always exchange a knowing look whenever they encounter people who discriminate against or treat other people as inferior beings.

Ligito always becomes very upset when anyone is discriminated against or treated as an inferior being! He is constantly telling that people who discriminate against other people, put others down or treat people badly are like croaking frogs. Adroru knows what Ligito means by this insult and always rolls on the floor with laughter when Ligito jeers, "Look at the bastards! They are like puffed up, ugly croaking frogs and they don't even see it!"

Adroru knows that every Kakwa despises and considers a frog as one of the ugliest and weakest animals on earth. She knows that if a Kakwa wants to insult someone or challenge someone to a physical fight, they only have to call the person a "frog", that frogs are ugliest when they are puffed up and croaking.

Adroru often chuckles as she observes frogs loudly croaking during her trips to the well. The croaking frogs always irritate her with their deep, hoarse, ugly and monotonous songs. They are always so puffed up and seem so pompous as if saying, "Look at us, aren't we the weakest, loudest and ugliest creatures on earth?"

The Airhostess had started speaking to Adroru in Afrikaans, then she had switched to a strange and heavily accented English that Adroru could hardly understand, when she realized that Adroru didn't understand a word of what she was asking.

"Where is your passport?" the Airhostess repeated in the heavily accented English, because Adroru could only produce a United Nations Travel Document issued through the office of the United Nations High Commissioner for Refugees in Geneva, Switzerland and not a real Passport as everyone had.

"I am a Conventional Refugee. I am using a United Nations Travel Document for travelling", Adroru responded to the question in "perfect" English that had a "tint" of "British Accent".

"Where are you from?" insisted the Airhostess.

"I am from Uganda", Adroru offered, wondering what the Airhostess was now thinking because Idi Amin had boasted about liberating Black South Africans by force and bombing Cape Town when he was in power. Adroru's aunt had also told her stories about South Africa when she and her husband were living in Lesotho. Her aunt's husband had been posted to Lesotho as Uganda's Ambassador to Lesotho during Idi Amin's regime and the two had taken periodic trips to South Africa.

During visits to her aunt in Kampala when she was attending Sacred Heart Senior Secondary School, the Catholic Boarding school for girls in Gulu, Northern Uganda,

Adroru's aunt had told stories about encounters with South Africans. During one visit, her aunt had recounted to Adroru and several of their extended family members how she and her husband went shopping to South Africa one day. As they were driving across the border into South Africa, they saw a car approach them from behind after they had driven off from the Border Post. A White Border Patrol Officer flagged them down and asked them questions. The Border Patrol Officer had been tipped by a colleague that the person in the car that had just pulled off was Uganda's Ambassador to Lesotho. According to her aunt, he had been curious to see what Ugandans looked like because of all the stories they had heard about "boisterous" Idi Amin. Ligito constantly told jokes about Idi Amin's threats to bomb South Africa and overthrow the Apartheid Regime by force. Amin even named one of his residences after Cape Town for that reason, Ligito said.

Ligito always chuckles when he remembers the times Idi Amin made a bunch of "Gilia" (White People) "kneel" before him and others carry him the way Black Africans used to carry White people in the colonial days. It was always a big joke when Ligito chanted, "Conqueror of the British Empire", "Conqueror of the British Empire", "Conqueror of the British Empire" the way the Newspapers screamed one time because Idi Amin gave himself that title.

Sometimes Ligito asserted while laughing that, the British deserved the rudeness they got from Idi Amin because they created him. He told that it was the fault of the British that "Awon'go Alemi turned out the despicable way he did".

"Awon'go Alemi was a great student though. He paid very close attention to lessons he learnt from the British and from the few stories he must have heard about Tole the Hare, even though he was born in Buganda and wasn't pointed towards Mountain Liru as Kakwa newborns are supposed to be, in Kakwa naming ceremonies".

Ligito often laughed hard as he said, "...But, But, Awon'go Alemi paid very close attention to stories about Tole the Hare that are shared by Temezi (Revered Elders) around the fire".

"Awon'go's opponents thought he was stupid but he outsmarted them and he had the last laugh!" Ligito regularly chuckled.

Tole is a character Adroru knows about from the countless Likikiris (stories and folklore passed down from generation to generation) she and her extended family share while spending quality time around the fire, after the family's evening meal.

Family members always take turns mimicking Temezi (Revered Elders) by telling countless Likikiris about animals, human beings and a world that existed a long time ago, before the "great grandparents" of the Kakwa tribe. Tole is clever and regularly outsmarts his opponents. Sometimes, he is a conniving trickster who doesn't think twice about deliberately hurting others. He could also be greedy - a characteristic frowned upon by most members of the Kakwa tribe.

As a young child, Adroru had always looked forward to spending quality time with her extended family around the fire and never tired of repeated Likikiris. She still enjoys spending quality time around the fire with her extended family. She had soaked and absorbed the lessons and wisdom contained in the stories about animals, human beings and the world that existed a long time ago, before the "great grandparents" of the Kakwa tribe. She had marveled at Tole's cleverness and used some of his "tricks" to gain an upper hand with child bullies at school, as Tole sometimes did with despicable bully animals.

However, like Ligito, Adroru despised and despises Tole's bad ways with a passion. Kakwa elders always emphasize that the Kakwa extended family system and its humanitarian principles are paramount. Even as they tell countless Likikiris that often centre on Tole and his mean, cunning, unscrupulous, conniving tricks and activities to intentionally hurt others, the elders incessantly preach about the importance of extracting from Likikiris only lessons that advance humanity. All Kakwa children understand the principles and values of the Kakwa extended family system – unconditional kindness and unconditional generosity.

Everyone always laughs when they remember the day Idi Amin took over power from his predecessor Apollo Milton Obote in a Military Coup and Ligito mouthed while providing eyewitness accounts of the jubilation on Kampala streets:

"You should have seen them. It was as if they were possessed by evil spirits."

"Dancing for Awon'go Alemi of all people as if they have nothing better to do!"

"These people never cease to amaze me. They always find a reason to dance."

"First they danced for Obote, now they are dancing for Awon'go. I have never seen people so unprincipled and confused! Somehow, they always seem to conveniently suffer from amnesia whenever a new President comes to power!"

On the day of the Military Coup by Idi Amin, everyone roared with laughter as Ligito continued, "People who dance every time there is a new President are nothing but Political Prostitutes."

"I will never kiss any President's arse no matter what tribe they are from."

"As far as I am concerned, all Politicians are a bunch of low level, power hungry nincompoops who have no regard for other human beings but themselves."

Ligito regularly uses the word arse when he is upset - the rude and impolite reference to buttocks by "Gilia" (White People). He often tells that "Gilia" refer to attempts to win a favour from someone by despicable means as "kissing arse".

"I will never understand Ugandans. They are unprincipled and mindless Political Prostitutes whose allegiances constantly shift for "dishonorable reasons"", Ligito constantly asserts.

Sometimes the girls in charge of dances in the Catholic Boarding School for girls that Adroru attended used to play English Records, which the whole school had learnt to sing and dance very well, including the waltz. Adroru always chuckles as she reminisces about her time at the Boarding School. She regularly remembers the girls screaming and singing all the songs in the feature film "The Sound of Music" as they waltzed in reckless abandon and jumped up and down the way Maria did in the feature film.

On one occasion while visiting Adroru at the Boarding School, Ligito mocked, "Look at them, jumping up and down like monkeys. Why do people wannabe "Gilia" when they can be better "being African?""

Ligito was referring to girls in Scottish costumes dancing to Scottish music and others dancing to Country Music. He uses the word "wannabe" to describe people who despise their African roots and want to be "Gilia" (White People).

He jeers that "any African who despises rich African cultures and African outfits and prefers to act and dress like "Gilia" all the time is a fool." He always continues, ""Gilia" have corrupted Africans into wanting to copy them in all ways - especially their bad and despicable ways!"

Adroru was still smiling and dialoguing in her head when the Airhostess handed her back her United Nations Travel Document.

"Are you a member of the African National Congress?" a nearby White male Steward had rudely interrupted the interrogation Adroru was getting from the Airhostess in the same strange and heavily accented English.

Adroru had said "no" but with a mischievous smile because she was thinking, "Are all Boers as stupid as you two?"

Ligito used the word Boers to refer to bigoted and racist South African Whites.

Adroru is convinced that Ligito would have had an altercation with the Airhostess and her male colleague because they had a terrible attitude with Adroru. She wished that she had travelled with Ligito this time because she knew that he would have shared more stories about the despicable Apartheid System. She knew that he would even have "made a scene" out of spite and to draw attention to the "stupid" Boers as he referred to the bigoted and racist South African Whites.

Ligito told that the African National Congress was the organization Nelson Mandela belonged to and that the African National Congress and other South African Freedom Fighters were hell bent on overthrowing the Apartheid System in South Africa and he was happy about that. He told that sometimes, members of these organizations who were living as refugees in neighbouring countries travelled back to South Africa for purposes of sabotaging the Apartheid Regime. Because of that, the Boers looked upon anyone who was a Conventional Refugee with suspicion, particularly people such as Adroru that carried United Nations Travel Documents.

Telling Idi Amin's Story

Before I met Jaffar Amin, I had heard a lot about Idi Amin through extended family members and reports written about him but I didn't have the opportunity to meet him or anyone as intimately associated with him as a son, in person. So, I was quite pleased to make acquaintance with Jaffar. Since our "first meeting" on the Internet, we have communicated extensively as I poked, pried, probed and asked very tough and annoying questions the same way Jaffar did with his father during their life in exile. The inquisitive, very bold and "fearless" Jaffar had taken his father on while they lived in exile first in Libya and then in Saudi Arabia. Imagine that!

For example, during many very warm father-son chitchats that Jaffar had with his father in Saudi Arabia, Jaffar fearlessly mouthed to his Dad, "Baba by you keeping quiet you are implying that all that trash they write about you is true." Needless to say, Jaffar's siblings and close family members were "horrified" by Jaffar's boldness but they knew that if anyone could take Idi Amin on, it was "fearless" Jaffar.

Jaffar was referring to the "nasty" "nasty" stuff that has been written about his father with all of the allegations of "horrific evil" committed by his father. He asked Daddy Amin for his side of the story because there are always two sides to "the same" story! While living in exile with his Dad in Saudi Arabia, Jaffar had poked, pried, prodded and asked his father very tough and annoying questions and Idi Amin obliged and spoke to his son from the heart. He provided never before heard and published answers.

"Dad always had ready answers for me," Jaffar laughed and reiterated one time.

"He would respond in a very Jewish manner with a question."

""Why do you think I send you to school, Hmmm? You answer them.""

You mean he didn't punch the daylights out of you? I mused and chuckled to myself when I recalled the narrative account Jaffar shared with me about his father walking into the "Whites Only" Officers' Mess in Jinja during Colonial Uganda and challenging Racism. The "bad behaviour" Idi Amin displayed on this occasion is something many Professional Boxers like him might do in total defiance of the fact that their hands are considered weapons in many instances and therefore criminal to use if they hate and despise discrimination as much as Idi Amin did. The incident in question happened in 1959 and Idi Amin had been promoted to the Honourary Rank of Affende - the highest rank awarded to Black African members of the Kings African Rifles at the time.

"On this day, Dad dared to march into the 'Whites Only' Officers' Mess at 1st Battalion Jinja after getting tired of moving with a rank that did not hold water," Jaffar recounted.

"He moved up to the 'Whites Only' Officers' Mess instead of going to the Sergeants' Mess and ordered a drink. When the White Bartender told him off and "barked" for him to go to the Sergeants' Mess, he grabbed him by the collar and pulled him straight over the counter. He then let rip with a resounding right on the Englishman's chin, to the hushed silence of the whole room, full of shocked White Officers. The segregative rule was changed after this audacious incident and Dad was even invited to join the exclusive Jinja Rugby Club because he was "one of their own" as a Star Athlete and Rugby Player. So there you have it "Proactive Action" from Africa's most maligned Activist. He always said, "Action speaks louder than words."

While living in exile in Saudi Arabia, Jaffar wanted to get to the bottom of what happened during his father's rule in Uganda and why his Daddy was being called some of the worst names in human history, including being referred to as evil incarnate and the devil. He did get some answers from his father that he wishes to share after corroborating the answers with Temezi (Revered Elders) and information gathered through Personal Accounts, Secondary Sources, The Internet, Library and Archival Research. He includes many of the answers in his book projects.

I couldn't contain my excitement at the opportunity to tell "everything" about Idi Amin as Jaffar and I laughed about funny encounters he and his siblings had growing up as Idi Amin's children. It was the same way Ugandans used to laugh as they had funny encounters with Idi Amin and mimicked the way he talked. Jaffar and his siblings have a myriad of standing jokes about their Dad like the time his brother Ali nicknamed him Bahrain and his sister Halima shared a funny incident that occurred during a family trip to Mecca for Juma (Friday) Prayers while living in Saudi Arabia. Some of these stories and jokes will be told later in the series.

Regarding the Bahrain nickname, Jaffar offered, "Dad would head furiously for the Communication Services in Jeddah and call the Bahrain BBC Bureau, vehemently explaining the issue of the Expropriated Property relating to the Asians he ordered out of Uganda in 1972. He insisted that the Asians had been fully compensated for the Properties they left behind even though no one paid any attention to his honest explanations and protests regarding how unfair he was treated and perceived in the 'Asian saga.' Then he would gather us around to listen to the Focus On Africa News at 19:00 East African Time, until it became a standing joke amongst the inner circle of siblings and Ali Nyabira Kirunda code named Dad Bahrain."

I have continued to communicate with Jaffar - now as a partner in telling his father's story, comparing notes and correlating facts. I am especially pleased to hear Idi Amin's story from "the horse's mouth" so to say and there are a lot of "horses" that are now willing to come forward with "all" the truth. I have joked with many of these "horses" while asking for reassurance that they have their facts straight and they won't back out when the going gets tough.

As with all contentious stories ripe with Learning Opportunities, there will be players that will not want "all" of the truth told. That is why I am intrigued by Jaffar's determination to enlist Temezi (Revered Elders) and close associates of his father, along with other people, in telling his father's story in its entirety, in spite of the "rude" interpolations that have characterized his telling of the story to date.

I am particularly referring to the "media obsession" with telling only the "slanted" aspect of Idi Amin's story that relates to his 8-year rule in Uganda and the rudeness with which Jaffar is often interrupted after he graciously agrees to give media interviews relating to his father's story. Ligito, the controversial character in my book projects would say the rude interruptions and misleading insertions to Jaffar's statements amount to mindless gossip. He would mouth, "Anyone who doesn't listen to the entire story before 'shooting' from the mouth is a fool" and I agree. You will know how "lippy" and controversial Ligito is when you get to read my writings relating to him which include sections titled "Controversial Ligito Speaks".

I have great admiration for Jaffar's bravery which is a prerequisite for my "Storytelling" projects because they are meant to emulate the way "Controversial Ligito" himself often pokes, pries, probes, asks very tough and annoying questions, "digs deep" and likes all of the truth exposed. In my quest to "tell the whole truth", I always insist that subjects of my "Storytelling" projects have their facts straight. This is because I have utmost respect for the rule of law and strongly believe in the principle, "Everyone is innocent until proven guilty beyond reasonable doubt".

Jaffar Amin is determined to tell another side of his father's story and he won't "crawl into a hole" as other people would! It takes someone of solid character "to be counted." Jaffar's "audacity" to want to give a differ-ent slant to his father's story in spite of the "din" arising from the "messy" and "convoluted" articles that can be found everywhere on the Internet amounts to "being counted". Try googling "Idi Amin Dada" and you will see what I am talking about!

Soon after the release of the hit movie "The Last King of Scotland", Jaffar boldly stepped forward from the obscurity enjoyed by many of his siblings and family members and introduced himself as Idi Amin's son. That time, I again chuckled and thought *oh my God, now he really wants to take a lot of bulls by the horns*! However, I am reassured by the fact that like me, Jaffar Amin has utmost respect for the rule of law and he also strongly believes in the principle, "Everyone is innocent until proven guilty beyond reasonable doubt" which is what will be the guiding principle for this project.

Every time I googled "Jaffar Amin" at the time the hit movie "The Last King of Scotland" hit the movie theatres I couldn't believe the myriad of articles that came "tumbling" down! Throughout my own poking, prying, probing and asking Jaffar the same tough and annoying questions he asked his father during their life in exile, Jaffar has remained objective, which speaks volumes to what a brave, fair and fine person he is. Not once, did he become defensive when I mimicked Ligito in uttering some of the very same statements made by Idi Amin's antagonists – many of the ones Ligito made that prompted Jaffar to "fire" me an email to introduce himself as Idi Amin's son and "set the record straight".

He would always stick to his famous statement "Our father had his faults. I do not see the period of his rule in Uganda with "rose-tinted glasses." However, we need to counter-balance history with all the truth!" Sometimes he sounds like a broken record but I fully understand his standpoint. Jaffar wants to tell another side of his father's story and I am happy to partner with him in telling that side of Idi Amin's story in Kakwa Adiyo narration style and format.

Jaffar and I have agreed that uncovering "all" the layers relating to his father's story, is the only way the world will get a balanced and accurate account of the "famous" and "infamous" Idi Amin and the series Idi Amin: Hero or Villain? His Son Jaffar Amin and Other People Speak is a great place to start. Beginning with this series, we will tell Idi Amin's story from a completely different perspective and not the same old "slanted" narrative that has been rehashed "to death" without providing Learning Opportuni-ties and telling "the other side" too. Our objective is to use the story as a Learning Opportunity.

Many Revered Temezi (Elders) who realize that they have nothing to lose that they haven't already lost will be actively engaged in the series, along with other people who have "jumped onto the band wagon" and are guided by the same principle we will be working with. The guiding principles "Every accused is innocent until proven guilty" and "Everyone is innocent until proven guilty beyond reasonable doubt" are strictly adhered to and respected in all my "Storytelling" projects and the series Idi Amin: Hero or Villain? His Son Jaffar Amin and Other People Speak is no exception.

Long after Idi Amin's demise on August 16, 2003, "tongues are still wagging" about him as numerous people continue to be undecided about whether he was a Hero or a Villain to the core. We are acutely aware that there are "zillions" of people on both sides of the debate, which is why we look forward to facilitating effective discussions about the conflicting characterization and learning from the discussions! Accounts by people on both sides of the conflicting characterization of Idi Amin as a Hero and Villain abound, as do the lessons ingrained in the story.

As Jaffar put it, "Without a doubt, Awon'go made an indelible mark in the world". Awon'go is one of Idi Amin's Kakwa names and his mother fondly referred to him by it. I also prefer to use that name because traditionally, all Kakwa names have very deep meanings and Kakwa children such as Idi Amin who are named after controversial life circumstances often eerily grow up to be what is implied in their Kakwa names.

I always "fume" when people ask me where I am from and go, "Hmmm, Idi Amin" after I tell them I was born in Uganda. They do this as if "Idi Amin" is the only thing there is to know about Uganda. However, I realize that the attitude arises from the fact that indeed "Awon'go made an indelible mark in the world" with the conflicting characterization of Hero and Villain at the same time and the "convoluted" and "slanted" accounts that have characterized the telling of his story to date.

I hate that question. I regularly grumble to family members and friends every time I encounter people who ask me where I am from. Then they "put me in a box" because I am from Idi Amin's Kakwa tribe! Ligito would say, "Anyone who asks a total stranger where they are from without first having 'intelligent' conversation to know the person better and provide context to the question is a stupid person with no social skills." I must say, I agree!

He would also call anyone stupid who judges a person by the way they look, their tribe, their race, their religion and other characteristics and not by their character. I agree with that too! I know for a fact that other Ugandans have been and continue to be subjected to the same simple-mindedness. So are myriads of other people around the world. Ligito would say, "Shame, shame, shame on everyone who judges individuals by tribe, race, religion and other characteristics and not by their character!"

A controversial and conflicted legacy

I have never come across a story with so many "twists and turns." I always gush to family members and friends when they inquire about how Jaffar Amin and I are doing "sorting through" his father's convoluted, conflicted and controversial story and legacy. I must say I find aspects of Idi Amin's story intriguing even though I regularly have bouts of very deep sadness accompanied by gut-wrenching sobs and wails for the victims and bereaved families of those who were callously murdered before, during and after his rule in Uganda. The brutal murders were some of the worst forms of evil in the history of humankind and one would have to have a very calloused heart not to experience very deep sadness in reading accounts of the horrific and unconscionable murders.

Sometimes I cry while laughing about some of the "things" Idi Amin did and managed to "pull off" - like the time he duped the British Royal Family and Secret Service by "inviting" himself to the Queen's Silver Jubilee in London, setting off a scramble by the British Secret Service to set up a fully armed response team to counter his unwelcome arrival in London! However, after "formally" "taking off" from Entebbe Airport with a troupe of 200 tribal dancers, Idi Amin made a detour, then he returned to Uganda. He was laughing hard because he had successfully duped and "taunted" the British for the sins of colonialism and imperialism yet again!

Then there was the time he "forced" the Ganda language on the United Nations and addressed the Assembly in it as the Chairman of the Organization of African Unity (OAU). This he did in total defiance of United Nations rules regarding "Official Languages". During his trip to New York to address the United Nations, he poked fun at the United States of America for the sins of the African Slave Trade by flying in a dance troupe to dance for him and show off African beauty and talent on American soil. While staying at the Waldorf-Astoria Hotel in New York that time, he gave a Black American cleaning lady a 10,000 dollar tip to ease her suffering from the racism he detested and talked about the flabbergasted look he got from the lady for a long time to come!

One of the most dangerous of all the "things" Idi Amin did was showing up at the War Frontline to see things for himself as the war between Uganda and Tanzania that resulted in his ouster was progressing. That time, he waved at members of the Tanzania Peoples' Defence Force that were engaged in intense battle with his own troops. The Tanzanian forces were well aware that it was Idi Amin waving at them but instead of shooting him, the soldiers excitedly waved back!

Upon arriving home that time, Idi Amin could not stop laughing at the spectacle of shocking combatants into inaction. The dumbfounded soldiers must have recounted their close encounter with the "notorious" Idi Amin for a very long time!

Ligito would laugh and say, "Awon'go Alemi was just like Tole the Hare" - the cunning character in the countless Likikiris (stories and folklore passed down from generation to generation) that Kakwa Temezi (Revered Elders) share while spending quality time with younger family members. Tole regularly "pulled off" "things" other people would never imagine or even think of!

In telling Idi Amin's story, we won't negate all of the horrific stories that have been told about him to date or "gloss over" them, out of respect and very deep compassion for victims and families who were bereaved because of the horrendous atrocities committed during his rule in Uganda. However, there will be a lot more information about what actually happened during Idi Amin's rule in Uganda than what has been reported to date and Jaffar Amin won't be the one "disseminating" this information and "telling all" either. He will just focus on what he knows as Idi Amin's son, especially through his own experience and personal accounts.

We will endeavor to share only true accounts and not fictional ones! Readers and participants will have opportunities to "jump in", make corrections, share information known to them as participants would in an Adiyo Narration Process. They will have opportunities to compare these accounts with the fictionalized accounts in "The Last King of Scotland" and other articles, books and films about Idi Amin that have been circulated since he started "behaving very badly". This Introductory Edition of the series Idi Amin: Hero or Villain? His Son Jaffar Amin and Other People Speak is a precursor to projects planned for the purpose of telling and uncovering Idi Amin's story in its entirety, layer by layer.

From the very first time he entered this world, "kicking" and "screaming" as a baby, to the time he ascended to the highest position in the land of Uganda and beyond, Idi Amin's life was punctuated with controversies and dramas very few historical figures can lay claim to. His "kicking" and "screaming" as a baby earned him the notorious Kakwa name Awon'go which means various things depending on the context, including and not limited to one who is loud or makes a lot of noise. It can also mean one whose life is characterized by "noise" as in the "noise" that followed Idi Amin's birth because of a contested paternity and the "din" that has persisted about him to this day – long after his demise on August 16, 2003.

According to accounts told by Idi Amin's family and his son Jaffar Amin, Idi Amin "screamed" and cried a lot as a baby beginning with the time his mother Aisha Aate Chumaru performed a self-delivery and the infant Amin landed onto a pile of hailstones, setting off a resounding scream. However, he shared a very deep and special bond with his mother especially after being subjected to an ancient Kakwa "Paternity Test" involving an infant being abandoned in a jungle full of wild and dangerous animals for three or four days. If the infant survived the harsh elements of nature during the three or four-day ordeal, paternity would be "confirmed" beyond reasonable doubt. Imagine that!

In the case of Idi Amin, he didn't only survive the controversy surrounding his contested paternity and wild animals foraging for food and prey in a perilous African jungle for four days as an infant, but he lived to tell the story! He lived to ascend to the highest position in the land of Uganda - dominating the headlines of the 1970s with unprecedented controversies. Unbeknown to the global community at the time, Idi Amin was being true to the Kakwa tradition relating to Kakwa children like him who are named after controversial life circumstances often eerily growing up to be what is implied in their Kakwa names.

I know that tradition and have experienced it with my own name and the names of family members within my extended family. Like Idi Amin, my own Grandpa was named Awon'go and he never shied away from "very loudly" challenging injustice, like the time he challenged his stern uncle Sultan Ali Kenyi as a youngster.

Sultan Ali Kenyi, a Kakwa Chief who served in the Colonial Administration was one of four Sultans appointed by Colonial Administrators during the colonization of Sub-Saharan Africa. Sultan Ali Kenyi who was also a Hereditary Chief and perhaps the most notorious, influential and towering Ugandan Kakwa Chief in the first half of the 20th century was highly respected by the Colonial Administrators. He was both revered and feared by his subjects the Kakwa. According to accounts by Temezi (Elders), Sultan Ali Kenyi had no tolerance for dissent and administered lashings that left dissidents squirming in pain for weeks - even months.

According to accounts by family members, the Sultan Ali Kenyi had ordered his nephew my Grandpa Awon'go to hand over a goat to White colonial authorities for less than the price Grandpa deemed fair and Grandpa protested and refused to hand over his goat. This "bad behaviour" "horrified" Grandpa's parents because it would have earned him a lashing, which Grandpa was fully aware of! Luckily, Grandpa was exempted from the lashing because he was Sultan Ali Kenyi's nephew. That day, Grandpa was ordered by his uncle Sultan Ali Kenyi to leave with his goat immediately instead which he did, while getting a "scolding" from his parents. My Great Grandpa apologized to Sultan Ali Kenyi for his son's "rudeness".

I always chuckle when I remember an account relating to my Grandpa walking into our local church screaming at the top of his lungs as the congregation was bowed in prayer. He stopped everyone in their tracks because he "needed" an injustice to be rectified before the congregation resumed prayers. My Grandpa was a devout Christian and he personified the Kakwa teaching and practice of unconditional kindness and unconditional generosity at all times but he never blinked when "screaming" at people as he scolded them for being unjust! He was very loud every time he did that and people knew when they had crossed a line and understood and excused his "outbursts!" They actually respected and loved him for being forthright, fair and unafraid to challenge injustice.

According to family members and Jaffar Amin, Idi Amin's mother Aate regularly told events surrounding the unusual "Paternity Test" Idi Amin was subjected to as an infant. She told that her infant son Awon'go survived the jungle because of Lemi (Just Cause or Justice) and because Nakan, a "sacred" snake, wrapped itself around him for warmth and protection as it would do around its own eggs and young offspring - Yikes!

Idi Amin's second Kakwa name Alemi is consequently derived from the Kakwa word Lemi (Just Cause or Justice). Moreover Awon'go Alemi was born during a heavy downpour of tropical rain which is considered an omen by many Kakwa people.

My initial reaction to Aate's story about Nakan the "sacred" snake wrapping itself around her infant son Idi Amin for warmth and protection while he endured the Deadly "Paternity Test" was horror and revulsion. However, I began to understand where she was coming from when Jaffar provided some context to Serpent Worship in the Kakwa tribe and other societies around the world.

"The commentary by Margaret Akulia is typical to anyone who comes across the controversial arena of Serpent Worship" Jaffar interjected and asserted before adding, "Yet the Adi (Tale) was strictly speaking my grandmother's words to her beloved son in line with her cultural beliefs."

Jaffar clarified that Islam has increasingly taken ultimate priority in the upbringing of the Dada family. However, their animist past history is still recounted by Temezi (Tribal Elders) of their Adibu Kakwa clan especially during clan and tribal ceremonies which I had occasion to witness while growing up in Ko'boko (Ko'buko).

To validate his grandmother Aate's story about Nakan the "sacred" snake protecting his father as an infant in the perilous jungle, Jaffar shared a story that occurred in the 1980s in Ko'boko (Ko'buko), home of the Kakwa tribe of Uganda during a Lokita (Kakwa Communal Harvesting Season Event). The story is included in a subsequent part of this Introductory Edition.

A learning opportunity

As we uncover the layers and the series unfolds, we will endeavor to avail audiences with opportunities for learning about and discussing "the good, the bad, the ugly and the evil" as they relate to Idi Amin's conflicted legacy, for contrast, balance and proper discussion. It is hoped that a section of the series devoted to "combing" through and discussing articles, books and films about Idi Amin that have been presented by various parties as "all" of the "truth" about Idi Amin will give readers the opportunity to differentiate between fiction and fact. So, welcome aboard the "ship" that will navigate Idi Amin's story in its entirety and from a different and factual angle!

Who was Idi Amin? How did he end up on the slippery path that led to him becoming one of the most reviled figures in history? How did this happen after being held in very high esteem by his British superiors in the Kings African Rifles (KAR), a multi-battalion British colonial regiment raised from the various British "possessions" in East Africa from 1902 until independence in the 1960s? How did Idi Amin end up being so "despised" after initially being hailed "Jogoo! Jogoo!" ("Hero! Hero!") by colleagues on the eve of the coup that catapulted him to the pinnacle of power in Uganda? How could anyone be so reviled after being cheered by large crowds of Ugandans and being recognized by governments around the world?

On January 25, 1971, Idi Amin became the Commander-in-Chief of Uganda, "The Pearl of Africa" and ruled it up to April 11, 1979 when he was overthrown and forced to live in exile, first in Libya and then in Saudi Arabia. From the time he was subjected to the ancient Kakwa "Paternity Test" involving him being abandoned in a jungle for four days as an infant, to the time of his demise in Saudi Arabia, on August 16, 2003, Idi Amin's lifestory was destined for the "Box Office".

At the time of his demise in Saudi Arabia on August 16, 2003, a lot had been written about Idi Amin, some of it captured in Documentaries and made into Feature Films. The most recent attempt at telling Idi Amin's story at the time of compiling the Introductory Edition of this series was the fictionalized novel and hit movie "The Last King of Scotland", starring Forest Whitaker who won a much deserved Oscar for the role. However, nothing compares to accounts by Jaffar Amin, his siblings, immediate family members and intimate friends of Idi Amin who have now become Temezi (Tribal Elders) and have nothing to lose that they haven't already lost, by providing the most accurate accounts of Idi Amin's story.

This Introductory Edition of the series is aimed at providing sufficient information to begin discussing questions raised by Idi Amin's "famous" and "infamous" rule in Uganda, along with his legacy. The most notable questions include: Have book authors and filmmakers that have attempted to tell the story of Idi Amin to date really delved deep enough to uncover everything there is to know about Idi Amin? Have they told everything there is to tell about him and what actually happened during his rule in Uganda?

"No", says Jaffar Amin, Idi Amin's son, who continues to regularly insist, "Our father had his faults. I do not see the period of his rule in Uganda with "rose-tinted glasses." However, we need to counter-balance history with all the truth!"

Jaffar is not alone in wanting all of the truth uncovered and told. Temezi want the truth uncovered as do other people, including myself because I strongly believe that knowing and telling all the truth can be great for learning, for future generations, for not repeating the same mistakes and for healing!

In this unprecedented series devoted to telling Idi Amin's story in its entirety and not just aspects of the story, I engage his son Jaffar Amin and other people in candid conversation about Idi Amin's life and legacy. For Jaffar, I also engage him in candid conversation about what it was like growing up as Idi Amin's son. Even though I was unjustly victimized many times over because I belonged to Idi Amin's Kakwa tribe, my role in the series will be that of Neutral Moderator and Facilitator for two opposing sides with strong arguments in support of standpoints about Idi Amin being a Hero or Villain.

Despite a terribly "soiled" reputation and being dubbed "the Hitler of Africa", "Villain", "Mad man", "Control Freak", "Paranoid Schizophrenic" and many other names, there are people who view Idi Amin as a hero and others who find his lifestory fascinating. Furthermore, people who knew Idi Amin intimately, before the curse of the colonial game of "Russian Roulette" played by Uganda's colonizers the British came home to roost on the day he "ascended to the highest position in the land", insist that Idi Amin was a nice man. But, there are also "dissenting" voices – ones that view Idi Amin as a villain to the core!

One is forced to ask, what happened to change a man described by Major A.E.D Mitchell a superior of Idi Amin's in the Kings African Rifles as "very quiet, well mannered, respectful and loyal?" What happened to a man of whom another superior in the Kings African Rifles Iain Grahame writes in 1958, "As a platoon commander, however I found him (Idi Amin Dada) first-class. It is always his unit that has the best esprit, discipline and standards of field training…?"

The following reflections by different people are a small sample that illustrates the conflicting characterization of Idi Amin as a Hero and a Villain at the same time:

Winifred a Ugandan national writes that Idi Amin is the only true Ugandan President that loved and cared for his people. He loved Black people all over the world. He brought Sir Edward Mutesa's body back home to rest. He made the British Asians get back the right to settle in the U.K that had been denied to them by the British government. He banned calling mixed children half-castes (abakyotara). Winifred adds that as Jaffar says, Idi Amin made us proud of our skin. He made the first Ugandan millionaire. He gave Mafuta Miingi. He fought Apartheid in South Africa. Indeed he is the greatest. "I'm sorry for those who died in his time, but those responsible for the killings are still at large, not Amin", expanded Winifred before concluding, "Jaffar Amin, thank you so much for bringing back our man Idi Amin Dada. I never thought I would live to witness this. Mungu Iko!"

Joseph, a member of the Kakwa tribe in the Sudan writes, "Amin was a hero. He was very instrumental in helping the Anya Anya 1 when he was the Army Chief of Staff. Doing what he did was very risky". Joseph goes on to recount how helping the Anyanya involved delivering arms and ammunitions to very remote areas located around the Uganda – Sudan border, using military helicopters. Joseph adds that he and many people from the Kakwa tribe in the Sudan regard Amin as a real hero of modern Kakwa history because he aided the Southern Sudan cause. Joseph is speaking about the First Sudanese Civil War that occurred between 1955 and 1972.

Jonathan inquires about how Idi Amin spent his time after he was forced to flee to the Arab Lands. "I find his lifestory quite fascinating and I think he must have felt quite sad about the situation in Uganda after he was forced to flee", Jonathan offered before continuing, "I am an American, but I lived in Scotland in 1970-71, where I went to high school. I too, became fascinated with all things Scottish."

Neil directs a note to Jaffar Amin saying that his "old man" met Jaffar's "old man" before he became President and as far as he knows, Jaffar's old man was a very liked man.

Roland writes, "I just watched The Last King of Scotland and it was very interesting" before adding, "Is there a way to e-mail Mr. Amin's son directly?"

Hellen a Brazilian writes that she lived in Uganda for a couple of years and recently watched the movie "The Last King of Scotland" and decided to know more about Idi Amin... "...I am very impressed with your work, and I've been doing some research and found out that not everything in that movie is true, which to me was very disappointing, especially the way they exposed Kay Amin in an affair with a doctor that seems to not exist.. There is so much I would like to ask."

Christopher, an American writes, "I have no particular question, I just wanted to tell you that I never realized The Last King of Scotland was a work of fiction supposedly based on "true" events. It has become obvious it was marketed as to have people believe it was an entirely accurate (albeit slanted) depiction of a misunderstood man in a very unstable place in a very uneasy time. I find this to be unfortunate. I would've preferred to learn about the REAL Idi Amin. I wish you the best."

The voices that view Idi Amin as a Villain are just as numerous. Again, we have provided a small sample only below but will share more as the series unfolds:

A Journalist writes: "Amin was renowned for brutally, snuffing out troublemakers. He seized power in 1971 and subjected Uganda to a reign of terror, ordering the killing of hundreds of thousands of people and expelling the country's Asian community."

Jenny, a Ugandan living in the UK writes, "My father was arrested by Amin's police on a plane at Entebbe airport and physically thrown off the plane on the runway. This happened in front of my mum and us children and we were all crying thinking he would be killed". Jenny shares how her father was taken to the police barracks, beaten and "unofficially" released by a policeman who recognized him. Because of this experience, Jenny's family fled Uganda in a convoy of English families with her father posing as a driver. "We ran a gauntlet of drunken soldiers waving guns who were shooting people for no reason. We never lived in Uganda again", Jenny adds.

Ansuya, an Asian with roots in East Africa writes, "My family was in Kenya at the time Idi Amin took control of Uganda. The impact of his actions were felt in Kenya and Tanzania as many Indians felt that their days were numbered in East Africa. My parents decided it was time to move out of Kenya." Ansuya also recounts how many of her relatives were forced to leave Uganda including an uncle in his 90s who had to leave to go to India with Ansuya's aunt who was bed-ridden. Ansuya talks about the sadness felt by a lot of people she knew who were forced to leave their possessions and relocate to England, India or Canada with only one suitcase.

Simon, a Ugandan writes, "I recall the date vividly. I was an 18-year old A-level student at Old Kampala Secondary School. The Radio Uganda announcement of the coup was read by Warrant Officer II, Sam Wilfred Aswa, followed by Major General Idi Amin himself, who gave his reasons for the coup, in halting English". Simon recounts how the statement issued by Idi Amin on the day of the coup was followed by a statement from Erinayo Wilson Oryema, Inspector General of Police at the time. He writes that Mr. Oryema informed Ugandans that he had recognized the military government. "In the meantime, the slaughter of Acholi and Langi officers and men had started on a large scale in the army barracks. For the rest of Uganda, the nightmare was only beginning!" Simon concludes.

Alan, another Ugandan writes: "As a 12-year-old boy I remember the day very vividly. The sounds of guns shooting in the air, normal programming on radio Uganda was all of a sudden cut off and all you could hear was military band music. After a few hours, an army officer came on the air, did not give his name or anything. He just said in a thick northwest Ugandan accent: "The government of Uganda has been taken over....I repeat the government of Uganda has been taken over and any interfering force will be crushed."" Alan recounts how he ran from his house to the main road because he felt that something big was going on. He saw speed-ing military vehicles loaded with troops that would sometimes beat anyone who had a shirt or dress bearing a picture of Milton Obote. Alan shares how he still vividly remembers the events of that day and opines that Idi Amin left a sad legacy because Uganda has never been the same since.

Background information for the series

Material and information taken and excerpted from Jaffar Amin's book projects, reflections by other people and other projects relating to Idi Amin provide background information for the series. It is supplemented with never before shared information about the life of the private Idi Amin as experienced by Jaffar and his siblings, immediate family members and conversations with intimate friends and associates of Idi Amin who have now become Temezi (Tribal Elders).

If you think you know Idi Amin and have already heard it all, wait till you get immersed in the series and related projects! Backup information and additional material for the series was gathered through Personal Ac-counts, Secondary Sources, The Internet, Library and Archival Research.

In the Introductory Edition, highlights of the "Life Tour" of Idi Amin Awon'go Alemi Dada (1928-2003) are provided to begin discussions relating to Idi Amin being a Hero or Villain. A future section of the series titled, "No Holds Barred Q & A Forum" will include contributions made by individuals who have something to say in relation to Idi Amin being a Hero or Villain. Whenever possible and appropriate, Snippets of History will be included in parts of the series, to provide context. There will also be sec-tions that include contributions made by individuals who have something to say in relation to the novel and hit movie "The Last King of Scotland" and various articles, books and films about Idi Amin that have been circulated since he started "behaving very badly."

Contributors will be asked to "dissect" the various articles, books and films about Idi Amin that have been circulated since he started "behav-ing very badly" and then respond to a Partial List of Questions for Discus-sion. They are encouraged to convey their thoughts about the articles, books and films about Idi Amin through their contributions.

Readers are encouraged to compare details in this series and related projects with details contained in the various articles, books and films about Idi Amin that have been circulated and presented to date then ask questions and participate in discussions. The objective is to provide a more thorough understanding of themes and issues raised by Idi Amin's legacy, while separating fact from fiction.

The future section of the series titled, "No Holds Barred Q & A Forum" will be included for information and discussion purposes only. Consequently, opinions and "allegations" that may be contained and conveyed in contributions will not necessarily reflect the views of Jaffar Amin, me as a Facilitator, Co-compiler and Co-writer or any entity or individual associated with the series and related projects.

Through the future section of the series titled, "No Holds Barred Q & A Forum", it is hoped that a little more light will be shed on how Idi Amin's image became so tarnished after initially being hailed "Jogoo! Joggo!" ("Hero! Hero!") by colleagues, being cheered by large crowds of Ugandans and being recognized by governments around the world.

Unless otherwise indicated, contributions to the future section of the series titled, "No Holds Barred Q & A Forum" may also be made anonymously in order to encourage the honesty that comes with anonymity – a factor deemed necessary for this contentious series!

Because the principle "Every accused is innocent until proven guilty" is strictly adhered to and respected, care and due diligence have been taken to minimize misrepresentations, misappropriations, errors, inaccuracies and infringements while providing opportunities for learning and gaining insight into what actually happened before, during and after the slippery path that led to Idi Amin Dada becoming one of the most reviled figures in history. Care and due diligence will continue to be taken as the Narration Process proceeds and the series unfolds.

After reading the Introductory Edition of the series, readers are encouraged to become involved in the debate and discussions about the "famous" and "infamous" Idi Amin by contributing their own opinions or just reading and hearing other people's contributions through various methods and formats. As this is a series that will unfold on an ongoing basis, contributions are being compiled and incorporated into subsequent parts of the series and related projects on an ongoing basis.

Letting the introductory edition "go"

In my characteristic "obsession" with getting all the facts right, the correct usage of English Grammar, the correct spelling and the correct style of writing, I was going to insist that we keep "checking", writing and rewriting the Introductory Edition until I was satisfied that it was "impeccable". However, I realize that it will take "forever" to do that and we might never get to a point where it is "impeccable" enough by my standards, to "release it."

Jaffar Amin has been gently "nudging" me to "Let the Introductory Edition go as it is".

In the characteristic baritone voice he inherited from his father Idi Amin, he has said:

"It is a series and we will have opportunities to correct inadvertent errors, misrepresentations and inaccuracies as the series unfolds."

"Sase, let me take the blame for the mistakes", he would laugh knowingly, because he is aware that my "obsession" with the correct usage of English Grammar, the correct spelling and the correct style of writing resulted from being "whipped in the arse in Primary School" as Ligito would laugh.

Ligito was vehemently opposed to children in Primary Schools being caned on the buttocks by teachers who insisted that all the pupils speak only English at school or be whipped hard on the buttocks.

He would often jeer:

"I can't believe Ugandan Primary School Teachers go along with "Colonial Policies" to whip children in the arse for making mistakes in the English language of all languages. What a bunch of nincompoops and stupid robots!"

Pupils were not allowed to speak any African language at school and they had to have no English spelling mistakes either or they would be whipped even harder.

I only relented to Jaffar Amin's gentle "nudging" when he pointed out that we were telling his father's story in Kakwa Adiyo narration style and format which includes other participants "jumping in to make any corrections or to state a forgotten issue". He reiterated that as the series unfolds, we would make any corrections and add information as Kakwa Temezi (Revered Elders) would in an Adiyo Narration Process.

That was when my "stubbornness" and "defiance" as a "Seasoned Advocate" for "underdogs" "kicked in" and I said:

Okay Lun'gase. Let's do it! Let's "put the Introductory Edition out there" as it is and see what it "stirs up".

The usual mischievous smile lingered on my lips as I said this because I know that "telling" Idi Amin's story "differently" is "challenging" the "status quo" and as an Advocate for "underdogs", I thrive on "challenging" the "status quo". Furthermore, telling the story the way Jaffar and I have embarked on is being audacious because it involves "refusing" to "conform" to the way the story has been told to date and "forcing" audiences to have a proper Debate and Discussion instead of accepting "gossip" as the "gospel truth!" I like being audacious because it sets me apart as a "Lead Dog" and in the case of "telling" Idi Amin's story, it gives me an opportunity to assert and argue as Ligito would that "Idi Amin didn't just happen. He was "created!"" It takes audacity to make such a bold statement and present the story in such a way that readers and participants are "forced" to confront and deal with issues related to "creating" Idi Amin instead of "sweeping" them "under the carpet" as has been the case to date!

Ligito would let off that uniquely African swear-expression done by pulling in air between closed lips and jeer "Enough of the mindless gossip and slanted accounts! It is now time to break the vicious cycle and uncover the rot that created Awon'go Alemi in the first place."

As I continued smiling mischievously, I recalled times I challenged and asserted that the "Academic and Literary Worlds" should stop being so strict about writing rules and accept "other people's" ways of writing and telling stories as valid too! I was very stubborn in asserting that considering "other people's" ways of writing and telling stories as inferior was Discrimination and Exclusionary, which prompted one of my Professors to tell me that I wouldn't survive in the "Academic and Literary Worlds". I had "agreed" with the point of view while silently musing, "Watch me!" with the characteristic mischievous smile family members and friends have learnt to discern, lingering on my lips. Some of my family members and friends know that smile so well that they regularly laugh and tease, "I know that smile!" Sometimes they do this while winking and wondering what I might have "up my sleeve" now.

Notwithstanding my "stubbornness" in wanting to "force" the "Academic and Literary Worlds" and the global community to accept "other people's" ways of writing and telling stories as valid too, I wish to state again that we apologize in advance for inadvertent errors, misrepresentations, misappropriations, inaccuracies and infringements. We will endeavor to make corrections in subsequent Editions and parts of the series as appropriate and as the Narration Process proceeds and the series unfolds.

Snippets of history

Centuries before Idi Amin was born, there were a myriad of activities and events in the global arena that set the stage for what would happen in Uganda before, during and after his rule. To present his story as if it occurred in a vacuum and without any connection to these activities and events is to rob the global community of lessons contained in the history of humankind from time immemorial. It is to negate the experiences of peoples all over the world that continue to "groan" under the very same "oppressions" that "created" Idi Amin, including but not limited to racism, colonialism, neocolonialism, classism and tribalism.

As a result, we deem it appropriate to include in the Introductory Edition of the series Idi Amin: Hero or Villain? His Son Jaffar Amin and Other People Speak, Snippets of History comprising of activities that occurred and events that unfolded in parts of the world, centuries before Idi Amin was born. In our humble opinion, these activities and events have a direct link to what unfolded in Uganda before, during and after his rule. Even though these activities and events occurred and unfolded centuries before he was born, we feel that they cannot be separated from the slippery path that led to Idi Amin becoming one of the most reviled figures in history. In fact, several of these activities and events were in our further humble opinion, the "culprits" that "created" him!

However, in order not to detract from the focus of the series, snippets only of historical activities and events are outlined and provided as an Appendix to this Introductory Edition of the series. We recommend that readers read the Snippets of History before delving into Idi Amin's story as they shed light on the story and enhance readers' understanding of themes that will emerge throughout the series.

Highlights of the snippets include but they are not limited to information on:

1)   The Age of Exploration, which was a period between the 15th century and the 17th century when Europeans initiated travels around the world in search of new trading routes and goods such as gold, silver and spices.

2)   Opening Resource Rich Africa to Western exploration and the systematic exploitation of its vast wealth through full-blown colonization.

3)   Africa as the so-called "Dark Continent" and attitudes to its exploration.

4)   Colonialism, the Colonization of Sub-Saharan Africa and the "full-fledged" greedy "Land grabbing Scheme" also known as "The Scramble for Africa" – "the proliferation of conflicting European claims to

African territory during the New Imperialism Period, between the 1880s and World War I in 1914".

     5)   The Lands that would become Uganda and Idi Amin's home.

Permit me to make a few comments about the last point above as I feel it is very crucial in understanding some issues that have a direct bearing on Idi Amin's story.

A most notable occurrence in these lands was the busyness and activities that ensued following realization by Europeans that Africa was a "gold mine" and its so-called "savage" Natives needed to be "tamed" to effectively exploit and "siphon" its vast resources. Excerpts adapted and taken from Jaffar Amin's writings titled "Eons of Plunder" and "Ki-Koloni" illustrate this busyness. The excerpts focus on events that unfolded in lands situated along the Nile from Egypt to the Kingdom of Buganda which along with other lands and upon colonization eventually became Uganda and Idi Amin's home.

As part of the activities that preceded and accompanied the colonization of the lands that would become Uganda and Idi Amin's home, we also introduce a snippet on "The Kasanvu system of coerced Labour". This was an exploitative system of "forced" and "cheap" labour that would haunt communities exploited through the system for generations to come. The snippet relating to this exploitative system of "forced" labour was also excerpted from notes, writings and reflections by Jaffar Amin that are adapted and taken from self-explanatory sections titled "Eons of Plunder" and "Ki-Koloni". As with all the Snippets of History included in this Introductory Edition, additional information outlining details relating to "The Kasanvu system of coerced Labour" will be provided as the series unfolds. However, it is important to note that this exploitative system of "forced" and cheap labour "sealed" the fate of millions of Ugandans who have continued to be labeled as inferior by bigoted Ugandans. This is because through the system, their regions of origin were designated as "labour reserve areas" and their people were exploited for cheap "menial" labour and consequently considered inferior by a "class crazy" society.

"The Kasanvu system of coerced Labour" is the very same exploitative system whose consequences have dogged Uganda for decades and manifested themselves as Tribalism and Classism on very many levels. It is also the very same system that was so despised by Idi Amin that anger arising from experiencing the form of "oppression" and other injustices might have made him:

Manhandle a bigoted White Bartender at a "Segregated" "Whites Only" Officers' Mess during colonial Uganda, as recounted by Jaffar Amin.

"Dupe" the British who allegedly assisted him in taking over the Government of Uganda from Apollo Milton Obote and "installed" him as the President of Uganda because they thought he was stupid and could be manipulated, by declaring war on colonialism, neocolonialism and "Imperialism" instead.

Act the way he did after he became the President of Uganda.

"It was as if Dad wanted to spite British Newspapers that had sung his praises and "screamed" "insults" at his predecessor Apollo Milton Obote immediately following the Military Coup that catapulted him to the position of President of Uganda. It was also as if Dad wanted to take it upon himself to mete out punishment to the British for the "sins" of the colonialism the Organization of African Unity he addressed in May 1973 aimed to redress", Jaffar has offered in narrative accounts relating to actions by Idi Amin.

In his notes, writings and reflections adapted and taken from self-explanatory sections titled "Eons of Plunder" and "Ki-Koloni", Jaffar Amin writes:

The latter half of the 19th century witnessed extensive travels to the Kingdom of Buganda by Arab Slave and Ivory traders and European Explorers. While these travels were occurring, concurrent events were also unfolding in lands situated along the Nile, including the Lado Enclave, historical home of Dad's Kakwa tribe. The Lado Enclave included "chunks" of present day Southern Sudan, parts of present day Congo and parts of present day Northern Uganda. Because the Nile has been the lifeline of Egyptian civilization and culture for millennia, events unfolding in Egypt at the time profoundly impacted tribes residing in the Lado Enclave. Furthermore, there was intense interest in properly mapping the Nile, which flowed through the Kingdom of Buganda and discovering its source. As a result events occurring along the Nile and the Lado Enclave inevitably became intertwined with events occurring in the Kingdom of Buganda - considered a possible "custodian" of the source of the Nile at the time.

The Lado Enclave was the home of the Kakwa tribe and other tribes of present day Congo, Sudan and Uganda before the tribes were thoughtlessly split through senseless demarcations during the "full-fledged" greedy "Land grabbing Scheme" that became known as "The Scramble for Africa". A history of this land will give fresh insights and understandings into the oppression known as colonialism, how it gave rise to Idi Amin and why he acted the way he did! As a result of being split into three during the period that became known as "The Scramble for Africa", the Kakwa tribe now exists as a fragmented community in Uganda, the Congo and the Sudan.

I still get amused when I recall times I was growing up in Ko'boko (Ko'buko) and witnessed Kakwa people crisscrossing the three countries of Uganda, the Congo and the Sudan to visit family members and relatives without the least bit of care for "Official Travel Documents". They were oblivious to the fact that they were considered foreigners in parts of the Kakwaland as they traversed the countries of Uganda, the Congo and the Sudan to be with family members and relatives.

Ligito had a lot to say about that and we reiterate again that opinions and "allegations" contained in his statements do not necessarily reflect the views of Jaffar Amin, me as a Facilitator, Co-compiler and Co-writer or any entity or individual associated with the series and related projects.

He always laughed as he recounted how interesting it was to watch an occasional lone "Border Patrol Officer" get flabbergasted and "blank" looks from members of the Kakwa tribe that seemed to quip, "Passport? What Passport?"

He would say:

"It serves the "Border Patrol Officers" right for enforcing the senseless demarcations!"

However, in relation to elusive dissidents and insurgents around the world who are able to cross multiple "International Borders", commit the worst forms of atrocities then "run" back to their "multiple countries" without being detected or caught, Ligito would say:

"Now you know why thugs around the world are able to "waltz" in and out of various countries, maim and murder people at will without being detected or caught."

"These thugs are able to hide behind family members and relatives in multiple countries because tribes were thoughtlessly split through senseless demarcations during the oppression known as colonialism."

"Look at what happened during Awon'go's rule in Uganda. Look at what happened in Rwanda in 1994. Look at what is happening to the Acholi people of Northern Uganda. Look at what is happening in the Congo. Look at what happened in Kenya after the 2007 Presidential Elections. Look at what is happening in Afghanistan. Look at what is happening in all the other dissident and insurgent infested countries in Africa, Asia, the Middle East and other countries around the world?"

Ligito would add that he was referring to:

Assertions made by Idi Amin himself and others that Ugandan exiles in neighbouring countries used to cross over into Uganda and murder prominent Ugandans so that it looked like Idi Amin and his operatives were committing the brutal murders.

Assertions that thousands of Hutus in neighbouring countries crossed over into Rwanda and participated in the Rwandan Genocide of 1994 where hundreds of thousands of Rwanda's Tutsis and Hutu political moderates were massacred en masse by Hutus.

Allegations that there are parties that are "colluding" to systematically annihilate the Acholi people of Northern Uganda by design. That the thugs these criminals are using to commit the genocide that has not been given the serious attention it deserves also by design are able to elude capture because they can "waltz" in and out of various countries and "blend" in with local populations.

Allegations that thugs from neighbouring countries "waltz" into the Congo and join forces with fellow thugs from their tribes to commit reprehensible crimes that include raping babies, men with AIDS intentionally raping and infecting women and men and committing other horrific atrocities.

Allegations that thugs originating from neighbouring countries joined others in Kenya and went on a violent rampage in several parts of the country after Mwai Kibaki was declared the winner of the Presidential Election held on December 27, 2007. According to reports, supporters of Kibaki's main opponent Raila Odinga of the Orange Democratic Movement alleged that the Elections were rigged and the thugs took advantage of the situation to commit some of the worst forms of atrocities under the pretext of "protesting" for so-called "Democracy".

Suggestions that it might be impossible to win the war in Afghanistan that was waged in response to the horrendous and unconscionable attacks made on the United States of America on September 11, 2001 without a different strategy. This is because members of Al-Qaeda and the Taliban can "waltz" in and out of Afghanistan and crisscross the two countries of Afghanistan and Pakistan at will, as the war continues to cost thousands of precious lives.

All the stories about dissidents and insurgents in countries in Africa, Asia, the Middle East and other parts of the world who use senseless border demarcations created by colonial powers to commit acts of violence.

The fact that it is impossible to defeat thugs around the world who take advantage of demarcations that were made during the period of colonialism that separate same peoples, without strategies that take the implications of the arbitrary demarcations into consideration.

The fact that thugs will continue to "waltz" in and out of various countries across "International Borders" and commit horrendous atrocities without being brought to justice because the oppression of colonialism has come back to bite people in the arse.

"What a bunch of lunatics and cowards. What a bunch of deranged and sorry excuses for men," Ligito would insult before letting off that uniquely African swear-expression done by pulling in air between closed lips and jeering:

"If they are so damn tough, why do they sneak around instead of facing their powerful opponents and actual enemies like real men? Why do they always go after helpless babies, children, women, the elderly and unarmed civilians instead of being men enough to face the armies they purport to be fighting?"

Historical information relating to activities and events that occurred in the global arena and in the lands that would become Uganda before and after Idi Amin was born is critical to understanding the forces that "created" him! Consequently, we hope that you have read the Snippets of History outlined in the Appendix to this Introductory Edition and trust that the information will enhance your understanding of the story. If you haven't done so yet, we encourage you to do so before immersing yourself in Idi Amin's story as the snippets serve the purpose of illuminating many factors that were responsible in part and in full for his convoluted, conflicted and controversial legacy!

Have a great learning experience!

"Our father had his faults. I do not see the period of his rule in Uganda with "rose-tinted glasses." However, we need to counter-balance history with all the truth!" (Jaffar Amin)

Grandpa's childhood

As a child in the 1800s my Grandpa Amin Dada Nyabira Tomuresu was adopted by and lived with a maternal aunt, Asungha Yasmin. According to stories narrated to me by my two aunts Awa Araba Deiyah and Awa De and other family members, Asungha was initially married to an Englishman who worked in the Southern Sudan colonial administration but the marriage ended. Following the demise of her marriage to the Englishman, Asungha married a Sikh Indian who served in the colonial police force.

Grandpa's father Nyabira belonged to the Adibu Likamero Kakwa clan and his mother Atata belonged to the Godiya-Gombe (Kelipi) Kakwa clan. Atata's mother Apayi hailed from the Ponyona Kakwa clan. She was the daughter of Gugumbi. Atata gave birth to the first born Rajab Yangu and the second born was Grandpa Amin (Andrea) Dada, who was named after his grandfather Dada lo Morobu. She also gave birth to a daughter Apayi who was betrothed to the Paranga in Ole'ba County, Maracha District. However, she never begot children in Paranga.

According to the stories I was told, Grandpa's father Nyabira Tomuresu rejected his wife Atata, forcing her to abandon the family home and return to her childhood homes among her paternal relatives the Godiya-Gombe (Kelipi) and maternal relatives the Ponyona.

As Grandpa's mother Atata left her husband's homestead, following the rejection, she was so angry that she dumped the cradle protecting the young Grandpa in a tree trunk. Her actions prompted Grandpa's thirteen-year old brother Rajab Yangu to stand guard over the toddler the same way Moshe's sister did when the Israelites were being oppressed in Egypt and Moshe's mother placed him in an Ark and hid him among reeds by the bank of the Nile River.

Like the time Moshe's sister continued to watch over baby Moshe until Pharaoh's daughter came to baby Moshe's rescue while on her way to have a bath in the Nile River, Grandpa's 13 year old brother Yangu stayed guard until their maternal uncles the Godiya-Gombe (Kelipi) came to their rescue. When the incensed war host from the Godiya-Gombe (Kelipi) clan arrived to fight the Adibu Likamero clan over my Great Grandpa's mistreatment and rejection of their daughter Atata, they were able to rescue the child. Both Grandpa and his 13year old brother Yangu were then taken to live amongst their maternal uncles the Godiya-Gombe (Kelipi).

Grandpa's brother Yangu later joined the Army of Sultan Ali Kenyi, a Kakwa Chief who served in the Colonial Administration. One of four Sultans appointed by Colonial Administrators during the colonization of Sub-Saharan Africa, Sultan Ali Kenyi who was also a Hereditary Chief and perhaps the most notorious, influential, and towering Ugandan Kakwa Chief in the first half of the 20th century was highly respected by the Colonial Administrators. He was both revered and feared by his subjects the Kakwa. According to accounts by Temezi (Elders), Sultan Ali Kenyi had no tolerance for dissent and administered lashings that left dissidents squirming in pain for weeks - even months.

During his tenure as Sultan and Chief of the Kakwa, Ali Kenyi culti-vated a friendship with Major Chauncey Hugh Stigand, OBE - a very gallant officer and capable Administrator who served in the colonial era including service in the Lado Enclave. The Lado Enclave is an area that had been designated as such by the colonialists and it included all of the Kakwa Tribe which spans present day Uganda, the Congo and the Sudan. As a result of being split into three during the period that became known as "The Scram-ble for Africa", the Kakwa tribe now exists as a fragmented community in Uganda, the Congo and the Sudan.

While serving as a Colonial Administrator in the Lado Enclave, Ma-jor Chauncey Hugh Stigand (1877-1919) had a particular fondness for Kenyi's Kakwa tribe. He was a remarkable man who spent considerable time hunting and traveling in the Lado Enclave. A posthumous book by him, considered one of the best books on the British Empire provides in depth information about the Lado Enclave.

Major Stigand's involvement in the Lado Enclave and events that occurred in relation to the Lado Enclave during the period that included the colonization of Sub-Saharan Africa will be explored in further detail as the series Idi Amin: Hero or Villain? His Son Jaffar Amin and Other People Speak unfolds. However, it is noteworthy to include here that activities that occurred in relation to the Lado Enclave had profound implications for Dad.

After Grandpa's mother Atata returned to live among her paternal relatives the Godiya-Gombe (Kelipi) and maternal relatives the Ponyona following the rejection by her husband Nyabira, Grandpa's maternal aunt Asungha was singled out to look after the young Grandpa. She left for the Sudan to join her English husband with the young Grandpa and adopted him as her own son. Grandpa's mother Atata didn't resist the adoption of Grandpa by her sister Asungha as such arrangements are common and even encouraged in most African tribes.

However, Asungha's marriage to the Englishman would end and force Asungha to return with the young Grandpa to her clan the Godiya-Gombe (Kelipi) Kakwa clan. Following her return, Asungha married the Sikh Indian who served in the colonial police force. Asungha and her husband the Sikh Indian had no children. So, they adopted and brought up Grandpa as their son.

Asungha's Sikh Indian husband was later transferred to Nsambia Police Barracks, Kampala, Uganda where he and Asungha lived, along with Grandpa. They took the young Grandpa to Nsambia Police Barracks in Kampala with them.

Regarding Asungha's unusual marriage to (cohabitation with) the Sikh Indian, the British hired Sikhs throughout the British Empire in the Armed Corps and the Police Forces. Because they are the most liberal amongst the natives of the Indian sub continent and they do not practice or abide by the horrendous caste system that views certain humans as untouchable at a religious and social level they were able to easily assimilate into local tribal communities. The Sikhs were able to have relationships based on mutual respect and even participate in intermarriages, unlike their bigoted other Indian counterparts.

When Asungha's husband the Sikh later retired from the Police Force, he set up and became part owner of a Bus business named Arua Bus Syndicate Company that plied routes in and around the West Nile region of Uganda and other parts of Uganda. At the time of writing the Introductory Edition of the book series titled Idi Amin: Hero or Villain? His Son Jaffar Amin and Other People Speak, their building had been taken over by Gateway Bus Services.

The information about Grandpa's childhood and adoption by his maternal aunt Asungha Yasmin is not available in the public domain. It is strictly Family History, which is always hard to come by like Dad's actual story. This information was passed down orally through the generations but Awa (Aunt) Araba Deiyah who was the oldest surviving child of Grandpa until her demise in 2008, was the one who told me this incredible story. So did her younger sister Awa (Aunt) De who is also fond of reminiscing about the past and they found a willing audience and listener in me because I want to learn about the past, Dad's family and Dad's full story.

I found the story relating to Grandpa's aunt Asungha marrying (co-habiting with) an Englishman and then a Sikh Indian most intriguing and can't help marveling at how brave she was because of the racism that was so rampant during that time!

Grandpa's conversion to Islam and service as a Colonial Policeman

According to Dad and other family members, before Dad was born, my Grandpa was a practicing Roman Catholic with the first name Andrea right up to and during the first decade of the 20th Century from 1900 to 1910. In 1910 however, Grandpa converted to Islam and changed his first name from Andrea to Amin. According to Dad and other family members, Grandpa was converted to Islam by Sultan Ali Kenyi the hereditary, notorious, influential, and towering Ugandan Kakwa Chief highly respected by the Colonial Administrators in the first half of the 20th century. In spite of Grandpa's conversion to Islam, many of our family members still practice Roman Catholicism and other Christian denominations.

At the time of Grandpa's conversion from Roman Catholicism to Islam, he had been conscripted as a Bugler in Sultan Ali Kenyi's Army. He served as a Bugler in the Sultan's Army from 1910 the year he converted to Islam until 1913 when he joined the Colonial Police Force and served as a Policeman at Nsambia Police Barracks in Kampala, Uganda from 1913 to 1914.

In 1914, Grandpa and others were forcibly conscripted into the Kings African Rifles - a multi-battalion British Colonial Regiment raised from the various British "possessions" in East Africa from 1902 until "Independence" in the 1960s.

After being forcibly conscripted into the Kings African Rifles, Grandpa served as a soldier between 1915 and 1921 and fought in the First World War (WWI), alongside colonial soldiers in Tanganyika which became part of present day Tanzania. Upon being honourably discharged from the Kings African Rifles in 1921, Grandpa and other veterans were allotted plots in a village in Arua, Uganda christened Tanganyika Village, after the veterans' successful Tour of Duty in Tanganyika.

The same year 1921, Grandpa rejoined the Colonial Police Force at Nsambia Police Barracks in Kampala but he maintained the plot he had been allotted at Tanganyika Village in Arua, in honour of his contribution to the First World War as a loyal soldier of the colonial powers.

When Dad was born in 1928, Grandpa had been transferred to the Shimoni-Nakasero Police Barracks where Dad was born.

My family's amalgamation with the Nubi (Nubians)

Grandpa and other family members' conversion to Islam and their involvement in the Kings African Rifles led many members of my family to develop close ties with the de-tribalised community referred to as the Nubi (Nubians). This community emerged from 19th century political upheavals in Africa that were linked to the colonization of Sub-Saharan Africa. Predominantly Muslim, this community, which spans present day Uganda, Kenya, Tanzania and other parts of Africa comprises of uprooted tribal populations whose ancestors were conscripted into colonial armies and used as mercenaries to subdue and conquer Indigenous Kingdoms in Africa.

According to an Article by the late Professor Omari H. Kokole titled "The 'Nubians' of East Africa: Muslim club or African 'tribe'? The view from within", while the "Nubi" are Muslim by faith, they do not constitute a "tribe". In the article which was featured in the Journal of the Institute of Muslim Minority Affairs in 1985 (6:2, 1985, pp. 420-448) Omari H. Kokole provides information about the "Nubi". He points out, "They have no indigenous language of their own, they do not have a tribal myth of origin of their own, they have no indigenous African names of their own and they do not have their own land or ancestral home."

It is important to note that this de-tribalised community is not the same as the Nubians or the Nuba of the Southern Sudan and Upper Egypt. However, the community comprises of uprooted tribal populations that came together in a unique "melting pot" as mercenaries for the colonial powers and their allegiance to what has been erroneously labeled as a "tribe" was cemented by their shared Islamic faith and loyalty to the colonial administrations. This "melting pot" would continue under the banner of the Kings African Rifles during the continuing colonization of Sub-Saharan Africa from 1902 until independence in the 1960s.

For the mercenaries that ended up in present day Uganda, the combined force of approximately 2,500 men were initially brought to a location near a lakeside Encampment later renamed Port Bell, along with their families. They resided in a garrison at Murchison Bay, which was eventually converted into Uganda's present day Maximum Prison at Luzira. The garrison where the mercenaries were initially placed was surrounded by so much forest that the troops remarked in colloquial Arabic, "Umon Jibu ina fil Ghaba!" ("They have brought us into a forest!"). The seashore port town of Gaba near Kampala got the name Gaba from this remark.

Due to the fact that the bulk of the mercenaries were recruited from African communities that had been colonized by the Arabs and the uprooted tribal populations were encouraged to ignore ethnic backgrounds and languages, colloquial Arabic became the de facto Lingua franca of the de-tribalised community referred to as the Nubi (Nubians). This continues to be the case to this day.

The mercenary Nubian troops that ended up in present day Uganda were eventually transferred to a location near the seat of political power at a swampy locale called Kitigulu in Entebbe, the initial colonial capital of Uganda. After a period in Kitigulu, the troops were finally transferred to the newly established Army Headquarters Barracks in Bombo in present day Luwero District in the Great Kingdom of Buganda.

With a donation from His Majesty Kabaka (King) Daudi Chwa of the Great Kingdom of Buganda, the troops built the Magnificent "Masjid Noor" in Bombo in the early 1900s. This mosque stands majestic to this day and it is arguably the oldest standing Brick and Mortar Mosque in Uganda.

Many members of the de-tribalised community referred to as the Nubi (Nubians) followed in the footsteps of their ancestors by pursuing careers in the Armed Forces of the respective countries where their ancestors ended and eventually became Naturalized Citizens of the respective countries. The ones who ended in Uganda were eventually amalgamated into the Kings African Rifles (KAR), then the Uganda Rifles (UR) and finally into the Uganda Army (UA) and Uganda Police (UP). For example by October 9, 1962, the day Uganda attained "Independence" from Britain, the Uganda Army and the Uganda Police Force were mainly manned by the Nubi (Nubians).

By January 24, 1971, the day before Dad took over power from Apollo Milton Obote in the Military Coup that catapulted him to the position of President of Uganda, the top four positions in the Uganda Army were manned by the Nubi (Nubians). Many of their counterparts in Kenya, Tanzania and other parts of Africa would follow the similar path of serving in the Army and Police Forces of the respective countries.

Like the de-tribalised community referred to as the Nubi (Nubians), my family's history with the Kings African Rifles dates back to the 19th century political upheavals in Africa that were linked to the colonization of Sub-Saharan Africa. During the time in 1914 when Grandpa was forcibly conscripted into the Kings African Rifles in order to fight in the First World War (WWI) alongside colonial soldiers, many other members of my family were also forcibly conscripted to fight in the same war.

Dad's family hails from Ko'boko, home of the Kakwa tribe in Uganda. However, the family settled in the Tanganyika Village of Arua after the First World War (WWI), following Grandpa's forcible conscription into the Kings African Rifles in 1914 and honourable discharge in 1921. This made it easier for family members to become amalgamated to the Nubi (Nubians).

Even though the bulk of my immediate family lived in Arua and Arua became the family's primary abode, Grandpa and other family members encouraged regular trips back to Kakwaland to continue to maintain the family's Kakwa roots. However, despite these efforts, many family members continued the process of amalgamation with the Nubi (Nubians) with colloquial Arabic becoming the widely spoken language by members of my family along with the Kakwa language and other languages.

The West Nile region of Uganda: a recruiting ground

From the time it was colonized, the West Nile region of Uganda was a fertile recruiting ground for the Kings African Rifles. As a result, when the First World War (WWI) and the Second World War (WWII) erupted, the Colonial Administration in Uganda recruited many soldiers from that part of Uganda including many of my family members. However, at the end of both wars, the few surviving soldiers were discharged and encouraged to re-enter farming as Kasanvu (coerced labourers), an oppressive system introduced by the colonial administration in Uganda in 1909. This history of Uganda will be explored in more detail in subsequent parts of the series, along with the colonization of Sub-Saharan Africa including the economic structure of the Uganda Protectorate, which eventually became present day Uganda. However, in order to sustain the oppressive Kasanvu system, the Colonial Administration designated the West Nile, Ma'di and Acholi regions of present day Uganda as "labour reserve areas" for the then British Protectorate and the Lake Victoria region plantation owners between 1909 and 1912. That was the beginning of a common "Kasanvu Sharecropper Heritage" shared by people from the West Nile, Ma'di and Acholi regions of present day Uganda and it would haunt communities from these regions for generations to come.

The West Nile region of Uganda was officially proclaimed a region of Uganda by Sir Frederick Jackson on May 29, 1914, Mr. A. E. Weatherhead became the first District Commissioner and went on to construct the Weatherhead Park Lane Golf Course in Arua Town by 1916. Mr. Weatherhead was nicknamed Anjereke'de by the Lugbara because of his short stature. Prior to May 29, 1914, the West Nile region was part of the Lado Enclave discussed in more detail in a subsequent part of the series.

In "compliance" with the oppressive system of "coerced labour", many people in the West Nile, Ma'di and Acholi regions understood that the only way out for them was as sharecroppers. It was the only profession that was open to most people from these regions, with the exception of Muslim Nubians who had the privileged tradition of the Armed Corps in the Kings African Rifles, following in the footsteps of their ancestors. This privilege dated back to an agreement between Salim Bey, a "Nubian" Army Officer and Captain Lugard, a British Soldier, Explorer of Africa and Colonial Administrator in the 1890s and it will be explored further in subsequent parts of the series.

The West Nile, Ma'di and Acholi regions of present day Uganda were designated as "labour reserve areas" for the then British Protectorate and the Lake Victoria region plantation owners during the same period Grandpa served as a Bugler in Sultan Ali Kenyi's Army. Despite resistance from the local populations in the West Nile region, my Grandpa and his older brother Rajab Yangu and others were forcefully conscripted into the Kings African Rifles in 1914. The forced conscription was made towards the Great War efforts in Tanganyika. My Grandpa and his older brother served in the First World War until 1919.

Grandpa's job at the District Commissioner's office

After his service in the First World War, Grandpa rejoined the fledgling Uganda Police in 1921 at Nsambia Police Barracks - the scene of his childhood under his Paternal Aunt Asungha Yasmin of the Godiya-Gombe (Kelipi) Kakwa clan. Following service at the Nsambia Police Barracks, Grandpa served at the former Shimoni and Kololo Barracks' before being allocated a job at the District Commissioner's office in Arua Township upon retirement from the Uganda Police.

Grandpa's first son, Dad's older brother Ramadhan Dudu Moro Amin was born to Grandpa and Grandma Aisha Aate in 1919. Then a daughter was born in 1925 but she passed away as a toddler and then Dad was born in 1928 at Shimoni Police Barracks in Kampala, where Grandpa was stationed as a Police Officer. By the time Grandpa retired from the Police Force in 1931 and accepted the job at the District Commissioner's office in Arua Township, he and Grandma had shifted to Kololo Police Barracks in Kampala.

After serving in the First World War (WWI) and being honourably discharged, a lot of the surviving soldiers settled and became peasants or indentured labourers in the Madhvani and Metha Sugar Plantations in the South. Others settled around Bombo among the Baganda (Ganda) tribe of Uganda. This trend would continue after the Second World War (WWII).

With the exception of Grandpa who felt it was beneath him to become a Kasanvu (coerced labourer), many members of my family joined the "settlers". Several followed in the footsteps of surviving soldiers that became peasants or indentured labourers in the Madhvani and Metha Sugar Plantations or settled around Bombo and assimilated into the Baganda (Ganda) tribe of Uganda. Grandpa chose to retire in the Tanganyika homestead in Arua that was allotted him after his successful Tour of Duty in Tanganyika, instead of settling in Buganda before rejoining the Colonial Police Force.

Madhvani and Metha are Asian families that have lived in Uganda for generations and owned sugar plantations and other businesses that employed Indigenous Ugandans until Dad asked the Asians to leave Uganda in 1972 after he took over power from Apollo Milton Obote in the Military Coup in 1971. After Dad's government was toppled in 1979, some Asians returned and picked up from where they had left off in 1972.

Embracing Islam and the Nubi (Nubians)

By the time several of my extended family members were discharged from the Kings African Rifles after the First World War (WWI) and "settled" as peasants and indentured labourers, the bulk of my family had fully embraced Islam. Owing to their strong affiliation to the Islamic faith, many members of the Kakwa community in Arua and other parts of Uganda have continued to be equated and associated with the de-tribalised Muslim community referred to as the Nubi (Nubians) and my family was no exception.

Many members of my family had fully amalgamated with the de-tribalised community way before Dad was born, including Grandpa and

Grandma. Following Grandpa's conversion from Catholicism to Islam he fully embraced Islam and immersed himself in its teachings.

Family members that had fully amalgamated with the de-tribalised community referred to as the Nubi (Nubians) were encouraged to ignore our Kakwa ethnicity and culture and identify with the Ummah (Community of Muslim Believers) instead and speak only colloquial Arabic. However, the majority of members of my family continued to hold onto our Kakwa roots and the Kakwa language, including Grandpa and Grandma.

The funniest form of an attempt to ignore our roots was by Amodo (Mzee/Elder) Rajab Yangu Grandpa's older brother who would perform ablution on Fridays. He would put on his "Friday best" and set off but every time he met a neighbor or family member that called him by his tribal name Yangu, he would turn back in disgust expressing aloud, "Astaghafurl, Allah/God forbid. Do not call me with that heathen name" and head back home to perform ablution again.

Hilariously this would sometimes happen three to four times on one eventful Friday, to the amusement of the lot, for some turned it into a game, to see how many times he would turn back with that exclamation, "Astagha-furl Allah/God forbid. Do not call me with that heathen name" and go and perform ablution to cleanse himself of his sacred indigenous Kakwa name. Instances of this self denial are encouraged and rampant to this very day, amongst so-called Nubians who reject their ethnicity wholesale.

Even though many of my family members had also fully assimilated into the Baganda (Ganda) tribe of Uganda and learnt to speak the Baganda language like the natives of Buganda, they continued to adhere to the Kakwa culture and Kakwa traditions. Temezi (Elders) consistently taught youngsters the Kakwa language and encouraged trips to Ko'boko to contin-ue to be exposed to Kakwa culture and Kakwa traditions. All children taught by Temezi always knew that the adage "Blood is thicker than water" is strictly adhered to in the Kakwa culture. The majority of members of the Kakwa tribe know you don't dare violate that teaching even if you belong to separate religions such as Islam and Christianity – two dominant religions practiced by members of the Kakwa tribe.

The de-tribalised community referred to as the Nubi (Nubians) is discussed in more detail in subsequent parts of the series, along with the significant role this community played in influencing Dad's lifestory and "writing" his script. This is because my family's "amalgamation" to this community raised a lot of issues and created a lot of problems for Dad. It had a direct bearing to events that unfolded in Uganda before and during Dad's rule in Uganda.

However, suffice it to say that the Nubi community is a truly triad cultural society combining the territorial imperative of the ongoing scrabble for Africa, the so-called "Dark Continent" which was imposed by the colonialists. Our Sufi Futuwah of the Al-Qadriyah Order and our individual ethnic origins came together in this unique "melting pot" under the Armed Forces of the emerging British Protectorate following the demise of the Belgian Monarch Leopold II, discussed in more detail in a subsequent part of the series. We have always been the Cavalry and the Vanguards in the Armed Corps and for my immediate family it was and is a family tradition.

However, despite our shared Islamic faith that was emphasized as the glue that should keep us together, it was divisions in our individual ethnic groups that precipitated Dad's overthrow and fall in April 1979. Our individual ethnic groups comprising of many different tribes in Uganda, the Congo, Sudan, Kenya, Tanzania and other parts of Africa would contribute to the "mess" that would become Dad's responsibility because he was the Head of State. The "mess" would play itself right under Dad's nose because he went along with the emphasis on the "melting pot" philosophy and gave many "impersonators" the benefit of a doubt while they went about murdering Ugandans at will.

A shared heritage of exploitation as cheap labour

It is interesting to note that as Uganda was evolving from a Protectorate to a Nation and the West Nile region of the country was officially proclaimed as part of the Protectorate in 1914, the present day Kigezi Province of Uganda was also being annexed from the former German Protectorate. After the First World War, it was proclaimed under similar circumstances to the proclamation of the West Nile region also in 1914. Consequently, the so-called Northern Hutus (Bakiga) were also incorporated into the new Protectorate. Moreover this area also became a fertile ground for the recruitment of Kasanvu to work the coffee plantations, cotton plantations and the Madhvani and Metha Sugar Plantations in Lugazi and Kakira. During this time, the Colonial Administration went as far afield as Urundi (present day Burundi) and Rwanda to recruit additional indentured labourers.

Between 1921 and 1929 the majority of indentured labourers were recruited from the regions of West Nile, Ma'di, Acholi and from the former

Belgium colony of Urundi and Rwanda. This is another "Kasanvu Share-cropper Heritage" that would also haunt communities from these latter regions for generations to come. This common "heritage" will also be discussed in more detail in a subsequent part of the series. However, suffice it to know that from the mid1920s onwards the system of indentured labour continued to grow. By the late 1940s when Middleton and Southhall's field work began, many men and women from the West Nile region of present day Uganda had spent time working in "the south", where they formed the second largest migrant group, after the so called "Balalo" from present day Burundi and Rwanda.

Because of the designation of the West Nile, Ma'di, Acholi and for-mer Belgium colony of Urundi and Rwanda as "labour reserve areas" by the colonial administration, individuals from these communities played the role of cheap, unskilled immigrants in Uganda. They formed the lowest stratum in society and were considered an under-class by a "class crazy" system until the tables were turned beginning with Dad's ascent to the highest position in the land. The common "Kasanvu heritage" between the "Balalo" who formed the bulk of Uganda's indentured labourers and the people of West Nile, Ma'di and Acholi formed the basis for the access gained into the Kings African Rifles by Grandpa and subsequently by Dad. The father of Ugan-da's President Yoweri Museveni gained access to the Kings African Rifles on the same basis.

Kasanvu migratory history and data relating to the West Nile region

With regards to Kasanvu migratory history and data relating to the West Nile region of present day Uganda, mass relocation also took place mainly due to famine between 1918 and 1921. This was brought on by the perennial onset of locust invasions, outbreaks of communicable diseases like meningitis, sleeping sickness, guinea worms, leprosy and rinderpest amongst people and livestock. Moreover infant mortality rates which have always been high in West Nile enhanced the urge to migrate. This was com-pounded by a negative tendency arising from cultural suspicions and rampant sorcery and superstitions. During the outbreaks, which occurred in the colonial period between 1933 and 1937, a staggering estimate of 60,000 labourers left the West Nile region of Uganda for Southern Uganda but out of this only approximately 44,000 ever returned.

Half of the above included Lugbara, Ma'di, Alur and Bari speaking Kakwa and Kuku from the out laying border areas of the Congo and Sudan.

Today, Uganda's Kayunga District is predominantly composed of the Kuku ethnic tribe and recent arrivals of members of the Dinka tribe in the new millennium between 2000 and 2009.

In 1937 alone, over 14,000 men migrated in search of jobs in other areas of the Protectorate before Uhuru (Independence 1962). By 1951 and 1952 the numbers were between 12,000 and 15,000, rising to over 18,000 by the year 1953 according to the Colonial Labour Report.

Because of the migratory patterns that have existed since the West Nile region of Uganda was designated a "labour reserve area", there has been an "Underdevelopment" dilemma in the Northwestern region. A worrying trend indeed showed that on average, over 35% of the able-bodied people were absent from West Nile for periods ranging from between 8 months and 2 years, causing untold psycho-social problems amongst the West Nile community at large. Examples include broken marriages, single motherhood and numerous other problems. The ethnic composition of Kasanvu from the West Nile region of Uganda included Alur, Aringa, Lugbara, Kakwa, Kuku and Ma'di Moyo/Adjumani. The rampant exploitation of human resources led to the persistent "Underdevelopment" of the West Nile region of Uganda. By Uhuru ("Independence") Day October 9, 1962, the West Nile Province and Karamoja Province were the least developed regions of Uganda. Over 45 years later in the 21st century, the very same two regions were still the least developed regions in Uganda by far.

Dad's birth and allegations of infidelity by Grandma

In 1928, as my Grandpa Amin Dada Nyabira Tomuresu set off from Shimoni Police Barracks Nakasero, for prayers offered in remembrance of the Islamic festival Eid Al-Adha amongst the Nubian Muslim shanty settlement on Kibuli Hill, a mystical hailstorm and shower engulfed the city.

Dad's brother, my uncle Ramadhan Dudu Moro, who was 9 years old at the time accompanied Grandpa on this Islamdom's holiest day in 1928. He regularly shared childhood memories of the day and the festivities that surrounded this religious festival celebrated by Muslims worldwide. I was pleasantly surprised to hear the very same tale from Fred Guweddeko a renowned Scholar and Researcher at Makerere University in 2007 when I gave my very first interview to the Sunday Mirror of UK. Eid Al Adha is one of only two recognized Holy days in Islam and it is celebrated on the 10th day of Dhul Hijja.

Dhul Hijja is the twelfth month in the Islamic calendar and it is the month during which Muslims with means go for Hijja - a cleansing ceremony that lasts for 10 days. It is during this month that pilgrims from around the world congregate at Mecca to visit the Kaaba - the most sacred site in Islam. On the tenth day of the cleansing ceremony, one is said to be as clean spiritually as the day one was born.

Muslims do not believe in original sin and children inheriting the sins of the parents. Thus on this date and following this cleansing ceremony, whatever sins one has committed are cleansed in the eyes of God. From then on, Muslims are supposed to abide by the teachings of Islam relating to good deeds and actions. The 10th day following the cleansing ceremony is called Eid Al Adha and it is the holiest date in the Islamic calendar. As a result, there are always festivities that abound on the day.

The 1928 Eid Al Adha day stuck to my uncle Moro because it was also the day his notorious kid brother Awon'go my Dad was born!

Earlier that morning, my Grandma Aisha (Asha) Chumaru Aate born in 1903 and aged 25 at the time, had begun experiencing slight labour pains but dismissed them as nothing out of the ordinary. So, she had gone about her chores as usual until the labour pains increased in intensity.

As a renowned expert in Holistic Medicine and a very experienced Cultural Midwife, Grandma Aate soon realized that this would be the day her baby would finally make its entrance into the world. However, she hid the fact from everyone and performed a self-delivery, much to the surprise of the Dada family members and friends, including Grandpa who had continued to entertain thoughts that he might not be the father of the baby his expectant wife was carrying.

Grandpa had continued to listen to vicious rumours spread by gossiping Ganda (Baganda) and Nubi (Nubians) alleging that King Daudi Chwa of the Great Kingdom of Buganda fathered the baby Grandma was carrying and not him.

The vicious rumours came about because at the time of Dad's birth, Grandma's clients included the Nnabagereka Irene Druscilla Namaganda, wife of His Majesty King Daudi Chwa of the Great Kingdom of Buganda who ruled from 1897 to 1939.

Nnabagereka means "Our Mother or Queen" in Luganda the language of the Baganda tribe of Uganda and that is how Grandma always referred to Queen Irene Druscilla Namaganda as she recounted stories about their friendship and interactions she had with both the queen and her husband King Daudi Chwa. Nnabagereka Irene Druscilla Namaganda and Grandma had cultivated an unusually close and endearing relationship after the queen was told of the exceptional skills of a certain Lugbara Holistic Medicine Woman (my Grandma) in her kingdom and Grandma treated the queen for infertility.

The queen had spent the better part of five years without conceiving, which was a terrible predicament at the time because of the fact that King Daudi Chwa would not have a direct heir to the Buganda throne. However, after the queen sought Grandma's Holistic Medicinal Services in the early 1900s and Grandma administered her fertility herbs to the queen, she conceived and bore both Princes Mawanda and Mutesa II.

Prince Mutesa II was born in 1924 four years before Dad was born and he ruled the Great Kingdom of Buganda from 1939 the year of his father King Daudi Chwa's demise until his own demise in 1969. Mutesa II was also the President of Uganda from 1963 to 1966.

Queen Irene Druscilla Namaganda was so grateful to my Grandma for her gift of conception that she demonstrated this gratitude in more ways than one including sharing the very close and special relationship she had with Grandma. Because of the unusually close relationship my Grandma and the queen shared, Queen Irene Druscilla Namaganda's husband King Daudi Chwa also became very fond of Grandma.

However, Grandma's close and special relationship with the Ganda Royal Family would bring some misunderstandings before and after Dad was born, when some unscrupulous Ganda and Nubians persisted in spreading the rumours that the Kabaka Daudi Chwa fathered Dad in the late 1920s. It was the view of gossiping Ganda and Nubians that Grandma and King Daudi Chwa were too close for comfort. The gossips were adamant in assertions that Grandma's friend Irene Druscilla Namaganda's husband King Daudi Chwa had an intimate sexual relationship with Grandma and fathered Dad.

Our family's amalgamation with the de-tribalised community re-ferred to as the Nubi (Nubians) along with its assimilation into the Ganda tribe of Uganda started to come back to "haunt" us long before Dad was born. It was how Grandpa and Grandma became "entangled" with gossip-ing Ganda and Nubians.

Needless to say, the allegations of infidelity by Grandma were false because the relationship between Grandma and the King and Queen of the Great Kingdom of Buganda at the time was purely platonic. It resulted from the gratitude relating to the precious gifts of Princes Mawanda and Mutesa II after Grandma treated the queen for infertility. The King was also very interested in the "Yakanye Order", a secret society imported into Uganda by the Nubi (Nubians), which Grandma was affiliated to and served as its Priestess.

However, the allegations of infidelity by Grandma cast enough doubt for Grandpa to reckon at the time preceding Dad's birth, "May be, just may be the baby Aate is carrying is not mine after all!"

Grandma as a "Yakanye Order" Priestess

The "Yakanye Order" was a secret African society that reportedly used sacred water and other mystical powers to instigate and win insurrec-tions and wars. According to its adherents, the society had been very successful before, during and after the 19th century political upheavals in Africa that were linked to the colonization of Sub-Saharan Africa, among other things. Since Grandma was a part of this secret society and served as its Priestess, King Daudi Chwa wanted to acquire the use of the society's powers because his reign from the demise of his father Kabaka (King) Mwanga had been one of political impotence and humiliating frustration.

The King had a fondness for the Nubi (Nubians) who had wrested Bunyoro land to Buganda during tribal wars that were part of the 19th century political upheavals in Africa linked to the colonization of Sub-Saharan Africa. He was interested in the "Yakanye Order" as he wanted to acquire its powers. The King was also attracted to the revolutionary aspects of the "Yakanye Order".

More in depth reading is required to obtain a full understanding of the history of Uganda including wars between the Great Kingdom of Buganda and Bunyoro and how King Daudi Chwa had a fondness for the Nubi (Nubians) who had wrested Bunyoro land to Buganda. Additional historical information will be provided in a subsequent part of the series for purposes of continuing to provide context to Dad's story and the history of Uganda. However, according to historical accounts, Kabaka Daudi Chwa was installed by the British Colonial Administration to the throne as a 6-day old child following the death of his father Kabaka Mwanga. He was Kabaka in name only for many years even though he ruled Buganda for 42 years from 1897 to 1939 the year of his demise.

During his rule, the Ganda Priesthood would often wonder how the Nubi (Nubians) and Lugbara managed to gain power militarily through the "Yakanye Order" and how their king could acquire those powers. Moreover the King would have gained the information about the "Yakanye Order" that Grandma belonged to from his subjects as the information continued to flourish at King George Garrison Jinja which Grandma frequented and "all roads seemed to lead to Grandma Aisha Aate's shrine". In Buganda while Grandma was the High Priestess of the "Yakanye Order" amongst the Kings African Rifles Nubians, word of her prowess got through to the "embattled and politically impotent Kabaka Chwa."

The Baganda believe that the Kabaka should be the supreme being amongst them, yet the colonialists through Sir Apollo Kagwa the Regent continued to usurp his powers in the interest of the great power, Great Britain. King Chwa was aware of the Yakanye troubles in the West Nile region of Uganda and the Ramogi Uprising and the Nubian inspired Maji Maji uprising in Tanganyika which were versions of the insurrections instigated by members of the "Yakanye Order". Therefore he too was interested in genuine Independence which is what the secret "Yakanye Society" that Grandma belonged to wanted for African tribes and communities.

As one of its Priestesses, Grandma was well versed with the "Yakanye Order" and she had information King Daudi Chwa wanted. So, the relationship between the King and Grandma also had a hint of political affirmation - attaining genuine Independence.

My Grandparents' shaky marriage and Dad's name Awon'go

Grandma was a second wife to Grandpa and traditionally, the Lugbara and Kakwa tribes of Africa have had very close associations and intermarriage assimilations. This is how my Grandma, a combined Lugbara/Kakwa from the Okapi-Bura/Rikajo/Leiko Kojoru clan of the Lugbara Tribe in Ole'ba County, Maracha-Terego District, Uganda ended up marrying my Grandpa, a Kakwa from the Adibu Likamero clan of the Kakwa tribe in Ko'boko District also in Uganda. A huge and mystical looking tree stands in our compound at Tanganyika Village in Arua as if to bear witness to the intermarriage between Grandma, a Lugbara and Grandpa, a Kakwa, even though every compound in Arua seems to have this strange phenomenon of Twin mango trees.

Awon'go as Grandma always fondly referred to Dad was the third child born to Grandma. Grandma had previously given birth to uncle Moro Dad's brother who accompanied Grandpa to the Eid Al-Adha Prayers the day Dad was born then a daughter who died as a toddler and finally Awon'go my Dad.

Grandpa had three other wives besides Grandma Aate with whom he had other children and according to accounts by family members, there were a lot of wrangles between the wives. Mariam Poya was the first wife and she was from the Gimoro/Kuluba Kakwa clan. She was married to Grandpa when she was 12 years old. She had four miscarriages before the birth to her of Dad's sister Araba Deiyah in 1925. Because of Mariam Poya's miscarriages, Grandpa decided to marry a second wife – my Grandma Aisha Aate. Grandma was from the Okapi/Rikazu clan and she was 16 at the time of her marriage to Grandpa. In 1919 she gave birth to her first born, my uncle Baba Ramadhan Dudu Moro. Her second born was a daughter who died as a child and her third born was my Dad Idi Amin Dada. Grandpa had a third wife by the name Iyaya from the Anjevu/Midia Kakwa clan and a fourth wife at a future time by the name Amori from the Kendio/Bori Kakwa clan.

After Dad was born and in spite of doubts Grandpa continued to entertain about Dad's paternity, he gave him the Islamic name Eid phonetically pronounced "Idi" by indigenous Africans and Kakwa on the very day he was born on May 30, 1928. This was because Dad's birth coincided with the ending of the Islamic Haj Celebrations marking the Islamic festival known as Eid Al-Adha.

According to the Gregorian Christian calendar used by most historians, Dad was born on Wednesday, May 30, 1928 at 4:00am at the Shimoni Hill Police Barracks, in Nakasero, Kampala, Uganda during a heavy downpour of hailstorm which is considered an omen by the Kakwa. Many sources use the Ethiopian Julian calendar in citing Dad's date of birth instead of the Gregorian Christian calendar, which would make the date of birth May 17, 1928 instead of May 30, 1928. According to the Islamic Calendar however, Dad's date of birth is 1346 Dhul-Hijja 10th Weekday Yawm Al-'Arb'a' at 04:00 because the day and time of his birth also coincided with the 10 day of Dul Hijja Al Hijriyah of that year 1928.

Contrary to false autobiographical accounts being circulated about Grandpa being a peasant, he was serving as a Colonial Policeman at the Shimoni-Nakasero Police Barracks when and where Dad was born in 1928. As well, Dad was not born in Ko'boko as many people that purport to be "experts" on his lifestory have claimed although we do hail from that very district in Uganda and it is close to our hearts.

Even though there are still slums in the area, Kibuli Hill where the Nubian Muslim shanty settlement was located in 1928 the year Dad was born, is now a flourishing suburb of Kampala the Capital City of Uganda. Many of Uganda's Nubian Muslims still reside at the same location.

Traditionally, all Kakwa names have very deep meanings and the names given to many Kakwa infants reflect circumstances and situations the infants are born into. Many times, the infants are named after events and very controversial life circumstances, as Dad would be. True to their names, some of these infants eerily grow up to be or live what is implied in their Kakwa names as Dad would. They often grow up to follow a path and live a life that mimics the names they were given as infants.

Dad was named Awon'go, which can mean the noise and "din" arising from backbiting, false rumours and false allegations. In Dad's case, the "noise" arising from being talked about during and after his rule in Uganda is a typical example of a Kakwa child growing up to "live" their name. This is because the name Awon'go can mean various things depending on the context, including but not limited to one that cries, is loud or makes a lot of noise. It can also mean the "noise" and "din" arising from backbiting, false rumours and false allegations - as was and is the case with the relentless gossip and false allegations that have continued long after Dad's demise.

It was also the case with the unending gossip that continued in relation to allegations that King Daudi Chwa of the Great Kingdom of Buganda fathered Dad and not Grandpa. Additional gossip by Grandpa's first wife added fuel to the fire!

In addition to the relentless gossip about King Daudi Chwa of the Great Kingdom of Buganda fathering Dad and not Grandpa, before Dad was born, there was constant backbiting by Mariam Poya, Grandpa's first wife. She claimed at one point that a man from the Amunupi Kakwa clan was Dad's father. Another time, Grandpa's first wife Mariam Poya accused Grandma of bearing the child of someone from the Monodu Kakwa clan. On other occasions Mariam Poya accused Grandma of having born the child of the Nubians from the Morru quarters in Arua.

Grandpa's senior wife Mariam Poya had become resentful of Grandma after having four miscarriages and giving birth to daughters who were considered inferior to sons in "ancient" Kakwa society. That fueled the spate of acrimony against her co-wife who had already borne a son Ramadhan Dudu Moro Amin to their husband Amin Dada Nyabira Tomuresu.

Moreover Grandma Aisha Aate was not one to stay home as an enterprising woman. She was constantly up and about with her good friend, the Baluchistan Indian mother of Colonel Sulieman Bai of Arua Township who grew up to be very close to Dad and stayed on in Uganda after Dad asked the Asians to leave Uganda in 1972. The close relationship between Sulieman Bai's mother and Grandma and their work as entrepreneurs fueled the rumor mills amongst the Nubian community because they frown on women being entrepreneurs and being out and about instead of staying home as "nice" and "respectable" Nubian wives and women are supposed to.

According to Dad and several of my family members, Colonel Sulieman Bai of the Baluchistan Sect and Dad shared their mothers' breasts when they were babies. Apparently when Bai's mother went off to forage for food at the local markets, she would leave Bai with Grandma Aisha Aate who would not hesitate to nurse the young Indian Baluchi child. When Grandma Aisha herself headed out to forage for food, Mama Sulieman would do the same with Dad as a baby.

Dad and Sulieman were both babies when their mothers developed a very close friendship and the close friendship that included breast feeding each other's babies would also characterize the close relationship Dad and Sulieman shared as adults.

Grandma gave Dad's older brother the Kakwa name Moro which in this context means insults because of the persistent insults she received from her rival Mariam Poya, Grandpa's first wife. The insults began long before Dad was born and continued long after he was born. However, Grandpa gave him the beloved name Dudu for being his first born son.

In addition to the insults borne by Grandma, there were also constant accusations of witchcraft, which was allegedly the reason Grandma's second born died as a toddler in 1925. In 1928, when Dad was born, Grandma deemed it appropriate to give him the Kakwa name Awon'go.

According to my beloved mother Mangarita Nakoli Bulima whom Grandma recounted the story of Dad's birth to and other Dada family members, as she performed a self-delivery and gave birth to Dad with no one else in attendance, her newborn son landed onto a pile of hailstones. This set off a resounding scream that reverberated around the Shimoni Hill Police Barracks where Grandpa was serving as a Colonial Policeman and Dad was born.

The mystical hailstorm and shower that had engulfed the city of Kampala as my Grandpa and Uncle Ramadhan Dudu Moro set off for the Eid Al-Adha prayers and festivities had increased in intensity. At the very hour Dad was born, the tropical hailstorm and hailstones were coming down with such intensity as if to announce the birth of a mystical child. Many Kakwa still believe that it is an omen for a child to be born during a hailstorm as Dad was.

Grandma told my mum and many Dada family members that Dad cried so excessively the day he landed onto the pile of hailstones as an infant that she gave him the Kakwa name Awon'go. However in accordance with Kakwa naming tradition she meant for Dad's name Awon'go to have a deeper meaning than a screaming infant.

True to his name Awon'go, Dad continued to cry excessively as a baby but he and Grandma shared a very close relationship and they had a very strong bond. Dad adored Grandma completely and it was always obvious during family gatherings! Grandma could do no wrong in Dad's eyes and she was the only one who could scold him without him answering back or being angry. True to his Kakwa name Awon'go, Dad also grew up to be and live what was implied in his Kakwa name. He lived the meaning of the name Awon'go to the fullest extent in relation to the "noise" arising from being "talked" about during and after his rule in Uganda. The "noise" and "din" arising from backbiting and false rumours followed Dad throughout his life and it translated into relentless "high tech" gossip and "lynching" that has continued long after his rule in Uganda and his demise on August 16, 2003.

The location of Dad's birth was the very same place where a round-the-clock construction and subsequent erection of the International Conference Centre in Kampala and Nile Mansions Hotel (Serena Hotel) occurred in 1975 ready for the screaming child's very own hosting of the Organization of African Unity (OAU).

The OAU was predecessor of the African Union, established on July 9, 2002 and formed as a successor to the amalgamated African Economic Community (AEC) and the Organization of African Unity (OAU).

As the Chairman in 1975, Dad hosted the Annual Conference of the Organization of African Unity in Uganda. At the conference, he shocked and amused delegates by sharing that he was born at the very site of the Conference Centre.

Infant Dad, Nakan the "sacred" snake and a Deadly "Paternity Test"

After Dad was born, the gossip and rumours about his paternity persisted until Grandpa requested for and asked Elders of his Adibu Likamero Kakwa clan to subject him to a Deadly "Paternity Test" as an infant. The unusual and dangerous ancient Kakwa "Paternity Test" which is no longer practiced involved an infant being abandoned in a jungle full of marauding wild and dangerous animals for four days if the infant was a male and three days if the infant was a female. This is because the Kakwa tribe determines a child's destiny after three to four days for the umbilical cord usually has to drop before a Kakwa infant is given a name. During the unusual "Paternity Test", if the infant survived the perilous jungle, then the child would be welcomed as a legitimate Progeny. In Dad's case, he was abandoned at the foothills of the Kakwa Legendary Mountain Liru (Mountain Gessi) for four days!

Events surrounding Dad's birth were regularly re-enacted by Grandma and other family members at family gatherings. I vividly recall a time in 1994 when Dad's uncle Siri'ba of the Piza Kakwa clan re-enacted the events of Dad's birth at a family gathering in Kawempe Kiyindi Zone in Kampala:

"Amin Dada was a particularly stern character and at the time of Awon'go's birth, he had reasons of his own for not accepting the infant Awon'go as his own", Dad's uncle Siri'ba regularly told. "Consequently, he demanded from amongst Elders of our Adibu Likamero clan of the Kakwa tribe that the infant Awon'go be taken into the jungle around the slopes of Mountain Liru and left there for four days! This was in compliance with a Kakwa tribal tradition where an infant whose paternal heritage was in dispute was taken into the jungle and left there for three days if it was a female child and four days if the infant was a male child".

"Amin Dada would only accept the infant Awon'go if it survived the cruel ordeal in the jungle. So, the Kakwa Elders from our Adibu Likamero clan relented and took the infant Awon'go into the Ko'boko County jungle around the slopes of Mountain Liru and left him there for four days! On the fourth day, when the Elders came for the child it was still alive!"

"Like an Avenging Angel, your Abuba (Grandma) Aisha (Asha) Aate strode with fury in front of her husband and the Adibu Likamero Kakwa Elders", recounted Dad's uncle Siri'ba. "At the next assembly, she placed an ancient Kings African Rifles (KAR) Rifle on the ground and pronounced a solemn curse on her husband Amin Dada Nyabira Tomuresu. She proc-laimed, "If this child is not yours and is of a Munubi, Monodu or of the Amunupi as you claim, let him languish in poverty and misery. But, But if he is of your blood, then let him prosper and succeed in this world to the highest position in the land and may you, his Father, not see of his wealth and prosperity"".

According to Dad's uncle Siri'ba, Grandma then stepped over the KAR Rifle to invoke this powerful curse. The assembly was awestruck by Grandma's curse since just the fact that the infant survived the jungle was good enough for justice to the mother and child.

This occasion made it impossible for my grandparents to live to-gether again as husband and wife. Grandma and Grandpa returned to Kampala from Ko'boko where the "Paternity Test" had taken place and attempted to live at Shimoni-Nakasero and Kololo Hill Police Barracks as husband and wife but their marriage had disintegrated beyond repair.

The rumors relating to Dad's Paternity were enough of a big deal for Grandpa to subject him to the unusual and dangerous ancient Kakwa tribal "Paternity Test" involving him being abandoned in a jungle full of maraud-ing wild animals for four days. It was also enough of a big deal for my grandparents to separate permanently and subsequently divorce after the then Policeman my grandfather Amin Dada Nyabira Tomuresu was trans-ferred from the Shimoni-Nakasero Police Barracks to the Kololo Hill Police Barracks and retired from the Police Force in the 1930s.

With regards to the Deadly "Paternity Test" that could have cost Dad his life as an infant, Grandma regularly told Dad and other family members that Nakan the Legendary seven headed Serpent ("sacred" snake) had saved Dad. Nakan is also said to have been the source of the sacred water used by the powerful "Yakanye Order" that Grandma served as Priestess for. Grandma insisted that Nakan had come to Dad and wrapped itself around Dad for warmth, as it would do around its own eggs. "Nakan placed its head on the crown of baby Awon'go's head for the duration of the ordeal", Grandma always emphasized.

Grandma's maternal uncles from the Leiko-Kozoru Kakwa clan gave Dad the name Alemi, derived from the Kakwa word Lemi. In this context it means Justice because of Dad's disputed paternity, resulting Deadly "Paternity Test" involving him being abandoned in a jungle full of wild animals and his incredible survival after four days. The name can also mean Just Cause.

In addition to "living" the Kakwa name Awon'go, Dad would also grow to "live" the Kakwa name Alemi, given by his maternal uncles. An example of Dad living the Kakwa name Alemi includes the time he evaded capture on Obote's orders and possible death and took over the government of Uganda from Obote in a Military Coup. Many Kakwa infants subjected to the same Deadly "Paternity Test", which has long been discarded, never survived the "Test"!

A similar "Paternity Test" to the one that Dad was subjected to existed amongst the Lan'go Diang (Cattle keepers), our distant cousins. In their case, they would place an infant with a disputed paternity in front of the gate of a kraal and then open the gates in the morning and let out hordes of cattle. If the child survived being trampled by the cattle, then the child was theirs! I refer to the Lan'go Diang as our distant cousins because Kakwas belong to the Eastern Plains Nilotic Dialect but we find ourselves amongst the Sudanic Lugbara speakers because we are said to have split around Kapweta, near Lake Turkana (Lake Rudolf) during early migration.

Thus began Dad's long journey from an infant abandoned in a Kakwa jungle, to "the highest position in the land" as Grandma Aisha Aate predicted. I had the pleasure of residing with Grandma Aisha Aate briefly as a child until her demise during the second week of August 1969 - a year and a couple of months shy of the day in January 1971 when Dad ascended to "the highest position in the land."

Dad defied the Deadly "Paternity Test" and grew into a strong lad, six foot four inches tall. He outshone his contemporaries by his physical prowess and leadership qualities and "defied" all odds to ascend to the position of President of Uganda on January 25, 1971. His was a very long journey punctuated by very many twists and turns – a journey that ended in Jeddah, Saudi Arabia, the Holy Land of Islam, where he died of kidney complications in 2003 and was buried in the same Holy Land. Without a doubt, Dad Awon'go made an indelible mark in the world!

The Adibu have a song which contains the lyrics "Dada na moro ku Lemi..." ("Dada I fight with Just Cause...") and most members of the Kakwa tribe know the song as the Adibu song. It is now associated with the January 1971 take over by Dad as he was reacting to a pending unfair arrest and possible execution which he overcame by taking over the government of Apollo Milton Obote in a Military Coup. Dad also regularly told us stories about his birth to the Adibu Likamero Kakwa clan and Grandma's account to him relating to Nakan (Yakan) the Legendary seven headed Serpent ("sacred" snake) that saved him as an infant.

The tale is amazingly similar to a Meso-American legend of Lord Quetzal (Ku'Kaham) relating to a prophet abandoned in a similar manner. The Meso-American legend talks about the feathered serpent, which also finds the abandoned Meso American Prophet and does a similar protection or preservation act, which saves the prophet. Yet Dad, in all his wanderings on God's Earth or Grandma Aisha (Asha) Aate, whose sphere of knowledge was strictly cultural, would never have known of the legend.

Moreover, Major Dudu Alias Adume my Kayo (Elder Cousin) from our Wangita Hereditary Line corroborated this tale. He said that the Temezi (Elders) from their Adibu Likamero clan actually encountered Nakan, the legendary seven headed Serpent ("sacred" snake) still wrapped around the infant Dad when they came to check on the results of the "Paternity Test". On seeing the "sacred" snake, the elders felt all was lost only for the "great" python to unwind its great length and gracefully slither away into the jungle on the Kakwa Legendary Mountain Liru. According to Dudu Alias Adume, the Elders were so astonished at this mystical event that they all nodded to each other, uttering, "Behold the Mata (Chief)" as they approached the baby who kept marking time with his feet in mid air like someone riding an inverted tricycle.

Over the years, people recounted Dad's ordeal in the jungle on the slopes of Mountain Liru with all the Adiyo (oral historical narrative account of history, events of the past) drama that is distinctive in Kakwa storytelling. During the years Dad was President of Uganda, many would chuckle and laugh:

"Don't joke with Awon'go!"

"Can you believe that the seven headed Serpent on the Kakwa Legendary Mountain Liru was actually found guarding and protecting him as an infant?"

"Even the Temezi were shocked when they came after four days to check if Awon'go was still alive as an infant".

"What can anyone possibly do to someone who was guarded and protected by a snake as an infant?"

"Ugandans have no idea what Awon'go was subjected to and they will never know because many think he is joking when he talks about some of the things that happened to him".

To this day, many Kakwa believe in Nakan and attribute mystical powers to the "sacred" snake. Others are still involved in serpent worship despite the influences of Christianity and Islam - the two major religions practiced by the bulk of members of the Kakwa tribe. A case in point occurred during a Lokita (Kakwa Communal Harvesting Season Event) in the 1980s in Ko'boko.

That time, one Muhammad Kamuje's wife placed their newly born son under the shade of a mango tree in full sight of the family. The family was busy in the field and did not realize that a fully-grown python was in the branches of the mango tree under which the baby was placed. Unnoticed by the family, the snake alighted and encircled the baby in a wall of shimmering serpent flesh - "protecting the child" as if it were its own eggs. Muhammad looked up from his efforts in the field only to rush towards the baby horrified at the sight of the enormous snake.

He came rushing with deadly intent to kill the serpent he felt was in the process of crushing his beloved infant son, only to be stopped by the concerned shout from his elderly mother who was also in the field.

"Don't, don't, that is our sacred snake", screamed Muhammad's mother.

"It is looking after its own. Don't!"

Not convinced, Muhammad approached slowly and to his amazement, the huge python systematically unwound itself and gracefully slithered away into the bush. The father rushed to his infant son who lay peacefully on the shawl with a certain "static warmth" still emanating from the recent mystic visitor. Muhammad's infant son was safe and sound and he grew up to tell that story!

My grandparents' broken marriage and Dad's formative years

Between 1928 and 1931 when Dad was aged 1 to 3 years, he lived with both his parents at Shimoni-Nakasero and Kololo Hill Police Barracks where Grandpa continued to serve as a Colonial Police Officer. Grandma had returned to Kampala from Ko'boko after the Deadly "Paternity Test" Dad was subjected to and attempted to continue living with Grandpa at Shimoni-Nakasero and Kololo Hill Police Barracks. However, the relationship between Grandpa and Grandma was strained and it had disintegrated to a point of no return. So, when Dad was four years old, my grandparents split.

My grandparents' marriage could not withstand the continuing and persistent false allegations that King Daudi Chwa or others fathered Dad and not Grandpa. It could not withstand the Lan'ga na Da (stepping over the Kings African Rifles Rifle) ritual that Grandma performed at the assembly following the "Paternity Test" Dad was subjected to, to invoke the powerful curse she pronounced on Grandpa. Moreover, Grandpa's first wife Mariam Poya continued the relentless gossip about other men being Dad's father. So my grandparents separated and subsequently divorced.

The separation and subsequent divorce between my grandparents had happened despite the exoneration by Elders of Dad's Paternal Adibu Likamero clan of the Kakwa tribe and the Deadly "Paternity Test" Dad was subjected to as an infant and survived!

My grandparents had attempted to continue living together before and after the "Paternity Test" but when they shifted to Kololo Hill Police Barracks where Grandpa had been transferred to, Grandma decided to leave.

In 1932, Grandpa retired from the Colonial Police Force and returned to live in Tanganyika village in Arua, Northwestern Uganda where he had been allotted a land to build a home in a homestead christened Tanganyika Village after his service in the First World War (WWI). The residence had been allocated to Grandpa as a Returnee Kings African Rifles soldier from the World War I campaign and war against the Germans in Tanganyika and he had resided there intermittently with his wives and children. Following his retirement and move back to Arua, Grandpa served in the District Commissioner's Office in Arua until the 1940s.

Between 1932 and 1936 during the time Dad was aged 4 to 8 years, after Grandpa retired to Tanganyika Village in Arua, he attended Arua Muslim School under the care of his stepmother Mama Poya where he now resided. By this time, his own mother my Grandma had completely given up the ghost of her marriage to Grandpa and headed for Semuto in Buganda to live among her relatives who had retired from the Kings African Rifles. Mariam Poya had no recourse but to look after the child of her rival because Muslim culture insists that the children remain with the father after a divorce. So, Dad's older brother Ramadhan Dudu Moro was living in his father's house as well.

While Dad lived in Arua, Grandma only sent some Sheikhs from Bombo to try and enroll young Dad in Sheikh Mahmood's Madrasa for Garaya (School of Qur'anic Studies/Readings) having finished Primary 4 at Arua Muslim School. So Dad actually spent more time as per Islamic tradition with families of the Sheikhs between the late 1930s and early 1940s because his parents were devoted to the teachings of Islam.

Arua Muslim School where Dad attended school during his formative years was also known as Muhammadian Primary School. This is a reference made by Christians who insist on calling us followers of Muhammad Muhammadians. This they do even though we insist that we are Muslims and do not follow Muhammad but the revelation from God the Almighty Creator that was entrusted in his hands. All colonial designations used the derisive title Muhammadian which was a favourite name calling by Orientalists (those who study Eastern Culture as opposed to Occidentalists who study Western Culture). Arua Muslim School had an academic syllabus that included and stressed the teachings of Islam.

Several of Dad's classmates and schoolmates at Arua Muslim School became close associates of his after he ascended to the highest position in the land of Uganda on January 25, 1971 and they remember him well. Among them was a Naturalized Munyoro OB (Old Boy) classmate called Kiiza and his sister Nyakayima who became Dad's flame in his teenage years, right up to his first stint in the Colonial Army. However, when Dad came to Grandpa to seek consent to marry Nyakayima, Grandpa refused to accept the marriage. He complained that Nyakayima's mother was an Alur and that they were fond of "night dancing" activity (Jokjok or witchcraft) – an allegation that persists in some circles to this day. Nyakayima's brother Kiiza and Dad attended Primary One right up to the limit of Primary Four together. It was the official stipulated level allowed by the Colonial Administration for Muslim schools.

According to family members, Grandpa rejected Nyakayima as Dad's choice of a bride because he had issues with a neighbour of Alur stock who was a notorious "night dancer" and was fond of targeting his

eldest son, Dad's brother Ramadhan Dudu Moro for nocturnal strangula-
tion. Family members regularly recounted how Grandpa put a stop to the
activities of the Alur "night dancer" neighbour who regularly hounded and
"strangled" my uncle Moro at night as a young lad using Jokjok (witchcraft).
The incessant activity did not bode well for Grandpa so he took off towards
his Godiya cousins of the Godiya Bura who resided in Oci'ba Parish at the
time and requested for a solution. One of Grandpa's Godiya cousins was a
renowned "Jokjok Catcher".

That very night on one of her nocturnal forages, the Alur neighbour
somehow could not extricate herself from right in front of the hut in which
Ramadhan Dudu Moro Amin was soundly asleep. In the morning, an
amazing sight met the early risers who had come out to sweep the compounds as they did every morning. The women started to cause an alarm
calling the man of the homestead. "Magoo! Magoo! Amonye (Father)!
Come and see this spectacle!" they exclaimed.

Grandpa grabbed his cane knowing very well what the outcome of
the commotion outside his hut was, for standing frozen in front of his son's
hut was the culprit - stark naked and in a trance like state, unaware of the
commotion surrounding her! Approaching her slowly in the hushed silence
of the multitude that had gathered to watch the spectacle, Grandpa simply
tapped the culprit with his walking stick and her eyes blinked back into
reality only to gaze into the hostile faces of the whole Jiako village in Arua.
Realizing the danger she was in, she dropped to her knees in front of
Grandpa when he asked, "What should I do with you?" The women quickly
brought a kanga (a wrap around cloth) to cover her shame while she
continued to plead her case.

The issue was resolved with a heavy fine and ever since that incident, no one has ever had the courage to wonder aimlessly on the Amin
Dada homestead apart from the time the whole of West Nile was emptied
during the 1979-1986 civil strife in Uganda. It was because of this experience that Grandpa came to the "blanket" conclusion that the Alur were
fond of "night dancing" activity (Jokjok or witchcraft).

Almost 25-30years after his eldest son's woes with an Alur, he
couldn't accept that his second born son picked interest in "these people's
maidens". His answer was a resounding no! He was adamant that he would
not accept his son's choice.

In Nubian culture the father usually makes the first choice of wife
for the son, the second, third and fourth choices are his own after that. So
Dad gave up his marriage to Nyakayima. However, he remained close to his

classmate Kiiza an unacknowledged Electrician who would have two notable encounters with Dad at future dates before and during the time he was President of Uganda.

"At the time, the up and coming Idi Amin came to my workshop with his gramophone so that I could repair it", Kiiza recounted to me when I started researching Dad's story and talking to Temezi (Elders).

"However, when the repair was done Idi came in, picked up the machine and as he attempted to walk out, I asked for my money only to get an Nkonzi/Ngolo (knuckle rap) on my head".

According to Kiiza, he went crying to his Dad but he wasn't able to do anything. Years later when his OB Dad was in power, they met when Mzee (Elder) Kiiza was patiently waiting for a hair cut.

Grandma's continuing association with the Buganda Royal Family

After the divorce between my grandparents, Grandma lived with her relatives who had retired from the Kings African Rifles and were living in Bombo, Semuto-Luwero, on the outskirts of Kampala, the Capital City of Uganda. Queen Irene Druscilla Namaganda and King Daudi Chwa continued to be thankful for the gift of life of the two Princes Mawanda and Mutesa II. So, Grandma continued her close association with the Royal Family. Born after Grandma administered Fertility Herbs to the queen, the two Princes held a very special place in Grandma's heart. The relationship between Grandma and the King and Queen was so close that the Kabaka Daudi Chwa even built for Grandma a house in Kitigulu at a marshy site just as you approach the Ugandan city of Entebbe some 26 miles from Kampala.

Surprisingly, upon my arrival from a one week trip to Tripoli, Libya on September 15, 2009, I was informed by the brother of the Cultural Prime Minister of the Lugbara Chiefdom that the whole Kitigulu, Entebbe marshes where the Nubians reside was leased by Dad for 99 years! The brother of the Cultural Prime Minister of the Lugbara Chiefdom also resides in Kitigulu, Entebbe and owns the land adjacent to the land in question.

The relationship between Grandma and the Royal family will be explored in more detail in subsequent parts of the series. However the Kabaka had a homestead on the way to Nsamizi Hill overlooking the Old Airport and Kitoro Trading Centre in Entebbe and Grandma and Dad were always welcome there.

King Daudi Chwa continued to have fondness for the Nubi (Nubians) after Grandpa and Grandma divorced, and he continued to be an ardent visitor to Grandma's shrine to continue to learn about the "Yakanye Order". The focus of the "Yakanye Order" was to expel foreigners and it started with a bitter experience against the Arab slavers, the Azande Empire and the Makaraka/Kakwa hegemony over the Sudanic tribes. Thus even though tribes like the Lugbara were aware of the bitter collusion Kakwas like the Sultan of Gulumbi and Sultan Ali Kenyi had in selling them to Arab slavers, they went to the same Kakwa to acquire the powers of the "Yakanye Order". They went to Kakwa lineages that had their strong roots in the Ole'ba section of the highland Lugbara who trace their maternal lineage to the Midia, Godiya, Padombu, Okapi and other Kakwa clans.

Ironically, Grandma's son (my Dad) would be the one that would fulfill the aspiration to attain genuine Independence on behalf of his Foster Parent King Daudi Chwa when he launched his notorious so-called Economic War in 1972. The saying goes that "Idi Amin opened our eyes". It still reverberates amongst Indigenous Ganda and other Ugandans to this very day. This has happened even though Dad was derailed from implementing his agenda for Uganda and other African countries to attain genuine Independence by his detractors, saboteurs and subversive elements that came in and out of Uganda at will and brutally murdered Ugandans during his rule, to tarnish his reputation.

Allegations and rumours that King Daudi Chwa of the Great Kingdom of Buganda was Dad's father and not Grandpa persist to this day, in dubious Baganda and Nubian circles. Many Ganda and Nubians continue to "whisper", "Idi Amin was a Muganda and not a Kakwa".

Some Ganda admirers of my Dad who consider him a hero have boldly stated, "He is one of our own!" They even boast of Dad having similar authority, power and dominion to mighty Buganda Kabakas of old such as Suna, Mutesa I and Mwanga. "Just look at the parallels", they insist after reading and listening to oral historical accounts offered about Suna, Mutesa I and Mwanga, by people in the know.

More extensive information about the "Yakanye Order" will be provided and explored in subsequent parts of the series, along with an understanding of how my father built an inter-linking system. However, it is important to note that since Uganda attained "Independence" from Great Britain, there have only ever been three systems in Uganda. These systems are Uganda People's Congress, which came up with the Common Man's Charter (Autocratic African Socialism), Aminism (Nationalist Martial

Absolute Rulership) and National Resistance Movement (Pragmatic Marxism, preceded by Anarchy in the 1979-1986 period). Prior to "Independence" there was the Colonial Administration (Monarchists).

On a visit to the RABITA (Arabic Acronym for World Islamic League, the Islamic Charitable Foundation of Saudi Arabia) offices in Kampala and upon my introduction, the Ugandan Director intimated to having known that Dad once stayed at Mengo during his childhood. Very conversant with the history of Dad's stay at Mengo, Kitigulu and at King Daudi Chwa's Entebbe residence, overlooking Kitoro with a good view of the Airport, the Director told me about Dad's life as a child. He confirmed that after my grandparents' marriage ended, Grandma continued her relationship with the Ganda Royal Family and Dad was always welcomed at the Royal Palace.

King Daudi Chwa ruled Buganda from 1897 to 1939 the year of his demise. His son Mutesa II who succeeded him after his demise in 1939 was the Kabaka (King) of Buganda from 1939 until his own demise in 1969. Mutesa II was also the President of Uganda from 1963 to 1966 when he fled for his life and lived in England until his demise.

Grandma's second marriage to Mzee Ibrahim

While living in Buganda with her relatives who had retired from the Kings African Rifles, Grandma married Mzee Ibrahim, a retired ex-services man. After Grandma married Mzee Ibrahim, her contact with the Ganda Royal Family became minimal. This was also the time she and Dad ventured into Central Uganda and began experiencing severe poverty. By this time, Dad was now living with Grandma on a more permanent basis.

It seems that with the demise of Kabaka Chwa, so did Grandma's influence at the King's Palace. Moreover Queen Druscilla went on to marry a Reverend to the consternation of the Ganda Lukiko (Buganda Parliament).

I believe that the allusion to Grandpa being a peasant by Dad's detractors came about with Dad's venture into Central Uganda in the footsteps of his mother who was now living with her new mate Mzee Ibrahim. For after Primary Four in the bosom of his father's secure home in Arua and a short stint with the Ganda Royal Family, Dad started his adventures in Bombo-Luwero District, Kawolo-Lugazi District and Buyukwe-Kayunga District after Grandma married Mzee Ibrahim and the rest is history!

Dad and Grandma lived at Semuto-Luwero for 4 years, from 1937 to 1940 when Dad was between the ages of 9 and 12 years old. While living at Semuto-Luwero Dad would sometimes live and work at the Metha Sugar Plantation in Kawolo, Lugazi, Uganda, as a Kasanvu (coerced labourer), to supplement Grandma's meager income. Grandma was still practicing Holistic Medicine and Cultural Midwifery but her clients were now few and far in between.

Dad's immersion in the teachings of Islam

When Dad finished Primary Four at Arua Muslim School, Grandma sent a delegation of Nubian Ulama (Learned Religious Scholars) to convince Grandpa to release Dad into the hands of the famous Sheikh Mahmood and his Madrasa and Grandpa relented.

Dad started out in Semuto where Grandma made intermittent visits then he moved to Mzee (Elder) Yusuf Tambu's home in Bombo, which is just across from Masjid Noor on the Kampala-Gulu Highway. Dad became neighbours with Abdul Qadir Aliga, a fellow student in Garaya (School of Qur'anic Studies/Readings) who would go on to become a renowned Sheikh.

By 11 years, Dad had progressed to the Khanqah (Islamic Centre), which is the equivalent of a Catholic Mission in Kawolo. This had happened while Grandma had also moved from Entebbe to Kawolo and finally to Bundo-Kidusu - about 15 miles from Kawolo on the outskirts of the vast Sugar Cane Plantation and out growers. It is on the old Jinja Road that skirts the lakeshores of Lake Victoria.

After leaving Dad in the care of the Sheikhs at Semuto-Luwero for 4 years, Grandma had eventually permanently shifted to Lugazi and finally, to the place called Bundo-Kidusu in Buyukwe Mukono District on the Old Kampala Road. It was at Bundo-Kidusu that she established her roots and my family finally settled. Even after her demise, the Baganda in the area recognize the land as hers and keep requesting for her grandchildren to come and reclaim it. It is ironic that I was the last of Dad's children to live at that residence for Grandma's death found me residing with her at Bundo.

When Mutesa II succeeded his father Daudi Chwa as King of Buganda in 1939, Dad was 11 years old. He had just fulfilled the obligations in the Al Qadiriyah Kankah in Bombo by going to make a formal Koranic Recital in Kawolo, Lugazi, Uganda, in front of a multitude of Ulama (Learned Religious Scholars). Muhammad Fataki, 13 years old at the time witnessed the rite of passage of 11 year old Dad and Abdul Qadir Aliga as Alim al Qur'an (memorizer or those who have managed to memorize a sizable chunk of the Holy Qur'an at a very young age).

In 1939 when Dad was 11 years old, he impressed Muslim clerics by his impeccable skills in reciting the Koran - so much that many of his classmates continued to heap praises before, during and after his rule in Uganda. It was a formal requirement for young lads to recite the Koran in front of a multitude of Ulama in fulfillment of obligations in the Al Qadiriyah Khanqah (Centre) in Bombo. The word Ulama, which means "Learned Persons" is derived from the Swahili words Mwalimu (teacher), those with learning ("Ilm") - Swahili - Ililimu. On this occasion, Dad travelled to Kawolo, Lugazi to make the formal Koranic Recital.

Sheikh Muhammed Fataki of Gulumbi remembered that day very well for he was a 13-year old boy at the time. He distinctly remembered that Dad was given the task of reading and asked to choose a recital and he of his own accord chose the extremely long Sura Al-Karf (one of the verses in the Holy Qur'an), which he recited to the astonishment of the learned Ulama. Dad and Abdul Qadir Aliga who became a Sheikh excelled in Qur'an memorization and won many accolades throughout their pre-teen years. To Aliga, Islamic priesthood beckoned but for Dad the attraction of the Kings African Rifles (KAR) Military Barracks was most comfortable.

The Al-Gadariyah had Madrasas in Semuto, Bombo's Masjid Noor and the Nubian Settlement in Kawolo. As pupils progressed, they were sent onwards to the next Khanqa (Centre).

Dad's progression at the age of 11 found him in Kawolo deep in the Sugar Plantations and it was here that he had a stint doing manual labour as a sharecropper among other low paid sharecroppers and labourers. Other than the Armed Forces for Nubians, it was the only work available in the area for Nubians and other people classified as lower class by Uganda's "class crazy" society at the time.

In Garaya (School of Qur'anic Studies/Readings), when one entered the Khanqa one went and stayed with the Holy men. That was how Dad joined Sheikh Mahmood's family in Semuto in 1941 and enrolled in the Garaya Islamic School at Bombo (Al-Qadriyah Darasah Bombo (Al-Qadriyah Khanqa, Masgid Noor Bombo)), Uganda, under Sheikh Mahmood. Thereafter Dad lived at Mzee (Elder) Yusuf Tambu's also in Bombo. Over the next three years, the Islamic scholar Sheikh Mahmood tutored Dad.

While at Bombo, Dad had also attempted Primary School, sporadi-cally combining this with the Garaya (School of Qur'anic Studies/Readings) he had become immersed in. During the time Dad was fulfilling the formal requirement for young lads to recite the Koran in front of a multitude of Ulama in fulfillment of obligations in the Al-Qadriyah Khanqa (Centre) in Bombo, Grandma was away in Entebbe. After Entebbe, she shifted to Kawolo District in Uganda where she eventually resided with her new mate Mzee Ibrahim in Bundo-Kidusu in Buikwe District.

The "Arabinization" of indigenous African Muslims

Additional information about the obligations in the Al-Qadriyah Khanqa which Dad did at 11 years in Bombo by going to make a formal recital in Lugazi in front of a multitude of Ulama will be provided in a subsequent part of the series, along with information about the Ulama. However, below is information about the "Arabinization" of Indigenous African Muslims, personified by Sheikh Muhammed Fataki of Gulumbi.

Sheikh Muhammad Fataki of Gulumbi has been praised for possess-ing vast knowledge in the history of both the Kakwa and Ulama. He became so immersed in Islam that he actually followed in the footsteps of his great grandfather by sending children to Khartoum in Northern Sudan to be "proper" Muslims – the same way Christians would send their child-ren to Christian Mission Schools. Staunch Kakwa Muslims and Muslims from neighbouring tribes send their children to the best Muslim schools in the Sudan to become "fully fledged" members of the Muslim Ulama, which frowns upon one identifying with tribe instead of Islam, yet the Prophet Muhammad was very comfortable with kin and ancestry.

Nevertheless, the likes of Ja'far Bin Abi Talib the prophet Muham-mad's cousin who led the Emissary of fleeing Muslim refugees to Ethiopia and their descendents discouraged identifying with tribal kin and ancestry in favour of identifying with the Ummah (Community of Muslim Believers). The same thing happened with Umar Bin Khatub the second Khalif after Abu Bakar who was the first Muslim Ruler after the Prophet and their descendants. Umar Bin Khatub and his descendants covered and traversed the African region spanning the shores of the Atlantic in Senegal right up to Port Sudan in an effort to convert Indigenous African tribes into Islam. The great Malian kingdom and other kingdoms were Muslim Empires.

Somehow when the likes of Ja'far Bin Abi Talib's descendents went on their missionary trips into the Sudan proper and Umar Bin Khatub's descendants went on their missionary trips to the Bilad Al Sudan (Land of the Blacks), they had a hidden agenda. Their conquest seemed to concentrate on us Indigenous Africans relinquishing our African Heritage and adopting Arab names. Becoming Fadhil Al Mullah, Salim Bey, Idi Amin, Muhammed Abdul Wahab, Jaffar Amin and many other Arab names was in line with the effort to relinquish rich African names in favour of Arab names.

Dad's exploitation as a Kasanvu and mistaken identity as a foreigner

Dad's family's exploitation as Kasanvu (Cheap Labourer(s)) began decades before he was born. This was when the colonial state in Uganda introduced the Kasanvu system and designated the West Nile, Ma'di and Acholi regions of present day Uganda as "labour reserve areas" for the then British Protectorate and the Lake Victoria region plantation owners. It was a system that was designed to keep coerced labourers as an underclass in perpetuity and my family was one of the families caught in this vicious circle of poverty and Kasanvu system of coerced labour.

The labour migration of adult males from the West Nile and Ma'di regions of present day Uganda to work in sugar and cotton plantations located in the Lake Victoria region continued during Dad's childhood. In line with the age-old southward trekking of West Nilers in search of Jobs and "greater" economic opportunities in Buganda and Busoga, a lot of our tribe mates settled and became peasants or indentured labourers in the Madhvani/Kakira and Metha/Lugazi Sugar Plantations in the South. In the process of looking for so-called "greener pastures" they unwittingly continued to "conform" to the designation of "labour reserve areas" for the British Protectorate and the Lake Victoria region plantation owners by the Colonial Administration.

I strongly believe that Dad began despising Uganda's Elitist System during the time he lived and worked at the Metha Sugar Plantations in Kawolo, Lugazi, Uganda. As a young lad, he worked intermittently as a Kasanvu in this Sugar Cane Plantation owned by Ugandan Asians, along with several of my family members.

Furthermore, Dad and the other Nubi (Nubians) were denied educational opportunities because they were considered foreigners when nothing could be further from the truth. This error in labeling Dad as a foreigner would persist when:

"Many Ugandans and much of the rest of the world believed that Uganda was, by and large, under the ruthless rule of an alien during the period between January 25, 1971, and April 11, 1979, when Id Amin was President of Uganda" (Omari H. Kokole).

According to Dad, he participated in riots organized by the Nubi (Nubians) to protest the injustice of being denied education. This had happened when he was twelve years old. During these riots, Dad was injured and arrested but released.

The above incident was corroborated by renowned researcher Fred Guweddeko, who wrote about Dad being arrested at 12 years old and the arresting officers releasing him because was too young to face charges. This is also the specific time thoughts of joining the Kings African Rifles loomed large in Dad's mind.

Fred Guweddeko and I have had a lot of discussions about Dad and he has done a lot of research which along with various other material relating to the debate about whether Dad was a hero or villain to the core, provides background information for the section of the series titled "Other People Speak". His articles are available in the public domain for anyone wishing to "dissect" them and offer related opinions.

The demonstrations Dad participated in were against the colonial policy that restricted Nubians and Muslims from furthering their education beyond Primary Four unless they joined a Mission school, which was contrary to Islamic requirements and teachings. One Christian Teacher who so happened to be the father of Honourable James Baba, who held various portfolios under the government of Yoweri Museveni was one of the pioneers of further studies at Bombo.

Dad's gig on the SS Yoma, a World War II navy ship

By the time Dad was born in 1928, our family had been heavily "invested" in the Kings African Rifles (KAR), the multi-battalion British Colonial Regiment raised from the various British "possessions" in East Africa from 1902 until independence in the 1960s. So, it was only natural that he would aspire for a career in the Armed Forces. Over the years, the Kings African Rifles had employed more members of my immediate and extended family and become a career path Dad would also aspire to as a child. As Dad searched for better opportunities, he would periodically spend time at the Al-Qadriyah Darasah Bombo and work as a Kasanvu at the Metha Sugar Plantations, like several members of our immediate family.

At 12 years old, Dad landed a gig in the Kitchen Mess of the Kings African Rifles aboard the Navy Ship named SS Yoma during the Second World War. According to him and others, he started his career in the Kings African Rifles in 1939 when he landed the gig at the Kings African Rifles Kitchen Mess as a Kitchen help. He would eventually join the Fighting Unit.

Sheikh Muhammad Fataki Dad's colleague at the Garaya (School of Qur'anic Studies) confirmed that the year after Dad received accolades for his unparalleled skills in reciting the Koran, he was in Bombo when he heard that Dad and Sul Wayi Wayi and some others had joined the Kings African Rifles. Sul Wayi Wayi is a nickname for Dad's Associate Captain Ismail Khamis.

Dad's gig in the Kings African Rifles Kitchen Mess took him aboard the Navy Ship SS Yoma during the World War II years. He told us a lot of stories about his encounters on the Navy Ship SS Yoma, which plied the following sea route and back between the World War II years in consecutive order:

Mombasa Port

Cape Town

Madagascar (the mysterious Island nation in the Indian Ocean off the Southeastern Coast of Africa)

Mombasa Port

Mogadishu

Djibouti

Aden

Port Sudan

Suez Canal

Dad, Ronny Bai of the Piza Leiko Kakwa clan and Ozo of the Ayivu Lugbara clan in Jiako village were conscripted into the Kitchen Mess of the Kings African Rifles on the very same day in 1939, along with a Munyoro colleague. They couldn't stop talking about working as Kitchen Help aboard the Navy Ship SS Yoma during the Second World War (WWII).

Dad's claims about having participated in the Second World War (WWII) have most often been ridiculed by all and sundry, especially his detractors. However, I had a most touching meeting with Ronny Bai of the Piza Leiko Kakwa clan on July 7, 2007 and he put the matter to rest. During that meeting, Ronny Bai corroborated and confirmed Dad's story about having participated in the Second World War (WWII). He said that he along with Dad, were two of three people recruited to work in the Kitchen Mess and aboard the Navy Ship SS Yoma during the Second World War on the same day in 1939.

The meeting between Rony Bai and me took place at the Funeral Gulomo Ceremony (Kakwa tribal ceremony honouring and telling the story of the dead) of my uncle the late Flight Captain Amule Kivumbi Amin. On that occasion, Ronny Bai specifically asked to see and have a word with me at Turupa Parish in Ko'boko. He proceeded to give me an account of how he joined the Armed Forces at the very time that Dad and Ozo joined - amazingly in the year 1939!

According to Ronny Bai, the following were their Conscription Numbers when they were recruited to work in the Kings African Rifles Kitchen Mess:

N-14610/Idi Amin Dada-Kakwa/Lugbara

N-14611/Ozo-Ayivu of Jiako Village

N-14612/Ronny Bai-Kakwa

The three veterans had sequential conscription numbers and Ronny Bai confirmed that they indeed all joined the Kings African Rifles on the very same day in 1939.

I was honoured by the fact that Temezika (an Elder) Ronny Bai saw it fit to ask to have a word with me on that day July 7, 2007 at Turupa Parish in Ko'boko - the date of my Paternal uncle Amule Kivumbi Amin Dada's Gulomo Ceremony.

After my conversation with Elder Ronny Bai I was now convinced beyond doubt about stories Dad used to tell us about his encounters during the Second World War (WWII). Dad used to reminisce about working in the Kitchen Mess of the Kings African Rifles during the Great War and how they were stationed aboard the American triple storied Navy Ship SS Yoma. According to Dad and Rony Bai, the trio worked until the end of the Great War in 1945.

According to Ronny Bai indeed he and Dad were all stationed on the triple-deck Navy Ship, which was under the East Africa-Overseas American (Allied) 44th Battalion, 27th Division USA under the coalition (Allied Forces Coalition Against Hitler). The ship was initially under the command of CO General Smith, who was later replaced by General Damilion upon his death. General Damilion's 2IC (Second in Command) was one Major Ray.

I put Ronny Bai through a grueling random examination (interrogation) Stazi fashion in order to properly corroborate the evidence he was giving and it turned out that he and Dad and others indeed joined the Kings

African Rifles as Kitchen Mess Help in 1939 under the Conscription Numbers listed above. This had happened while Dad was a lanky under age Youth.

The Former "Cold War" East German Secret Police Force was renowned for "effective" interrogation tactics. Uncle Wani Diloro of the Bari tribe used to show us his style of corroborative tactics to find out what someone knows or does not know. He was one of those sent to East Germany by Dad, to train as a Secret Service Agent. I tend to use the style to glean information from people.

In the stories Dad told about the Second World War, he had claimed that during the war, he was on board a ship that was downed by a U-Boat and an American Destroyer rescued them. Records show that the Navy Ship SS Yoma was sunk on June 17, 1943 between the Port of Alexandra and the Libyan Coast. So, Dad's story definitely has some truth to it.

Moreover according to Dad, the rescue team had wanted to send them all the way to the United States of America! In jest Dad used to say, "All my seeds, all of you would have ended up being Niggers", the rude and unacceptable reference to African Americans by bigoted people. Dad would accompany this rude, derogatory and unacceptable reference to African Americans with his usual teary earth quaking laugh as if to say "stupid bigoted White people" who stole Africans and enslaved them in America for centuries.

Dad liked to crack jokes and laugh even though some of his jokes could be very annoying and in terrible taste. No one was exempted from Dad's jokes including us his children, family members, associates and foreign dignitaries. We just learnt to take them as they came.

The irony is that Dad himself was an Indentured Labourer and "Slave" in his own land even though many "Africans" in the Diaspora including African Americans "enslaved" for centuries, tend to differentiate between Indigenous Africans and the lost souls who ended up either in the Arabian Peninsula or the Americas by force. Dad regularly talked about the African Slave Trade and the deplorable conditions Africans were subjected to as they were being transported to the Americas to work as slaves.

Dad's conscription into the Fighting Unit of the Kings African Rifles

According to Elder Ronny Bai Dad's colleague who confirmed that he and Dad and others indeed worked in the Kitchen Mess aboard a troop carrier Navy Ship named SS Yoma during the Second World War, Dad tried to join the Fighting Unit of the Kings African Rifles (KAR) during their gig. However, he was considered under age. So after the gig, he came to stay with Abuba (Grandma) Dusman and Mzee (Elder) Khamis Walala of the Morodu Kakwa clan at Kawempe Kiyindi Zone in Kampala.

While living with Abuba Dusman and Mzee Khamis Walala, Dad landed another gig at the Grand Imperial Hotel in Kampala where he worked as a Bellboy of sorts. He landed the gig at the Grand Imperial Hotel between the ages of 17 and 18.

The Grand Imperial Hotel was one of the first hotels to be built in colonial Kampala and the only hotel that has been used by every governor of the colonial era. It would be at this hotel that Dad would meet a Scottish Officer, assert his interest in joining the Fighting Unit of the Kings African Rifles and be formally recruited into the Fighting Unit of the Colonial Army.

This is the scene of the account by Dad's biographer Judith Listowel when in 1946 Dad supposedly requested a Scottish Officer, in simple Kiswahili, "Sir I want to join the KEYA (KAR)". He was conscripted then under what would be used as his first official conscription number of N44428 and stationed at Magamaga for training. The rest is history!

According to Dad's Biographer Judith Listowel and on record, 1946 is the actual year in which Dad was recruited into the King's African Rifles (KAR). However as I outline above, by 1946, he had already had a gig and stint with the Kings African Rifles. He regularly told that he was conscripted into the Army in 1939 as has been corroborated by his colleague on the troop carrier Navy Ship SS Yoma, Mzee (Elder) Ronny Bai.

Furthermore, during his rule from January 25, 1971 to April 11, 1979, Dad once scouted a Munyoro work mate – another colleague who worked with him aboard the troop carrier Navy Ship SS Yoma in the Kitchen Mess. According to renowned Researcher Fred Guweddeko, while on a tour of the Bunyoro region as President of Uganda, Dad was making a

speech when he scouted the former work mate amongst the crowd. That
time, he proceeded to ask this work mate to come over and the man
confirmed that they had worked together on the triple-decker troop carrier
Navy Ship SS Yoma during the World War II years.

I was thrilled when Elder Ronny Bai told me that the following sequence of conscription numbers, which were the conscription numbers
assigned to the three of them do exist:

N-14610 / Idi Amin Dada-Kakwa/Lugbara

N-14611 / Ozo-Ayivu of Jiako Village

N-14612 / Roni Bai - Kakwa

The revelation by Elder Ronny Bai when he specifically asked to see
me as he paid his respects at the cultural funeral vigil for my uncle, the late
Flight Captain Amule Kivumbi Amin was unbelievably intriguing. This is
because it corroborated the many intriguing stories Dad told us about his
encounters aboard the triple-decker troop carrier SS Yoma. In Judith
Listowel's charming biography on Dad, she only quoted Dad's second
Conscription Number N-44428 as the first Testament of Dad's conscription
into the Kings African Rifles. It is the number that would be used as his first
conscription number and negate the fact that Dad joined the Kings African
Rifles Navy and worked in the Kitchen Mess way before he was enlisted
into the Fighting Unit in 1946.

Judith Listowel wrote the most attractive and favourable book about
Dad but in my opinion it doesn't matter that Dad worked in the Kitchen
Mess the first time he was conscripted into the Kings African Rifles. The
compelling evidence by a key witness and ex-service man about Dad joining
the Kings African Rifles in 1939 and participating in the Second World War
cannot be ignored even though Dad's detractors label his assertions as lies.

At the time of Dad's "official" conscription into the Fighting Unit
of the Kings African Rifles, the colonial Army had just returned from
Burma where up to 1,924 Africans had died during the Second World War.
However, this did not deter Dad from aspiring to join the Fighting Unit of
the Army anyway. On its return to East Africa from Burma, the 4th Battalion of the Kings African Rifles was stationed at Lan'gata Camp outside
Nairobi, Kenya and several of my extended family members who were still
in the Kings African Rifles were stationed there. From there, a recruiting
safari was sent out to Northern Uganda where it signed up a group of
Kakwa in 1946.

Temezi (Elders) regularly recalled and recounted the first official recruitment of Kakwa into Colonial Uganda's Army. It was performed by a

King's African Rifles Recruiting Safari at the Nyarilo (Ko'boko Headquarters) Football Ground in Ko'boko County.

As a part of the recruiting rituals, potential soldiers ran four times around the football stadium and eventually a certain Juma Kuri was enlisted. Juma Kuri is actually both a maternal cousin of Dad's from the Piza Kakwa clan and a paternal cousin on the Godiya Kakwa clan side. Grandma Aisha Aate's mother Dede had a half sister Kidde. Their mother Aba of the Kozoru Kakwa clan had a 2nd husband who hailed from the Piza Kakwa clan while Grandpa Amin's mother Atata hailed from the Godiya Kakwa clan.

On the day Juma Kuri was enlisted in the Kings African Rifles, three other candidates were also enlisted based on a strong physique, stamina, speed of reaction and an upright bearing. No intellectual or academic considerations played a part in the recruitment process.

While all the events of the Second World War were unfolding from 1939 to 1945 and African colonization was at its peak, Dad was growing into a strong lad - six-foot four inches tall. As a young lad, he outshone his contemporaries by his physical prowess and leadership qualities.

A year after the end of the Second World War, he began his long eventful career in the Fighting Unit of the Kings African Rifles – a career that preceded his ascend to the highest position in the land of Uganda. This happened as pronounced by Grandma Aisha Aate during the Lan'ga na Da (Stepping over the KAR Rifle) ritual she performed after the Deadly "Paternity Test" Dad endured as an infant and the accompanying "curse" she invoked and pronounced on Grandpa. Dad had served as a Kasanvu (coerced labourer) and landed gigs at a Kings African Rifles Kitchen Mess and the Grand Imperial Hotel before joining the Fighting Unit of the Kings African Rifles and ascending to the highest position in the land of Uganda!

When Dad worked at the Kings African Rifles Kitchen Mess, he had a different conscription Number from the one quoted by his Official Biographer Judith Listowel. Judith Listowel provides Dad's conscription date into the Kings African Rifles as 1946 but by 1946, Dad had already had a gig and stint in the Kings African Rifles and been given a Conscription Number. Dad started his military career in the Fighting Unit of the Kings African Rifles in 1946 and he was first stationed at the Jinja based B Company 4th Kings African Rifles (KAR) Battalion. According to him, during training they were stationed at Magamaga. There are two versions to Dad's conscription into the Kings African Rifles. One version that Dad regularly told in typical Kakwa Adiyo (oral historical narrative account of history and events of the past) narration style was that he was busy selling mandazi (doughnuts) on the streets when he was grabbed and forcefully conscripted by a Scottish man, at the probable age of twelve.

The second version that Dad's biographer Judith Listowel pens down is that Dad was a Bellboy of sorts at the Imperial Hotel when he requested a British officer to join the Kings African Rifles.

Regarding the correct version, the Scottish man who grabs him off the streets is more in line with the Kitchen Mess gig aboard the triple-decker troop carrier Navy Ship SS Yoma. This was from 1939 to 1945, when Dad was underage and turned down for recruitment into the Fighting Unit of the KAR. The "Bellboy version" is more in line with his recruitment into the Fighting Unit of the Army in 1946.

Renowned Researcher Fred Guweddeko talks of Dad being rejected for military service for being underage. However, the Listowel account falls in line with Dad's stay at Kiyindi zone at Mzee (Elder) Khamis Walala's homestead doing odd jobs including the stint at the Grand Imperial Hotel around 1945-1946 when he joined the Fighting Unit of the KAR.

For the "Bellboy version", people in the know recount that Dad smartly stood to attention and said in simple Swahili, "Sir, I want to join the KAR." According to them, the Safari Commander looked up at this huge figure with fine impressive physique, the tribal scars identical to others they had seen at Ko'buko (Ko'boko) during a "recruiting safari" sent out to recruit members of the Kakwa tribe into Colonial Uganda's Army at Nyarilo (Ko'buko's Headquarters) and said, "All right. Jump in the truck" – a 3-ton truck.

Thus began Dad's career in the Fighting Unit of the Colonial Army. His KAR-UR conscription Number in the Fighting Unit was N44428 and he started off his Military Career in the Fighting Unit of the Kings African Rifles in the E Company.

Dad had the thread-like faint incisions on his cheeks done for medicinal purposes among the Kakwa, but not the 111s referred to in Leopold's book. So this was an exaggeration and the same old same old unfair labeling and insults leveled against my tribe the Kakwa.

The 111 markings were prevalent amongst the Baka tribe of Sudan but not the Kakwa. Even Jaffar al-Numeri, the former President of the Sudan has those 111 scars and ironically the highest officials in the Northern Sudanese government bear the 111 marks. Yet in the past, it was the mark the slaver placed on their victims. So it is ironic that a lot of the rulers of the Sudan today bear this 111 mark on their cheeks. Dad would laugh and say, "It is great that the slaves have become the rulers!"

Dad's rise through the ranks of the KAR and Reflections

After conscription into the Fighting Unit of the Kings African Rifles (KAR), Dad rose steadily through the ranks of the Army. Many people have recounted how he and his army colleagues were put through very rigorous exercises, which included walking and running very long distances in very difficult terrain. According to them, Dad was always the best at these physically demanding and difficult Military Exercises. They report that during these exercises, he beat and left everybody else behind and would often sit under a tree and wait for his colleagues to "cross the finish line" long after he had done so. According to reports, Dad's excellence led some of his superiors to ask what he eats to make him so strong and he told them "millet and sorghum!" - two staple foods eaten by members of the Kakwa tribe and other tribes in Uganda and neighbouring countries. They are very nutritious and healthy.

Following is Dad's Tour of Duty in the Kings African Rifles and Uganda Rifles/Uganda Army from 1939 to 1979:

Army Number and Year
N-14610 (1939-1945 -Kitchen Mess)
N-44428 (1946-1961)
UO-03 (1961-1979)

While the Second World War (WWII) was progressing between 1940 and 1944, Dad worked at various odd jobs. As he journeyed from childhood poverty working as a Kasanvu slashing sugar cane at the Metha Sugar Plantations in Uganda, little did he know that the hard labour and hardship of being driven to exhaustion by "Indian Overseers" was preparing him for excellence in another physically demanding career - the Army. As he landed a gig at a Kings African Rifles Kitchen Mess including aboard a triple-decker troop carrier Navy Ship that took him to distant lands, little did Dad know that his lifestory and "script" had already been predetermined.

As Dad traversed such places as Mombasa Port, Cape Town, Madagascar, Mogadishu, Djibouti, Aden, Port Sudan and the Suez Canal in the Military Navy Ship SS Yoma as Kitchen Help during the Second World War, little did he know that the exposure was preparing him for bigger roles. Little did Dad know that this experience was preparing him for the "highest position in the land" as Grandma pronounced following the unusual "Paternity Test" on the foothills of the Kakwa Legendary Mountain Liru that could have cost him his life.

As Dad went about executing his duties as a Bellboy at the Grand Imperial Hotel in Kampala, little did he know that the job was unintended training for the humility and strict obedience necessary for a steady rise through the ranks of the army he would shortly be conscripted into. As Dad stood to attention while uttering in simple Swahili, "Sir, I want to join the KEYA (KAR)", little did he know that his conscription by the Recruiting Army Officer that same day was part of the script relating to ascending to the "highest position in the land of Uganda!" Little did Dad know that the powerful pronouncement made by Grandma after he was subjected to the unusual "Paternity Test", would begin to take form after his conscription into the Colonial Army.

Beginning with this chapter, I provide a sample of events that unfolded in Dad's life that fulfilled Grandma's powerful pronouncement and look forward to sharing additional information as the series Idi Amin: Hero or Villain? His Son Jaffar Amin and Other People Speak unfolds.

It is my hope that the series of events leading up to the beginning of Dad's career in the Kings African Rifles and his subsequent rise to "the highest position in the land" will motivate oppressed peoples to pull themselves by the bootstraps as Dad did. It is also my hope that oppressed peoples that are still "groaning" under the very same oppressions that "created" Dad will find the courage to break away from the shackles of those oppressions that have existed well into the 21st Century. A case in point is the fact that African countries still lack Economic Independence, decades after so-called "Independence" from colonial powers.

Dad tried to break the very shackles of Economic "Dependence" I allude to above, but he was systematically derailed from doing so by his detractors, saboteurs, subversive elements and other people determined to undermine his noble agenda! He wanted all people to be liberated from the shackles that resulted from the activities of ardent believers in the contemptible oppressions of colonialism and imperialism such as Cecil John Rhodes but his detractors and saboteurs wouldn't let him!

Cecil John Rhodes' dream indeed traverses (albeit in the ICT sector) the so-called "Dark Continent", from Cape Town to Cairo in multinational conglomerate shackles firmly back in place with marketing mantras which have replaced Soyinka's eternal Colonial Prayer with "commercials" that keep us glued to "Entertainment" - the new "religion".

Omujjassi (The Late Field Marshall Idi Amin Dada) served his country as a controversial absolute and supreme ruler under Martial Law from January 25, 1971 until he was militarily ousted from political power on April 11, 1979.

To us Kakwas he was bestowed with what we the Kakwa Ethnic Group call Lemi (Luck, Instinct or a Just Cause), for he seemingly transcended both cultural station in life and even educational criteria throughout his mercurial life. Right from the time he was born through to the time he ascended onto the Political Throne, he had unequalled power and dominion over his subjects. He wielded power like no other leader has or will ever wield, up to his demise in the Muslim Holy Land, where he unwittingly held centre stage again, upon his death on August 16, 2003.

This latent force "Lemi" carried this simple but effective man far, from a peripheral West Nile "indentured labourer community" living in the Kingdom of Buganda right up to the pinnacle of absolute power and dominion by God's will.

This journey was much longer than any leader has ever traversed other than maybe the likes of The Great Abraham Lincoln who was also from similar humble beginnings. Omujjassi traced his long journey from the bottom rung of a brutal embedded class and caste ladder, seemingly not only through time but also through civilizations and cultures. For Omujjassi seemingly managed to transcend impossible challenges at the height of colonialism, to be counted amongst "the Elite" on Uhuru ("Independence") Day on October 9, 1962.

The endearing imprint of his enormous footprint in the sands of time is the giving back to the Indigenous Africans what was theirs in the first place, for better or for worse. He did indeed dare to be Non-Aligned and managed to be Independent.

In 2007 as we celebrated the Commonwealth Heads of Government Meeting (CHOGM) in Uganda with fanfare, it was hard to explain a few things. Looking back, it was hard for the so-called sycophantic praise singers in intellectual circles across the so-called "Dark Continent" to explain to the magnitude of the common man's Under Class in today's structurally adjusted society:

1. Why all the best land is being freely given away to so-called "Investors".

2. Why they still enjoy Tax Holidays, courtesy of Uganda Investment Authority (UIA).

3. Why IMF and World Bank Policies are wolfishly only characterized to our common man's mind with the act of taking away and nepotistic favoritism.

4. Why an image of selling the family silver under the Privatization Scheme post 1986 is now more pronounced.

5. Why the Nation's Assets for example Uganda Airlines have been sold off, only to be replaced with the CHOGM inspired "Air Uganda", to capitalize on the windfall CHOGM expects to reap.

This Loan Shark character lingers and continues to haunt the citizens' collective Psyche with ample evidence such as the ongoing court case over the GAVI Fund Saga in the Ministry of Health. I dare say 8 years of the Omujjassi was characterized with giving back to the Indigenous Africans in 90 days what it took British Colonialism 60 years to subjugate, using the Anglican version of Catholicism to usurp social political power from the Indigenous African for over sixty years (1900-1972).

Omujjassi forcefully sought social and political redress or payback carried forward when he finally opened our eyes from Soyinka's lingering "Anglican Colonial Prayer." We found ourselves under a truly brutal colonial yoke, harnessed and chained firmly in collusion with our very own erstwhile so-called cultural leaders and the so-called Elite receiving breadcrumbs. These breadcrumbs included token titles like Highness instead of Majesty, both Honourary and landed (for example 9000 square miles), plus scholarships for their progeny, only to be humiliated internally like Sir Freddie, following banishment to the cold streets of London from the sagging overlords' table.

Ironically after the auspicious launch of the very first CHOGM in 1971 in Singapore when the Father of the Nation of Uganda Dr. Apollo Milton Obote challenged the status quo, Omujjassi was "unwittingly handed over power" on a Silver Platter by his British colonial masters. However, he made an about turn (face off) when he went on to continue to break these very chains symbolically when he launched his Economic War in 1972. This had happened one year after the auspicious Launch of the CHOGM Fan Club and being "handed over power" that some cynics allege was "taken away" from Obote because the very Obote challenged the status quo.

Some quite often continue to claim "Amin opened our eyes" and for this sacrilege in the eyes of the Anglicans he has roundly been condemned for eternity by all - especially individuals that support colonialism and its continuation by way of neocolonialism. His short reign compared to that of Yoweri Museveni was completely maligned in historical accounts, yet it achieved a lot for the underclass. In spite of that, his achievements have not been recognized by the very same Ugandan Parliament that is supposed to provide leadership in breaking the chains Omujjassi tried to break but denies his Al-Amin Family Presidential Emolument.

This indelible image of manhood remains of Omujjassi despite the fact that all his property lies in ruins after being destroyed during the 1979 retributive war of Liberation and all his other property is under Political Caveat. Nevertheless in the collective memory of the teeming masses of the so-called underclass the following knowledge exists:

1. Omujjassi dared to level the social and political playing field.

2. Although it will be compulsory for school going age children right up to our Legislators to partake in outdated and Bankrupt Marxist oriented political "indoctrination", it is ironic that the indigent Agrarian Society still retains a collective memory and experience of Omujjassi. This indigent Agrarian Society makes up 90% of most African populations and teeming masses in the case of Uganda. This has happened despite the fact that indeed politically indoctrinated UNEB textbooks continue to spew outdated Marxist Oriented sentiment to a generation that neither witnessed nor experienced Omujjassi. This is because 51% of the population is below the age of 14 and 9% are between the ages of 15 to 29 years old. Therefore they have only known one leader collectively and cumulatively for over 22 years in 2008.

3. By the year 2008 it was thirty years since the 1978 Kagera Fiasco that saw the back of Omujjassi. Yet no amount of name-calling and "Settler" inspired colonial mentality books and films like "The Last King of Scotland" can explain away the resurgent grinding poverty that exists today in the first decade of the 21st Century. No amount of name-calling and "Settler" inspired colonial mentality books and films can explain the glaring privileges of the resumed very few Cultural Leaders and Elites under their very successful reputed 6% Annual Growth target attempt to re-institute a Neo-Colonial Class and Caste System. Although the Neo-Colonial Class and Caste System are normal on the Indian Sub-Continent or even amongst the Hima-Tutsi/Bantu divide, it re-ignites and re-invigorates the weight of Neo-Colonialism.

4. This Latent undercurrent also threatens to revive Latent Pro-Indigenous Nationalist Tendency. Moreover if the strong undercurrent is misread by the prevailing Political Establishment, this genuine sense of deprivation can bring down whole systems in total. The Prevailing Political Establishments should treat this upsurge with due diligence and care. For it

has the potential to bring down well-laid out Structural Adjustment Programs which failed to take into account key Social-Political problems that had traditionally been left on the wayside by World Bank and IMF Policy Planners post 1979 but today these very same Social Political issues have taken an agenda of their own. Moreover these issues are A-Political in nature and cut across the north-south divide as genuine social political concerns of the citizens of Uganda.

The significance of CHOGM 1977 England was when Omujjassi was excluded for non-compliance and the CHOGM 1991 in Harare was when Mugabe was still the darling of the British realm for subservience to their "Subservience Protocol". Today he has become a Pariah for the "Colonial Master" is not amused. But do not be surprised when the successors to Mandela's Majority Rule Reign of South Africa will also have to swallow "The Poison Challis" of true nonalignment and realistic Independence bereft of our colonial master's dictates. But woe to the brave heart for he/she will also be shot down like Omujjassi of old who dared to challenge the status quo.

As we celebrated the resilience at the ongoing Bi-Annual CHOGM fan club which finally reached the shores of Lake Nyanja (Lake Victoria) in 2007 we should remember what Omujjassi tried to do. Ooh how the Omujjassi would rage to see the turn around the nation is going through back to his bleak childhood days as a Kasanvu doing "hard labour" in the Metha Sugar Plantations in the 1930s and 1940s! We are truly back in that bleak era socially and politically under a 21st century commercial serfdom with straps firmly back in place on Queen Victoria's inherited apron.

It is my hope that the global community will rise up to stop the "use" of oppressions by powers that be to "design" "slippery paths" similar to the one that was "designed" for Dad and led him to unwittingly become one of the most reviled figures in history.

President Obama of the United States of America will hopefully break the mould of the New World Order and view resource areas like Africa and the Middle East as equal partners in development at long last!

Drawing parallels between Dad and Toussaint Louverture

Dad's steady rise through the ranks of the Colonial Army and unlikely ascend to the most powerful position in Uganda would be a break away from the shackles of poverty and "slavery" on Uganda's Sugar Plantations that is only parallel to the successful revolt led by Toussaint Louverture who led a notorious revolt against inhuman and cruel slave owners in Haiti, beginning in 1791. The notorious revolt in Haiti, which began in 1791, would eventually go down in history as a lesson to be remembered for generations to come. The revolt was against inhuman and cruel slave owners who were determined to maximize profits without any regard for human life and dignity. It would also unwittingly earn Toussaint Louverture the leader of the revolt the conflicting characterization of hero and villain at the same time - the same way Dad has been characterized.

Like the Papa Dock Duvalient family who are descendants of the very same Toussaint Louverture who tried to rescue Haiti from the shackles of slavery, all that is remembered of the only successful revolt in the Americas was the Tom Tom Makut and the voodoo rituals.

False allegations that Dad believed in sorcery

At various times, a hostile media also focused on allegations that Dad believed in sorcery which is equated to the voodoo rituals attributed to Louverture's Haiti. The hostile media quite often confused the ingrained beliefs of henchmen like Lieutenant Colonel Malera who served under Dad and was innately an Animist from the Baka Ethnic group in Southern Sudan with present day animist tendencies vying for spiritual space with the powerful Born Again Christian crusades in Southern Sudan.

However, the best attempt at explaining Dad's Sufi Orientation which touched on Mysticism and was mistaken for sorcery was given by renowned Researcher Fred Guweddeko in an article by Moses Serugo titled "The myths surrounding Idi Amin" that appeared in the Ugandan Newspaper the Sunday Monitor on August 20, 2003. This had happened four days after Dad's demise. The false allegations contained in the Article are discussed elsewhere in the series Idi Amin: Hero or Villain? His Son Jaffar Amin and Other People Speak.

There have also been false allegations relating to Dad being a follower of Sai Baba an Indian Guru featured in a 1968 photograph. The photograph was taken with Dad and my two stepmothers Mama Kay and Mama Mariam. The allegations are a fabrication and the photograph was taken during a visit to Dr. Patel who was Dad's Physician at the time.

Baba, the "Afro" looking individual in the picture came to Uganda in 1968 invited by Dr. Patel, Dad's Physician at the time. They took the picture while Dad was visiting Dr. Patel, along with Mama Kay and Mama Mariam. Apparently Sai Baba is said to have informed every

Indian who would listen that, "Every foreigner would leave Uganda in 4 years." According to reliable sources, the Indian community took it like some joke and yet Sai Baba's "prophecy" came to pass in 1972 with the expulsion of the Asians from Uganda.

Mama Kay was expecting my brother Lumumba at the time and as an adult, he once came to me excitedly and informed me that they used to celebrate his birthday on January 25 but he went to the Birth Records and found that he was actually born on January 24, 1968. He even mentioned the name of the doctor who performed the delivery as Dr. Patel. So, contrary to false claims that the 1968 photograph featuring Sai Baba, Dad and my stepmothers Mama Kay and Mama Mariam is so-called proof that Dad visited Indian diviners, Dad posing for a photograph with Sai Baba was pure coincidence. It had happened during a medical visit to Dr. Patel by Dad in the company of Mama Kay and Mama Mariam. The photograph definitely shows that Dad was more cosmopolitan than the "bush craft evil man" he is depicted by the likes of Henry Kyemba and others intent on "dragging him through the mud" for wanting to liberate Ugandans, other "Africans" and oppressed groups.

Dad's tussle with a crocodile in Somalia and our Somali siblings

While spending quality time with our Dad at Paradise Beach, a private Island owned by Kabaka Mutesa during his reign or Cape Town, Munyonyo, he was always fond of requesting my siblings and I to massage him all over the body. It was always interesting to see how one of my brothers would concentrate on the shoulders, another on an arm each and some sisters on a leg each and two siblings would concentrate on the feet.

While we were massaging Dad as we always did one day in 1978, I noticed a scar on his leg and asked him about it in my typical inquisitive style.

"Oh, that scar", Dad laughed in his characteristic deep shoulder shake laugh. He then delved into the story of his encounter with a crocodile in Somalia. It was a story he had told numerous times before with all the Adiyo (oral historical narrative account of history, events of the past) drama that is distinctive in Kakwa story telling. My younger brother Siri'ba Kagera born that very year 1978 heard a slightly different version of the story, but it was in 1978 that my other siblings and I heard Dad tell it for the first time.

Dad didn't grow up in Ko'boko, home of the Kakwa tribe in Uganda. However, he had somehow managed to master the Kakwa storytelling and narration style that always mesmerizes Kakwa youngsters when Temezi (Elders) recount Adiyo and tell countless "Likikiris" (stories and folklore passed down from generation to generation) around the fire after the evening meal.

In 1949, Dad's 4th Battalion was sent on a Kings African Rifles Military Tour of Duty to Somalia and it stayed there until 1950. While there, he easily assimilated into the local Muslim community and went for swims in local rivers as the locals did.

However, a particularly horrifying incident happened to Dad in Somalia while taking a dip in a crocodile infested river. Dad had been warned by the locals not to swim in a particular crocodile infested river but he did not heed their warning and stubbornly jumped in anyway! According to Dad, a few minutes into the daring and defiant swim, a marauding crocodile grabbed him around the ankle line and dragged him for some distance. No one knows how Dad survived but somehow he got away!

According to the story account Dad told my younger brother Siri'ba Kagera and others, he recounted that as the fierce crocodile dragged him outwards, he instinctively went for his rifle and shot the reptile. Dad always bragged about his Lemi, which means luck in this context and told how he was lucky that the crocodile dragged him downstream and in a strong current or he would have been toss.

Dad told that the monster had not got a good grip around his famous World War II ration Catfish-like paratrooper degree boots, which possibly saved him from a deeper gash on his foot. Anyway, Dad did have a scar around his ankle to show for his "crocodile trouble". I know because I spotted the scar and was constantly reminded about "The Somalia Crocodile Adventure" during the "massage therapy" sessions my siblings and I administered to Dad.

My siblings commonly referred to Dad's encounter with the vicious crocodile in Somalia "The Somalia Crocodile Adventure" and never tired of the many versions Dad told with all the Adiyo drama that he mastered. Dad had a knack for trouble and always got away but he constantly cautioned us to be careful and not to always follow in his "naughty footsteps".

Key witnesses to this incident were Retired Lieutenant Musa 'Dimba and Captain Ismail Khamis nicknamed Sul Wayi Wayi who were bathing in the same crocodile infested river with Dad when the incident occurred. 'Dimba and Dad joined the Fighting Unit of the Kings African Rifles together and he comes from the Leiko Origa clan – the very same clan in which my Grandma's mother Aba Na Lokolondre resided. She had come to live there with her three children Juruga, Abiriya and my Grandma Aate.

According to 'Dimba's version of the same story, apparently just as the beast went for Dad around the waist, the rest of the people rushed out of the river naked fleeing to safety. The next thing 'Dimba saw was Dad emerging forcefully out onto the surface of the river. Then with strong strokes, he made for the riverbank, waded out and rushed for his rifle with the beast, giving chase out of the river. 'Dimba said Dad managed to shoot the crocodile and the last image 'Dimba saw was of a large and very dead reptile on the riverbank.

My siblings always laughed as we heard these different versions of "The Somalia Crocodile Adventure" but enjoyed the accounts as they were told in the Adiyo and Likikiri formats that are meant to engage, mesmerize and teach Kakwa youngsters history, life skills and valuable lessons.

Following another dramatic retelling of Dad's "Somalia Crocodile Adventure" 'Dimba surprised me by announcing and confirming that Dad left a daughter in Hargeisa to Mama Amina and a son to Mama Howra' Allah in Bale-tuen in 1949-1950! 'Dimba said he himself left a son and Captain Sul Wayi Wayi of Bombo left two children all in Hargeisa.

Mzee Ismail Khamis also known as Sul Wayi Wayi corroborated the events with a twist as to who had what. That was the time he even gave me the names of the two mothers my Dad fathered children with but claimed he did not father any child in Somalia. However he confirmed that Dad and possibly 'Dimba did. He remembered that Dad split from the mothers and their children when he was posted to Galakayo and onwards back to Gilgil and Nakuru by 1952.

Dad had told us that we had siblings in Somalia - a brother indeed born in Bale-tuen and a sister born in Hargeisa. He had also joked that he was in "cahoots" with one Captain Sul Wayi Wayi of Bombo Town Council. However, I was only convinced after 'Dimba reconfirmed the same account.

I often wonder where my two siblings are and fondly call the boy born in Bale'tuen Bale'tuen Amin Dada and the girl born in Hargeisa Hargeisa Utusi Amin. Utusi of the Mitamero Kakwa clan is our ancestor Wangita's mother.

While telling the story about my two siblings in Somalia, 'Dimba also shared that during the time they were in Somalia, Siad Barre who was President of Somalia from 1969 to 1991 was a Policeman in the Italian Somali Police and a good friend to Dad.

During their Strongman Reign in the 1970s Siad Barre told his "brother" Idi Amin the Bull Elephant of Africa:

"We admire your courage and stubborn independence but you have to pick sides. The Cold War is a different kind of war from the Second World War. Now you have to pick sides. Play them against each other but pick a side that will defend you".

According to dad, Siad Barre had intimated that dad was open to attack and added, "Look, right now I am with the Soviets. Al-Qadhafi is with the Soviets. Mengistu Haile Mariam is with the Soviets. Mobutu is with the Americans. Kenyatta is with the Americans. Nyerere is a Socialist. You have to choose a side."

It is interesting to note that Siad Barre later changed from the Soviets to the Americans.

Alas Dad went with Tito of Yugoslavia and his Non-Aligned Programme, not realizing that the "East" and "West" only gave respect to Tito of Yugoslavia because of his historical participation in the Second World War.

Dad claimed that during the Kagera War (Uganda's war with Tanzania) Siad Barre sent him some sophisticated bombs that caused rainstorms to set in when detonated in midair. I doubted it but was later told that there is a technical means by which rainstorms can be caused artificially.

According to Dad, the Americans protested the use of these weapons and threatened to join the war for it seems the weapons used some form of Plutonium content. Dad said these bombs were used over the northern regions of Tanzania by the TU-22 Bombers from Libya and his heavily depleted Mig 21 squadrons, to delay preparations for the final push against him in the so-called 1979 Kagera War of Liberation. Dad always looked towards Siad Barre with affection.

How Dad disobeyed British superiors to shoot Jomo Kenyatta

As an "exemplary, loyal and obedient soldier", Dad fought the Mau Mau in Kenya alongside his British Army Commanders. Of Dad as an Exemplary, Loyal and Obedient Soldier who followed strict orders from British Army Commanders to fight the Mau Mau in Kenya, two British superiors write:

"He was one of several NCOs who showed outstanding qualities of leadership, bravery and resourcefulness".

"Idi Amin was renowned for perfect eyesight."

"He was able to spot the Mau Mau at a distant mountain or gallery with his naked eye."

While on Patrol as a young soldier under British Commanders in Kenya during the Mau Mau Uprising, Dad saved the life of Jomo Kenyatta, the Father of the Nation of Kenya. On that day at a Roadblock specifically erected by the British Colonial Administration for purposes of "liquidating" Kenyatta, a trusted Indigenous Sergeant Idi Amin had been ordered by a White Officer to climb up to look under gunny bags for Jomo Kenyatta. This had happened as colonial soldiers hunted down Kenyatta for allegedly instigating the Mau Mau Uprising and they wanted him dead or alive!

That time, Dad did climb up the truck as ordered by his superior and located Kenyatta. He actually came face to face with Kenyatta but in a tense moment, he told the British officer, "There is no one up here Affende", while looking into the eyes of the reputed son of Kabarega.

At that very lethal of moments, when the English Officer inquired about whether there was anybody hidden in the litter truck, Dad's spur of the moment response was disobedience. "No sir, there is no one aboard", he repeated when the officer asked the question again.

Dad had said this while placing back the gunny bags protecting Kenyatta so that he could evade capture by the colonial soldiers.

When the White officer insisted that Kenyatta was on the truck, Dad dared him and said, "You come up and see for yourself"! "There is nobody up here."

"Okay" responded the British Captain.

Word had got to the Colonial Intelligence that the fugitive Kenyatta would indeed be on the very litter truck Dad was ordered to inspect at the Roadblock as a Junior member of the Kings African Rifles. Reliable sources had tipped Colonial Intelligence that Kenyatta would be hiding under the charcoal bags on the very truck.

However, Dad chose not to betray his mwananchi (fellow citizen) by revealing fugitive Kenyatta's presence on the truck. He defiantly disobeyed the order to capture Kenyatta and didn't divulge the secret relating to his disobedience to his superiors!

Later in the 1970s when war almost erupted between Uganda and Kenya after Dad became President of Uganda, Kenyatta quickly cooled and diffused the standoff when Dad revealed that he, Idi Amin was the Indigenous Sergeant who saved Kenyatta's life during the Mau Mau days. The revelation so shocked and amazed the old man that Kenyatta felt compelled to end the hostility that was occurring between Uganda and Kenya at the time. Being reminded of that lethal moment in time so shocked Kenyatta that, he called off the troop build up along the Kenya - Uganda border in time to avert a war between the two countries.

The fracas between Dad and Kenyatta had brought a build up of troops along the Kenya - Uganda Border and almost exploded into war but for Dad's revelation to Kenyatta about Kenyatta "owing him his life". The fracas had happened when Dad in his usual bombastic style reminded Kenyans of the old colonial territorial lines that included Nyasaland, Kisumu, Naivasha and Kalenjin territory in the Rift Valley right up to the Northern Frontier District and the shores of Lake Turkana (Rudolf) being Ugandan territory. Dad claimed that when he reminded Kenyans of the old colonial territorial lines, he was just reflecting on the historical past but not laying claim to the "controversial" land.

That time, Dad sent Captain Ismail Khamis nicknamed Sul Wayi Wayi with a personal reminder to Kenyatta about the incident at the Roadblock that could have ended Kenyatta's life. By recounting the events of that day, he was able to prove to Jomo Kenyatta beyond reasonable doubt that indeed he, Idi Amin Dada was the very Indigenous Sergeant who manned a Roadblock, which stopped the charcoal litter truck that was carrying him.

After Captain Sul Wayi Wayi conveyed the message from Dad, Kenyatta knew without a shadow of a doubt that Dad was the very Indigenous Soldier who was ordered by the White Officer to climb up the charcoal litter truck to see if he was on the truck. He knew that only someone who had climbed up onto the very truck he was in could ever have known this singular one-on-one event that would have put a stop to his activities to save Kenya from the clutches of the British colonizers.

As he evaded capture, Kenyatta was aware at the time that the British Colonial Administration was so determined to hang onto Kenya, especially the fertile parts of the country that they were willing to kill, main and massacre anyone who stood in their way.

The revelation to Kenyatta that Dad saved his life that fateful day brought on memories of his very personal terror of the very night he would have been killed by the colonial soldiers. Kenyatta recalled that he would have been dead but for that singular Indigenous African Soldier (Dad) who saved his life. The father of the Nation of Kenya remembered that he was supposed to be shot on sight.

During the Kenya/Uganda crisis in the mid-1970s, Dad relished the opportunity to remind Kenyatta of the one on one encounter they had when he as a Sergeant made the defiant decision to let him escape instead of obeying orders from his British superiors to capture and possibly shoot him.

Njoroge and Njuguna, our Kikuyu siblings

After Dad became President of Uganda, he would also publicly declare on a state visit to Kenya that he sought the whereabouts of Njoroge and Njuguna, progeny from his Mau Mau days. This is because while on his Tour of Duty in Kenya, Dad had several Kikuyu concubines with whom he also had children.

Dad and fellow soldiers entertaining Queen Elizabeth II in 1954

As a loyal soldier in the Colonial Army and servant of the Queen of England, Dad and his 4th Battalion were part of the festivities to welcome Queen Elizabeth II when she opened the Owen Falls Dam in Jinja, Uganda in 1954.

Dad's 4th Battalion of the KAR moved to Jinja for the visit of Queen Elizabeth II, of the Commonwealth. That year, the Queen travelled to Uganda to open the Owen Falls Dam.

During that visit, the Queen presented the units of the KAR in Uganda with new colours and the KAR entertained her. Dad and his men were everywhere with their starched uniforms and happy to be part of the festivities.

For the festivities, the KAR performed an excellent drill comparable to that of a Guards Battalion in Britain. Colonel Nott, Commander of the Jinja Battalion at the time had obtained dark green forage caps-dark green for the 4th Uganda Battalions, especially for the occasion of the Queen's visit.

Sir Andrew Cohen, the Colonial Governor in Uganda at the time, was present for the occasion.

Sir Edward Twinning, Governor of Tanganyika at the time also attended the occasion and he was entrusted to take the colours to Jinja's St. Andrew's Church.

Dad as an excellent athlete

From 1954 onwards, Dad excelled in athletics, including sprinting and winning the Heavy Weight Championships and the National Title. His physique was like that of a Grecian Sculpture.   No matter what form of Athleticism he turned his hand to, he excelled and he conquered. He won the 100 Yards and 200 Yards Sprints against no main opposition.

Dad regularly recounted how he ran a race in 9.97 seconds in the 1950s. However because Uganda was not a nation at the time and Great Britain did not have a similar assimilation policy in the colonies to that of France, he was not considered Olympic Roger Banister Material when he should have been.

Roger Banister was born on March 23, 1929 in Harrow, Middlesex, England. He is best known as the first human to run a sub-four-minute mile.

On May 6, 1954, Roger Banister ran the first timed sub-four-minute mile in history. A medical student at Oxford University at the time, Banister ran the mile in 3:59:4 at a local meet at Oxford's Iffley Road track. Always an amateur athlete, he retired from competitive running later that year and went on to become a prominent neurologist. His autobiography, First Four Minutes (later reprinted as Four Minute Mile), was published in 1955. Queen Elizabeth II knighted Roger Banister in 1975 (Source: Wikipedia, the free Encyclopedia).

The sprint records dipped under 10 seconds and 20 seconds only at the Famous "Black Empowerment Protest Olympics" of 1968 where two African American athletes Tommie Smith and John Carlos used the Olympics to stage a political protest. Their actions remain controversial to this very day as the two Olympiads raised their fists above their heads during an Awards Ceremony, giving the black power salute associated most closely with the Black Panthers - enraging Americans who saw the Olympics then as non political.

Dad was an anchorman in the running tug-of-war team and quickly put on the canvas conquering all opposition in the heavy weight championships. He later went on to win the National Title at this event and it would be nine years before he finally hung his gloves still undefeated!

In addition to becoming a Light-Heavy Weight Boxing Champion of Uganda and excelling as an athlete, Dad excelled as a Rugby Player.

Many Ugandans reminisced about Dad's sports accolades even after he retired unbeaten in the 1950s right up to 1960.

During Dad's dominance as National Light-Heavy Weight Boxing Champion, he had one cardinal rule - much in the mould of Sonny Liston and Mike Tyson. He loved to Knockout (KO) opponents and in later years he would advise the likes of the Beast Mugabi of Uganda and his generation to aim for a Knockout if Africans were to beat what he termed the rampant cheating by Judges at International Boxing Meets.

Dad's stay at the King George IV Jinja Garrison, which he would later rename Al-Qadhafi Garrison during his boxing career was memorable in every sense. Al-Qadhafi Garrison is the name Dad changed the 4th Battalion in Jinja to after he ascended to the position of President of Uganda, in honour of his friend Muamar Al-Qadhafi.

Dad was a great athlete of every sport and he trained hard at all of them. Reinforced by his superiors in the Army after joining the Uganda Army, he became "a fine and resourceful NCO" (Non Commissioned Officer).

Dad as a promising young soldier and acknowledged he-man

In 1954, as a promising young soldier who continued to show exemplary behaviour, Dad's British superiors in the Kings African Rifles sent him to a special training school in Nakuru, Kenya, along with his colleagues at the "A Company" of the Kings African Rifles. While serving at the "A Company", Dad had served and impressed his superiors with his skills and exemplary behaviour in all parts of the Battalion including Mortar Platoon, the Transport Company and the Signals Division.

At the special training school in Nakuru, Dad continued to show exemplary behaviour while gaining a certain degree of formal education including a basic knowledge of English. On the grounds that Dad stood head to shoulders above all the other students in every aspect apart from education, upon completing the special training school in Nakuru, an exception was made and Dad was promoted to Sergeant. Dad's rapid and steady promotion through the ranks of the army was a testament to the way his British superiors continued to view him as an exemplary soldier!

During Christmas celebrations one year, Dad smashed a huge concrete block with a sledgehammer as part of a Christmas party during which a local Indian conjurer was performing for the soldiers. Interestingly, as an acknowledged he-man of the Battalion at Jinja, Dad regularly demonstrated his physical strength and prowess.

Here is what Iain Grahame a superior of Dad's reported about that day:

"It was the occasion of a Christmas party and the services of a local Indian conjurer-cum-contortionist had been engaged. He was soon at his act, swallowing knives and electric light bulbs, producing geckoes and ground squirrels from every conceivable part of his anatomy and wrestling with an apparently lethal python. For the climax to his performance, an African assistant produced a huge concrete block and a sledge hammer, and the Indian then lay down on the ground, with the block on top of his chest, and invited anyone in the audience to come forward and smash it to smithereens. Even if anyone possessed the necessary strength, he assured them, no harm would come to himself."

All eyes focused on Dad.

Chuckling to himself and cheered on by the spectators and his fellow soldiers, he strode to the fore, rolling up his sleeves and flexing his muscles.

A sudden silence descended and everyone's attention focused on the puny-pale brown frame of the Asian. With a mighty heave, Dad hoisted the weapon high above his shoulders, paused momentarily and brought it down with a resounding thump on the block of concrete!

Grahame states:

"The concrete disintegrated in a shower of chips and gray dust, and we all rushed forward to see what had become of the frail little man. For a moment he lay quite still, eyes cast upwards to where deity presumably resided, then gradually his eyes rolled around and he began to recover. Amin, thereupon, dropped the sledge hammer, threw the Asian onto his shoulders and marched off to the African Sergeants' Mess, where a series of stiff drinks soon restored our intrepid entertainer."

Admiration for Dad from a British superior and a hindsight tribute

In 1954, Dad's British superior Iain Grahame offered, "still in 1954, a large proportion of the 4th Battalion KAR returned to Jinja along with one Sergeant Awon'go Idi Amin Dada, the acknowledged Atlas of the Battalion".

In 1955, Grahame returned to England but he didn't stop admiring Dad.

In a Hindsight Tribute to Dad's ability to pick up knowledge in Geography and resulting "mapping" skills by "Old Man About Town" F.D.R. Gureme, he once sincerely exalted Dad in his usual insightful and balanced style in an article in the "New Vision".

In the article, F.D.R Gureme stated that Dad's single handed effort at restructuring the provinces of Uganda and installing new districts to exact calculations of grid references on maps showed that his capacity to learn was his saving grace. Dad had demonstrated his skills in "mapping" during the time he was the Supreme ruler of the land of Uganda in the 1970s.

Dad's rapid promotions in the KAR, more praises and admiration

In 1958, Dad was promoted to Warrant Officer Platoon Commander (WOPC). In the same year, his superior Iain Grahame who had returned to Uganda to command the "B Company" wrote:

"As a Platoon Commander, however, I found him (Idi Amin Dada) first-class. It is always his unit that had the best esprit, discipline and standards of field training. In the simple methods by which we operated where the written word was kept to the minimum and where a natural eye for the ground was more important than the calculations of grid references on a map, his low intellect was only a minor handicap."

Iain Grahame had come back to Uganda and Dad was his Sergeant Major while a number of demonstrations were occurring in West Nile and Acholi.

Another British superior reflected:

"Idi Amin was very quiet, well mannered, respectful and loyal."

The day Dad defied and challenged racism during the colonial era

Even though Dad was very quiet, well mannered, respectful and loyal, he despised any form of injustice and "oppression" as demonstrated by an incident that occurred between him and a White Bartender during "segregated" Uganda.

It was 1959. Dad had been promoted to the Honourary Rank of Affende - the highest rank awarded to Black African members of the Kings African Rifles at the time. On this day, Dad dared to march into the "Whites Only" Officers' Mess at 1st Battalion, Jinja after getting tired of moving with a rank that did not hold water. He moved up to the "Whites Only" Officers' Mess instead of going to the Sergeants' Mess and ordered a drink. When the White Bartender told Dad off and "barked" for him to go to the Sergeants' Mess, Dad grabbed the Bartender by the collar and pulled him straight over the counter. He then let rip with a resounding right on the Englishman's chin, to the hushed silence of the whole room, full of shocked White Officers. The segregative rule was changed after this audacious incident and Dad was even invited to join the exclusive "Whites

Only" Jinja Rugby Club because he was "one of their own" as a Star Athlete and Rugby Player.

So there you have it. "Proactive Action" from Africa's most maligned Activist!

He always said, "Action speaks louder than words".

Major Ali Musa of the Morodu Kakwa clan a colleague and associate of Dad's corroborated the above incident.

A game of "Russian Roulette" with tribalism as a political tool

The British Colonial Administrators used Tribalism as a Political Tool. They promoted Dad and others to the ranks of Second Lieutenant in 1959 and organized Uganda Army Battalions along Tribal Lines.

In 1959, Dad (a Kakwa), Shaban Opolot (an Iteso) and Pierino Okoya (an Acholi) were promoted to the ranks of Second Lieutenant. Following these promotions, six Kings African Rifles Battalions were organized along tribal lines. The Northern Brigade was for the Nilotic Tribes and the Southern Brigade was for the Bantu Tribes. Such a tribal segregation extended to the company and sub-units as well.

In the same year 1959, a "charming and well-educated" Mukiga named Gus Karugaba was sent to Sandhurst, the British Royal Military Academy commonly known simply as Sandhurst. He was the only Ugandan Native sent to that prestigious Academy. It is where all British Army officers, including late entry officers who were previously Warrant Officers, as well as many from elsewhere in the world, are trained. The Academy opened in 1947 in the former Royal Military College (RMC) at Sandhurst. Karugaba thus became the first Ugandan Army Officer to train in England. Certain detractors claimed that Dad frustrated Gus Karugaba's career in the Uganda Rifles yet actually the blame rests at the door of his superior Shaban Opolot who had a running feud with the openly arrogant Mukiga officer.

When Dad beat cattle rustlers and earned a promotion to Lieutenant

Dad's stature soared the next year 1960-1961 when he beat the Cattle Rustlers of Karamoja, thus gaining the respect of the Karamojong. This action prompted Sir Crawford to promote Dad to the unheard of rank of Lieutenant in 1961. He was one of the very first Africans to attain that rank. His residence was shifted from Nalufenya Road in Jinja to Acacia Avenue,

Kololo in Kampala. This is where Uganda's elite and wealthy citizens and other dignitaries resided.

The "Congo Crisis" and dad's friendship with Patrice Lumumba

As a rising Army Officer, Dad became involved in the "Congo Crisis" which included a series of events that occurred in the Belgium Congo (now the Democratic Republic of the Congo) between 1960 and 1966. It was a period of turmoil that began with Congo's "Independence" from Belgium on June 30, 1960 and involved "revolutionaries" such as Patrice Lumumba, Moise Tshombe, Cyrille Adoula, Antoine Gizenga, Joseph Kasongo, Joseph Mobutu, Godefroid Munongo, Joseph Kasavubu and others. This period of turmoil included the brutal murder of Patrice Lumumba the first Prime Minister of Congo on January 17, 1961.

Factors that caused and fueled the "Congo Crisis" included an anti colonial struggle, a secessionist war, a United Nations peacekeeping operation and a "Cold War Battle" between the United States of America and the Soviet Union among many others. The "Congo Crisis" supposedly ended in 1966 months after Joseph Mobutu seized power from President Kasavubu on November 25, 1965. However, many of the factors that caused and fueled it had profound implications for the Congo and continued to play out decades after the "Crisis" supposedly ended, leading to the loss of thousands of lives in the Congo.

More in depth reading is required for a proper understanding of the history of the Congo, events that unfolded in the Congo before, during and after the "Congo Crisis", circumstances surrounding the murder of Patrice Lumumba and events that have continued to unfold in the Congo decades after the "Crisis". Consequently, additional information will be made available in sections of subsequent parts of the series including a section titled "Patrice Lumumba: The Murder of an African Hero". However, below is a very sketchy outline of selected events that are reported to have occurred during the "Congo Crisis" from 1961 to 1962, for purposes of only providing context to Dad's involvement in the "Crisis" and as a prelude to "fuller" information about the "Crisis".

As the "Congo Crisis" was unfolding, events continued to unfold in Uganda as well. Sketchy outlines of some of these events are also included here for purposes of only providing context to Dad's story and as a prelude to "fuller" information.

We apologize for inadvertent errors, misrepresentations and inaccuracies. However, as the series unfolds, we will make any corrections and add information as Kakwa Temezi (Revered Elders) would in an Adiyo Narration Process.

According to various reports:

On January 17, 1961, Patrice Lumumba was killed in a CIA-inspired "coup" and General Joseph Mobutu was installed as the new President of the Republic of Congo.

During 1961, in Belgium Congo, Tshombe was held for trial on charges of assassinating Lumumba, massacring the Baluba, conspiring with Belgium and counterfeiting (printing) Katangan currency. He was jailed for two months in Leopoldville.

Obote as a rising Political Leader in Uganda attempted to help the Congolese rebels avenge Lumumba's death through the Uganda-Congo border areas. He assigned Dad the responsibility of overseeing the operation and sent him to broker peace deals between the warring factions while implementing "Obote's agenda".

On June 22, 1961, Tshombe agreed that all his forces should be placed under the Congolese Army. He was then released, but on reaching his hometown, he vowed that Katanga would always remain independent. Meanwhile, a new Government was formed in Kinshasa with Cyrille Adoula, former Socialist Labour Leader as the Prime Minister, Gizenga as his Deputy and Joseph Kasongo as the new President of Congo. However, the problem of Katanga's secession was a thorn in the new government's flesh. Colonel Mobutu led 5,000 troops into Katanga but Tshombe's forces repulsed these troops. Mobutu's forces arrested up to 400 Whites and harassed women and missionaries.

On December 5, 1961 Tshombe toured Paris and New York while his Interior Minister Munongo clashed with UN troops and destroyed bridges, planes and railways. Munongo warned: "The UN may take our cities. There will remain our villages in the bush. All the tribal chiefs are alerted. We are savages; we are Negroes. So be it. We shall fight like savages with our arrows!"

On December 21, 1961, Tshombe finally signed an agreement, ending Katanga's secession at Kitona near Kinshasa. He recognized Kasavubu as President of the Congo and promised to put his gendarme under Central Government Control. Meanwhile, Adoula jailed Gizenga.

On December 23, 1961, Tshombe charged the ANC soldiers of killing 22 White missionaries at Kongo and he continued to use delaying tactics in fulfillment of the Kitona Agreement resolutions.

In December 1961, UN forces controlled much of Elizabethville.

On February 2, 1962, Adoula asked the UN for an all out crushing of Tshombe but Tshombe was reluctant to join Adoula's government because of being re-jailed or jailed like Gizenga.

Dad and Patrice Lumumba were very good friends. A man named Peter Ali Andia a Congolese from Aru who served in the Uganda Army from 1966 in the Military Band once told me a very revealing story about Dad's relationship with Patrice Lumumba. Andia later converted to Islam in the 1980s.

Andia said that on one of Dad's forays into Mable Nightlife, he pulled out of his pocket a black and white picture, which showed Dad standing side by side with the late Lumumba.

Dad kept asking Andia, the Congolese soldier then serving in the Uganda Army, "Who do you think this is?"

Perplexed and noticing the great leader, who had just been murdered not so long ago, he answered, "Patrice Lumumba".

"Yes, so you know how close we were. We were being supplied by the Communists to fight Colonel Mobutu's soldiers who were supported by the Belgians and the Americans", continued Dad before adding:

"Tshombe did not kill Lumumba. It was the Belgians who did him in. Tshombe was only an Imperialist Stooge, but Lumumba was too forceful towards the former colonial masters and America was worried of losing its holds on the Uranium mines to the Soviets if Lumumba continued to make open overtones to the USSR."

It is on released Intelligence records that the Great War Hero President Dwight Eisenhower once exclaimed in frustration, "Kill that Nigger!"

Dad's continuing rise in the KAR and the continuing tribalism

As Dad continued to rise through the ranks of the Colonial Army, the British colonial administration continued to organize Kings African Rifles/Uganda Rifles Battalions along Tribal Lines and Dad was caught smack in the middle of this "segregative" and "divisive" way of organizing Wananchi (fellow citizens).

On March 1, 1961, Dad had been commissioned Lieutenant and he served in the "C Company" of the Uganda Rifles under Major Hugh Rogers of the British Army.

The "C Company" was formerly charged with disarming a section of the cattle rustling Turkana Tribe. That was how Dad became involved in disarming them.

The company was sent with the Northern Frontier District (NFD) to help against cattle rustling and to disarm the Ngwatella section of the Turkana tribe.

The 5th Kings African Rifles under the command of Lieutenant Colonel A. P. H. Hartley commanded two of the three Platoons the operation was engaged in.

During this time, Dad also acted as Deputy Company Commander.

In future years, Dad's detractors who included former British Officers and Obote would falsely claim and accuse Dad of killing three Turkana tribesmen. These false accusations would be accepted as truth even though curiously on the said date in question, October 9, 1962, Uganda's "Independence" Day, Dad was on Official Duty with Major Rogers in Kampala for the Uhuru (Independence Day) Celebrations!

Iain Grahame, one of Dad's superiors, confirms that Dad was with his Commanding Officer in preparation for Uhuru.

Moreover during the previous year in 1960, Dad was the first Black African to receive the rank of Lieutenant for the very reason of restoring the pride of the Kings African Rifles after a White Officer was killed by the very same Cattle Rustlers.

Dad received accolades for his work in defeating the Cattle Rustlers and even got his Captaincy during Queen Elizabeth II's Birthday celebrations in July 1962.

It is therefore a mystery and strange to hear that, that very period was when a cloud hung over his head and allegations that he murdered Turkana tribesmen have been circulated by his detractors to tarnish his reputation.

Uganda's "Independence" from Britain and Dad's active involvement

A number of notable events occurred during 1962, in preparation for Uganda's "Independence" from Britain. More in depth information will be made available and these events and others will be explored in more detail in subsequent parts of the series. However, following is an outline of selected information for purposes of continuing to provide context to Dad's story and as a prelude to a "fuller" discussion about the history of Uganda. This "fuller" discussion is necessary to obtain a proper understanding of how Dad became entangled in Uganda's "Political Game of "Russian Roulette"" with Tribalism and what led to him unwittingly attaining the conflicting characterization of hero and villain at the same time.

For much of April 1962, Kabaka (King) Mutesa II and the Baganda Protestants accommodated the Uganda Peoples Congress (UPC) Party.

The King conducted indirect elections by means of the pro-monarchist Lukiko and Buganda assumed a "special status."

The Kabaka Yekka (KY) (the Kabaka alone) Party thus, provided all 21 seats to the National Assembly and the Uganda People's Congress (UPC) Party defeated the Democratic Party (DP) nationally by 37 to 24 seats.

Mutesa II, the British and Obote all desired a Protestant government over the Catholic Democratic Party by joining together in a "shaky coalition".

In 1962, British Officers commanded the Uganda Army (UA) while Ugandan Officers were being trained to assume responsibility for the Army.

The British promoted Ugandan Africans in the Kings African Rifles (KAR) only to the rank of Effendi.

This rank did not put the African officers at par with the British officers, nor were the Africans deemed ideal material for officer rank.

The Uganda Army's "primary mission" was "to defend Uganda's territorial integrity". Its "secondary mission" was "to assist the police in maintaining public order."

On October 8, 1962, President John F. Kennedy of the United States of America sent Prime Minister Obote a message on the occasion of the "Independence" of Uganda.

On October 9, 1962, Uganda attained "Independence" from Great Britain after nearly 70 years of colonial rule. As the designated Chief of Staff and the second highest ranked Indigenous African official in the Uganda Armed Forces under the then designated Army Commander Shaban Opolot at the time, Dad received the new Flag, which was to be hoisted on Uhuru Day (Independence Day).

He also received back the Union Jack, which was lowered on October 9, 1962 the day Uganda attained "Independence" from Great Britain.

Dad had been promoted to the rank of Captain and he was Second in Command of Uganda's Armed Forces and Chief of Staff under Captain Shaban Opolot. He had been promoted to the rank of Captain in recognition of his work in restoring the honour and prestige of the Kings African Rifles when he restored law and order in the Ugandan region of Karamoja as a Lieutenant.

That time, a British Captain was killed by the Cattle Rustlers in the Northern Frontier District which was a humiliating and devastating blow dealt to the Kings African Rifles by the Cattle Rustlers so when Dad restored law and order in that region, his work did not go unnoticed.

The Northern Frontier District extended from Moroto right up to the shores of Lake Rudolf (present-day Lake Turkana).

This would be the exact scene of a future confrontation in 1975 between the Kenya Army under Jomo Kenyatta and the Uganda Army under Dad when he reminisced about most of the west land in Kenya being part of Uganda because it was part of the Uganda Protectorate.

Dad made the July 1962 Queen Elizabeth II birthday list of honours and was duly promoted to Captain before Uganda's "Independence" on October 9, 1962. If he had indeed murdered 8 Turkana tribesmen as has been alleged by his detractors, why was he promoted to Captain in June-July 1962 when a cloud hung over his head for so-called "degooding" of 8 Turkana Cattle Rustlers?

Grandma's joy at watching Dad stand side by side with Obote

On Uganda's "Independence" Day, October 9, 1962 (Uhuru Day), an NCO hoisted Uganda's new Flag while Dad and Shaban Opolot participated in the festivities as Uganda's highest ranking Indigenous African Army Officers. Grandma Aate was ecstatic as she watched her son Awon'go (Captain Idi Amin Dada) stand side by side with Obote, the most powerful man in the land of Uganda on Uhuru Day 1962 (Independence Day 1962). The fact that her son was actually handed the new Ugandan Flag which was to be hoisted on Uhuru day brought back memories of the time in 1928 when Dad could have died on the slopes of Mountain Liru during the Deadly "Paternity Test" he endured.

As the Non Commissioned Officers (NCOs) under Dad's command did the actual hoisting of the beautiful new Uganda Flag, Grandma remembered the time in 1928 that Dad's uncle Siri'ba regularly recounted. The excerpt is reproduced below for ease of reference.

Recalling the Deadly "Paternity Test" Dad endured as an infant

"Amin Dada was a particularly stern character and at the time of Awon'go's birth, he had reasons of his own for not accepting the infant Awon'go as his own", Dad's uncle Siri'ba regularly told. "Consequently, he demanded from amongst Elders of our Adibu Likamero clan of the Kakwa tribe that the infant Awon'go be taken into the jungle around the slopes of Mountain Liru and left there for four days! This was in compliance with a Kakwa tribal tradition where an infant whose paternal heritage was in dispute was taken into the jungle and left there for three days if it was a female child and four days if the infant was a male child".

"Amin Dada would only accept the infant Awon'go if it survived the cruel ordeal in the jungle. So, the Kakwa Elders from our Adibu Likamero clan relented and took the infant, Awon'go into the Ko'boko County jungle around the slopes of Mountain Liru and left him there for four days! On the fourth day, when the Elders came for the child it was still alive!"

"Like an Avenging Angel, your Abuba (Grandma) Aisha (Asha) Aate strode with fury in front of her husband and the Adibu Likamero Kakwa Elders", recounted Dad's uncle Siri'ba. "At the next assembly, she placed an ancient Kings African Rifles (KAR) Rifle on the ground and pronounced a solemn curse on her husband Amin Dada Nyabira Tomuresu. She proclaimed, "If this child is not yours and is of a Munubi, Monodu or of the Amunupi as you claim, let him languish in poverty and misery. But, But if he is of your blood, then let him prosper and succeed in this world to the highest position in the land, and may you, his Father, not see of his wealth and prosperity.""

According to Dad's uncle Siri'ba, Grandma then stepped over the KAR Rifle to invoke this powerful curse. The assembly was awestruck by Grandma's curse since just the fact that the infant survived the jungle was good enough for justice to the mother and child.

Grandma's prediction about Dad prospering was unfolding right before her eyes as he continued to rise through the ranks of the Army. He would indeed "succeed in this world to the highest position in the land" a little over 9 years later following a coup against the very Obote he was standing side by side with on Uhuru Day 1962 - the ironies of Post "Independent" Africa!

The Uganda Flag, beautifully designed by Semei Matia Nyai

At Uhuru 1962, the Old British "Union Jack" was handed back to Dad in exchange for the new Uganda flag which was beautifully designed by Semei Matia Nyai a dedicated teacher at the time and very talented artist from the Lugbara tribe of Uganda in the West Nile region.

Many sources have erroneously credited Uganda's former Minister of Justice, Mr. Grace Ibingira for designing the Uganda Flag when nothing could be further from the truth. As indicated by various reports, Mr. Ibingira continued to wrongly take the credit for Semei Matia Nyai's work and this error has continued to be perpetuated.

Many people consider it unscrupulous that Mr. Ibingira continues to be credited for Semei Matia Nyai's hard work and they have equated the continuing status quo and "silence" over the matter to "thuggery", outright "theft" and "robbery". Semei Matia Nyai must be given the credit due to him for designing Uganda's beautiful flag and any Royalties that rightly belong to him. To continue going along with claims that Grace Ibingira designed the beautiful artwork for the Uganda flag and not Semei Matia Nyai is unfair and unjust. Just because Grace Ibingira was part of the upper echelons of power and Internal Affairs Minister at the time and Semei Matia Nyai was a "powerless" private citizen did not give the Government of Uganda the right to "steal" his Royalties. Moreover successive governments in Uganda – including Dad's government neglected to correct this injustice.

According to reliable sources, Mr. Ibingira just came up with the three colours Red, Blue and Black for the Uganda National Congress (UNC). The UNC was Uganda's first Political Party formed in 1952 and it merged with the Uganda People's Union to form the Uganda People's Congress (UPC) Party in 1960. The three colours of Red, Blue and Black that Mr. Ibingira came up with for the UNC were later adopted by the UPC Party, which Mr. Ibingira belonged to.

The circumstances surrounding the design competition for the new Uganda Flag which saw Semei Matia Nyai emerge as the eventual winner of the design contest were articulated in an Article by Fred Ouma that was featured in Uganda's Newspaper the New Vision on October 9, 2005. This was 43 years to the date on October 9, 1962 when Dad stood to attention beside his Commander in Chief Apollo Milton Obote as the Flag was hoisted.

Dad as a Captain and the time he adopted Grandpa's name Dada

At "Independence" time, Uganda's population was roughly 7 million and the former Kings African Rifles numbered roughly 1,000 men, with officers, training and equipment from Her Majesty's Government of Britain. The 4th Battalion became the 1st Battalion Uganda Rifles at Jinja.

By the time the Army in Uganda transitioned from the Kings African Rifles to the Uganda Rifles and finally to the Uganda Army, Dad had added and adopted Grandpa's name Dada as his last name. During the "British Empire Days", Dad's name used to only read Idi Amin but by Uganda's "Independence" from Britain, he had added Dada and was now going by Idi Amin Dada.

Dad was also given the Officer Number UO-03 while Shaban Opolot was given UO-01 and his Junior Okoya was given UO-02.

From then onwards, Dad's Army Number was UO-03 instead of the N44428 assigned him at the time of his Conscription into the Fighting Unit of the Kings African Rifles, during the "British Empire Days".

Dad was thus a Captain by Uhuru (Independence) day but in all publications many writers erroneously write that he was promoted to Captain in 1963, yet 1963 was when he was promoted to Major and was duly sent to Israel for Paratrooper Training.

King Mutesa II as the President and Obote as the Prime Minister

King (Kabaka) Mutesa II became the first President of post colonial and "Independent" Uganda and Obote became the first Prime Minister. The Duke of Kent had handed to Obote the Instruments of Independence and the Union Jack had finally been lowered at the Kololo Airstrip.

The Baganda rejoiced deliriously because their Kabaka had been honoured with the highest position in the land of Uganda. Bonfires were lit throughout Uganda and there was a lot of celebration.

Speaking to cheering and adoring crowds outside the Kabaka's Palace on Mengo Hill, Mutesa II announced, "Uganda is determined that she will never again become an extension of Europe."

Sir Edward Mutesa II born on November 19, 1924 was the Kabaka (King) of Buganda from 1939 until his death on November 21, 1969 and President of Uganda from 1963 to 1966.

Apollo Milton Opeto Obote born on December 28, 1924 was Prime Minister of Uganda from 1962 to 1966 and President of Uganda from 1966 to 1971 and from 1980 to 1985 when he fled into exile again after being deposed the second time. He died on October 10, 2005 and I attended his funeral in Akokoro in Northern Uganda, to pay my respects to him and his family. Obote was a Ugandan political leader who led Uganda to independence from the British colonial administration in 1962.

Uganda's Tribalism and the continuing game of "Russian Roulette"

Soon after "Independence" from Great Britain, Obote continued playing the game of "Russian Roulette" with Ugandan Politics that the British Colonial Administrators introduced. The British Colonial Administrators had used Tribalism as a Political Tool. They had promoted Dad and others to the ranks of Second Lieutenant in 1959 and organized Uganda Army Battalions along Tribal Lines. Obote continued the game when he sent Dad to Israel for Paratrooper Training as a Major.

Prince Mutesa II was born in 1924, four years before Dad was born. He ruled the Great Kingdom of Buganda from 1939 the year his father King Daudi Chwa died until his own death in 1969. Mutesa II was also the President of Uganda from 1963 to 1966.

In a previous section, I shared details about Nnabagereka (Queen) Irene Druscilla Namaganda, wife of His Majesty Kabaka (King) Daudi Chwa of the Great Kingdom of Buganda who ruled from 1897 to 1939.

I shared details about how the queen who is the mother of King Mutesa II sought my Grandma's Holistic Medicinal services in the early 1900s. Grandma administered her fertility herbs to the queen, which led to the conception of Princes Mawanda and Mutesa II.

In the same section, I also disclosed that Queen Druscilla was so grateful to my Grandma for her gift of conception that she demonstrated this gratitude in more ways than one, including sharing a very close and special relationship with Grandma.

Because of this unusually close relationship, King Daudi Chwa also became very fond of Grandma. He was an ardent visitor to her shrine at Bundo in Kidusu because of his wife Druscilla's relationship with Grandma and because Grandma belonged to the "Yakanye Secret Society" that I introduced in a previous section. The King wanted to acquire the powers of the "Yakanye Secret Society".

However, Grandma's close and special relationship with the Ganda Royal Family brought misunderstandings before and after Dad was born when some unscrupulous Ganda and Nubians persisted in spreading the rumours that the Kabaka Daudi Chwa fathered Dad in the 1920s and not Grandpa. This led to Dad being subjected to the Deadly "Paternity Test" outlined previously.

I reintroduce the above information in this section for ease of reference as I recount events below that would have a profound effect on Dad's relationship with the Ganda tribe of Uganda. Uganda's Politics had quickly disintegrated as the game of "Russian Roulette" gained momentum.

The consequences of the game that was initially introduced when the British colonial administration organized Uganda Army Battalions along Tribal Lines just before "Independence" began to manifest and rear their ugly heads in Ugandan Politics a few months into the so-called Independence from Great Britain.

The game was in full swing before "the footsteps of the British Colonial Administrators even dried up after "Independence"!" The "new form" of the game was reintroduced by Obote when Dad left for Israel for Paratrooper Training as a Major.

The "chickens" associated with the game would come home to roost on the day Dad took over power from Apollo Milton Obote by force, in the infamous military coup that catapulted him to power on January 25, 1971.

When Obote, the Americans and the Israelis started "grooming" dad

After Uganda attained "Independence" from Great Britain, Dad continued to rise steadily through the ranks of the Army and the Political Game of "Russian Roulette" continued!

From the ages of 34 to 44 years (1962 - 1971), Dad continued his career in the Armed Forces serving in the post colonial Administration in the Command Centre in Mbuya, his Uganda Army Number being UA No. UO-03.

However, something else started to happen. Obote began to "groom" Dad as his "Guard Dog" and travelled with him, "everywhere!" The year 1963 was also when the Americans and the Israelis started slowly "grooming" Dad.

In 1963, while a fellow Northerner named Onama was Uganda's Minister of the Interior, Obote promoted Dad from the rank of Captain to the rank of Major. He then travelled to Israel and took the new Officer Major Idi Amin Dada along.

While Dad and Obote were in Israel, Obote requested the Israeli government to "send a six man team from Israel, to carry out Primary Patrol Training in Uganda's Teso District".

Obote had turned down the arrangement by Colonel J.M.A. Tillet for British Officers to train the Uganda Army and instead retained them only as seconded officers.

Dad's superior Iain Grahame noted of Dad in his book about Dad: "The normally talkative Major [Amin] had the African gift of silence on subjects he did not wish to discuss and, therefore, he failed to tell Tillet about the Israel arrangement" (Grahame p.29).

Obote would later send Dad for the Paratrooper Training in Israel.

Dad as a continuing exemplary soldier and Obote's marriage to Miria

The same year 1963 an additional battalion was created to expand the Uganda Army (UA).

Dad continued to be an exemplary soldier and leader.

In an exercise held in the Northern Frontier District between the Uganda Rifles (UR), Tanganyika Rifles (TR) and the Kenya Rifles (KR) and some British units, where each battalion was represented by one company, Dad's "C Company" easily won the contest.

In 1963, Major (later, Lieutenant Colonel Rogers) left Uganda and Dad arranged a cocktail party for him. Dad daringly engaged the regimental band on British standards.

The same year 1963, Obote married his Muganda Secretary, Miria Kalule in a wedding that cost some 29,000 Pounds Sterling!

Dad's incredible "Rags to Riches Story"

Grandma Aisha Aate enjoyed the fruits of her son's efforts and steady rise through the ranks of the Armed Forces. She was very pleased to see her pronouncement at the assembly of Clan Elders that followed the Deadly "Paternity Test" Dad endured unfolding right before her eyes! Grandma "cheered Dad on" as he rose steadily through the ranks of the Army and lived the incredible "Rags to Riches Story" no one would ever have imagined. Dad made sure Grandma didn't miss out on the fruits of his concerted efforts to be the best soldier he could be.

My mother as a 9-year old Nursemaid for Dad and Mama Mariam

In 1963, Dad was now living in the Officer's Compound (Army House) with Mama Mariam (Sarah Mutesi Kibedi) who is considered Dad's first official wife even though Dad had another wife and concubines before her, namely Adili, a Kakwa, Mama Taban, a Lan'gi and many others.

My Iya (mother) Mangarita had at the time been hired and worked for Dad and Mama Mariam as an Ayah-Amah (Yaya, Nursemaid) to care for the newly born Mariam Aaliyah (Aliya) born on January 21, 1961. At the tender age of nine, mum had been hired to be Dad and Mama Mariam's nursemaid.

Mum had been hired to work as a nine-year old nursemaid for Dad and Mama Mariam two weeks after my sister Mariam was born on January 21, 1961 and she moved with Dad and Mama Mariam when Dad moved residences from Nalufenya in Jinja to Acacia Avenue, Kololo in Kampala.

Mama Mariam (Sarah Mutesi Kibedi) had managed to get mum through my Great Aunt Ssenga Nnabirye Lovisa, a good friend of Mama Mariam's with whom they used to train together at the Singer Sewing Factory in Jinja. Before this friendship, the very same friend had been in an intimate relationship with Dad before Dad befriended Sarah Mutesi Kibedi.

In fact, she (my Great Aunt) was the one who introduced Sarah Mutesi Kibedi to Dad when he came visiting her once. Alas, their friendship was to reach a misunderstanding because of their rivalry for Dad before they made up.

Fate/Luck (Lemi) was on Mama Mariam's side for even though she had three children from a previous relationship, Dad married her and she became his official first wife. By the time my sister Aaliyah was on her way, Sarah Mutesi Kibedi approached her former rival my Great Aunt, for assistance in finding a nursemaid. That was when my Great Aunt brought her nine year old niece (my mother) to look after Dad's legitimate children in the Officer's Compound – the Official 2IC's Army House Residence, Plot 13 Acacia Avenue Kololo, where he and Mama Mariam were now living.

Today that residence is an Officers' Mess and it was the scene of Brigadier Tumukunde's incarceration (House Arrest) at the turn of the century.

I recount the story of how my mother became one of Dad's women in a subsequent section of this Introductory Edition.

According to stories confirmed by Major Mududu a relative of Dad's, Dad cohabited with Bironi an Acholi wife while he was stationed in Nakuru in the 1950s.

By the late 1950s he was cohabiting with Taban Amin's mother, a Lan'gi and cousin to Obote.

By the time in 1960 when Dad continued to reside at the King George IV Barracks in Jinja, he had linked up with four women namely, Adili of the Nyooke-Bori Kakwa clan, my Great Aunt Nnalongo Nnabirye Lovisa, Nnamuwaya Kirunda and Mama Mariam (Sarah Mutesi Kibedi).

The first to vacate was my Great Aunt Ssenga Nnabirye Lovisa leaving the other three to fight over their man.

Sarah Mutesi Kibedi won with the birth of Aaliya Mariam on January 21, 1961 hence the name Mama Mariam which she became known by from then on.

The other two Adili of the Nyooke-Bori Kakwa clan and Nnamuwaya Kirunda gave birth to Uhurus ("Independence") in 1962.

While pregnant with my sister Maimuna, Dad had asked Adili to stay at the massive Kasubi style Hut he had built in Tanganyika Village but the pregnant maiden refused. She went to stay with uncle Sosteni instead before returning to her father's house to await the birth of her daughter.

A very pregnant Nnamuwaya also left because for the life of her, she felt that she could not share the Nalufenya Bungalow with her sister Sarah Mutesi Kibedi, for they were true sisters in the African sense and reference to First Cousins. Mama Mariam (Sarah Mutesi Kibedi) of the Ba-isemenha Soga clan is first cousin to Nnamuwaya Kirunda.

The victor Mama Mariam (Sarah Mutesi Kibedi) remained at the Nalufenya House which is the scene of a most poignant picture of the Matriarch (my Grandma) holding the two toddlers Ali Nyabira on the left and Maimuna Adili on the right. It is a 1963 photograph taken in front of Dad's Anglia saloon car.

Dad's painful comment to his women who departed was that if the children were his, then they would search for him.

In future years, reliable witnesses would recount how a "boozy" Dad came to the Nyooke compound where his wife Adili was residing and picked a young daughter Maimuna up and walked away leaving Adili (Mama Maimuma) crying. She never stopped regretting her decision not to live in Dad's Tanganyika compound as Dad asked her.

Rifts between Obote and Mutesa II over the Lost Counties

In 1963, rifts emerged between Obote and Mutesa II over the Lost Counties transferred to Buganda from Bunyoro nearly 70 years earlier.

Obote had "arranged" for Mutesa II to be elected President of Uganda for a period of five years taking the place of Sir Walter Court, the last British Governor. Mutesa II thus combined his traditional hereditary and monarchical position in Buganda with the functions of a constitutional head of state over the whole of Uganda.

Meanwhile, Catholics and Muslims in office felt discriminated against and rifts soon began to emerge between Obote and Mutesa II over Obote's insistence on the sensitive lost counties, which the British colonial government had transferred from Bunyoro to Buganda nearly 70 odd years earlier!

Obote insisted that a Referendum be held over the status of the sensitive Lost Counties, which the British Colonial government had transferred from Bunyoro to Buganda nearly 70 years earlier and Mutesa II was opposed to the Referendum.

The wild mutinies calmed down by Dad, prompting more promotions

In 1964 mutinies that were reminiscent of the one in 1897 that was instigated by the Nubian soldiers imported into the land that would become Uganda during the 1800s ran wild in the Uganda Army. Dad was the only one who could resolve these mutinies, calm the soldiers and persuade them to stop "revolting", earning him more high regard from his colleagues and British superiors in the Kings African Rifles.

In 1897, the mutinying Nubian soldiers shot their British Commanding Officer on the shore of Lake Victoria as I will outline in a section of a subsequent part of the series and the British Commanders didn't want a repeat of the 1897 event.

On January 17, 1964, Dad's British superior and Commanding Officer Iain Grahame had the following comments about the 1897 mutiny by the Nubian soldiers. Even he describes the pitiful conditions of the troops "(low pay, poor equipment and continued separation from families with constant campaigning against various insurgents within Uganda) as varying from virtual nakedness to operatic displays of cherry coloured trousers and blue-coloured coats laced with gold braid".

According to Iain Grahame in his book:

"They [the Nubian soldiers] shot their British Commanding Officer on the shore of Lake Victoria" (p.19).

"As is the case everywhere in Africa, loyalty to the Ugandan soldiers, meant in the first place, unswerving allegiance to their tribes and tribal chiefs [for state societies]. Secondly, it was to the Crown [the Queen], which in their eyes was represented by the administrative officers within their tribal areas and Europeans seconded to the regiment. National unity or pride was incomprehensible and consequently non-existent".

Following is an account of the mutinies that occurred in the Uganda Army in 1964 and catapulted Dad to an even higher status among his colleagues and superiors in the King's African Rifles, following a series of previous promotions based on his good conduct and impeccable service as a soldier.

A mutiny had been in the brewing when on December 17, 1963, Uganda's Minister of the Interior, Felix Onama, told KAR soldiers that they would receive no pay raise. This action precipitated the mutinies that would run wild in 1964.

On January 20, 1964, there was an army mutiny in the newly independent Tanganyika. African soldiers mutinied, demanding higher pay and "a faster Africanisation". The result of the mutiny enabled the African soldiers in Tanganyika to obtain considerable pay raises. This coup was extensively covered in the Uganda Press. Field Marshall John Okello, a Lan'gi by tribe led the Revolutionary Coup, which occurred in Zanzibar. Because of this coup, Obote anticipated trouble in Uganda and sent loyal troops to guard Entebbe and communications installations in Kampala.

On January 22, 1964 some elements in the Kenya Army (KA) mutinied. In Uganda, the Army still had one British Officer and one Senior Ugandan Officer (Opolot) above Dad. Meanwhile, the British Officers discovered two "subversive" letters allegedly written by two members of the 4th Battalion and the culprits were dismissed. The British thought that only a handful of men shared the views of the dismissed soldiers. They were wrong.

Relations between the British Officers and the young Ugandan Officers trained in Mons fast deteriorated. The same Ugandan Officers also held little or no respect for 8 young Ugandan officers trained in Israel.

On January 22, 1964, the same day the Kenya Army (KA) mutinied, the Minister of the Interior, Felix Onama announced considerable pay raises for the senior NCOs (Non Commissioned Officers). Onama had obtained the permission of the Cabinet for a pay raise to Warrant Officers (WO) and

Non Commissioned Officers (NCOs) but not for the other ranks of the Uganda Army. This was to be arranged later. Moroto or the Second Battalion was in the process of being formed, under the Command of Lieutenant Colonel Richard Groom with Major Shaban Opolot as his Second in Command. At this time, there were 2 African Majors, 14 Captains, 26 Lieutenants and 15 Cadets in Training. The troops, however, were dissatisfied because they had not received pay raises equivalent to those that had been granted to senior officers.

The next day on January 23, 1964, the First Battalion at Jinja mutinied and Felix Onama the Defence Minister was taken hostage after coming to Jinja to meet the demands of the mutineers relating to higher pay and rapid Africanisation. The soldiers detained Onama as well as the British NCOs. The Jinja barracks in Uganda had known about the coup in Tanganyika that occurred on January 20, 1964 in relation to a demand for higher pay and "a faster Africanisation", which may have prompted their own mutiny.

Several events occurred on January 23, 1964 as follows:

The men of the Headquarters Company Uganda Rifles at Jinja demanded to see the Commanding Officer (CO), Lieutenant Colonel J.B. Hamilton. Hamilton then addressed them through an interpreter. The CO had been in Uganda just six weeks and not had the time to learn Kiswahili the official language of the soldiers. After the speech, the men refused to disperse. The "ring" leader of the mutiny demanded to see the Prime Minister or the Minister of the Interior and Defence, Felix Onama.

At 4:00pm, Onama erroneously consistently described by Iain Grahame as "Dad's kinsman", and sometimes as uncle arrived with a Police Escort whom the Army beat up.

Onama was dragged from his car and thrown into the guardroom where soldiers conversed with him through their spokesman Corporal Paul, a Karamojong.

Eventually, Onama agreed to yield to their demands for a pay raise.

To celebrate the news, the soldiers took Onama to the canteen, broke it open and some got drunk with beer.

The Army Commander, Colonel Tillet and Lieutenant Colonel Hamilton later castigated Onama for caving to the demands of the soldiers saying:

"Do you realize what this means? You have given way to the men on every point and you let them get away with beating up your Police

Escort and manhandling yourself. This is the end of discipline. This is going to affect the whole future of Uganda."

After Onama the Minister of the Interior and Defence caved in to the mutinying soldiers, the British Paymaster Pay Clerks worked overtime to adjust wages and allowances for the mutinous Uganda Rifles.

Still unsure of what might happen next, the Signals Officer, Captain Roger Sherin telephoned Hamilton at Entebbe for reinforcements. Meanwhile, Obote asked for help from Nairobi and the First Battalion, Staffordshire Regiment and two companies comprising of 450 Scotts Guards and Troops. The 450 Scotts Guards and Troops landed in Jinja at midnight on January 23, 1964, to crush the uprising.

On January 24, 1964 at 4:45am, Major James Houston of the Army Headquarters, assisted by the Jinja Mayor, Councillors and the local Asian contractors helped transport and guide the Staffordshire Regiment to Jinja.

Later in the day on January 24, 1964, Cuthbert, a Muteso, Minister of Regional Affairs, addressed the mutinying soldiers at Jinja.

Following the mutiny, 30 Ugandan Army "ringleaders" were identified and thrown into jail. Many of the soldiers were dismissed from the Uganda Rifles after being paid wages.

Of the mutiny, Dad's superior Iain Grahame writes in his book:

"Throughout this period of trouble, very few African Officers or senior NCOs were to be seen. They were bewildered and frightened, very much on the side of the law and order against the mutineers. They were completely outnumbered and powerless, and therefore kept out of sight" (page 35-36). Most importantly, Major Idi Amin was nowhere near the scene of the disturbances. This is because Colonel Tillet had sent him on recruitment upcountry".

On January 25, 1964, Obote invited the Staffordshire Regiment to intervene in the mutiny at Jinja.

On January 26, 1964, Dad returned from his upcountry "recruitment campaign and safari" and intervened in the continuing mutiny.

As Grahame writes, when the mutiny was taking place in 1964, Dad was nowhere near the scene of the disturbances because Colonel Tillet had sent him on a "recruitment safari" upcountry in Northern Uganda. Captain Katabana had flown to Entebbe with the agreement of the Commanding Officer and the Army Commander to see Obote.

By evening that day, Dad was back.

That night, Tillet asked Dad what was happening at Jinja and Dad replied, "Nothing nasty will happen tonight."

Rumours soon flared out in Jinja that Dad would be the new Commanding Officer as he had been seen with the politicians who addressed the troops in the barracks minus the British Officers.

Soon, lists were drawn for Dad to assume the First Battalion (Jinja), and Opolot the Second Battalion (Moroto).

Dad summoned some of the British Officers and the Uganda Rifles troops and addressed them.

One British officer observed that:

"It was the most moving speech and a sincere one. Idi Amin dwelt on our [British-Uganda] traditional ties and fully expected us to rise to the occasion" (Grahame, p.37) and yet, Lieutenant Colonel Hamilton's reply was uncooperative and Dad got suspicious and angry. He began to adopt a different attitude. He contacted Opolot in Moroto and in a 20-minute conversation, not in Swahili, but in a Nilo-Hamitic language (Iteso) which Sherin, the Signals Officer did not understand, talked about the situation. Sherin's impression was that Dad and Opolot were discussing how to handle the situation.

I consider Dad's decision to speak to Opolot in Iteso Pan-Africanist pro-action in co-ordination with his Commanding Officer Major Opolot. They were both promoted to Lieutenant Colonel following the 1964 Mutiny.

On January 28, 1964, it was agreed that certain key British officers should stay in Uganda. These included Major J.W.C. Morgan (the Second in Command) who was to act in an advisory capacity, Captain Roger Sherin (as Signals Officer), Tony Parkin (as MTO), the Quartermaster and some other officers and senior NCOs.

It was agreed that Dad would take over the Battalion the next afternoon, after having addressed the men.

On Hamilton's orders, Captain Sherin was to announce to the assembled soldiers that if they laid their hands on Dad, they would be machine-gunned from the British Ferrets parked at each corner of the square. Captain Sherin made this announcement through a megaphone, standing unarmed in front of the men.

At 2:00pm, Lieutenant Colonel Idi Amin Dada (Dad and Opolot had just been promoted to Lieutenant Colonel) walked into the square. He turned around and barked at Sherin:

"What are you doing here?"

Sherin replied, "Sir I am going to tell them (the African soldiers) they will be shot if they attacked you."

But Dad quipped, "Get away. I want no part of your arrangements."

The soldiers applauded and Dad demanded of them the behaviour they learnt from the British. The two companies that mutinied were disbanded but Dad, in a characteristic style calmed the tempers of the others.

So, Dad was held in high esteem by the African army. He helped calm things down, restored order and he was held in high esteem. Massive increase in pay, spring beds instead of wooden ones were the concessions won by the soldiers.

Three weeks later, Dad ordered Captain Sherin out of Jinja for good saying:

"You (Sherin) have mislaid two signals. Don't answer back—you have two hours to pack."

Dad took over the Commanding Officer's office without difficulty and immediately restored order to the men. He proceeded to drive around the barracks in his staff car and at the same time, "he looked after his own Kakwa men and related West Nile tribesmen." He paid less and less attention to Major Morgan, his British advisor.

In future years, Dad would also regularly drive around in a show of solidarity with soldiers and Ugandan masses before and after becoming President of Uganda on January 25, 1971.

Dad's superior Iain Grahame opined that on January 29, 1964 at 2:00pm, "there was trouble in the Uganda Army because the Africans no longer wanted the British Commanders."

On January 30, 1964, at 7:00am, Dad had all 500 soldiers in the barracks playing in the Army playing field where he also taught them Rugby as a seasoned Rugby Player.

Dad was an excellent Rugby player, "the only Black African member of the Jinja Rugby Club where he was very popular" after the incident relating to the day he challenged the racism and segregation that was rampant in Colonial Uganda.

On that day, Dad had dared to march into the "Whites Only" Officers' Mess at 1st Battalion Jinja after getting tired of moving with a rank that did not hold water and defiantly ordered a drink. When the White Bartender scolded him for breaking the rules of segregation, Dad had started a physical fight with him that led to the rules of segregation being changed and a special invitation being issued for him to join the exclusive "Whites Only" Jinja Rugby Club.

Dad's promotion to the rank of Lieutenant Colonel in 1964 after he successfully stopped a mutiny in progress was purely on merit. It was because of his work relating to stopping the mutiny that he was promoted to that rank. As explained above and confirmed by Dad's superior Iain Grahame, Dad was nowhere during the mutiny but returned in time to stop it.

However, his detractors have falsely alleged that he was actually the one who engineered the mutiny. If Dad indeed engineered this mutiny, why was he promoted to Lieutenant Colonel after he successfully stopped it? Why was Dad honoured by the British if there was so-called high suspicion that he actually engineered the mutiny?

After the mutiny that Dad helped quench, Prime Minister Obote apparently misled the world and perhaps even himself about the gravity of the mutiny Dad assisted in quenching. He asserted that order had been restored and the guilty had been duly punished.

This was only partly true. The men obtained all they wanted, and the politicians were afraid of them. The soldiers had obeyed Dad and he was now confident he could keep it that way. Obote realized that Dad had power in his hands and he opportunistically relished the newly acquired potential realized in Dad and he had every intention of adding to it and exploiting it.

On March 3, 1964, the Staffordshires were withdrawn and the soldiers removed from Uganda. Meanwhile Obote conspired with Army Commander Tillet to have the Headquarters and "A Company" disbanded. At this time half of the Battalion was away stationed on the Kenya, Congo and Rwandan borders.

Obote openly advocating a one-party state

In 1964, Obote openly advocated a "one-party" state in Uganda and a one-party socialist state "free from the effects of what he saw as the "factional and tribal groupings" threatening the stability of the country".

The above statement was quoted in "The Daily Telegraph on January 7, 1974" in relation to the Military Coup by Dad on January 25, 1971.

Obote's so-called one-party socialist state "free from the effects of what he saw as the "factional and tribal groupings" threatening the stability of the country" was really a shift in strategy in the game of "Russian Roulette" with Ugandan Politics that began before Uganda attained "Independence" from Great Britain.

To achieve his one party state in Uganda, Obote needed the support of the army but the Army Commander, Shaban Opolot, who had recently married into the Buganda Royal Family, owed his loyalty to the Baganda and not to the Commander in Chief of the Uganda Armed Forces. So, Obote named Dad the new Commander of the First Battalion of the Uganda Rifles (UR).

A "very close" relationship between Dad and Obote developed while Obote continued to play "Russian Roulette" with Ugandan politics, the same way Uganda's colonizers the British did albeit using different strategies! He invited Dad to state functions and ordered that Dad be given a Mercedes Benz by the State.

During the year 1964, the opportunistic alliance between Obote and Mutesa II was dissolved, Obote having wooed significant members of the Kabaka Yekka (KY), (the Kabaka alone) Party to the Uganda Peoples' Congress (UPC) Party. The Majority of the KY crossed the floor of the National Assembly and joined Obote's UPC Party. Obote gave 5 posts to the ex-Kabaka Yekka men who crossed over to the UPC Party.

You will recall the number of notable events that occurred during 1962, in preparation for Uganda's "Independence" from Britain. This had included Kabaka (King) Mutesa II and the Baganda Protestants accommodating the UPC (Uganda Peoples Congress) Party. The King had conducted indirect elections by means of the pro-monarchist Lukiko and Buganda assumed a "special status." Kabaka Yekka (KY) (the Kabaka alone) thus, provided all 21 seats to the National Assembly and the UPC Party defeated the Democratic Party (DP) nationally by 37 to 24 seats. Mutesa II, the British and Obote had all desired a Protestant government over the Catholic Democratic Party by joining together in a "shaky coalition". During 1964, that "shaky coalition" "crumbled" as outlined above.

Dad's British superior Iain Grahame writes:

"The antagonism between the Protestant Kabaka and the Roman Catholic Benedicto Kiwanuka, which prevented the KY and the DP from forming an alliance, played right into Obote's hands."

In the above statement, Iain Grahame is alluding to the fact that the Kabaka Yekka (the Kabaka only) and Democratic Parties were both led by Baganda. However, the two parties could not form an alliance on the grounds of religion, which has been used as a ground to cause divisions among and discriminate against Wananchi (fellow citizens).

After the "shaky coalition" between Mutesa II's KY Party and Obote's UPC Party "crumbled", Obote became relentless in pursuing his "one-party" state and system in Uganda and one-party socialist state "free from the effects of what he saw as the "factional and tribal groupings" threatening the stability of the country". In 1964, while doing so, the UPC Party ousted John Kakonge, its pro-Communist Secretary General and Leader of the radical Youth Wing. In his place, the UPC Party elected Grace Ibingira.

During his continuing "Russian Roulette" like Courtship Dance with the KAR Old Guard, Obote continued to need the support of the Army but he was still suspicious of the Senior Army Officer Colonel Shaban Opolot who by virtue of marrying into the Buganda Royal Family was loyal to the Kabaka. So, he continued to see Dad as a replacement for Shaban Opolot and increasingly turned to him for help in implementing his not so hidden agenda.

According to Dad, around the same time, he began to dislike the Bantu because of their presumptuous superiority complex – their not so subtle treatment, consideration and perception of other Ugandans as inferior beings. However, he respected Freddie (Mutesa II) because like him, Freddie was an officer (actually Captain of the Grenadier Guards) - which meant that he was a good soldier. Besides, Dad hadn't forgotten the close relationship Grandma had shared with the Ganda Royal family on account of the precious gifts of Princes Mawanda and the very same Mutesa II.

A continuing close relationship with Obote and a "shower" of gifts

In his continuing need for the army to advance his political goals, Obote continued to increasingly turn to Dad for help. He continued to attract Dad and continued to invite him to state functions. Dad continued to enjoy the "gifts" given by Obote, including the Mercedes Benz Obote had ordered that Dad be given by the State and many other "gifts" including betrothal to Mama Nora Aloba Enin of the Royal Oyakori Lan'gi clan. It was the same clan who gave refuge to King Kabarega during the Nubian led wars of colonization commanded by Colonel Colville. The wars had forced the Bunyoro Babito Monarch to seek refuge amongst the Royal Lan'gi household of the Oyakori Lan'gi clan. Alas it was another number of years into the future before Mama Nora Aloba Enin gave birth to a son Alemi Aliga Issa in Tripoli, Libya in 1972 despite the fact that certain Lan'gi frowned on the union of Lan'gi and Kakwa.

In 1964, the Armed Forces Act of 1964 repealed a British Act of 1955. More Uganda Army expansion occurred and the Uganda Air Force was established.

A conference of Commonwealth Heads of Government and refugees

In July 1964, Obote attended his first conference of Commonwealth Heads of Government in London, as Prime Minster of Independent Uganda while other events were occurring in Neighbouring Sudan. Over 100,000 Refugees fled to Uganda, Kenya, Congo and Ethiopia. The Any-anya struggle in the Sudan had taken on a new meaning and sophistication as it acquired new weapons from renegade soldiers fleeing another war taking place in the neighbouring Belgium Congo (now the Democratic Republic of the Congo), during the "Congo Crisis".

The continuing "Congo Crisis" and Dad's friendship with Bob Astles

The "Congo Crisis" which included a series of events that occurred in the Belgium Congo between 1960 and 1966 and the brutal murder of Patrice Lumumba, the first Prime Minister of Congo continued and Dad was caught right in the epicentre.

As indicated in a previous section, more in depth reading is required for a proper understanding of events relating to the "Congo Crisis" and additional information will be made available in sections of subsequent parts of the series Idi Amin: Hero or Villain? His Son Jaffar Amin and Other People Speak. However, below is another sketchy outline of events that are reported to have occurred during the "Congo Crisis" this time from 1964 to 1966, for purposes of continuing to provide context to Dad's involvement in the "Crisis" and as a prelude to "fuller" information about the "Crisis".

As the "Congo Crisis" continued to unfold, events continued to unfold in Uganda as well. Sketchy outlines of some of these events are also included here for purposes of only providing context to Dad's story and as a prelude to "fuller" information.

We apologize for inadvertent errors, misrepresentations and inaccuracies. However, as the series unfolds, we will make any corrections and add information as Kakwa Temezi (Revered Elders) would in an Adiyo Narration Process.

In July 1964, the Simba (Lions) led by Christopher Gbenye staged a revolt against the rebel "government" of Tshombe in Katanga Province (now Shaba Province).

Between 1964 and 1965, Obote and his leftist friends sympathized with the rebels led by Christopher Gbenye.

Gbenye's Foreign Minister was Thomas Kanza and the Treasurer, Tony Nyate.

Both Dad and Obote had been admirers of Lumumba and believed that Lumumba had been murdered on President Kasavubu and Colonel Mobutu's orders, not according to their own informers, by Tshombe.

It was widely believed that Obote sent Dad inside the Congo to set up training camps for the Simba - which means Lions - the name adopted by the rebels for their struggle against Kasavubu.

It was claimed that Dad was entrusted to bring Gold, Ivory and Coffee to pay for arms and equipment and it appeared that the Defence Minister, Felix Onama, Dad, Obote, and Nekyon Adoko, Minister of Planning and Economic Development had the blessings of the "Congo Affair".

In 1964, many of the defeated Congo's Simbas fled across the borders into Godiya-Gombe in the Kakwa Congo County, Ko'buko (Ko'boko) in Uganda and to the Yei town in the Sudan, abandoning their weapons.

What a windfall for the Anyanya during the first Sudanese war! Free Weapons!

In 1964, refugees flooded Uganda from the Sudan because of the first war the Anyanya waged on the Government of Sudan.

During the "Congo Crisis", Dad developed a friendship with Bob Astles an ex-Royal Engineer in Kenya on whom the fictional character Nicholas Garrigan in the hit movie "The Last King of Scotland" is loosely based. Bob Astles had left the Kings African Rifles in 1952 and became an employee of the Public Works Department in Uganda. He also worked as a pilot and was told by Obote to fly Dad to the Congo for operations around the Katanga region during the "Congo Crisis."

While Bob Astles worked as Dad's pilot in the Congo, he was rescued by Dad from a Congolese prison when the White man was captured and thrown in prison by the Congolese one day.

In an interview posted on July 30th, 2006 which was conducted by Norman S. Miwambo of the Black Star News, a New York Investigative Newspaper, Bob Astles stated:

"When I was a pilot, I was told by Dr. Apollo Milton Obote to fly Amin to Congo for operations around Katanga regions. That was my first time and he liked me. We came to know each other but it was the president that had directed me to fly him to Congo"… "Get this right! In 1964, I was directed by Dr. Apollo Milton Obote's government to be Amin's pilot during the Congo crisis until my position was taken by Israeli pilots in 1966…" (Excerpted from http://www.blackstarnews.com/?c=122&a=2270).

The fictional character Nicholas Garrigan in the hit movie "The Last King of Scotland" is loosely based on Bob Astles' relationship with Dad. The film stars African American Forest Whitaker as Dad and James McAvoy as his Scottish adviser Nicholas Garrigan.

Bob Astles was Dad's British-born right-hand man. There are allegations that Dad ordered Bob Astles death whenever he got tired of his company but I remember Bob Astles well and I don't believe Dad ordered his death. They were chums.

Dad's continuing rise through the ranks of the army and accusations

Dad continued to rise through the ranks of the army and Obote continued to rely on him heavily, to forge forward with his "political agenda". Obote continued to come to the aid of the Congo rebels during the "Congo Crisis", assisted by Dad. However, accusations of financial gain by Dad, Obote and others from the "Congo Crisis" through corruption soon flared up.

These accusations would continue in future years, even after Dad took over power from Apollo Milton Obote on January 25, 1971. Following is a sketchy account of related events for context. Fuller information will be included in subsequent parts of the series:

In March 1964, Daudi Ochieng, a Ma'di, but adopted by the Acholis accused Dad of having his (Dad's) Bank Account at the Ottoman Bank swollen by money received through corrupt means.

Ochieng had met the Kabaka, Freddie (Mutesa II), at King's College Budo where they became friends. After Makerere, Ochieng went to Aberystwyth while the Kabaka went to Cambridge. According to a couple of sources, this close relationship between the two men would harbinger a controversy in the 1990s when some rebel Princesses in the Buganda Courts accused Ronald Mutebi of being Daudi Ochieng's son and not Mutesa's legitimate son.

Before Uganda's "Independence", Ochieng was working as an Agricultural Officer in Eastern Uganda.

In March 1965, the Acholi Daudi Ochieng, Deputy Leader of the Opposition produced photocopies of Dad's bank account for February 1965, with deposits of up to £17,000 – too high of a deposit in one single month according to him.

Ochieng brought the photocopies to Parliament and alleged financial gain from corruption in the "Congo Operations".

Ochieng called for an enquiry and recommended that Dad should be suspended from the army in the meantime. By this time, Dad was a Colonel.

In September 1965, Daudi Ochieng raised the issue of Dad's bank account deposits again and he again recommended Dad's suspension from the Army and from his position as Deputy Commander of the Army but Obote opposed the motion saying the investigations into the affair were nearly complete.

In yet another move, Ochieng alleged that Dad was training a secret Army in the Eastern Region to overthrow the Constitution - Obote's Government.

While all the hoopla about Dad's alleged misconduct and financial gain from the Congo Operations was going on, Obote, by his offers of office, induced the leader of the Parliamentary Opposition, Basil Bataringaya and 5 of his supporters to cross over to the UPC Party.

On January 31, 1966, Ochieng, again, with the support of the Kabaka, Chief Whip and the Leader of the Opposition, tabled a motion that Dad be suspended. Again the suspension was for his alleged "plunder in Gold, Ivory, Coffee and money from the Congo, and for sharing the proceeds with the Prime Minister (Obote), Onama and Nekyon Adoko".

"The amounts were £17,000 for Dad, £50,000 for Obote and the two Ministers each got £25,000, for a total of £125,000" declared Ochieng.

"The reason why Colonel Amin has not been subjected to the searching eyes of the law is because he is the man through whom few individuals in the Government are planning a coup to overthrow the Constitution", accused Ochieng.

However, Onama fought back saying, "These are the fabricated allegations - let Mr. Ochieng repeat them outside the National Assembly where he is not covered by Parliamentary Immunity and he will see what will happen."

On that day, January 31, 1966, Obote, on his part, cautioned against "fake prophets, self-seeking chiefs and self-righteous politicians" (Grahame, 49).

Obote was implicated in Ochieng's allegations of financial gain by corrupt means. He opposed the motion to suspend Dad and denied allegations in a Press Conference on February 13, 1966.

That day on February 13, 1966, having returned from his Northern Tour, Obote held a Press Conference at State House Entebbe. During that Press Conference he said, "I deny absolutely that I have received any money, gold, coffee or elephant tusks, or any gainful commodity out of the troubles last year along the Congo border. I have led the government with clean hands. This is frame-up to blacken my name—it is a frame-up by my enemies to persuade members of my own party to lose confidence in me."

During the Press Conference, Obote also defended Dad on the so-called Congo gold rush affair.

Dad's marriage to Mama Mariam and "feuds" between his parents

In 1966, Dad finally married Mama Mariam (Sarah Mutesi Kibedi) and the two consummated their marriage after cohabiting for six years from 1960 and becoming betrothed in 1963. My mother introduced to Mama Mariam by my Great Aunt in 1961 continued as the nursemaid to Dad and Mama Mariam's children.

There continued to be a rift between my grandparents and lots of "feuds" over the Deadly "Paternity Test" Dad endured as an infant and the pronouncement Grandma made after "the test" and Lan'ga na Da ritual she performed to evoke a curse on Grandpa. Dad was also caught right in the middle between my grandparents in their continuing feuds.

Grandma's pronouncement was continuing to unfold right before her eyes as Dad continued to ascend in power from the time he was conscripted into the Fighting Unit of the Kings African Rifles in 1946. In terms of seniority and obvious leadership qualities, Dad was a natural choice before Uganda's "Independence" from Britain for the Commanding Officer of the Uganda Rifles and subsequent leadership positions. So he continued his ascend in the ranks of the Army.

Grandma never forgave Grandpa for "listening" to the Ganda and Nubian gossips that alleged that Buganda's King Daudi Chwa fathered Dad. She never forgot Grandpa's demand for the "Paternity Test" involving Dad being abandoned in the Kakwa jungle on the slopes of the Legendary

Kakwa Mountain Liru as an infant because Grandpa disputed his paternity. She never got over the fact that Dad could have died during the "Paternity Test" as many Kakwa infants subjected to the same "Paternity Test" did.

According to family members, Grandpa once came for some assistance from his son but he was brutally accosted by Grandma. She came storming into the Army House Executive apartment in Kampala that Dad and Mama Mariam were residing in and reminded Grandpa that he had disowned Awon'go and therefore he had no right to even step into her son's house.

By then, Dad was an upward mobile Colonel in the Uganda Armed Forces.

Despite his parents' feuds, Dad stayed close to Grandpa and he was always the charming effect between his parents as they wrangled openly in his house.

Moreover the powerful curse Grandma evoked during the assembly following Dad's "Paternity Test" came to pass!

Mysteriously, by the time Dad was a Colonel, Grandpa was suffering from Tunnel Vision.

A quiet whisper in the Dada family circles was that Grandma's KAR Rifle proclamation had indeed come to pass.

Come to think of it in hindsight, amazingly deep in the era of outright segregation when no Black African was allowed beyond Buganda Road, Nakasero unless they were some kind of worker, maid and shamba boy (farm hand) Dad was living on Acacia Avenue in Kololo, Kampala. This was a High-class exclusive residential area inhabited only by Uganda's elite.

Dad had come a long way indeed through sheer determination from the days when he used to slash sugar cane as a Kasanvu (coerced labourer), at the Metha Sugar Plantations in the 1940s. This was happening in the era when the Indians resided in Kamwokya, which was some kind of microcosm of New Delhi, Mumbai or Kolkata.

Trouble from Tribalism and how my 14 year old mother saved Dad

As Dad continued his ascent to the most powerful position in the land, there was more trouble for him because the game of "Russian Roulette" with Ugandan Politics continued.

On February 22, 1966, Policemen entered the Parliament and arrested five Ministers namely Grace Ibingira, Balaki Kirya, Mathius Ngobi,

George Magezi and Dr. Ernest Lumu. All of the arrested ministers were Bantus and they were taken to Gulu in Northern Uganda.

After the arrest, Obote announced that he had assumed "all powers of Government because of his understanding of the wishes of the people for peace, order and prosperity."

On February 23, 1966, Obote put Shaban Opolot under Dad, and Dad took over the command of the Army and Air Force and assured Obote of the loyalty of the Ugandan troops. However, political crises soon erupted and Dad found himself right in the middle of the continuing crises including the "Mengo Crisis" of February 25, 1966 during which my mum, 14 years at the time saved Dad's life.

In a section of one of my book projects, I pay tribute to my mother who became entangled with Dad and "unwittingly" ended up being one of his many women, while working as a nursemaid for him and his official senior wife Mama Mariam.

In a section of a subsequent part of the series titled "Nakoli the Mulamoji", I introduce my mother Ms. Marguerita (Mangarita) Nakoli, born on February 12, 1952 at the peak of colonialism in Uganda and 6 years after Dad was conscripted into the Fighting Unit of the Kings African Rifles.

At the time of mum's birth, little did my maternal grandparents Princess Marie Celeste a Ba-Ise Ngobi "Mumbeda" and Eryakesi Bulima know what fate had in store for their precious daughter when fourteen years later she would become one of Dad's many women.

The section in the subsequent part of the series titled "Nakoli the Mulamoji" includes information on mum's clan, circumstances surrounding her birth, her childhood and events preceding her life as a nursemaid to Dad and his senior wife Mama Mariam. As well, it includes information about mum's life as a nursemaid for Dad and Mama Mariam.

Dad had continued to rise steadily through the ranks and he was now married to Mama Mariam who is considered by many as Dad's first wife when heavily armed soldiers sent by Lieutenant Colonel Oyite-Ojok came knocking on the door for Dad. Mum a 14-year old girl denied that he was home. Following is an account of the story relating to that day on February 25, 1966 that could have proved fatal for Dad. It is commonly referred to as the "Mengo Crisis":

During the "Mengo Crisis" of February 25, 1966, Dad conferred with the Kabaka Mutesa II who was still the Commander in Chief at Lubiri.

The Baganda panicked thinking Dad had come to arrest their King.

Later that evening, Obote announced the suspension of the Constitution "temporarily" and added that during his Northern Tour, "an attempt was made to overthrow the Government by foreign troops because of the selfish interests of a few individuals in high places."

Deep in the night, three 3-ton Military Bedford lorries trudged their way up to the Army House, Plot 13 Acacia Avenue, Kololo (Command Post Kololo). This was the Official Residence of the 2IC (Second in Command).

They trudged their way to Kololo with a mission to capture and destroy the newly appointed Commander in Chief, who was Dad. But, Dad, unbeknownst to any of the assailants was at home with the family. Fortunately, when the soldiers came knocking at the gate, one 14-year old Mangarita was at hand to open the door for them. With agitation, they inquired whether Dad might be around.

Whether it was "Lemi" or "Yakanye" or our "Tobura", something made Mangarita instinctively protective of her lot.

She exclaimed, "He has just left for Mbuya. Didn't you meet him on the way?"

The heavily armed soldiers made a hasty retreat and the three toners rolled off at great speed.

Shocked and with tears in his eyes, Dad came out of hiding quaking in relief and embraced Mangarita wondering what in the world came into her and gave her the cunning at that very lethal of moments. However, he seemed grateful for the reprieve and the moment strengthened his resolve. He rushed to his armory and started to arm himself then he set off for Loyal Troops towards Bombo Barracks.

Dad never forgot that incident and in fact re-enacted the whole scene to his mother, my Grandma when he also confessed that the young girl had conceived and was heavy with child – me!

Grandma never forgot that moment too and in Kakwa Tradition named me Remo (my Kakwa name), after an incident that might have befallen either my mother or my father. In effect my Kakwa name Remo was two-fold - the critical moments that confronted my father at the height of the Mengo Crisis and the lengthy time I was destined to stay in the womb, which I recount in a section below.

I have something to say about the understandable frown against child motherhood, which seems to be the norm in "African cultures" but is frowned upon in the so-called affluent West, yet according to a number of articles, Teen Child Mothers are on the rise in the affluent West.

In a subsequent part of the series, I will share my standpoint about teen mothers including an explanation on my heritage and how that early pregnancy derailed my mother permanently.

Obote's 1966 abrogation of Uganda's 1962 Constitution

On March 2, 1966, Obote assumed the power of President and Vice President and in a radio broadcast, alleged that the Kabaka Mutesa II had summoned foreign diplomats and requested troops to be sent to Uganda. Kabaka Mutesa II refused to acknowledge the truth of this rumour but insisted that "he believed that troops were being trained to overthrow the Constitution."

There would be more trouble between Obote and the Kabaka (King of the Baganda), in future months and years.

Meanwhile, Sir Clement de Lestang of the East African Court of Appeal with Justice Henry Miller of the Kenya High Court and Justice Augustine Saida of the Tanzanian Court of Appeal formed the Judicial Enquiry into the "Congo Affair". The allegations of corruption against Dad, Obote and others had continued. The findings of this trio of judges were published after Dad's coup in 1971 and its minutes were available to the public in most bookshops in Uganda.

On March 8, 1966, one of the key witnesses to the "Congo Affair", the Congolese rebel, General Nicholas Olenga testified, agreeing that sums of money had been deposited in Uganda banks in the names of various ministers and dignitaries, including Dad. The evidence of the ex-Ministers was also heard in camera.

In 1966, the Uganda Army numbered 5,700 men in four battalions and the Uganda Air force numbered 260 men.

In the same year 1966, Prime Minister Obote abrogated the 1962 Constitution. He declared a new constitution on April 15, 1966.

On that day, April 15, 1966, in a motion that passed by 55 votes to 4, Obote suspended the Constitution and declared himself President. He made this declaration on the grounds that it was his "understanding of the wishes of the people of this country for peace, order and prosperity".

Abolition of kingdoms in Uganda and the explosion of Tribalism

On April 17, 1966, Obote abolished the kingdoms much to the chagrin of pro monarchists.

Despite the overwhelming rejection of the old Constitution, the Buganda Parliament (Lukiko) passed a resolution rejecting Obote's new Constitution and re-affirming that the 1962 Constitution was still valid. Because of his reckless actions, Obote thus faced opposition from the Baganda, leading to political trouble and "The Kabaka Uprising" which is discussed in a section below.

The law firm of Messrs Abu Mayanja, Clark and Company was activated. Clark represented Dad, Onama and Nekyon in the continuing "Congo Affair" while Mayanja represented the Kabaka to claim that he was still the President and that the suspension of the 1962 Constitution by Obote was unconstitutional.

Under the provisions of the new constitution, Obote was the Executive President of Uganda. The Kabaka of Buganda as well as the kings of Busoga, Bunyoro, and Toro were barred from holding political office. At this time, Uganda's per capita income was a whopping $65, a substantial figure for Black Africans during that time.

Obote further claimed that the Kabaka had made an attempt to overthrow him in his absence from Kampala in February and that "some persons who held Government positions asked foreign missions for massive military assistance of foreign soldiers and arms." Obote then ordered the arrest of the Army Commander, Shaban Opolot and imprisoned the Iteso soldier. Opolot, who was married into the Buganda Royal Family, owed his loyalty to the Baganda.

Obote named Dad the new Commander of the Uganda Army and effectively dismissed Opolot who would languish in jail until Dad released him. Opolot's release would occur after Dad overthrew the same Obote who appointed him Commander of the Army in the military coup that catapulted him to the position of President on January 25, 1971.

On May 20, 1966, the Kabaka demanded that the Obote Government remove itself from Buganda soil within ten days. Two days later Obote ordered an attack on the Kabaka's Palace, with the intention of assassinating Mutesa II. This was the time Dad assisted the Kabaka Mutesa II to escape the "death trap" by Obote out of loyalty for the close relationship Grandma shared with his parents and what his father King Daudi

Chwa did for Grandma. Dad saved the Kabaka's life as he did Jomo Kenyatta's during his "Mau Mau days".

On May 22, 1966, Obote summoned Onama, Dad, Henry Kajubi and two other men of his inner circle to attack the Kabaka's Palace.

When Dad "botched" Obote's plan to assassinate the Kabaka (King)

On May 24, 1966 at 5:30am, the attack on the Kabaka's Palace commenced.

However, Dad told us that in the thick of battle he threw a smoke screen which shielded the Kabaka and the Kabaka escaped amidst a heavy shower by taxi where he and his ADC Captain Katende drove away to the Congo and then to Bujumbura in Burundi. From there, the Kabaka flew by an American plane to Brussels and by the BOAC to London where he lived in exile until his demise in 1969.

Dad's uncle Sosteni of the Piza Kakwa clan, a Military Transport Officer (MTO) was actually the person who drove the King and his ADC Captain Katende to safety.

Dad regularly told that his action was in memory of the close relationship between the Buganda Royal Family and his mother in the past.

In retrospect the deposed Monarch has never denied this public pronouncement by his presumed assailant or Obote's former Hatchet man - right up until his death in November 1969 at age 45.

Although proudly not acknowledged by the Baganda today, His Majesty Ronald Mutebi as he should rightly be addressed was looked after by Dad from the time his father's body was brought back to Buganda for burial right up to the day the so-called Liberators took power in 1979. Only then did the then Royal Highness and Heir face hardships during his stay in exile throughout the eighties.

After the Deadly "Paternity Test" Dad endured because of allegations that Kabaka Mutesa II's father Kabaka Daudi Chwa fathered Dad and not Grandpa, Grandma continued to have a strong relationship with the Ganda Royal Family.

As Dad rose through the ranks of the Army, Grandma regularly reminisced about past events to Dad who also held the Royal Family in high esteem because of the generosity and kindness Mutesa II's parents King Daudi Chwa and Queen Druscilla extended to Grandma, along with Dad.

Grandma was still revered in the Ganda Royal family for the Gift of the very King Mutesa II. The reverence for Grandma had continued in spite of the fact that my grandparents had separated when the then Police-man my grandfather Amin Dada Nyabira Tomuresu was transferred to the Kololo Hill Police Barracks in the 1930s from the Shimoni-Nakasero Police Barracks. Grandma had continued to enjoy the house King Daudi Chwa had built for her in Kitigulu at the marshy site just as you approach En-tebbe.

Dad knew about the tight relationship between Grandma and the Ganda Royal Family but Obote didn't. So, on May 22, 1966, when Obote summoned Onama, Dad, Henry Kajubi and two other men of his inner circle and ordered the attack on the Royal Palace, Dad decided to "craft" a plot that would assist the Kabaka Edward Mutesa II to escape the "death trap" instead.

A couple of witnesses were present when Dad threw the smoke screen, which shielded the Kabaka in the thick of battle and enabled him to escape the "death trap" by Obote. He did this so that the Kabaka could escape amidst the heavy shower by taxi where he and his ADC Captain Katende drove away to the Congo and then to Bujumbura in Burundi. Dad's uncle Sosteni, the Military Transport Officer (MTO) of the Piza Kakwa clan that was the actual person who drove the King and his ADC Captain Katende to safety regularly told of their escape.

According to Dad, the plan of attack was supposed to be a basic siege encirclement of the Lubiri wall. Dad decided on a frontal attack at the main gate along the Kabaka Njagala Avenue instead while leaving the Kisenyi wing unmanned. He stationed his Uncle MTO Sosteni there with the recounted taxi that was hailed by the diminutive Monarch and his ADC.

Thus in 1966, Obote used the Uganda Army to crush the "Kabaka Uprising" and the King escaped because Dad deliberately "botched" Obote's plan to assassinate him and the Kabaka fled into exile in Britain by way of the Congo, Burundi and eventually to London.

Unbeknownst to Obote, Dad was the one who let the Kabaka Mu-tesa II escape.

The same month Obote ordered the attack on the Kabaka's Palace in May 1966, he instructed the GSU (General Service Unit) and the Secret Service to walk loose in Buganda. He imposed a State of Emergency in Buganda, further antagonizing the Baganda.

That same year 1966, Obote sent a secret memorandum to all Afri-can Heads of State explaining what was happening in Uganda. He said:

"On 23 May, in preparation for the final showdown, arms were handed to tribesmen at the Kabaka's Palace. Roads leading to the capital

were dug up and roadblocks erected. The railway line was broken up thirty-
five miles from Kampala in both directions. The telephone to Jinja and
Nairobi was cut, and attacks were staged on police stations."

Obote claimed that that's when he realized on May 23, 1966 that he
was faced by a full-scale rebellion and ordered the attack on the Kabaka's
Palace.

According to various sources, "The real issue however, was money
as two checks valued at £9 million were transferred to the Kabaka and
banked in London, to pay for his (Kabaka's) Palace Guards".

Dad's continuing steady rise, other events and a tussle with robbers

Following the 1966 crisis, Dad was promoted to full Colonel and
Brigadier Opolot was dismissed and imprisoned by Obote for siding with
the monarchists.

Dad had been the Chief of Staff from 1962 and Shaban Opolot had
been the Army Commander.

Following the crisis, Dad became the Army Commander and Okoya
his Chief of Staff.

In July 1966, Sayed Sadiq Al-Mahdi became the Prime Minister of
the Sudan. Soon, Obote visited Sadiq in Khartoum in order to discuss the
Anyanya situation in the Southern Sudan. The war in the Sudan had
continued and Obote was "unfriendly" to the Anyanya.

On August 24, 1966, Obote defied democracy and took the oath of
Office as Uganda's Executive President.

Meanwhile, Dad's "Rags to Riches Story" continued. However with
the riches, came a security problem – Kondos (armed thugs). Following is a
related story Dad regularly told us about how he fought off Kondos.

By the year 1966, Dad was doing very well economically. According to him, he was doing so well in life that he even managed to contract
Israeli friends to build him triplicate Bungalows on his Free Hold Plot
33/35 Sir Daudi Chwa Road, Mbuya Hill enroute to the Uganda Army
Mbuya Military Hospital. However, because of his economic wealth, Dad
also became a target of Kondos (armed thugs) that had become a phenomenon in Uganda.

By this time Dad had been relocated to Plot 10, Prince Charles
Drive, Kololo, the Official Residence of the Army Commander, which he
called "The Command Post."

While reminiscing about his adventures in 1966, Dad once almost cracked our ribs laughing when he related an incident that happened to him at the height of their "Gold Dust Twins" era in the 1960s.

Dad had related this incident in 1983 at our former Macarona home with his newly wedded bride Nnasali Nightie (Mama Chumaru) present.

At the time of the attack by the armed thugs, Dad had also acquired for himself a Beamer (BMW) with rectangular headlamps - possibly the 2001 or 2000 model. According to Baba Diliga an uncle from the Bori Kakwa clan, the car was given to Dad as another present by Milton Obote.

I still remember the plush burgundy leather seats and the overtly extensive aerial on the side.

Unfortunately, this equivalent of the 2001 M3 (BMW) was the target of eight Kondos (armed thugs) that Dad fought off single handedly. One particular night, they managed to corner Dad and ordered him out of the car not realizing that they were confronting a battle hardened Kings African Rifles Veteran.

Dad reenacted the fight sequence to devastating effect at our first Residence on Macarona Street in Jeddah, while we lived in exile in Saudi Arabia. He did this with all the Adiyo (oral historical narrative account of history, events of the past) drama that is distinctive in Kakwa story telling.

According to him, he came out of the Beamer headlong into the midriff of the ringleader. Then instinctively, he used the equivalent of what looked to me while we were all roaring with laughter like the "Thai Boxing Knee Up" at every opportunity he met any of the thugs. He made a dash for a slope with some thugs in hot pursuit. He stopped in mid stride, struck backwards with what to me was a back kick at the approaching thugs. All in all, he managed to single handedly demobilize all eight Kondos.

The incident actually came out in the Uganda Argus! At the time in Kampala, thefts, blackmail, and kondoism or armed robbery had reached new heights and rampancy. Luckily for Dad, the kondos in those days specialized in machetes rather than the present day thugs who use AK47s. Whenever I recall this incident, the Ragga hit with the line "Whose got the Key to my Beamer" comes to mind!

As Dad was telling the story of his encounter with the armed thugs, we kept screaming "lies, lies" ("wongo, wongo") in Kiswahili and Dad kept saying "haki, haki" ("honest, honest") also in Kiswahili. "You go and check the Makerere National Archives", he offered. The incident was reported in the Uganda Argus.

Dad's love affair with cars

Dad's love affair with cars was legendary. He owned the hybrid Citroen/Maserati SM with the distinctive UVN 945 Number Registration Plate. After Dad became President of Uganda, Al-Qadhafi also gave him a fabulous Metallic Emerald Green Mercedes Benz 300 Coupe, with those distinctive stacked up double headlamps. He was given a 1974-75 model Cadillac Eldorado Convertible as a bonus when he bought two brand new 707 Boeings and a Lockheed Hercules C-130 Cargo Transporter Plane which he paid for in cash. He is also on record as having once bought eleven Mercedes Benz 600 Pullman Stretch Limousines on a single day!

Dad would come storming down the highway in the Mercedes Benz 300 Coupe, from a weekend outing in Munyonyo/Gaba or at Paradise Beach on the way back to State House Entebbe with Elekinwa's latest hits at full blast on the car Stereo. I enjoyed these breathtaking romps back home with the single escort 504 Estate trailing miserably.

Dad used to terrorize his wives and girlfriends in his amphibian "Amphicar" we christened "Anfuka" [child-speak sic] motor car, by driving right into the lake with our mothers on board screaming their heads off.

The last I heard of that very particular mode of transport "Amphibian car" is that one of the Blik family members has enthusiastically restored it to running condition.

Dad was obsessed with both Land Rovers and a beige 1st Generation Range Rover with 20" Rims and BF Goodrich Rubber on and he participated in Rallies with the cumbersome Flagship 604 Peugeot. He also owned a Winibago Camper Van given to him by some Kuwaiti nationals who apparently travelled with the Camper all the way from Kuwait.

The one endearing image of Dad to my very personal Hip Hop/New Jack Swing influenced perspective is the snapshot of him self-driving a drop top military Jeep Renegade during the 1971 take over. New Jack Swing Beat indeed! Yap! Yap!

The peculiar circumstances of my 13-month gestation

When I finally met my mother in 1986 after being taken away from her at the tender age of three, she told me a very peculiar genesis story of events surrounding my birth. Mum claimed to have conceived (missed her period) in February 1966, so she was supposed to give birth to me by

October 1966. However, the water did not break that month! Amazingly, the pregnancy progressed into the year 1967!

The unusual circumstances of my 13-month gestation created more trouble for Dad and it earned him a scolding by Grandma.

In Luo culture, I would have been named Okunu because like the proverbial Adibu Bull Elephant, I spent the better part of one year and one month for good measure in my mother's womb. Thus at age 15 did the then child mother release her burden into the world - a stone's throw away from Mpumude the hilltop last stand of the Kabarega who had been allowed to return to his home land. His body was transported to Bunyoro for burial.

My maternal Great Aunt Nnalongo (Mother of Twins) Nnabirye Lovisa was distraught with worry for the child mother, as mum was only fourteen years old upon conceiving me and lived with it right into the tender age of fifteen in 1967, for she was born on December 2, 1952. So, Ssenga (Aunt) as we fondly call her rushed with her niece to Abuba (Grandma) Aisha (Kabaka) Aate Bint Buda in Kidusu fearing for her niece's life. Grandma was commonly referred to as Kabaka because a lot of the Kakwa and Nubian Elders had nicknamed her Kabaka due to her enormous size and close association with the Buganda Royal Family in the early 1900s.

Grandma received my mum and Great Aunt with care and under-standing. She made a spot inspection and put mum to rest. She then sent for Dad whom she lambasted about the matter but she also requested for transport from him to a fellow shaman in Kamuli District who specialized in Qur-anic verse (Faliq) incantations.

It is heartening to know that Dad did not deny the deed although it was my mother Mangarita's word against his since his senior wife had hired mum as an Aya (nursemaid) for his legitimate children. According to mum, this fellow shaman was actually a leper and upon arrival, mum approached the shrine with the natural apprehension of a fifteen-year old girl.

According to mum, the date was March 8, 1967. This date is forever etched in her mind's eye because of what transpired after she and Grandma arrived at the fellow shaman's shrine. The shaman told mum that the reason for her delay in giving birth was due to a wronged rival who because of not ever having produced a male offspring for Dad had deemed it necessary to stop this pregnancy in its tracks. Mum was awestruck with what to her mind was a strange certainty amongst these strange seers.

"Who could know the gender of the expected child?" mum reflect-ed.

The shaman then continued to tell mum that the rival had bought a black bull and she had sacrificed it for this purpose.

The shaman proceeded to write Qur-anic scripts on seven pieces of paper. Then he lit a candle on a stand and handed the seven scripts to mum. He solemnly requested that mum pray and wish for whatever her heart desired then place each piece of paper to the candle and let each piece burn completely without letting go of the burning piece!

Mum closed her eyes and wished her blessed wish for the safety of her first child, me! Then she placed the first piece of script towards the burning candle and watched it burn slowly. As it approached her fingers, she felt the excruciating pain but held on for dear life. Strangely enough she claims that the tips of her fingers were numb by the time the burning got to the second piece, then the third and fourth, right through to the seventh.

After what seemed like a lifetime, mum looked up with pride at the shaman who solemnly informed her that she would give birth after seven days! Surprisingly there was no trace of burning when mum delicately rubbed the tips of her fingers!

Grandma took mum back to my Great Aunt in Wanyange with the good news. Upon arrival, she massaged mum's swollen stomach with a concoction of oils and medicinal herbs to ease the pressure.

While doing so, Grandma recounted the story about Dad's birth as I outline in the section relating to Dad's childhood. Mum regularly recounted how Dad landed onto a pile of hailstones as a newborn which set off a resounding scream that reverberated around the Shimoni Hill Police Barracks where Grandpa was serving as a Colonial Policeman and Dad was born.

As I recounted in the section on Dad's childhood, the mystical hailstorm and shower that had engulfed the city of Kampala as my Grandpa and Uncle Ramadhan Dudu Moro set off for the Eid Al-Adha prayers and festivities had increased in intensity. At the very hour Dad was born, the tropical hailstorm and hailstones were coming down with such intensity as if to announce the birth of a mystical child. Many Kakwa still believe that it is an omen for a child to be born during a hailstorm as Dad was.

Grandma told my mum and many Dada family members that Dad cried so excessively the day he landed onto the pile of hailstones as an infant that she gave him the Kakwa name Awon'go. However in accordance with Kakwa naming tradition she meant for Dad's name Awon'go to have a deeper meaning than a screaming infant as I detail in the section on Dad's childhood.

My birth during a heavy downpour of hailstorm, just like Dad's

That fateful day, March 15, 1967, mum was rushed to Bugembe Hospital where she gave birth between 6:00am and 8:00am, during a heavy downpour of hailstorm, just like the time Dad was born! She gave birth to me, a 3.50 kgs bouncing baby boy, after an incredible 13 months in the womb!

Sadly in a lot of African countries, 12 years marks the moment girlhood supposedly moves into womanhood - too young to push for the hip bones are still developing and too naïve to understand their very own body. However the harsh reality of Africa is that many end up in early marriages and pregnancies. Alas that was the fate of my mother although I was delivered when she had just crossed the 15-age threshold.

Years, later, I had a wrangle with mum over the date of my birth since my passport and all my official documents read October 27, 1966. Yet here she was in 1986, claiming I was actually a year younger. At that time I retorted that:

Considering the length of time I stayed in the womb and her actual confirmation that I was due in October 1966, then in all probability, fate and my renowned stubborn nature deemed it that on paper I would always have been born on October 27, 1966.

Mum even recalled that Dad lambasted her years before apparently when I was about to begin school for having lost my vaccination and birth certificates. She claims that she never went back to Bugembe Hospital to collect them being so young at the time and considering the number of years that had passed she doubted that such records still existed.

On paper including school documents, which cannot be changed, my date of birth is October 27, 1966. However in 1986 when I came to see my mother in September, she claimed my incredible stay in the womb between February 1966 and March 15, 1967 and further claimed that I was numerically one year younger despite having spent one year and one month in the womb.

My own "Paternity Test" conducted by Grandma of all people

After my birth, Grandma herself subjected me to a different but equally lethal "Paternity Test" as an infant - the way Dad was! Like father, like son, my own birth, heritage and paternity was contested and Grandma of all people subjected me to another unusual "Paternity Test".

Following is how events surrounding my contested paternity unfolded:

My heritage came into doubt (like Dad's!) when the first lady of the house Mama Mariam (Sarah Mutesi Kibedi) raised a storm claiming "any of the house boys and cooks could have fathered the new born bastard" – me!

Another Kakwa tradition is a thoroughly mystical test, which is enacted by the concerned members of the family to confirm the heritage of the child. As shaman Grandma Aisha Aate confronted my mother with the accusation laid by the chief wife, she ominously informed her that if the child was not one of their own, then the child would leave her shrine a corpse!

Mum said she could not change her resolve when her Great Aunt who was in attendance pressured her to preserve what to her was a beautiful child and "leave these mystical people alone". Abuba (Grandma) Aisha Aate asked mum thrice and she was adamant since I was a virgin birth in the most biological sense of the word. At 14, mum had never known a man and Dad's liaison was her initial loss of innocence and it led to my conception.

For my "Paternity Test", Abuba (Grandma) Aate started to chant incantations and she raised her ebony rod into the air and behold Nakan, the great python appeared and encircled the child - me! According to Grandma, it was the very same "sacred" snake that had come to Dad and wrapped itself around Dad for warmth as it would do around its own eggs during the Deadly "Paternity Test" Dad was subjected to as an infant because of his contested paternity.

You will recall that according to Grandma, the "sacred" snake had placed its head on the crown of Dad's head for the duration of Dad's "Paternity Test". I have no reason to dispute Grandma's claims that it was the same snake that mysteriously appeared when my heritage also came into doubt.

These scenes continued to greatly horrify my Great Aunt who again urged mum to take me and leave. However, before mum and Ssenga (Auntie) could scoot out of Grandma's shrine, Abuba (Grandma) gleefully raised the ebony rod then placed it forthright in front of her----in effect the great snake disappeared and she then proclaimed my name "Osman Remo".

At that moment, after she had confirmed my lineage through another "strange" "Paternity Test", my Grandma cradled me, rocked and danced with joy and gleeful laughter. She sent for Dad who came after three months, making a fracas more so out of relief than anything. Grandma and Dad loved me unconditionally and I loved them right back!

The novelty or even in some circles what was considered to some an oddity brought out a most poignant statement from a Reviewer who had read the Associated Press Interview I gave in 2007 following the release of the feature film "The Last King of Scotland". The Reviewer had made statements such as "Jaffar Amin actually makes one feel sorry for Idi Amin Dada". That is when I realized that as a son born in 1966 and having continuously lived under various roofs and in the warm bosom of this "strict but loving man," I had a different experience of Idi Amin.

On hindsight and in many respects, the above statement was leveled at Forest Whitaker's outstanding performance, which presented a softer side of the hard image of Idi Amin Dada.

This is what gave me the impetus to explain further what I had been writing about my father since 2001 when he discovered that he had diabetes, following a fainting incident while driving his ubiquitous White Caprice Classic Chevrolet Station Wagon. Considering his image to my mind of invincibility, the actual incident was hushed up but I was greatly shocked to find out about it. For I was last in Jeddah in 1990 and moved to jotting down on word document in my free time all I ever remembered that he had told me, which started in dire earnest in 2001, when we also lost Major Moshe Abdi'Nebbi his Younger brother to Diabetes too.

As I explained in a previous section, traditionally, the names given to Kakwa babies reflect circumstances and situations the babies are born into. The names can mean different things depending on the context. In my case, Grandma gave me the Kakwa name Remo to reflect the fact that my parents and I escaped death numerous times. Examples include the time when my father and mother could have been killed during the "Mengo Crisis" and numerous other times my father was a "marked" man as he rose steadily through the ranks of the army, after Uganda attained "Independence" from Great Britain.

Another time was when my mother and I could have died because I stayed in the womb for more than 9 months. The final time was when Grandma confronted my mother with the accusation laid by Dad's chief wife, Mama Mariam (Sarah Mutesi Kibedi) about the fact that I was not Dad's child and ominously informed her that if I wasn't Dad's child, I would leave her shrine a corpse. Like Dad, I survived this "strange" and equally Deadly "Paternity Test" and lived to talk about it!

The last I ever heard of Grandma's famous ceremonial ebony rod was that it was confiscated by Sister Genevieve of Namagunga Primary School when she found it amongst the artifacts of my Grandma's heir, my elder sister Farida Akulu Dawa. Dawa was attending the prestigious Missionary School, St Mary's Namagunga Primary School at the time and the Nuns would have none of the mystical stories and "nonsense" represented by Grandma's ceremonial ebony rod.

Alas, the name Osman (Uthman) given to me by Grandma after I survived her "Paternity Test" never caught on as a Muslim name since everyone called me either Tshombe, a name I write about below or Remo in my toddler years.

Years later after Dad had ascended to the position of President of Uganda on January 25, 1971 and in his drive for Islamization, I was deemed as one of his children without proper Islamic names. So, a list was sent to a panel of Kadi (Muslim Judges) under the leadership of the 1st Mufti at his newly created Uganda Muslim Supreme Council.

After perusing the list of Islamic names, the likes of Sheikh Sharif Idris gave me the name Jaffar, phonetically pronounced Jaafar but quite often mistakenly pronounced Jafari by Indigenous Kakwa and Black Africans.

How I got the name Tshombe like the Congolese Revolutionary

Following is how I got the name Tshombe at Hussien's house in Wanyange, like the Congolese Revolutionary/Rebel discussed in the section relating to the "Congo Crisis" which included a series of events that occurred in the Belgium Congo (now the Democratic Republic of the Congo) between 1960 and 1966. As outlined in the section introducing the "Congo Crisis" it was a period of turmoil that began with Congo's "Independence" from Belgium on June 30, 1960 and involved "revolutionaries" such as Patrice Lumumba, Moise Tshombe, Cyrille Adoula, Antoine Gizenga, Joseph Kasongo, Joseph Mobutu, Godefroid Munongo, Joseph Kasavubu and others. This period of turmoil included the brutal murder of Patrice Lumumba the first Prime Minister of the Congo on January 17, 1961.

The day Dad finally came to Grandma's - 3 months after she sent for him following my "Paternity Test", he put me in his staff car, an Austin Albion Station wagon. Then he drove with me, along with mum to the present day Qadhafi Garrison, former King George IV 1st Battalion Jinja, where all his buddies were at the Officers' Mess. Mum was quite frightened by the hoopla atmosphere amongst these warriors but Dad wanted to show me off to his colleagues.

At this particular gathering of warriors, there were presumptuous statements like "Duplicate!" "Junior!" and so on and so "force" as Dad was inclined to pronounce the word "forth" from the likes of Sulieman Hussien, Tito Okello and Juma Ndege. These warriors were apparently present the day Dad came to Grandma's, put me in his staff car and drove with me to the Officers' Mess at present day Qadhafi Garrison and never stopped reminiscing about that day. In fact, after the Officers' Mess, they all headed for their watering hole at Hussien's house in Wanyange where it was deemed fitting to give me a name separate from the Kakwa name Remo that my Grandma had given me.

Officers being Officers, names of Revolutionaries such as Nkrumah, Lumumba, Kenyatta, Abdul-Nasr, Sengor, Tshombe and others were written on pieces of paper and placed in a bowl.

According to Dad my hand was placed in the bowl and as is a natural reaction for an infant, I made a grab for the bits of paper. Apparently my first choice was Tshombe which was not well received considering their recent tour of duty in the Congo in relation to the "Congo Crisis".

Dad put back the piece of paper and re-mixed the bits.

Amazingly my hand was placed in the bowl again and I grabbed again. Shockingly the same name Tshombe came up.

Dismayed and filled with wonder, they put the paper back in the bowl and mixed the bits of paper one more time! My hand was placed into the bowl again and to the utter amazement of everyone, I grabbed Tshombe for the third consecutive time!

At that time, they all conceded defeat and accepted that name!

Dad recounted this incident while we were coming out of a newly built shopping mall on Macarona Street in Jeddah after we had fled into exile and he had encouraged me to enter the Raffle Draw having piled several trolleys full to the brim with groceries and other stuff. The Raffle Draw was for a brand new Mazda Station Wagon in 1984.

Dad said the above to me while claiming in the presence of his newly wedded wife Mama Iman Chumaru Nnasali Kigundu, "You have always been lucky. You can win the car!"

Mum tells the story of how I got the Pet name Tshombe differently. She claims that two choices came up between Lumumba and Tshombe and Dad settled on Tshombe having himself picked Tshombe from the bowl and her or Hussein having chosen Lumumba.

"The officers finally settled for the father's choice" recounted mum.

I kind of like Dad's version of how I got the Pet name Tshombe since it gives me a much-needed Mystique! However it was also fitting that at Colonel Hussien Sulieman of the Nubian Alur's Wanyange house, he would second the name Tshombe. For in the Alur Language, "Chombe" means "There are no men in the house but you try". This was very much in line with the Adibu Likamero sooth-sayers implication that I would be the first child to restart the male progeny, following a string of Girl-Children to the Al-Amin Family between 1961 and 1966.

Dad's marriage to Kay, the continuing war in the Sudan and Triblism

In 1967, Dad married Mama Kaysiya (Kay) at the Registrar's Office, much to the chagrin of the Bride's Father, who felt disappointed that he was not consulted about the marriage. Kay's father Archdeacon Adroa was troubled by the marriage and disappointed that Dad and Kay decided on a "kangaroo wedding" instead of the usual formal request for a girl's hand in marriage. The request is usually first directed through the Father of the Bride or other Tribal Elder as required by tradition and culture.

Another reason for Archdeacon Adroa's displeasure was the fact that he was from the Paranga clan of the Lugbara Tribe and Dad's family both on the mother and father's side have strong first generation links to that very Adroa family and that of Brigadier Wilson Toko. Brigadier Toko was a close associate of Dad's.

Kay was considered a cousin of Dad's and in most African countries marriages between cousins is not allowed. A marriage between Dad and Mama Kaysiya without a "cleansing" and "blessing" ceremony by Clan and Tribal Elders because they were considered family was thus prohibited.

I believe that Dad and Kay realized that the Father of the Bride and other Elders would not have allowed their marriage, hence their "kangaroo wedding". Besides, my sister Kidde was well on the way when Dad and Mama Kay made the decision to get married.

The after party was a society event that attendees remembered and talked about for a very long time. Erinayo Oryema was best man at the wedding. It is ironic that being cousins and therefore "illegally married" according to Dad was the very same reason he gave when he divorced Mama Kay in 1974, among other reasons.

Meanwhile the first Sudanese war was continuing in the Sudan and Dad continued to be involved. He assisted the Anyanya in Southern Sudan against the Arabs in the North even though the majority of the Arabs were Muslims like him.

In May 1967, Mohammed Ahmed Mahgoub became Prime Minster of the Sudan and he vowed to crush the Anyanya rebellion in the Southern Sudan, which had continued unabated. Dad was very instrumental in aiding the Anyanya in their war to defeat the Northern Sudanese government.

The same year 1967, Obote made a move to "the left" and "unconstitutionally" changed Uganda's Constitution.

That year 1967, Dad was promoted to Brigadier General.

Obote successfully orchestrated a change of Uganda's Constitution, which designated the President as the Commander in Chief of the Uganda Army and only he could declare war if authorized by the National Assembly. He also announced a "move to the left" with a view to rapid "Africanisation." The 1967 Constitution became effective immediately.

Beginning the same year in 1967, Obote started to rely heavily on his Lan'gi and Acholi tribesmen in the Uganda Army instead of Dad.

This was a systematic "Plot" to get rid of Dad as he did Shaban Opolot, the Iteso Army Officer that had married into Buganda Royalty and was still languishing in jail after being imprisoned by Obote.

As events were unfolding in Uganda under Obote, the historic East African community was signed in 1967. Obote as the leader of Uganda, Nyerere as the leader of Tanzania and Kenyatta as the leader of Kenya signed the historic East African Community and all three countries agreed to unite under the Banner of the East African Community.

However, after Dad took over power from Apollo Milton Obote, the East African Community stopped functioning in 1972 on account of tensions between Dad and Julius Nyerere. It was eventually dissolved in 1977.

A promotion, my brother Moses and Obote's Common Man's Charter

In 1968, Dad was promoted to the rank of Major General. Some detractors alleged that he was also promoted to the position of top Commander of the Army and the "Air Force." They further allege that "this promotion was a reward from Obote and that after this promotion, Dad started to establish considerable loyalties within the army". They also allege that "he used his smuggling proceeds and creative use of military assets to recruit members of his own tribe as well as Muslims from the West Nile area near the all-Islamic northern Sudan border".

This is a false allegation because as of 2009 the majority of Kakwa, Lugbara, North Western Uganda and the whole of Southern Sudan were Animist Christians and not Muslims.

In the year 1968 during which Dad was promoted to the rank of Major General, his beloved son my brother Moses was finally born to the long awaiting Mama Sarah Mutesi Kibedi, better known as Mama Mariam. Grandma Aate had constantly harangued Mama Mariam for bringing four daughters in a row while having had one son and two elder daughters before she met Dad.

In the meantime, Obote forged forward with the Common Man's Charter, which stipulated that 60% of Ugandan companies needed to be owned by Indigenous Ugandans. This would affect the Bus Company that had been set up and partly owned by Grandpa's aunt Yasmin Asungha's Sikh husband. As outlined in the section on my grandfather, when Asungha's husband retired from the colonial Police Force, he set up and became part owner of a Bus business named Arua Bus Syndicate Company that plied routes in and around the West Nile region of Uganda and other parts of Uganda.

According to Anthony Butele, in 1968 he and the Honourable Felix Kenyi Onama took over ownership of Arua Bus Syndicate Company from the previous owners. According to him, that time, 80% of the company was transferred from Mr. Gudwal Singh to Mr. Felix Kenyi Onama and 20% was transferred from Rambi Singh to him Mr. Anthony Butele.

Mr. Gudwal Singh retired in 1968 after a tip from Felix Kenyi Onama about the Common Man's Charter, which stipulated a 60% indigenous ownership to 40% foreign ownership. According to sources, at the time of completing the Introductory Edition of Idi Amin: Hero or Villain? His Son Jaffar Amin and Other People Speak, Mr. Gudwal Singh was living in Julanda town in Punjab State, India.

An associate of the Singh Family Muhindra Singh Puyi was a renowned Singh who married a local Ma'di Maiden just like the forefather of Gudwal Singh who was the most likely person who married Grandpa's aunt Yasmin Asungha of the Godiya-Gombe Kakwa clan. For the records show only one to two Singh Families have owned the Arua Bus Syndicate Company. As outlined in the section on my grandfather, Yasmin Asungha, Grandpa's aunt adopted him as a child and she and her Sikh husband who served in the Colonial Police Force brought him up as their child. When Asungha's husband the Sikh later retired from the Police Force, he set up and became part owner of a Bus business named Arua Bus Syndicate

Company that plied routes in and around the West Nile region of Uganda and other parts of Uganda.

When the "Cookie" between Dad and Obote "crumbled"

In 1969, the "Cookie" between Dad and Obote "crumbled" which would lead to a rift from 1969 to 1970 and sad split in 1970 that led to the Military Coup on January 25, 1971. The unity between 1964 and 1969 was both poignant and painful following the future split in 1970. However, initially Dad was a willing servant throughout Obote's "ideological suicide". This "ideological suicide" started in 1966 when Obote abrogated Uganda's 1962 Constitution, declared a new Constitution on April 15, 1966 and announced that he had assumed "all powers of Government because of his understanding of the wishes of the people of Uganda for peace, order and prosperity."

On April 17, 1966, Obote abolished the kingdoms, which infuriated Pro Monarchists. That is why by the time on December 13, 1969 when Obote made a trip to Ko'boko, accompanied by Dad, angry Pro Monarchists had reportedly "hatched" a plot to assassinate him six days later on December 19, 1969.

On December 13, 1969, Obote in the company of Dad and Erinayo Oryema the Head of Police opened the Airstrip at Ko'buko (Ko'boko), home of the Kakwa tribe in Uganda. According to accounts by witnesses to the event, it was a colourful event celebrated by thousands of Kakwas who congregated at the Airstrip and danced to their heart's content while singing praises to their fellow Northerner Obote, who "boldly" led Uganda to "Independence" from Great Britain.

"It was interesting to watch Kakwa young, old and very old "Youth Wingers" risk their lives to protect their leader Obote as he descended and ascended the plane" recount witnesses.

"They did this by linking hands to create human fences and shields and then surrounding their leader to ensure that no foe got close to him".

"During that event, the Kakwa could not sing enough praises about Awon'go, Aate's son from the Adibu Likamero Kakwa clan who had defied all odds to rise to the highest rank in the Uganda Army".

However, for many Kakwa and Aringas, this would be the last time they would see Obote until 1980 as the "Cookie" between Dad and Obote began to totally "crumble" a mere 6 days after this colourful event and Dad was eventually forced to overthrow his "master" on January 25, 1971. This is because on December 19, 1969, an assassination attempt was made on Obote and a lot of fingers pointed at Dad even though Dad was not involved in the insidious "Plot".

It later came to light by their own admission that it was a Ganda (Muganda) monarchist who attempted to assassinate Obote, the most reviled Head of State in the eyes of the Ganda. Buganda monarchists have made revelations and claims and even wrote lengthy records in Newspapers in the 1990s and the new Millennium, of having been the perpetrators of the attempted assassination of Obote but Dad was unfairly blamed for it!

According to Dad, the "blame game" and false allegations were orchestrated by senior Lan'gi and Acholi officers as part of the continuing systematic "Plot" to get rid of him as Obote did Shaban Opolot and replace him with fellow Lan'gi and Acholi tribesmen. Uganda's continuing tribalism and game of "Russian Roulette" was very much at play!

According to Dad, both Obote and Adoko had sought to continue to divide the army along tribal lines in the footsteps of the colonial British Administration. They put highly trained fellow Lan'gi in key positions and created a "rival army" around the Cabinet Office by bringing and using senior officers who turned on their fellow officers. Trouble had been brewing within the Officer Corps.

Obote continued to rely heavily on his Lan'gi and Acholi tribesmen in the Uganda Army instead of Dad but he needed Dad for the trip to Ko'boko because he didn't wish to risk antagonizing Dad's tribespeople the Kakwa.

An assassination attempt and Obote's Common Man's Charter

On the evening of December 19, 1969, Obote was fired upon and wounded in the face as he left Lugogo stadium at the end of the Annual Delegates' Conference of the Uganda People's Congress Party. While Obote was whisked away to hospital, his Vice President John Babiiha declared a State of Emergency. All parties were dissolved except Obote's Uganda People's Congress. Predictably, the immediate reaction of imposing a nationwide emergency for an indefinite period was to give Adoko increased freedom to arrest, imprison and deport at will.

Unfortunately at the time, Obote went on to falsely allege that during the evening of the assassination attempt on his life by the Muganda monarchist, Dad had run away from his house. He also falsely alleged that it was Brigadier Pierino Yere Okoya the number two Commander of the Army, a fellow Luo who drove from Jinja (50 miles away) to Kampala, to assure the Uganda Army that they should remain in their barracks, in order not to cause deaths. At this time, Brigadier Pierino Yere Okoya, Second in Command of the Uganda Army went along with the false accusations made about Dad being behind the assassination attempt on Obote's life even though he and Dad were very close friends. They shared a common Kasan-vu heritage growing up in Uganda's Sugar Plantations.

In the heat of the moment, Okoya claimed that Dad was connected with the shooting of Obote, which was treason and punishable by death. However, he would later recant the above statement and he and Dad would continue their close relationship. Dad never forgot the first time he met Okoya as a teenager when Grandma Aate introduced him during the time they lived in Bundo-Buyukwe County just off the Old Jinja - Kampala Road.

Grandma had said to Dad, "My son I want you to look after this boy. He will look after your back". Hence a strong friendship was born between Dad and Okoya.

I strongly believe that even Obote knew that it was not Dad who planned or carried an assassination attempt on his life that fateful December 19, 1969. However, he stayed silent to continue to sow the seeds of division on the basis of tribe and ethnicity. Because of the false allegations relating to the assassination attempt on Obote, Dad and Obote's relationship was compromised beyond repair.

Meanwhile, inflation was highest in two years, and the "common man" was becoming ever poorer. In 1969, Obote published the Common Man's Charter, which drew on Tanzania's Arusha Declaration of 1967. It was supposed to empower the "common man" however, the opposite happened!

As all the events related to the assassination attempt on Obote's life were unfolding, someone was "hatching" an evil plot to murder Dad's friend and colleague Brigadier Pierino Yere Okoya so that it looked like Dad did it! What a very sad "state of affairs" in "post "Independent"" Uganda!

Grandma's death in August 1969 seemed to have sealed Dad's fate for according to Dad, soon after that the headlong confrontation with Akena and his "stooge" Oyite-Ojok came home to roost. According to Dad, Akena and Oyite-Ojok were "hell bent" on getting rid of him at any cost.

The time I was taken away from my mother

Grandma had demanded I stay with her when I was weaned at age three whence I was taken to her homestead at Kidusu in Mukono District. I lived with her briefly from the tender age of three, right up to her demise.

I distinctly recall how she used to rear amamu (pigeons/doves) at her Homestead. I also remember Grandma's ventures into mysticism, which are legendary - forever associated with the Kings African Rifles and fearfully respected by all that knew her.

A lot of the Kakwa and Nubian Elders continued to use Grandma's nickname "Kabaka" which she had acquired due to her enormous size and close association with the Buganda Royal Family in the early 1900s.

Following Grandma's demise in August 1969 - the very same month her beloved son my Dad would also succumb to the great equalizer on August 16, 2003, instead of being returned to live with my mother I was taken to live with Aunt Akisu. My stay with Aunt Akisu would be very brief because she too succumbed to the great equalizer in 1970.

My mother cried a great deal when I was "ripped" from her at the tender age of three and taken to live with Grandma and then Aunt Akisu after Grandma's demise but she had no recourse. She never recovered from the pain of my being taken away from her at that tender age.

My mother, Ms. Marguerita (Mangarita) Nakoli was born on February 12, 1952 at midnight. She is of the Balamoji tribe, a sub-section of the Basoga tribe and of the Bantu ethnic group. Her grandfather, Daudi Balwa Kiwomu, is of the Ba-Ise-Muwaya clan while my maternal grandmother, Marie-Celest (Eryakesi Bulima's wife), comes from the Ba-Ise Ngobi clan. Marie-Celest's mother is from the Ba-Mbeda Royal Babito clan from Bunyoro Kitara.

As I introduced in a previous section, mum was born at the peak of colonialism in Uganda and 6 years after Dad was conscripted into the Fighting Unit of the Kings African Rifles. At the time of her birth, little did my maternal grandparents Princess Marie Celeste a Ba-Ise Ngobi Mumbeda and Eryakesi Bulima of the Ba'Ise-Muwaya clan know what fate had in store for their precious daughter when fourteen years later she would become one of Dad's many women.

I have more in-depth Memoirs and Reflections that are included in sections of subsequent parts of the series Idi Amin: Hero or Villain? His Son Jaffar Amin and Other People Speak and other projects that provide more information about my mother.

This information includes tributes to my mother Mangarita Nakoli and how she became entangled with Dad and "unwittingly" ended up being one of his many women, while working as a nursemaid for him and his official senior wife Mama Mariam.

In other projects, including Memoirs, Reflections and Spoken Words, I share additional details about my birth and the pain mum experienced over my being taken away from her at the tender age of three. I also have sections devoted to "singing" special praises to my mother, Ms. Marguerita (Mangarita) Nakoli because of challenges she endured after unwittingly becoming one of Dad's "wives" by default. In addition, I reflect on how I was "deprived" of her motherly love when I was taken away from her at the tender age of three.

As I introduce in a previous section, the section in the subsequent part of the series titled "Nakoli the Mulamoji" includes information on mum's clan, circumstances surrounding her birth, her childhood and events preceding her life as a nursemaid to Dad and his senior wife Mama Mariam. As well, it includes information about mum's life as a nursemaid for Dad and Mama Mariam.

My Iya (mum) has borne hardship since the day I was taken away from her with almost Herculean strength of character, despite the "LOT" like circumstances she found herself in.

In 1986, during a visit to my mother at which she told me the very peculiar genesis story of events surrounding my peculiar birth, mum told me of a vision she had in a dream in 1969. In that vision she saw herself calf deep at the Owen Falls Dam in Jinja, Uganda. Just as she turned around, she saw me at age three (the age I was taken away from the child mother) being taken away behind her standing waist deep in the water.

Mum always felt that the vision signified hardship. Yet, others have told me that any vision with water and a bridge crossing and the like signifies wealth! That vision was right back in 1969! In Falik (Muslim Mysticism) dream interpretations, any dream involving water and bridges signifies riches.

Despite my being taken away from her to live with Grandma, mum had a lot of respect for Grandma. The two shared a special bond as Grandma and I would. So she had gone to the Funeral Vigil and burial of Grandma Aate at Masjid Noor all the way to Arua where Grandma rests to this day.

Grandma and Aunt Akisu's deaths and my transfer to the Katabarwas

Grandma Aate died in 1969 but she had told her son on her deathbed that she was proud of what he had achieved against all odds and that she had lived long enough to see him achieve the impossible. She said, "In whatever you do make sure Lemi (instinct, luck, absolute truth) is on your side then you will overcome every obstacle."

Grandma's demise seemed to mark the point of no return between Obote and Dad as their relationship continued to disintegrate. While I lived with Grandma briefly from the tender age of three, the relationship between Dad and Obote continued to "crumble". It was almost as if Obote was "shooting himself in the foot." The curse of the game of "Russian Roulette" that Obote had inherited from the British and continued to play for so long with Ugandan politics was beginning to come home to roost!

After Grandma's death, I was relocated from Bundo in Buikwe County to Awa (Aunt) Akisu's homestead in Kayunga, Bugerere but alas my stay there would also be a short one for my beloved aunt died shortly afterward.

I distinctly remember the very day Aunt Akisu had felt cold inside her house and had asked to be brought out and as was normal she had been brought out. Joseph was still suckling at the time and he was close by. At four years of age, I too was very close to her.

One of the elder girls kept coming to check on Aunt Akisu intermittently and on one of the trips, she reacted when she felt no movement. Her concern immediately ran through Joseph who started to cry in reaction to the wailing of the girl who ran around wailing for everyone to come.

My most memorable view was of Joseph crying on top of his mother's stomach while I sat right next to the dead body. Joseph continued to wail until an Elder insisted that we children be removed. The body was then covered with a Swahili Kanga sheet.

The very next day, a brand new Land Cruiser arrived with Sergeant John Katabarwa in tow and uncle Diliga in the driver's seat. At the back were hordes of my older siblings from King George IV Garrison Primary Boarding School, Jinja. We had been clothed in brand new suits - mine was lime green in colour and Joseph's was brown, to await the passage to Kampala.

One of the children in the Station Wagon, a beautiful girl suddenly called my name. "Tshombe, come let us go." John also encouraged us and Joseph and I took courage and came out. The beautiful girl who called my name "Tshombe" and urged me to get into the Station Wagon was Mariam Aaliya Idi Amin Dada. I received a warm welcome from my elder sister Mariam Amin who seemed to know who I was. Dressed in our "Idi Best Suits" ("Sunday Best Suits") that time, I had duly nudged Joseph and we had climbed into the Station Wagon and joined Dad's other children.

I could hear inquiries inside the car as inquirers asked, "Who are they?"

The inquirers seemed to settle on us being the children of the late Akisu, which brought some sympathy but my beautiful sister Mariam Aaliya offered, "He is our brother", referring to me. I got hostile stares from Taban and Maimuna and this set the scene for the rest of my life. My siblings Bebi and Farida were more curious than anything but I had immediately noticed both the curious and hostile stares from Taban and a fiendish nonchalant glance from Maimuna. Otherwise Farida, Bebe and Amina were anxious to know who the little ones were - all dressed up!

The chief wife Mama Mariam was not in the car when Sergeant John Katabarwa and uncle Diliga picked Joseph and I from Aunt Akisu's home. She was at Command Post Plot 10 Prince Charles Drive Kololo and so were my other stepmothers Mama Kay and Mama Nora.

Upon our arrival at the Old Wing, Plot 10, Prince Charles Drive where Aunt Akisu's Funeral Vigil was to take place, more inquiries were made by several people at the funeral who thought I was Aunt Akisu's son. However, Mama Mariam kept insisting, "No, this is Mangarita my nanny's child. Don't you remember her?"

After we arrived at the Old Wing, Plot 10, Prince Charles Drive we spent the whole day there. I kept pretty much to myself or with Joseph who got the majority of sympathy and attention. What remains in my mind's eye was when the decision to transport Aunt Akisu's body with a Military Leyland or Bedford bus came and it was parked up front on Prince Charles Drive.

Dad had instructed that all children at King George IV Garrison Primary School would have to return with the Land Cruiser back to school. I thought I would be taken along with Joseph who would continue to Arua but I was separated and put in the care of John and Joyce Katabarwa our Tutsi Foster Parents. This day was the formal hand over of me Tshombe to Sergeant Katabarwa and Joyce in 1970. I was relocated to the new setting of the Jinja Military Barracks on that day which was where most of Dad's children were housed.

I had met John and Joyce before because they were always at Ab-uba's (Grandma's). All of Dad's illegitimate children were under his care including Amina Amin, Taban Amin, Maimuna Amin, Ali Amin, Macho-mingi Amin, Sukeji Amin and Geriga Amin. So were his legitimates like Mariam Amin, Farida Amin and Bebi Amin.

The errand that day was for Sergeant Diliga and Sergeant Katabarwa to pick up Dad's children who resided at King George IV Military Barracks and those at Aunt Akisu's Homestead in Kayunga, Bugerere and bring them to the Old Wing, Plot 10, Prince Charles Drive. It was where Aunt Akisu's Funeral Vigil would take place. After the Funeral Vigil, the children were to be returned to Jinja where they would continue living under the care of Sergeant John Katabarwa and Joyce, with me as a new addition.

The July 1971 mutiny or guerilla attack in Jinja against Dad's gov-ernment as well as the 1972 attack on Mbarara found us at Sergeant Kata-barwa's.

After Aunt Akisu's Funeral Vigil, Katabarwa started to round up the Al-Qadhafi Garrison boarders. Suddenly they noticed that the lanky 13-year old Taban was missing.

"Where is Taban?" inquired John.

The soldiers started to look for him. Taban tried to hide inside the Leyland Bedford Military Bus which had been parked in front of the Army Commander's residence. Diliga found him stuck tightly under one of the rows of chairs in the Military Bus.

You should have heard the screaming that ensued.

"I want to go and bury Akisu" Taban kept repeating and howling down the place.

It took Diliga and John all their might to get him out and the entou-rage heading for Arua boarded and the convoy of cars took off.

Taban spent the whole night wailing on the steps of the Old Wing Command Post until we left for John Katabarwa's that very night in the very same 1st Generation Land Cruiser.

We really loved Aunt Akisu and somehow with all the hostility he exuded, I remember distinctly approaching Taban and sitting next to him for we were told to wait for the Land Cruiser 1st Generation Model that would take us back to Jinja to John Katabarwa's.

Dad accompanied Aunt Akisu's body and Funeral Procession to Arua that day in 1970.

It would also be the day Dad's friend Okoya and his wife were gunned down in cold blood and persistent false allegations heaped on Dad.

The person who had begun "hatching" the insidious and evil plot to murder Dad's friend and colleague Brigadier Pierino Yere Okoya so that it looked like Dad did it had very sadly succeeded.

There were strong recriminations that Aunt Akisu of the Pizale Kakwa clan who was Grandma's sister Abiriya's daughter died because she had usurped her junior mother's "Yakanye" powers and responsibility as shaman without the consent of the Okapi clan. According to the Okapi clan, Aunt Akisu usurping Grandma's "Yakanye" powers was what led to her death. The Okapi so believed in these recriminations that the Elders of the clan insisted that Aunt Akisu's body would not be allowed to be buried in the ancestral home, which led to Dad deciding to bury his sister on his homestead in Tanganyika Village, Jiako in Arua. The fact that Aunt Akisu was married into the Lokora Kakwa clan was overlooked when the decision was made to bury her at Dad's Arua Jiako Residence next to the Aerodrome.

According to eyewitness accounts, Nakan, the "sacred" snake appeared just as my aunt was laid to rest inside the tomb. A sudden gust of wind whipped up a dust storm, which quickly turned into a whirlwind. It headed directly into the tomb and then whipped up a vortex skywards while heading upwards. Several hundred people including soldiers were shocked to see the tail end of a large serpent heading upwards in the whirlwind. Some even started shooting at the ascending serpent. Several people including Awa (Aunt) Deiyah recounted this scene to me.

The last simplified attempt at an explanation was by our Elder from the Ayivu Lugbara tribe Mzee Doka Bai. He explained it in the simpler version I have chosen to write above, for we Africans have this innate propensity to heighten the drama surrounding probably large mounds of dust from the grave that suddenly appeared to look like a serpent as it ascended up into the heavens.

Shocked at the omen, Dad immediately left and he did not stay at his homestead after the Christian funeral but boarded a plane back to Kampala instead for the most critical confrontation with his Commander in Chief Apollo Milton Obote. That confrontation would decide his destiny for the Part One Order was ringing with the recent assassination of Brigadier General Okoya.

The murders of Dad's friend Okoya and his wife and false allegations

Aunt Akisu's burial and funeral was taking place when the tragedy of Dad's friend Okoya's shooting came through. Dad was in Arua burying Aunt Akisu when Okoya was shot. However, despite the personal tragedy of the death of Aunt Akisu that Dad was having at his very own door step, rumours and false accusations that Dad murdered Brigadier General Okoya abounded and unfairly hung like a noose around his neck despite his persistent plea of innocence to the deed.

Following are events relating to the cold blooded murder of Pierino Okoya, the Second in Command of the Uganda Army in January 1970 and the false allegations that Dad murdered him, along with a glimpse into a future Mystical Gathering and Reconciliation Ceremony. During the future Mystical Gathering and Reconciliation Ceremony, Okoya's father "pointed the fingers" at someone else and exonerated Dad from the false allegations of murdering his son.

Immediately following the assassination attempt on Obote on December 19, 1969, a curfew was imposed on Kampala and several politicians were implicated and detained.

Later, in January 1970, Brigadier Pierino Yere Okoya and his wife were shot dead just outside Gulu. All fingers pointed at Dad in spite of the fact that the Acholi Army Officer Pierino Okoya was killed along with his wife, at his Layibi home while Dad was in Arua for the burial and funeral of my aunt Akisu.

Dad had been flown to Arua by an Acholi pilot and not by the Israelis or Bob Astles as usual. He had gone to Arua to attend the funeral of our aunt Akisu with whom I lived briefly after Grandma's demise.

In other words, Dad was in Arua when Okoya was murdered.

More political chaos, a reflection on a curse and a future ceremony

All hell broke loose as Uganda descended into more political chaos. There was trouble in the army as false allegations and accusations that Dad committed the murders of Okoya and his wife persisted. Obote instituted an inquiry into the killings of Okoya and his wife, which eventually came to naught.

However, Okoya and his wife were buried along with a sheep in a curious ceremonial burial which stipulated that all the foot tracks around the burial ground would be swept into the twin graves after the burial ceremony, to cement the curse. In future years, Okoya's father would exonerate Dad of his murder and that of his wife and point the fingers at "someone else".

Mysticism abounds in and at all levels of African culture just as in a bizarre ritualistic curse, the two victims Okoya and his wife were buried in a seated position. Then a 100kg sack of sesame (simsim) seeds was placed inside the grave with the bodies. Then the coup de grade - a living ram was placed in the grave as well and buried with the bodies. After that, a solemn curse was placed and pronounced that whomever killed the couple should suffer retribution to the number of sesame seeds in the two sacks.

Ironically the Acholi seem to have borne the brunt of suffering and death throughout the 1970s during Dad's rule in Uganda, the 1980s following Dad's overthrow and the 1990s during the war that has raged on in Northern Uganda well into the 21st century.

Moreover, to compound issues, both Tito Okello, a Former President and colleague of Dad's before the coup by Dad against Obote and Okoya's very own father came out strongly to exonerate Dad of the death of their Gallant Son. This happened when a ritualistic version of "Omato Oput" ceremony was done on the shore of a sacred river, in part to lift the curse of the 200 kgs sesame seeds. In the 1990s, former president Tito Okello Lutwa publicly claimed that "It was not Idi Amin who killed Okoya".

The fact that Okoya's father even exonerated Dad from the death of his son, Dad's Chief of Staff in 1970 during a version of an "Omato Oput" cleansing ceremony between the Acholi and the people of West Nile was very welcome news to Dad while we lived in exile. He had continued to deny the false allegations that he killed Okoya before, during and after his rule in Uganda.

When we lived in exile in Saudi Arabia, Dad had followed events that unfolded in Uganda with interest and known about the version of "Omato Oput" cleansing ceremony.

Jason Avutia who professes to be the Agofe (Paramount Chief of the Lugbara) and other representatives from the tribes of the West Nile represented the people of West Nile during this famous "Bent Spear" ceremony where both sides bent spear blades as a sign of reconciliation between "bitter enemies." Dad sent Baba Diliga to attend the ceremony.

The "Omato Oput" (Bent Spear Ceremony) took place under the auspices of the then President Tito Okello. He realized the importance of the matter and it explained the reasons why he was willing to hold peace talks in Nairobi with President Museveni with Kenya's President Arap Moi as the host. The "Bent Spear Ritual" is well known and it is used as the only example of a genuine Cultural Reconciliation between two bitter enemies that has ever been initiated in Uganda's history. In all articles in the public domain this singular event is very well known.

My brother Machomingi who is the nephew of Tito Okello was in Kampala during the time of the "Omato Oput" ceremony organized by his Uncle Tito Okello. His late mother used to joke to her husband (Dad) and say that, "Now that we are in power, let us show you how it is supposed to be done."

Dad once came back from his lengthy international calls with the above jest from Mama Macho Okello. He kept laughing and implied that "After all they have sought the assistance of the Former Uganda Army to consolidate power."

He also intimated the above after the incident that occurred when his brother-in-law and then Vice President Brigadier Gad Wilson Toko was appointed as the second most powerful man in the Tito Okello regime following the "Omato Oput" ceremony. Brigadier Gad Wilson Toko was the very same rush uncle who got up and slapped the then Guerilla Leader Yoweri Museveni in Nairobi. It is a surprise that Museveni forgave such a rude affront and physical assault on his person considering reports that he doesn't normally forgive his enemies and individuals that undermine him.

Jason Avutia who has been referred to as a self proclaimed Agofe (Paramount Chief) of the Lugbara wrote a book on the matter, which is in the public domain. His Excellency Former President Tito Okello's comments exonerating Dad were in Uganda's Newspaper the Monitor.

All human rights organizations use the above historical attempt at reconciliation in response to a Cultural Curse that was placed in 1970 as an example. It is similar to the controversial "jumping over a slaughtered Dinka Bull" proposal that was reportedly made to exonerate Museveni from the issue of the slain SPLA Leader John Garang.

Reconciliation is of the utmost importance because most people in Northern Uganda realize that the North has been maligned by design and the only solution is reconciliation first before any development can become successful. Just at a micro level, West Nile remains perennially divided because of historically sewn seeds of division.

Two revelations relating to the brutal murders of Okoya and his wife

According to Dad, two revelations occurred in relation to the brutal murder of his friend Okoya. The first revelation relates to Dad being placed under house arrest following Okoya's murder while it appeared that members of the General Service Unit looked for opportunities to murder him too. The second revelation related to a decision by Okoya to inform Dad about being bribed to murder Dad and unwittingly becoming a "marked man" himself because he "foiled" the insidious "Plot".

"Okoya you keep the money and thank you for informing me" Dad had offered when Okoya informed him about the plan for Okoya to be the "hit man" that would get rid of Dad.

Dad had said this not knowing that Okoya would pay the ultimate price for "looking after his back". As outlined in a section above, Dad never forgot that first meeting with Okoya when Grandma introduced him to Dad and said, "My son I want you to look after this boy. He will look after your back".

It is unbelievable how anyone can be so evil as to "hatch" such a callous "Plot" and brutally murder an innocent man and his wife over a mere position in the Army but let God be the Judge.

That fateful year in 1970 at the very hour of the political fall out between Dad the then Army Commander and the 1st Executive President of Uganda Dr. Apollo Milton Obote, Dad was placed under virtual house arrest. The virtual house arrest followed the mysterious death of the 2IC (Second in Command) Brigadier General Okoya and it occurred after Dad's return from the burial of his sister which happened at the very time Brigadier Okoya was being buried. Dad's "absence" from Okoya's burial was "misconstrued" as an affront to the late Okoya by the Luo circles that had open animosity towards Dad and continued to be "hell bent" on getting rid of him.

According to Dad, he once left the vicinity of the enclosure of his BMW and was accosted by a unit of the General Service Unit who were posted on the Kololo Airstrip end of Prince Charles Drive and on the Lahona Academy side of Prince Charles Drive. The likes of Mujahid remember Dad storming past the gate with a General Service Unit car in hot pursuit while he frantically indicated to the Quarter Guards to open the gate.

That time, Dad said he sped past and took the Lower Kololo route, swerved up again to Prince Charles Drive and by this time he found the Plot

10 gate open. He stormed in and instantly scrambled to the balcony on the ready "sniper fashion" just as the General Service Unit car passed by with lethal looking Luo Officers snarling at the Quarter Guards who were now all ready for their Commander's instructions. This had happened while Dad, the Army Commander crouched in a lethal mood - a hack back to his sniper days in the Mau Mau war.

This was the very balcony Dad had once threatened to hurl his favourite son Moses from in 1969. It was also the very balcony Obote would spend quality time at with the Amin family, tacking into roasted beef or goat meat and washing it down with his favourite tipple when relations were still "good" between him and Dad.

My brother Moses Kenyi's arrival into the world was a blessing and it fulfilled a prediction made by Elders from Dad's Adibu Likamero Kakwa clan that Dad would have five sons in a row beginning with me, but alas his birth also marked the road to "Political Schism" between Dad and his Commander in Chief Dr. Apollo Milton Obote.

The whole Dada family witnessed the most memorable and devastating scene of Dad threatening to hurl my brother Moses from the balcony when he came out onto the balcony at Plot 10, Prince Charles Drive (Command Post). That time, he threatened to throw the newly born child over the balcony while directing a statement to Mama Mariam (Moses' mother):

"After all these girls, you now claim this is my son?"

Dad was falling into the age old tragedy of disowning one's own blood in this recurrent theme in the Adibu Likamero Kakwa clan which had almost become a ritual for he too was rejected in 1928. His father Amin Dada Nyabira Temeresu (Tomuresu) before him was also rejected by his own father Dada Nyabira some +70 years before and just two years earlier the very same Mama Mariam had rejected me in 1967. She had alleged that I was not of the Dada Family but the progeny of one of the shamba boys (gardeners) or cooks. Dad seemed to be paying Mama Mariam back in kind for that personal insult but he was duly stopped by his mother's looming figure on the very balcony.

When everybody else was cowering away and petrified from the raging fury on the balcony, Grandma quietly and authoritatively asked for her grandson Moses. Dad relented, seeing her positive acceptance of Moses. Grandma gave Moses the Kakwa name Kenyi (one born among or following girl siblings), for he had followed a long line of girl child siblings from Nawume, Jennifer, Aaliya (Aliya), Akulu, Anite and Akujo. Moses was destined to be Dad's favourite child and he was also given the name Moshe (Moses). Later on in Saudi Arabia, he was given the name Abdul Mohsen.

That time, the General Service Unit realized the danger they were in while trying to look up towards a fortified location and sped away from the scene. Mujahid, one of Dad's original Escorts recounted the incident above and my older brother Taban Amin who remembered the incident from inside the Command Post reiterated the same series of events. It was a very tense moment indeed as the relationship between Dad and Obote continued to disintegrate.

While residing at our Al Safa residence in Jeddah, Saudi Arabia after Dad's government was overthrown, Dad clearly remembered the convening uproar and intrigue relating to the hot pursuit by the lethal looking members of the General Service Unit. He also recalled the precursor to the tragedy of Okoya and his wife's brutal murder. Dad regularly recounted the events that might have led to Okoya being targeted for assassination while expressing deep sadness at the way he and his wife were innocently murdered.

Apparently, deep in the night, Brigadier General Okoya approached his Commanding Officer and childhood chum from their Kasanvu days in the Asian Sugar Plantations in Kawolo, with an urgent message at his residence on Plot 10 Prince Charles Drive Kololo (Command Post). Because of the close and strong friendship Okoya and Dad shared, Okoya could come and go from Dad's residence as he pleased, even in the middle of the night.

"Affende, I have just been from a top secret meeting with His Excellency. I am afraid this is grave news, Affende. His Excellency has requested I assassinate you! He even gave this money", Okoya had told Dad, pulling out the money.

Flabbergasted, Dad got an instant flashback to the first time he set eyes on the then teenage boy introduced to him as Okoya by his beloved mother Aisha Aate Chumaru in Bundo-Buyukwe County just off the Old Jinja - Kampala Road.

As outlined in previous sections, Grandma had said to Dad, "My son I want you to look after this boy. He will look after your back".

"Now this very 1970, incredibly, his beloved mother's foretelling had come to pass!" reflected Dad.

"For here was the very same young boy now the second most powerful person in the Armed Forces. Now the 2IC (Second in Command) and a Brigadier General the young boy had come a long way indeed from the bleak existence of our fore fathers whose only prospects were as sharecroppers in the Metha and Madhvani Sugar Plantations in Kawolo and Kakira" Dad continued to reflect.

Dad fondly remembered this brash upstart colleague of his who drove all the way from Jinja in a fury and confronted his Commanding Officer after the assassination attempt on Obote by a Pro Monarchist from the Baganda tribe of Uganda on the evening of December 19, 1969. In the heat of the moment, Dad's friend Okoya had scolded that Dad was a coward for leaving the Head of State in dire straits following the attempted assassination of Obote.

Okoya had openly stated, "It was cowardice not standing by His Excellency", following the 1969 Lugogo Stadium attempt to assassinate the 1st Executive President of the 1st Republic of Uganda by a Buganda Monarchist. Okoya even went along with accusations that Dad was behind the assassination plot.

To date, a lot has been written and analyzed by the media both local and foreign about events that unfolded after the assassination attempt on Obote on December 19, 1969. The media took that singular incident/confrontation between Dad and Okoya as the precursor to what befell Okoya, for they saw it as an open affront to Dad by his Junior Officer. However, they did not realize that from an insider's perspective the two comrades in arms always confronted each other in the very same frank manner as only true friends do without any sense of rank, formality or animosity.

This was much in the amusing manner in which Major General Otafire is fond of publicly confronting his Commander in Chief Yoweri Museveni without any fear of a backlash. That is what true friends do!

After all the recrimination against Dad, he went on to muse, having sought the safety of his loyal soldiers in the Malire Mechanized Battalion Lubiri from threats by UPC stalwarts like Akena and the whole UPC political wing, "Now it had come to this kweli kabisa? Hmmmm".

Dad felt a grave and deep sense of betrayal by his Commander in Chief and Head of State of the 1st Republic of Uganda, for he placed loyalty and patriotism above all else and himself from his KAR days. Although second to his love of family, he was even a Bona Fide UPC card holder for God's sake, with the famous picture of him in the UPC batik print shirt that got maximum circulation.

A most principled action by Dad in relation to the second revelation relating to the brutal murder of Okoya was Dad's grave decision to let Okoya keep the bribe he had been given for purposes of murdering him.

"Okoya you keep the money and thank you for informing me" Dad had offered as outlined in a section above.

Dad's confrontation with Obote

According to Dad, an astonishing event happened the very next morning, when Dad almost resigned to his fate in eccentric medley put on his military shirt without his Major General applets. He wore mufti weekend khaki shorts and was bare footed without his shoes when he walked into Obote's office uninvited!

Like a condemned man, Dad got into his cream BMW with his handgun (Pistol) and headed from Kololo towards Nakasero and the August House Parliament Building where the President's Office was located. This shocking spectacle is remembered by all who were there that day for Dad strode into the Parliament Building and headed straight for the President's office. He did this without any restrictions from those who were too used to his frequent arrivals at the very office on other occasions like the Planning of the Storming of the Lubiri Palace in 1966 during the "Kabaka Rising" ordered by the very Obote.

That time, Dad was ushered into the presence of His Excellency President Apollo Milton Obote by sheer force of presence without consultation first. The President was shocked at the arrival of Dad, the person who had apparently been scheduled to be killed by Okoya, the night before.

Tension thickened in the air as Dad solemnly declared, "Your Excellency, I have come to you, for you want me dead. Here shoot me" Dad said placing the imposing handgun and his Major General applets as a sign of resignation on his Commander in Chief's Presidential desk top.

According to Dad, too shaken to respond and searching for words, the Father of the Nation remained silent with bitter realization written all over his face.

"What is the meaning of this?" he finally stammered, feeling the silent intimidation exuding from his Army Commander.

Dad, who could have very easily turned the gun on Obote at that moment but chose not to out of loyalty and principle replied, "They say you want me dead. Here I am. Shoot me."

This incredible event, not often repeated or reported in the public domain, was the First Standoff and First Reprieve for Dad and it marked the end of the unofficial House Arrest warrant which according to Dad seemed to have been engineered by Obote's cousin Akena Adoko. Unfortunately, this would not be the last House Arrest warrant on Dad.

Sadly this incident also marked Okoya the 2IC out for what has turned out to be the third most damning accusation against Dad after the Ben Kiwanuka "disappearance" and the "Luwum deaths". All of these deaths and others allegedly committed or ordered by Dad should be properly investigated through an Independent Truth and Reconciliation Commission because Ugandans and the global community deserve to know all the truth.

Shortly after the confrontation between Obote and Dad, a Part One order came through requesting Okoya, the 2IC to prepare for an unexpected and unscheduled Military Course abroad. This Order did not pass via the Army Commander's desk but through the Ministry of Defense without the vetting and approval of the Army Commander (Dad) who was still under a cloud of suspicion from the UPC 1st Republic for "trumped up" allegations.

Okoya's so-called journey for an unexpected and unscheduled Military Course abroad was not to be because he was brutally murdered before taking the so-called journey when he went upcountry to his home village in Acholiland. The day of Okoya's brutal murder, he and his wife were cut down by a sniper's bullet in cold blood just as the wife took his bathing water out to the bathroom. When Okoya reacted to the resounding shots that killed his wife by coming out to see the calamity, he was cut down in a hail of bullets as well. There are allegations that one renowned Uganda Rifles marksman called Oryem from the Acholi tribe of Palabek in Southern Sudan who was stationed at Masindi Artillery Regiment was the Sniper responsible for cutting down Okoya and his wife. However, an Independent Truth and Reconciliation Commission is the place to arrive at the actual truth.

Obote's policies and his role in allegedly undermining the Anyanya

Dad has been unfairly and sometimes solely blamed for implementing several of Obote's policies relating to the Common Man's Charter and Africanisation which is why it is important to obtain information about and understand some events that preceded the Military Coup against Obote on January 25, 1971.

In January 1970, Obote began plans to hasten the Africanisation of commerce, trade and industry in Uganda which Dad implemented when he asked the non Ugandan Asians to leave after he took over power in Uganda and was unfairly solely blamed for.

There were over 40,000 Asians, who held British passports in Uganda when the Ugandan Government under Obote announced plans to hasten the Africanisation of commerce, trade and industry in January 1970.

During 1970, the Labour Minister E.Y. Lakidi said that the government of Uganda intended to dismiss 80,000 Kenyan and Tanzanian workers to make room for Ugandans in skilled and semi-skilled employment.

In 1970, the war continued in the Sudan and Obote undermined the efforts of the Anyanya because of loyalty to Nimeiry. According to the New York Times of January 2, 1970, 40 to 50 Arab troops were killed at Torit in a battle of unusual size. The Christian Monitor of January 4, 1970 reported a massacre in which entire villages were wiped out - at least 212 in the 1969 attacks at Kaya and Torit. The Anyanya attacked government positions at Kaya.

In 1970, in what may perhaps be deemed the final straw with Obote for Ugandans, Obote further angered Ugandans by what has now become known as his Nakivubo Pronouncement relating to socialism. The pronouncement slid the country further into socialism. Obote then put the Indian tycoon, Jayant Madhivani, to be head of the new state-run Exports and Imports Department.

On May 1, 1970, a new Immigration Act relating to non-Ugandan Asians was due to effect. Under its provisions, non-Ugandan Asians would be required to possess one of a variety of entry permits if they wished to remain in the country.

As the relationship between Dad and Obote continued to disintegrate, I continued to reside in Jinja under the care of our Tutsi Foster Parents Sergeant John Katabarwa and Joyce. As outlined in a previous section, following Grandma's demise, Dad had transferred me to the care of his maternal sister Akisu, daughter of Grandma's sister Abiriya in Kayunga, Bugerere that very month of August 1969. However, my aunt would also succumb to death in 1970 and be buried right inside Dad's leased homestead next to the Aerodrome (Airstrip) in Arua.

I was then transferred to live with Sergeant John Katabarwa and Mama Joyce who acted as my Foster Parents. Sergeant Katabarwa did his master's bidding of looking after Dad's illegitimate children who could not step into Dad's Acacia Avenue and Command Post residences during the years before he became President of Uganda in 1971. So we were left in the hands of his key Lieutenants and other Officers.

That very year 1970, my sister Zahra Araba Omari Amin was born to Anuna Omari, a Telephone Switchboard Operator in Gulu who was the daughter of a Lugbara Opi/Sultan Fadhil Mullah Bondo of Erewa in Arua District on July 8, 1970.

By the end of 1970, Dad's relationship with Obote had disintegrated beyond repair. Unbeknown to Obote and his entourage at the time, the hostility would provide the "perfect" setting for Dad's coup against him on January 25, 1971 and the fulfillment of Grandma's prediction relating to Dad rising to the "highest position in the land".

When Obote suspended Independence Day Celebrations in 1970

Lemi, Tobura or pure luck was on Dad's side for Obote in an about-turn face decided to suspend the observance of Independence Day Celebrations on October 9, 1970 and send his Army Commander Dad to represent him at the burial of Gamal Abdel Nasser of Egypt.

A lot of people have failed to understand the significance of suspending the celebrations of Uganda's "Independence" in 1970. They have also failed to understand the significance of the omen of what was to come one year after the death of Okoya, for Dad took over power from Apollo Milton Obote on January 25, 1971. This was exactly one year to the date his sister Akisu and Okoya died on January 25, 1970! This eerie occurrence can only be explained through the mysticism that followed Dad throughout his life.

The "fortunate" reprieve of Obote sending Dad to represent him at the burial of Gamal Abdel Nasser of Egypt raised unexpected opportunity for the Kakwa native in the land of the Pharaohs. This is because even though the Commander-in-Chief Obote unexpectedly "chose" Dad to lead the Ugandan delegation to the funeral of one of Africa's and the Arab world's greatest Revolutionary "by design" a number of events would unfold in Egypt that would "seal" Dad's fate.

So, in September 1970, Dad led the Ugandan Delegation to Egypt to attend the funeral of Gamal Abdel Nasser on October 1, 1970, despite the so-called "dark clouds" hanging over his head.

Gamal Abdel Nasser was the second President of Egypt from 1956 until his death in 1970. Abdel Nasser inspired anti-colonial and pan-Arab revolutions in Algeria, Libya, Iraq and Yemen and played a major role in founding the Palestine Liberation Organization (PLO) and the international

Non-Aligned Movement, which Dad would champion and subscribe to before, during and after his rule in Uganda.

Despite the cloud hanging over his head regarding the false allegations levied upon him about allegedly murdering Okoya and his wife and other allegations, Obote sent Dad as head of the Ugandan delegation to Cairo to attend the funeral of Gamal Abdel Nasser held on October 1, 1970. The funeral was one of the largest in history, attended by an estimated seven million people because of what Gamal Abdel Nasser represented to Arab People. He is considered the father of Arab nationalism, just like Kwame Nkrumah is considered the father of African nationalism.

The mystical events involving Dad that occurred in Egypt

While Dad was in Egypt attending Gamal Abdel Nasser's funeral, the reason Obote "chose" him to lead the Ugandan delegation to the funeral despite being under "house arrest" became clear. This is because in Dad's absence, Obote quickly proceeded to do three things, namely rounding off the Okoya enquiry, appointing Brigadier Sulieman Hussien as Army Commander and appointing his fellow Lan'gi Lieutenant Colonel Oyite-Ojok as Adjutant and Quarter Master General. However, Dad's "Lemi" or "Tobura" was always with him because unbeknown to Obote and his entourage at the time, a number of "mystical" events occurred while Dad was in Egypt. The "mystical" events would "overpower" the continuing "conniving" that Dad said went on behind closed doors in relation to "getting rid" of him.

As in the case of the false allegations that it was Dad who planned or carried an assassination attempt on Obote's life that fateful December 19, 1969 I strongly believe that Obote knew that it was not Dad who murdered Okoya and his wife. However, he stayed silent to continue to feed the false allegations that were systematically levied on Dad.

According to Dad, on hindsight, Dr. Apollo Milton Obote had hoped in part to get the opportunity to rearrange the Uganda Army High Command along ethnic lines. This Dad said Obote was planning to do to suit the reverberating "din" and clamouring demands from the Lan'gi-Luo Sorbonne trained and Sandhurst drop outs and young Turks like Lieutenant Colonel Oyite-Ojok and the General Service Unit Chief Akena Adoko. According to Dad, Akena Adoko who was the real power behind the "Luo throne" had increasingly become openly hostile to the prominent position Dad continued to hold in what they saw and termed "their" Government.

As Obote and his entourage continued to "scheme" and "craft" a plot to get rid of Dad, they had no idea they were up against Dad's "Lemi" or "Tobura" and the mysticism that followed him throughout his life. Following the "mystical" events that involved Dad while he was in Egypt, the Kakwa son returned unexpectedly from Cairo and all plans against him were frozen but not forgotten by Obote.

While Dad was in Egypt attending Abdel Nasser's funeral, a couple of "mystical" events occurred in relation to the age old "fight" between the descendants of Abraham's children Isaac and Ishmael and Dad unwittingly became a pawn. The "mystical" events were connected to Dad's very strong relationship with Israel at the time while also being part of the Ummah (Community of Muslim Believers). The events unfolded right before Dad's eyes like a scene out of a Hollywood movie and he was both "tickled" and overwhelmed by them.

According to Dad, as Obote and his entourage continued to "scheme" and "craft" a plot to get rid of him in his absence, Mossad Agents were "secretly" clocking their every move and putting a few plans in action. Dad claimed that the Israeli Mossad duly sent a Female Agent who flew in from New York as part of the Press Corps to cover the Funeral of Abdel Nasser to warn Dad and convey instructions from "higher up". According to Dad, unbeknownst to him, he had been earmarked for leadership by the Judeo Western powers that be as early as 1963 when he went for Paratrooper Training in the Jewish Holy Land and by 1964 following the Uganda Rifles (UR) Mutiny at the 1st Battalion King George IV Barracks Jinja.

The "mystical" events that unraveled while Dad was in Egypt attending Abdel Nasser's funeral are little known in the public domain but they were what Dad would reminisce about that Autumn (Fall) season endlessly at the dinner table at our Al Safa Residence in Saudi Arabia. The events would have far reaching repercussions on the revolutionary transition from Abdel Nasser to his eventual successor and rubble rouser from the most unexpected of corners in the African and Middle Eastern region at large.

According to Dad, the Mossad followed his every move. However, unbeknownst to their Agents, two singular events took place secretly in relation to the Ummah (Community of Muslim Believers) while he was in Egypt.

Dad's secret meeting in Egypt with Crown Prince Faisal

During an informal gathering that occurred within the course of the day in the vicinity of the mosque after our obligatory five prayers, Crown Prince Faisal Bin Abdul Aziz expressed and admired and indeed intimated to Dad great admiration. He conveyed to Dad that he was proud of the fact that a Muslim was the Head of the Military Establishment in Uganda which was a predominantly Christian Country. During this first meeting, Crown Prince Faisal Bin Abdul Aziz arranged for another secret meeting to take place between him and Dad before his departure for Jeddah after the Funeral of Gamal Abdel Nasser.

According to Dad, he was greatly affected and moved by the insight and keen interest shown by the de facto King of Saudi Arabia in the ongoing build up and frenzied Zionist operations in Uganda and the Sudan. When he addressed the issue with Dad, a frenzied construction of a state of the art large haulage Airbase was taking place at Nakasongola Military Air Base in Uganda - dead centre in the heart of Africa. Realization came thick and fast as the King asked Dad a typically provocative Muslim Question:

"You call yourself a Muslim Eid Al-Amin when you as Army Commander let your land be used for Zionist Hegemony over the Arab Muslim Nations in Africa and the Middle East? Have you ever sat down and asked yourself why Uganda would need a sixteen capacity simultaneous takeoff runway, for F4 Phantom Jets on your land, if not but to be a southern hemisphere rear base to enable the illegitimate Jewish state to attack Arab Muslim countries from the southern Hemisphere? Ask yourself sincerely......"

Perplexed, Dad said he sat back and reflected on the revelation since he had often wondered at the astronomically Juggernaut construction activity that continued apace in Nakasongola Military Airbase unabated by economic woes or Uganda's incapacity to afford such a White Elephant project. Moreover Uganda did not have the financial clout and only had miniscule Israeli Fuga Jets and Bombers. The notion of what purpose the Airbase would be for had continued to cross his mind so this insight by King Designate Faisal Bin Abdul Aziz put his mind to rest.

Alas on hindsight today the Airbase has been turned into a Bullets Munitions Factory manned by North Koreans and the very Dad was lambasted by the very Western media for building a "White Elephant deep in the middle of nowhere".

The King continued to forcefully place the seed of his Islamic Agenda on schedule to a willing fellow Muslim. When he felt Dad was open to his wise suggestions and the effects of the revelations were indeed succeeding, he asked Dad to realize his great potential as a Muslim Leader and Muslims should always work together he intimated. Then he added, "And we should always show allegiance to our creed and defend the Ummah".

The Dye had been cast and it was to be sealed some two years into the future on King Faisal's only travel to Sub-Saharan Africa on his momentous visit to Uganda. It would bring an end to Dad's perception by Israel as a Reliable Helmsman (HAGAI NE'EMAN). This would happen despite a second revelation and another event that is not in the public arena relating to the female Mossad Agent allegedly flown from New York to warn Dad and convey instructions from "higher up" in order to continue solidifying his relationship with Israel.

Dad's secret meeting in Egypt with a beautiful female Mossad Agent

According to Dad, he met up with the female Mossad Agent who had come specifically from New York to inform him of the intended plans of Obote against him while he was in the land of the Pharaohs attending the funeral of a descendant of Abraham's son Ishmael. What an unbelievable sequence of events!

"Just as I alighted at my official hotel following the funeral service of Gamal Abdel Nasser, I was cordially accosted by an enchanting Mediterranean lady of unspecified origins, who requested for a private meeting" Dad told.

Intrigued by the beautiful lady's interest in him Dad accepted and invited her for dinner. He was baited when she claimed to have been sent by Colonel Baruch Balev an intimate chum of Dad's at the time who had been instrumental in coordinating all cordial military activity and bilateral relationships between Israel and the 1st Republic of Uganda since 1963. That had also been the year Dad was promoted to the rank of Major and sent for a tour of the defense facilities in the Judeo State. Dad later attended a Paratrooper Training in the Judeo Holy Land as well.

The beautiful lady intimated to Dad that she was sent on an urgent mission from New York to meet him and convey an urgent message from Colonel Balev. She told Dad that his life was in danger and that Obote was rearranging the High Rank military structure so he should urgently return to

Uganda but he was not to use the direct route to Entebbe. The beautiful lady said Dad should head via Gulu Airbase, which had a strong presence of Israeli Trainers. They were training the Ugandan Pilots on the Vector tail winged Fuga Jet Fighters/Bombers.

According to Dad, he received instructions for the DC4 (DAKOTA) to first land in Gulu before continuing to Entebbe Airport possibly via the Jinja Airstrip. Dad said he was to continue to Entebbe Airport after meeting and getting a briefing from Israeli Military Instructors who would guide his every movement from the time he touched down in the country. The beautiful lady told Dad that Obote was intending to accuse and finalize the implication of the murder of Brigadier General Okoya and the loss of funds from the Uganda Ministry of Defense Coffers towards funding his Mabira Units training and armament which was unearthed by Aggrey Awori.

Dad was momentarily dumbfounded by the enormous political interest in his person from all corners of the geo-Political Protagonists. Being at the very epicenter both alarmed and tickled his enormous ego, while he continued to listen to this petite Guardian Angel sent from God's Chosen People as his late mother Aisha Aate Chumaru was fond of calling Moshe's People. It was interesting how Dad's kid brother Adinebi Amin was given the name Moshe too, when he went for Battle Tank Training in Israel.

Grandma's warning for Dad to "Never forsake the children of God"

Dad had reflected over the "mystical" events that unfolded in Egypt while sadly recalling the events of the last year 1969 when Grandma died around mid August. That time, the Israeli Paratroopers' Regiment sent a team specially from Israel with a garland of flowers which was parachuted over Arua Town trailing colours of smoke with deft accuracy. There was also a lone Paratrooper who landed exactly next to Grandma Aisha's grave near Masjid Noor on Rhino Camp Road and placed the garland of flowers on her grave. It was a technical marvel to all that witnessed the event apart from the one event involving another Paratrooper who was supposed to land at Dad's residence some one mile away from Grandma's grave. This Paratrooper overshot and landed on the roof of Mzee Doka's House just across the Jiako road at Tanganyika Village, Arua instead. A multitude had gathered at Mzee Doka's house for Grandma's funeral and witnessed the strange spectacle, which became a talking point for a long time.

The above show of sympathy and support was a strong bonding which Colonel Baruch Balev knew would touch the soul of this stern but simple Kakwa Soldier he had learnt to respect despite most people's under estimation of his potential and he genuinely held Dad in high esteem. Now here he was again in 1970, scheming and directing his life and destiny towards Power and Dominion.

As the "mystical" events were unfolding right before Dad's eyes, he still remembered his mother's warning to him:

"Do not forsake the children of God my son, never forsake the children of God."

Dad would lament this point during his 24year stay in Jeddah, even whilst continuing to show staunch support for the Arab Islamic cause.

Dad's realization that he had to pick sides in the "tussle"

Dad realized that he had to pick sides in this Isaac/Ishmael tussle at a spiritual level, which was in contrast to his intransigence towards picking sides in the Political East/West "Cold War" conflict during his reign as President of Uganda between 1971 and 1979.

I always thought Dad should have called the encounter with the beautiful female Mossad Agent, "The Spy who loved me". The enchantress later intimated a possible ruse, that she was a niece to General Moshe Dayan when Dad expressed admiration for the 6day war hero. Just before Dad left the land of Ramesis II, they both took a day off and went sightseeing at the mysterious Sphinx and Great Pyramids. One thing led to another and they found themselves in each other's arms. Conception was instant.

The beautiful female Mossad Agent left for New York and Dad headed back for the second confrontation with his Commander in Chief and Head of State of the 1st Republic of Uganda via Gulu Airbase, Jinja Airstrip and finally the old Entebbe Airport.

Ploys by the descendants of Isaac and Ishmael to "use" Dad

The "mystical" events that unfolded in Egypt would be the beginning of systematic ploys by the feuding factions of descendants of Isaac and Ishmael to "use" Dad as a tool to advance their agendas in relation to their "fight to the death".

Dad's arrival back in Uganda from attending Abdel Nasser's funeral

Dad had sent word when he alighted in Gulu to all loyal officers to await information about his intended arrival. This had happened while the General Service Unit Operatives had "officially" rushed to Entebbe Airport awaiting his arrival on the official DC 4 (DAKOTA).

When the plane touched down at the Old Airport in Entebbe, the pilot was surprised by the heavily armed presence he received at the tarmac, only to tell them that he had left the Army Commander at the Gulu Airbase inspecting the facility. When Dad finally touched down at Entebbe his loyal officers led by one Captain Mustafa Adrisi met him at the tarmac. Then he was escorted with a heavy convoy to Kampala.

To cap it all, Dad then feigned Rheumatoid pains and was thus transported to the President's Office in a wheel chair. He was seeking the sympathy vote from his Commander in Chief when he came in as an invalid, to the astonishment of the Head of State according to one Abdul Latif who was part of the escorting team to the August House the very next day of Dad's arrival.

A standing ovation by university students and continuing events

On October 7, 1970, Dad, Obote, Kenyatta and Nyerere attended an Inauguration Ceremony at Makerere University to make the university the University of East Africa. During that time, Obote became a Chancellor of the university.

At the Inauguration Ceremony, the students gave Dad a standing ovation after Obote had already arrested several politicians and begun investigating the death of Okoya while Dad was still in Cairo. Dad was supposed to be arrested on his return from Cairo but he returned and remained unharmed.

On October 9, 1970, Obote cancelled Uganda's 8th Independence Celebrations allegedly because of Gamal Abdel Nasser's death. It appeared however, that despite the trip to Egypt for Abdel Nasser's funeral, Dad was under "house arrest" and Obote was planning against him but he did not wish to risk antagonizing the army.

During October 1970, Steiner an Israeli mercenary allegedly helped train the Sudanese Anyanya in collaboration with Dad on Uganda soil. Steiner was arrested by the police in Uganda while trying to re-enter Uganda because of this allegation and he is quoted to have told the police that the Ugandan "Chief of Staff" helped him in his activities of training Anyanya from Uganda. However, it was really the late Brigadier Sulieman Hussien appointed by Obote as Army Commander while Dad was in Egypt for Abdel Nasser's funeral who helped Steiner in his activities relating to training the Anyanya.

It has been claimed that on December 19, 1970, Bar Lev the head of the Israeli Military Mission in Uganda was in Nairobi enroute to Israel. However, on December 20, 1970, Bar Lev returned to Kampala allegedly to plot the overthrow of Obote.

According to Dad, on January 11, 1971, Obote called him to his office and informed him of two things - the Report of the murder of Brigadier Okoya and his wife at Gulu and the Auditor-General's Report which alleged that Dad's Ministry of Defence had overspent £2,691,343.

On January 16, 1971, Dad held a Press Conference reiterating that there was a plan by Obote to have him (Dad) arrested by Obote's men.

On January 24, 1971, Obote flew to Singapore to attend the Commonwealth Conference while the head of the General Service Unit, Akena Adoko flew to London.

During the evening of January 24, 1971, Obote rang up the Officers' Mess at Jinja Barracks to instruct a trusted Aide believed to be Lieutenant Colonel Oyite-Ojok to arrest Dad and his immediate "underlings". However, a certain Kakwa Sergeant Major named Musa was said to have intercepted the message.

Meanwhile, Dad was wild duck shooting upcountry unaware of what was about to change his life and that of Uganda, until he was fortunately tipped off by a lady friend in the President's Office.

Unbeknownst to Obote, the rift between him and Dad was to be the "perfect" setting for the fulfillment of the pronouncement made by Grandma Aisha Aate way back when Dad was an infant. A "friendship" gone terribly wrong would in effect be the force that would aid Dad's ascent to the "highest position in the land" of Uganda as pronounced and predicted by Grandma Aisha Aate after the Deadly "Paternity Test" Dad endured as an infant. The survival of the ordeal Dad endured on the slopes of the Kakwa Legendary Mountain Liru as an infant seemed to have become the norm as Dad survived one "liquidation plot" after another!

The day Dad overthrew Apollo Milton Obote in a military coup

On January 25, 1971, Dad overthrew Apollo Milton Obote in a Military Coup, while Obote was in Singapore attending a Conference of Commonwealth Heads of State and Governments. Obote had eventually moved forward with his plan to get rid of Dad so he had relayed orders to his loyal Lan'gi officers to arrest Dad and his key Army supporters.

Over the years, Dad had bittersweet memories of the coup against Obote and it is to Mama Sauda Nnalongo that he owed his personal survival because she was the one who leaked word of the impending "plot" and plan to arrest Dad to him. Mama Sauda Nnalongo of the Babito of Bunyoro was one of Dad's women and at the time of the coup she was expecting twins that she delivered on April 4, 1971 - over two months after Dad's ascent to the "highest position in the land".

Some claim that it was Moses Ali who was then a Lieutenant at the Malire Station at Lubiri who saved Dad's life. However according to Dad, Moses Ali was a very reluctant participant who thought and acted like the teacher he was training to be in the 1960s. He said Mama Sauda Nnalongo was indeed the one who informed him of the impending doom and not Moses Ali. She got word of the telegram from Singapore and without hesitation secretly informed her man.

Unbeknownst to the "arresting team", Dad then instinctively swung into preemptive action. He decided to strike first and on January 25, 1971, while Obote was out of the country at a Commonwealth Conference of Heads of Government meeting in Singapore a coup was staged by the Army and Dad was declared President.

Dad relied on the Crack Team of Israeli and Sandhurst trained Junior Officers who had had their training in the Jewish Holy Land and Great Britain, to secure the key installations and garrisons across the country. On hindsight Dad didn't realize that the preemptive move would turn into a counter coup like some scene out of a Tom Cruise WWII German movie.

He quickly sought the loyalty of Pangarasio Onek in King George IV Garrison Jinja. Then he sought the loyalty of Erinayo Oryema who was the Head of Police at the time and had shown reluctance to go along with the plan to issue an arrest warrant against Dad when he attended the meeting that Obote convened before his departure to Singapore.

There are allegations that Dad's coup against Obote was backed by Israel and Britain both staunch supporters of Dad at the time of the coup but following is an outline of immediate events surrounding the day of the Military Coup by Dad on January 25, 1971:

On January 25, 1971 at 2:00am, while most of the residents of Uganda were sleeping, Dad ascended to the "highest position in the land" of Uganda as pronounced and predicted by Grandma Aisha Aate after the Deadly "Paternity Test" he was subjected to as an infant.

The Kakwa son, Awon'go Idi Amin Dada, in a Dramatic Re-affirmation of "Rembi's Mystical Legacy" took over the Government of Uganda with the help of loyal troops.

Although the coup was largely bloodless, Dad's Biographer Judith Listowel claims that "two Canadian Roman Catholic priests, Father Jean Paul Demers and Father Gerald Perrault, were killed at Entebbe".

Things had come to a Head and Obote's counter move against Dad while attending that fateful Singapore Conference of Commonwealth Heads of State and Governments in 1971 were not Luo led but entirely Nubian led.

Army Chief of Staff Brigadier Sulieman Hussien, Air Force Chief of Staff Juma Musa and Buganda Police Chief Constable Sulieman Dusman were supposed to arrest and presumably liquidate Dad who was Commanding Officer right up to January 26, 1971.

Obote's "scheme" culminated in a century old affirmation of "Rembi's Mystical Legacy", when my father took over power from him. Indeed, Dad's mercurial rise during his military career from Private right through to Major General on the eve of his Coup D'etat is a testament to the Lan'ga na Da or "Stepping over the KAR rifle" ritual by my grandmother. That curiously "Yakanye-like" ritual was indeed a blessing in disguise.

Grandma was not present to witness the Coup D'etat that saw her son Awon'go Alemi ascend to the "highest position in the land" of Uganda as she pronounced after the Deadly "Paternity Test" Dad endured as an infant. She had died in August 1969, one year and a few months shy of the day she had looked forward to all her life. However, Dad had been content with the knowledge that Grandma had given him full blessings throughout his life and on her deathbed. He had been content with the knowledge that he had been by her side on the day of her demise and they had had the intimate conversation about the fact that she was proud of what he had achieved against all odds.

Dad had been very happy with the knowledge that Grandma had lived long enough to see him achieve the impossible and even partaken in the fruits of his incredible success. He was never going to forget Grandma's counsel regarding Lemi when she said, "In whatever you do make sure Lemi (justice, just cause, instinct, luck, absolute truth) is on your side then you will overcome every obstacle".

It is comforting to know that Dad later properly reconciled with Grandpa, after a cleansing ceremony facilitated by Elders from Grandma's Okapi-Bura/Lenya Clan of the Lugbara Tribe and Grandpa's Adibu Lika-mero Clan of the Kakwa tribe. Dad relented and after the ritual cleansing ceremony (which took place when Dad had achieved the impossible and had already become President of Uganda), Grandfather, the senior Amin Dada, was able to visit and actually stay with his son.

Dad placed his father at the Entebbe Lodge overlooking the lake front Entebbe Zoo which has now been transformed into a Wildlife Research Centre of sorts. Thus, until his death in the mid-1970s, Grandpa at least tasted his "Prodigal Son's" wealth. We used to be ushered towards the new wing at Entebbe Lodge to formally greet our Grandpa.

The rest is history as they say!

In future sections of the series, we include accounts by Temezi (Elders) who speak about events that unfolded in Uganda before, during and after Dad took over power from Apollo Milton Obote on January 25, 1971. In those sections, Temezi (Elders) who were associates of Dad and others provide details and shed light on a lot of things.

The part of the series involving Temezi will provide a proper account of events that unfolded before, during and after Dad took over power from a previously close "friend" Apollo Milton Obote on the eve of January 25, 1971 and why.

The Military Coup by Dad against Obote bore an eerie resemblance to a mutiny that occurred seven years before in 1964 around the same dates as the Military Coup that catapulted Dad to the position of President of Uganda.

As I recounted in a previous section, in 1964, mutinies ran wild in the Uganda Army and Dad was the only one who could resolve these mutinies, calm the soldiers and persuade them to stop "revolting". This action earned him more high regard from his colleagues and British superiors in the Kings African Rifles and it was replaying itself right before his eyes.

During the similar mutiny in 1964, the First Battalion at Jinja mutinied and Felix Onama the Defence Minister was taken hostage after coming to Jinja to meet the demands of the mutineers relating to higher pay and rapid Africanisation.

On January 25, 1964, Obote invited the Staffordshires to intervene in the mutiny at Jinja.

On January 26, 1964, Dad returned from his upcountry "recruitment campaign and "safari"" and intervened in the continuing mutiny.

As Grahame writes in his book, when the mutiny was taking place in 1964, Dad was nowhere near the scene of the disturbances because Colonel Tillet had sent him on a "recruitment safari" upcountry in Northern Uganda. Captain Katabana had flown to Entebbe with the agreement of the Commanding Officer and the Army Commander to see Obote. By evening that day, Dad was back. That night, Tillet asked Dad what was happening at Jinja and Dad replied, "Nothing nasty will happen tonight."

Rumours soon flared out in Jinja that Dad would be the new Commanding Officer as he had been seen with the politicians who addressed the troops in the barracks minus the British Officers. Soon, lists were drawn for Dad to assume the First Battalion (Jinja), and Opolot the Second Battalion (Moroto).

Dad summoned some of the British Officers and the Uganda Rifles troops and addressed them.

One British Officer observed that:

"It was the most moving speech and a sincere one. Idi Amin dwelt on our [British-Uganda] traditional ties and fully expected us to rise to the occasion" (Grahame, p.37).

The above story line relating to Dad's take over of Obote's government through a similar mutiny seemed to say, "Let's do this all over again but this time in honour of "Rembi's Mystical Legacy"!"

After the Military Coup by Dad, there were celebrating, cheering, optimistic and admiring crowds. There was jubilation, hero worship, ecstatic merry-making amongst the Baganda and the people of West Nile. They could not believe this upstart winning - just like France beating Brazil at the Paris World Cup. After that win, Ugandans came out in droves around Nsambia screaming their heads off in the 1990s.

Many Ugandans welcomed the Military Coup by Dad on January 25, 1971 and vowed undying allegiance. Others took a more cautious "wait and see" approach. On the whole however, large crowds of Ugandans rejoiced deliriously. They demonstrated their support for Dad by flooding the streets of Kampala, "dancing" and "singing" to their hearts' content.

That memorable day, Dad became the Commander in Chief of Uganda, "The Pearl of Africa," the Head of State of the 2nd Republic of Uganda and he ruled Uganda from that January 25, 1971 until April 11, 1979 when he was overthrown and forced to live in exile with several of my family members, including me. We first lived in Libya and then in Saudi Arabia where Dad died on August 16, 2003.

Following are highlights of events that unfolded during Dad's rule in Uganda from January 25, 1971 to April 11, 1979.

Dad's "cold feet" about becoming President and a gun to his head

Following are highlights only of events that occurred during the first year of Dad's rule in Uganda from January 25, 1971 to February 1972:

On that momentous day, January 25, 1971, an amazing incident happened. Realizing that in his haste to defend himself against Obote's Master Plan, he had incredibly taken over ultimate power, a certain reluctance came to Dad's heart and he was sincere enough to voice his doubts to his trusted men.

One Juma Oka nicknamed Butabika was so infuriated with Dad's doubt in destiny that he pulled out his gun and placed it on his Commanding Officer's temple. Then he demanded that Dad strengthen his resolve and realize their achievement of successfully bringing about change in Uganda or he would shoot him. Juma also reminded Dad of the hoopla that was still going on in the streets of Kampala, which continued to teem with people chanting "Amin, Our Saviour, Amin, Our Saviour."

The Lugbara Warrant Officer Class II, Asuwa, later read out the 18 reasons given by the 2nd Republic of Uganda for taking over the government of Apollo Milton Obote in a Military Coup. The soldiers had hurriedly drafted the 18 points for staging the coup and read them on Radio Uganda. They had added a 19th point to convey that the prevailing reason for the coup was to "prevent a bad situation from getting worse". According to the 19th point, the soldiers had asked Dad to take over temporarily and their instruction to him was to prevent the dangerous situation from getting worse.

It is important to note that it was not Dad who read the 18 points on Radio Uganda but one of the mutinying soldiers. It is also important to note that the 18 points were written before Dad joined the coup and was unwittingly pronounced President of Uganda.

Our ride to safety in an APC and Dad's "disappearance"

When Dad took over power from Obote in 1971, I was five years old and living with Joyce and Sergeant John Katabarwa my Tutsi Guardians at King George IV Military Barracks in Jinja. This Barracks was later renamed Al-Qadhafi Garrison by Dad at the height of his support for the Arab Peoples beginning in 1972.

Dad wanted to ensure that we were safe from events that were unfolding in relation to the coup so we were placed in an Armoured Personnel Carrier (APC) and taken to our home in Arua in Northern Uganda. The mothers were in Dad's Staff Car (Austin Albion) while we made the rear in the Armoured Personnel Carrier, driven by our cousin Abdul Latif, son of Awa (Aunt) Khamisa Senya. Dad's sisters Awa (Aunt) Deiyah and Awa (Aunt) Senya regularly recalled and recounted that trip. Many of my siblings remember that trip well.

Awa (Aunt) Deiyah Araba also regularly recounted my brother Ma'dira's birth at the exact hour Dad took over power from Apollo Milton Obote in the Military Coup. Hence the name Ma'dira, which in this context means, "Kill Him" in the Lugbara language. Awa Deiyah Araba was with Mama Kay at Arua Referral Hospital on the day and hour the announcement was made on January 25, 1971 that her husband had captured power. At that very hour she released a healthy bouncing baby boy to whom Awa Deiyah gave the Lugbara name Ma'dira which is an equivalent of my Kakwa name Remo, for word had come through that Dad had been murdered on January 24, 1971.

He had disappeared from sight with the likes of Ratib Mududu and Hussein Diliga vigilantly on high alert at his side as he secretly coordinated the counter maneuver against Akena Adoko and Oyite Ojok - Senior Officers that had been charged with the responsibility of arresting Dad. Dad, Ratib and Hussein actually spent the twilight hours at a very pregnant Nnalongo Sauda's residence, which was just behind one of Dad's residences, Plot 10, Prince Charles Drive, with a gate as the only access to his beloved's residence. The residence was located opposite the present US Ambassador's residence on Kololo Hill Drive.

The whole family had endured 24 long hours of claims and counter claims that ran the gauntlet that Dad had indeed been killed. So, it was a blissful hour when Adam came into the world with incredible Lugbara Polo (Ululation) resounding the length and breadth of West Nile, just as the Baganda gathered a joyful storm, the likes of which had never been seen before. Ironically, this joyful storm would be matched by the same scene of jubilation 8 years later on April 11, 1979 when Dad was overthrown.

A warm welcome and "insults" to Obote from Britain

On the day Dad took over power from Apollo Milton Obote, convoys and convoys of soldiers and locals from in and around Bondo Army Barracks flocked in the thousands to our homestead in Tanganyika Village, as witnessed by all that momentous day. The merrymaking and incredible jubilations were unprecedented. Wave after wave of jubilant soldiers from Bondo Barracks inundated the Tanganyika residence to show solidarity with the new Lugbara-Kakwa Head of State, as recalled by Sergeant Peter Andia of the Keliko (Kaliko) and Midia Clan. They trace their lineage to Jaki. Sergeant Peter Andia later converted from Christianity to Islam in the 1980s and changed his name to Ali Andia.

Immediately following the coup, Dad said something to the effect: "The men of the Uganda Armed Forces have placed this country in my hands by entrusting me with its government. I am not a politician, but a professional soldier. I am, therefore, a man of few words and I have been very brief throughout my professional life. I have emphasized that the military might support a civilian government that has the support of the people and I have not changed from that position… I will take this task, but on the understanding that mine will be a caretaker administration, pending an early return to civilian rule. Free and fair elections will also be held in the country, given a stable security situation. Everybody will be free to participate in the election. For that reason, political exiles are free to return to this country and political prisoners held on unfounded charges will be released forthwith. All people are to report for work as usual. Further information and direction will be made as the news arrives. Long Live the Republic of Uganda".

Dad's first affirmations were clearly from the heart and lacked the abrasive paranoid delusions that crept in under constant struggle against determined foe over the next eight hard-fought years.

Many Ugandans, Britain, Israel and the International Community warmly welcomed Dad. Britain and Israel were Uganda's allies at the time. Britain, Israel and the United States of America were some of the first governments to recognize Dad's regime and it is alleged that British intelligence operatives remained alongside Dad as "mentors" until the relationship failed.

As he indicated in his first speech to Ugandans, Dad advised that his rule was only temporary and he would hand over the country back to civilian rule as soon as possible – a model of Western Democracy.

Obote faced certain death if he returned to Uganda after the Military Coup and so he flew from Singapore and landed first at Nairobi and then at Dar es Salaam where he vowed to fight back and reclaim his presidency from Dad. Julius Nyerere granted Obote asylum in Tanzania.

Julius Nyerere had attended the 1971 Commonwealth Summit in Singapore during which Dad toppled Dr. Apollo Milton Obote and according to sources, he left the meeting early to go to India on a state visit. It was while he was on the way to India that the news of the Military Coup by Dad against Obote came through. Sources have reported that while on his state visit to India, Julius Nyerere attempted to convince Kenya's former President Jomo Kenyatta to grant deposed Obote asylum but he was unsuccessful. That was how Obote ended up in Tanzania. According to Dad, Julius Nyerere then began a campaign to have him isolated by several African Heads of State and he succeeded with some.

Meanwhile, in London, England, the editorial of The Daily Telegraph had this headline:

"Good Riddance to Obote", while The Times observed that the reign of Obote "was no longer worth protecting." The Times added that Obote's government was "—hostile to British interests [sales of arms to South Africa], contemptuous of Europeans... ethnically divisive and potentially so unpopular that no British Government would be able to shore it up, let alone wish to be associated with it."

Dad's inaugural Cabinet Committee on internal security

In January 1971, Dad's inaugural Cabinet Committee on Internal Security was chaired by Basil Bataringaya, Minister of Internal Affairs and it was decided that Steiner be deported to Germany. Steiner is the Israeli mercenary who allegedly helped train the Sudanese Anyanya in collaboration with Dad on Uganda soil. You will recall that in October 1970, Steiner was arrested by the police in Uganda while trying to re-enter Uganda and he is quoted to have told the police that the Ugandan "Chief of Staff" helped him in his activities of training Anyanya from Uganda. However, it was really the late Brigadier Suliemaan Hussien the Nubian Alur at whose house in Wanyange I was given the name Tshombe who helped Steiner but the blame was erroneously placed on Dad that time.

Jubilation at the Kololo Airstrip as Dad released political prisoners

On January 28, 1971, there was jubilation at the Kololo Airstrip as Dad released more than 50 political prisoners from Luzira Prison, including the 5 Ministers and the former Commander Brigadier Shaban Opolot previously detained by Obote in 1966.

Dad embraced the former detainees and told them:

"In a few minutes you will be free and will join the rest of the people of Uganda. You are joining them at a time of great excitement and joy. There is no room for hatred and enmity, only for love and friendship between us all."

Finally, he said, "Uganda will remain in the Commonwealth and I wish to state my warm appreciation for Britain's preparation of Uganda for independence".

You will recall that on February 22, 1966, Policemen entered the Uganda Parliament and arrested five Ministers namely Grace Ibingira, Balaki Kirya, Mathius Gobi, George Magezi, and Dr. Ernest Lumu. All of the arrested ministers were Bantus and they were taken to Gulu. After the arrest, Obote announced that he had assumed "all powers of Government because of his understanding of the wishes of the people for peace, order and prosperity."

You will also recall that on April 15, 1966 in a motion which passed by 55 votes to 4 Obote suspended the Uganda Constitution and declared himself President on the grounds that it was his "understanding of the wishes of the people of this country for peace, order and prosperity." Obote further claimed that the Kabaka had made an attempt to overthrow him in his absence from Kampala in February and that "some persons who held Government positions asked foreign missions for massive military assistance of foreign soldiers and arms." Obote then ordered the arrest of the Army Commander Opolot and imprisoned the Iteso soldier. During that period, Obote named Dad the new Commander of the Uganda Army. Opolot and all the individuals imprisoned by Obote had languished in jail until January 28, 1971 the day referred to above when Dad released them.

Dad's decree to establish a Defence Council

On February 2, 1971, Dad issued a decree to establish a Defence Council, which essentially put in his hands the control of Parliament and local government.

Allegations have been made that Dad's Islamic and military background determined the character of his rule. He is said to have instituted an Advisory Defense Council composed of military commanders and that he placed military tribunals above the system of civil law, appointed soldiers to top government posts and supporting agencies and even informed the newly inducted civilian cabinet ministers that they would be subject to military discipline. "Uganda was, in effect, governed from a collection of military barracks scattered across the country, where battalion commanders were the local warlords" claimed a Newspaper Article.

However, Republic House was manned by Sandhurst trained Officers like Charles Arube, Major General Emilio Mondo and Major General Isaac Lumago all of whom were Christians. In addition, two so-called local warlords namely Maliyamungu and Elly Aseni were also Christians.

The only semblance of a warlord was Malera's 20,000 strong Anyanya forces that were inculcated into the Uganda Army to placate the 1972 Peace Agreement between Sudan and the Anyanya I Forces. Malera was expelled from Uganda following an attempted coup in 1974. Dad said the coup was led by the then Chief of Staff Charles Arube in cahoots with Isaac Lumago, Justice Opu, Elly Aseni and other Christian Kakwas disgruntled by the prevalence of the Baka tribes of the Sudan in Dad's Military Administration. He said the Christian Kakwa Army Officers were also disgruntled with the break in relationship between Dad and Israel, which had occurred a mere one year and two months into his government.

Dad had absorbed the Sudanese into his army during the period between 1972 and 1979 when there was Peace in the Sudan after the signing of the Addis Ababa Agreement. However, this Peace in Southern Sudan was broken when in the 1980s John Garang resumed the bitter war, which lasted until the Comprehensive Peace Agreement was signed between Omar Al Basher and John Garang.

Praises and bringing the body of King Mutesa II for a Royal Burial

In February 1971, Dad's stand against communism was hailed in the Daily Telegraph. A caption read, "from Africa, one commonsense voice has come through loud and clear, and it is that of General (now President) Amin, who assured that Uganda would certainly not leave the Commonwealth."

On February 2, 1971, the British Government of Edward Heath formally recognized Dad's government. Several African countries also recognized the military regime except Tanzania, Zambia, the Sudan and Nigeria who remained loyal to Obote.

After events settled down, Machomingi, Sukeji, Joseph Akisu and I remained with Alias of the Drimu Kakwa clan. My cousin Atiki looked after us until we were returned to Joyce and Sergeant John Katabarwa in Jinja where we rejoined my older brother Taban and my other siblings at the Barracks Primary Boarding School.

On February 20, 1971, in the first of only two "self-appointment" ranks, an announcement declared:

"The officers and men of the Armed Forces and Air Force promote Idi Amin Dada to Full General".

On the same day, an amendment was made to end the curfew imposed by Obote earlier. In addition, an announcement was made that Dad would be President for 5 years and that during this time all political activities would be suspended.

Immediately following the Military Coup by Dad against Obote, Dad extended a warm gesture to the Baganda and began facilitating the return of the body of their Kabaka, King Mutesa II for burial in Uganda. While doing so, he assured Prince Ronald Mutebi, heir to the Buganda throne at the time that he was safe to return to Uganda.

A Ministerial Committee was immediately announced to organize the return and burial of Kabaka Mutesa II's body. The Committee was composed of Abu Mayanja, a Muganda as its Chairman (Mayanja was one of Obote's former detainees), Wanube Kibedi (Dad's wife Mama Mariam's younger brother), J.H. Gesa, J.M.N. Zikusoka, Lieutenant Colonel O'bitre-Gama (a Maracha) and Charles Oboth Ofumbi (a Jopadhola).

Dad also announced that the Katikiro of Buganda, Mayanja-Nkangi and the former Buganda Attorney General, Mpanga, were free to return to Uganda on tickets to be borne by the new government. Princess Mpologoma, the ex-Kabaka's sister, detained by Obote was also released on Dad's orders.

In March 1971, Dad assured the 16-year old Ronald Mutebi who by direct descent was the Kabaka of Buganda upon his father's demise, of his safety in Uganda. Before his overthrow by Dad, Obote had declared that Mutebi would be arrested if he ever set foot in Uganda.

Moreover, Dad confirmed that Mutebi would once again be allowed to perform the sacred rite of symbolically covering his father's grave with bark cloth before his official burial.

On March 31, 1971, the embalmed body of the Kabaka, Mutesa II was returned to Uganda for burial at Kasubi, the site of the Royal Tombs.

There was an Undecided Postmortem in relation to Kabaka Mutesa II's death and allegations that Obote sent someone to poison the Kabaka Mutesa II while he lived in exile in England, which grieved the Baganda and continued to fuel the hatred many Baganda had for Obote. As outlined in a previous section, the continuing hatred of Obote by pro-monarchist Baganda is reported to have prompted the assassination attempt on him that occurred on December 19, 1969 and was unfairly blamed on Dad.

In 1971, Dr. Hugh Johnson, a Pathologist at the London Hospital personally performed some very extensive tests regarding the autopsy of Mutesa II, the deceased Monarch of Buganda. The Department of Forensic Medicine at the London Hospital stated:

"We looked for a very large and extensive range of drugs and poisons ... we looked for basic drugs. The only significant finding was that of alcohol, in very large quantities in the body. The respective amounts in mm per alcohol were as follows: blood level 408; urine 444; liver blood 302 absorbed [unabsorbed] stomach contents, 406".

According to the Autopsy Report, the levels of alcohol found in the Kabaka's body were extraordinarily high!

Dad's assistance to Obote's family and a heartwarming homecoming

In 1971, Dad assisted Obote's father Opetu in Akokoro and looked after Mrs. Miria Kalule Obote and her children, accommodating them at the former International Hotel (now Sheraton Hotel Kampala) before their reunion with Obote in Dar es Salaam.

Chief Justice, Sir Dermont Sheridan retired in the same year and Dad appointed Benedicto Kiwanuka in his place.

Dad and some members of his first cabinet embarked on an extensive tour of the country soon after taking over the government. During this extensive tour across Uganda that took place in 1971, Dad explained to his countrymen the reasons for the coup on January 25, 1971.

At a home coming function and poignant event held in Ko'buko (Ko'boko) County organized by Elders of the Kakwa tribe, including the Church of Uganda Pastor in Godiya, 'Birizaku, Reverend and Archdeacon John Dronyi, Dad was the Chief Guest. The "Prodigal Son" was welcomed as the President of Uganda by a host of Clan Elders of the Kakwa tribe, in fulfillment of Grandma's legendary stepping over the Kings African Rifles ritual way back in the late 1920s.

It was heartwarming to note that a similar but gloomy assembly of Elders of Dad's Adibu Likamero Kakwa clan that happened 45 years ago had come full circle under happy circumstances!

During the occasion to welcome Dad as the President of Uganda in Ko'boko, the Reverend and Archdeacon John Dronyi greeted the new Head of State in the following fashion:

"Son of Uganda, Your Excellency General Idi Amin Dada, President of the Second Republic of Uganda, Ministers who have come with you, the D.C. of West Nile, the Chief of Ko'buko and his staff, Ladies and Gentlemen".

"I thank God that [He] has opened the way for you, Son of Uganda, Your Excellency General Idi Amin Dada, President of the Second Republic of Uganda to come among us now. Praised be the God of heaven. For when the Uganda Army enabled you to come to power over Uganda on January 25, of this year, you resolved to put God first and yourself after him, and you uplifted Our Uganda motto: For God and My Country. Long Live Dada to reign over us."

Grandma would be singing praises to Allah at that pinnacle moment in her beloved son's life although she was not alive to witness it "Allah Yar Hamu."

The beginning of resistance, sabotage and propaganda against Dad

In April 1971, Obote, with the blessing of the Chairman of the Sudanese Revolutionary Council, Jaffar Nimeiry of the Sudan, moved to the Sudan and called for his Luo tribesmen to join together, to overthrow Dad's regime. This would be the beginning of the resistance and sabotage that was instrumental in tarnishing Dad's reputation and eventually leading to his fall and defeat.

Lieutenant Colonel Oyite-Ojok, along with 2,000 Luos and Itesos joined the training team (camp) as guerrillas at Owiny Kibul in Acholiland on the Sudan side of the border. The same month April 1971, the General Service Unit (GSU) was dissolved and several of its members were arrested. The apparent persecution of Acholis and Lan'gis intensified in direct response to Obote's call to arms by his tribesmen and many of them acting on that call.

Contrary to allegations that Dad systematically set out to murder Ugandans from the Lan'gi and Acholi tribes of Uganda, Dad's army acted in self defense but this would form the basis of unfounded allegations that Dad systematically targeted and killed innocent civilians. The above accounts were mere propaganda to raise hatred against the martial rule of the 2nd Republic as corroborated by articles that exist in the public arena.

False allegations in the public arena continued to characterize the propaganda that began with Obote regrouping his troops in the training camp in Sudan. The allegations accompanied Dad's rule in Uganda and they were blindly accepted as truth.

In May 1971, Dad offered 1 million Uganda Shillings (£56,000) for Obote, dead or alive, and 500,000 for each of Sam Odaka, Obote's Foreign Minister, and Akena Adoko who were in Dar es Salaam at this time in what would come to be recognized as his distinctive bombastic style. This included an offer to liberate Black South Africans from the shackles of racism by force. In his soon to be renowned bombastic style, Dad offered to travel to South Africa in order "to get a first hand account of the conditions there."

The "Detention Decree", foreign trips and a "plot" by saboteurs

On May 5, 1971, the Attorney General of Uganda announced an ill conceived "Detention Decree" enabling the Minister of Internal Affairs to detain any person who had "conducted or was conducting himself in a manner dangerous to peace and good order". The decree was supposed to last until March 1973 but it did not. Thus began Uganda's presumed slide into anarchy and dictatorship under Dad.

Meanwhile there was business as usual as Dad prepared to take trips to Britain and Israel. As this was happening, saboteurs began "hatching" and implementing insidious plans "crafted" to make Dad look like a whimsical murderer or someone who ordered brutal murders.

On July 1, 1971, Dad proceeded to meet the Queen in London. The British Elite continued "admiring him" as a "gentle giant" opposed to communism even though they would revoke their strong support for Dad one year later in 1972 when Dad stopped towing the puppet line of Subservience Protocol. Also in July 1971, Dad visited Israel and was received by Israel's Prime Minister Mrs. Golda Meir.

During his visit to England, Dad told the Queen about England being the only place he knew he could buy size 14 British shoes - probably his favourite "Church" shoes.

According to Dad, the Queen was beside herself and she was truly amused by the remark by her former subject who was part of the Guard Patrol when news came through in Kenya of the death of her father and her ascension to the British Throne. Dad was fond of reminding anyone of that little known fact.

A short-lived "honeymoon" with Israel and our Jewish twin brothers

While on the trip to Israel, the Israelis presented Dad with an Executive Jet dubbed "Jet Commander." Israel also promised to sell Dad arms for up to $1 million while Britain agreed to supply Anti-Personnel Carriers (APCs) worth the same amount and to train fifty Ugandan officers.

Alas the honeymoon was short lived between the two nations of Israel and Uganda! Dad's erstwhile New Mentor Al-Faisal from Black Arabia (Saudi Arabia) was positioning himself on the distant horizon to replace the Israelis. His most loyal brother-in-arms Al-Qadhafi from the Magrib shores of Libya was also preparing to make his indelible mark on Dad's Psyche. This would come to the forefront after Dad and Al-Qadhafi's February 13-14, 1972 declaration of Indigenous Independence less than a year after the warm reception he received from Israel in July 1971.

The provocative question that King Faisal asked Dad during their secret meeting in Egypt in 1970 while attending Gamal Abdel Nasser's funeral would come home to roost in 1972 when Dad expelled the Israeli's from Uganda. As outlined in a previous section, that day, the King had asked Dad a typically provocative Muslim Question:

"You call yourself a Muslim Eid Al-Amin when you as Army Commander let your land be used for Zionist Hegemony over the Arab Muslim Nations?…"

The honeymoon with Britain would last a little longer but eventually wear off as well when Dad became "wayward", stopped "listening" and being a loyal servant and began "taunting" the British in the most unthinkable ways.

Dad had very friendly relations with both Israel and Britain considered friends of Uganda and Dad until the relationships failed. In fact in the early years of Dad's regime, the British Ambassador would sit in the cabinet meetings and the Israeli Ambassador was a regular figure at Dad's cocktail parties. Furthermore, the British press loved Dad and praised him, often referring to him as the 'Gentle Giant'.

You will recall that in 1963, Dad was sent to Israel, despite being a Muslim. He had gone to Israel to take a Paratrooper Training course. While in Israel, Dad established strong relationships with members of the Israeli Elite. These relationships continued after Dad took over power from Apollo Milton Obote. The same relationships enabled Dad to supply arms to the Anyanya during the war in the Sudan between the predominantly Christian south and the predominantly Muslim North.

Prior to Dad's visit to Israel good news came his way around the American and French Independence days in 1971 when he had already achieved the impossible and was already the Head of State of the 2nd Republic of Uganda. That time, the Israeli Embassy sent him a "Private and Confidential" Post consisting of news about the birth to him of Jewish twin boys by the beautiful female Mossad Agent he had a secret meeting with in Egypt when he attended Gamal Abdel Nasser's funeral in 1970. According to Dad, his very close friend at the time, Colonel Baruch Balev sent him the "Private and Confidential" Post consisting the good news about our Jewish twin brothers.

You could almost see Dad's usual perplexed joy at knowing he had scored as he set eyes on pictures of the "Twin Bundles of Joy". "Twins!" he had thought to himself while reflecting that these were his second set of twins, for another woman who had also saved his life by warning him about another impending arrest this time immediately preceding the coup had also given him twins!

Dad could not help reflecting on the time in 1970 when he attended the funeral of Gamal Abdel Nasser in Egypt. He hadn't forgotten the beautiful female Mossad agent who asked to have a private meeting with him and intimated that she was sent on an urgent mission from New York to meet him and convey an urgent message from Colonel Balev. As outlined in an earlier section, the female Mossad agent had told Dad that his life was in danger and that Obote was rearranging the High Rank military structure so he should urgently return to Uganda but he was not to use the direct route to Entebbe. One thing had led to another and the results were the beautiful set of Jewish twins featured in the photograph he was now staring at in utter disbelief.

Dad's girlfriend Nnalongo Sauda who warned him about his impending arrest by Obote's High Command immediately preceding the Military Coup had given birth to a boy and a girl on April 4, 1971. Previous to that, Mama Kay had given birth to Ma'dira at the very hour Dad captured power on January 25, 1971. Now the mysterious lady – the beautiful female Mossad agent who also saved his life from Obote's "schemes" had placed the icing on the cake with Twins from the Judeo Holy Land!

In Uganda, the Baganda gave Dad the Honourary title Ssalongo, which is a title given to fathers of twins while the title Nnalongo is given to the mothers. Dad's title of Ssalongo would stick for the rest of the other sets of twins that followed over the next eventful years.

The unconscionable murders of two Americans by saboteurs

While Dad travelled overseas, two Americans, Nicholas Stroh and Robert Siedle, one a Journalist the other a Makerere University Sociology Professor died mysteriously at Mbarara. Dad was accused of ordering their killings but he said he did not.

During the same month July, 1971 Dad sent his brother-in-law, Wanume Kibedi, the brother of Mama Mariam who was in Washington DC at the time, to offer compensation to the families of Nicholas Stroh and Robert Siedle, who died in Mbarara in 1971.

The deaths of the two Americans would be the beginning of false allegations levied against Dad that would be blindly accepted as truth without the allegations ever being brought before a Court of Law. Dad used to lament that he only ruled Uganda for one day because Ugandan exiles started subversive activities the very second day of his rule. According to Dad, these subversive activities included Ugandan exiles operating within Uganda, kidnapping and murdering prominent Ugandans and foreigners so that it looked like Dad's operatives were committing the brutal murders.

According to Dad, the Ugandan exiles operating within Uganda were responsible for the brutal murders of the two Americans Nicholas Stroh and Robert Siedle. Judge David Jeffreys Jones, a Welshman presided over the inquiry of the "disappearance" of the two Americans and according to him, "It is obvious that the Americans have died an unnatural death".

These two tragic losses should be properly investigated through an Independent Truth and Reconciliation Commission because as I outlined in a previous section relating to a false allegation that Dad murdered a colleague and close friend, Brigadier Okoya, Ugandans and the global community deserve to know all the truth.

Coup attempts and closing Obote's Guerrilla Camp at Owiny Kibul

On July 20, 1971, Lieutenant Colonel Valentine Ochima, an Alur, whom Dad had promoted to Colonel and Secretary of the Defence Council and Acting Security Officer, attempted a coup against Dad because of rivalry with Charles Arube, a Kakwa. Dad had placed Charles Arube in charge of the Army during his absence in England.

Also, V. A Ovoyi, a former Obote Minister was arrested after being accused of ordering the deaths of several civilians in Arua.

The guerrilla Camp at Owiny Kibul in Southern Sudan established by Nimeiry and Obote for purposes of training an army with the intention of overthrowing Dad's regime and reinstating Obote was closed. This decision was aided by a "communist-inspired coup attempt" in Khartoum in July 1971. Nimeiry also feared that Dad, in association with the Israelis, was helping the Anyanya from Uganda against his regime. It is worth noting that Obote had been anti-Anyanya and therefore pro-Nimeiry until his overthrow by Dad on January 25, 1971 hence his good relationship with Nimeiry.

Our return to Jinja from safety in Arua after Dad's coup

After spending a memorable period at the Tanganyika residence with Alias of the Drimu Kakwa clan and his wife and my elder cousin Atiki, we were returned to Jinja to continue living with our Foster Parents, Sergeant John Katabarwa and his beautiful Tutsi wife Joyce. It was during our stay with Alias and his wife and my elder cousin Atiki that someone took a photograph of me with mucous caked all over my face. Over the years, Dad would relentlessly tease me about that picture. I hated the teasing so much that when we lived in Saudi Arabia, I "stole" the picture from where Dad kept it and got rid of it.

I now wish I had kept that infamous picture because I would now consider it as a priceless memorabilia of my childhood. My sister Sukeji was also in the picture and she was looking towards the Aerodrome right behind our 5-acre plot. She was probably looking out for her grandfather Chief Philipo Wani Diloro who according to Atiki was fond of sending raiding parties to abduct his granddaughter because he wanted her to stay with him at his Jiako Homestead in Arua. Alias and his wife and Atiki were under strict orders never to allow that to happen.

After we left Arua, we were all sent to King George IV Garrison to continue living with Sergeant John Katabarwa and his wife Joyce.

Sukeji, Machomingi, Joseph Akisu and I left Arua just as the mangoes began to ripen in June/July. We left for King George IV Garrison in the company of Sergeant John Katabarwa and Sergeant Diliga. The two drove us all the way to Jinja into the care of Mama Joyce Katabarwa when the 1971 danger was deemed to have subsided and the whole country had been pacified and secured only for the July fracas to rear its ugly head at the Jinja Barracks. The Barracks was soon to be renamed Al-Qadhafi Garrison.

Since the demise of my dearly beloved grandmother in August 1969, this nomadic lifestyle dogged my toddler years until 1973 when I was finally reunited with my Dad under the care of my step mother Mama Kay Amin.

The 1971 attack on the Jinja Barracks and a tribute to the Katabarwas

In July 1971, there was an attack on the Jinja Barracks by Ugandan exiles intended on defeating and overthrowing Dad's regime. Some insurgents tried to attack and take over the barracks but they were repelled.

Acting in self-defense, Dad's soldiers repelled the attackers but this would also form the basis of unfounded allegations that Dad systematically targeted and killed innocent civilians. The above accounts were continuing propaganda to raise hatred against the martial rule of the 2nd Republic as corroborated by articles that exist in the public arena.

The report regarding the insurgents who attacked the Jinja Barracks in July 1971 was made by the then Chief of Staff the Late Charles Arube of the Kaliwara Kakwa clan when Dad was still the darling of the British and had gone for a visit to London. According to Dad, Colonel Sulieman Bai of the Baluchistan Sect who was in the Uganda Army and Hussein Musa of the Bori Kakwa clan of the Police Special Branch, secured the King George Jinja Barracks in the July 1971 attack.

Colonel Sulieman Bai was a Baluchistan Muslim but his relationship with Dad went a long way. As I recounted in the section on Dad's childhood, Colonel Sulieman Bai and Dad shared suckling when they were babies. During the time they were both babies, when Bai's mother went off to forage for food at the local markets, she would leave Bai with my Grandma and Grandma would not hesitate to nurse baby Sulieman. When it was Grandma's turn to go out to forage for food, Sulieman's mother would also not hesitate to nurse Dad as a baby.

In a previous section, I recounted that Grandpa's aunt was married to a Sikh and she along with her husband adopted Grandpa. I also alluded that the Sikhs are the most liberal amongst the natives of the Indian Sub Continent and they do not abide by the horrendous Caste System that views certain humans as untouchable at a religious and social level. That is why Indigenous Ugandans and other Africans lived and continue to live in harmony with them.

Despite the "animosity" that arose between Dad and the Asians he asked to leave Uganda in 1972 after he took over power in the Military Coup, my family was closer to people of Indian origin than most people know.

The July 1971 attack on the Jinja Barracks found my siblings and I at the Barracks. I was at the Boarding School with Sergeant John Katabarwa, our Tutsi Foster Parent, when it happened. It was terrible and I still shiver at the recollection of the attack. The barrage felt like a pile driver chipping away at the dormitory walls. The attack would be the beginning of a number of attacks aimed at overthrowing Dad's regime.

Dad and Sergeant John Katabarwa were childhood friends. They shared a common Kasanvu (coerced labourer) heritage as Kakwa-Lugbara-Balalo exploited as Kasanvu in Uganda's Sugar Plantations. John Katabarwa was very loyal to Dad as were many others. However, Dad's worst problem was going back to his former youth to pull his childhood chums to come and enjoy the fruits of his success because many of them turned against him and were responsible for his downfall!

As my Foster Parents, I have a lot of memories growing up with Sergeant John Katabarwa and Mama Joyce. Doing his master's bidding of looking after his illegitimate children was a very honourable thing to do. These were Dad's children who could not step into the Acacia Avenue and Command Post residence during the pre-1971 years and after.

After the July 1971 attack on the Jinja barracks, my siblings and I were sent to a Primary School near a Catholic Seminary in Mbarara but Mbarara would also be attacked in September 1972, while we were at school there. The same thing that happened in Jinja in July 1971 happened after we were transferred to Simba Barracks in Mbarara with Colonel Fadhul and my father's uncle, Major Sosteni, Chief MTO (Military Transport Officer) of the Uganda Army. The September 17, 1972 invasion and attack on Mbarara got us at the Boarding School in Mbarara.

Brigadier General Ali Fadhul was the Commanding Officer of the Barracks in Mbarara and he was jailed by Yoweri Museveni in 1986. Uncle Sosteni is Dad's uncle and he was actually the one who drove the Kabaka all the way from Bulange right up to the Rwanda Border in 1966 during the "Kabaka Uprising."

Dad's speeches to Ugandan Asians

In September 1971, Dad telephoned the British Government to prepare to receive a Ugandan delegation.

From December 7 to 8, 1971, Dad called a large conference in the International Conference Centre in Kampala drawing Asians from across the whole nation instead of just those of the various religious groups.

In a diplomatic tone, Dad said:

"Your Excellencies, Honourable Ministers, delegates, ladies and gentlemen. As you are aware, this is one of the conferences, which the government has called to this centre to discuss the problems facing the different groups of persons in Uganda. Some four weeks ago, we had the Muslims, and only a week ago we had the Bishops of the Church of Uganda, Rwanda and Burundi.

This particular conference has been convened as a follow-up of the many public statements and letters in the press complaining against the Asian community in this country. My aim is to ensure, like a father in a family, that understanding and unity between the different communities in this country are established on a permanent basis. Through the policies of the colonial government, you received special treatment which gave you a chance to establish yourselves firmly in all the main towns and trading centres in the then Uganda Protectorate.

Your community made use of this policy by establishing its own commercial and trading organizations, which played a big part in the economic life of the nation. And this is big but, first, the Uganda government made available to Ugandans and even to non-Ugandan Asians training in local and overseas educational institutions. Some had received government assistance. For instance, between 1962 and 1968, the government sponsored 417 Asians for training as engineers. To date, however, only 20 of the 417 Asians work for the government. Within the same period, the government sponsored 217 Asians to train as doctors, but today no more than 15 of these doctors are working for the government. Of 96 lawyers, only 18 were serving the government.

Moreover, even those who went into government service soon resigned for selfish reasons mainly because they would be transferred away from Entebbe, Kampala, Jinja or Mbale. Many of them had business interests on the side, outside the civil service, such as shops, garages and transport businesses, from which they received considerable sums of money. Many Asians referred to the Africans, whom they employed as labourers and servants or maids as nugu (black monkeys)."

For much of 1971, Dad toured the whole country. While in Fort Portal, he told the Asians:

"In some of the towns where I have addressed rallies, I found Europeans with us but not Indians. And yet, the members of the Indian community in Uganda are larger than that of any other people. The only bad feeling inside all Africa, all Black Africa, to Indians is because you cut your community off completely.

You do not co-operate or join together with Africans in social activities either here, or in Nairobi or in any other place. This is the secret feeling of Africans I am telling you today".

Dad intimated that the Asians had cheated the Africans albeit "legally". They had exploited them. They had charged them insidious interest rates. They had lived inaccessible lives in which there was no room for Africans and they spoke languages - Gujarati or Hindustani or Punjabi - which Africans could not understand.

Earlier during the colonial regime, Lugard advocated the importance of the Asians:

"…being unaffected by the climate, much cheaper than Europeans, and in closer touch with the daily lives of the natives than it is possible for a white man to be".

"They would form an admirable connecting link (under closer supervision of British officers)", Lugard had expanded.

In 1971 Obote had actually ridiculed the Asians saying:

"We'll say in time that we want them to leave and they will just have to leave."

The explanation in effect was actually in the UPC pipeline which was why as a follow-up to this proposal at the rally in Fort Portal in 1971 Dad told the Asians his only sad feeling toward the Indians was because:

"…You cut your community off completely. You do not co-operate or join together with Africans in social activities either here or in Nairobi, or in any place…."

This indeed was a Clarion Call that ironically would be echoed decades later by a British Labour Minister in the 21st Century when trying to explain the ongoing riots and insecurity amongst the South Asian Community in Britain.

Propaganda and continuing efforts to defeat and overthrow Dad

As 1971 came to a close, business continued as usual but so did Obote's efforts to defeat and overthrow Dad's government.

On December 28, 1971, Dad announced that the former Obote sympathizers had been transferred to Mutukula.

On January 5, 1972, Lieutenant Colonel Hugh Rogers, Dad's old friend arrived at Entebbe to head military training in Uganda. Dad met him at the Command Post.

On January 17, 1972, Dad announced that Obote's former sympathizers detained at Mutukula had been released.

On February 4, 1972, Dad told the press that 15 of the detainees had overpowered their guards and escaped to Tanzania.

On February 5, 1972, Tanzania denied that Ugandans had crossed into her territory.

On February 9, 1972, 15 "Ugandan Refugees" told journalists at Pangale Camp in Tanzania that Acholi and Lan'gi troops numbering 5,000 had been murdered since Dad took over. They detailed that there were 510 military detainees and a number of former General Service Unit men. They also alleged that Anyanya Squads composed of Kakwa and Sudanese tribesmen had executed many of the Luos.

These allegations led Rogers and anyone acquainted with the Uganda Army before Dad's coup to wonder about the figures after confirming that statistical records in the War Office showed only about 3,500 Lan'gi and Acholi had served in it. So it seemed that the 15 refugees were lying when they said that 5,000 Lan'gi and Acholi had been expelled from the Uganda Army and that they (the Refugees) were the only tribesmen surviving. The facts indicated that a number of Acholi and Lan'gi soldiers were still serving in the Uganda Army, as Rogers could see for himself and he discounted the horror stories of the refugees as crude propaganda.

The above stories would continue to form the basis of unfounded allegations that Dad systematically targeted and killed innocent civilians. The propaganda to raise hatred against the martial rule of the 2nd Republic of Uganda as corroborated by articles that exist in the public arena became relentless.

False allegations in the public arena such as what is contained in the paragraph below were the norm during Dad's rule in Uganda:

"In one incident, thirty-two officers were placed in a cell and blown up with dynamite. A survivor of one of Amin's prisons described how bullets were conserved and the nuisance of sharpening swords was avoided by strangling the prisoners and finishing them off with sledge hammers to the head. Amin's soldiers were sent to Akokoro, Milton Obote's native village, and killed everyone they could find. As many as 6,000 of the army's 9,000 officers were executed within The Butcher's first year of power".

It is interesting to note that some 5,000 soldiers whom the Uganda People's Congress Party mouth-piece claimed to have been massacred in 1971 by Dad reappeared in 1979 as the Liberation Soldiers who overthrew Dad's rule in 1979! This occurred to the relief and consternation of their relatives who had feared they had all been massacred by Dad as falsely reported by a media that was "hell bent" on tarnishing Dad's reputation.

The beginning of Dad's friendships with King Faisal and Al-Qadhafi

In 1972, Dad established close friendships with King Faisal Bin Abdul Aziz Al-Saud of Saudi Arabia and Muamar Al-Qadhafi of Libya. The seeds for these friendships had been sown in 1970 when Dad attended the funeral of Gamal Abdel Nasser, the second President of Egypt.

As outlined in a previous section and reproduced here for ease of reference, two years before these friendships blossomed, Apollo Milton Obote sent Dad to represent him at the burial of Gamal Abdel Nasser of Egypt. Obote had "chosen" Dad to lead the Ugandan Delegation to the funeral despite the so-called "dark clouds" hanging over his head over false allegations that he murdered his friend and colleague, Brigadier General Okoya and his wife and other "trumped up" allegations. However, while Dad was in Egypt attending Gamal Abdel Nasser's funeral, the reason Obote "chose" him to lead the Ugandan delegation to the funeral despite being under "house arrest" had become clear. In Dad's absence, Obote had quickly rounded off the Okoya enquiry, appointed Brigadier Sulieman Hussien as Army Commander and his fellow Lan'gi Lieutenant Colonel Oyite-Ojok as Adjutant and Quarter Master General.

Notwithstanding the "conniving" that Dad said went on behind closed doors in relation to "getting rid" of him, a number of more overpowering events unfolded in Egypt that related to his rock solid relationship with Israel at the time while also being part of the Ummah (Community of Muslim Believers). Despite the fact that the Commander in Chief Obote unexpectedly "chose" him to lead the Ugandan delegation to the funeral of one of Africa's and the Arab world's greatest Revolutionary "by design", the trip to Egypt raised unexpected opportunity for the Kakwa native in the land of the Pharaohs instead. The events that unfolded in Egypt "sealed" Dad's fate and they were the "prelude" to Dad's friendships with King Faisal Bin Abdul Aziz Al-Saud and Muamar Al-Qadhafi.

The break in Dad's rock solid relationship with Israel

Prior to Dad's "shift in allegiances" from the descendants of Isaac to the descendants of Ishmael in their age-old "fight to the death", he had a rock solid relationship with Israel.

You will recall that the first two countries visited by Dad after he took over power from Apollo Milton Obote in 1971 were Britain and Israel. In July 1971, Dad visited Israel and he was received by Israel's Prime Minister Mrs. Golda Meir along with an admiring Colonel Balev and his colleague General Moshe Dayan.

While on the trip to Israel as related in an earlier section, the Israelis presented Dad with an Executive Jet dubbed "Jet Commander". Israel also promised to sell Dad arms for up to $1 million while Britain agreed to supply Anti-Personnel Carriers (APCs) worth the same amount and to train fifty Ugandan officers.

Alas the honeymoon was short lived between the two Nations of Israel and Uganda for Dad's erstwhile New Mentor Al-Faisal from Black Arabia (Saudi Arabia) was positioning himself on the distant horizon to replace the Israelis. His most loyal brother-in-arms Al-Qadhafi from the Magrib shores of Libya was also preparing to make his indelible mark on Dad's Psyche. This would come to the forefront after Dad and Al-Qadhafi's February 13-14, 1972 declaration of Indigenous Independence less than a year after the warm reception he received from Israel in July 1971.

The provocative question that King Faisal asked Dad during their secret meeting in Egypt in 1970 while attending Gamal Abdel Nasser's funeral would come home to roost in 1972 when Dad expelled the Israeli's from Uganda. As outlined in a previous section, that day, the King had asked Dad a typically provocative Muslim Question:

"You call yourself a Muslim Eid Al-Amin when you as Army Commander let your land be used for Zionist Hegemony over the Arab Muslim Nations?…"

Dad had very friendly relations with both Israel and Britain as has already been pointed out but the relations soured in 1972. During that year, Dad went on Pilgrimages to Makkah, Saudi Arabia. While on a trip to Makkah to join other Muslims around the world as they congregated at Makkah to visit the Kaaba – the most sacred site in Islam, he made a stopover in Libya and visited with Muamar Al-Qadhafi. Following the visit, Dad's relationship with Israel worsened very swiftly, as he took up with Muamar Al-Qadhafi and King Faisal Bin Abdul Aziz Al-Saud of Saudi

Arabia and consolidated relationships with the two Muslim brothers. Dad would maintain these close relationships until his government was overthrown in April 1979 and beyond. While he was at the pinnacle of power in Uganda in the 1970s, he enjoyed support from Muamar Al-Qadhafi and King Faisal Bin Abdul Aziz Al-Saud and other Arab countries.

The close friendships between Dad and Muamar Al-Qadhafi and Dad and King Faisal Bin Abdul Aziz Al-Saud would ensure a safe passage for our family first to Libya and then to Saudi Arabia where we led an opulent lifestyle after Dad was overthrown in 1979. However, the relationships would create a significant rift between Dad and Israel. The damage to the once warm and cordial relationship Dad and Israel shared would be irreparable. The relationship would disintegrate to a point of no return. While living in Saudi Arabia after his government was overthrown, Dad would also devote himself to Islam and be accorded the highest honour in Islam on the day of his demise on August 16, 2003. I share a few details of our life in Libya and Saudi Arabia in subsequent sections relating to our life in exile.

According to information provided by Dad and other sources, following is a sketchy outline of what transpired in 1972 with respect to him crossing over to the "Arab" side of the age-old feud between the descendants of Ishmael and the descendants of Isaac and other events. The sketchy outline is for purposes of continuing to provide context to Dad's story and as a prelude to "fuller" information.

In February 1972, Dad went on a Pilgrimage to Makkah, which turned out to be a glorious occasion in Saudi Arabia following a mystic rainfall that Muslims in Saudi Arabia remember to this day. After the Pilgrimage to Makkah, Dad was called Al Hajj Idi Amin Dada, in compliance with the Islamic Rules of Pilgrimage to Makkah. Dad was also given a new Private Jet and the key to unlimited assistance "Wathiya" from the Saudi Royal family. On this occasion, he was encouraged to discard the Executive Jet dubbed "Jet Commander" that had been given to him by Israel when he had visited Israel in 1971 and had been warmly received by Israel's Prime Minister Mrs. Golda Meir along with Colonel Balev and General Moshe Dayan and other Israeli Elite.

Unbeknown to Dad at the time, accepting the key to unlimited assistance "Wathiya" from the Saudi Royal Family and discarding the Executive Jet dubbed "Jet Commander" that had been given by Israel, was the beginning of being definitively caught between the warring descendants of Abraham's Children Ishmael and Isaac. The action by Dad would be in direct opposition to the gesture of warmth and endearing friendship that Israel extended to him over the years.

Drawing the lines and "dragging" Ugandans into the age-old war

The lines had been drawn and Dad had inadvertently "dragged" Ugandans into the age-old war between two perpetual enemies and warring factions determined to fight to the death to claim supremacy, legitimacy and land. In future years, Dad would continue to be caught in this vicious war and be way in over his head as the descendants of the two "sons of Abraham" continued to wrangle openly and involve "everyone" in their fight.

The teaching to abide by the adage "Blood is thicker than water"

Kakwa people know and abide by the adage "Blood is thicker than water". Traditionally, members of the Kakwa tribe know and don't dare violate that teaching even the ones who belong to the two religions of Islam and Christianity - the two dominant religions practiced by members of the Kakwa tribe. Kakwa Muslims who are unwavering supporters of the Arab people and Kakwa Christians who are unwavering supporters of the people of Israel have always lived together peacefully despite their "silent" support for the two warring factions.

They always know that Kakwa people don't dare fight because they belong to different religions. Dad was well aware of the teaching by Kakwa Temezi (Elders) to value blood relations over relations arising from religion and he even practiced it. However, I don't believe that he thought through the serious implications of his "jumping onto the band wagon" of the perpetual conflict between the descendants of Ishmael and Isaac. I don't believe he considered the seriousness of inadvertently being "dragged" into a war that would escalate into the event referred to as "The Entebbe Raid", earning him many enemies along the way. I outline this "Raid" in a subsequent section.

A reflection on Dad's relationship with the Israelis

The Israelis acknowledge the good relationship they had with Dad before King Faisal Bin Abdul Aziz Al-Saud of Saudi Arabia and Muamar Al-Qadhafi of Libya came into the fray and I know Dad secretly lamented the split with the children of God as Grandma used to refer to the Israelis.

Her point of reference was the teachings she received from being a practicing Catholic before she converted to Islam and immersed herself in its teachings as Grandpa and many members of my family did.

As outlined in previous sections, Grandma told Dad, "Do not forsake the children of God my son, never forsake the children of God" but alas a budding love relationship with the Israeli Nation was cut short at the roots.

King Faisal's gift to Dad of the original Lear Jet "Gulf Stream II"

King Faisal Bin Abdul Aziz Al-Saud gave Dad the original Lear Jet "Gulf Stream II", free of charge. He intended it as a replacement for the Executive Jet dubbed "Jet Commander" that the Israelis gave Dad.

Dad never took the gift of the Lear Jet as his own, but preferred to refer to it as Ugandan State property. After his overthrow, the NRM Government pawned off the still functional Lear Jet and a GIII was bought in its stead.

During Dad's visit to Saudi Arabia for the Pilgrimage, he was also invested by King Faisal Bin Abdul Aziz Al-Saud with the highest Islamic Order – A Palm Tree Medal he would begin to wear to every occasion. The Palm Tree Medal was always pinned close to Dad's top button on all Military Dress he wore and discernible amongst a collage of other medals he collected from every Arab Islamic country he paid a visit to, following his visit to Saudi Arabia. Dad was honoured with accolades and faithfully honoured those who revered him by pinning their numerous accolades onto his broad chest, to the amusement of the Western Media. The Western media misinterpreted and conveyed this action by Dad as self aggrandizing behaviour and failed to note that the medals were to display the unwavering support he had for Arab people and Arab lands after severing ties with Israel.

A Diplomatic Relationship with Libya and Joint Communiqué

On February 12, 1972, Roman Catholic Archbishop Mgr. Emmanuel Nsubuga, the Anglican Archbishop Dunstan Nsubuga and the Chief Khadi of Uganda, Sheikh Abdularazak Matovu, flew with Dad to Libya.

On February 14, 1972 Dad and Muamar Al-Qadhafi signed and issued a Joint Communiqué in Tripoli relating to their unwavering support for the Arab People. This Joint Communiqué was actually Dad's declaration of Genuine Independence for Uganda, Africa and its Diasporas.

The Communiqué read:

"The two Heads of State undertake to conduct themselves according to the precepts of Islam. They assure their support to the Arab peoples in their struggle against Zionism and Imperialism for the liberation of confiscated lands and for the right of the Palestine people to return to their land and homes by all means".

Dad's audacious declaration in support of the Arab Peoples would permanently seal the "enmity" he now had with the People of Israel.

Following the Joint Communiqué signed and issued by Dad and Al-Qadhafi, Libya and Uganda decided to declare Diplomatic Relations and Al-Qadhafi accepted a formal invitation from Dad to visit Uganda at a date to be fixed later.

Al-Qadhafi assured Dad not to be intimidated by the Israelis and Zionists following the Joint Communiqué they issued, declaring support for the Arab peoples' rights and just struggle against Zionism and Imperialism. Because of the now strong relationship they shared, Al-Qadhafi in turn, appealed to Dad as an older, wiser man, to go and talk to the President of Tchad, Francois Tombalbaye. Al-Qadhafi was at war with Tombalbaye because of Tombalbaye's mistreatment of the Berber and Arab inhabitants of the northern area of Tchad. The Berber and Arab inhabitants of Tchad are Muslims who lived in the Tibesti Mountains and they called themselves the Tchad Liberation Front. Dad flew to Fort Lamy from Tripoli and after two days, he returned to Tripoli triumphantly with the news that Al-Qadhafi wanted.

In this euphoric atmosphere, Al-Qadhafi offered Dad financial aid on a much larger scale and on much better terms than Uganda had been receiving for some time. He became one of Dad's strongest allies and even promised Dad military assistance. Later that year 1972, Dad extensively toured the Middle East and returned with £40 million, which he received "with no strings attached" because he was "one of their own!"

On February 23, 1972, a ten-man Libyan delegation arrived in Uganda headed by Major El Maheidy.

On February 28, 1972, Uganda and Libya signed an agreement on economic and cultural co-operation.

In commemoration of their friendship, Dad changed the name King George IV, 4th Battalion of the Former Kings African Rifles Jinja Garrison to Al-Qadhafi Garrison. At the time of writing the Introductory Edition of

Idi Amin: Hero or Villain? His Son Jaffar Amin and Other People Speak, Al-Qadhafi had visited Uganda under President Yoweri Museveni and was charmed to know he had a garrison still bearing his name.

In February 1972, Dad summoned the Israeli Ambassador to Uganda and accused the Israelis of subversive activities. In future weeks, he would ask all Israeli citizens to leave Uganda.

Dad's cabinet and high command on March 14, 1972

On March 14, 1972 at 10:00am, the cabinet of Dad's Military Regime looked as follows:

H.E. General Idi Amin Dada, President and Head of the Military Council - by this time, Dad was a Full Four Star General following the first of only two "self-appointments" on February 20, 1971.

1. Hon. J.M. Byagagaire, Minister of Public Services and Local Administration;

2. Hon. Y.A. E'ngur, Minister of Culture and Community Development;

3. Hon. Dr. J.H. Gesa, Minister of Health;

4. Hon. A.K. Kironde, Minister of Planning and Economic Development;

5. Hon. W.O. Lutara, Minister of Commerce, Industry and Tourism;

6. Hon. W.L. Naburi, Minister of Information and Broadcasting;

7. Hon. P.J. Nkambo Mugerwa, Attorney General;

8. Hon. Lieutenant Colonel O'bitre-Gama, Minister of Internal Affairs;

9. Hon. F.L. Okware, Minister of Agriculture, Forestry and Co-operation;

10. Hon. E.W. Oryema, Minister of Mineral and Water Resources;

11. Hon. E.B. Rugumayo, Minister of Education (he defected in 1973);

12. Hon. E.B. Wakhweya, Minister of Finance;

13. Hon. Wanume Kibedi, Minister of Foreign Affairs. Kibedi defected to London in 1973 and Colonel Michael Ondoga, formerly Ambassador to Moscow in 1971, took over the post of the Foreign Minister;

14. Hon. Engineer J.M.N. Zikusoka, Minister of Works, Communications and Housing.

Major Hussein Malera with the distinctive One Eleven slashes on his cheeks similar to those on Jaafar Al Numeri and the majority of descendants of slavery in the Sudan headed the Military Police. The One Eleven Ethnic mark was to haunt the so-called Amin Regime for all those that were considered in the higher echelons of power were associated with this mark. Yet Kakwas per se do not indulge with the One Eleven slashes, but do mark the temples with faint slashes for medicinal purposes. Dad did not have these so-called 111 slashes and anything said about him having the 111 slashes which were Arab slaver's markings were deliberate exaggerations meant to shed him in a terrible light and make him look like a maniacal foreigner intended on destroying a foreign land. Dad only had the faint Kakwa slashes made for medicinal purposes.

In his book titled A State of Blood, Henry Kyemba described Malera as "the most vicious man I have ever met."

The Public Safety Unit was headed by Ali Toweli a Nubian from Bombo in Uganda and Kibera in Kenya and Mohammed Hussein was head of the Criminal Investigations Unit (CID). The State Research Bureau (Centre) was headed by Lieutenant Colonel Francis Itabuka assisted by Major Farouk Minawa, a Nubian from Bombo with strong ethnic ties to Nubians in Dar-es-Salaam, Kibera and Mombasa in Kenya.

On March 14, 1972, Dad cancelled a planned visit to Egypt and the Sudan. He abolished the post of the Chief of the Defence Forces and instead created three new posts namely (1) Army Commander (2) Air Force Commander and (3) Paratrooper Commander.

The Addis Ababa Agreement for Peace in the Sudan

On March 17, 1972, the Addis Ababa Peace Agreement was signed between the rebel Anyanya movement of the Southern Sudan, led by General Joseph Lagu and the national Government of the Sudan headed by Jaffar Nimeiry. Henceforth, Obote transferred his troops from Owiny Kibul in the Sudan to a new and larger training camp at Handeni in Tanzania.

According to Dad and other sources, following the Addis Ababa Agreement that ended the First Sudanese War, frenzied activity occurred amongst Obote's humiliated Lan'go-Luo Sorbonne and Sandhurst trained Young Turks. They had to vacate their camp at Owiny Kibul in Southern Sudan where they had been supported by the Sudanese government to overthrow Dad while he "broke bread" with Israel.

Dad was in the process of severing ties with Israel and solidifying relationships with the Ummah (Community of Muslim Believers) instead so the two "warring" Muslims Dad and Jaffar Nimeiry saw it fit to end their hostilities. By 1972, Al-Qadhafi had brokered a Peace Deal between them, leading to a more cordial relationship between the two historical enemies. To "seal" the Peace Deal brokered by Al-Qadhafi that year, Dad and Jaffar Nimeiry opened and met over the Nimeiry Bridge on the Kaya River linking the Ora'ba and Kaya border towns of Uganda and Sudan respectively. This was a gesture of reconciliation and a sign of the cessation of hostilities between the two Muslim brothers.

Jaffar Nimeiry had never forgiven Dad for the direct support he provided to his fellow tribesmen in the Sudan during the southerners' insurgency led by Joseph Lagu from the Yei region of Sudan. The Northern Sudanese leader knew and dreaded Dad's ascension to the throne and his renowned long standing strong Israeli connections, which helped train and arm the Anyanya I insurgents in their long running War of Liberation from Arabinization and serfdom. Therefore he was willing and able to pragmatically support Obote's defeated troops after Dad took over power in the Military Coup. However, Al-Qadhafi showed concern about the possibility of two Muslim leaders confronting each other and like Faisal Bin Abdul Aziz Al-Saud of Saudi Arabia had done earlier, sought to lure Dad the newly installed Head of State of the 2nd Republic of Uganda to "permanently" cross over to the "Arab" side. Dad's potential had clearly been discernible by all who ever met him since his Kings African Rifles days in the 1940s and 1950s.

As the name denotes, the Addis Ababa Agreement was signed in the Ethiopian capital of Addis Ababa in the presence of Ethiopia's Emperor Haile Selassie.

The Addis Ababa Agreement, also referred to as the Addis Ababa Accord was signed to end the first Sudanese Civil War which occurred between 1955 and 1972 over a demand by insurgents in Southern Sudan for more regional autonomy. The first Sudanese War was also known as Anyanya I. The term "Anyanya" had been coined from the Amadi word Inyinya meaning poison. Amadi is a tribe in Southern Sudan.

According to reports, at the signing of the Peace Agreement in March 1972, Abel Alier signed the Agreement for the Government of the Sudan while General Joseph Lagu signed it on behalf of the Anyanya. Aggrey Jaden, a Pojulu by tribe was supposed to have been the one to sign the agreement on behalf of the Anyanya but being less educated than Lagu and not being a military graduate, Jaden thought it wise for Lagu to sign the agreement on behalf of the Anyanya instead.

The Addis Ababa Agreement lasted from 1972 to 1983 when it broke down resulting in the civil war between John Garang's Sudan People's Liberation Army (SPLA) and the Government of the Sudan. The relative peace that had followed the signing of the Agreement in March 1972 was disrupted when the former president of Sudan Jaffar Nimeiry imposed Shari'a throughout the country including the very Southern Sudan that had fought for Autonomy but settled for semi Autonomy with the signing of the Agreement.

Shari'a is the body of Islamic religious law and legal framework within which the public and private aspects of life are regulated for those living in a legal system based on Islamic Principles of Jurisprudence. Shari'a deals with many aspects of day-to-day life, including politics, economics, banking, business, contracts, family, sexuality, hygiene and social issues.

17 years of bloodbath had come to an end finally - or so it was thought in March 1972 when a somewhat uneasy agreement was signed between the rebel Anyanya movement of the Southern Sudan and the national Government of the Sudan but war would erupt again in 1983.

The Addis Ababa Agreement that ended Anyanya I did not completely address the reasons that had caused this first war in the first place. As a result, war erupted again between Northern Sudan and Southern Sudan, a mere decade after the signing of the Agreement.

Eye witnesses reported watching and participating in mass demonstrations in Juba, the capital city of Southern Sudan leading to the Second Sudanese Civil War, with crowds repeatedly chanting "Kokora" (which means division in the "Bari languages") and "Nimeiry, we want separation" in Arabic. The "Bari languages" include the Kuku, Bari, Kakwa and Pojulu languages among others.

The Second Sudanese Civil War is commonly referred to as Anyanya II and it lasted from 1983 to 2005. The two conflicts that occurred in the Sudan between 1955 and 2005 are sometimes considered one conflict with an eleven-year cease-fire and hiatus separating the two wars.

According to Dad, following the signing of the Addis Ababa Agreement in 1972, he used his 20,000 strong tribes-mates from the Sudan who could not go back to the Sudan or chose to stay in Uganda, to expand his army. This arrangement had also been part of an agreement between himself and Jaffar Nimeiry as Muslim brothers. Instead of letting the former Anyanya I soldiers "roam about with no purpose" after the end of the First Sudanese war, Dad integrated many of them into the Uganda Army and actually sent a substantial number for extensive military courses abroad.

This decision boosted his army to a resounding 45,000 strong by the time his government was overthrown in 1979.

Meanwhile Dad's exiled former mentor Dr. Apollo Milton Obote was forced to transfer his loyal troops from Southern Sudan to the northern region of Tanzania following the uneasy Peace Agreement between President Jaffar Nimeiry and General Joseph Lagu and the agreement between Dad and Jaffar Nimeiry as Muslim brothers.

Dad's 180-degree turn against Israel

Dad's change in allegiances from the Israelis to the Arabs was to precipitate a melt-down of the Israeli-Uganda special relationship starting with the immediate and "shocking" expulsion of all Israeli firms and citizens from Uganda by Dad. The melt- down would culminate in the 1976 Israeli Hostage saga dubbed "The Entebbe Raid" which is outlined in a subsequent section.

The opportunity for Dad to "permanently" cross over to the "Arab" side arose when Dad made an unexpected extended visit to Israel in July 1971 to meet Golda Meir of Israel and onwards to England to meet Queen Elizabeth II with a special request for heavy armory.

Alas! Dad's requests for armaments were rejected by supposed allies Israel and Great Britain. Feeling dejected, he made a pre-arranged but undisclosed detour to Cairo where he met a high profile amalgamation of the Arab League's Leadership. They had picked up concern laid out in The Times Magazine around a question relating to the enormous build up of activity at Nakasongola Airbase in Uganda.

The combined echelon of the Arab League Leadership intimated King Faisal Bin Abdul Aziz Al-Saud's previous 1970 pronouncement and grave concern when he quizzed:

"You call yourself a Muslim Eid Al-Amin when you as Army Commander let your land be used for Zionist Hegemony over the Arab Muslim Nations in Africa and the Middle East? Have you ever sat down and asked yourself why Uganda would need a sixteen capacity simultaneous takeoff runway, for F4 Phantom Jets on your land, if not but to be a southern hemisphere rear base to enable the illegitimate Jewish state to attack Arab Muslim countries from the southern Hemisphere? Ask yourself sincerely……"

During Dad's undisclosed detour to Cairo, he was able to meet the following Arab leaders:

Anwar Al-Sadat of Egypt

Hafez Al-Assad of Syria

Muamar Al-Qadhafi of Libya

Deep down, Dad felt an overwhelming sense of betrayal from those he felt intimately loyal to, namely Britain and the Jewish Nation. So, despite his mother's plea to "never forsake the children of God", at this critical juncture Dad was all ears to the illustrious group of Arab League Heads of State. He was convinced that they would honour his request for armaments after his supposed allies Israel and Great Britain rejected the request. That time, Dad was able to make an unscheduled detour to Libya which culminated in the Joint Communiqué and declaration between the Peoples' Great Jamahiriyah of Libya and the 2nd Republic of Uganda on February 13 –14, 1972.

As a now more committed "African Muslim", Dad miraculously managed to quell and foster an "uneasy truce and peace agreement" between Libya and the Republic of Tchad, to the amazement of his Host Al-Qadhafi. Pumped up with revolutionary fervor, Dad then made his return journey to Uganda. From that time onwards, the world was in for an Apple Cart Suplex upset from the least expected of Wrestling Ring Corner since they felt they had installed "Big Daddy" on the throne. They expected nothing short of dogged loyalty and Subservience Protocol from the Kakwa native whom they thought they knew so well!

As a bonus for crossing over to the Ummah (Community of Muslim Believers) and "Arab" side, Dad was given his second most favourite mode of transport between 1972 and 1979 by Saudi Arabia – the original Lear Jet "Gulf Stream II". It was second only to his famous SM Citroen Maserati, a metallic Green Mercedes Benz 300 SE Coupe, which was given by Al-Qadhafi.

Having completely crossed over to the "Arab" side of the age-old tussle between the descendants of Ishmael the Arabs and the descendants of Isaac the Israelis, Dad took a very hostile stance towards the Israelis. He severed his relationship with Israel after taking up with the Ummah (Community of Muslim Believers) and "vowing" to be a devout Muslim from then onwards:

On March 23, 1972, Israel firmly denied interference in Uganda's Internal Affairs following an accusation by Dad. However, despite the denial, Dad called for all Israel military instructors to leave on the grounds of "subversive activities."

On March 25, 1972, Dad cancelled all arms deals with Israel and stopped work on civilian construction contracted by Israeli companies, including the Arua Airport.

On March 27, 1972, Dad ordered all Israeli firms to leave Uganda.

On March 30, 1972, Dad ordered the Israeli Embassy to be closed.

On March 31, 1972, Israel published the true number of her citizens working in Uganda (149 with their wives and children, 470 in total).

Dad's marriage to Mama Madina, a fellow Muslim

On March 26, 1972, Dad married Madina Najjemba, a fellow Muslim and Traditional Muganda Dancer from a renowned Dance Troupe known as "The Heart Beat of Afrika." Madina became Dad's fifth wife, despite having three children from a previous relationship. From then onwards, Dad only married Muslim women. Two years later, he would divorce all his Christian wives for various reasons.

Thus far, he had had four official wives. The first was Adili a Kakwa of the Nyooke-Bori Kakwa clan (Mama Maimuna), Sarah Mutesi Kibedi - the second wife, a Musoga of the Ba-isemenha clan, Mama Kaysiya (Kay) Adroa - the third wife a Lugbara of the Paranga clan of Maracha, and Nora Aloba Enin - the fourth wife a Lan'gi of the Royal Oyakori clan. Like Taban Amin's mother with whom Dad co-habited in the 1950s Nora Aloba Enin Dad's fourth official wife was Apollo Milton Obote's cousin.

By the time Dad married Madina Najjemba, he still had the other three wives namely, Sarah Mutesi Kibedi, Kaysiya (Kay) Adroa, Nora Aloba Enin – all Christians. However, two years later in 1974, he would divorce all three wives over Radio Uganda (Uganda Broadcasting Corporation). Adili, Dad's Kakwa wife left the marriage before my sister Maimuna was born.

According to Radio Uganda at the time, an announcement was made to the effect "Madina has been given to Idi Amin in appreciation of his generosity to the Baganda and because of the love he has shown to them."

Dad had continued to show kindness and love to the Baganda and their Royal Family despite having misgivings about Baganda having superiority complex and looking down upon other Ugandans. He laid down fair rules in dividing his attention with his wives, giving them equal amounts of clothes and luxuries. Since he became Head of State, Dad had taken them in turn to State functions and ceremonies. In his speeches, especially to his troops, he repeatedly said, "It is a man's duty to divide his love fairly among his wives and to make them feel wanted and happy."

In Islam we have controlled polygamy limiting men to four wives, but Africans have no limits. So much so that Mutesa I one of the Kings of Buganda beat the Legendary King Solomon for though Solomon had 700 wives, Mutesa I had 1000 wives! He entered the Guinness book of records!

The birth of my brother Aliga Alemi Amin to Obote's cousin Nora

In the meantime, my brother Aliga Alemi Amin was born to his mother Mama Nora Enin Aloba of the Royal Oyakori Lan'gi clan in Tripoli, Libya on April 1, 1972. Because Nora was Apollo Milton Obote's cousin and Dad narrowly escaped death by "justly" taking over the government of Uganda from Nora's cousin Obote through a Military Coup, Dad's maternal uncles the Leiko Kozoru Kakwa clan also gave my brother Aliga the Kakwa name Alemi. It was the same name Dad was given when he survived the Deadly "Paternity Test" he was subjected to on the slopes of the Legendary Kakwa Mountain Liru as an infant. A ritual cleansing ceremony was also performed before the birth of our brother Aliga Alemi Amin.

The time the last Israelis left Uganda and continuing events

On April 8, 1972, the last Israelis left Uganda. According to Dad, the Israelis claimed that Uganda owed them £9 million for airports, training equipment and economic losses.

The rest of April and May 1972 were relatively quiet months in Uganda. However, on April 15, 1972, Uganda and Britain signed an agreement on military training.

On April 19, 1972, Dad announced that Libya agreed to (a) Build two hospitals in Uganda (b) Train Ugandan pilots and technicians and (c) Provide instructors for the Uganda Armed Forces.

On April 28, 1972, a full training team from Britain led by Colonel Rogers arrived in Uganda.

In May 1972, a Saudi delegation headed by the Director-General of the Islamic World Union arrived in Kampala where a Supreme Muslim Council was to be set up in Uganda.

At the end of May 1972, an Iraqi delegation visited Uganda and Dad called for the establishment of a regional military alliance for Arab and African States because "all the seas around the African continent belonged to African or Arab nations", he asserted in his distinctive bombastic style. It was around this time in 1972 that Dad started to passionately embrace the African cause as well. He had despised colonialism but he hadn't been as vocal and public about it until this time in 1972. So, in June 1972, he made it public that he was going to the Organization of African Unity (OAU) Conference in Rabat, Morocco.

The OAU was predecessor to the African Union (AU) and its aims included promoting the unity and solidarity of African states, acting as a collective voice for the African continent and eradicating all forms of colonialism. Both the OAU and the AU will be explored in more detail in subsequent parts of the series, Idi Amin: Hero or Villain? His Son Jaffar Amin and Other People Speak. However, on June 10, 1972, Dad left for Rabat and stopped in Tripoli to visit with his staunch supporter Muamar Al-Qadhafi. He left Charles Oboth Ofumbi as Acting Vice President in his absence.

On June 18, 1972, Dad was back from the Organization of African Unity (OAU) Conference in Rabat, Morocco.

Rumours of a coup and Dad's return from an Arab Tour

Meanwhile, it was rumoured that individuals from the Lugbara tribe were "planning" to overthrow Dad's regime.

On June 23, 1972, Dad was back in Kampala from an Arab Tour and he came home with £40 million "with no strings attached" because he was a Muslim brother.

On June 29, 1972, Dad left for Egypt and from there proceeded to Algeria, Tunisia, Syria, Jordan, Saudi Arabia and the Sudan to visit with Arab and Muslim Heads of State.

On July 1, 1972, Colonel Roger's British Training Team consisting of 4 Company Commanders and 12 NCOS (Non Commissioned Officers) began a military course for the Uganda Army. Lieutenant Colonel Francis Nyangweso, the Army Commander opened the course in Jinja, which ended on August 25, 1972.

On July 2, 1972, Dad saw Al-Qadhafi in Tripoli as he flew from Bonn, West Germany.

On July 6, 1972, a Palestine Liberation Organization (PLO) delegation visited Uganda and the delegation was entertained in the vacated Israeli Embassy.

At the end of July 1972, Dad announced that Al-Qadhafi had granted Uganda £3.4 million and pledged Libya to buy Uganda coffee and cotton to the tune of £11.6 million a year.

Friendships with African leaders and an agenda for two causes

Dad had friendly relationships with many African leaders including Jean-Bédel Bokassa of the Central African Republic and Siad Barre of Somalia. As he strengthened friendships with many African Heads of State, he continued to forge forward with his agenda for the African cause alongside his agenda for the Arab cause. However, his relatively consistent - perhaps the most consistent aspect of his policies as President of Uganda was his most controversial anti-Israeli/Anti Zionist orientation and strong Pro-Palestinian/Pro-Arab stance since meeting with Malik Faisal Bin Abdul Aziz Al-Saud of Saudi Arabia in the 1970s. This fateful act continued to pay off even after his turbulent overthrow in April 1979. Dad enjoyed the privilege of being a life-time guest of the Royal Family's hospitality and generosity partly in return for his dedicated pro-Arabism.

The loyal Kings African Rifles soldier whose father was converted to Islam by Sultan Ali Kenyi at the turn of the 20th century now resides in the heartland of Sunni Islam, the ancestral home of the Messenger of Allah, the original Dar-El-Islam among fellow Believers. Dad was supremely aware, despite several disclaimers as to his ability to effectively rule Uganda under an embargo for eight years! Since our Kakwa tribe was a tiny fraction of approximately 150,000 strong in a population of over 14 million at the time, it did therefore make political sense to Dad to cultivate additional constituencies including his very own Ummah (Community of Muslim Believers).

As I stated in a previous section, before Grandpa was converted to Islam, he was a practicing Roman Catholic. His first name was Andrea right up to and during the first decade of the 20th Century from 1900 to 1910. His full name at the time was Andrea Dada son of Nyabira, who in turn was the son of Dada of the Adibu Likamero Kakwa clan. Grandpa was converted to Islam by a fellow Kakwa with the title Sultan Ali Kenyi of the Drimu Kakwa clan of Ko'buko (Ko'boko) - perhaps the most notorious, influential, and towering Ugandan Kakwa Chief in the first half of the 20th century. One of four Sultans appointed by the Colonial Administration, Sultan Ali Kenyi who was also a Hereditary Chief was highly respected by colonial administrators and both revered and feared by his subjects the

Kakwa. He had no tolerance for dissent and administered lashings that left dissidents squirming in pain for weeks - even months. During his tenure as Sultan and Chief of the Kakwa, Ali Kenyi cultivated a friendship with Major C.H. Stingard who had a particular fondness for Kenyi's Kakwa tribe.

Dad's stance to cultivate additional constituencies including his very own Ummah because our Kakwa tribe was a tiny fraction of approximately 150,000 strong in a population of over 14 million at the time was directly parallel to the Petrol Dollar Era in the 1970s. He was precisely in power during the heyday of OPEC (Organisation of Petroleum Exporting Countries) during the period 1971 to 1979 and as an organisation OPEC is overwhelmingly Muslim in composition. The Aid distribution behavior of OPEC or OAPEC (Organisation of Arab Petroleum Exporting Countries) has tended to be to help firstly fellow Arabs and secondly fellow Muslims and thirdly fellow so-called third world countries, provided there is some evidence of support and sympathy for the Arab cause. Under Dad and despite the fact that Muslims remain a minority in Uganda, Uganda benefited considerably from OPEC sources. This was because Dad was a Muslim Head of State who was also staunchly Pro-Palestinian as well as a dedicated and consistent friend of Arabs - once he had made the decision to break ties with the Israelis in 1972.

Dad had once trained as a paratrooper in Israel and continued to wear Israeli Wings to his last days at the helm of power but the relationship with Israel had disintegrated beyond repair.

I liken Dads' split with the Israelites to Muhammad Ali's schism with Malik Al-Shabbaz considering the extremely close relationship they had.

One time, Dad related to me how he survived a helicopter crash with an Israeli pilot and they instinctively decided to become "blood brothers", by severing themselves and mingling each other's blood in remembrance of their ordeal.

As outlined in previous sections, another close blood-tie Dad had in Israel was a claim he had of having fathered twins with a female Mossad agent who fortunately fell for him in Cairo during the time he attended the funeral of Gamal Abdel Nasser in Egypt in 1970.

I fondly call my two unknown siblings Izrael Adule and Israel Dombu and their mother apparently has a lineage to Moshe Dayan who was a General when Dad visited Israel in 1971. Israel and Dad had very strong relationships at the time.

While we lived in exile in Saudi Arabia, I often wondered and actually asked Dad if he would like to meet up with these children but he bluntly told me off and said that these kids were nothing more than enemies as far as he was concerned. I was taken aback, much in the same way I felt when the famous Boxer Muhammad Ali commented that anyone who crossed Elijah Muhammad, the Supreme Minister of the United States based "Nation of Islam" from 1934 until his death in 1975 deserved what they got more or less. At the time I asked Dad about our Jewish siblings, I still felt the distinct nostalgic longing for the good old days.

Despite the outward support for the Arab people and the Ummah (Community of Muslim Believers), it was obvious that Dad was in conflict within himself about his relationship with Israel. The irony of it all was that as Dad continued to openly support the Ummah, he never ever severed relationships with members of our family who were Christians. He was consistent in adhering to the teaching by Kakwa Temezi (Elders) to value blood relations over relations arising from religion and he even practiced it. That is the reason why he used to label the false claims about him persecuting Christians in Uganda during his rule as pure "Parapaganda" (Propaganda). It was part of the ongoing slander and conspiracy meant to shed Dad in a terrible light and bring him down. Like all the false allegations relating to Dad, the false allegations about Dad persecuting Christians would be blindly accepted as truth without anyone ever investigating how close and intimate Dad's relationships were with Christian family members, Christian associates, other Ugandans who were Christians and other Christians elsewhere.

As a matter of fact, in 1972, Dad in his usual bombastic utterances wanted two of his sons to become Roman Catholic Priests and they were already in Roman Catholic Seminary. Come to think of it by this time, I together with the following had been relocated from Al-Qadhafi Garrison in Jinja and sent in the company of our Foster Parent Sergeant John Katabarwa to live with Grandpa Sosteni:

1. My sister Sofia Sukeji
2. My younger brother Khamis Machomingi and
3. Our cousin Joseph (Yusuf) Akisu

Until these new living arrangements, we had resided with our Foster Parents Sergeant John Katabarwa and his wife Joyce. At the time we moved in with Grandpa Sosteni, he was stationed at the Simba Battalion in Mbarara. While residing at Grandpa Sosteni's, we attended Preschool at a Catholic Seminary School near Ntare Senior Secondary School and spent most times watching Celluloid Films. If Dad hated and persecuted Christians as it has been falsely alleged, he would never have sent us to Christian Mission Schools more so daring the likes of Al-Amin Mazrui to convert two of his biological children Tshombe (me) and Machomingi to Christianity.

Liberating Ugandans and Africans and the "Asian Saga"

By the end of July 1972, Dad started having ideas about how to liberate Ugandans and the rest of Africa from the "shackles" of colonialism. It was an African cause he had decided to embrace with passion a year and a half into his rule in Uganda!

On August 4, 1972, he went by helicopter to the Air and Sea Borne Battalion at Tororo where he made the historic announcement:

"I am going to ask Britain to take some responsibility for all Asians in Uganda who are holding British passports because they are sabotaging the economy of the country. I want the economy to be in the hands of Ugandan citizens, especially Black Ugandans. I want you troops to help me protect the country from saboteurs. There is no opportunity in Uganda for people who have decided not to take up local citizenship, especially people who are encouraging corruption", Dad "thought out loud" again in his distinctive bombastic style. The soldiers clapped, cheered and "screamed" in agreement!

As this announcement was being made, Foreign Minister, Uncle Wanume Kibedi (Dad's wife Mama Mariam's brother) was on his way to the Caribbean Islands and to the United States of America to visit President Nixon.

In subsequent statements, Dad announced that the expulsions of the mainly 80,000 Asians in Uganda would occur within 90 days because "they are milking the cow without feeding it". Dad accused the Asians of "receiving considerable sums of money". He also accused Asian doctors of refusing "to go upcountry to places like Gulu, Soroti, Apac, Atutur, Iganga and to Butambala Hospitals."

"That is the question of your refusal to integrate with the Africans in this country. It is particularly painful in that seventy years have elapsed since the Asians came to Uganda. But, despite the length of time, the Asian community has continued to live in a world of its own to the extent that the Africans in this country have, for example, hardly been able to marry Asian girls.

A causal count of African males who are married to Asian females in Uganda shows only about six such couples. And even then, all the six married themselves when they were abroad and not here in Uganda. The matter became even more serious when attempts by Africans within Uganda to fall in love and marry Asian girls had in one or two occasions even resulted in the Asian girls committing suicide. This happened when their parents discovered that the girls were in love and intended to marry Black Africans."

Dad went on to catalogue Asian mal-practices which he said included smuggling, corruption, bribery, price discrimination against African traders and evasion of income tax by keeping two sets of books with one in Gujarati and Hindustan which African Tax Collectors could not read.

On August 5, 1972, Dad repeated his statement concerning the expulsion of the Asians in Uganda on a nation-wide address giving Britain an ultimatum to remove all Ugandan Asians entitled to British passports - about 80,000 of them, within 3 months - by November 8, 1972. Dad promised to summon the British High Commissioner in Kampala, Richard Slater, to ask him to arrange for the removal of the affected Asians.

At the same time, Dad announced that he had decided to buy out the Uganda British American Tobacco (BAT) Company's processing plants because the owners, along with the Asian community, were sabotaging the economy. The BAT Chairman in London at this time was R.P. Dobson. At the announcement by Dad, its Territorial Director, Patrick Sheehy said, "The very profitable plant employs about 650 people and we have always had good relations with President Amin."

On August 5, 1972, on hearing about the impending expulsion of the Asians from Uganda, Daniel Lane, Under Secretary at the Home Office in London angrily stated:

"We are already a crowded island and immigration must and will remain strictly controlled."

But Dad replied, "Asians have always wanted to make the biggest possible profit with the least investment. They milked the cow but they did not feed it to yield milk."

"They prevented African farmers and businessmen from learning their skills and sabotaged the economy by profiteering, hoarding currency, frauds and similar offenses."

At a Motor-Rally later in Kampala, Dad reiterated, "My decision is final."

In London, Uganda's Foreign Minister at the time, Wanume Kibedi, Dad's brother-in-law, equally fully shouted, "The Asians must go - but Uganda citizens will not be affected. The problem we are determined to solve is this one involving Asians who decided not to take citizenship, but they have been hoping to stay on year and year, making a good living, sending money abroad and preventing our Ugandans - especially Black Africans from getting ahead in commerce and industry".

On August 8, 1972, Dad said, "I am determined to teach Britain a lesson over the Asians. I received divine guidance before I took my action. I had a direction in which God told me to effect the expulsions. Responsibility for the situation rests only with the British Government", Dad announced tongue in cheek!

On August 9, 1972, Geoffrey Rippon, the Chancellor of the Duchess of Lancaster flew to Kampala to persuade Dad to change his mind but he was advised by Ugandan officials that "His Excellency has an extremely tight programme; he could only see Rippon on August 15, a Tuesday".

The British Officer, Iain Grahame Dad's superior during their Kings African Rifles days, visited Dad. He speaks perfect Swahili having stayed in Uganda for 17 years. Dad told Iain Grahame that his so-called conversation with Geoffrey Rippon had been awful, for he had not understood one word of what Rippon had said. Iain and his ex-Sergeant Major (Dad) then had a heart to heart private discussion about Dad's defiant and at the time very daring decision as President of Uganda to expel the Asians mainly from India, Pakistan and Bangladesh that November 1972 with the bombastic ninety-day notice.

Wanume Kibedi the Foreign Minister at the time was also critical of Rippon's visit to Kampala, accusing Britain of "economic blackmail" and of using arrogant and insulting behaviour towards Uganda. He said, "As the British in their arrogance would not increase the number of vouchers for Asians, Uganda decided to teach them a lesson."

Iain Grahame, Dad's former Commanding Officer, perhaps discreetly encouraged by the British Government, attempted to persuade Dad to change his mind about the Asians and to revoke the Expulsion Order. In fact he used a variety of tactics including the use of an Acholi Proverb he and Dad both knew but to no avail. Iain tried a different tack "Motmotocyero Munupoto" which means slowness prevented the European from falling but Dad would not change his mind about the Wahindi (Indians). They had to go, he determined!

In fact, before the deadline of November 8, 1972, Dad decided to increase the Asian Expulsion List to include even "Professional Asians." On August 19, 1972, he decided that he was expelling all Asians and it didn't matter if they were British, Ugandans, Kenyans or Tanzanians.

A certain Kisimba Masiko, President of the NUS (National Union of Students) allegedly sent a "Memorandum" to Dad protesting the expulsions. Meanwhile, business continued as usual.

On August 22, 1972, Dad hosted a dinner in honour of the Sudanese Foreign Minister Mansour Khalid, where he announced that "Those Asians with the correct documents will stay". Anil Clark of the Legal Firm Messrs Mayanja, Clark and Company was expelled. Some Senegalese, Gambians and Sierra Leonians, posing as security officers, were arrested.

According to Dad, when the time came for the Asians to leave, every Asian was allowed to take £1,500 and the rest of the funds over a period of time. The airlift had been completed well before the November 8, 1972 deadline stipulated by Dad.

It is common knowledge that "non-citizen" Asians used to have a hard time in other African countries including such countries as Kenya and Tanzania. Memories and scenes of their expulsion in 1968 abound yet no one talks about that. Moreover, Dad's predecessor Apollo Milton Obote had begun "hatching" a "plot" to expel the "non-citizen" Asians from Uganda before Dad took over power from him even though Dad has been solely blamed for implementing several of his policies relating to the Common Man's Charter and Africanisation. Dad inherited this "agenda" from Obote and "charged" right ahead with it when he implemented it in 1972 in his newfound passion to "reverse" the "sins" of colonialism and imperialism!

According to reports, there were over 40,000 Asians, who held British passports in Uganda when the Ugandan Government under Obote announced plans to hasten the Africanisation of commerce, trade and industry in January 1970. As it is evident, a year before Dad took over power from Apollo Milton Obote, plans were in place to hasten the Africanisation of commerce, trade and industry in Uganda. Dad simply implemented these plans when he asked the non-Ugandan Asians to leave.

In the series, Idi Amin: Hero or Villain? His Son Jaffar Amin and Other People Speak, there will be opportunities to explore and discuss issues raised by Dad's expulsion of the Asians from Uganda in 1972 including the February 14, 1972 Joint Communiqué he issued with Al-Qadhafi in Tripoli. According to Dad, the Joint Communiqué he issued with Al-Qadhafi was actually his declaration of genuine and actual Independence for Africa – a "stubbornness" and "audacity" that contributed to his "High Tech Lynching" by a "powerful" media.

I strongly believe that it is of utmost importance for Ugandans of all backgrounds including Asians and Black Africans to discuss and resolve issues that led to the expulsion of the Asians from Uganda by Dad so that history does not repeat itself! I believe that such discussions if properly facilitated will promote lifelong learning and bring about much needed healing that in my opinion hasn't occurred. I don't believe it is constructive to "sweep" issues related to the expulsion of the Asians from Uganda by Dad "under the carpet".

My siblings and I have a myriad of standing jokes about Dad - like the time my brother Ali nicknamed him Bahrain. While we lived in exile in Saudi Arabia after Dad's government was overthrown, Dad would furiously head for the Communication Services in Jeddah and call the Bahrain BBC Bureau, vehemently explaining the issue of the Expropriated Property relating to the Asians he ordered out of Uganda in 1972. Then he would gather us around to listen to the Focus On Africa news at 19:00 East African Time, until it became a standing joke amongst the inner circle of siblings and my brother Ali Nyabira Kirunda code-named him, Bahrain.

Dad insisted that the Asians had been fully compensated for the Properties they left behind even though no one paid any attention to his honest explanations and protests regarding how unfair he said he had been treated and perceived in the Asian saga. According to him and other people, the 80,000 Asians whom he expelled from Uganda were compensated to the tune of 1 Billion dollars.

There are many significant issues relating to the Asian Expulsion from Uganda by Dad which will be discussed as the series Idi Amin: Hero or Villain? His Son Jaffar Amin and Other People Speak unfolds. However, an article that appeared in the Ugandan Newspaper the Sunday Monitor on February 24, 2008 provides "food for thought". It provides background information that is useful in exploring issues raised by Dad's expulsion of the Asians from Uganda in 1972 and the claim that the 2nd Republic of Uganda under Dad's command actually compensated the departed Asians to the tune of 1 Billion Dollars. The article claims that many of the Asians who departed from Uganda in 1972 were unscrupulously and scrupulously compensated twice.

I invite audiences to contribute to the ongoing debate and discussion about this "thorn in the side" of Asian and Black African Ugandans alike. We must explore how colonialism, classism and other factors were responsible for the state of affairs that led to the expulsion of fellow Ugandans and how it affected our collective psyche so that such an event never happens again!

"Behaving very badly" towards "colonial masters" and other events

With the expulsion of the Asians, Dad started "behaving very badly" towards the British, Uganda's former colonial masters. Armed with his agenda for the Emancipation of Africa and its Diasporas, he stopped "listening" to the British and began "taunting" them in unthinkable ways including "insulting" the Queen. This was the very same Queen Dad had bragged about before and had a warm conversation with when he went on the Official visit to England in July 1971 following his coup against Apollo Milton Obote in January that year.

If you will recall, during Dad's visit to England that time, he told the Queen about England being the only place he knew he could buy size 14 British shoes. According to Dad, the Queen was beside herself and she was truly amused by the remark by her former subject who was part of the Guard Patrol when news came through in Kenya of the death of her father and her ascension to the British Throne. Dad was fond of reminding anyone of that little known fact.

Colonel Rogers who was in charge of the British Training Team consisting of 4 Company Commanders and 12 NCOS (Non Commissioned Officers) that began a military course for the Uganda Army on July 1, 1972 was first on the list of White British citizens to be "taunted" by Dad.

On August 28, 1972, Dad addressed the Rogers training team at Jinja and inspected the Barracks but he had something "up his sleeve".

On August 31, 1972, Rogers took off on a week's leave in Nairobi.

On September 7, 1972, Rogers returned to Jinja.

On September 13, 1972, Rogers arranged to meet Dad but at 8 O'clock on Radio Uganda, it was announced that the British Training Team was to leave Uganda by Friday, September 17, 1972.

Meanwhile, business continued as usual and Dad made several appointments to high positions in the Military. For example, he appointed Lieutenant Colonel Mohammed Ali the Commanding Officer of Masindi. This officer later became the Deputy Commander of the Uganda Army.

As Dad was busy consolidating his power through the army, Ugandan exiles were busy "plotting" to overthrow his government.

On September 15, 1972, at 2:00am, three Africans "hijacked" an East African Airways DC-9 Plane from Dar es-Salaam under the very noses of the Air Controllers and Airport Security. The plane was to transport from Kilimanjaro in Tanzania, 80 heavily armed guerrilla commandos to secure Entebbe and eradicate Dad's Air Force. But on approaching the runway at Kilimanjaro, the pilot failed to turn a switch which would disconnect the non-skid mechanism and on landing, all the wheels locked, bursting all four tires. There were no spare tires at Kilimanjaro and the commandos could not take off. The invasion attempt had failed! As members of the Kakwa tribe would say in relation to the Kakwa word Lemi, "Lemi lika lo'bu nye ilode!" In this case, this phrase very loosely translates into "The operation failed because Good Luck/Justice was on our side or the guerrilla commandos were not justified in their attack that is why their operation failed."

Meanwhile, the United States Senate held up $3 million because of Dad's "pro-Hitler/Anti Semitic" telegrams. By this time, he had fully embraced the Arab cause in the age-old tussle between the descendants of Ishmael, the Arabs and the descendants of Isaac, the Israelis. Libya supplied Dad with 5 American-built Hercules transport planes and equipment.

The September 1972 invasion by Ugandan Exiles and a reflection

On September 17, 1972, it was reported that Tanzanian troops had invaded Uganda and they had captured the towns of Kyotera, Kubuto and Kalisizo after crossing the border at Mutukula. According to Dad and others, apparently, Yoweri Museveni, Apollo Milton Obote, Julius Nyerere, some of the exiled Asians, Oyite-Ojok and Tito Okello (Oyite-Ojok and Okello being former members of the Kings African Rifles like Dad) in association with the Tanzanian Defence Forces launched an attack against his troops at Mutukula and Mbarara.

According to Dad and others, Obote had been deceived by two rumours: (1) That Yoweri Museveni had irrefutable evidence that as soon as the guerrillas advanced on Mbarara, many in the Simba Garrison would accept him (Obote) as leader. (2) That there were considerable defections at Entebbe from the Uganda Army and Air Force.

According to Dad, some three thousand invaders came in from Tanzania and they were actually singing with a thought that the populace would turn against the 2nd Republic under Dad. Dad said they were crushed.

Suspicion rose to fever pitch when the 1972 Mutukula invasion by Ugandan exiles failed in September 1972. The invasion that had taken place from Tanzania by the combined FRONASA (Front for National Salvation) and Kikosi Ma'lum (Special Forces) fighters fell into swing but they were unsuccessful in their plan to defeat Dad's government.

According to Dad, on September 19, 1972, Obote's invading troops were badly beaten back - suffering many casualties and injuries. Following this invasion by Ugandan guerrillas based in Tanzania, Uganda and Tanzania almost went to war. However, Siad Barre of Somalia brokered a Peace Deal between the two countries.

In 1972 Dad attended Somalia's Revolutionary Army Day and according to him, President Julius Nyerere of Tanzania hastily took off for home to avoid meeting with him at Mogadishu.

Alas, Yoweri Museveni's ill-fated attack on Dad's government found me at the Catholic Seminary at Ntare, a location near the famous Ntare Secondary School in Mbarara District. Most of the fighting was at Kitagata but the seminary was on the outskirts of Mbarara. It had a Preschool and Primary School next to the Cathedral which my siblings and I attended.

I will always remember scenes from the 1972 invasion and a memorable stay at the Catholic school near Ntare when the ill-planned attack came through from Mutukula. According to various reports, the combined FRONASA (Front for National Salvation) and Special Forces (Kikosi Ma'lum) insurgents even attacked Ntare secondary school! For what strategic reasons nobody knows other than "liberating it from Amin" symbolically may be but there were no soldiers stationed at the famous school where Museveni spent his formative years with his old chum Eriya Kategaya.

I distinctly remember the similar fracas of unbelievable noise from gunfire and all students quaking under their bunco spring beds. The same thing that had occurred during the July 1971 invasion by the same forces while my siblings and I resided with Sergeant John and Joyce Katabarwa in Jinja was occurring again!

I recall uncle Luka, Baba Diliga and Cousin Agele Akisu coming in full combat fatigue in a drop top Military Jeep Renegade with a mounted MMG gun on the front Bonnet to see if my siblings and I were all right. That sight took me back to the days we lived with Luka and the late Abuba (Grandma) Aisha Aate in Kidusu. I remember I used to copycat Luka as he did his military exercises in front of Grandma's porch.

I also recall my childish wonderings while at the Seminary School about whether the White man with the long snow-white beard (probably a member of the White Fathers' Missionaries) who used to drive by daily in a white Peugeot 202 was God. I remember glancing back with awe at my cousin Joseph (Yusuf) Akisu and saying, "Look that must be God." I must have got the notion from the frescos and the like splattered inside the Cathedral where Joseph (Yusuf) used to receive Holy Communion.

I once joined him in the row in front of the priests by kneeling patiently. Joseph did get the Body and Blood of Christ but mysteriously the Priest passed right over my head and moved on to the next worshipper! He was definitely in the know that this was the President's son and a Muslim but for the child that I was, I was "bloody" furious but not furious enough to blurt out why? to the Priest. All I could think of when we left the Cathedral was ask Joseph, How did it taste like? Huh? Huh?

What amused me most about this institution were the hilarious romps down the hill. We children used to roll up tightly inside Truck Tires and play. "Roller Coaster" indeed, way before Alton Towers or Disney World meant anything to me. The dusk bath time when children would line up along the murram road towards the Cathedral all busy bathing out of plastic basins were also memorable.

Dad's disintegrating relationship with Britain

Towards the end of 1972, Dad's relationship with Britain began to disintegrate the same way his relationship with Israel did – but not as rapidly!

On September 17, 1972, Donald Stewart, a British businessman was arrested and placed in prison.

Around the same time, Dad ordered the expulsion of the correspondents of major British papers in Uganda, namely John Fairhall of the Guardian, Christopher Munnion of the Daily Telegraph, John Harrison of the Daily Express, Donald McCullin of the Sunday Times, and Andrew Torche of the Associated Press.

As Dad was getting ready to intensify his "bad behaviour" towards Uganda's former colonial masters the British, planes donated by Libya arrived in Kampala on September 22, 1972.

On November 6, 1972, Newsweek claimed that the Dutch Bishop of Jinja Joseph Willigers "was arrested and taken to Makindye Military Prison, where he was stripped naked and held for 24 hours without food or water".

In his continuing determination to "free" Uganda from the "clutches" of its former colonial masters the British and the effects of colonialism, Dad summoned John Hennings the Acting British High Commissioner in Kampala and asked him for details of all British citizens in

Uganda and their families. He was given a figure of 7,000 nearly all of whom were Technical Personnel.

On November 7, 1972, Dad declared that "The expulsion of the non-citizen Asians was over the Economic War we have declared." He would expand on this statement by saying that he wanted Uganda's economy in the hands of its citizens and not foreigners who don't have Uganda's best interests at heart. According to reports by Dad's associates, immediately following the Asian Exodus, "Uganda's foreign exchange earnings rose to a healthy £12 million." Meanwhile, Britain was plagued with Labour Strikes.

Continuing support for the Ummah and consolidating Islam

In 1972, Dad continued his agenda to demonstrate his support for the Ummah (Community of Muslim Believers) and to promote Islam in Uganda. That year, he visited the late Badr Kakungulu at his Kibuli Mosque with a proposal to build a large Mosque which Muslims from all over Uganda could call their own. They stood on the Kibuli hillside looking at the expanse of Kampala and its famous 7 hills. The new Head of State of Uganda (Dad) then commented to his Royal Highness, "This looks like the best place for the Headquarters of the Muslim Supreme Council" he intimated.

However taken aback by the abrupt visit from Dad and feeling threatened, his Royal Highness bravely answered "Etaka te Tundilwa" ("Land is never sold"). Dad shrugged his shoulders and said, "Okay". Then he strode to his awaiting SM Citroen Maserati and took off to his Official Parliament Presidential Office at Parliament Building. According to Dad, the next time he and the late Badr Kakungulu would collide would be during the infamous 1976 Nsambia grenade attack on his life that killed his driver Musa after the Police Pass Out of the new Recruits.

That time, Dad requested his Permanent Secretary to find out through the Town Clerk and the Land Board if there was any land in the city that was available for his grand designs. Luckily the response was positive from the Permanent Secretary. Apparently the Lease on Fort Lugard had expired and was ready for the taking. Overjoyed, Dad called up his chum Qassim Ramadhan, nicknamed "No Parking". Qassim acquired this nickname because he was the smallest Rugby Player who played as a Forward during their Rugby Playing days. He was a little rum and used to wade into the others at the Jinja Rugby Grounds. This was the same place Dad took them to play after the 1964 mutiny he helped stop. He got the nickname for his ferocious Defense and bringing down attacking wingers from the other teams. Qassim Ramadhan ("No Parking") was then Governor of southwestern Uganda.

Dad and Qassim Ramadhan then drove up to Kapere's deserted House on the hill. Lord Lugard was called Kapere by the Baganda for he favoured the checkered short sleeved shirts.

High up on Old Kampala Hill overlooking the Business District Centre, Dad asked "No Parking" in Kinubi (the language of the detribalised community referred to as the Nubi (Nubians)) - looking towards Namirembe Hill, "De be ta munu?" ("Whose house is that?") "No Parking" answered, "Church of Uganda". Dad arched his head round over to Rubaga and made the same inquiry. "Catholic Church", responded his most trusted Aide.

Dad then pointed across the expanse of the Buganda Road Bus Park over to the Hindu Temple, which was built brick by brick without using steel or concrete right up to the height of three storeys. Then down towards the Ismailia Mosque, occupied by the newly installed Muslim Supreme Council right below where they stood and lamented:

"All the other faiths have a national place where they gather, yet we Muslims only have places of worship that belong to individuals".

The above happened because Buganda is the land of Overloads and Serfs since the "1900 Agreement" - the very few haves and the majority serfs who are the have nots - Kibuli, Wandegeya even Speedika in Ntinda.

"Why can't we have a place where Muslims from Karamoja, Arua, Bushenyi, Kabale or even Mbale and Tororo can call their own? Insha Allah this will be the spot right here where we plant the Liwa (Banner) of Islam. We will plant the Banner proclaiming La Illah Illah Allah Muhammad Rasul Allah right here where the British planted the Union Jack," Dad intimated with profound determination glinting in his eyes. He ensured a 99-year Lease was processed.

As if to give a very public nod of approval for Dad's passion to be a champion of Islam, a most memorable and rare event took place when Malik Faisal Bin Abdul Aziz Al-Saud of Saudi Arabia made a show of support to Dad by visiting Uganda in the early seventies. While on this trip, Dad gave the King of Saudi Arabia a tour of the Magnificent Masjid Noor in Bombo. He also organized an impromptu Picnic at a Picnic site near the Mabira Forest on the way to Jinja.

You will recall that this Magnificent Masjid was build by the detribalised community referred to as the Nubi (Nubians) that emerged from

19th century political upheavals in Africa that were linked to the colonization of Sub-Saharan Africa. During the 19th century, the original mercenary community that was predominantly Muslim was transferred to the newly built Army Headquarters Barracks in Bombo in present day Luwero District in the Great Kingdom of Buganda.

As introduced in previous sections and discussed more fully in subsequent parts of the series, Idi Amin: Hero or Villain? His Son Jaffar Amin and Other People Speak, the Vanguard Mercenary Troops of the New Protectorate Army under the Command of Colonel Colville, settled in Bombo under a donation from His Majesty Kabaka (King) Daudi Chwa of the Great Kingdom of Buganda. They built the Magnificent Masjid Noor in Bombo in the early 1900s. The structure holds so much majesty and historical significance that it impresses everyone who has the privilege of entering it.

Because of our Islamic roots, many members of my family became amalgamated with the de-tribalised community referred to as the Nubi (Nubians) and referred to themselves as such. In the early years of his youth, Dad attended Garaya (School of Qur'anic Studies/Readings) at this location so he was well acquainted with the structure.

During his visit to Uganda, Dad showed King Faisal Bin Abdul Aziz Al-Saud around the Magnificent Mosque and the Late King was mesmerized and his confidence strengthened when he beheld this ancient structure in the most unexpected of places. The King marveled at the Magnificent Masjid Noor during his visit to Uganda in 1972 and never stopped talking about it.

When Dad gave the late King a personal tour of the ancient structure in 1972, he also went on to introduce his former Madrasah classmates. Amongst these classmates, the most famous one was the adept Sheikh Abdul Qadr Aliga. Of course the other one was Dad himself. Both Sheikh Abdul Qadr Aliga and Dad were trained in the esoteric practices at this Khanqah where they won honors in their youth in Alim Al Qur-an (the Quranic Scholar), in the 1930s and 1940s under the guardianship of the late Sheikh Al-Rajab.

Dad remarked that the most touching moment during King Faisal Bin Abdul Aziz Al-Saud's visit was when he arranged an impromptu picnic for the King en-route to Jinja. Dad surprised him by setting up a picnic at a site located in the middle of the now endangered Mabira Rain Forest on the right hand side shoulder of the forest as you head to Jinja from Kampala.

Actually to this day, if one makes an effort, you can see this particular picnic site on your right shoulder as you proceed to Jinja. The site has concrete park benches strewn around the blissful locale which always reminds me of scenes from "Snow White and the Seven Dwarfs" when she had managed to evade her step-mother with gentle cascades of sun rays with tiny gold dust particles lighting up the forest floor.

Malik Faisal Bin Abdul Aziz Al-Saud was so taken in by the wonderful surroundings and the scene so overwhelmed him that he remarked to his host:

"This surely must be how heaven must look like Allaaah!"

Dad was ecstatic and truly touched by the King's remarks and the praise showered on the beauty of his homeland and country Uganda by his illustrious and most honourable guest. That same year, he had made two pilgrimages to Mecca and met King Faisal Bin Abdul Aziz Al Saud and other leaders of several Muslim countries who had also come to Mecca. During the King's visit, he praised Dad's measures against Israel and promised Dad assistance in strengthening Islam in Uganda.

The late King Faisal Bin Abdul Aziz Al-Saud never forgot Dad's unwavering support for the Arab People, along with his visits to the Kingdom of Saudi Arabia and the impromptu picnic he set for his VIP guest when he visited Uganda in 1972.

Years later while reminiscing about his past at our Al Safa residence in Saudi Arabia, Dad recalled the picnic at Mabira Rain Forest while lamenting the loss of what he claimed to have had - a beautiful voice! Dad claimed that he lost his beautiful voice following a brutal Illegal Hook by an unscrupulous Zania (South African) Boer Frontlines Man in a Rugby Match in the 1950s.

He was then the only Indigenous Rugby player allowed to use the facility at the Jinja Rugby Club at the height of colonial segregation following the incident relating to him challenging the racism and segregation that was rampant in colonial and "segregated" Uganda at the Officers' Mess in 1959.

As I recounted in a previous section, Dad had dared to march into the "Whites Only" Officers' Mess at 1st Battalion Jinja after being promoted to the Honourary Rank of Affende - the highest rank awarded to Black African members of the Kings African Rifles at the time. He got tired of moving with a rank that did not hold water and moved up to the "Whites Only" Officers' Mess instead of going to the Sergeants' Mess and ordered a drink. When the White Bartender told Dad off and "barked" for him to go to the Sergeants' Mess, Dad beat up the Bartender, forced a change in the segregative rule and got invited to join the exclusive "Whites Only" Jinja Rugby Club because he was "one of their own".

Dad claimed that after the brutal illegal hook by the unscrupulous Zania Boer Frontlines Man in the Rugby Match, which he considered as a deliberate attempt by the Boer Frontlines Man to put him out and in his place as a Kaffir, he never again regained that beautiful voice - hmmmm!

Kaffir was a word used by bigoted South African Whites during the time South Africa practiced the reprehensible Apartheid System of segregation to refer to Black Africans.

Dad's 1973 "Dream Speech" at the Organization of African Unity

In May 1973, Dad attended and addressed the Organization of African Unity (OAU) Summit in Addis Ababa, Ethiopia.

Established in 1963 by 37 "Independent" African nations, the OAU was formed to promote unity and development, defend the sovereignty and territorial integrity of members, eradicate all forms of colonialism, promote international cooperation and coordinate members' economic, diplomatic, educational, health, welfare, scientific and defense policies. At the time of its formation, the OAU was synonymous with Pan-Africanism, a term generally used for African movements whose aims include unifying "Africans" and eliminating colonialism and white supremacy from the African continent. Among several things, the OAU mediated internal and external disputes involving Member States and it played a significant role in ending Apartheid in South Africa, which became the 53rd OAU Member State in 1994.

The African Union (AU), established in 2002 by the OAU states is a successor to the OAU. The AU has been commissioned with more powers to promote African economic, social, and political integration and a stronger commitment to democratic principles. It also aims to promote unity and solidarity among African states, act as a catalyst for economic development and promote international cooperation, among other things. The OAU had similar goals to the AU but the AU is more economic in nature and it has a stronger mandate to intervene in conflicts occurring on the African continent between Member States, as one of its objectives is the promotion of peace, security and stability in Africa.

The 53 African states that were members of the OAU are also members of the African Union, which includes a Pan-African Parliament, inaugurated in 2004. The Pan-African Parliament also known as the African Parliament is the legislative body of the African Union. After its inauguration in 2004, the Pan-African Parliament agreed to create a peacekeeping force, which has since been actively involved in peacekeeping efforts in various parts of Africa.

The Organization of African Unity, Pan-Africanism and the African Union will all be explored in more detail in subsequent parts of the series, Idi Amin: Hero or Villain? His Son Jaffar Amin and Other People Speak, along with how they evolved and what the future holds for Africa and its Diaspora's in relation to them. In particular, the involvement of descendants of Africans "stolen" from Africa during the "African Slave Trade" in the Emancipation of Africa will be given special consideration, as the success of Africa and its Diasporas is intimately connected to the Emancipation of All "African Peoples" around the world! However, suffice it to state here that Dad really embraced the OAU's aims relating to promoting the unity and solidarity of African states, acting as a collective voice for the African continent and eradicating all forms of colonialism and many other aims. He wanted Africa and its Diasporas liberated from all the "chains of oppression" but his saboteurs and detractors would not let him implement the noble vision he had!

Throughout his rule, Dad faced intense and unprecedented sabotage that started immediately after he took over power from Apollo Milton Obote in January 1971. As outlined in a previous section, Dad used to lament that he only ruled Uganda for one day because Ugandan exiles started subversive activities the very second day of his rule. According to him, these subversive activities included Ugandan exiles operating within Uganda, kidnapping and murdering prominent Ugandans and in some cases even foreigners, so that it looked like his operatives were committing the brutal murders.

As if the sabotage by Ugandan exiles wasn't enough, a powerful media soon began "lynching" Dad when he couldn't be "controlled". They did it the same way African slaves who dared to run away, defy or challenge "rules" imposed on them during the "African Slave Trade" were lynched. However, Dad's "lynching" was done by making unsubstantiated allegations against him and putting them in print or film for "everyone" to blindly accept as truth. The form of "lynching" was intended for "anything" and "everything" written, said and depicted about Dad to be the "gospel truth". Dad's saboteurs, detractors and a powerful media thus succeeded in undermining and stopping his efforts to liberate "oppressed groups" until he fell without accomplishing the noble vision he had.

During his address to the OAU Summit in Addis Ababa in 1973, Dad articulated his dream for Africa while listing some of Africa's problems and how they might be solved. He took a Pan Africanist stance and argued for many of the solutions to Africa's problems. The solutions Dad proposed and implemented for Africa's problems during his rule will be discussed in subsequent parts of the series, Idi Amin: Hero or Villain? His Son Jaffar Amin and Other People Speak.

However an article by Bamuturaki Musinguzi titled "Amin's dream for Africa" which includes information about what Dad said during his address to the Organization of African Unity in Addis Ababa, Ethiopia in May 1973 provides insight into Dad's passion for the liberation of Africa. The article was published in 2006 and it conveys many of Dad's thoughts and actions relating to his vision for Africa.

At the 1973 OAU Summit in Addis Ababa, Ethiopia, Dad spoke in his usual bombastic manner. He wanted true Independence for "African People" everywhere and in subsequent "conversations" and speeches, he would assert in his usual bombastic style:

"Let me tell you!" "Africa is for Africans."

"We want true Independence for all Peoples of Africa".

"Africa is Strong!" "Africa is Independent and Self-sufficient."

"We need to understand the need to come together!"

Every time issues relating to the Emancipation of Africa and its Diasporas came up, Dad became as passionate, animated and bombastic as he did at the 1973 OAU Summit in Addis Ababa, Ethiopia. The thoughts conveyed by him in his address to the Organization of African Unity in May 1973 speak for themselves!

In subsequent parts of the series, Idi Amin: Hero or Villain? His Son Jaffar Amin and Other People Speak, there will be opportunities to discuss (1) The solutions "presented" by Dad at the OAU Summit in Addis Ababa, Ethiopia in May 1973 and thereafter, for the liberation of Africa, (2) Assertions he made in his address to the OAU Summit in Addis Ababa, Ethiopia in May 1973, (3) Excerpts from the book referred to by Bamuturaki Musinguzi in his article titled "Amin's dream for Africa," (4) Assertions he made about Africa in subsequent "conversations" and speeches, (5) Actions he took as Head of State of Uganda to realize the solutions he envisioned and presented for Africa's problems, along with the consequences of his "audacity" to "publicly" push for and pursue those solutions and (6) Any other issues relating to his legacy.

Dad's salute to Julius Nyerere and Apollo Milton Obote

Dad respected Julius Nyerere tremendously as the Father of the Nation of Tanzania and a major force behind the Pan-African movement and the Organization of African Unity, both of which Dad fully subscribed to. He recognized and appreciated the fact that Julius Nyerere was very instrumental in leading his country to "Independence" just as Apollo Milton Obote did in Uganda.

Contrary to popular belief, Dad respected Apollo Milton Obote as well and considered him the Father of the Nation of Uganda. Like Dad, Obote has been characterized as a hero and villain at the same time. However, despite the conflicting characterizations of Obote, Dad respected him and subscribed to his ideologies as a Nationalist, Pan-Africanist and Socialist.

There will be opportunities to explore the relationship between Dad and Obote in more detail as the series, Idi Amin: Hero or Villain? His Son Jaffar Amin and Other People Speak unfolds, along with Obote's contribution to Uganda and the conflicting characterizations of hero and villain. However, until a rift developed between them leading to a sad split in 1970 and the Military Coup on January 25, 1971, Dad and Obote were inseparable!

Dad respected Julius Nyerere for labouring for the Unification and Emancipation of the African continent and the Elimination of colonialism and white supremacy from the African continent. He admired Julius Nyerere's rejection of tribalism and all forms of racial and ethnic discrimination. Julius Nyerere was a strong advocate for economic and political measures in dealing with the apartheid policies of South Africa and overthrowing White supremacy in present day Zimbabwe, South Africa and Namibia and Dad completely agreed with this standpoint. However, by May 1973 when Dad and Julius Nyerere both attended the OAU Summit in Addis Ababa, Ethiopia, there was "hostility" between the two of them following the September 1972 invasion of Uganda by Ugandan exiles operating from Tanzania.

In Dad's point of view, the hostility between him and Julius Nyerere, arose because Julius Nyerere granted Obote asylum in Tanzania after Kenya's Jomo Kenyatta refused Nyerere's request for Kenyatta to grant the deposed Ugandan President asylum in Kenya. As outlined in a previous section, sources have reported that after Julius Nyerere got news of the Military Coup by Dad in Uganda against Apollo Milton Obote in January 1971, he attempted to convince Kenya's President Jomo Kenyatta to grant deposed Obote asylum but he was unsuccessful. That was how Obote ended up in Tanzania. According to Dad, Julius Nyerere then began a campaign to have Dad isolated by several African Heads of State and he succeeded with some.

At the time of the OAU Summit in Addis Ababa, Ethiopia in May 1973, there was a sour relationship and an ongoing conflict between Julius Nyerere and Dad. Among other reasons, Dad felt that Julius Nyerere had sanctioned the invasion of Uganda by the Ugandan exiles operating from Tanzania in September 1972 and he considered this an act of aggression and declaration of enmity by Julius Nyerere.

As outlined in a section above, Pan Africanism and the Organization of African Unity will be explored in more detail in subsequent parts of the series, Idi Amin: Hero or Villain? His Son Jaffar Amin and Other People Speak. The work of the African Union which succeeded the Organization of African Unity (OAU) will also be explored further, along with the related visions of Julius Nyerere, Kwame Nkrumah of Ghana and other Gallant sons of Africa. However, suffice it to state here that as one of the founders of the OAU in 1963, Julius Nyerere was very devoted to the success of the OAU and he was in agreement with what Dad articulated during his address to the OAU Summit in Addis Ababa, Ethiopia in May 1973 in relation to the aims of the OAU.

The fruits of Julius Nyerere's efforts to promote peaceful co-existence among the communities and tribes of Tanzania are evident in present day Tanzania and they will also be explored in subsequent parts of the series, Idi Amin: Hero or Villain? His Son Jaffar Amin and Other People Speak, in relation to how Tanzania can be a model for other African countries. The country of Tanzania has also been a model for political stability, which is credited to Julius Nyerere and the reasons for the political stability are worthy of exploration and replication. Julius Nyerere's mass literacy campaigns and institution of free and universal education are models for Africa, along with the emphasis on social and economic equality and the need for Tanzania to become economically self-sufficient. These will also be explored, along with any related issues.

Despite the hostility that existed between Dad and Julius Nyerere at the time of the OAU Summit in Addis Ababa, Ethiopia in May 1973, Dad passionately subscribed to ideas advanced and implemented by Julius Nyerere. That is the reason why he said he extended a hand to Julius Nyerere during the Summit, for the two countries of Tanzania and Uganda to exist peacefully. According to Dad, he also wanted peace with Julius Nyerere after beating him twice at the "Political Game".

Dad said he had successfully resolved the Anyanya issue in the Sudan, which forced Julius Nyerere's friend Apollo Milton Obote's soldiers to vacate Southern Sudan. It was his own Reconciliation with a sworn enemy

Jaffar Nimeiry that prompted Obote's Special Forces (Kikosi Ma'lum) to leave Sudan and precipitated their redeployment to Northern Tanzania. The enmity between Dad and Jaffar Nimeiry had arisen because of the First Sudanese War between Northern Sudan and Southern Sudan and Dad's active participation in aiding the Anyanya forces with the help of Israel. After Dad reconciled with Jaffar Nimeiry as Muslim brothers, Obote had to move his soldiers away from Southern Sudan. As outlined in an earlier section, Muamar Al-Qadhafi showed concern about the possibility of two Muslim leaders confronting each other and by 1972 he had brokered a Peace Deal between Dad and Jaffar Nimeiry, leading to a more cordial relationship between the two historical enemies.

Dad said he had also successfully repelled the "Mutukula War" in 1972 during which Ugandan exiles invaded Uganda through Mutukula and Mbarara. They attacked Mutukula in September 1972 and according to Dad they were wiped out. So, Dad said he went to the 1973 OAU Summit in Addis Ababa, Ethiopia in May 1973 in a triumphant mode.

According to Dad, Julius Nyerere's mistake then was to underestimate his capacity to judge and think through issues of state. He believed that Julius Nyerere based his assessment of him as a "Politician" on his friend Obote the Ugandan exiled leader's assessment of his former presumed "uninformed" "Hatchet-man" turned Head of State Dad. According to Dad, Julius Nyerere only came to respect and understand his capacity to think through issues and implement solutions at a future time in 1975 when he galvanized the Frontline States against South Africa. This included the building of an African United Armed Corps and an Armory which was unwittingly placed in Tanzania post the 1975 OAU Summit that would take place in Uganda with Dad as its Chairman, two years after the 1973 OAU Summit in Addis Ababa, Ethiopia. Dad regularly lamented about how Julius Nyerere utilized this very armory against his Uganda Army during the war between Uganda and Tanzania that led to his ouster in April 1979.

Despite Dad's offer of a hand to Julius Nyerere during the OAU Summit in Addis Ababa, Ethiopia in May 1973, the conflict between Dad and Julius Nyerere continued. A full-blown war would erupt between Tanzania and Uganda a few years later, which would lead to his ouster as President of Uganda.

Dad used to lament that he trained a lot of the ZANU (Zimbabwe African National Union), SWAPO (South West Africa People's Organization), ANC (African National Congress) and other soldiers that fought the racially segregative regimes in Zimbabwe, South Africa and Namibia, leading to the regimes' eventual collapse. However, some of these soldiers turned around and were involved in the 1979 push to throw him out of Uganda. Ironic!

The ZANU, SWAPO, ANC and other soldiers that Dad said he trained were part of the African United Armed Corps which was unwittingly placed in Tanzania post the 1975 OAU Summit that would take place in Uganda with Dad as its Chairman. The African United Armed Corps was instituted for purposes of overthrowing White supremacy from the African continent and supported by Pan-Africanism and the OAU, both of which Dad was a champion for.

A champion for causes and a conflicted relationship with Britain

In 1973, Dad continued demonstrating his unwavering support for Arab people and the Ummah (Community of Muslim Believers). Sometime that year, he gave a Press Conference in Damascus, Syria and voiced that unwavering support. The Arab and Muslim cause was one he had fully embraced by the year 1973.

As Dad publicly championed the cause of the Arab people and the Ummah, he also publicly championed the cause of Africa and its Diasporas. He pursued his agenda for the Emancipation of Uganda and the rest of Africa and its Diasporas with a passion and made many decisions consistent with what he eloquently articulated when he attended and addressed the Organization of African Unity (OAU) Summit in Addis Ababa, Ethiopia in May 1973.

After Dad "picked up" and fully embraced Pan-Africanism and the "African" cause, he had a very conflicted relationship with Britain, Uganda's former "Colonial Master". That conflict manifested itself as a series of "very public" "bad behaviours" by Dad towards Britain and its citizens while he continued to "praise" them in private and love all things British.

Dad's very first "very public" "bad behavior" directed at Britain and its citizens was the expulsion from Uganda in 1972 of Asians who either held British Passports or were entitled to British Passports. That time he decided to nationalize the Uganda British American Tobacco (BAT) Company's processing plants and went on to assert that he bought the BAT Company because the owners, along with the Asian community, were sabotaging the economy. He had given a 90-day bombastic notice for Asians to leave Uganda after accusing them of sabotaging the economy of Uganda and declaring that he wanted the economy of Uganda to be in the hands of

Ugandan citizens, especially Black Ugandans. This very first "very public" "bad behavior" had happened barely two years into Dad's rule in Uganda and a little over a year to the month in July 1971 when he received a very warm welcome from Britain during his first official foreign trip as President of Uganda.

It was as if Dad wanted to spite British Newspapers that had sung his praises and "screamed" "insults" at his predecessor Apollo Milton Obote immediately following the Military Coup that catapulted him to the position of President of Uganda. It was also as if Dad wanted to take it upon himself to mete out punishment to the British for the "sins" of the colonialism the Organization of African Unity he addressed in May 1973 aimed to redress.

As outlined in a previous section, following the Coup against Apollo Milton Obote on January 25, 1971, in London, England, The Daily Telegraph editorial had this headline:

"Good Riddance to Obote", while The Times had observed that the reign of Obote "was no longer worth protecting." It had added that Obote's government had been "—hostile to British interests [sales of arms to South Africa], contemptuous of Europeans... ethnically divisive and potentially so unpopular that no British Government would be able to shore it up, let alone wish to be associated with it."

In February 1971, Dad's stand against communism had been hailed in The Daily Telegraph. A caption had read, "from Africa, one common-sense voice has come through loud and clear, and it is that of General (now President) Amin, who assured that Uganda would certainly not leave the Commonwealth."

On February 2, 1971, the British Government of Edward Heath had formally recognized Dad's government.

After his ascent to the "highest position in the land" of Uganda and a "honeymoon" period with Britain, instead of conforming to "expectations" intimated in the British Newspapers and continuing to bask in their "praises", Dad seemed to want to do the total opposite! He seemed to have had a total change of heart towards Britain. He declared war on "Imperialism" instead and Uganda's Asian community became a pawn and the first to be unwittingly caught in the crossfire!

Dad started advocating for and implementing the very same policies and plans that had "alienated" his predecessor Apollo Milton Obote from Britain and led to the British Newspapers "insulting" him, following the Coup against him in the first place. It started to become clear that Dad was not going to live up to what Britain and others who allegedly "hand-picked" him to replace Apollo Milton Obote "expected".

By May 1973 when Dad attended and addressed the OAU Summit in Addis Ababa, Ethiopia, he had made a 180-degree turn against Britain. After the "thunderous" cheers he received from inside and outside the Africa Hall during the OAU Summit in Addis Ababa, Ethiopia, Dad seemed very eager to use his position as President of an "Independent" African country, to champion and take the cause of the OAU to a new level!

Like a "bad marriage" waiting to end in a divorce, Dad seemed to want Uganda to be completely independent from Britain while "needing" Britain's "approval" at the same time. He never stopped reminiscing about his Kings African Rifles days and "bragging" about being part of the Guard Patrol when news came through in Kenya of the death of Queen Elizabeth II's father King George VI and her ascension to the British Throne in 1952. He never stopped talking about his close friendships with British Superiors in the Kings African Rifles and the mutual respect and admiration they had for each other.

However, many times, Dad would fondly refer to the British as loyal friends of Uganda while also "berating" them for colonizing Uganda, parts of Africa and many countries of the African Diaspora. It was always confusing to listen to him praising the British while also "taunting" them every time an opportunity presented itself - like the time Britain experienced "economic challenges" in 1973.

Dad's "Save Britain Fund" and "plots" he attributed to others

In 1973, Dad tongue-in-cheek launched the "Save Britain Fund" on Old Kampala Hill during which he also pledged £600 of his own money "to save and assist Britain our former colonial masters from economic catastrophe", he "lamented". In addition to other offers, he offered to fly over a load of Matooke (green bananas).

A mentor, Yuga Juma Onziga remembered that day vividly as he was physically there and so was Princess Elizabeth Bagaya of Toro who served as Dad's Minister of Foreign Affairs at some point.

On December 1, 1973, Britain cancelled all aid to Uganda as it was experiencing its own economic woes. After asking the Asians to leave Uganda, Dad had nationalized many foreign-owned firms including those owned by Britain.

Britain, Uganda's former colonial master was experiencing economic difficulties resulting from the oil crisis of the early 1970s and Dad was responding to an appeal by Britain for the International Monetary Fund to bail the country out. Many people have suggested that Dad was at pranks and jests aimed at deliberately annoying Britain but several excerpts and telegrams indicate otherwise:

"...And so it was in December 1973, when Her Majesty's diplomatic staff in the Ugandan capital of Kampala telegrammed London to pass on an offer to save the UK from financial ruin from General Idi Amin Dada." (Excerpted from an Article titled "Despot planned 'Save Britain Fund'" by Dominic Casciani, BBC News at the National Archives - http://news.bbc.co.uk/2/hi/africa/4132547.stm).

"In the past months the people of Uganda have been following with sorrow the alarming economic crisis befalling on Britain."

"The sad fact is that it is the ordinary British citizen who is suffering most. I am today appealing to all the people of Uganda who have all along been traditional friends of the British people to come forward and help their former colonial masters."

At one point, Dad offered to Whitehall, "Today, 21 January 1974, the people of Kigezi District donated one lorry load of vegetables and wheat. I am now requesting you to send an aircraft to collect this donation urgently before it goes bad. I hope you will react quickly so as not to discourage Ugandans from donating more."

Needless to say, Britain declined Dad's bombastic offers.

Full of continuing Pan-African zeal, Dad continued his efforts to rule Uganda and implement his noble vision. However, according to him, the "conspiracies" and "plots" by Ugandan exiles, to "soil" his reputation, increase subversive activities in Uganda and bring down his rule intensified. Dad was consistent in asserting that Ugandan exiles operating within Uganda kidnapped and murdered prominent Ugandans and in some cases even foreigners so that it looked like his operatives were committing the brutal murders. According to him and other people, the State Research Bureau, which he instituted to oversee matters of "State Security", was completely "infiltrated" by subversive elements residing inside and outside Uganda and he didn't seem to be able to do anything about the problem!

As 1973 began and unfolded, many individuals he regarded as close associates "crossed over" to the "conspirators" and "saboteurs'" side and began "colluding" with them to "soil" his reputation. Some sources said that many of these individuals provided so-called "credible information" to a biased and hostile media that "lynched" Dad for refusing to be "controlled."

"In essence, these so-called close associates of Idi Amin and "reliable" witnesses aided the "conspirators" in their relentless "schemes" and efforts to defame Idi Amin and bring down his government", offered one source.

Theories and rumours abound about why and how "conspirators" and "saboteurs" succeeded in bringing down Dad's government but an Independent Truth and Reconciliation Commission is the place to arrive at the actual truth. Likewise, an Independent Truth and Reconciliation Commission is the place to arrive at the actual truth relating to why two Ministers in Dad's government, namely Edward Rugumayo and Wanume Kibedi defected in 1973.

However, according to reports, in 1973, the defecting Minister Edward Rugumayo anonymously wrote a 5,000-word document, specifying the "things" Dad had done and urging that the Organization of African Unity (OAU), the United Nations (UN) and the Commonwealth should condemn Dad (Smith, 101). Rugumayo later signed the anonymous letter, which listed nine points about Dad as follows:

"1. That he is an illiterate soldier who became President of a modern state. 2. That he comes from the minority Kakwa tribe. 3. That he is a member of a minority religion Islam, which accounts for less than 6 % of all Ugandans. 4. That he is of low intelligence. 5. That he is medically unfit and suffering from a hormone defect. 6. That he is a racist, tribalistic and a dictator. 7. That he has no principles, moral standards or scruples. 8. That he will kill or cause to kill anyone without hesitation as long as it serves his interests, such as prolonging his stay in power or getting what he wants such as a woman or money. 9. That he is an incorrigible liar with no moral or political standards whose word cannot be relied upon and of whom the only prediction which can safely be made is that he is unpredictable."

The Formal Campaign by the defecting Minister Edward Rugumayo, for the Organization of African Unity, the United Nations and the Commonwealth to condemn Dad paled in comparison to the murder of Ugandans by subversive elements operating inside and outside Uganda that Dad and others said was occurring. Dad used to lament that innocent Ugandans died at the hands of the very same Ugandan exiles that provided information to a biased and hostile media that aided the exiles in falsely implicating him in the murders the very exiles committed or orchestrated.

The systematic and horrific murders would become so common that everyone pointed the fingers at Dad as the Head of State of Uganda but according to various reports, other people committed the brutal murders that cost so many lives. Dad had "failed" to protect Ugandans as their Head of State and completely lost control of the state machinery instituted to protect Ugandans. Only an Independent Truth and Reconciliation Commission will "uncover" the whole truth, including Dad's "failure" to guarantee the security and safety of all Ugandans.

Opinions offered by others about Dad's "failure" to protect Ugandans and in some cases foreigners from being murdered in Uganda as the country's Head of State and allegations contained in various reports about other people committing the brutal murders that were solely blamed on Dad are recommended readings. They will be great additions to the background information for the section of the series titled "Other People Speak", along with other material relating to the debate about whether Dad was a hero or villain to the core.

Wanume Kibedi, Dad's official first wife Mama Mariam's younger brother was Uganda's Foreign Minister till the spring of 1973 when he defected. According to Dad, during the spring of 1973, after his brother-in-law Wanume Kibedi defected, he joined the Ugandan exiles in their continuing "conspiracies" and "plots" to "soil" his reputation, increase subversive activities in Uganda and bring his government down. Dad lamented that Wanume Kibedi did this despite benefiting tremendously from his "Rags to Riches Story" and steady rise to the top. In a strange twist of fate, Dad said Wanume Kibedi became one of his staunchest enemies despite benefiting from his relationship as dad's brother-in-law.

Others have voiced, "In essence, Wanume Kibedi bit the hand that fed him because after putting him through Law School in London and taking care of him as a brother-in-law, Idi Amin had appointed him as Uganda's Minister of Foreign Affairs".

According to some reports, Wanume Kibedi deliberately made false and exaggerated claims about murders committed during Dad's rule in order to "soil" Dad's reputation and bring down his government. For example, he claimed that between 90,000 to 100,000 people had been killed in Uganda by September 1972 following the Tanzanian invasion of Uganda by the combined FRONASA (Front for National Salvation) and Kikosi Ma'lum (Special Forces) troops.

It is unclear why Wanume Kibedi allegedly decided to join the "voices" that intensified their efforts to make sure the false claims about the so-called hundreds and thousands of people murdered during Dad's rule in Uganda became "facts," but there are many theories and rumours surrounding his sudden "change of heart". As I suggested earlier, these theories and rumours are best handled by an Independent Truth and Reconciliation Commission.

Wanume Kibedi's 180-degree turn against Dad came as a total shock to Dad considering the fact that he was one of Dad's cheer leaders less than a year before his so-called "revelation" that between 90,000 to 100,000 people had been killed in Uganda by September 1972. As Dad went about implementing his 90-day bombastic notice to expel Asians that either held British Passports or were entitled to British Passports, the very Wanume Kibedi had equally fully shouted, "The Asians must go - but Uganda citizens will not be affected. The problem we are determined to solve is this one involving Asians who decided not to take citizenship, but they have been hoping to stay on year and year, making a good living, sending money abroad and preventing our Ugandans - especially Black Africans from getting ahead in commerce and industry".

Wanume Kibedi had also accused Britain of "economic blackmail" and of using arrogant and insulting behaviour towards Uganda. He had said, "As the British in their arrogance would not increase the number of vouchers for Asians, Uganda decided to teach them a lesson."

So, Wanume Kibedi's defection didn't make any sense to Dad. He could only guess the real reasons behind it and go along with the theories and rumours that abound about the surprising defection.

The irony is that the false claims about Dad murdering or ordering the murder of hundreds and thousands of innocent people have since been disputed by reputable sources. However, these false figures continue to be presented as "facts". They continue to perpetuate the irreparable damage that led to Dad becoming one of the most reviled people in history but an Independent Truth and Reconciliation Commission is the place to arrive at the actual truth.

My first day at State House and meeting Mama Kay

As the "plots" by Ugandan exiles to "soil" Dad's reputation and increase subversive and murderous activities inside Uganda continued in 1973, I and several of my siblings continued to reside with Grandpa Sosteni at the Simba Battalion in Mbarara. We resided there while continuing to attend

Preschool at the Catholic Seminary School near Ntare Senior Secondary School.

After the July 1971 invasion of the Al-Qadhafi Garrison in Jinja by Ugandan exiles, we had been relocated to Mbarara to live with Grandpa Sosteni. We had resided at the Al-Qadhafi Garrison with our Tutsi Foster Parents Sergeant John Katabarwa and his wife Joyce until then. Following the July 1971 invasion, we were sent in the company of Sergeant John Katabarwa to live with Grandpa Sosteni.

After a stay with Grandpa Sosteni in Mbarara, Dad decided to gather us and bring us to live at his Official Residences with his official wives, beginning with Nakasero Lodge in Kampala where Dad's second official wife Mama Kay (Kaysiya) resided.

I will never forget the first day I met my beloved stepmother Mama Kay (Kaysiya).

Following the stay at Grandpa Sosteni's in Mbarara, I and several of my siblings were brought to join Mama Kay at Nakasero Lodge in Kampala. This had happened after Dad came back from a tour of the Soviet Union with Mama Kay and my two siblings Lumumba and Kidde and it was the time I was permanently reunited with my Dad and began living life as the President's Son.

I had not noticed Mama Kay during Aunt Akisu's Funeral Vigil in 1970, just as I had not noticed Dad. So, this was the formal introduction par se.

Before we met Mama Kay for the first time, we were picked up from the Seminary where we were going to school and taken to Grandpa Sosteni's house in Mbarara. Our stay at Grandpa Sosteni's house sticks to mind because while there we spent the whole day watching celluloid cinema on a Projector. We did so together with Grandpa Sosteni's children Muhammed, Nigo and the rest until instructions were left with the CO (Commanding Officer) of Simba Battalion in Mbarara Ali Fadhul to drive "the survivors" of "The Mutukula Attack" namely, I Remo, Sukeji, Machomingi and Joseph, to State House Entebbe.

Brigadier General Ali Fadhul was the Commanding Officer of the Barracks in Mbarara and he was put in jail by the government of Yoweri Museveni in 1986 but later released in 2009.

Grandpa Sosteni is the same person who actually drove Kabaka Mutesa II all the way from Bulange right up to the Rwanda Border in 1966 during the "Mengo Crisis". He posed as a Taxi Driver during the infamous invasion of the Kabaka's Palace that was ordered by Obote in

1966. Grandpa Sosteni posing as a Taxi Driver was a plan "hatched" by Dad so that the Kabaka could escape the "death trap" ordered by Obote that year.

Thus I, Sukeji, Machomingi and Joseph Akisu boarded Ali Fadhul's famous Light Blue Peugeot 504 and left for Entebbe State House. I have lasting memories of that day.

My first impression was the gonja bananas and lots of roast meat and chicken that we ate along the way. The second impression was being ushered into this enormous hallway between the biggest elephant tusks I had ever seen. When we arrived at State House Entebbe, I had immediately become aware of these large pieces of elephant tusks that formed an arch at the entrance. In future years, my siblings and I would argue amongst ourselves about whether they were or weren't mammoth tusks.

We moved into the waiting room right under the oak staircase. Then we were led up the oak staircase to the Presidential Wing, where we were met by Mama Kay's cousin Marta, who ushered us into the Presidential Nursery Wing which was located just off the Private Presidential Lounge.

In the Nursing Quarters all eyes focused on a chubby baby Adam Ma'dira our brother whose birth had ushered in Dad's reign on January 25, 1971. Marta had just been dressing him. What struck us immediately was seeing the still healing "I" shaped rosy scar dead centre on his face. I asked what happened and was told that it was an accident at the swings.

Ma'dira is my brother who was born on January 25, 1971 at the very hour our father took over power from Apollo Milton Obote, hence the Lugbara name Ma'dira, which is derived from the word "kill" in the Lugbara language. As we had entered the Nursing Quarters, the toddler was seated on the bed being wrapped in nappy/diaper. I had immediately noticed the nasty scar running the length of his forehead and we all asked with concern what had happened.

We were all concerned when we were told that Ma'dira had been hit while playing at the swings at the bottom of the Colonial Mansions Garden. We later went on a tour, around the fishpond, which is featured in the 1974 French Documentary on Dad titled, "General Idi Amin Dada: A Self Portrait" where he gathered the same brood during the shoot.

We got a chance to explore and play at the Colonial Mansions' vast gardens before lunch. We were happy to spend time exploring the vast gardens right down to the scene of my brother Ma'dira's accident at the swings which were located at the furthest point of the Colonial Mansion. Unbeknownst to the parents who blamed the Nursemaid Marta, my beautiful elder sister Mariam Aaliya (Aliya) Amin was the actual culprit. It was an innocent accident and it happed as the culprit explained it to us. She accidentally swung the swing chair into her baby brother's face but the blame was placed on Nursemaid Marta, Mama Kay's cousin.

While we were exploring State House Entebbe, word came that we were to be taken to Plot 10/11 Prince Charles Drive, Kololo, Kampala, the current location of the North Korean Embassy, for that was where Dad wanted to meet up with his children who had survived the attack in Mbarara. This had happened before we could tuck in lunch. Word came for Ali Fadhul to bring the children from Mbarara to 11 Prince Charles Drive which had been annexed to Command Post Plot 10, for His Excellency wanted to see the children who got caught up in the war zone.

So off we went with John Katabarwa our Tutsi Foster Parent and Ali Fadhul in his famous Light Blue Peugeot 504 which had brought us all the way from Mbarara. Commanding Officer Ali Fadhul drove us all the way to Kololo and finalized his personal errand by dropping our lot at Nakasero Lodge afterwards.

As we entered the New Wing on Prince Charles Drive, all eyes fell on Dad's amazing SM Citroen Maserati. It was Dad's favourite grand tourer. With my keen interest in cars, the SM Citroen Maserati was one of the first things I set eyes on that memorable day when I first came to know who my father was.

I was last at this same location on the other side of the chain-link fence in Command Post Old Wing the night of the Funeral Vigil of Awa (Aunt) Akisu following her death in January 1970. That day, my brother Taban tried to evade the eagle eyes of Sergeant John Katabarwa and the vigilant attention of Sergeant Diliga who found him under the Military Bus chairs. Taban had come out of there like a magnet which keeps popping back on the metal, trying his best to stick to the door handles at the entrance to the bus screaming, "I want to go to the burial of Akisu", repeatedly wailing down the place. This had set off increased wailing inside the house from the mourners who had come to Aunt Akisu's Funeral Vigil.

The next significant gathering at this location would be in 1979 on our outward journey into exile to Libya after Dad's government was overthrown.

In 1979 this Kololo home would be the scene of our final gathering and also the orgy of destruction when UNLA (Uganda National Liberation Army) soldiers destroyed stacks and stacks of our family photos. In fact there is a famous photo showing all our photo albums, strewn all over the living room which we saw in the Magazine titled DRUM while we lived in exile.

Dad's "African Chili Prank" on my siblings and I

We were led up the stairs and into the famous living room with stacks and stacks of family photo albums that lined one whole wall. Dad was an avid photographer and he loved taking pictures.

On this initial meeting I approached my father only understanding then that I was being introduced to him. I greeted him in the traditional Nubian way where you place the hand of someone you respect and revere on your forehead then you kiss the hand. The rest followed suit but all our eyes were on the roasted chicken laden plate on the low coffee table in front of Dad.

We sat down and Dad jokingly asked Fadhul how the children survived the attack, for the combined FRONASA (Front for National Salvation) and Kikosi Ma'lum (Special Forces) troops had attacked Ntare Secondary School in a misguided attack on a civilian target which had no significance at all. Apollo Milton Obote accounted for that incident on the Uganda Peoples' Congress Party website.

When Dad obviously noticed our keen interest in his plate of roasted chicken, he offered, "You want?" in Kiswahili. We all nodded with enthusiasm then he offered us the roasted chicken. We all scrambled for a piece and walked back to our seats as we greedily munched in. I immediately reacted to the sting of the African chili. So did Sukeji and Machomingi. Only Joseph Akisu seemed able to take it.

As I immediately looked up, my father was engaged in one of his tearful earthquake laughs - mirthful, is how Reporter Adam Luck described it in a Sunday Mirror Interview I gave after the release of the Fictional Feature Film "The Last King of Scotland". However, to me it was a naughty, jolly prankster mode for "Big Daddy" as Dad has often been referred to. My siblings and I were not amused by Dad's "African Chili Prank" at all!

As I shared in a previous section, Dad liked to crack jokes and laugh even though some of his jokes could be very annoying and in terrible taste. No one was exempted from Dad's jokes including us his children, family members, associates and foreign dignitaries. We just learnt to take them as they came.

He used to play the same "African Chili Jokes" on fellow officers, like once when they were having dinner and Moses Ali looked away for a second. Dad poured a load of Tabasco Sauce into his juice and according to Major Mududu, when the Finance Minister took a swing at his drink he immediately regurgitated reacting to the sting - setting off bouts of laughter from the cabinet. This had happened as Dad and his colleagues were having a meal on a mat. Muslims eat informally, on a mat - four to a tray "communal duwas".

So here was my very first recollection of who my father was, although previously, the whole family had gathered at this same location for the Funeral Vigil of my aunt Akisu when she died in Kayunga, Bugerere in 1970. It was during my brief stay with her, following Grandma Aate's demise. Joseph Akisu and I were actually at her side when she breathed her last breath.

Meeting my brother Lumumba for the first time and our life with Kay

The decision to place us in the care of Mama Kay at Nakasero Lodge in Kampala was concluded after the sweet and sour experience we had with Dad's "salt and hot chili prank". We were placed in Fadhul's car again and he was asked to finalize his errand and drop us at Nakasero Lodge.

I was mystified to find Marta and Adam Ma'dira had arrived there too. To my childish mind, I couldn't explain how Marta and Ma'dira got there too. How Marta and Ma'dira got here baffled my "toddler mind" but then suddenly I sighted the most influential member of this huge family just as he came winging round the circular tarmac on a metallic chopper bike. He came towards the front of the Ivy covered Colonial Nakasero Presidential Lodge - the scene of another photograph with our family pictures strewn all over after Dad's fall in 1979. It was my kid brother Lumumba Juruga and he was unaware that we were brothers.

I remember his happy go lucky attitude was a real attraction from the beginning, which was in contrast to my age mate, his maternal sister Kidde who exuded grumpiness from the word go. When we, new arrivals became aware of her metallic green chopper bike which was parked at the front porch having just been assembled by someone, she came onto the stone kitchen stairs and grumbled up a storm in a foul mood, expressing ownership and letting us know full well that we had no rights to ride her bike….Hmmm! The two sorts of welcome set the trend in my life inside my father's family circles all my waking life.

This was the very first moment I met up with my rival namesake Lumumba, for we had taken up names of Political Rivals from the Congo – rivals who were involved in the "Congo Crisis" I introduced in an earlier section. Lumumba and Kidde had actually accompanied their mother Kay and Dad to the USSR where their uncle Ondoga was Uganda's Ambassador and they were bought metallic chopper bikes while there. Lumumba's bike was red while Kidde's was metallic green. We actually arrived just when Lumumba was winging down the circular driveway on his and Kidde had left hers on the lawn.

With excitement, our attention was taken with the brand new bikes, which had just been uncased. Just as Lumumba suggested we ride Kidde's bike, the owner came out of the kitchen in a foul mood claiming ownership and refusing anyone to touch her bike. This set the tone to our relationship – me, Machomingi, Joseph and Sukeji. Lumumba was always the welcoming one.

Mama Kay was always strict and very pregnant with Mao Ari'dhi while Kidde was always in a foul mood. The Nursemaid Marta, Kay's cousin was the brightest star on the horizon. She cared for every stray cat (Illegitimates) like her own and she was loved back by all of us.

After we were placed with my stepmother Kay, my younger siblings were placed at Nakasero Nursery just adjacent to Nakasero Primary School and opposite the French Ambassador's residence. I for my part was placed in Primary One with remedial lessons at Makerere Kindergarten next to Mary Stuart Hall. At six years old, I was placed in Primary One at Nakasero Primary School while the rest were placed in Nursery. However because of my slow uptake, Mama Kay arranged for Nasur Izaga who was a driver then to always drop me off at the Kindergarten school just next to Mary Stuart Hall at the Makerere University Campus.

Nasur Izaga was later promoted to Lieutenant Colonel by Dad. He was an Old Boy from Tanganyika Village and one of the favoured Drivers and Escorts before he was given a commission and later a Battalion to command. He was one of the "Brutus" Officer corps who compromised in 1979.

I enjoyed the afternoon to dusk drives to the Kindergarten school next to Makerere University, the special lessons and back drives which formed a romantic back drop and slide show in my mind's eye. Nasur Izaga, the Chauffeur at the time seemed to have access to any car in the State

House (Eagen Mansions) Garage. He used to change vehicles on a daily basis and I used to enjoy the variety for he seemed to have a vast choice of cars to choose from in the Presidential Garage at the Eagen Mansions Basement, just off the Kampala Train Station off Station Road. One day it was a Benz, the next day it was a BMW. The rest of the kids looked on as I was taken.

I once came across an article by the Headmistress of the Nursery recalling that she had taught Idi Amin's children. I knew she was talking about me and I had thought of taking my young ones to the same school. However, I had second thoughts because I did not at the time want to bring attention to myself.

I was heartened when in the 1999 article about the Kindergarten the Headmistress recalled having taught Idi Amin's children. This had happened just when my son Remo II was starting school. After I became a Dad myself, I intended to take my children to the very same Kindergarten too but changed my mind, not wanting to bring too much attention to myself at the time.

Mama Kay genuinely cared about our education.

Uncle Ajule's wedding and the Christmas Party of 1973

The other events that actually coincided with Mama Kay's last stay with us was Uncle Ajule's Wedding in 1973 and the Christmas Party of 1973 when she invited the whole Nakasero Primary School to the Presidential Lodge because she was on the Nakasero Primary School Board.

The whole Idi Amin family was at Ajule's wedding, which was held at Entebbe Lodge, where Grandpa resided. The Christmas Party followed in December and it was held at Nakasero Lodge where we were residing with Mama Kay. She invited the children at Nakasero Primary School because all her children went to school there and she was on the Board, as First Lady.

The luxury of the Ajule's wedding sticks to mind. I was amazed to find massive, black, strange looking cars packed outside - very ceremonially long Black Cars, which I later found out were the old Colonial Governor's entourage "Silver Cloud/Shadow Rolls Royce".

Dad was in a "honeymoon mood" with his new flame Mama Madina - the undertone reason for the three simultaneous divorces he gave to his other wives that was just around the corner in 1974. It was to Madina's residence at Command Post that we were taken to meet Dad at Plot 10/11

Prince Charles Drive before meeting and being left with Mama Kay. This was the location Dad played the "Hot African Chili Prank" on us!

On the day of Uncle Ajule's wedding, I was asked to ride in the very car carrying Mama Kay and her children, which was a privilege. She pointed at the space in front of her and asked me to sit on what seemed to me the floor. She laughed when I consented saying "No, no" because she was not suggesting that I sit on the floor at all. Then Marta magically pulled up folding chairs, which seemed to come out of the floor. That was where Mama Kay meant for me to sit.

We headed for Entebbe Lodge where the Reception was to take place while the rest headed for the church service at a Church of Uganda church that was a stone's throw away from Nakasero Lodge. Between the Reception and the After Party, we took a glorious ride in the Ancient "Silver Cloud/Shadow Rolls Royce". I never could tell the difference but I enjoyed the ride. The bride and bridegroom came to the Reception in a Citroen DS.

Memorably on Christmas 1973, I played the biblical character Joseph, Ayikoru Adroa played Mary, Lumumba Amin, Joseph Akisu and Lumumba Adroa were the three wise men and Machomingi and Kidde were the angels while Alice, Tileku and the rest made up the shepherds.

At the Christmas Party in 1973, the whole of Nakasero Primary School was invited to the Nakasero Presidential Lodge. I enjoyed playing Joseph and watching my cousin Ayikoru Adroa playing Mary. With her Tutsi looks, she really looked the part.

Lumumba Amin, Lumumba Adroa and Joseph Akisu looked great playing the three wise men. Tileku, Alice and Sukeji were very funny playing the shepherds while Machomingi and Kidde shone as the Angels.

The play was performed in front of a host of dignitaries and it was shown on Uganda Television. However, what amused the guests were the angels, for it seemed they started to cry because they had been asked to keep their hands raised for the longest of times while the short play "Silent Night" was enacted. The two angels caused laughter for they had to keep their arms in the air for a long time. It hurt and I am told Kidde and Machomingi were actually seen shedding tears on National Television. I on my part was strictly told with my fake beard to keep my eyes on Baby Jesus - one of my sister Kidde's dolls in Frances Ayikoru's arms.

This was the luxurious lifestyle that I was introduced to that year from the relatively rural life that was my previous life under the care of Grandma Aate, Aunt Akisu and Dad's key Lieutenants. So this was when I was permanently brought to live with Dad.

New Year's Day 1974 with Mama Kay

New Year's 1974 rolled in while we were asleep and I was woken by the two mothers either Ayikoru's Tutsi mother or Aunt Penina dancing with Mama Kay doing the "Lindy Hop" famous dance. The ornate gramophone was in my room and so was Dad's Israeli Motorola Radio. We saw encouragements from the mothers who asked us to join in. The rest of the children came from the other rooms as I continued to jump up and down on the expensive spring mattress, unaware of the significance of New Year's Day.

What sticks to mind was mum's (Mama Kay's) black and white Polka dot dress popping at every twirl. Round and round they went. The tune I distinctly remembered was "Listen to your leaders." The "B" side was "Black and White let's get together", by Sonko or some other famous Ganda singer from the 1960s.

1974 was here and Mama Kay had bought me purple corduroy, which squeaked every time I took a step in my brand new Startrite shoes, causing laughter from the invited guests. "Here goes flat footed Tshombe!" I was some kind of mascot that Mama Kay fondly showed off to her friends.

Dad's second official wife, my stepmother Mama Kay was the only one who was comfortable with her husband's "stray children". I joined her in 1973 and enjoyed her warm acceptance for the short duration she was with us after we met her. I have very fond memories of her because she had a very warm and very kind disposition.

While we stayed with Mama Kay, she continued to be assigned the responsibility of overseeing our schooling. So, in 1974, she sent my siblings and me to study at an Elite Boarding School in Kigezi District – one of the best in the country! Studying at Elite Schools would be a trend that would continue throughout my childhood – first as the President's son and then while we lived in exile after Dad's government was overthrown.

Going to Boarding School and Mama Kay's farewell

The day we left to go to Boarding School, we set off for Kabale Preparatory School in the company of Issa Sebbi who was then a Permanent Secretary in the President's Office. By 1979, he was a Cabinet Minister.

Mama Kay's Farewell will forever be carved in my mind. We were off to Kabale Preparatory School and I remember being told where we were setting off to. I was apprehensive about Wazungu (Caucasians) but Mama Kay calmed my fears.

"They are alright. You will be okay. Who else is going? You, Lumumba, Machomingi and Sukeji" she consoled and offered.

My next question was What about Joseph?

"Next year, he will join you", Mama Kay promised but it was never to be because that decision was left to another.

That same year 1974, Dad divorced Mama Kay along with two of my stepmothers Mama Mariam and Mama Nora.

I was shocked at the sudden separation between me and Joseph Akisu. He was the one person second only to Luka Yuma, son of Stephan Yuma, son of Geriga, son of Abiriya elder sister to Grandma Aate and Juruga son of Buda that I knew and liked the most in my short stint in life. Unfortunately the discernible line was that Tshombe, Lumumba, Sukeji and Machomingi would be going to a school run by Wazungu (Caucasians) in a distant land much further than my cherished Mbarara. It was high up in the mountains called Kigezi at a town called Kabale.

We set off with the Permanent Secretary Ismail Sebbi early in the morning with RSM (Regimental Staff Sergeant) Kapere at the steering wheel and arrived dead tired at eight in the evening.

Miss Hayward, the muzungu (White) lady at Boarding School

I was pleasantly surprised when the muzungu (White lady) called me by my Kakwa name Remo. The last persons to call me that were Grandma and Aunt Akisu. I had now got used to being called Tshombe but thoughtfully Dad had insisted on Remo Amin. The Muzungu in question and the next Avatar in my life was Miss Hayward. We phonetically pronounced her name Haywood. She was the very same age I remember Abuba (Grandma) Aisha Aate and I instantly bonded with her.

Sebbi had introduced me by the name Tshombe, which I had never liked at the time but Miss Hayward called me Remo. So I was thus back to my favoured name in memory of Grandma Aisha Aate who used to talk to me in Kakwa and only called me by my Kakwa name Remo.

Miss Hayward as my Ad-hoc surrogate mother

Miss Hayward became my Ad-hoc surrogate mother between 1974 and 1979 for even after we returned for holidays I was personally never returned to Nakasero Lodge where Mama Kay had resided. This is because the bitter 3 simultaneous divorces had taken place and we were all placed in State House Entebbe where Mama Madina had relocated to, having taken the First Lady role from Mama Mariam. The Adroa Children (Mama Kay's children) from Kabale Preparatory School and Namagunga cried until they were allowed to go and visit their mother who resided in an apartment just below Hotel Equatoria in Kampala. My brother Mao was still suckling then.

Alas I never set eyes on my beloved Mama Kay again until the grave event surrounding her death that very year 1974, during our second term holidays. Mama Kay died on August 13, 1974 and I miss her a great deal! By the time she died, Dad had divorced her and she had moved on.

In 1974, after Dad divorced his three wives namely Mama Mariam, (regarded as Dad's first official wife), Mama Kay, (Dad's second official wife) and Mama Nora, (Dad's third official wife), he remained with only Mama Madina (formerly a dancer). Dad said Madina was given to him by the Baganda as a token of appreciation for the support he showed the Baganda and their King, Kabaka Ronald Muwenda Mutebi II.

According to Dad, he publicly divorced Mama Mariam, Mama Kay and Mama Nora in 1974 on charges of involvement in unlawful business deals. In addition Dad claimed that Mama Kay was his cousin and the Elders did not sanction their marriage so he had to divorce her.

Although the details of this public divorce remain sketchy, many Ugandans listened "in amusement" as Dad issued the public divorces over Radio Uganda, christened Uganda Broadcasting Corporation after he took over power in 1971. The public divorces were in fulfillment of Islamic Divorce Law.

Dad had married his 1st official wife Sarah Mutesi Kibedi (Mama Mariam) in 1966. He had married his 2nd official wife Kay (Kaysiya) Adroa in 1967. He had married his 3rd official wife Nora Enin Aloba in 1972. He had married his 4th official wife Madina Nnajjemba in 1972. The three wives that Dad divorced in 1974 namely, Sarah Mutesi Kibedi (Mama Mariam), Kay (Kaysiya) Adroa and Nora Enin Aloba were all Christians. His 4th official wife Madina Nnajjemba was a Muslim. After Madina, Dad only married Muslim women.

Allegations that Dad murdered Mama Kay as well as her brother

There have been allegations that Dad murdered Mama Kay after suspecting that she had committed adultery. There have also been allegations that Dad murdered Mama Kay's brother Michael Ondoga earlier in the year 1974, after appointing him to the position of Minister of Foreign Affairs. However, Dad was completely absolved by Mama Kay's father Archdeacon Adroa and Elders from both sides of the family, of the accusations that were laid at his door in relation to the two deaths.

According to reports in the "public arena", Mama Kay's brother Michael Ondoga was kidnapped and murdered by the callous Ugandan exiles and their subversive elements operating within Uganda after the making of the 1974 French Documentary on Dad titled "General Idi Amin Dada: A Self Portrait". The cold blooded murder of Michael Ondoga is said to have been part of the continuing relentless and deliberate "schemes" by the Ugandan exiles, to "soil" Dad's reputation and make him look like a whimsical murderer. These callous Ugandan exiles allegedly kidnapped and murdered prominent Ugandans and in some cases even foreigners, so that it looked like Dad's operatives committed the brutal murders.

During the making of the French Documentary, Dad allegedly rebuked Michael Ondoga while having a meeting with his Cabinet Ministers that was featured in the French Documentary. Sources suggest that the alleged very "public rebuke" of Michael Ondoga by Dad, gave the callous Ugandan exiles and their subversive elements operating within Uganda a "setting" to kidnap and murder him.

"It was a perfect setting for their twisted minds and evil schemes", some sources have asserted. However, as in many other cases, an Independent Truth and Reconciliation Commission is the place to arrive at the actual truth about events surrounding Michael Ondoga's unconscionable death.

With regards to Mama Kay's death, according to renowned Researcher Guweddeko, at the time of her death, Dad had divorced her and she had moved on. Following the divorce, Mama Kay had an affair with a medical doctor named Mbalu Mukasa and got pregnant. In the meantime, Dad and Mama Kay made up and she became afraid of what he would do if the pregnancy came to light so she requested for an abortion. In an article by Fred Guweddeko, he writes:

"The doctor was hesitant because the pregnancy was at an advanced stage - seven months and three weeks. But Kay insisted.

She died from heavy bleeding during the abortion. The doctor panicked.

He figured that if he made her death look like a typical Amin handiwork, he could get the fingers to point in that direction.

So he cut off her limbs put her torso and severed limbs in the boot of his car and then tried to dispose off the body. After failing to do so, Mbalu tried to kill his family with a drug overdose and committed suicide" (Fred Guweddeko).

The following statement made by Kay's father Archdeacon Adroa at a gathering of representatives from my Dad's family and Kay's family corroborates Fred Guweddeko's account in relation to the doctor:

"Please do not add misfortune to another misfortune, I was at my daughter's in Kampala on the day she set off of her own accord with her doctor friend. I was in the house with her mother and Marta. Please desist from blaming my son-in-law or the Adibu. We are also related for Idi Amin married his cousin. Let us not add misfortune to the misfortune we have suffered" (Archdeacon Adroa, Kay's father).

Relentless and deliberate "schemes" to "soil" Dad's reputation

According to Dad, in 1974, his detractors and saboteurs continued their relentless and deliberate "schemes" to "soil" his reputation and make him look like a whimsical murderer. By this time, Dad's very own brother-in-law Wanume Kibedi, his official first wife Mama Mariam's bother had completely crossed over to the saboteurs' side.

As if it wasn't enough that he deliberately made false and exagge-rated claims in 1973 about there being between 90,000 to 100,000 people killed in Uganda by September 1972 following the Tanzanian invasion of Uganda by Ugandan exiles, Wanume Kibedi went one step further and made an unthinkable allegation. That year 1974, Wanume Kibedi deliberate-ly started a false rumour that Dad sacrificed his sister Mama Mariam's son, my brother Moses Kenyi and ate him in a ritual to prolong his rule in Uganda.

This lie by Wanume Kibedi about his nephew, my brother Moses would persist and be used to give credence to lies that Dad was a cannibal. It would also contribute to the "slippery" path that led to Dad becoming one of the most reviled figures in history in the eyes of people who blindly went along with the biased accounts of a powerful media that began "lynch-ing" Dad when he couldn't be "controlled".

As I stated before, it is unclear why Wanume Kibedi decided to join the "voices" that intensified their efforts to make sure the false claims about the so-called hundreds and thousands of people murdered during Dad's rule in Uganda became "facts". However, there are many theories and rumours surrounding his sudden "change of heart". As I suggested, these theories and rumours are best handled by an Independent Truth and Reconciliation Commission.

My brother Moses grew up to be a 6'6" Nicolas Anelka lookalike but the damage had already been done. Not even his maternal uncle Wanume Kibedi would recant his deliberate "plot" to "soil" Dad's reputation. According to Dad and others, that is exactly how he and his fellow detractors and saboteurs wanted it.

My brother Moses was alive and well, yet even his own mother in exile believed the lies deliberately spread by her brother that her son had been sacrificed and eaten by his own father!

Sarah Mutesi Kibedi of the Ba-Isemena Basoga Ethnic Group is Moses' biological mother. She is the one who is also known as Mama Mariam.

According to Dad and other people, for political and other reasons, Mama Mariam's younger brother Wanume Kibedi duped his elder sister who had put him through school right up to the elevated status of Foreign Minister no less - using her husband's resources. He made her sign an Affidavit that her son had been sacrificed and eaten by his own father.

To convince the Kibedi family that the reports relating to Dad cannibalizing my brother Moses were false and the same relentless negative propaganda Dad was being subjected to, he rounded up Moses and his older sisters from the same womb. Then he sent a large convoy to Busembatiya where they found Moses' Funeral Vigil.

You should have seen the elation on the grandparents' faces when their grandson who is a spitting image of Prince Menha arrived. Moses was then given that illustrious name Menha of the Babito Bunyoro Kitara Kingdom. Nightie, a relative of Mama Mariam's checked Moses for birthmarks as she had worked as a Nanny for Dad and Mama Mariam and accompanied them to Britain and Israel during Dad's State Visits there in July 1971.

Moses' maternal grandparents gave him the Princely name Menha from the Spiritual Ba-isemenha clan of Busembatiya following the acrimony surrounding the false accusation that his father had sacrificed him and eaten him as published by his illustrious Uncle Wanume Kibedi, the former Foreign Minister of Uganda. Wanume Kibedi had "fallen out" with his brother-in-law Dad and he had convinced his elder sister who had been unceremoniously divorced by Dad on radio the same year 1974 to also run into exile. Therefore when the rumors came through from London to

Busembatiya, the Kibedi family elders actually set up a mourning vigil to
honour the memory of their grandchild Moses.

On hearing this, Dad gathered a lorry truck full of essential com-
modities and all his children from Mama Mariam (Mariam Aaliya (Aliya),
Farida Akulu Dawa, Bebi Anite, Akujo Kadara, Moses Kenyi, Halima Atta).
Then he put them under the care of John Musoga, a former Waiter who
Dad placed in the army. John Musoga later became the person who replaced
Captain Dumba as the Protocol Officer responsible for us Dad's children.
Dad placed my brother Moses Kenyi in a Mercedes Benz with his biological
sisters in tow and they set off in a long convoy of expensive German
machines for Busembatiya where they found a Funeral Vigil and hordes of
crying Bantu relatives.

Tears of sorrow turned into tears of joy when an apparition of their
favourite grandchild stepped out of the motorcade, for behold Prince
Menha had finally arrived. Moses takes after his maternal ancestor Prince
Menha of the Royal Babito Dynasty of Runya-Kitara. The grandfather and
the whole of Busembatiya rose up in joyful wonder.

The likes of Nightie who used to look after Moses checked him for
discernible birth marks and injuries that occurred while in her care and the
grandparent consented and accepted the painful reality, naming the child
Menha "who has come back to us!" Then he amazingly started to curse his
own children Sarah Mutesi Kibedi and Wanume Kibedi in London for
misleading him. He gratefully accepted the gifts from the child's father and
the merry making started. The Ba-Isemenha danced for their resurrected
King Menha for surely Prince Menha had come back to the Ba-Isemenha.

For security reasons, Dad insisted that Moses and his sisters return
that very day for he did not want anything untoward to happen to his
favourite son after the confirmation that indeed this was Moses Kenyi
Menha Amin.

Tragically, it was from then on that it became a necessity for Dad to
move around with Moses to each and every occasion if only to drown out
the "din" of false accusations from the hostile world media that he had
sacrificed and eaten his favourite son. That explains the constant presence
of Moses by Dad's side after the false allegation and blatant lie by his own
maternal uncle Wanume Kibedi. If anything, it was to reassure the mother
who was far, far away in London that her son lived. Alas she only believed it
when my brother Moses Kenyi set out across the English Channel from
Paris where he resided, to London where she resided in 1995 for he too had
felt a strong loyalty towards his father and he had resented the act of

tarnishing Dad's name by his own maternal family members. It was only in 1995 that Moses Kenyi sought out his mother and initiated a "Reconciliation" of sorts, as a grown man!

As I said before, there are a lot of theories and rumours surrounding why Wanume Kibedi "crafted" the "schemes" relating to the false and exaggerated claims he made in 1973 about there being between 90,000 to 100,000 people killed in Uganda by September 1972. There are also a lot of theories and rumours surrounding why Wanume Kibedi "crafted" the "scheme" relating to his unthinkable lie about Dad sacrificing and eating his nephew, my brother Moses Kenyi. However, as I suggested before, an Independent Truth and Reconciliation Commission is the place to arrive at the actual truth.

Dad and others believed that one of the reasons Wanume Kibedi "crafted" or went along with such "schemes" was because he was a member of Apollo Milton Obote's UPC (Uganda People's Congress) Party. Most Basoga are UPC diehards and Wanume Kibedi had attained a certain level of masked contempt for a person who in his eyes got everything by sheer luck of the draw, leave alone that he was actually put through school and lodging, by the very man he despised.

The whole of the Ba-Isemenha clan and the Basoga tribe can substantiate the story relating to Wanume Kibedi fabricating a story about my brother Moses being cannibalized by Dad. We have no less than 7 mothers ("wives" of Idi Amin Dada) with children from that very ethnic group in the Dada Family, including my mother. Mama Mariam, Mama Kirunda, Mama Tshombe, Mama Kagera, Mama Kenneth, Mama Fatuma Nabirye and others all hail from the Basoga tribe of Uganda. They are many.

Moses' mother Mama Mariam did not knowingly sign the false Affidavit that her son had been sacrificed and eaten by Dad and she honestly believed the false fabrications by her brother Wanume Kibedi. She was coerced with the accusation that her son had been eaten and only confirmed the blatantly false allegations later when it was too late. The damage had been done and Dad's detractors and the hostile and powerful Media had "run with it!"

At the time of completing the Introductory Edition of Idi Amin: Hero or Villain? His Son Jaffar Amin and Other People Speak, my brother Moses who was allegedly sacrificed and eaten by my Dad was safe and sound and resided in France.

When we lived in exile in Saudi Arabia, Dad sent Moses and several of my brothers to study in France and me and other siblings to study in England.

The 1974 French Film Documentary on Dad

In 1974, the French Documentary made about Dad titled, "General Idi Amin Dada: A Self Portrait" was shown extensively around the world. During the making of the film, Dad made statements that were taken out of context. Several of his statements were labeled as nonsensical. However, they came to pass.

In the Documentary, Dad made a lot of "audacious" statements such as:

"The Black people of America must be the President of the United States of America". "They must be the Secretary of State."

This is because he wanted all people of African Descent to feel confident and proud of their heritage and he succeeded in doing so for Ugandans.

Dad's predictions and so-called "nonsensical ramblings" regarding an African American President and Secretary of State came to pass!

He always mouthed that "Black people are more brilliant than any other race". He did this to the horror of people who worried that such statements would lead to additional backlash against him and other Ugandans but he didn't care about making such "audacious" statements "on camera".

Many of Dad's statements have been labeled nonsensical because he conveyed them in English - a language he didn't care for but was "forced" to communicate in because of colonialism. Dad was very eloquent, very articulate and very fluent in a number of African languages and if he was afforded the opportunity to convey his statements in one of these languages, his statements would have had the clarity he intended.

The 1974 French Documentary and other films about Dad will be great additions to the background information for the section of the series titled "Other People Speak", along with other material relating to the debate about whether Dad was a hero or villain to the core. A discussion is encouraged as the series, Idi Amin: Hero or Villain? His Son Jaffar Amin and Other People Speak unfolds!

My life as the President's Son

As the President's Son, I was always out and about in the Presidential Mansions. From the day in 1973 when I was permanently united with my father and started living life as the President's Son, I never stopped marveling at the Presidential Mansions. From the day we were ushered right through to the stone pillars into the Oak Laden Reception Area at State House Entebbe, I became mesmerized by what was to become my life until Dad was overthrown in 1979.

After the 1972 invasion by the Ugandan exiles, Dad had asked that several of my siblings and I be brought from Mbarara to the Former Colonial Mansion (State House Entebbe) then taken to his residence in Kololo, Kampala that he named Command Post. That day, I had immediately become aware of the elephant tusks at the entrance to State House Entebbe and never tired of admiring them throughout my life as the President's Son.

Over the years between 1974 and 1979 and especially in 1974 during the first, second and third term holidays under the care of Mama Madina, we children would debate whether the elephant tusks at the entrance to State House Entebbe were mammoth tusks or normal elephant tusks. They were very large and encased or booted in a square oak stand with brass trim. As a kid, I also took note of the manufacturers of the "Silent Ghost" front door.

Between 1999 and 2005, I once mentioned this fact to a KARAOKE singing friend of mine - a Presidential Brigade Guard named Lieutenant Peter Otim and he was surprised when I mentioned "Silent Ghost". He laughed because it was the type of detail only those who have been to the State House in Entebbe would notice.

I told Lieutenant Peter Otim that I used to spend most of my time aimlessly playing the grand piano in the formal dining room, whiling my time spooning through the rows and rows of Sheffield Silver Cutlery. I told him that sometimes I would browse through Magazines like TIMES, Newsweek and The Economist and rows and rows of leather bound books in the Old Study. I also told him that other times, I would follow Mugarura who was fond of siphoning (pilfering more like) quality Liquor/Scotch Whisky for his own consumption from the Colonial Gravel Cellar in the under belly of the original colonial building. I caught him once and asked if Dad or visitors were coming since he had three or four bottles at hand. Mugarura was the Chief Finance Officer and everyone who ever worked in

State House Entebbe during Dad's rule knows him. He was basically responsible for paying all the workers' wages and he had access to the cellars.

Spooky places indeed for the rest of the family but I seemed to be attracted to this "Old English" furnishing and setting. It was ironic considering that I was from a rural background after my life with Grandma Aate and Aunt Akisu in Kayunga, Bugerere.

Every First Term, Second Term and Third Term Holiday between 1974 and 1979 we would be placed at Lake Victoria Primary School in Entebbe. That was when we would meet up with Timothy Kalyegira who also went to school there. Somehow the Boarding and Day School never synchronized so for extra coaching, we ended up in Lake Victoria Primary School. However because of the issues surrounding Moses (the false allegations and lies about him being sacrificed and cannibalized by Dad), he was kept longer at Lake Victoria Primary School but later insisted on joining us at Kabale Preparatory School permanently.

State House Entebbe was always the gathering point but we resided at or visited all of Dad's residences during his time as President of Uganda:

Command Post where Mama Madina resided from 1972 to 1979;

Nakasero Lodge Main House where Mama Kay resided from 1971 to 1974;

Nakasero Lodge New Wing where Mama Nora resided from 1971 to 1974;

Entebbe Lodge where Mama Mariam resided from 1971 to 1974.

Mama Sara Kyolaba whom Dad married in 1975 preferred Nakasero Lodge. However, the two - Mama Sara Kyolaba and Mama Madina later jointly shifted to State House Entebbe which has a better defence position following attempts by insurgents to raid Dad's Kampala residences.

Events in neighbouring countries and another coup attempt

As Dad continued to hang onto power amidst the sabotage and propaganda intended to bring him down, he continued to follow events in neighbouring countries.

Earlier in 1974, there had been a visit to Juba, Southern Sudan by the Emperor Haile Selassie of Ethiopia, to celebrate the Anniversary of the signing of the Addis Ababa Accord and continuing peace in the Sudan, which Dad was instrumental in bringing about.

Emperor Haile Selassie of Ethiopia had arrived in Juba the Capital of Southern Sudan to celebrate the Anniversary of the signing of the Addis Ababa Accord, which he had witnessed in March 1972. The colourful event was attended by hordes of crowds that were hopeful about the continuing peace in the Sudan.

Meanwhile, a rift had developed between Dad and Senior Christian Army Officers from Dad's Kakwa tribe, which had led to a coup against Dad in January 1974. According to Dad, two issues created the rift, with the first being Dad's broken relationship with Israel after being a loyal friend, strong supporter and ally for years and fathering twins with an Israeli Secret Service (Mossad) Agent. The second issue was the integration and appointment of Sudanese Anyanya in top positions following the signing of the Addis Ababa Accord in 1972.

Dad claimed that deep down the Christian Kakwas felt he made a wrong choice where the Israelis were concerned. He claimed that they felt that he should have kept what to them was a watertight engagement with the battle hardened Israelis to the very end - much in the mould of the Warrior Kakwas of old.

According to Dad, this factor came to a head in January 1974, when three Battle Hardened Kakwa Christian Army Officers along with a Justice plotted a mutiny against him. They were Charles Arube from the Kakwa clan of Kaliwara in Ko'buko (Ko'boko), Elly Aseni from the Kakwa clan of Godiya in Ko'buko (Ko'boko), Isaac Lumago from the Kakwa clan of Isoko in Ko'buko (Ko'boko) and Justice Opu from the Kakwa clan of Ludara in Ko'buko (Ko'boko). According to Dad, the four Kakwa Christian Army Officers probably acted under instructions from either the Soviets or even the Israeli Mossad, leading to the attempted coup in January 1974.

The rift that developed between Dad and the Senior Christian Army Officers from his Kakwa tribe over his decision to appoint Sudanese Anyanya in top positions following the signing of the Addis Ababa Accord would persist and contribute to his downfall in April 1979.

According to Dad, the issue mainly centered on the Sudanese Anyanya I contingent that he absorbed into the Uganda Army following the end of the First Sudanese War in 1972. Since the "warring factions" had just signed a Peace Agreement in Addis Ababa, the Indigenous soldiers felt affronted by the presence of Sudanese in top positions. Examples included Moses Ali, Lieutenant Colonel Malera, Gore, Taban Lupayi and others. The fact that most of them were top Flight Officers who got their training in Great Britain and Israel was secondary to their concerns.

Dad said the involvement of Justice Opu in the coup attempt pointed to Constitutional concerns about the prevalence of Kenyans, Tanzanians, Rwandese Tutsi, Sudanese and Congolese in the Security Services. The likes of Isaac Maliyamungu were most likely to bring in contingents of Congolese Kakwa from Jaki County in the Congo. Taban Lupayi would bring in Pojulu from the Sudan. Moses Ali brought in Bari from the Sudan.

Dad and his associates used to joke that the Rwandese Tutsis emptied out of the Refugee Camps and into the officers' homes as wives and their brothers ended up being recruited into the security services as far back as 1968. "This was by design!" they intimated.

Following is a sketchy outline of the attempted coup against Dad by Charles Arube, Elly Aseni, and Isaac Lumago, the three Battle Hardened Kakwa Christian Army Officers from Dad's Kakwa tribe as recounted by Dad:

Exactly three years to the time of the coup that catapulted Dad to power on January 25, 1971, there was a rumoured attempted coup by Charles Arube the Army Chief of Staff, that occurred between January 23 and 24, 1974. Arube was allegedly angry that in his absence in Moscow, a Muslim was put in his place. He was referring to the appointment of Lieutenant Colonel Malera who is an Animist and not a Muslim. Colonel Malera was one of the Sudanese soldiers absorbed into the Uganda Army following the end of the First Sudanese War.

I once asked Dad what could have turned Arube a close family member against him and Dad's answer was painful to hear. He re-enacted his phone call to Arube during which he asked Arube why Arube felt the need to take power from him.

According to Dad, Arube answered him that it was better for an educated Christian Kakwa to rule Uganda. According to Dad, he then proceeded to remind Arube of how close Arube's family was to ours and how he looked out for Arube and our uncle Luka and treated them like his own blood brothers. Dad reminded Arube that he promoted Arube to the position of Chief of Staff, in memory and recognition of his family relation with us.

"After all this, how can you turn against me surely?" Dad had concluded the phone conversation.

With tears in his eyes, Dad claimed that he then called our uncle Luka who had just returned from Libya to set up the Uganda Marines Corps at Bugolobi Barracks.

In July 1971, Dad had daringly left his 6-month regime in the capable but young hands of Sandhurst trained Brigadier General Charles Arube when some insurgents tried to storm the King George IV Garrison in Jinja. So he was disappointed that Charles Arube broke their trust and tried to take over the Uganda government from him through a Military Coup.

According to Dad, it was after a training course in the USSR that Charles Arube attempted to take over leadership from him through the Military Coup in January 1974 in connivance with Dad's uncle Elly Aseni, Justice Opu and Isaac Lumago. This would be a Christian Kakwa inspired coup attempt that was precipitated by dissatisfaction with the way Dad severed relationships with Israel and how Lieutenant Colonel Malera one of the Sudanese brought into Dad's army was handling the command of the Military Police.

Dad told us that during the mutiny instigated against him by the Senior Christian Army Officers from his Kakwa tribe, our uncle Luka kept insisting on knowing his location and where he was. However, Dad insisted that Luka take his Crack Marine Troopers and secure the key locations which had been taken over by troops loyal to Charles Arube, Elly Aseni and Isaac Lumago, again, all Christian Kakwas.

It was only after uncle Luka came back to Dad with affirmative confirmation of having re-taken the capital that Dad was able to inform him that he was at the Makindye Lodge overlooking the city. Dad claimed that he could see Armoured Personnel Carriers roaming the streets of Kampala at the height of the attempted Coup D'etat.

This was an incident that raised concern among Temezi (Elders) from the Kakwa tribe because for generations, Blood Ties have taken precedence over Religious Ties in the Kakwa tribe. Dad just felt that Charles Arube had been influenced from "outside" by the British, Russians and the Israeli Mossad. He was convinced that Charles Arube, Elly Aseni, Isaac Lumago and Justice Opu would never have wanted him dead if they had not been influenced by "outsiders."

The Foreign Press reported that up to 30 Kakwa soldiers were killed at Makindye including Brigadier General Charles Arube, soon after returning from a Training Mission in Moscow with Isaac Lumago. However, there are also unconfirmed but undisputed accounts relating to suspicions that Charles Arube committed suicide by self-inflicting a gunshot wound after realizing the consequences of the mutiny and coup he and the other Senior Christian Army Officers from Dad's Kakwa tribe had instigated. An Independent Truth and Reconciliation Commission is also the place to arrive at the actual truth about events surrounding Charles Arube's sad and untimely death.

According to Dad, even if Arube urgently wanted him killed, he had underestimated both the powers that he had over the soldiers and his personal courage. Indeed, Dad, dressed in his pajamas, immediately came out and spoke to the soldiers, ordering them to unload their weapons and return to the barracks. He then put on his uniform, got into his own vehicle and drove to all the trouble spots where peace was quickly restored. It was a typical display of his innate leadership and fearlessness in the face of adversity.

According to reliable sources, Elly Aseni was spared the wrath of the irate soldiers because he came from Dad's Paternal Uncles the Godiya Kakwa clan. Following the coup attempt, he was magnanimously given the Ambassadorship of the USSR by Dad while Isaac Lumago was eventually given the Ambassadorship of Lesotho. Rumours abound about Isaac Lumago's father approaching my Grandpa Amin Dada Nyabira and the two of them together talking to Dad about sparing Lumago's life.

According to Dad, he sent the people from his own Kakwa tribe for Specialist Training abroad but they would come back from Russia or the United States of America thinking they were better educated than him and start getting ideas that they wanted to rule. Dad said that the superpowers started creating tensions between him and his trusted Lieutenants to get at him.

During Dad's rule in Uganda, there were constant threats of coups. However, he said that he stamped down on these coups because he had a very good intelligence service that had been set up by the United States of America and the USSR and before that by the Israelis and the British.

In 1974, Lieutenant Colonel Hussein Malera, Commanding Officer of the Military Police in Makindye was ordered out of Uganda to the Sudan his birthplace by Dad. Originally from the Baka tribe in the Yei River District, Lieutenant Colonel Malera left Uganda for the Sudan in a massive convoy of cars and trucks. The trek was a spectacle to behold and Dad's associates regularly recounted circumstances surrounding the "deportation" ordered by Dad.

The sentence to death of Denis Hills and "kneeling" British citizens

Events that unfolded in May and June 1975 in relation to the arrest and trial of Denis Hills, a British Sociology Lecturer at Makerere University, Uganda would go down in history as some of the most memorable events that occurred during Dad's rule in Uganda. The situation was made worse by the fact that Dad's relationship with Britain had become "strained" after a series of "bad behaviours" by Dad towards Britain and its citizens and a "disappointing" turn of events where Britain's "expectations" of Dad were concerned. Dad seemed to be giving Britain and the other parties who allegedly "hand picked" him to replace Apollo Milton Obote a run for their money with his "unexpected" "waywardness"! Nevertheless, Britain continued maintaining Diplomatic Relations with Uganda, its former colony.

Opinions abound as to why Britain continued a "strained" relationship with an "ungovernable" Dad and these opinions are recommended readings for the section of the series titled "Other People Speak", along with other background information. However, despite the "bad behaviours" Dad exhibited after the "honeymoon" period with Britain, many British citizens continued to reside and offer their services in Uganda including Denis Hills, the British Sociology Lecturer at Makerere University.

According to various reports, Denis Hills was arrested, tried by a Military Tribunal and found guilty of treason for his book "The White Pumpkin", which is critical of Dad and his regime and the initial Book Manuscript described Dad as a "pagan tyrant". To many British citizens Dad was no longer the 'Gentle Giant' "they" "praised", immediately following the Military Coup against his predecessor Apollo Milton Obote in January 1971. Like Denis Hills, they exercised their right to free speech and didn't shy away from voicing their negative opinions about Dad. However, for Denis Hills, his right to free speech and voicing opinions about Dad would become a nightmare that would haunt him for a very long time.

According to reports, Dad's intelligence got word of the contents of Denis Hills' initial Book Manuscript and arrested him. It is reported that Denis Hills was first acquitted of all charges by a Ugandan Magistrate but later tried by a Military Tribunal that found him guilty of treason and sentenced him to death by firing squad on June 21, 1975. The reference to

Dad by Denis Hills as a "pagan tyrant" was what precipitated the charge of treason against him.

The British Government panicked and sent Lieutenant General Sir Chandos Blair and Dad's former Commanding Officer Iain Grahame to plead for clemency. According to reports, Queen Elizabeth II sent Dad a personal appeal to spare Denis Hills' life. Dad seized this as another "perfect" opportunity to "taunt" Britain and its citizens "for the sins of colonialism."

Upon arriving in Uganda, the two envoys Lieutenant General Sir Chandos Blair and Dad's former Commanding Officer Iain Grahame proceeded to Arua to meet Dad. They were accompanied by Colonel Sabuni, one of Dad's officers. Dad was very open to the meeting with the two British envoys but he had "something up his sleeve!"

Iain Grahame described what happened next:

"Bucking low to avoid the thatch (Amin's hut), we entered as instructed kneeling before the President. Inside, a quite remarkable sight greeted our eyes. Close to the opening was a two-man television crew one of whom was holding a battery operated light that was directed towards the far end of the hut. There sitting on an enormous curved wooden throne was his Excellency the President of Uganda. He was wearing the largest Mexican sombrero that I have ever seen, blue pinstripe bush jacket and trousers, a Christian Dior scarf and the inevitable size fourteen of brown shoes."

In Kakwa culture and other cultures of Uganda and Africa, kneeling before anyone is considered the utmost sign of reverence. It also occurs when someone is begging for mercy. Dad obviously set the scene described by Iain Grahame so that the two British citizens could "kneel before him".

I can only imagine how hard Dad must have laughed in private at the fact that he had successfully "duped" and "orchestrated" two Wazungu (White men) to "kneel before him". It would have been the very same tearful earthquake laugh he was engaged in when he played the "African Chili Prank" on my siblings and I the day he offered us chili laden roast chicken after noticing our keen interest in the chicken. It had been the very first time several of my siblings and I got to know Dad and began living in his official residences as the President's Children. That time, we didn't find Dad's "African Chili Prank" as funny as he thought it was and the two British envoys may not have found the deliberate "set up" by Dad for them to "kneel before him" funny either.

During the meeting between Dad and the two British envoys Lieutenant General Sir Chandos Blair and Dad's former Commanding Officer

Iain Grahame, he presented Lieutenant General Blair with assorted bows and arrows and Iain Grahame with the musical instrument, Nanga. He also gave Lieutenant General Blair the manuscript of Denis Hills' book. That day, Dad entertained Lieutenant General Blair and Iain Grahame to a typical Kakwa delicacy of bowels of goat meat, kon'ga (edible white ants) and "the skin of some lungfish [popularly known in the West Nile by the name aboke] from the Nile."

Iain Grahame commented, "I made a bee-line for the ants, one of my favourite traditional African delicacies."

On June 10, 1975, Dad stipulated six conditions that had to be fulfilled before Denis Hills could be spared the firing squad:

"The British stop all malicious propaganda against me, the Government and the people of Uganda mounted in Britain and international news media. Expel all Uganda exiles presently in Britain who are spreading unfounded rumours against Uganda. The British media must stop their fruitless campaigns against Uganda by trying to persuade other friendly countries not to give any technical or other material assistance to Uganda and at the same time trying to persuade potential tourists not to come to Uganda. Stop and desist from making wild and useless reports that Uganda is in a state of chaos."

Dad's concerns were confirmed by the fact that while attending the Commonwealth Conference in Kingston, Jamaica, the British Prime Minister himself made some unfortunate reference that Uganda could not afford to host the forthcoming summit of the OAU (Organization of African Unity) Heads of State and Government.

"They must be prepared to sell to Uganda all the spare parts of military equipment which Uganda bought from Britain, such as Saladin armoured cars and Ferret scout cars, and any other spare parts for British military hardware bought by Uganda. The British Prime Minister or the Queen, who is the Head of the Commonwealth, must give me a written confirmation of the conditions enumerated above and the Defence Council has directed that this confirmation must reach Kampala ten days from tomorrow".

The spectacle deliberately set up by Dad that involved Lieutenant General Sir Chandos Blair and Iain Grahame "kneeling before him" as they bucked low to avoid Dad's thatch became a standing joke among Ugandans as they laughed about Dad's "audacity" to continue "taunting" their former colonial masters. Some Ugandans laughed even harder as they regularly recalled Dad pulling off yet another "stunt" by "setting up" fourteen Ex-

Services British men who joined the Uganda Army to "kneel before him" as they "pledged" to take up arms for Uganda. Many Ugandans thought the spectacles were funny but others found them in terrible taste!

The spectacles involving Lieutenant General Sir Chandos Blair and Iain Grahame "kneeling before Dad" and the very public "reverence" and "declaration of loyalty" by fourteen Ex-Services British men who joined the Uganda Army in a so-called "pledge" were jokes Dad mocked in private as he laughed hard!

No one needed to kneel to "pledge" to take up arms for Uganda. Dad just wanted to "reverse" the Master-Servant "roles" that existed between the British and Ugandans because of colonialism. As I stated before, in Kakwa culture and other cultures of Uganda and Africa, kneeling before anyone is considered the utmost sign of reverence.

"Idi Amin wanted to humiliate a couple of White British citizens as 'punishment' for the 'sins' of colonialism and the African Slave Trade, which Britain participated in before 'championing' its end," many people have intimated.

It would be interesting to hear what others have to say about the spectacles and the reasons why fourteen Ex-Services British men joined the Uganda Army in the first place and endured the "humiliation" Dad subjected them to. There will be opportunities for related discussions as the series Idi Amin: Hero or Villain? His Son Jaffar Amin and Other People Speak unfolds.

According to accounts, in July 1975, General Mobutu of Zaire (Congo) and others urged Dad to hand over Denis Hills into the hands of the British Foreign Secretary James Callaghan in Kampala. Present at this historic moment and hand over was Jim Hennessy, the British Ambassador in Uganda at the time. Before the formal hand over to James Callaghan, Denis Hills had to apologize fully to the President of Uganda - Dad.

At the Command Post, one of Dad's residences and in front of Representatives of the British Press, Lieutenant General Sir Chandos Blair and Iain Grahame drank large quantities of Uganda's favourite alcoholic drink, Uganda Waragi. Their actions later gave rise to a jest throughout Uganda's bars, schools and other places of social gathering.

Instead of asking for a Waragi, Ugandans would simply ask for a "Double Blair" or "Neat Blair". The local press also reported that after gulping down so much Waragi, Lieutenant General Blair was too drunk to walk, so he had to be supported.

Dad's tiff with Jomo Kenyatta, the President of Kenya

In June 1975, Dad had a tiff with Jomo Kenyatta, President of Kenya at the time, after he announced that large parts of Southern Sudan and Western and Central Kenya were historically part of Uganda. This announcement created tensions between Dad and President Jomo Kenyatta who deployed troops and armored vehicles along the Uganda - Kenya border.

During Dad's tiff with Jomo Kenyatta, Kenyatta refused to allow Uganda's imports to pass through Mombasa, including Petroleum Products. This caused a lot of hardship for ordinary Ugandans even though Libya's Al-Qadhafi intervened by flying petrol to Entebbe Airport directly.

During the Kenya/Uganda crisis, Dad reminded Kenyatta of the time he saved his life during the Mau Mau uprising in Kenya. As is common in the Adiyo narration style and format we are using to tell Dad's story, reproduced below for ease of reference are excerpts from a previous section outlining events relating to that time:

While on Patrol as a young soldier under British Commanders in Kenya during the Mau Mau uprising, Dad saved the life of Jomo Kenyatta, the Father of the Nation of Kenya. On that day at a Roadblock specifically erected by the British Colonial Administration for purposes of "liquidating" Kenyatta, a trusted Indigenous Sergeant Idi Amin had been ordered by a White Officer to climb up the truck to look under gunny bags for Jomo Kenyatta. This had happened as colonial soldiers hunted down Kenyatta for allegedly instigating the Mau Mau uprising and they wanted him dead or alive!

Dad did climb up the truck as ordered by his superior and located Kenyatta. He actually came face to face with Kenyatta but in a tense moment, he told the British officer, "There is no one up here Affende", while looking into the eyes of the reputed son of Kabarega.

At that very lethal of moments, when the English Officer inquired about whether there was anybody hidden in the litter truck, Dad's spur of the moment response was disobedience.

"No sir, there is no one aboard", he repeated when the officer asked the question again.

Dad had said this while placing back the gunny bags protecting Kenyatta so that he could evade capture by the colonial soldiers.

When the white officer insisted that Kenyatta was on the truck, Dad dared him and said, "You come up and see for yourself! There is nobody up here."

"Okay" responded the British Captain.

Word had got to the Colonial Intelligence that the fugitive Kenyatta would indeed be on the very litter truck Dad was ordered to inspect at the roadblock, as a Junior member of the Kings African Rifles. Reliable sources had tipped Colonial Intelligence that Kenyatta would be hiding under the charcoal bags on the very truck.

However, Dad chose not to betray his mwananchi (fellow citizen) by revealing fugitive Kenyatta's presence on the truck. He defiantly disobeyed the order to capture Kenyatta and didn't divulge the secret relating to his disobedience to his superiors!

So in 1975, when war almost erupted between Uganda and Kenya, Kenyatta quickly cooled and diffused the standoff when Dad revealed that he, Idi Amin was the Indigenous Sergeant who saved Kenyatta's life during the Mau Mau days. The revelation so shocked and amazed the old man that Kenyatta felt compelled to end the hostility that was occurring between Uganda and Kenya at the time. Being reminded of that lethal moment in time so shocked Kenyatta that, he called off the troop build up along the Kenya - Uganda border in time to avert a war between the two countries.

The fracas between Dad and Kenyatta had brought a build up of troops along the Kenya - Uganda Border and almost exploded into war but for Dad's revelation to Kenyatta about Kenyatta "owing him his life". The fracas had happened when Dad in his usual bombastic style reminded Kenyans of the old colonial territorial lines that included Nyasaland, Kisumu, Naivasha and Kalenjin territory in the Rift Valley right up to the Northern Frontier District and the shores of Lake Turkana (Rudolf) being Ugandan territory. Dad claimed that when he reminded Kenyans of the old colonial territorial lines, he was just reflecting on the historical past but not laying claim to the "controversial" land.

That time, Dad sent Captain Ismail Khamis nicknamed Sul Wayi Wayi with a personal reminder to Kenyatta about the incident at the roadblock that could have ended Kenyatta's life. By recounting the events of that day, he was able to prove to Jomo Kenyatta beyond reasonable doubt that indeed he, Idi Amin Dada was the very Indigenous Sergeant who manned a Roadblock, which stopped the charcoal litter truck that was carrying him.

After Captain Sul Wayi Wayi conveyed the message from Dad, Kenyatta knew without a shadow of a doubt that Dad was the very Indigenous

Soldier who was ordered by the White Officer to climb up the charcoal litter truck to see if he was on the truck. He knew that only someone who had climbed up onto the very truck he was in could ever have known this singular one on one event that would have put a stop to his activities to save Kenya from the clutches of the British colonizers.

As he evaded capture, Kenyatta was aware at the time that the British Colonial Administration was so determined to hang onto Kenya, especially the fertile parts of the country that they were willing to kill, main and massacre anyone who stood in the way.

The revelation to Kenyatta that Dad saved his life that fateful day brought on memories of his very personal terror of the very night he would have been killed by the colonial soldiers. Kenyatta recalled that he would have been dead but for that singular Indigenous African Soldier (Dad) who saved his life. The father of the Nation of Kenya remembered that he was supposed to be shot on sight.

During the Kenya/Uganda Border crisis, Dad relished the opportunity to remind Kenyatta of the one-on-one encounter they had when he as a Sergeant made the defiant decision to let him escape instead of obeying orders from his British superiors to capture and possibly shoot him.

Dad also publicly declared on a state visit to Kenya that he sought the whereabouts of Njoroge and Njuguna, progeny from his Mau Mau days. This is because while on his Tour of Duty in Kenya, he had several Kikuyu concubines with whom he also had children.

The declaration of Dad as Life President, a promotion and reflections

In 1975, Dad made the second and final self-military appointments - second only to his initial promotion to Full General in February 1971, during the first year of his Presidency. That same year 1975 the Defence Council announced the declaration of Dad as Life President of Uganda and promoted him to Field Marshall.

Regarding Orders, Honours, Decorations and Medals awarded to Dad after Uganda became "Independent" from Britain on October 9, 1962 and after Dad became President of Uganda, Dad always wanted to succeed as a soldier and he worked hard at it. Even in the colonial times, he rose steadily through the ranks despite the fact that his formal education was minimal. In the eyes of his British superiors and as far as their direct supervision was concerned, Dad's British training and steady progress in the Army ended during the 1964 mutiny outlined in a previous section. This was because he listened less to their advice and took full reign of the military when he was promoted to Lieutenant Colonel in 1964.

Regarding Dad's titles, which have been ridiculed by his detractors, Dad got and deserved the Distinguished Service Order (DSO) through his over 17 years in the Kings African Rifles from 1946 to 1962. After Uganda attained "Independence" from Great Britain in 1962, Dad received rapid promotions from Major in 1963 to Major General in 1968. The only self-appointments under the so-called Military Council that was instituted during Dad's regime from 1971 to 1979 were promotion to Full General in February 1971 and Field Marshall in 1975.

Dad was one of the first Indigenous Africans to receive the True not Honourary Officer Rank of Lieutenant in 1959-1960 and he was a Captain before "Independence". Moreover, as the highest ranked Indigenous African and Chief of Staff at the time Uganda attained "Independence" from Great Britain, Dad received the new flag, which was to be hoisted on Uhuru Day (Independence Day). He also received back the Union Jack, which was lowered on October 9, 1962.

Major Iain Grahame's book about Dad provides a rare and true picture of what Dad received as per British Standards. Major Iain Grahame was one of Dad's superiors during the time he served under the British Colonial Administration.

Dad carried titles such as His Excellency President for Life, Field Marshall, Al Hadj, Doctor Idi Amin Dada, VC, DSO, MC, Lord of All the Beasts of the Earth and Fishes of the Sea and Conqueror of the British Empire (CBE), in Africa in General and Uganda in Particular. Regarding these titles, many of which have been ridiculed, Dad relished the CBE in jest to Queen Elizabeth II. Field Marshall was in homage to Montgomery.

The King of Beasts is just another of those "Settler" mentality Pub jokes thrown around by Journalists who knew they could become "fact" in print, for "anything" goes with "defenseless" Idi Amin. He rarely broke the silent barrier until I came along after his demise to try and correct some of the misconceptions and outright lies that have been told "over" and "over" and "over" again!

Dad as Chairman of the OAU and his marriage to Mama Sarah

Between July 28, 1975 and August 1, 1975, the Organization of African Unity (OAU) Summit took place in Kampala and Dad was Chairman. He organized and made the Summit into such a colourful event that many of his associates and other Ugandans "bragged" about it for a very long time.

Prior to the Summit, there were construction projects all over the place as Dad wanted to make a lasting impression on delegates. Some of the resulting projects include the present day Conference Centre and the Serena Hotel (Formerly Nile Mansions Hotel). During the OAU Summit, delegates laughed as Dad repeatedly said, "I was born on this very spot". Many thought that Dad was at his usual pranks and jests but he was dead serious this time because he was indeed born at the very location of the Conference Centre and the Serena Hotel (Formerly the Nile Mansions Hotel) in Kampala in 1928.

Despite Dad's sincere attempt to tell delegates to the Organization of African Unity Summit, "I was born on this very spot", a lot of the media and even Ugandans dismissed this fact as another "wayward" attempt by Dad to be funny. Dad liked to jest but he was very serious in asserting that he was born at the location of the International Conference Centre in Kampala and Nile Mansions Hotel.

To this day, many people cannot imagine the Kampala of the 1920s, let alone the fact that Dad's parents lived there that time and he was born at the very location of the International Conference Centre and the Nile Mansions Hotel in Kampala.

In the same year 1975, Dad married Sarah Kyolaba a so-called go-go dancer from the Suicide Mechanized Unit Jazz Band in Masaka. The marriage was a lavish affair televised over Uganda Television and it coincided with the OAU Summit in Uganda that was chaired by Dad. The Reception was held at the same location and hall where the OAU Summit was held. Many associates of Dad's and Ugandans remembered the lavish reception for a long time. The Palestine Liberation Organization's (PLO's) Yasser Arafat was the Best Man at Dad and Sarah Kyolaba's wedding. There are claims that Dad married Sarah the Islamic way then he was forced to repeat the Wedding during the OAU Summit.

I have recollections of many dignitaries hosted by Dad and will always remember the time The Nation of Islam dignitaries came to Uganda on Dad's invitation during the OAU Summit in 1975.

Mobutu, with all his Afro-Jazz Bands and the likes of Mpongo Love, Orchestra Veve and Orchestra Lipua Lipua, Pure Raz Mataz impressed me a great deal! This is because like most Ugandans, I loved Congolese Music as a child. I still do and believe that it is one of the best demonstrations of African talent. Dad couldn't get enough of it!

Visits by "Black Empowerment" and Arab Nationalist Groups

The state visits by "Black Empowerment Groups", including The Nation of Islam under Louis Farrakhan (based in the USA), The Black Panthers (based in the USA), the PLO and other Arab Nationalist Groups during the 1975 OAU were among the most memorable occasions that occurred in 1975.

Dad's invitation to "Black Empowerment Groups", originating from the United States of America was for purposes of his agenda to call on the Black Peoples in the American Diaspora to unite. He emphasized unity for Black people way back, just as he was uniting the Frontline States against Apartheid and their perceived notion that Israel was an Apartheid state too, which won him the landslide UN Resolution 3379 between 1975-1992 that I write about in a section below.

That year 1975, the Leader of The Nation of Islam, Elijah Muhammad died and one Abdul Haleem Farrakhan was the one who led the delegation to Uganda for the OAU Summit in Kampala in place of Wallace. Many people couldn't get over how The Nation of Islam dignitaries came to Uganda on Dad's invitation during the OAU Summit when something like that had never been done before. However, Dad had an agenda to unite Black people in the United States of America and the OAU afforded an opportunity for him to implement that agenda.

Dad was obsessed with liberating African people everywhere from oppression. He never stopped asserting that African people everywhere needed to be liberated. For example, he continued to constantly rave about how "the Black people of America must be the President of the United States of America" and how they "must be the Secretary of State." It is a statement he repeated "on camera" in the 1974 French Documentary titled "General Idi Amin Dada: A Self Portrait."

Fond memories of the bald Black American cameraman

I still remember and have fond memories of the bald cameraman with the beautiful bride-to-be. They were part of Louis Farrakhan's entourage to the OAU Summit in Uganda in 1975.

That time, Dad lined us his children at Nile Mansions Hotel (Serena Hotel) and went through a formal introduction of all of us. The beautiful lady who had on the original Whoopi Goldberg beads 1970s style - way before Whoopi showed up on the radar screen in 1975, repeatedly asked with marked wonder:

"All your children?"

"Yes" responded Dad.

I was at the very end of the row and I could see the bald-headed husband-to-be grinning from ear to ear, right next to her. It is funny that I ended up with the very same Isaac Hayes close shave.

In 1989, while living in exile in Saudi Arabia, I asked Louis Farrakhan's Chief of Staff about this golden couple after running into Louis Farrakhan and his entourage in Saudi Arabia. Even Dad was surprised at how I could remember the event with The Nation of Islam dignitaries.

I told Dad that it was because of the groom's bald head - a style I wear today. They actually got married either in Uganda or Morocco. The two lovebirds actually traversed the country filming. I pray I can get footages of their travels, for they kept taking photos of the whole "brood" - priceless Colour Photos in 1975.

We got used to Technicolour way back, as per the coloured pictures Dad was fond of taking with his favourite Maroon Leather Embossed Aluminum Polaroid Camera.

By the time the satellite was up and running at Mpoma, Kololo, Soroti and Ombaci Relay Stations, Dad had brought in the earliest versions of Toshiba Colour Televisions. He had also brought in Sony Video Decks and the works, from Dubai.

Actually my paternal uncle Ramadhan Amin and his Pakistani associate Abdul Sattar were the pioneers of the Dubai route for Dad's Uganda Airlines plied the route. It still had the concession under the Monika QU (Uganda Airlines) with direct flights to Jeddah, Riyadh, Dubai, Abu Dhabi, Kuwait City, Karachi and other places and for the record Dad actually acquired the pioneer versions of Cellular Telephones, which prompted his number to be changed from 2241 to 20241.

Dad traversed the country with the colloquially called Simu Ya Upepu (air phone or what is termed wireless). He was fond of gadgets.

Dad's spear throwing jest with his Black American friends

The scene of the bald cameraman with the beautiful bride-to-be who was part of Louis Farrakhan's entourage asking Dad if we were all his kids was also the same scene where Dad playfully hurtled towards the cameraman with a spear and launched it at his feet in jest. I remember the day very well because the cameraman actually brought down his camera to nervously look at where the spear had landed.

That time, the whole 30 yard line up of children laughed with glee, knowing Dad was up to no good as usual but also show-bouting to his Black American friends and the OAU dignitaries. I was present that day and witnessed Dad's mischief as he show-bouted to his Black American friends and the OAU dignitaries and regularly reflected on what was going on in their minds as they interacted with Dad. That time, Dad also wanted to demonstrate Acholi dances, which he loved.

Dad's "spear throwing" jest and other interactions with dignitaries to the OAU Summit in Kampala that year were shown on colour televisions across the world. He realized that it was his chance to show-bout progress. This was the very time he got the Pioneer Cellular Telephone that was relayed to the earth station in Mpoma, Kololo and Ombaci and across the world, while the Nakasero and Soroti Relay Radio Stations relayed radio across the world. The Green Channel was the very first FM Radio Station.

Dad was great as a father. He was proud of us his children and he loved to show us off to dignitaries. He accepted, gathered and took care of all of us, including ones born out of wedlock like me.

I share details about Dad as a father in another project titled "My Father Idi Amin Was Daddy To Us: Jaffar Amin Speaks In Memoirs, Reflections And Spoken Words", along with the dynamics of growing up in a household with more than one mother.

Recollections by Mzee Kiiza, a childhood friend of Dad's

Mzee Kiiza was a classmate of Dad's from his days as a child at Arua Muslim School. An unacknowledged electrician, he had two encounters with Dad that he never forgot. At the time of the encounter he talks about below, he still hadn't forgotten the day in Dad's early life when Dad as an up and coming big man came to Kiiza's workshop with his gramophone so that Kiiza could repair it.

"When the repair was done, your Dad came in and picked up his gramophone and as he attempted to walk out, I asked for my money only to get an Nkonzi/Ngolo (knuckle rap) on my head", Kiiza recounted. Then he added, "I went crying to my Dad who wasn't able to do anything".

During the occasion Kiiza recounted below which happened after his OB (Old Boy) Dad was in power, Dad and Kiiza met when Kiiza was patiently waiting for a haircut.

"In walked Idi with his two favourite children Moses and Mwanga" Kiiza offered.

"Just as I wanted to sit in the Barber's Chair, your Dad said", "Kiiza let the children take a cut" before grumpily adding, "or do you want another Nkonzi hmm?"

"As Idi Amin walked out with your brothers Moses and Mwanga towards the SM Citroen Maserati he said, "By the way Mzee Kiiza, tomorrow let us meet at Kabibi's in Old Kampala and I will come with the money I owe you for the gramophone repair"".

Shocked that the Head of State remembered that old incident, the next day Mzee Kiiza was at the President's Flames House when the MS Citroen Maserati Sports Car took the corner into the residence. Then with relish Dad took out 100 thousand shillings and handed it to his OB (Old Boy) Kiiza. He also asked Kiiza to go to my uncle Diliga who would allocate for him a consignment of cement, which he used for his Construction Projects.

An inversion of roles: Caucasian men "carrying Dad"

Ugandans who were at hand at the time will never forget the day in 1975 during the Organization of African Unity (OAU) Summit when Dad orchestrated an "inversion of roles". That day, Bob Astles, Dad's friend and ex-Royal Engineer on which the fictional character Nicholas Garrigan in the hit movie "The Last King of Scotland" is loosely based and a couple of European businessmen living in Uganda at the time carried Dad to a Reception on a litter. One of the businessmen was a British named Robert Scanlon.

In this exercise, a Swede walked behind with a parasol, a long stick that he held over Dad's head, while Bob Astles walked alongside the group. What a spectacle it was! Caucasian men, carrying a Black African! A hilariously true inversion of roles!

The Caucasians in this jestful event were also laughing because they were not forced to carry Dad. They did it willingly.

Dad relishing the opportunity to showcase Uganda and a reflection

During the 1975 Organization of African Unity Summit in Kampala, Dad relished the opportunity to showcase Uganda as a very beautiful country. He gave dignitaries to the Summit a tour of Ugandan landmarks and interesting features, including a statue erected in his honour.

The statue was placed on the grounds of the Cape Town Villas Hotel. Like Saddam Hussein's statue during the Iraqi War, it was smashed to the ground after Dad's government was overthrown in 1979.

While the festivities of the Organization of African Unity (OAU) Summit were taking place in Kampala, Uganda, Yakubu Gowon, Head of State of Nigeria at the time got a call that Murtala Mohammed had taken over power in a Military Coup in Nigeria. Like Apollo Milton Obote before Dad, he too would be forced to live in exile.

Other dignitaries who attended the OAU Summit in Kampala that year included President Bokassa of the Central African Republic.

Dad's obsession with piling on the medals came after the visit by President Bokassa during the OAU Summit in 1975. That is when those funny round and flowerish medals from the Arab Islamic countries started appearing just below the neat row of British Accolades. He used to just have the Israeli Paratrooper Wings and a multi colour cloth parchment accolade. The "Arab Medals" first started "popping up" post the 1973 Arab - Israeli war.

The Arabs had seen Dad's commitment during the 1973 war between Israel and the Arab Islamic World. It was the very first time the Arabs united since the days of Salahudeen (Saladin).

Because of his unwavering support for the Arab people, the "Petrol Dollars" supported Dad's regime until his fall in 1979.

The participation of Uganda in the 1973 war against Israel when they suffered their only defeat against the combined Arab Islamic Nations brought Dad a lot of prestige and Honours from Arab countries.

The Medals started to pile up and the incessant Tours of the OIC (Organisation of Islamic Conference) countries rolled. Every reception was concluded with the award of the highest accolades, which Dad insisted on sticking onto his No.1 Military Dressage Coat.

The Nubi (Nubians) gave Dad the Pet name (Abu Jarara) meaning Father of Buttons in Kinubi, the language of the Nubi (Nubians).

The Western Media laughed at the spectacle but like the typical WWII "Red Poppy" day in England where Veterans proudly wear the "Red Poppy", Dad continued to wear his buttons given by Arab countries and he didn't care about being ridiculed. For he had an Islamic constituency he was well aware of and he cultivated the Network.

Today we Muslims stand at 1.5 Billion and we are expected to reach 2 Billion by 2020.

Dad was playing to a gallery and both sides knew the count, the casualties and the honors won or lost.

Dad's clarity at the 1975 OAU Summit and "walking the talk"

As Dad did in previous Organization of African Unity (OAU) Summits, he was very clear in articulating his messages relating to Africa and the Diasporas - True Independence for all "Peoples of Africa", self sufficiency, the need to come together and etc, etc. As the Chair that year, Dad was as bombastic as ever during the 1975 OAU Summit in Kampala and he "walked the talk!" It is worth mentioning that a number of significant events occurred in 1975 during his tenure as Chairman of the OAU, namely the successful Emancipation of five African countries.

During the year 1975, the African countries of Angola, Cape Verde, Comoros, Mozambique, Sao Tome and Principe gained "Independence" under Dad's Chairmanship, in fulfillment of his "Dream Speech" at the OAU Summit in May 1973 in Addis Ababa, Ethiopia. Seychelles, Djibouti and Zimbabwe followed suit in 1976, 1977 and 1980 respectively. Interestingly Namibia and South Africa were the only outstanding "Liberation Objectives" he did not achieve as he set out to do when he articulated a "Liberation Plan" during the articulate speech he gave at the OAU Summit held in Addis Ababa, Ethiopia in May 1973. However, I venture to say that his efforts contributed to Namibia gaining "Independence" in 1990 and Indigenous South Africans being freed from the shackles of Legalized Racism in 1994 at last!

Dad's audience with the Pope in Rome and his support for Christians

On September 11, 1975, Dad had an audience with the Pope in Rome. Many people mocked his visit to the Pope that year but he wanted to demonstrate his support for Christians.

Dad was very supportive of Christians and he had very close family members, friends and associates who were very committed Christians. As I shared previously, in 1972, Dad in his usual bombastic utterances wanted two of his sons to become Roman Catholic priests and they were already in Roman Catholic Seminary. If he hated and persecuted Christians as it has been falsely alleged, he would never have sent us to Christian Mission

Schools. Nevertheless, an Independent Truth and Reconciliation Commission is the place to arrive at the actual truth about persistent claims that Dad persecuted Christians in Uganda. It is also the place to arrive at the actual truth about the following assertion by an observer who obviously views Dad as a hero in the debate raging on about whether he was a hero or villain to the core:

"Idi Amin's detractors and "saboteurs" lied about him actively persecuting Christians in Uganda! It was the same relentless Propaganda that included so-called "facts" "crafted" to defame him and bring down his government!"

Addressing the UN, a "flamboyant defiance" and Resolution 3379

In November 1975 Dad travelled to New York to address the United Nations as Chairman of the OAU (Organization of African Unity) that year.

In a "flamboyant defiance and audacity" at the Airport in New York, Dad's favourite Dance Troupe "The Heart Beat of Afrika" danced for him! He had sent the Dance Troupe ahead of him so that they could dance for him, entertain and welcome him on American soil at the Airport, while "flaunting" the beauty and talent of Africa. This "flamboyant defiance and audacity" by Dad on American soil caused a lot of laughter, even though some people were annoyed by it.

Dad said it was his way of poking fun at the United States of America for the evils and "sins" of the African Slave Trade. He said he wanted to remind Americans that "Africans" are the brightest and most talented human beings on earth and they made and built the United States of America. So Americans better treat Black Americans better than they have been doing for centuries.

By the time Dad travelled to New York to address the United Nations in 1975, the once strong relationship he had with Israel had become irreparable. It had disintegrated beyond recognition.

As Chairman of the OAU (Organization of African Unity) in 1975, Dad addressed the United Nations in Luganda, one of many Ugandan languages he was very articulate and very eloquent in. On that occasion, he chose to defy United Nations rules respecting languages accepted as Official Languages at the United Nations and spoke in Luganda.

During Dad's speech at the United Nations in New York, he was very instrumental in passing UN Resolution 3379, equating Zionism with Racism and Apartheid.

The arising Resolution stood the Test of Time from 1975 to 1991 when George Bush Senior sought an Alliance to fight against Saddam Hussein. At the time of the passing of UN Resolution 3379, Africans came together as one to protect their "wayward" Chairman Dad.

Dad caused a murmur at the United Nations when he spoke in Luganda, a language he mastered while growing up among the Baganda people of Uganda. When he defiantly forced the Luganda language on the United Nations in New York in 1975 and gave an address in Luganda, he was very clear in articulating his points.

As Chairman of the Organization of African Unity that year, Dad felt it was necessary to clearly articulate his position at the United Nations in relation to UN Resolution 3379, without the constraints of language. He was always aware of his constituency.

He had already set up the International External Service of the Uganda Broadcasting Corporation and knew that the people that mattered were listening. Dad was speaking directly to his constituency and Luganda was actually the one language he spoke fluently. Even the Baganda were stupefied and elated to hear him speak their language on the world stage, for Swahili was the preeminent language - actually the only language with a translatable service at the United Nations.

Dad could also speak Swahili fluently but he chose to speak in Luganda. Many Baganda and other Ugandans cheered and laughed about Dad's "audacity" to force Luganda on the United Nations while other people were very annoyed by this form of "waywardness".

Younis Kinene, Uganda's Ambassador to the United Nations at the time had to be the "Impromptu Translator" for Luganda back to English. I can only imagine what must have gone through Younis Kinene's head as his "wayward" Head of State put him in the awkward position of "Impromptu Translator", with no warning whatsoever.

Dad was making a statement. He understood the significance of the occasion and he did not wish to be compromised. He understood that he represented Africa at that moment as the Chairman of the OAU and he was aware of the significance of the occasion and necessity for eloquent articulation.

Dad's humble upbringing and crowd pleasing style resonated with the teeming masses. This style stemmed from his gift of speech. He had the astonishing ability to lead a Nation due to his extraordinary fluency in at least a dozen Indigenous African languages. His memory for words, for people and places never ceased to amaze his former Kings African Rifles Commanding Officer Major Iain Grahame. He spoke directly to the people in a language they understood. The essence of good communication in today's ICT generation is the ability to get your message across. This factor is quite often ignored by his detractors, but it is the most indelible testament as to why he continues to resonate with the majority of the now revived underclass ("Common Man") under this structurally adjusted society in the 21st century.

I would venture to say that Dad did very well in attempting to communicate in English. I doubt that many people would perform so well if they were "dumped" in a hostile environment and expected to pick up and communicate in a language they had no interest in learning or mastering. I know they would sound just as "nonsensical" to Native Speakers. However, the irony of Dad's so-called "nonsensical" statements is that they came to pass with the appointments of Colin Powell and Condoleezza Rice as United States Secretaries of State and the election of Barack Obama as President of the United States of America.

I am particularly referring to "audacious" statements Dad made during the making of the 1974 French Documentary titled "General Idi Amin Dada: A Self Portrait." He had boldly stated:

"The Black people of America must be the President of the United States of America".

"They must be the Secretary of State."

A tussle between Dad's bodyguards and an Assassin in New York

At the United Nations in 1975, Dad articulated that Zionism was equal to Racism, in a 10-minute speech following a 90-minute speech by Younis Kinene, Uganda's Ambassador to the United Nations at the time.

Zacharia Fataki from Gulumbi, a descendant of the notorious Chief of Gulumbi was Dad's Bodyguard in 1975. He regularly recounted the story of a tussle with an assassin, who was armed and in a "no arms area". It was suspected that the assassin was attempting to assassinate Dad while on the trip to New York.

Idi Osman of the Lurunu Kakwa clan who was Uganda's Ambassador to the United States of America at the time can also provide detailed accounts.

Younis Kinene can provide further key accounts about the whole event including Dad's visit to New York, his speech to the United Nations and how Africans came together as one to protect their "wayward" Chairman Dad.

It was a strange solidarity indeed in light of the strong protest from the American Ambassador who was determined to put Dad in his place so to speak and in a bad light. Dad believed that the US Ambassador was very upset because Dad managed to convince all the African States, the Soviet Bloc and South American countries to vote for UN Resolution 3379.

Support and preparation for UN Resolution 3379

Preparation for UN Resolution 3379 began long before the Organization of African Unity (OAU) Summit in Uganda. There were a lot of determined stakeholders involved in its passing. Hence there was a lot of support for it.

By the time the OAU Summit in Uganda came around, Dad had been promoted to Field Marshall - one of the highest positions in the Military. In 1971, he had been denied the position of OAU Chairman because of the Military Coup against Apollo Milton Obote. However, by 1975, he had built enough clout to be recognized as a formidable force in the passing of UN Resolution 3379.

The Prime Minister of Great Britain at the time declared during a Commonwealth Conference in Kingston, Jamaica that Uganda could not hold the OAU Summit that year. However, what he did not realize was that the Arab Islamic Countries were determined to pass UN Resolution 3379 and it involved galvanizing the "Third World States" into a Bloc Vote and putting their money where their mouths were. This was the Era of the Petrol Dollar and Dad had become the de facto spokesperson. The Arab countries ensured that he was successful in facilitating the passing of UN Resolution 3379 because they wanted it passed.

Dad evidently responded to being the de facto spokesperson and the African countries closed ranks to give him the votes he needed along with a standing ovation in the World Assembly when he successfully passed UN Resolution 3379, equating Zionism with Racism. However, little did Dad know that this resounding success would precipitate the Hostage Saga popularly known as the "Entebbe Raid" that would occur in Uganda, nine months after the passing of UN Resolution 3379.

The Africans came together as one to protect their "wayward" Chairman and to demonstrate their support for the Organization of African Unity (OAU). It was a strange solidarity indeed in light of the strong protest from the American Ambassador who was determined to put Dad in his place and in bad light so to speak.

A reflection on Dad's medals and honours and his opposition to Israel

Like Kings African Rifles (KAR) of old, which he truly was, a misplaced sense of grandeur somehow got the better of Dad. For when he invited Bokassa in 1975 to come and lay the foundation stone for the Old Kampala Mosque and the University of Islam at Enjeva, he was still leaving the Number One dress bereft of the grandiose medals he piled up post 1975. He had also become an "outcast" amongst the "Western World" so his trips were limited to the OIC (Organisation of Islamic Conference) countries. At every stop, Dad was given medals and honors, which he piled onto his suit jacket. In fact he would affectionately ask Mrs. Emilio Mondo to do the needful and sew them on for him. She once told her beloved daughter Esther Mondo:

"You see all those medals? I painstakingly sewed them all - the lot of them".

Dad's opposition to the Jewish State of Israel that he was once very close to could not have been any clearer when he lobbied hard, for the passing of UN Resolution 3379. As I stated in a preceding section, he became the de facto spokesperson for the Palestinian People and he did manage to successfully facilitate the passing of UN Resolution 3379 equating Zionism with Racism. However, nothing prepared him for the Hostage Saga popularly known as the "Entebbe Raid" which would occur nine months after the successful passing of UN Resolution 3379 and forever seal his fate in the age-old tussle between Abraham's children Ishmael and Isaac.

As fate would have it, the Saga would play itself right in Uganda and cost the lives of innocent Ugandans unwittingly caught in the crossfire and "dragged" into the age-old war between two warring factions determined to fight to the death to claim supremacy, legitimacy and land! As I alluded to in a previous section, the lines had been drawn when Dad ended his relationship with Israel and took up with the Arabs and the Ummah (Community of Muslim Believers).

I often wonder how Grandma Aisha Chumaru Aate would have responded to Dad's "unexpected" 180-degree turn against Israel and direct opposition to the Jewish State if she had been alive. I also wonder if Dad remembered her words to him regarding the children of God as she referred to the people of Israel.

As outlined in previous sections, Grandma had warned, "Do not forsake the children of God my son, never forsake the children of God." As Dad went about arguing and lobbying hard for the passing of UN Resolution 3379 at the world's highest assembly, I wonder if Grandma's words had "flashed" through his mind, even for a split second.

Dad's opening of Uganda House in New York and a 10,000 dollar tip

While in New York, Dad opened and commissioned Uganda House, a monument attributed to him. He had financed and built the 13 storey building from scratch in the world's Number 1 Business District. He had also bought Prime Property around the world for Uganda and not for himself, including Prime Property in the United Kingdom, France and right next to the Vatican in Rome.

Upon Dad's return home from New York, he once told the family that the CIA had even the cleaning ladies as spies. He said he got fond of one Black American cleaning lady and gave her a very large tip. He had said to the lady, "I know you are suffering under the white man, but you have this. It will help you", while relishing the look of shock on the woman's face when he handed her 10,000 US dollars in cash!

The incident tickled Dad so much that he would laugh hard as he re-told the story numerous times – his teary earth-quaking and chesty laughs.

Dad never got tired of reminiscing about that Waldorf-Astoria Hotel incident. The next time I saw the very hotel located in Manhattan was in the movie Trading Places, starring Eddie Murphy.

What went through my mind when I watched Trading Places was the grandeur of the place! It was a "Rags to Riches Story" of a Black man who made good. The story was similar to Dad's story - a former Kasanvu (coerced labourer) rising to the position of President of Uganda. Dad loved watching Trading Places and "enjoyed" the reversal of fortunes in the movie.

Dad's "Economic War" and his encounter with a struggling Ugandan

As Dad reminisced about his successful trip to New York, Uganda's economy continued to deteriorate for ordinary Ugandans. During Dad's rule in Uganda, the economy deteriorated as a result of boycotts and economic sabotage by subversives. Issues that came up because of the economic sabotage and how they impacted ordinary Ugandans will be explored in subsequent parts of the series, Idi Amin: Hero or Villain? His Son Jaffar Amin and Other People Speak, along with other people's standpoints. However, following is an account relating to Dad's encounter with a "struggling" Ugandan.

Dad was out and about in the beige VW Registration Number UUU 017 when a motherly lady hailed the buggy and he stopped. She got in and asked to be dropped off at Kawempe Kiyindi Zone. On their way, she started to bitterly lament the effects of the "Economic War" on the citizens and concluded that Idi Amin Dada was a bad man.

Unbeknownst to her, she was lamenting directly to the very man incognito!

"There is no sugar, no salt and the basic minimum since the Indians left", lamented the motherly lady.

When they got to her homestead, her husband was at hand to welcome them in shock, knowing the famous UUU 017 buggy. He was surprised to see his wife come out of the famous buggy.

She thanked the driver profusely and took her groceries out of the front boot of the buggy.

Just as the mystery man drove off, the husband asked his wife, "Do you know the man who just dropped you off?"

"No but he is a very good man".

"That was the President of the country Idi Amin Dada."

"Mama Nyaboo nfudde!" the woman slumped to the ground in shock, lamenting of her impending death, in the Ganda language. She explained to her husband how she had lamented the state of affairs in the country not knowing she was talking to the very person she harangued. As a family they decided to vacate their house that very night and headed to their home village in Mubende.

Just as Dad got home, he called up Permanent Secretary Balinda to find out how he could help the lady acquire a business. Then a search party was sent to convey the good news only to find that the whole family had disappeared.

Dad insisted they be found and when the good news was explained to the neighbours, Dad's search party was able to locate the family.

To this day, the lady lives an affluent lifestyle but cannot for her life stop explaining the fear that went through her when she realized she had been insulting a whole President to his face.

I have been asked why Dad didn't identify himself to the woman and why he wasn't upset. I have also been asked if the "subversive elements" in the State Research Bureau who Dad said were "colluding" with the Ugandan exiles would have killed this lady and her family if they had been privy to this incident, to continue to "smear" his reputation and make it look like he ordered the deaths as he said. Here is what I have to say:

We are discussing the Platinum lining of how Dad ruled. He had a private side, which a lot of people saw. This private side should not be mixed with the propaganda efforts that truly buried his reputation. I noted that in the CTV interview I gave after the release of the hit movie "The Last King of Scotland". He had a simple way of dealing with his subjects.

Every Muslim who has been to Madrasa studies which starts at the age of 4 onwards will tell you of Khalifa Al Rashid who used to go around his Empire incognito and hear the problems of the masses, then come back and institute changes during the Caliphate of Baghdad.

People claim we do not have an ideology but we do - not Nubian but Islamic. "Lowu kana murran isma kalam" ("However bitter the words, listen to my words"), is a common saying in Islam.

We are sincere and sincerity is a virtue. That is what kept Dad in power, for even his very tribes mates, the Kakwas were plotting his downfall, based on the factor Nubian Kakwas and Baris said "Uwo agara weni?" ("In which school did he study?").

Dad once lamented that with the Embargo, the "Economic War" was a harder war to win than say the success of the 1972 "Mutukula Invasion".

Today the famous Registration Number UUU 017 has turned up in the hands of the brightest prospects in the Ugandan Music Industry. Maurice Kiirya is the proud owner of the Registration Number UUU 017 and wherever he goes with the famous buggy the old folks ask him where he got the Field Marshall's car from. They all seem to know it from memory and in a sense it shows that they were aware of his movements but no one tried to harm him except the Ugandan exiles and the "subversive elements" they "planted" inside Uganda.

Dad used to consistently say, "I do not need security, the citizens will protect me". He repeated this statement several times between 1971 and 1979, especially after the "Nsambia Grenade Attack". He believed in Patriotism for what it was worth.

Dad was a Nationalist at heart. He loved our culture, our traditions and the way we dress. He knew that true Independence is the act of releasing the country from the harness and shackles of colonialism and slavery. He was fully aware that given a chance, the Indigenous people can take up responsibility and full ownership of our country.

Dad gave his famous telephone line 2241- 20241 to everyone and actually, he had the Pioneer Cellular Telephone 20241 from Marubeni or some Japanese firm, which he drove around with in his Maserati. He was on tap to anyone who sought his help and was fond of turning up at village funeral vigils or parties, uninvited.

The man knew each and every nook and cranny of the country he ruled and traversed it without Escorts. He moved around in his Beetle VW car with Registration Number UUU 017. For long distance trips, he had the Bell Agusta Helicopter PAW 01 and 02 with which he moved around to distant places like Kigezi and Karamoja.

Dad would request all the doctors to assemble at a specific time, ask them to list their names at the door, find out their needs and respond immediately. Some doctors missed out on brand new cars because they thought the ubiquitous list was a "death list". Some still lament for they had written fictitious names and could not then come up and claim their prize.

Horrific murders occurring in rapid succession

In 1976, Dad was still full of Pan-African zeal, anti-colonialism and support for Arab People and the Ummah (Community of Muslim Believers) when a number of horrific murders occurred in Uganda in rapid succession. It was as if Satan had taken up residence in the country in order to unleash his demons in full force!

A very dark cloud had continued to hang over Uganda from previous years including the time in January 1970 when Dad's friend and colleague Brigadier General Pierino Yere Okoya and his wife were brutally murdered in cold blood!

Between 1969 and 1970, according to Dad, someone or a group of people "hatched" an insidious and evil plot to murder Okoya and his wife and then made it look like Dad committed the brutal murders. However, Dad was persistent in his pleas of innocence and completely exonerated and absolved of the two deaths.

At a Traditional "Reconciliation Ceremony" called up and organized by the father of Dad's friend, the late Brigadier General Okoya in 1985, Okoya's father invited all tribes from the West Nile region of Uganda, who together with the Acholis (Okoya's tribes mates) converged on a sacred Acholi riverside gathering. As part of the Traditional "Reconciliation Ceremony", a ram was slaughtered. Okoya's father then gracefully stood up and solemnly declared to the dignitaries that "Amin did not kill my son. The blame lies elsewhere"!

Similarly, in the 1990s, Tito Okello Lutwa, a Former President of Uganda and colleague of Dad's before the Military Coup in January 1971 that turned friends into enemies, exonerated and absolved Dad of the callous murder of Okoya and his wife. Upon returning from exile and without being prompted or any need to support a sworn enemy like Dad, Tito Okello Lutwa had boldly stated that he knew who killed Okoya and that it was not Dad after all. Furthermore, Dad was attending the funeral of my aunt Akisu in Arua the very same time Okoya and his wife were murdered. So, he was nowhere near the scene of the brutal murders.

However, the fact that Okoya's father pointed the fingers at "someone else" and a former colleague of Dad's - an "Insider" who despite becoming an avowed enemy after the 1971 Military Coup, exonerated and absolved him, is still completely ignored by a hostile media that continues to "lynch" Dad.

Dad had very strong alibis on the day Okoya and his wife were callously murdered but a "lynching" media continues to go along with "hidden agendas" perpetuated during his rule that were intended to make him look like the whimsical murderer he has been "painted" to date! This blatant disregard for truthful, responsible and ethical journalism aided the real culprits and perpetrators of the murders in Uganda to "walk" scot-free.

The need for an Independent Truth and Reconciliation Commission

It is not my place to investigate the so-called hundreds and thousands of murders Dad allegedly committed or ordered. However, if Ugandans and the rest of the world wish to uncover the actual truth relating to the callous murders that occurred in Uganda during Dad's rule, an Independent Truth and Reconciliation Commission is one of several avenues to pursue. For obvious reasons, I cannot be the one leading the creation and implementation of such an Independent Truth and Reconciliation Commission.

On the other hand, if Ugandans and the rest of the world wish to continue to be like the Proverbial Ostrich that has its head in the sand and let the real culprits "take their "secrets" to the grave", then let God be the Judge as Dad used to say. However, "burying heads in the sand" and neglecting to dig deeper than the simplistic manner, narrow and single mindedness that has characterized the telling of Dad's story to date, dishonours the memories of individuals who were callously murdered or "set up" to be murdered during Dad's rule in Uganda.

Letting the real culprits responsible for the so-called hundreds and thousands of murders that Dad allegedly committed or ordered "get away with murder" is the worst form of injustice to the victims and families that were bereaved during the murderous activities that went on in Uganda when Dad was President. For closure, the bereaved families deserve to know the whole truth about what actually happened to their loved ones and who actually murdered them in cold blood!

When we lived in Saudi Arabia, after a heated argument with Dad about false allegations contained in a Book, Newspaper or Magazine that I read to him and believed until he explained what really happened, Dad used to say, "God will be my Judge!" I used to challenge and argue with Dad a lot about allegations made about him, which I believed until I heard his painful explanations.

I realized then that I had misjudged him and gone along with everything and anything written about "defenseless" Dad, which is the view of most people who have ever read anything about him. It is exactly how the "lynching" media wanted it because Dad's form of "lynching" was done by making unsubstantiated allegations against him and putting them in print or film for "everyone" to blindly accept as truth. His form of "lynching" was intended for "anything" and "everything" written, said and depicted about him to be the "gospel truth" even if some of it was taken out of context and outright lies.

It was exactly how the real culprits wanted it because to succeed in their callous "schemes" to murder innocent people in Uganda, they needed all fingers to point at Dad. They needed all eyes to focus on Dad so that no one looked their way and discovered that they and not Dad were the ones murdering or ordering the murder of people in Uganda.

I have regularly said, "Everything goes with "defenseless" Idi Amin", for because of a powerful media that systematically "lynched" Dad, most of the world was "blindly" against him and didn't consider that something else could have been going on in Uganda. Dad didn't stand a chance at an objective evaluation of his rule in Uganda or a fair "trial" in a proper Court of Law for murders he allegedly committed or ordered.

He didn't have any equally powerful alternative media at his disposal, to counter the biased reporting that characterized the "telling" of his story or stories related to events that unfolded in Uganda during his rule. With the exception of authors like Iain Grahame his superior in the Kings African Rifles and his Biographer Judith Listowel who did everything in their power to stay factual, the "mainstream" media just went along with "lynching" Dad. It went along with orchestrating a "din" that made it impossible for "anyone" to defend him or tell his story from a different angle.

There are other authors and journalists who have been objective, fair, truthful, responsible and ethical in their writing and reporting on Dad but to date, they have been "crowded" out by the ones who "lynched" and continue to "lynch" him. Their articles and books are recommended readings for the section of the series titled "Other People Speak" and some will be made available through the series. As well, a number of films that tell Dad's story objectively, fairly, truthfully, responsibly and ethically are underway and they will also be recommended for the section of the series titled "Other People Speak".

Most of the world still believes that Dad committed or ordered the murders that were perpetrated by others in Uganda during his rule and he did realize that he was up against formidable "kangaroo courts" that had already found him guilty beyond so-called "reasonable doubt". So, all he could say was "God will be my Judge".

Unfortunately, the "findings" of these "kangaroo courts" persist to this day and no one has bothered to look at an alternative explanation for the senseless and insidious murders that occurred in Uganda during his rule or the motives behind the "kangaroo courts." Needless to say, "kangaroo courts" are unjust, unfair and they totally go against the legal principle relating to everyone being innocent until proven guilty beyond reasonable doubt! If everyone is entitled to that principle, why should Dad be the exception?

As I have intimated numerous times, Dad is the only person who has ever been judged and found guilty by an ill informed "public" and "jury" without the matter ever reaching a proper Courthouse. I am speaking about the "convoluted" writings and all resulting films "designed" and deliberately "crafted" to provide a lopsided picture of my father. I am referring to all the writings and films that have been presented as so-called "truth" and "facts" and used by a Court of Public Opinion to pronounce a guilty verdict on Dad without a "shred" of evidence or proof beyond reasonable doubt.

Dad's "lynching"

According to sources, after Dad was allegedly "hand picked" to re-place Apollo Milton Obote in the Military Coup that catapulted him to the position of President of Uganda on January 25, 1971, he was expected to go along with everything dictated to him by the alleged "meddlers" in Ugandan Politics. However, Dad was not stupid even though many of the people who allegedly "hand picked" him thought he was!

In their preoccupation to "lynch" Dad because he started doing as he pleased, many of the people who instituted some of the "lynching" didn't even realize that the callous culprits were hiding behind the "din" that resulted from their "lynching" of Dad, to murder people in Uganda. They didn't even realize that the real culprits were "piggy backing" on their "lynching" of Dad to commit the worst forms of atrocities in Uganda.

The relentless and "deafening" "din" that accompanied Dad's "lynching" gave the real culprits free reign to implement their callous "schemes" in Uganda. It was the "perfect" setting for them to murder people in Uganda or "set up" prominent Ugandans to be murdered without anyone "noticing" and exposing their evil "schemes".

According to Dad and others, some of the culprits responsible for "framing" him for the murders they themselves committed also went to the biased and hostile media with so-called "credible evidence" to "implicate" him. They said the culprits did this so that Dad's continuing "lynching" could be justified and attention could be taken away from their evil "schemes" and the fact that their so-called "credible evidence" would lead objective, attentive and "sharp" Investigators right back to them!

Objective, attentive and "sharp" Investigators would know that their so-called "credible evidence" was "tainted" and "corrupted" to the core but alas there didn't seem to be a single Investigator interested in giving Dad the benefit of a doubt and properly investigating false allegations made against him. It wouldn't have taken long for an intelligent Investigator to realize that claims made against Dad about murdering or ordering the murder of so-called hundreds and thousands of people in Uganda were outright lies!

As outlined in a previous section, the media "lynched" Dad the same way African slaves who dared to run away, defy or challenge "rules" imposed on them during the "African Slave Trade" were lynched.

Stop blaming Dad for "everything"!

To the individuals who continue to believe biased and false accounts about my father that are still "making the rounds" through articles, books, films and ignorant personal opinions, you are continuing to be like the Proverbial Ostrich that has its head in the sand. By continuing to bury your heads in the sand, you are letting the real culprits continue to "walk" scot-free or "take their "secrets" to the grave".

To the ones who continue to believe that Dad was "guilty as charged" and refuse to properly "dissect" so-called "credible and reliable evidence" "presented" against him, you are letting the actual perpetrators of the murders in Uganda make a mockery of legal systems instituted to protect human kind. By continuing to believe the "findings" of the "kanga-roo courts" that have persisted in their "judgment" and "pronouncement" of Dad as guilty despite a lot of new evidence exonerating and absolving him, you are allowing the real culprits to make a "laughing stock" out of the global community!

To the ones who are adamant and convinced that all allegations made against Dad that are in print or film are the "gospel truth", you need to know that something more insidious was going on in Uganda before he was President, during the time he was President and long after he was overthrown. By being so adamant about your opinions, you are dishonoring the memories of the people who were callously murdered by others during his rule in Uganda.

To all Ugandans and the rest of the global community, do your own independent research and make your own conclusions because even the "mindless" Proverbial Ostrich that has its head in the sand gets it out of the sand at some point!

Dad was not one to "bump people off in the dark", someone else did

For anyone who will be brave enough to open up a South African Style Independent Truth and Reconciliation Commission for Uganda, you need to know that Dad was not one to "bump people off in the dark" the way the people who murdered "countless" individuals in Uganda did. So, he was not the one who was "bumping people off "secretly"" or ordering people to be "bumped off "secretly"" during his rule in Uganda. As in the brutal murder of his friend Okoya and his wife in January 1970, the fingers point elsewhere!

Furthermore the murderous Maoist style Marxist tactics that were so rampant in Uganda during his rule were not his style at all!

He always adamantly refuted the American style (Nagasaki-Hiroshima) scorched earth policy of wiping out whole villages, which he considered as a Maoist style. So, other people who subscribe to the reprehensible style and tactics were responsible for the callousness that went on in Uganda during his rule.

Dad was as bombastic in private as he was in public and he did not mince his words!

If he had a "tiff" to settle with anyone, he confronted the person directly and didn't "sneak around in the dark" or "go behind their back" to "bump them off "secretly"" as the real culprits did in Uganda.

If Dad was angry or unhappy with you, you would be the first person to know it because he would speak to you immediately and directly, like the time he confronted Apollo Milton Obote after learning from his friend Okoya that Obote had allegedly secretly paid Okoya to kill him. He would be very loud and clear about it and want everyone to hear what he had to say. They would also know what he planned to do about it.

That time, Dad had put on his military shirt without his Major General applets, worn mufti weekend khaki shorts and walked into Obote's office bare footed and uninvited! Tension had thickened in the air as Dad solemnly declared, "Your Excellency, I have come to you, for you want me dead. Here shoot me" Dad had said placing an imposing handgun and his Major General applets as a sign of resignation on his Commander in Chief's Presidential desk top.

According to Dad, too shaken to respond and searching for words, the Father of the Nation had remained silent with bitter realization written all over his face.

"What is the meaning of this?" he had finally stammered, feeling the silent intimidation exuding from his Army Commander.

"They say you want me dead. Here I am. Shoot me", Dad who could have very easily turned the gun on Obote at that moment but chose not to out of loyalty and principle had replied.

Dad despised "secret schemes"

Dad despised "secret schemes" because he considered them cowardly.

He also considered "sneaking behind anyone's back" cowardly and detestable – very much in the mould of a common Kakwa tribal tradition to confront your enemies directly and allow them to defend themselves.

Dad would not "secretly" murder so-called hundreds and thousands of people in Uganda as has been alleged.

If Dad wanted a person dead, he would tell them directly and everyone would know about it but he would not stop the person from "running" for their life, provided the person was not a convicted prisoner, sentenced to die by hanging or firing squad.

He did not participate in the "secret schemes" instituted and implemented by the real culprits that "sneaked behind people's backs" and "secretly" murdered people in Uganda during his rule.

The fingers for the gruesome atrocities committed during Dad's rule in Uganda that continue to be unfairly blamed on him wholesale point elsewhere!

Dad would execute people "found guilty" in full public view

Dad was very much a product of colonialism with anti-insurgency training and action, like the time he was involved in hunting down the Mau Mau in Kenya, alongside his British Army Commanders. So if he suspected people of "plotting" to overthrow him, he was more likely to hunt them down and parade them before the public, as the colonial British soldiers did with members of the Mau Mau in Kenya. He would not "secretly" get rid of alleged so-called "coup plotters" as the perpetrators of the murders in Uganda did during his rule.

In terms of dealing with "treason" or anyone who was "plotting" to overthrow his government, Dad was more likely to utilize his ill conceived Military Tribunal to "judge" perpetrators and put ones who were "found guilty" on Firing Squad. He would let everyone know that he was executing a person or people "found guilty" of "treason" and even encourage the public to watch the execution.

Dad would execute people "found guilty" of "treason" in full public view, not "secretly" as the real culprits responsible for the so-called hundreds and thousands of murders that Dad allegedly committed or ordered did when they executed their innocent victims.

The public executions of people "found guilty" of "treason" would be very much in the mould of our Islamic public execution method and practice under Shari'a. Like the colonial British soldiers in Kenya in the 1950's who displayed captured members of the Mau Mau insurgency publicly as a deterrent, the public execution method used under Shari'a is also thought to act as a deterrent.

Shari'a is the body of Islamic religious law and legal framework within which the public and private aspects of life are regulated for those living in a legal system based on Islamic Principles of Jurisprudence. Even though Uganda was not an Islamic State, Dad adapted the "brutal" methods of Shari'a when he sanctioned the unnecessary and unacceptable Firing Squads that occurred during his rule.

Unlike the real culprits who committed the murders that occurred in Uganda during his rule, if Dad wanted to execute anyone on the grounds of "treason", he would not "secretly" "get rid" of them the way the real perpetrators of the murders that occurred in Uganda did. Dad would let "everyone" know about his intentions to execute anyone accused and "found guilty" of "treason" or "plotting" to overthrow his government.

It would be like the time in May and June 1975 when he sanctioned the arrest, trial by his ill conceived Military Tribunal and intended execution by Firing Squad of Denis Hills, a British Sociology Lecturer at Makerere University, Uganda. That time, Denis Hills was arrested, tried by the Military Tribunal Dad instituted during his rule and "found guilty" of "treason" for his book The White Pumpkin, which was critical of Dad and his regime. The initial Book Manuscript described Dad as a "pagan tyrant".

Unlike the Political Assassins and murderers who "sneaked around" "in the dark" to "lay traps" and callously murder innocent people in Uganda during his rule, Dad was very public about his plans to execute Denis Hills or others accused of "treason". This was his style and it was how Britain became involved and successfully pled for clemency on behalf of Denis Hills as I outlined in a previous section.

So the "sneaking around" and "secret" murders that occurred in Uganda during his rule were other people's work!

Contrary to popular belief, Dad was fair and forgiving

Contrary to popular belief, Dad was also fair and forgiving and he was not the whimsical murderer "painted" in biased articles, books and films. He gave people multiple chances to explain themselves and even let so-called enemies escape, like the time he allowed Jomo Kenyatta to escape as colonial British soldiers hunted him down and gave orders to shoot him on sight for allegedly instigating the Mau Mau insurgency.

That time, Dad was ordered by a superior to climb up a truck and inspect it to see if Jomo Kenyatta was on the truck. He did climb up the truck and actually came face to face with Kenyatta but in a tense moment, he told the British officer, "There is no one up here Affende", while looking into the eyes of the reputed son of Kabarega.

At that very lethal of moments, when the English Officer inquired about whether there was anybody hidden in the litter truck, Dad's spur of the moment response was disobedience.

"No sir, there is no one aboard", he repeated when the officer asked the question again.

Dad had said this while placing back the gunny bags protecting Kenyatta so that he could evade capture by the colonial soldiers.

When the White officer insisted that Kenyatta was on the truck, Dad dared him and said, "You come up and see for yourself"! "There is nobody up here."

"Okay" responded the British Captain.

Dad demonstrated the same fairness and forgiveness in 1971 when he assisted Apollo Milton Obote's father Opetu in Akokoro and looked after Mrs. Miria Kalule Obote and their children - accommodating them at the former International Hotel (now Sheraton Hotel Kampala) before facilitating their reunion with Obote in Dar es Salaam. This he did despite having become a staunch enemy of Obote and "putting a prize on his head" after the Military Coup. It was Obote he wanted captured not his father, Miria or their children. So, he spared no expense in assisting them and letting Miria and the children join Obote in Dar es Salaam, where Obote had taken Political Asylum.

I venture to say that, the callous murderers who "framed" Dad would not have been as fair and kind as Dad was!

According to Dad, in 1974, following a coup attempt by Charles Arube, Elly Aseni, and Isaac Lumago, three Battle Hardened Kakwa Christian Army Officers from his Kakwa tribe, he confronted all three Army Officers directly and demanded an explanation for their actions. Then he gave Elly Aseni the Ambassadorship of the USSR and Isaac Lumago the Ambassadorship of Lesotho at a future time. That time, Dad was sad to learn that following his confrontation with Charles Arube, Arube reportedly committed suicide by self-inflicting a gunshot wound after realizing the consequences of the mutiny and coup he and the other Senior Christian Army Officers from Dad's Kakwa tribe had instigated.

I am certain that the callous murderers who "framed" Dad would not have been as forgiving and fair as Dad was after the coup attempt by Charles Arube, Elly Aseni, and Isaac Lumago and they would not have rewarded Elly Aseni, and Isaac Lumago with Ambassadorial posts!

The Maoist style Marxist tactics was not the way Dad did things

The Maoist style Marxist tactics that involve political assassinations and the murder of key prominent officials and personnel was not the way Dad did things. This style and tactics characterized the callousness with which Dad's friend Okoya and his wife were murdered in January 1970 and the callousness with which people were murdered in Uganda during Dad's rule. So the fingers point elsewhere!

As was the case at the Traditional "Reconciliation Ceremony" organized by Okoya's father in 1985 during which he completely absolved Dad of the brutal murders of his son and daughter in law in 1970, the fingers relating to the brutal murders that occurred in Uganda during Dad's rule point elsewhere. That time, Okoya's father had gracefully stood up and solemnly declared to dignitaries who attended the Traditional "Reconciliation Ceremony" that "Amin did not kill my son. The blame lies elsewhere"!

There had been other politically motivated murders in Uganda before the brutal murders of Dad's friend Brigadier General Okoya and his wife in January 1970. However, the particular murders of Okoya and his wife which Dad was falsely accused of committing but completely exonerated and absolved of, would mark the beginning of a form of callousness in Uganda that seemed to take a turn for the worst in the year 1976.

Dad became the President of Uganda on January 25, 1971 - exactly one year to the time the new form of callousness began in Uganda in January 1970 when Okoya and his wife were brutally murdered. He was not the one who committed the murders but the callousness with which the murders were committed characterized the brutal murders that occurred in Uganda during his rule.

The same callousness continued and characterized murders that were committed in Uganda long after Dad was overthrown on April 11, 1979.

Questions to ask and issuing a challenge

If Dad was the one who "master-minded", murdered or ordered the murder of so-called hundreds and thousands of people in Uganda during his rule as widely alleged, why did the exact same callousness continue long after he was overthrown and no longer the President of Uganda?

Who were the real culprits of the callous murders perpetrated in Uganda during Dad's rule?

Are there "serial killers" still on the loose in Uganda "roaming about" the country "undetected" and free to systematically murder at will as they did during Dad's rule because Dad was wrongly "convicted" in their place?

If that is the case, should people in Uganda be very afraid of these "serial killers" as they continue their "insidious", systematic but now "more discreet" "killing sprees", decades after Dad's government was overthrown?

Should Ugandans be very concerned that the same "serial killers" continued and continue murdering people in Uganda using "more discreet" methods after their "scapegoat" Idi Amin was overthrown on April 11, 1979?

Should the "cold case files" on the unsolved "mass" murders and "disappearances" that occurred in Uganda during Dad's rule be reopened for proper investigation and resolution?

Don't we owe it to the memories of the murder victims to reopen the "cold case files" and definitively solve the "murder mysteries" that callously took their lives in Uganda during Dad's rule?

Don't we owe it to the bereaved families to reveal the actual truth relating to the brutal murders of their loved ones so that they can get some closure?

I am issuing a challenge to Ugandans and anyone who believes in true justice to advocate for the proper investigation of what really went on during Dad's rule in Uganda.

I am issuing a challenge to people interested in solving the "Jigsaw Puzzle" relating to the questions above and other related questions to open the "Pandora Box."

I also encourage other people to speak about the issue of Dad allegedly murdering or ordering the murder of so-called hundreds and thousands of people in Uganda during his rule.

To the media outlets, Journalists and Film Producers that went along with "lynching" Dad and continue to do so, do the right thing now!

Tell Dad's story objectively, fairly, truthfully, responsibly and ethically.

As I have regularly insisted, our father had his faults. I do not see the period of his rule in Uganda with "rose-tinted glasses". However, we need to counter balance history with all the truth!

I strongly believe that there are a lot of lessons to be learnt from my father's story. As a result, issues raised by the story should be studied, discussed and written about in more depth instead of "glossing over" them in the simplistic way the issues have been studied, discussed and written about to date.

I strongly believe that Dad's story needs to be told entirely, objectively, fairly, truthfully, responsibly and ethically in order to derive benefit from the story including preserving the lessons provided by the story for future generations. However, like I intimated before, it is not my place to investigate the so-called hundreds and thousands of murders Dad allegedly committed or ordered but bereaved families and Ugandans especially deserve to know all the truth!

Let us stop history from repeating itself in Uganda or anywhere else in the world for that matter!

Providing context to the horrific murders that occurred in 1976

Prior to 1976, a number of brutal murders had been committed in the very same Maoist style Marxist tactics that characterized the murder of Dad's friend Okoya and his wife. Dad was blamed for these murders but he was adamant that he didn't commit them.

The horrific deaths that occurred prior to 1976, which Dad denied perpetrating or ordering and the many others that occurred during his rule are best handled through an Independent Truth and Reconciliation Commission. However, I deem it necessary to reproduce and repeat information relating to a partial list of some of the murders allegedly committed or ordered by Dad below, for ease of reference and to provide context to the horrific murders that occurred in Uganda in rapid succession in 1976.

As outlined in previous sections:

After the coup that catapulted Dad to the position of President, his first Foreign Trips were to Britain and Israel. As he prepared to take these trips saboteurs began "hatching" and implementing insidious plans "crafted" to make him look like a whimsical murderer or someone who ordered brutal murders. While Dad travelled overseas, two Americans, Nicholas Stroh and Robert Siedle, one a Journalist the other a Makerere University Sociology Professor died mysteriously at Mbarara. Dad was accused of ordering their killings but he said he did not.

The deaths of the two Americans would be the beginning of false allegations levied against Dad that would be blindly accepted as truth without the allegations ever being brought before a Court of Law.

According to Dad, the Ugandan exiles operating within Uganda were responsible for the brutal murders of the two Americans Nicholas Stroh and Robert Siedle. Judge David Jeffreys Jones, a Welshman presided over the inquiry of the "disappearance" of the two Americans and according to him, "It is obvious that the Americans have died an unnatural death." These two tragic losses should be properly investigated through an Independent Truth and Reconciliation Commission.

In July 1971, there was an attack on the Jinja Barracks by Ugandan exiles intended on defeating and overthrowing Dad's regime. Some insurgents tried to attack and take over the barracks but they were repelled. Acting in self-defense Dad's soldiers repelled the attackers but this would also form the basis of unfounded allegations that Dad systematically targeted and killed innocent civilians.

On February 9, 1972, 15 "Ugandan Refugees" told journalists at Pangale Camp in Tanzania that Acholi and Lan'gi troops numbering 5,000 had been murdered since Dad took over. They detailed that there were 510 military detainees and a number of former General Service Unit men. They also alleged that Anyanya Squads composed of Kakwa and Sudanese tribesmen had executed many of the Luos.

These allegations led Lieutenant Colonel Hugh Rogers, Dad's old friend and colleague during the time they served together in the Kings African Rifles and anyone acquainted with the Uganda Army before Dad's coup to wonder about the figures. This they did after confirming that statistical records in the War Office showed only about 3,500 Lan'gi and Acholi had served in it. So it seemed that the 15 refugees were lying when they said that 5,000 Lan'gi and Acholi had been expelled from the Uganda Army and that they (the Refugees) were the only tribesmen surviving. To that day, a certain number of Acholi and Lan'gi were serving in the Uganda Army, as Rogers could see for himself, and he discounted the horror stories of the refugees as crude propaganda. The above stories would continue to form the basis of unfounded allegations that Dad systematically targeted and killed innocent civilians.

False allegations in the public arena such as what is contained in the paragraph below were the norm during Dad's rule in Uganda:

"In one incident, thirty-two officers were placed in a cell and blown up with dynamite. A survivor of one of Amin's prisons described how bullets were conserved and the nuisance of sharpening swords was avoided by strangling the prisoners and finishing them off with sledge hammers to the head. Amin's soldiers were sent to Akokoro, Milton Obote's native village, and killed everyone they could find. As many as 6,000 of the army's 9,000 officers were executed within The Butcher's first year of power".

It is interesting to note that some 5,000 soldiers whom the Uganda People's Congress Party mouth piece claimed to have been massacred in 1971 by Dad reappeared in 1979 as the Liberation Soldiers who overthrew Dad's rule in 1979. This occurred to the relief and consternation of their relatives who had feared they had all been massacred by Dad as falsely reported by a media that was "hell bent" on tarnishing Dad's reputation.

On September 17, 1972, Ugandan exiles invaded Uganda and they captured the towns of Kyotera, Kubuto and Kalisizo after crossing the border at Mutukula. According to Dad, on September 19, 1972, the invading troops were badly beaten back - suffering many casualties and injuries. Dad's soldiers acted in self-defense. However, their actions would also form the basis of unfounded allegations that Dad systematically targeted and killed innocent civilians.

According to reports, after defecting as Uganda's Foreign Minister during Dad's rule, Dad's brother-in-law Wanume Kibedi deliberately made false and exaggerated claims about murders committed during Dad's rule. He claimed that between 90,000 to 100,000 people had been killed in Uganda by September 1972 following the Tanzanian invasion of Uganda by the combined FRONASA (Front for National Salvation) and Kikosi Ma'lum (Special Forces) troops.

There have been allegations that Dad murdered my stepmother Mama Kay after suspecting that she had committed adultery. There have also been allegations that Dad murdered Mama Kay's brother Michael Ondoga earlier in the year 1974, after appointing him to the position of Minister of Foreign Affairs. However, Dad was completely absolved by Mama Kay's father Archdeacon Adroa and Elders from both sides of the family, of the accusations that were laid at his door in relation to the two deaths.

According to reports in the "public arena", Mama Kay's brother Michael Ondoga was a victim of the callous Ugandan exiles and their subversive elements operating within Uganda. They allegedly kidnapped and murdered prominent Ugandans and in some cases even foreigners, so that it looked like Dad's operatives committed the brutal murders. According to these reports, Michael Ondoga was kidnapped and murdered by the callous Ugandan exiles and their subversive elements operating within Uganda after the making of the 1974 French Documentary on Dad titled "General Idi Amin Dada: A Self Portrait". The cold blooded murder of Michael Ondoga is said to have been part of the continuing relentless and deliberate "schemes" by the Ugandan exiles, to "soil" Dad's reputation and make him look like a whimsical murderer.

During the making of the French Documentary, Dad allegedly rebuked Michael Ondoga while having a meeting with his Cabinet Ministers that was featured in the French Documentary. Sources suggest that the alleged very "public rebuke" of Michael Ondoga by Dad, gave the callous Ugandan exiles and their subversive elements operating within Uganda a "setting" to kidnap and murder him.

"It was a perfect setting for their twisted minds and evil schemes", some sources have asserted. However, as in many other cases, an Independent Truth and Reconciliation Commission is the place to arrive at the actual truth about events surrounding Michael Ondoga's unconscionable death.

With regards to Mama Kay's death, according to renowned Researcher Fred Guweddeko, at the time of her death, Dad had divorced her and she had moved on. Following the divorce, Mama Kay had an affair with a medical doctor named Mbalu Mukasa and got pregnant. In the meantime, Dad and Mama Kay made up and she became afraid of what he would do if the pregnancy came to light so she requested for an abortion. In an article by Fred Guweddeko, he writes:

"The doctor was hesitant because the pregnancy was at an advanced stage - seven months and three weeks. But Kay insisted.

She died from heavy bleeding during the abortion. The doctor panicked.

He figured that if he made her death look like a typical Amin handiwork, he could get the fingers to point in that direction.

So he cut off her limbs put her torso and severed limbs in the boot of his car and then tried to dispose off the body. After failing to do so, Mbalu tried to kill his family with a drug overdose and committed suicide" (Fred Guweddeko).

The following statement made by Kay's father Archdeacon Adroa at a gathering of representatives from my Dad's family and Kay's family corroborates Fred Guweddeko's account in relation to the doctor:

"Please do not add misfortune to another misfortune, I was at my daughter's in Kampala on the day she set off of her own accord with her doctor friend. I was in the house with her mother and Marta. Please desist from blaming my son in law or the Adibu. We are also related for Idi Amin married his cousin. Let us not add misfortune to the misfortune we have suffered" (Archdeacon Adroa, Kay's father).

In 1974, Dad's brother-in-law Wanume Kibedi deliberately started a false rumour that Dad sacrificed his sister Mama Mariam's son, my brother Moses Kenyi and ate him in a ritual to prolong his rule in Uganda.

This lie by Wanume Kibedi about his nephew, my brother Moses would persist and be used to give credence to lies that Dad was a cannibal. It would also contribute to the "slippery" path that led to Dad becoming one of the most reviled figures in history in the eyes of people who blindly went along with the biased accounts of a powerful media that began "lynching" Dad when he couldn't be "controlled".

My brother Moses grew up to be a 6'6" Nicolas Anelka lookalike but the damage had already been done. Not even his maternal uncle Wanume Kibedi would recant his deliberate "plot" to "soil" Dad's reputation. According to Dad and others, that is exactly how he and his fellow detractors and saboteurs wanted it.

My brother Moses was alive and well, yet even his own mother in exile believed the lies deliberately spread by her brother that her son had been sacrificed and eaten by his own father!

Dad's protests and our heated arguments in Saudi Arabia

As protested by Dad, the Maoist style Marxist tactics that involve political assassinations and the murder of key prominent officials and personnel was not the way he did things. However, he continued to be blamed for the murders that were obviously being committed by others who subscribe to the style and tactics which is unjust, unfair and totally goes against the legal principle relating to everyone being innocent until proven guilty beyond reasonable doubt!

During our heated arguments in Saudi Arabia, Dad stood and based his arguments on the grounds that, "they" fought him, he fought back, but he did not kill innocent people and he left all Judgment to Allah.

He always said that, "They took up arms to fight me using low level intensity warfare and Maoist style Marxist tactics that involved Political Assassinations of key prominent officials that were blamed on me but I did not commit the murders or order them".

I believed Dad's assertions relating to other people committing the so-called hundreds and thousands of murders that he allegedly committed or ordered in Uganda. I believed his assertions that other people were responsible for the "secrecy" and "sneaking around" that characterized the callous murders that were perpetuated during his rule in Uganda because he did not condone that style but I am not excusing him for the brutal murders!

He was the Head of State of Uganda at the time so he bore ultimate political responsibility by omission and in a way he gave the callous murderers the "brushes that were used to paint him" as a whimsical murderer. Dad lost total control of the State Research Bureau that he instituted and made it possible for thugs to infiltrate an institution that should have defended and protected the sanctity of life in Uganda.

Instead of defending and protecting human life, thugs and rogue officials within the State Research Bureau "colluded" with callous murderers and went along with "schemes" designed to kidnap and murder people in

Uganda at whim. These thugs would not have succeeded in their callous "plots" if Dad had done things differently.

Besides, the Rule of Law should have prevailed and not the ill-conceived Military Tribunal and Military run State Research Bureau and "Public Safety" Unit he instituted.

That being said, an Independent Truth and Reconciliation Commission is one of several avenues needed to get to the bottom of what actually happened in Uganda during Dad's rule, in additional to other avenues deemed appropriate under the circumstances. However, like I intimated before, I cannot be the one to lead the creation and implementation of such an Independent Truth and Reconciliation Commission.

I also cannot be the person to prompt and encourage the real culprits and individuals with information about the callous murders that occurred during Dad's rule in Uganda, to come forward instead of "taking "secrets" to the grave". However, I am aware that other people have been speaking out in Dad's defence and encourage a proper, honest and truthful debate about events that unfolded during his rule in Uganda, along with sharing factual information not the fiction that has "crippled" and "discouraged" proper discussion and learning, by design.

As I alluded to in a previous section, the irony is that the false claims about Dad murdering or ordering the murder of so-called hundreds and thousands of innocent people have since been disputed by reputable sources. However, these false figures continue to be presented as "facts". They continue to perpetuate the irreparable damage that led to Dad becoming one of the most reviled people in history but an Independent Truth and Reconciliation Commission is the place to arrive at the actual truth.

Many mistakes like the ones Dad made have been common throughout the African continent and other "Third World" countries that have suffered and continue to suffer from the ravages of colonialism. That is why I am looking to encourage younger generations of First Sons and First Daughters of African leaders and leaders of other "Third World" countries to correct the mistakes made by their parents who bore ultimate political responsibility for their countries, especially after "Independence" from colonial masters. I strongly believe that by working with communities and institutions in their respective countries, these First Sons and First Daughters can play an important role in facilitating learning from their parents' mistakes.

I also encourage oppressed peoples that are still "groaning" under the ravages of colonialism and the very same oppressions that "created" Dad to speak out and learn from the lessons offered by his life.

In addition, I encourage all Peoples of the World who are opposed to all forms of oppression to become allies in attaining justice for all!

Anarchy in "The Pearl of Africa" and Dad's lamentations

By 1976, Uganda once described by Winston Churchill as "The Pearl of Africa" had disintegrated into a form of anarchy its colonial masters the British would never have imagined when they handed over the Union Jack to Dad as a Senior Officer in 1962, on Uhuru Day (Independence Day).

Dad had continued to lament that he only ruled Uganda for one day because Ugandan exiles started subversive activities the very second day of his rule. He had continued to lament that innocent Ugandans died in the hands of the very same Ugandan exiles that provided information to a biased and hostile media that aided the exiles in falsely implicating him in the murders the very exiles committed or orchestrated. As outlined in previous sections, according to Dad, the subversive activities by the Ugandan exiles included the exiles operating within Uganda, kidnapping and murdering prominent Ugandans and in some cases even foreigners, so that it looked like his operatives were committing the brutal murders.

Dad was not a saint but many sources have corroborated his lamentations!

A couple of individuals who believe that Dad was a hero and not the villain others believe him to be have said:

"To continue to put all the blame on Idi Amin for so-called hundreds and thousands of murders he allegedly committed is to allow the actual culprits to continue to "walk" scot-free and carry on their evil "schemes". I agree with Jaffar Amin that it is unjust, unfair and it totally goes against the legal principle relating to everyone being innocent until proven guilty beyond reasonable doubt!"

"Allowing the actual perpetrators of the vicious crimes that occurred during Idi Amin's rule to "walk" scot-free is an injustice that must not be tolerated by the global community".

"Let us honour the memories of Ugandans and foreigners who were callously and brutally murdered during Idi Amin's rule to tarnish his reputation by "telling" and learning all the truth about what actually happened and if possible charge the perpetrators with criminal offenses including crimes against humanity!"

As outlined in a previous section, the form of callousness that characterized the murder of Dad's friend Okoya and his wife intensified during his Presidency and continued long after he was gone. Dad's government fell on April 11, 1979 but the callousness continued.

The form of callousness that characterized the brutal and systematic murder of Ugandans and foreigners alike in Uganda was the environment that existed in 1976 when a number of horrific murders occurred in Uganda in rapid succession.

As outlined in an earlier section, prior to 1976, a number of equally horrific murders had occurred in Uganda. However, 1976 seemed to usher in a renewed form of murderous Maoist style Marxist tactics that were despised by Dad and not his style at all!

Brutally murdering and "bumping people off in the dark" started to happen again in more earnest in 1976.

Dad did not practice these "stealthy", unfair, cowardly and insidious methods so there are other explanations, which anyone who doesn't wish to continue to bury their heads in the sand like the Proverbial Ostrich can research and investigate in more depth in order to uncover the actual truth.

Below is a partial list and sketchy outline of events that occurred in Uganda in 1976, including murders that were committed in rapid succession, beginning in early 1976.

All of these brutal murders were allegedly committed or ordered by "defenseless" Dad, the perpetual "scapegoat" used by the real killers to hide their murderous rampages and the brutal murders they committed in Uganda between January 1970 and April 11, 1979 when their "scapegoat" Dad was finally overthrown. However, Dad denied committing these murders.

The murderers had become more vicious in their "killing sprees" when they murdered Dad's friend and colleague Brigadier General Pierino Yere Okoya and his wife in cold-blood in January 1970 and "framed" Dad for the vicious murders, in an attempt to get rid of him. However, by 1976, the vicious killers had become more evil in their determination to get rid of Dad and the ways they murdered innocent people.

They continued to "frame" Dad for their callousness by "flaunting" their "tainted" and "corrupted" evidence against Dad, as the world stood by and supported them blindly.

They finally succeeded in getting rid of their "scapegoat" Dad nine years later on April 11, 1979 but why did they have to viciously and callously murder so many innocent people in the process?

Couldn't they have "crafted" a different way that didn't involve murder, since they were so "crafty"?

The callous murders of three people and demonstrations

On February 15, 1976 Esther Chesire, a Kenyan female student attending Makerere University, Kampala at the time was reported to have "disappeared". A relative of Kenya's former President Arap Moi, Esther Chesire was allegedly kidnapped and murdered by Dad's operatives.

On March 6, 1976, a Makerere University Law Student, Paul Sserwanga, a Muganda by tribe was allegedly killed on orders from Dad.

The murder of Paul Sserwanga had occurred less than a month after Esther Chesire's "disappearance" and it precipitated a string of Public Demonstrations by Makerere University students against Dad's government which led to a series of unpleasant events involving members of Dad's security forces and the students.

In response to the student demonstrations, Dad addressed the university community, expressed concern over the loss of life and promised to appoint a Commission of Inquiry, which he did.

This was not the first time Dad had addressed Makerere University students.

In happier times, he had addressed students and they had paid close attention to his speeches. However, like other Ugandans, many would be amused, chuckle and laugh as they listened to their "wayward" President make points especially as Chancellor of Makerere University. Others would mimic the way Dad talked to Ugandans in his state addresses and the way he walked. They would do this while laughing hard - away from prying eyes and attentive ears, for fear of being reported to members of the notorious State Research Bureau or its more evil, vicious, subversive and "colluding" "impersonators" as the truth has now come out!

From March to August 1976, Professor Bryan Langlands, an Englishman with 23 years on the Makerere teaching staff served as Chairman of the Commission of Inquiry into the Makerere "disturbances" as events related to the string of Public Demonstrations by Makerere University students against Dad's government became known. He was appointed by Dad first chairman of the Commission of Inquiry into the Makerere "disturbances" and he reported nearly twenty students missing but quickly added, "even this number may be too high" and that for reconstructions suggested there may have been no deaths at all.

There have been reports that as the inquiries into the Makerere "disturbances" progressed, Dad's operatives "manhandled" and subsequently murdered a Makerere University lady warden by the name Mrs. Theresa Nanziri Mukasa-Bukenya and her unborn baby, in the most brutal manner imaginable.

Dad denied involvement in the "disappearance" of Kenyan student Esther Cheshire and the brutal murders of Paul Sserwanga and Mrs. Theresa Nanziri Mukasa-Bukenya who was expecting a child at the time of her brutal murder by the "serial killers".

There have been many versions of the stories relating to the "disappearance" of Kenyan student Esther Chesire, the brutal murder of Paul Sserwanga, the student demonstrations and "standoffs" with Dad's security forces and the brutal murder of Mrs. Mukasa-Bukenya. However I can only say again that, the actual truth is best handled by an Independent Truth and Reconciliation Commission or Investigators interested in uncovering the actual truth about the sad events.

As I alluded to before, letting the real culprits responsible for the so-called hundreds and thousands of murders that Dad allegedly committed or ordered "get away with murder" is the worst form of injustice to the victims. For closure, the bereaved families deserve to know the whole truth about what actually happened to their loved ones and who actually murdered them in cold blood!

By coming forward, the real culprits and individuals with information about the "disappearance" of Esther Chesire and the callous murders of Paul Sserwanga and Mrs. Theresa Nanziri Mukasa-Bukenya will be honouring the memories of these three individuals. They will also be honouring the memories of others murdered in cold blood before, during and after Dad's rule in Uganda - not to mention clearing their consciences!

According to various reports in the "Public Domain", Mrs. Bukenya was the Warden of Africa Hall where Esther Chesire, the Kenyan student who "disappeared" resided and she was supposed to testify before the Commission of Inquiry into the Makerere "disturbances" the day after she was murdered. According to the reports, Mrs. Bukenya's killers kidnapped and murdered her and her unborn baby on June 23, 1976, the eve of the day she was to testify.

Allegations that Dad ordered Professor Langlands "deported"

There have also been reports that the very Professor Bryan Langlands, the Englishman whom Dad appointed to serve as Chairman of the Commission of Inquiry into the Makerere "disturbances" was "kidnapped" and threatened with murder by unidentified "killer squads". According to these reports, he was then given 48 hours to leave Uganda, which he reportedly did on July 29, 1976. The "killer squads" who "kidnapped" Professor Bryan Langlands are alleged to have been Dad's operatives but Dad denied any involvement in the alleged "kidnapping" and so-called 48 hour "Deportation Order".

I would not put it past the evil, vicious, subversive and "colluding" "impersonators" of members of the notorious State Research Bureau that Dad and others said infiltrated the State Research Bureau to "craft" the "scheme" relating to "kidnapping" and "ordering Professor Langlands deported". It makes no sense at all that Dad would appoint Professor Langlands and then order his kidnapping, murder and deportation by giving him 48 hours to leave Uganda!

Even though many people want to believe that Dad was stupid, he was not that stupid!

Theories about "impersonators" being responsible for murders

I would not put it past the evil, vicious, subversive and "colluding" "impersonators" of members of the notorious State Research Bureau that Dad and others said infiltrated the State Research Bureau, for being the ones that "crafted" the "disappearance" of Kenyan student Esther Chesire either. Furthermore, the atrocious and horrendous murders of Paul Sserwanga and Mrs. Theresa Nanziri Mukasa-Bukenya matched the murderous Maoist style Marxist tactics that Dad despised and attributed to others during his rule in Uganda.

False allegations that Dad massacred university students

In March and April 1976 and subsequent months, the news about the Makerere "disturbances" was widely reported in the International Newspapers. There were allegations that Dad's operatives massacred some students.

According to Dad and others, what happened in relation to the Makerere "disturbances" was that some students insulted the then Minister of Education Brigadier Barnabas Kili while others smashed Dad's portrait and the Vice Chancellor at the time failed to restore calm. So, the University Administration summoned the soldiers to restore calm. According to sources, the following day, everyone including the students and the professors turned up for exams but the BBC (British Broadcasting Corporation) reported 20, 80, 100, 200 students missing without giving who, if anyone was missing.

While the story of the Makerere "disturbances" was breaking, Ali Mazrui, Head of the Department of Political Science and Dean of the Faculty of Social Science at Makerere University who had been with his wife and children in Uganda for 10 years, was in Dar es Salaam with Obote. Ali Mazrui refuted reports by media outlets and wrote:

"A massacre in front of the main building of the only university of a country situated in its capital city, seemed unlikely to remain unnoticed to all but British observers. Even the Kenyan newspapers, next door to Uganda, seemed to be citing only British sources..." Ali Mazrui offered that there was indeed an invasion of the university by soldiers who seemed to have been invited by university authorities because of the student unrest. He confirmed that the soldiers did go out of hand – beating, kicking and injuring some students with rifle butts. However, no one was killed and no girls were raped or mutilated.

More reflections and other people speak

Various sources have corroborated lamentations Dad had about the state of anarchy in Uganda in 1976 including boldly intimating that:

"The Ugandan exiles and their subversive elements operating within Idi Amin's State Research Bureau kidnapped and murdered Kenyan student Esther Chesire and subsequently murdered Paul Sserwanga and Mrs. Theresa Nanziri Mukasa-Bukenya so that it looked like Idi Amin ordered the unthinkable and brutal murders but he didn't".

The sources further boldly intimate that:

"The exiles and their subversive elements operating within Idi Amin's State Research Bureau took advantage of the Makerere "disturbances" to intensify and advance their evil agendas until Idi Amin fell which is what they wanted all along."

I am hoping that Ugandans will advocate for and constitute a Truth and Reconciliation Commission and there will be many objective Investigators interested in uncovering the actual truth about events that unfolded in Uganda during Dad's rule. If that was to happen, the brutal and evil nature of the atrocities committed by others between January 1970 and April 11, 1979 will necessitate utmost sensitivity in bringing the truth to light, for the sake of the bereaved families!

The "disappearance" in Uganda of Kenyan Makerere University student Esther Cheshire and the murders of Paul Sserwanga and Mrs. Theresa Nanziri Mukasa-Bukenya were probably the beginning of Dad's slow but sure descent to total defeat!

According to him, the "conspiracies" and "plots" by Ugandan exiles, to "soil" his reputation, undertake subversive activities in Uganda and bring down his rule increased in intensity.

The chickens associated with Dad's opposition to Israel

As if the evil and unconscionable "disappearance" of Kenyan Makerere University student Esther Chesire and murders of Ugandans Paul Sserwanga and Mrs. Theresa Nanziri Mukasa-Bukenya were not enough, barely one week following the brutal murder of Mrs. Bukenya and her unborn baby on June 23, 1976, something unexpected happened. The chickens associated with Dad's opposition to the Jewish State of Israel came home to roost!

As outlined in a previous section, Dad's opposition to the Jewish State of Israel that he was once very close to could not have been any clearer when he lobbied hard, for the passing of UN Resolution 3379 at the United Nations in New York, on October 2, 1975. Speaking in his bombastic style, he had emphasized, "We have to ensure UN Resolution 3379 passes today! Tell me why Palestine cannot gain National Status. This is their land!"

Dad had become the de facto Spokesperson for the Palestinian People and he did manage to successfully facilitate the passing of UN Resolution 3379 equating Zionism with Racism. However, nothing prepared him for the Hostage Saga popularly known as the "Entebbe Raid" which would occur nine months after the successful passing of UN Resolution 3379 and forever seal his fate in the age-old tussle between Abraham's children Ishmael and Isaac.

The "Raid" on Entebbe by Israelis

On the night of July 3, 1976 and the early morning of July 4, 1976, there was a "Raid" on Entebbe by the Israeli Elite Special Forces. They "raided" Entebbe to rescue fellow Israelis taken hostage by the Popular Front for the Liberation of Palestine (PFLP) on Air France Flight 139 at Entebbe Airport in Uganda. While this "Raid" was taking place, Dad was in Mauritius handing over the OAU (Organization of African Unity) Chairmanship to that country's leader. He had held the Chairmanship of the OAU from 1975 when the summit was held in Kampala, Uganda.

Sometimes referred to as "Operation Thunderbolt", the "Raid" has been dramatised in films such as Victory at Entebbe (1976) directed by Marvin J. Chomsky and Raid On Entebbe (1977) directed by Irvin Kershner, among others. Books on the "Raid" include William Stevenson's Ninety Minutes at Entebbe and Yoni's Last Battle: The Rescue at Entebbe by Iddo Netanyahu.

Additional information will be provided as the series Idi Amin: Hero or Villain? His Son Jaffar Amin and Other People Speak unfolds. However, Dad told us that he was actually supposed to be hijacked in a daring mid air operation by the Israelis upon his intended return from Mauritius where he had gone to hand over the OAU (Organization of African Unity) Chairmanship. Upon being hijacked he was supposed to be escorted to Israel. However, Dad got wind of the event from General Lumago, a Kakwa who was Ambassador in Lesotho.

Apparently the Gulf Stream II (G II) that was given to him by the Saudi Royal Family in 1972 was ordered by him to take off almost vertically from Mauritius Airport at top speed, without leveling off then come down like a roller coaster ride to Entebbe Airport right away. This was to avoid Phantom Jets from either the Israeli or the American Aircraft Carriers. This is a highly technical outmaneuver few are familiar with but pilots do it to hasten flight time. Dad got home before the Israeli attack and he had already got to State House Entebbe when the attack started.

The likes of his pilots like Atiku, Abusala, Amunya and Kiiza of the Bunyoro Babito Royal Kingdom were Fighter Pilots trained in the USSR. When Pilots make scramble liftoffs from an airport being bombed or under attack, they normally do 60-45 degree liftoffs. They maintain that angle until they achieve maximum elevation (Altitude). Then they either level off or descend. Since the elevation between Seychelles and Uganda was sufficient to start descending towards Entebbe Airport, in effect it looked like a Roller Coaster ride – up, then down and landing.

A "Conversation" with Major General Isaac Lumago

In a series titled Serving Amin that was published and posted online in Uganda's Newspaper the Sunday Monitor on June 5, 2005, Isaac Lumago talked to Tabu Butagira about the senior positions he held in Dad's administration. In the Article captioned "Foreign commanders let down Amin, says Maj. Gen. Lumago", Isaac Lumago confirmed that he had warned the Uganda Army of the impending "raid" on Entebbe. According to Isaac Lumago, at the rank of Colonel, Dad appointed him Minister of Industry and Power in 1975. Following is what he had to say in connection with the "raid":

"After putting things in the ministry right within four months, I was appointed an ambassador to Lesotho but accredited to seven other countries in southern Africa. This was in 1976".

"It was while in Lesotho that I informed the Ugandan army that Israelis were coming to raid the Old Entebbe Airport to rescue passengers, most of whom were Israeli, taken hostage by Palestinians aboard an Air France Boeing aircraft from Paris to Tel Aviv".

"I had undertaken extensive and high profile intelligence training with the Mossad in Israel, CIA in America and the KGB in Russia. This is how I got the confidential information before hand that the Israelis were coming to raid Entebbe Airport to rescue their hostages".

In the Interview with Tabu Butagira, Isaac Lumago shared that army officials did not heed his warning about the impending "raid" by the Israeli Elite Special Forces.

"This was not our war. It was a fight between the Palestinians and the Israelis. As far as I was concerned, there was no need for our soldiers to get involved in it", offered Isaac Lumago. He clarified that he did not call to inform the Uganda Army so that they could fight the Israelis but he called them so that they could relocate the hostages away from the airport and prevent it from being destroyed.

Being "taunted" at Kabale Preparatory School after the "Raid"

I was at Kabale Preparatory School in Kigezi District when the "Raid" occurred. Just as I came out of the outdoor bog house, Ian Bitwire, brother to Wilber Bitwire rushed up to me and asked me "What is your father's name?" I answered Idi Amin. "Another?" he prompted, I said Dada. "What else?" I said those are his names. Then Ian Bitwire started listing the titles "DSO, blah, blah, blah". Those are not names I blurted.

He started laughing while uttering "Bure Kazzi" ("Useless") then he pulled out the Newspaper footage showing a row of burnt Mig 21s and made the historical pronouncement of the Zionist "Operation Thunder" to me. Shocked and dreading the implications while a group gathered, ironically one Andrew Bemba the son of a Sergeant in the Uganda Army (UA) attending a Posh School no less...who had lost 20 soldiers during the "Raid", asked, "Was he killed?" With great anticipation from the assembled crowd, Ian answered "No", setting off regrets from the lot of them. "Aaaaaaaaaaaaaaaaah eeehyeeee!" they lamented in Bantu Fashion, about the fact that Dad hadn't been killed in the "Raid". They did this with regret.

That is when I released a weary smile and left them discussing the issue. Hahahahaha, hmmmmmmmmmmmm! I still laugh and muse in my head about Dad's ability to evade capture or murder.

Dad's 180-degree turn against Israel and our Jewish siblings

I have often been asked for an opinion about Dad's 180-degree turn against Israel after being a loyal friend, strong supporter and ally for years and fathering twins with an Israeli Mossad Agent and following are some thoughts and reflections I have shared. I encourage readers to read thoughts and reflections by other people that will be included as background information for the section of the series titled "Other People Speak". However, as I explained in a previous section, Dad felt that since our Kakwa tribe was a tiny fraction of approximately 150,000 strong in a population of over 14 million at the time, it made political sense to cultivate additional constituencies within the Ummah (Community of Muslim Believers).

In his opinion, there was no better way to pursue this agenda than to demonstrate unwavering and total support for Arab People who form the bulk of the Ummah. However, it was always interesting to watch the dynamics in my multi-religious family as members emphasized strong family ties over religious ties. This happens within the entire Kakwa tribe where numerous families are also multi-religious and they do not manifest the least bit of conflict because they belong to different religions – some even convert back and forth and partake in each other's celebrations. As an example, Grandma Aisha adored the people of Israel. She called them God's chosen people and her point of reference was the Bible because like Grandpa, Grandma was also a Christian before she converted to Islam and some ideas never leave your mindset.

Regarding Dad's strong relationship with Israel before his 180-degree turn, we actually have Jewish twin brothers born in 1971. If anything I believe Dad secretly lamented the split between himself and the Israelis because he had some lifelong friendships with individual Israelis but I guess the pursuit of a strong relationship with the Ummah precluded "double dealing" for Dad.

Dad always talked about how a lone Israeli Paratrooper skydived with a wreath with smoke trailing behind and laid it on Grandma's grave the time she died in 1969. This was when the relationship between Dad and the Israelis was still good - a most poignant salute by Colonel Balev to his friend Idi Amin's mother. It is ironic that Dad and Balev would "meet" again as antagonists and not friends under a brink man ship scenario during the Hostage Taking and "Raid" on Entebbe in 1976.

I have often reflected on my Jewish twin brothers fathered by Dad and sometimes wonder where they are. Then I guess that they are probably soldiers of some sort. Successful soldiers no less, since the mother is related to Moshe Dayan no less, and having a father like Idi Amin no less!

Whether people like it or not, Dad was an exemplary soldier – the best!

My siblings and I would definitely be open to the idea of trying to locate and meet our Jewish twin brothers by an Israeli mother as Dad used to show us letters our Jewish brothers wrote him every birthday from 1972, a year after they were born in 1971. The letters were accompanied with cherub twins smiling to the camera. Their mother dutifully sent these pictures to the twins' father my Dad.

The last word about our Jewish brothers came in 2008 from an Israeli expatriate who claimed that one of the twins joined his mother's profession as a Major in the Israeli Secret Service Mossad while his twin brother is also a Major in the Israeli Air Force. I have always fantasized about inviting my Jewish brothers to Uganda. It would be touching to invite them to Mount Liru, "the true place where the Jewish Prophet Moshe disappeared".

I have regularly reflected on my Jewish Siblings as well as my other siblings whom I have never met. I have dubbed these siblings "Falasha Twins" and "the Lost Boyz" respectively. Poignantly Annual

Birthday celebration photos and letters kept streaming from the "Falasha Twins'" mother. However, they were sorrowfully first confined to Bomb and Poison Squad Letter Experts in the State Research Bureau, awaiting the all clear before they were sent to Dad's Permanent Secretary Balinda at the President's Office between 1971 and 1978 and the fall of their father from grace in 1979.

According to Shaban Abdul Tem, pictures and photographs in time of caramel coloured smiling twins facing the camera at various stages of growth were regularly sent to Dad between 1973 and 1978. God bless Nnalongo (mother of twins) for she kept sending the pictures and the children's letters to "Big Daddy" as Dad is often referred to by the time they were old enough to scratch out a few sentences to a father they would never know. Interestingly and simultaneously in Posh Schools strewn across the country, siblings of the twins I affectionately call Mikhael Adule Amin and Jibril Dombu Amin, went through the age long ritual of also writing letters to parents. They conveyed their thoughts and personal interests and usual childish requests. The Posh Schools strewn across the country that my siblings and I attended included such schools as Gayaza Primary School, Budo Primary School, St Mary's Namagunga Primary School, Namilyango Primary School and Kabale Preparatory School where I attended.

Hankering for the past after one of the lengthy revelations that characterized my conversations with Dad at our Al-Safa residence in Saudi Arabia in the 1980s, I once asked Dad where he thought my Jewish siblings were and he unexpectedly gave me a resounding rebuke. I liken his response to that of Muhammad Ali's response to the schism (parting of ways) between the Late Elijah Muhammed and the Late Malik El Shabaz (Shabab People's King) a.k.a. Malcolm X.

I was reliably informed in 2008 that one of my Jewish siblings followed his mother's profession into the secret services Mossad while the other followed his father's love affair with Aeronautics into the Israeli Air Force. They were apparently both at the rank of Major no less. Although the existence of these siblings is not common knowledge, Dad was fond of reminiscing about them to family members at both our former Makarona residence in Jeddah and at the Al-Safa residence in Jeddah near `Souk Suriyah. That is where I got the gist to adlib into English the events as they unfolded.

Dad even told the tale to Israel's bitter enemies the Palestinians who were very close to the family in the nineteen eighties, at the height of the events surrounding Sharon's desecration of Lebanon and the horrific events at Shabra and Shatila refugee camps. Nevertheless they considered the fact that Dad was able to conceive with that "Proud Jewish Race" as Philosophical and Poetic Justice since they felt Dad was being used and manipulated in the past but he was the one who had the last laugh. I never liked to look at it from that politicized angle but felt a need at family level to get in touch with these Semitic siblings of mine and maybe introduce them to our highly misunderstood Nilo Hamitic (Plains Nilotic) Heritage.

Gathering my siblings and a prayer for a Jewish-Muslim Peace Pact

I have taken up the task of gathering my siblings - the lost tribe of the Adibu Likamero Kakwa clan. Our oldest sibling Baba born in 1948, lives in Vancouver, Canada. A Somali brother born in Balet'uen in 1950 and a Somali Sister in Hargesia the same year are somewhere. Our lost Kikuyu Elders Njoroge and Njuguna born in 1951 and big brother Kazimoto born in 1952 all need to come into the Al-Amin family fold as Temezi (Elders) in order to complement the Official Heir and First Son Taban Idoru Amin who was born in 1958. Our brother Kazimoto prefers to live in Torit. We are truly a multinational family.

I ask my siblings wherever they might be to take time off and get in touch or pay a visit to their Paternal Homeland West Nile "The Heart Beat of Africa." They will be warmly welcomed and at the age of +38 years they are old enough to decide.

Whatever the misunderstanding between these two Nations in the past, I strongly believe that my grandmother's dying wish should be fulfilled through my Jewish twin brothers - the two Angels I have named Mikhael Adule Amin and Jibril Dombu Amin. This should happen as a fulfillment of a 21st century Jewish-Muslim Peace Pact between the children of Ishak and Ishmael (Isaac and Ismail) at a spiritual level. Let us keep Armageddon at bay a little longer I pray Insha Allah (God Willing).

How Dad became entangled in the "Entebbe Raid"

Dad felt the occasion was his chance to gain the spotlight on the world stage as a peacemaker. Alas! The world saw him as someone perilously pandering to the whims of terrorists! He lost 27 soldiers including the seven hostage takers.

Regarding the question who was responsible for "painting" Dad as someone perilously pandering to the whims of terrorists and what the

reason/motivation was behind the "painting", the 1974 French Documentary on Dad titled, "General Idi Amin Dada: A Self Portrait" brought out a lot
of issues. The Documentary was meant to explain Dad's views to the
world. However, what comes across very strongly is his strong Anti-Zionist
stance.

It is evident that the makers of the 1974 French Documentary
turned the Documentary into an Anti-Zionist film instead of what Dad
thought it was going to be – a broader explanation of his views to the world!

Thus the dye had been cast prophetically with hostages taking over
an Airline he had jokingly suggested on silver screen during the making of
the Documentary two years earlier in 1974!

An assassination attempt on Dad's life

Soon after the "Entebbe Raid", there was an assassination attempt
on Dad. We were actually at Entebbe State House when it happened.

Dad had converted the old colonial clay Tennis Court into a dusty
Basketball Court where we played.

When Dad came with the Newspaper showing the injured and dying
Musa his Half-Caste driver, we were very saddened and scared. Following
the Grenade Incident (assassination attempt on Dad's life), he shifted the
Basketball Court from the Tennis Court to a secure area near the old
swimming pool, since the court is right next to the road leading to Nsamizi.

On the fateful day in 1976 when someone attacked Dad's Jeep Re-
negate, he was about to enter the co-driver's seat when he instinctively told
the late Musa that he would drive after they pass out of the new Police
Recruits. That change in sitting arrangement saved Dad's life but Marhum
(Late) Musa died that day.

I remember Dad talking of how the unclipped shrapnel grenade
landed with a thump on his back before it lobbed to the side exploding and
fatally injuring Musa his Half-Caste driver. According to Dad, apparently the
one who hurled the deadly weapon had not waited long enough, having
unhinged the lever before they lobbed the grenade. Dad survived that
incident and drove the Jeep with deflated back tires on the metal rims all the
way from Mukwano Road, Nsambia to Mulago, wobbling all the way to
safety.

Like many Kakwa and Nubians, Dad was fatalistic. He had a strong
belief in Al-Qadar-Predestination. Some mystical beliefs based on the
"Yakanye Order" that my Grandma was Priestess for still did and do persist.

The "Order" believed that someone could not be killed by the gun once they had been cleansed with the "Yakanye Water". Dad even stood in front of his troops after the Nsambia grenade assassination attempt in 1976 and mystically announced, "No bullet can harm me. You can bring a full magazine and empty it in my chest and nothing will harm me." Following an injury he sustained in the Kenyan Jungles during the Mau Mau war, my mystical Grandma Aate had told Dad that he would not be harmed by bullets and he believed it.

A more organized effort to overthrow Dad's government

In 1976, a conference of Ugandan exiles in East and Central Africa was convened in the Zambian capital Lusaka. The meeting set up the Uganda National Movement (UNM) and elected John Barigye, the eldest son of the Muga'be of Ankole as chairman and Yoweri Museveni as Minister of Defence, based in Tanzania.

Later, Edward Rugumayo, the Minister who defected from Dad's cabinet in 1973, succeeded John Barigye as the leader of UNM (Uganda National Movement). New branches of UNM later opened in Nairobi and more Ugandan exiles joined.

Meanwhile hostilities had continued in the Sudan against Nimeiry of the Sudan. In July 1976, an abortive coup took place against Nimeiry, which would continue to sow the seeds of instability in the Sudan.

Life at Kabale Preparatory School

While living life as the President's children my brothers and I enjoyed studying at the best Elite Boarding Schools in Uganda. We would always reminisce about our life at Kabale Preparatory School especially our encounters with Miss Hayward.

I vividly remember the occasion when Miss Hayward the School Matron came and said, "Remo, come quickly. Your father has come for a visit. He is supposed to open Mr. Betwire's Mansion just across the Rugarama Hill and next to the Golf Course in Kabale. Hurry up and get dressed".

That time, I did a crazy thing. I started to open the bottom of my trouser for it was what the rest of the kids would tease me about as "Katema mbide" rising well above my ankles. It made me look pretty funny for downstairs, we were always stuck out in Startrite shoes.

With my flat feet and Daffy duck gait I was always laughed at. So I felt that if I could cover my feet I would look better.

Miss Hayward came back for me as the rest were already in the car. "Remo where are you?"

Her eye went straight for the deed I had done.

"You stupid child why?"

I thought you would iron it, I said.

"I will not, you stupid little child. You will go to your father looking like that."

It was too short. No, it wasn't. It was fine, I dialogued in my head.

Miss Hayward gave me her usual smack on the nape, which always stung but was not as brutal as in sounded.

"Go on off. You go."

She managed to come out smiling with this sulky Remo and I dived in the back of the 450 SEL.

The driver Kapere or someone asked in Kiswahili, "We na chelewa wapi?" "His Excellency na ngoja sisi." He was scolding me for being late and making Dad wait.

My younger brothers gave me the knowing look as if to say "Absent-minded Tshombe as usual!"

We got there just in time for Dad to come back from the occasion at the Betwires.

There was the Proverbial Bull waiting for the First Family, for even on the long helicopter trips, he always timed the flight to get us in time for lunch at White Horse Inn, Kabale before we were taken by the hotel vehicles back to Kabale Preparatory School. Sumptuous it was. Then Dad got some cameraman who had acquired the latest I think AGFA prints from Dubai/Abu Dhabi, to take a picture of the "Famous Five" - the ones the sooth-sayers/Elders from Dad's Adibu Likamero Kakwa clan had predicted about, while Grandma Aate smiled joyfully. The sooth-sayers/Elders from Dad's Adibu Likamero Kakwa clan had predicted the arrival of five sons for Dad in succession, beginning with me!

The White Horse Inn, Kabale, was formerly owned by the Ismailia Asians (the Somani Brothers) that Dad expelled out of Uganda in 1972.

So we continued to study at the Elite Boarding School – the best in the country, from the time in 1974 when Mama Kay sent my siblings and I to study in Kigezi District. Mama Kay was close to the missionaries and she valued good education and Dad was not against Christian Missionary Schools for he understood how because of past stringent rules amongst

Muslims, their children like him missed out on education after the 4th Grade or Primary 4 level.

Singing a "Gospel Song" for Dad

Dad once asked us to sing him a song so we lined up in front of him and belted out a Gospel Song. After we finished the song, he sat there stone-faced and the whole lot of us looked at each other expecting the usual clapping one gets at school only for him to lament:

"Muna yimba nyimbo la wa Kafir" ("You are singing the songs of unbelievers").

We all looked down in shame following the rebuke.

"Apana mbaya, he muzuri" ("This is not bad, it is good"), Dad tried to cheer us up with his favourite jest about his Christian family members.

"Wa kina Baba Siri'ba wana yimba kama nyinye" ("Those of Baba Siri'ba sing like you boys") Dad offered, referring to his Christian uncle Siri'ba and other Christian family members he held in high regard and had very close relationships with.

"Tuku Te Te Te Tendereza Yesuuuuuu", Dad imitated his Born Again Christian uncles and other Born Again Christian family members praising Jesus (Yesu) in a Luganda song sung by many Born Again Christians in Uganda, before finishing it with a volcanic shoulder-shaking laugh.

Luganda is the language of the Baganda tribe of Uganda and Dad and many of his family members spoke it fluently from living in Buganda.

My stepmother Mama Madina who was also Muslim born and bred had commented, "Ndiyo (Yes). They are singing Christian songs".

Following the rebuke by Dad for singing a Gospel Song, he got onto his "Air Phone" and called Mzee (Elder) Barnabas Kili, the Minister of Education and asked:

"Where can I get a Muslim teacher within Kabale? I do not want you to transfer someone. Get me a Primary School Teacher who is a Muslim and can teach my children Garaya (Qur'anic Studies/Readings) within Kabale Preparatory School. I do not want them teaching my children Sunday school. They will find time to practice our religion, do you hear me?"

Brigadier Barnabas Kili the Minister of Education found a Kiga by the name Zakaria. Unfortunately he would later claim in the book by Cameron titled, "The Rise and Fall of Idi Amin" that he was forced to come and teach the Idi Amin children against his will. Regardless of his future claims, Zakaria was a very good Geography teacher and even impressed the British missionaries who thought this was a ploy of Idi Amin's to introduce Islam to Kabale Preparatory School through the back door. However, the only children who were Muslims at the school were us, the children of Mzee Yusuf Odeke the CO (Commanding Officer) of Simba Battalion, an Acholi, Conrad Nkutu, who was known as Abdul Nkutu son of Shaban Nkutu and Minister Marjan's son who became a Medical Doctor. He arrived at the school in 1979 and was actually left there when Dad evacuated us during his impending fall in 1979.

The first thing we said when Dad sent a Platoon to rescue us during the war that led to his ouster was that we had left Yusuf Odeke's son Saidi Odeke and Marjan's 6 year old son behind. Dad was shocked but by the grace of God the missionaries looked after the boy and he went on to become a doctor. Every time I meet Marjan Jr. I repeat his favourite childish song "Kunene kookoo nene". He would also repeat that to the amusement of all.

Saidi Odeke was my classmate and managed to be vacated to the Congo after Dad's fall where he eventually linked up with his family.

In 2008 I was surprised to see a gentleman called Yusuf Odeke in the Kony Peace Talks (The Peace Talks between the Lord's Resistance Army and the Government of Uganda) contingent that came to Arua. I almost felt or sensed that it might be Saidi, for his father died in exile and I have always asked after Saidi Odeke. They were Acholi Muslims and his father was one of Dad's strongest Commanding Officers who was respected by all and sundry.

Being bullied and bonding with Miss Hayward and the workers

While we were studying in Boarding School at Kabale Preparatory School in Kigezi District, Uganda, my siblings and I were bullied and tormented because we were Dad's children. It was a terrible experience but I never once snitched to Dad about being bullied but waded into battle with boys much older than myself instead.

Kabale Preparatory School was run by Protestant Missionaries from England. The likes of Sulieman Geriga, Muhammad Luyimbazi, Mariam Aaliyah (Aliya), Maimuna Moding Adili, Issa Aliga, Adam Ma'dira, Mau Muzzamil, Abd'Nasr Mwanga, Moses Kenyi and Asha Aate Mbabazi Al-Amin later joined the original five at Kabale Preparatory School between

1974 and 1979. The original five included Lumumba Juruga, Sophia Sukeji, Machomingi Khamis and me Tshombe Remo.

I must say I gained the most educational experience that far at that particular institution while still in my motherland, Uganda and on hindsight, it seems my deceptively gangly height confused a lot of people right from the word go in 1974 while I attended Primary 2.

At that tender age, I was even given the derogatory nickname Alfonse by one effeminate fellow by the name of Ian Musoke. He considered himself God's gift to all and sundry and he continued to whip me with a stick for no particular reason on my first day at school, other than for hating Nodolos (Northerners) as he was fond of calling us. Ian was quite different from his older sibling Jonathan (Jonti) Musoke who got along with everybody.

Sadly Alfonse stuck as a nickname, only to be replaced with the derogatory name Duma, an over-age character in one of the school textbooks. I also got into a lot of fights with older boys mistakenly hell bent on giving punishment to "Big Daddy's" (Dad's) children in the aftermath of the September 1972 invasion mounted by Ugandan exiles in Tanzania.

Unfortunately, I also got the tag name "Bully" as a result of these persistent scraps. However, somehow whenever the matter got to Miss Hayward the School Matron, I would explain the incident and disturbingly it always revolved around an affront, abuse, malicious joke - call it what you may, leveled against Dad, our ethnicity, tribe or religious sect. I have always been a no holds barred kind of guy and never held back but I would wade into battle with boys much older than myself.

For whatever reasons known only to her, Miss Hayward somehow believed me and she could see the tree from the woods so to speak. She became my Ad-hoc Foster Mother between the ages of seven and twelve. So much so that I became her favoured child. This led my colleagues to ominously warn me, "When you leave for Secondary School you will not have a Miss Hayward to defend and protect you".

I was attracted to grandmother types because of my strong connection to Grandma Aisha Aate. Miss Hayward sensed the attraction and realized I was the picky type who chose friends carefully.

I also tended to hang around Mr. Wilson, the Head Cook at Kabale Preparatory School in the kitchen or with the Kiga maids when they were doing the laundry – just like I did while at State House Entebbe.

Hanging out at Odhiambo's office at State House Entebbe

At State House Entebbe, I would hang out at Odhiambo's office. He was the Chief Stockman at State house. He was like a Quartermaster General in the Military. I would sit for hours in his office quietly asking for an apple and he would say they were finished.

I would say I saw them in the fridge when Onyango went to bring out the leg of goat from the freezer. Then he would say, "I am writing a report. If you keep quiet until I finish, I will get you one." Odhiambo was very kind and when he finished writing the report, he would indeed get me an apple.

Dad was not a cannibal

Many people have persisted in their lies, false allegations and unsubstantiated malicious reports that Dad was a cannibal but nothing could be further from the truth. The fridges at Dad's various residences were always open to everyone and the cooks would have been the first people to discover any human remains and pieces allegedly eaten by Dad. We, Dad's children as well as his wives, girlfriends and all the workers at State House would have discovered these so-called human pieces Dad allegedly ate because we could go anywhere we wanted at all of Dad's residences. There were no restrictions whatsoever on where we could or could not go.

According to an interview reportedly given by one of Dad's cooks Mr. Otonde Odera, he was quoted to have said:

"Take it from me that Amin was never a cannibal. I took care of his kitchen and refrigerator for years. There was nothing strange…."

Our dog Kadogo

Right outside Odhiambo's door, across the paved patio overlooking the Children's Wing was where Kadogo as we chose to call it was caged. On one of Dad's visits to Ethiopia, he was given a tiny Chihuahua, which was fond of attacking us we thought whenever we scrambled to the State House garage area.

Odhiambo later told me, "Kina taka ku cheza nanche, wona mikiya yake kina dingika" ("It only wants to play with you. See how its tail wags").

"Hiyo ni alama ya umbia kama kime furayi" he added referring to the fact that a dog acts that way when it is happy.

I eventually took courage, faced the little dog with its pop-eyes and gradually stopped fearing the little monster. I got the rest to lose that fear as well until our little brother Mwanga became a great fun of the little Chihuahua.

One time, instead of heading toward a small gate into the garden to release itself, Kadogo went the other way into the grand dining room and let rip with some unspeakable bog on the expensive red carpet.

Mwanga spied it and let out an alarm, "Kadogo kime kunai kwa carpeti!" ("Kadogo has excreted on the carpet!")

Onyunde one of the workers at State House Entebbe was able to clean up the mess. Then we all started up a song led by Ruba son of Ali Lopuli Amin that was popular at the time but we changed the lyrics to:

"Kadogo ali fanya, ali fanya? ali fanya vitendetooo kwa carpti, kadogo ali fanya, ali fanya? ali fanya vitendooo kwa kapeti."

The song related to Kadogo letting rip with the unspeakable bog on the expensive red carpet and it became his best friend Mwanga Amin's song for he would repeat it over and over again every time he saw the tiny Chihuahua.

Spending time at the Strike Force Presidential Guards' offices

Other times I would head for the Strike Force Presidential Guards' offices, which were next to the former Governor's offices on the second floor with a conduit that took one past the Children's Wing and they would find me seated behind the Governor's Chair, my father's at the time.

"We na fanya nini hapa, baba asha amuka?" ("What are you doing here, is your Dad awake?")

Sijuyi (I don't know).

"Usi aribu kitu chyochyote huna sikiya, ndiyo", a Guard would instruct me about not wrecking anything while I explored my father's office in my typical inquisitive character.

I loved looking at ancient pictures of the Original State House, which was built with a complex thatched roofing style prevalent in the British Indo China region - with a vast verandah. There was a second picture showing the present State House right up to 1979 with its distinct Edwardian Style architecture. It had the very same vast verandah where cocktails used to take place and was now the very same place where we had our breakfast, lunch and supper from, but in the evenings we would spend time chasing bats, which hung amongst the pillared rafters.

From the manicured gardens and the verandah, we would haul dark mud and pebbles at the bats, causing untold vexation with the cleaners. We got a resounding warning from Mama Madina once, not to ruin the beauty of the place or we would be sent to live in the haunted Entebbe Lodge. This would usually quickly quieten us.

Grandpa's home at Entebbe Lodge

Entebbe Lodge was known to be haunted, for like a scene from "Daktari", the whole building was full of Hunting Trophies at every turn. It was the scariest place to my mind as a child. At every turn, you would meet the three feet high stump of an elephant leg, a wall covered with a Zebra skin, Buffalo heads mounted on the wall, bush back in the next, Impala on the next and all sorts of spears. Rungus and the like crisscrossed each wall in a professionally done way but the fear and rumor amongst mystical Africans was that the place was haunted.

If I could, I would buy that mansion and restore it to its former glory and make it an ornamental hotel for it has the best view of the Lake and the zoo just below. Dad's Amphicar was always packed in the vast garage at the back, which came out toward the original Parliament and Protectorate Administrative Building just across the road heading down to the zoo.

Moreover, it was where Grandpa lived with Abuba (Grandma) Amori and our cheeky baby aunt Ajonye whom I was fond of slapping which would bring Grandpa out with his shiny sheathed walking sword. He would pull it out with flare and faint as though he was going to run it through me and then laugh a cough retching laugh.

One could see the affection in this British Aristocratic looking man and I only wish we had insisted on living with him before his demise in 1976. One wonders what stories he would have told us, peppered with his favourite swearing expression "You Fuckin You - hehehehe" - a true Kings African Rifles soldier!

I will never forget the time in 1973 when Entebbe Lodge was the scene of the second largest gathering of the Idi Amin family. It was when all the mothers were requested to bring their brood to see Mama Madina in 1973 when she brought Baby Mwanga to be blessed by Grandpa Amin Dada Nyabira.

That day, we set off with Mama Kay and her whole bunch of rascals who had just arrived from Mbarara and she kindly went about introducing the whole lot, only to find the flat footed floogy had set off on his usual village romps. They found me at Major Dumba's Lodging behind the main house and I was quickly passed through the kitchen wing, past the amazing stuffed animals on the wall into the grand living room with rows and rows of French windows and miles and miles of chairs.

"There you are Tshombe" Mama Kay had said with relish. "Come and greet your mother."

I thought she meant my real mother only to see rows and rows of beautiful women who had their eyes fixed on me in my brand new purple corduroys which squeaked as I waddled to the nearest lady they had pointed at. They all seemed to be carrying babies while Mama Kay was highly expectant with my brother Mao Ari'dhi.

There was Mama Nora with Fatuma in her arms. I greeted her in the Nubian way, which seemed to amuse the whole lot, for I was taught by Grandma Aate to do that. Mama Kay implied the reason I greeted so respectfully. Then I moved onto Mama Madina who had baby Mwanga in her arms. Then suddenly the sniggering got louder for I was finally directed towards Mama Mariam who was also carrying baby Halima in her arms. All along she had been eyeing me in a fascinated manner rather than hostility and I innocently placed her hand on my forehead, the Nubian way then kissed it, which seemed to please her. I was then directed to our Arua contingent where my elder cousin Atiki who had looked after us during and after the Military take over by Dad in 1971 resided.

There was a long contingent of a Nubian dressed lot who had noted the respectful manner in which I greeted elders and not the haughty out-stretched arms way typical of First Sons and First Daughters. All of Dad's sisters had come, namely Awa Deiyah, Awa Senya, Awa Daa and Awa Rafah. Grandpa's wife Amori and Grandpa himself was there.

In a sense it was also my first formal introduction to Dad's family, which occurred during the formal introduction of Mwanga Alemi Abdul Nasser Amin born to Dad's fourth official wife Madina Amin.

During the blessing ceremony for my brother Mwanga, I struck a jovial rapport with my sister Bebi Anite with whom I would run the length and breadth from her mother Mama Mariam's Executive Room to the Children's Wing and back again. The room was next to the Pantry and Kitchen Wing. At one point she passed through the door on her way back to her mother and as I set off after her I bumped into a girl with the same height and simply embraced her saying got you, only to get a resounding slap.

I shut my eyes asking, Why do you slap me? only to get another resounding slap. I let rip with one of my own only to focus on the person in front of me and realized it was someone else.

Sorry I thought you were Bebi.

My older sister Maimuna Adili only let off that uniquely African swear-expression done by pulling in air between closed lips. "Squeak", I heard.

Somehow Lake Victoria Primary School always lagged behind in letting children off before the end of third term or so it seemed. So, the very next morning, the whole house was a hive of activity with children preparing to head for school. This had happened while the Nakasero Lodge, Kampala contingent were on some kind of holiday treat.

Hanging out with the workers at State House

At State House, I was also fond of and would hang out with the "Signalers" like Michael, Tom Bayiga, Mzee Kivumbi and the rest. Sometimes you would find me with Mzee Zziwa the Chief Chauffeur with his list of drivers like Alioni, Kapere and Nda. Other times, I would be with the Technicians like Richard who were always busy installing or assembling American Communication.

Sometimes Zeeglar would turn up while I was there and I later realized that he was the very person who was sent to us in Kabale so that he could test Communication Equipment Dad had just acquired from the Americans. That time, Dad had asked that my brother Lumumba be brought to the White Horse Inn in Kabale where the Communication Equipment was located and I tagged along. During the testing of the Equipment, Zeeglar gave Dad and us the derogatory call signs "SNOWFLAKES 1" (Dad), "SNOWFLAKES 2" (Lumumba) and "SNOWFLAKES 3" (me).

During Zeeglar's visits to State House Entebbe, he even brought in Zodiac inflatable boats, which the Technicians took hours on end inflating. They usually had problems placing the plywood compacted floor panels together.

I would spend hours hanging out and wondering around State House only to be pulled away by Onyunde who would say, "Master Tshombe, your brothers are finishing the food. You are always late."

Sometimes I would ask him to bring my food over or I would go and eat with them in the kitchen.

They would whisper, "Captain Mateos would not be amused to find Master Tshombe eating with the workers in the kitchen."

I would tell them:

But even Dad eats with you in the kitchen sometimes.

Then they would nod in consent.

Most of the workers were Jaluos from Barack Obama's homeland in Nyanza Land and they had been working at State House since the days of the Governors of the Protectorate.

"Whuyu mtoto iko na kichawa cha waze" ("This child has the head of the elders"), they would say. So it was like this at Kabale Preparatory School.

Hanging out with the diggers and a chase by the Reverend's dog

I would follow the Bakiga diggers to the slopes of Kabale Preparatory School for the school had a sizable chunk of land surrounding the school and we were situated right next to the residence of the Reverend of Kigezi. He was the head of the soon to be one hundred year old Church in 1977 which was built in 1877 and he had a fierce dog that looked like a cross between a hyena, a greyhound and an African wild dog. Paulo his son was fond of letting the fierce dog chase the school kids especially we Muslims, for we left our Juz Aa'mah recitals and prayers after 5:30pm and we would spend hour on end before supper wondering around.

We found what we called Hyena scavenging for bones one evening near Mzee Wilson's kitchen and the whole of the Idi Amin brood and Saidi gave chase. We started from the main house past P4, P3, P2, P1, Miss Read the Headmistress' office past P6 and P7 - right across the net ball ground and towards the green hedge of the Reverend's house.

Then suddenly, Paulo came out and in perfect Swahili he menacingly asked the whole lot, "Muna sumbuwa Simba kwanini?" ("Why are you bothering Simba?") "Eehe?" He asked us twice and Simba sort of turned around with a similar menacing look. Then Paulo said "Simba, kamata hawo!" ("Simba, catch them!").

My brothers scrambled as Simba gave chase with its swift greyhound prance. Each of us started diverting at stages. Some went down towards the Warren Dormitories. Moses rushed into Miss Read the Headmistress' office in alarm. Then I realized that I was the only one coming down the runway towards the main house with Simba snapping at my feet, only for Paulo to give a command from a distance.

I had some two metres distance from Simba when it turned behind on the passage by P3 and the guava tree and headed round towards P5 and the big girls' dormitories right round, coming out near Miss Read's office and back towards the net ball grounds.

All I remember was Mr. Wilson the Head Cook coming out with concern and asking, "What is wrong?"

I kept muttering and saying, Hyena! Hyena! – hehehehe, I still laugh every time I remember our mischief. That incident taught me a lesson!

A lot of things went through my mind when Miss Hayward, being a qualified Matron, gave us a lengthy lecture about the effects of rabies.

"Do not play around with stray dogs even if that is the Reverend's dog. Some of them do not treat their guard dogs. What will your father say if he heard you were bitten by that fierce dog, hmm?"

Wading into battle with hordes of bullies

I never once snitched to Dad about the unbearable insults and punishments we received on a daily basis. I stubbornly fought my silent battles against hordes of students who felt they were doing their part in the relentless fight against Dad's regime by tormenting innocent children!

It was more often than not that deep in the night I would be traumatized by the late Wilber Bitwire, a pure Mukiga and son to Dad's supposed friend with a thump from a loaded and hardened pillow!

From those I thought of as friends, images in time are of terrifying shadows sneaking out of the dormitory - "Kuyekera" guerrilla warfare indeed. Wilber only stopped this torment when ironically my father was invited to come and open his father's hilltop mansion just across the valley from Rugarama hill where the Missionary School was located as I recounted in a section above.

From the time of the visit, the whole of Kabale identified his father with my father's regime so he became conscious of attacking us.

Britain's formal break in relationships with Uganda, cynics speak

On July 28, 1976 Britain formally broke off Diplomatic Relations with Uganda. The straw that broke the camel's back and the reason why Britain said "Enough…we are out of here" was because of Dad's close association with Russia. Dad associating with Communist Russia was a "waywardness" Britain simply couldn't tolerate!

Dad had also started to target British Nationals whom he felt were in Uganda as spies in earnest and he had "taken off his gloves" so to say. So on July 28, 1976, Britain formally broke off Diplomatic Relations with Uganda.

Dad had continued to "behave badly" towards Britain and its citizens. He had continued to seize opportunities to "taunt" Uganda's former colonial masters, to the horror of everyone who feared more reprisals against him and Uganda. However, British citizens had continued to reside in Uganda.

Britain however, continued to support Dad in various ways including maintaining and "allowing" a shuttle that used to transport "goods" between Britain and Uganda to fly back and forth. The "goods" transported between Britain and Uganda included Whisky for Dad's Army. It was as if they "turned the other way" as Dad continued his "waywardness!"

According to reports, Britain's attitude to "turn the other way" where Dad was concerned persisted even after they broke off Diplomatic Relations with Uganda. Uganda's former colonial masters continued to "allow" the shuttle that transported "goods" including "Hard Liquor" between Britain and Uganda to fly back and forth.

It will be interesting to read and hear what other people have to say about that because some cynics have suggested that:

"Britain needed to keep Idi Amin's soldiers in a drunken stupor so that they could continue to control them from a distance!"

However, the formal end of Dad's relationship with Britain was like a "nasty," "nasty" divorce on both sides. It was the same thing with the Israelis in 1972!

After Dad's friendships ended with Israel and Britain, relationships with both countries became very tumultuous to say the least.

Many cynics suggest that Dad was the darling of the colonial rulers until he showed that he really preferred to be independent.

Others have suggested that the Brits and Israelis acted like a divorced spouse who does not accept that a relationship has ended, but so did Dad, for he still looked up and expected acceptance from especially Britain. This had happened even after Dad took up with the Arab and Islamic World.

"Was it the Israelis or the British or the Americans that "hand picked" Idi Amin to replace Apollo Milton Obote or all of them equally?"

quizzed a cynic who was adamant and very bold about allegations that Britain, Israel and America "hand picked Dad" and thought he was stupid!

Dad himself confirmed that he was indeed "hand picked" and supported by all three parties because they thought he was stupid and could be controlled.

"It was hard to discern who was more angry at the "divorces" and responsible for the "slander" against Idi Amin that precipitated his fall!" offered another cynic.

"Until the fall out, the British, Israelis and Americans were Idi Amin's mentors and he was their "darling'. Then he turned his back on them!" a third cynic suggested.

According to many cynics, it was like the saying "hell has no fury like a woman scorned". They were referring to Dad scorning the British, Israelis and Americans – the people that allegedly "hand picked" him but I will let "Other People Speak" about the "bold" allegations.

Other cynics have suggested that as a very angry jilted spouse would do, Israel, Britain and America, the parties that allegedly "hand picked" Dad began "fabricating" "things" to get back at him but I will let "Other People Speak" about that as well!

"The systematic "slandering" had begun many years back and a hostile media had jumped on the "bandwagon" but it intensified in 1976," insisted another cynic.

"Idi Amin's saboteurs and the subversive elements allegedly operating inside and outside Uganda definitely had "a feast" as they capitalized on the "Slander" that ensued from the angry "jilted lovers" after Idi Amin's "divorces" with Israel, Britain and America, the parties that allegedly "hand picked" him", offered another cynic.

"The saboteurs and subversive elements had Idi Amin exactly where they wanted him and the "world" couldn't have made it any easier for their evil and sick minds to continue murdering Ugandans and even foreigners at will!" volunteered another cynic.

The media accused Dad of a lot of different things when all he was doing was pursuing his agenda for Pan-Africanism, anti-colonialism and support for Arab People and the Ummah (Community of Muslim Believers).

According to Dad, before he stopped listening to the British, they had high regard for him as indicated in the following statements:

"British officers described him as "...a splendid (rugby) player with nothing but bone from the neck up, and needs things explained in words of one letter." Sadly, the Brits would go on to say of Idi: "He's a splendid and reliable soldier and a cheerful and energetic man, an incredible person who certainly isn't mad - very shrewd and cunning.""

According to Dad, the change came about when he went against Israel and the West. Then the name calling, character assassinations and false accusations started to rear their heads.

A plane crash with British guests and a search and rescue by Dad

On January 29, 1977, a Ugandan Twin Otter aircraft with 18 people on board, including Judith Listowel Dad's Biographer and 14 other British guests of Dad's crashed in bad weather in Southern Sudan.

On January 31, 1977, the crashed plane was located and its occupants were unharmed and flown back to Kampala. Despite the broken relationship between Dad and Britain, he personally led the successful search to locate the crashed plane carrying his Biographer Judith Listowel and 14 other British guests and in turn got a rare thank you from Britain.

The relationship between Dad and Britain had continued to deteriorate as he continued his "waywardness". Dad continued to "behave badly" towards Britain and its citizens, seizing any opportunity to "taunt" Uganda's former colonial masters.

However, as indicated in a preceding section, despite Dad's continuing "bad behaviour" towards Britain and the broken Diplomatic Relationship with Uganda, Uganda's former colonial masters continued to support him in various ways. This included maintaining and "allowing" the shuttle that transported "goods" including "Hard Liquor" for Dad's Army, between Britain and Uganda to fly back and forth. As well, "die hard" British citizens like Bob Astles, Dad's friend on whom the fictional character Nicholas Garrigan in the fictional hit movie "The Last King of Scotland" is loosely based and others continued to reside in Uganda.

Dad's great taste and love for everything British

Dad had great taste and love for expensive clothes, shoes, cars and everything British. He loved to dress well and made sure his children dressed well too. He was particular about his clothes and had a Butler named Odero to deal exclusively with his wardrobe. Odero was a Steward/Butler by the time we got to State House Entebbe. Onyango was the cook then and like Odero said in an interview that hopefully put to rest the mean spirited rumours being circulated about Dad being a cannibal, he and the rest of the workers at State House can testify to the fact that Dad was not a cannibal. Oyunde and Ishaka (Issac) were the waiters while we lived at State House Entebbe. Odhiambo was the Stockman.

Dad had to have cravats and he was obsessed by them. I don't know the difference between Louis Vuitton, Hermes or Dior, but Dad could tell the difference at a glance. He had hand-made shoes flown in from Britain and anything else British, if it was well made. This passion extended to his car collection, which included Land Rovers, Range Rovers and Rolls-Royces, with the exception of a Mercedes Benz 300 coupe that he received as a gift from Libya's Muamar Al-Qadhafi which was a particular favourite.

Another plaything of Dad's was an amphibious car. He would take his wives or girlfriends out in it and head towards a lake. The girls would start screaming as they thought they were going to drown but the car just floated and this tickled Dad.

Dad loved laughing and jesting

We enjoyed lots of laughter with Dad and regularly recalled the time in 1975 when he jested with his Black American friends during the OAU (Organization of African Unity) Summit in Kampala. He loved doing the Acholi Welcome Dance, which resembles the Maori Welcome Dance. He loved jesting and one of his favourite jokes was to run at people with a spear the way Acholi dancers do in imitation dances. Dad would throw the spear so that it landed at people's feet like the time he did with the bald camera-man during the OAU (Organization of African Unity) Summit he chaired in Kampala in 1975. It was just a joke and not meant seriously. I likened Dad to the famous boxer Muhammad Ali because he had the same sense of mischief. I hated and still hate it when people called and call my father a buffoon when what they referred to as buffoonery was really Dad jesting around.

Dad's playfulness and mischief was legendary. He was a playful and mischievous man and he liked to laugh. No one was exempted from his mischief and jests including us his children, family members, associates and foreign dignitaries. Media outlets labeled many of Dad's jests as buffoonery but he meant them for laughs even though some of the jests could be very annoying and in terrible taste. We just learnt to take them as they came, like the time he played the "African Chili Prank" on several of my siblings and I. It was in 1973 and the first day we were formally introduced to Dad and begun living life as the President's Children.

As outlined in a previous section and reproduced here for ease of reference, we were led up the stairs and into the famous living room with stacks and stacks of family photo albums that lined one whole wall. Dad was an avid photographer and he loved taking pictures.

On this initial meeting I approached my father only understanding then that I was being introduced to him. I greeted him in the traditional Nubian way where you place the hand of someone you respect and revere on your forehead then you kiss the hand. The rest followed suit but all our eyes were on the roasted chicken laden plate on the low coffee table in front of Dad.

We sat down and Dad jokingly asked Fadhul how the children survived the attack, for the combined FRONASA (Front for National Salvation) and Kikosi Ma'lum (Special Forces) troops had attacked Ntare Secondary School in a misguided attack on a civilian target which had no significance at all. Apollo Milton Obote accounted for that incident on the Uganda Peoples' Congress Party website.

When Dad obviously noticed our keen interest in his plate of roasted chicken, he offered, "You want?" in Kiswahili. We all nodded with enthusiasm then he offered us the roasted chicken. We all scrambled for a piece and walked back to our seats as we greedily munched in. I immediately reacted to the sting of the African chili. So did Sukeji and Machomingi. Only Joseph Akisu seemed able to take it.

As I immediately looked up, my father was engaged in one of his tearful earthquake laughs - mirthful, is how Reporter Adam Luck described it in a Sunday Mirror Interview I gave after the release of the Fictional Feature Film "The Last King of Scotland". However to me, it was a naughty, jolly prankster mode for "Big Daddy" as Dad has often been referred to. My siblings and I were not amused by Dad's "African Chili Prank" at all!

Dad liked "flaunting" us his children

We enjoyed the way Dad "flaunted" us his children to Ugandans. It was the same way he "flaunted" us to all dignitaries that visited Uganda - like the time he did during the State Visits by King and Queen Sihanouk of Cambodia and the then Crown Prince Sihanouk and the "Black Empowerment Groups" including the Nation of Islam and the Black Panthers. He would take us with him in his Mercedes cars, when he went out to the various Ugandan provinces and districts.

Dad would take with him a child or children from local mothers to show his loyalty to the area. When addressing constituents, Dad would often say, "This is your child" - like the time he went to open the Kibimba Rice Scheme in Busoga District. He took me with him because my mother comes from the area and so does my younger brother Moses' mother Mama Mariam. I remember my young brothers Moses and Mwanga being dressed in mini military uniforms on these trips, as I myself donned a safari suit.

When I was nine years old in 1975, Dad took us to Angola. It was a really nice day trip. He was friends with a CIA Agent Zeeglar, who had new equipment from the US, including planes for our trips.

Dad's Presidential Basketball Team and invitations to musicians

Dad had a colourful Presidential Basketball Team, which included him because Basketball was another sport he loved. He would watch films of the Harlem Globetrotters and then organize games with his troops. Dad was 6 foot 4 inches, but most of my brothers towered over him as grown men. I am the shortest at 6 feet 1 inch and when we lived in Saudi Arabia, he used to joke that we would make a great Basketball Team.

Some famous Chinese lady singer by the name Ken Ken came to Uganda one time and one of the functions was a Basketball game against the Presidential Strike Force Team which included Ruba Ali Amin who was nicknamed "Sungura" (Rabbit) and Mama Sarah Kyolaba, Dad's wife.

Dad loved to invite singers and musicians and many times Congolese musicians would visit Uganda upon his invitation. He pursued a strong relationship with Mobutu Sese Seko who encouraged Congolese and other Africans to "flaunt" their culture and music when he renamed the Congo Zaire and encouraged every Congolese to wear mostly African attire.

A prank on me by Zeeglar the CIA Agent

In 1977 on what turned out to be a hilarious affront to Dad on hindsight, he once sent out a Southern American technician with his customized fully loaded Beige Range Rover, decked out with 20" alloy rims and the latest military two-way Communication Equipment. I later realized that the Southern American technician was Zeeglar, the CIA Agent working within the "Uganda Security System".

Dad had apparently wanted to test the long-range capacity of the new Communication Equipment. So he sent the entourage all the way from

Entebbe to Kigezi District where my siblings and I were studying, with specific instructions to speak with my younger brother Lumumba from the White Horse Inn location in Kabale. This was the best Hotel in Kabale and it was where we met Dad every time he paid a visit to Kabale.

A Peugeot 504 Estate had arrived on Rugarama Hill at Kabale Preparatory School to pick up my brother Lumumba but fortunately for me, I was around and the Bodyguard obliged and allowed me to tag along. We headed for the White Horse Inn where this glorious Utility Car was parked with the longest aerial I had ever seen. We met up with this Confederate sounding American who swiftly gave instructions to us - Lumumba in particular as ordered by Dad.

He said, "Your papa's call sign is "SNOW FLAKES 1". You will be "SNOW FLAKES 2", and You might as well be "SNOW FLAKES 3"", nodding his head towards my direction. Throughout the charade he played on me, he had an amused look on his face!

So, Lumumba started, ""SNOW FLAKES 2" calling "SNOWFLAKES 1". Do you read over?" That deep Baritone voice came through from Entebbe loud and clear "Roger "SNOWFLAKES 1" reading you loud and clear" then Dad switched into Swahili, "Lumumba nyi nyi iko namunagani?" ("Lumumba, how are you all?"). Lumumba answered like we would normally do on the phone that we were alright. Dad then switched off the Communication Equipment at his end since the test was alright to him but excited as I was, I tried out my call sign, "SNOWFLAKES 3" calling "SNOWFLAKES 1". Do you read over? I repeated this over and over and the "redneck" had an enormous grin on his face until he said, "Your Papa has switched off now".

It took me three to four years in the future in the 1980s and a whole lot of classical "gone with the wind" type of romantic Deep South novels, to get to know and to connect the "SNOWFLAKES" "call sign" to its actual derogatory meaning - Nigger, Coon, Golliwog etcetera. The Deep South novels included the Great Frank Yerby's Classic "The Man from Dahomey" and the Sequel "A Darkness at Ingram's Crest". Anyway, the "redneck" had his fun and he was paid handsomely for the Communication Equipment!

Our target practice and Dad's thrill at the Vietcongs

Throughout his rule in Uganda, Dad insisted on all his children's combat readiness. I have often reflected on our "Target Practice" and a scary incident that could have been fatal.

Between 1975 and 1979, we had a shooting range at one of our residences and all of us the President's Children were taught how to shoot and how to strip an AK-47. My father liked us competing against each other to see who could dismantle the weapon quickest. My record was nine seconds.

Dad's insistence on all his children's combat readiness started around the same time he tested the Communication Equipment sold by the "red neck", under Baba Luka Youm's instructions. Luka was then head of Dad's Striking Force Bodyguards, a name Dad thought up when he was setting up his Presidential Basketball Team. The attire was quite distinct - a white T-shirt with the Uganda Emblem the Court of Arms and Striking Force printed on Blue, Zairoise Kamanyola camouflage combat pants and original "Chuck Taylor" Converse Basketball shoes, ages before Snoop Dogg made it compulsory Hip Hop G-Funk Wear in the nineties.

We started target practice using what Luka called Black French Automatic Pistols that were apparently standard issue for Mirage Fighter Pilots in the French Air Force. I found them cumbersome to grasp especially since it had a strong Rodeo like kickback when you let rip with some shots at the target range. I much preferred what we kids called the Chinese Star Automatic, much in the mould and a possible reproduction copy of the famous Walther PPK a.k.a. 007 fame. We also preferred the Soviet-made Gargantuan Automatic, which had a fancy holster that could be attached to the bat of the pistol turning it into a rifle of sorts.

After Dad was overthrown, we learned to strip and reconstruct AK47s under strict timing drills by Sharif Sacaba Sacayonso Sacayoyo son of a gun Taban at our Makarona Residence in Jeddah. It was the time I was between the ages of 13 and 18. Taban was in and out of Saudi Arabia and last there when Khalid died and Fahad became the King. We next met in Uganda.

I remember by the time we went into exile, I had reached an adept fluency of 9 seconds! - to strip, reconstruct, chamber check, load the full metal jacket magazine and lock the safety cache, which must have been some kind of record then because I got some sidelong grudging looks from my siblings. Being older and bigger helped too I guess.

This is what thrilled me the most at Cape Town Villa in the 1970s one particular day. Actually, it was the first day we came up to shoot with the AK47s with quaking hands, while standing upright with a heavy rifle pressed into my shoulder blades. Somehow, I managed to pay attention to the instructions on how to breathe when getting ready to pull the trigger and somehow I managed to hit the Bulls Eye of the stationary picture of a charging soldier from amongst the shots during that target practice. First time lucky? I don't know! However, we progressed a little higher up the slope at Dad's Munyonyo get away christened Cape Town Villa just on the side of the tarmac track leading to the peer and this time lay down on the prickly alfalfa grass. Somehow, or other, the Female Bodyguard Mariam who was supervising my target practice set the position at "rapid fire" instead of single shots and I let off a barrage of "rapid fire" and then frightfully chucked the rifle away from me in fear.

A harsh scream came from Luka, "Never, never throw a rifle like that!"

I kept pointing at the Lady Bodyguard in accusation. Thankfully, she calmed me down, readjusted the firing position and I resumed my target practice.

Then suddenly out of the blue and from a higher point above the tarmac road where we were, we reacted to thunderous cracks from an AK47 rifle and there he was. Dad was in a relaxed sniper's sitting stance, shooting at our targets from a greater elevated position amongst the ancient bolders up on the hill! I must say we did enjoy those bouts into manhood.

Dad would show us an exercise he would do to steady his nerves and thus improve on his target skills, insisting on staying under water for the longest time possible then coming up for breath when we were out swimming. Horning our skills was his insistence on familiarization of the gun, much in the same manner Communist Vietnam trained the young.

Dad was thrilled by the Vietcong's ability to soundly defeat the Americans in 1975 in a protracted war. Long before I personally became obsessed with General Vo the Supreme Army Commander of the Vietcong and much earlier than the vaunted NRM (National Resistance Movement) policy of Mchakamchaka in the 1980s and 1990s.

Dad was a great swimmer like the time he jumped in the swimming pool during the making of the 1974 French Documentary on him titled, "General Idi Amin Dada: A Self Portrait" and he would tell us, "Whoever can hold his breath under water for two minutes wins 100 shillings". He said it would help us be good marksmen.

The deaths of Archbishop Janan Luwum and two Ministers

The deaths of Archbishop Janan Luwum, an Acholi Clergy, Erinayo Oryema an Acholi Government Minister and Oboth Ofumbi, a Jopadhola Government Minister were the final nail in Dad's "Political Coffin." The deaths had occurred as the real culprits responsible for the so-called hundreds and thousands of murders that Dad allegedly committed or "ordered" during his rule in Uganda continued to wreak havoc in Uganda.

In this section, I introduce the sad circumstances surrounding the deaths, which were a continuation of the murder of innocent people during Dad's rule in Uganda – a painful, shameful and horrific part of Uganda's history. I introduce this section here to continue encouraging dialogue about that horrific part of Uganda's history, for purposes of obtaining closure and healing for victims and/or their families and learning from history. Instead of offering my own standpoint and/or leading related discussions, I deem it more appropriate to let other people convey sentiments shared by many through the section of the series titled "Other People Speak" and generating discourse.

Since Archbishop Janan Luwum's death was the beginning of Dad's "speedy" fall from the "highest position in the land", I provide a sketchy outline below which relates to the circumstances that surrounded his sad and untimely death, along with the sad and untimely deaths of Erinayo Oryema and Oboth Ofumbi. I obtained this information from the "public domain" and encourage further reading and research.

As I have repeatedly asserted, Dad had his faults. I do not see the period of his rule in Uganda with "rose-tinted glasses". However, we need to counter-balance history with all the truth. It is my strong opinion that information shared by other people about the sad circumstances surrounding the deaths and the murder of innocent people during Dad's rule in Uganda along with various views and standpoints will have more credibility than my own. So, please read Dad's story then participate in the section of the series titled "Other People Speak", as the series unfolds.

On February 2, 1977, Dad staged a full official and diplomatic gathering at the Nile Mansions Hotel (Serena Hotel). The Chief of Staff of the Uganda Army at the time, Colonel Maliyamungu had his eyes fixed to the incriminating text in a frightening concentrated stare, to ensure that not one word was left out.

According to reports:

On February 5, 1977, arms were found in Luwum's Namirembe residence at about 1:00 a.m. in the morning.

On February 17, 1977, Archbishop Janan Luwum, an Acholi Clergy, Erinayo Oryema an Acholi Government Minister and Oboth Ofumbi, a Jopadhola Government Minister died in a "car crash" as they were being taken to Luzira Prison. One Juma Onziga remembered this event very well because later that evening, he walked along the Kampala Road to the Kampala International Hotel (now The Sheraton Kampala Hotel) and stayed up to about 2:00 am in the night. According to him, he did not notice anything unusual.

There are still a lot of unanswered questions regarding the sad circumstances surrounding the deaths of Archbishop Janan Luwum and the two Government Ministers. Luwum and Dad were chums and often traded jokes and enjoyed each other's company. Oryema and Dad were also very close. In fact he was Dad's Best Man when Dad married Mama Kay in 1967 and they were still close on the day Dad took over power from Apollo Milton Obote in January 1971. As Head of Police at the time of the Military takeover, he gave a statement recognizing Dad's government.

In 1977, the deaths of Luwum and the two Government Ministers brought about worldwide outcry against Dad's regime. The deaths of the Archbishop and the two cabinet ministers were reacted to in various terms worldwide. "Murder", said the All Africa Conference of Churches. "Assassination", said the International Commission of Jurists. "Unswallowable", said The Vatican. The Tanzanian Daily News quoted "authoritative" sources in Kampala: the victims were "tortured and interrogated in front of government officials", and as for the Archbishop, "his body was dumped in Lake Victoria." The Daily Mail added that "Dad punched the 52-year old Archbishop and then shot him twice." The Daily Telegraph of February 17, 1977 gave a different picture. It relied on a "finding" by its Nairobi correspondent saying, "...asked what should be done with the plotters (the Archbishop and the two Ministers), the soldiers roared, "Kill them, Kill them today". "But the President shouted at them (the soldiers) to cool down their tempers" and promised a fair trial before a Military Tribunal for all those arrested. But, Smith claimed that "the two had been shot twice at close range. The Archbishop had been shot through the mouth and had three or four bullets through the chest. The two Ministers had been shot in the same way, but only in the chest and not in the mouth. One of them, Erinayo Oryema, also had a bullet wound through the leg". (p. 203)

On February 19, 1977, the Uganda Ministry of Information and Broadcasting published Obote's War Call to the Acholis and Lan'gis.

Dad's naughty but expensive jest on the British Royal Family

In 1977, Dad played a naughty but expensive jest on the British Royal Family and Secret Service. He "planned" to attend the Queen's Silver Jubilee in London with a troupe of 200 tribal dancers and then "decided" to "cancel" the trip.

He formally flew off from Entebbe International Airport having been seen off by his High Command and "swamped" by Reporters intended on writing about the fact that he was an unwelcome guest at the Queen's Silver Jubilee in London.

Unbeknownst to Reporters, the British Royal Family and Secret Service at the time, Dad took off in the G2 Presidential Jet that had been given by the Saudi Royal Family but headed for Gulu and Khartoum instead and then he returned to Entebbe. He was laughing hard as he did this – the same chesty laugh that accompanied a question posed to him by a French Reporter who compared him to Hitler on that boat ride at Kabarega Falls in the 1974 French Documentary on him titled, "General Idi Amin Dada: A Self Portrait."

According to Dad, his naughty but expensive jest set off a scramble by the British Secret Service to set up a fully armed response team that was supposed to counter the "danger" of his "imminent" and unwelcome arrival in London. Dad laughed hard because he had successfully "duped" Uganda's former colonial masters the British yet again and he thought this was very funny.

Dad was a playful and mischievous man

As I shared before, Dad was a playful and mischievous man and he liked to laugh while jesting - like the times he would run at people with a spear the way Acholi dancers do in imitation dances. One of Dad's favourite jokes was to run at people with a spear the way the Acholi dancers do. During the OAU (Organization of African Unity) Summit in 1975, Dad threw a spear that landed at the feet of the bald cameraman who was part of the delegation representing the United States based Nation of Islam but it was just a joke and not meant seriously. He had a lot of friends among the Acholi and Lan'gi tribes before and after Uganda's Political Game of

"Russian Roulette" with Tribalism came home to roost and needlessly cost so many Ugandan lives. He spoke both languages very fluently and I have siblings from mothers who come from the Acholi and Lan'gi tribes.

Dad was very fluent in the Acholi language and spoke it frequently. I remember when he went to lay the Foundation Stone at the Kitgum Mosque. As usual he went with a child from the region and shocked the indigenous Acholi by speaking in fluent Acholi at the height of the uproar over the Luwum death in 1977. Luwum was from Kitgum and he and Dad used to speak and trade jokes in Acholi.

That time, he asked the people assembled in a lengthy speech on UTV (Uganda Television), "They say I am your enemy and I kill your sons and daughters. Would I surely bear children like Machomingi (Macho) Okello? Hmmm? You ask yourself. Children from enemies normally develop into lepers".

Then Dad brought my brother Macho in front of his people. Macho was then obliged to push the wheelbarrow for some distance until they got to where the Foundation Stone for the mosque was to be laid. My brother Macho is directly related to the former and late President of Uganda Tito Okello Lutwa and his son Okello Oryem.

Deporting Americans and the title Conqueror of the British Empire

In 1977, two hundred or so Americans were deported out of Uganda but this was later revoked. Idi Osman was Uganda's Ambassador in London at the time.

In 1977 Dad attended the OAU (Organization of African Unity) Summit in Gabon and he announced that he "is the Conqueror of the British Empire (CBE)" and he was widely applauded.

Henry Kyemba's book about Dad titled A State of Blood

In 1977, Henry Kyemba, a Musoga who had served in Dad's government under various ministries and as Principal Private Secretary and Cabinet Secretary till 1977 wrote the book titled A State of Blood which was and has been regarded as truth to this day. However, information has come to light to dispute some of the allegations and assertions made in the book.

Henry Kyemba's book will be a great addition to the background information for the section of the series titled "Other People Speak", along with other material and Articles relating to the debate about his book and whether Dad was a hero or villain to the core. However, in 1977, Henry Kyemba (a Musoga) supported false allegations made by his fellow Bantu ex-Minister, Wanume Kibedi, Dad's brother in-law.

In his so-called authoritative book on Dad, Henry Kyemba supported false claims made by Wanume Kibedi about the number of murders committed during Dad's rule. In 1973, Wanume Kibedi made deliberately false claims that between 90,000 to 100,000 people had been killed in Uganda by September 1972 following the Tanzanian invasion of Uganda by the combined FRONASA (Front for National Salvation) and Kikosi Ma'lum (Special Forces) troops. Those were the same figures Henry Kyemba quoted in his book titled A State of Blood and they are the very same figures many "kangaroo courts" have quoted as they "presided" and continue to "preside" over Dad's "trial". However, mimicking his fellow Musoga Wanume Kibedi, Henry Kyemba based his assessment on the rather strange presumption that a boatman at Owen Falls Dam worked full time removing corpses from the Nile.

Eager to bring his casualty figures up to date, Kyemba further calculated that the same (rather weary) boatman would have removed 40,000 dead bodies but added that "this figure does not include those that must have been eaten by crocodiles or swept away through the dam - at least another 10,000!" Moreover, Owen Falls Dam was only one of three dumping areas according to Henry Kyemba. Multiplying the Owen Falls Dam numbers by three gave a total of 150,000 dead by mid 1977- QED.

A carping point, crocodiles had been rare in the area of the Owen Falls Dam for many years. This led Dad's former superior Iain Grahame to ask: "But how easy was it for anyone to demonstrate with any accuracy the extent of the killings that took place? In Uganda the facts came mainly from dissident elements in Dar es Salaam and later Nairobi, who would have been only too happy to give to hordes of journalists (many of whom had never set foot in the country) all manner of massacre and grisly details. Murders and mutilation are, sadly, manna to the media, and to those involved in covering events in Uganda these ingredients were certainly not lacking. What few observers however attempted to point out was that repression is common to all dictatorship".

A book on Dad by Iain Grahame, Dad's superior during their service in the Kings Africans Rifles will also be a great addition to the background information for the section of the series titled "Other People

Speak", along with other material relating to the debate about whether Dad was a hero or villain to the core.

My recollection of Henry Kyemba before he ran into exile in 1977 with reportedly between 1-36 million $US of Ministry of Health funds meant for buying medicinal drugs was on the occasion of Mama Madina's home coming from Egypt where she had gone for the treatment of her detached retina. We the family had all gathered at the Tarmac in front of the Gulf Stream II Jet at Entebbe International Airport and casually, Kyemba asked us children if we had any welcoming song we were going to sing to our mother. He even suggested a common welcoming song in Luganda, "Nze sanyu se mama oku balaba" but alas we were not familiar with the lyrics and were content to have hugs and kisses without the formality or Protocol that he thought the occasion demanded. Then we all headed for the VIP Lounge and onwards to the awaiting fleet of cars.

Henry Kyemba fled the country in May 1977 and returned to Uganda after Dad was overthrown in 1979. Following involvement in the National Resistance Council and positions he held as minister in various portfolios, he has now been relegated to the sidelines despite trashing Dad and making false allegations in his book about Dad's rule in Uganda titled A State of Blood. Henry Kyemba's book has been widely accepted as "the truth" and "the book" to quote and refer to when lying about what really took place in Uganda during Dad's rule!

Dad's Relationship with Al-Qadhafi

In 1977, Dad continued his involvement as an ally of the Arab World, attending the Afro Arab Conference on August 7, 1977and visiting Al-Qadhafi in Libya.

The strong relationship between Dad and Al-Qadhafi went back to the time in February 1972 when they signed a Joint Communiqué in support of Arab Peoples. As outlined in a previous section and reproduced here for ease of reference, the Joint Communiqué was actually Dad's declaration of Genuine Independence for Uganda, Africa and its Diasporas.

The Communiqué had read:

"The two Heads of State undertake to conduct themselves according to the precepts of Islam. They assure their support to the Arab peoples in their struggle against Zionism and Imperialism for the liberation of confiscated lands and for the right of the Palestine people to return to their land and homes by all means".

Dad's audacious declaration in support of the Arab Peoples would permanently seal the "enmity" he now had with the People of Israel.

Following the Joint Communiqué signed and issued by Dad and Al-Qadhafi, Libya and Uganda decided to establish diplomatic relations and Al-Qadhafi accepted a formal invitation from Dad to visit Uganda at a date to be fixed later.

Al-Qadhafi assured Dad not to be intimidated by the Israelis and Zionists following the Joint Communiqué declaring support for the Arab peoples' rights and just struggle against Zionism and Imperialism. Due to the now strong relationship they shared, Al-Qadhafi in turn appealed to Dad as an older, wiser man, to go and talk to the President of Tchad, Francois Tombalbaye. Al-Qadhafi was at war with Tombalbaye because of Tombalbaye's mistreatment of the Berber and Arab inhabitants of the northern area of Tchad. The Berber and Arab inhabitants of Tchad are Muslims who lived in the Tibesti Mountains and they called themselves the Tchad Liberation Front. Dad flew to Fort Lamy from Tripoli and after two days, he returned to Tripoli triumphantly with the news that Al-Qadhafi wanted.

In this euphoric atmosphere, Al-Qadhafi offered Dad financial aid on a much larger scale and on much better terms than Uganda had been receiving for some time. He became one of Dad's strongest allies and even promised Dad military assistance. Later that year 1972, Dad extensively toured the Middle East and returned with £40 million, which he received "with no strings attached" because he was "one of their own!"

Like Dad, Al-Qadhafi had a "Rags to Riches Story" which is probably one of the reasons they got along so well.

Trouble for Dad with infighting, cronyism, rivalry and opposition

Beginning in April 1978, there was trouble for Dad as there was infighting, cronyism, rivalry and opposition to his rule in Uganda. Dad alas seemed to falter in his control of the armed forces as mounting "friction" occurred in the Uganda Army, leading to his ouster on April 11, 1979.

In April 1978, Dad relieved a close associate Brigadier Moses Ali of his post as Minister of Finance and accused the Adjumani native of nepotism in the distribution of newly acquired Honda Accord and Honda Civic cars. The cars were officially supposed to sell for Uganda Shillings 30,000 but Moses Ali was reportedly selling them to some individuals for as much as Uganda Shillings 120,000. Henceforth, Brigadier Moses Ali targeted Dad as an important enemy. However it was in the purported loss of 40 million US Dollars meant for the construction of the Grand National Mosque that the real animosity stemmed from.

Brigadier Moses Ali is an uncle to my half Bari sister Sukeji whose mother hails from Juba and is the daughter of Mzee (Elder) Wani Diloro. Over the years, he has been associated with every tribe in the West Nile region of Uganda – Nubi, Bari, Gimara, Alur and Ma'di.

"Nubian culture" and the homogeneous nature of Islam, plus the number of wives he married lent legitimacy to the tribes he was associated with in Adjumani District which has a large contingent of Indigenous pre-"Independence" Bari who settled in the former Moyo District.

At about the same time, Dad had trouble with several other members of his Military Government. For example, Isaac Lumago, the Chief of the Armed Forces at the time was criticized. Dad dismissed Nasur Ezega, Commanding Officer of Masaka and Abiriga 99 of Masindi Artillery Regiment (both members of the Aringa tribe) from the Armed Forces. Additional information will be provided in subsequent parts of the series. However, the ongoing trouble dad was having with members of his Military Government provided opportunities for his critics, saboteurs and detractors to build a case against him.

Then in late April 1978, Mustafa Adrisi, the Vice President of Uganda at the time from the Aringa-Kakwa clan of Gisara was injured in a car accident. Some members of the Aringa tribe interpreted this as the final plot by Dad's regime and people from the Kakwa tribe "to rid the Aringa tribe of all individuals in important and top positions in Dad's government!"

These sentiments almost led to a major revolt by members of the Aringa tribe in Dad's Army. The chickens associated with the game of "Russian Roulette" with Ugandan Politics that had existed since the colonial administration organized the army in Uganda along tribal lines almost came home to roost again. Uganda's Tribalism almost reared its monstrous head and exploded in the Army yet again!

Following the car accident, Mustafa Adrisi was taken to Cairo for treatment in the company of Haruna Abuna. He did not return to Uganda until December 1978, at the height of mounting border incidents between Uganda and Tanzania that escalated into the full blown war that led to Dad's ouster on April 11, 1979. They joined my elder brother Ali Juma Bashir who was undergoing extensive preservation of a shattered leg following a shooting incident involving smugglers on Lake Victoria as he was part of Dad's Elite Marines Anti-Smuggling Unit.

We were able to meet our brother Ali Juma Bashir after Dad's government had been overthrown. We were already in Tripoli, Libya when he joined us there upon his release from the hospital in Cairo. Cairo is only an hour's flight from its neighbouring Arab Islamic country of Libya by Libyan or Egyptian Airlines.

The war between Uganda and Tanzania that led to Dad's ouster

Events relating to the war between Uganda and Tanzania that led to Dad's ouster on April 11, 1979 will be explored in more detail under the section of the series titled "Other People Speak". However, suffice it to say that relations between Dad and Julius Nyerere had continued to deteriorate, despite the time in 1973 when Dad extended an offer of the hand to Julius Nyerere at the 1973 OAU (Organization of African Unity) Summit in Addis Ababa, Ethiopia. At the time of the OAU Summit in Addis Ababa, Ethiopia in May 1973, Julius Nyerere and Dad had difficulties in their relationship and an ongoing conflict.

As outlined in previous sections, conflict had developed between Dad and Julius Nyerere immediately following the Military Coup that catapulted Dad to the position of President of Uganda on January 25, 1971 and Julius Nyerere granted Apollo Milton Obote political asylum in Tanzania.

In September 1972, Ugandan exiles had invaded Uganda through Tanzania and Dad felt that Julius Nyerere sanctioned the invasion. He considered it an act of aggression and declaration of enmity by Julius Nyerere.

Between September 1972 and October 1978, tensions had continued to build up between Dad and Julius Nyerere with the threat of war continuing to be imminent. Units of Dad's army were regularly placed on high alert in readiness for war and suspicion ran rampant. Most people in Uganda were always aware that as long as Dad was the President, it was just a matter of time before a full-blown war erupted between Uganda and Tanzania.

Stories and first hand accounts by Army Veterans and other individuals who were intimately involved in the ongoing conflict and the subsequent full-blown war between Uganda and Tanzania abound and they will be made available through the section of the series titled "Other People Speak". However, beginning in 1978, tension between Uganda and Tanzania increased with rumours of an impending attack on Uganda by Tanzania running wild! This led members of Dad's High Command to call for an immediate attack on Tanzania, which eventually happened in October 1978.

Before the attack, the Chui and Simba Battalions were rumoured to have mutinied over pay also in October 1978.

At this time, Dad made his biggest mistake and as it turns out, the final disastrous gamble by sanctioning the attack on Tanzania and occupying its territory - although on hindsight a close associate of his by the name Juma Oka was at the epicentre of this most unfortunate of blunders. He was nicknamed Butabika.

Juma Oka, nicknamed Butabika is the same Army Officer who put a gun to Dad's head back in 1971 when Dad became reluctant about taking over the Presidency following the Military Coup against Apollo Milton Obote on January 25, 1971.

Loyalty to his own forces led Dad to not openly clash with the invaders led by Juma Oka Butabika, although privately he was furious about the incident as he was ill informed about it when he sanctioned the attack!

According to reports, on October 27, 1978, sporadic border clashes and attacks ensued at the Border Town of Mutukula between the Uganda Army and the Tanzania People's Defence Forces. Then on October 31, 1978, the Uganda Army crossed into the Kagera Salient and attacked Tanzania. Juma Oka Butabika, one of Dad's officers, led the initial attack. He is reported to have phoned Dad and claimed that Tanzanian troops had invaded Uganda, which forced him to take charge of Ugandan soldiers stationed at the border areas in order to repel the Tanzanian invaders.

According to reports, Dad fell for the information given by Juma Oka Butabika and sanctioned more attacks on Tanzania.

After the attacks by Juma Oka Butabika, Dad went on air and declared "a world record" of twenty-five minutes in capturing some 700 square miles of Tanzanian territory. He announced that his government had annexed the Kagera salient.

Following the border clashes and attacks on Tanzania, there was widespread looting, rape, murder and destruction of unimaginable proportions in the Border Towns of Tanzania.

More details have now emerged about the circumstances surrounding the war between Uganda and Tanzania. These include allegations that Dad and his senior officers were given false and misleading reports by saboteurs and subversive elements operating within the State Research Bureau in order to start a war between Uganda and Tanzania so that Dad could be overthrown.

There are also allegations that others and not Dad or his senior officers orchestrated vicious atrocities on innocent civilians in Tanzania following the attack by Juma Oka Butabika which was sanctioned by Dad and made it look like Dad and his senior officers sanctioned these atrocities.

They allegedly did this so that Tanzania could be "pushed" to the limit and declare an all out war on Dad's government to defend itself and its citizens and to completely overthrow Dad.

In essence, the people making the allegations suggest that Dad, Juma Oka Butabika and Dad's other senior officers were duped into attacking Tanzania under false pretences and on false information that was given deliberately so that they could attack Tanzania and start a war. In addition, the same saboteurs and subversive elements allegedly went on to commit the most gruesome atrocities.

Some critics have boldly stated: "The widespread looting, murder and destruction in the Border Towns of Tanzania that followed the clashes between Tanzanian and Ugandan soldiers and the attacks by Uganda on Tanzania were committed by the same saboteurs and subversive elements that operated within Uganda and murdered innocent Ugandans throughout Idi Amin's rule. They did this to continue to tarnish Idi Amin's reputation and make him look like a maniacal murderer. They are cold hearted killers who were only interested in achieving their own agendas."

Needless to say, the horrific atrocities committed against innocent Tanzanian civilians provoked Julius Nyerere and his government to declare war on Dad. These atrocities indeed pushed Tanzania to the limit and necessitated the country's military to defend its innocent citizens against murders and other atrocities allegedly committed by others and not Dad's soldiers.

Moreover, powerful governments around the world had allegedly gone along with the propaganda that was ongoing against Dad and fully supported Tanzania and the exiles in their bid to overthrow Dad's government.

Allegations relating to the war between Uganda and Tanzania will be explored in more detail under the section of the series titled "Other People Speak" along with additional details on the war. However, in response to the "careless" "blunder" by Juma Oka Butabika, one of Dad's senior officers, soldiers comprising of Tanzanians, Ugandan exiles and mercenaries launched an attack on Mutukula.

They were determined to overthrow Dad's government and the Ugandan exiles were about to realize the objectives of the meeting they held in 1976 in Lusaka, Zambia to lay a more systematic strategy for overthrowing Dad. Uganda and Tanzania were now entangled in an all out war. The casualties would be many and the damages immeasurable!

Meanwhile, roughly 10,000-15,000 mainly young Uganda Army recruits passed out at Ngoma, northwest of Bombo and prepared to fight the guerrillas.

Having recently obtained armaments from the Soviet Union, Tanzania was more than prepared for the war against Dad and angry and determined enough to want to not only drive the so-called invaders out of Tanzanian territory but to completely overthrow Dad. So in November 1978, Tanzania launched a counter-attack on Uganda and on December 9, 1978, the country's President Julius Nyerere announced that the Tanzanian army had had a victory. He told Tanzanians that Dad's soldiers had been driven out of Tanzanian soil.

A Key Note: Actually, after the attack sanctioned by Dad and the announcement that his government had annexed the Kagera salient, nations from the OIC (Organization of the Islamic Conference) convinced him to withdraw back to the original borders that existed when each country achieved "Independence." Dad had done that but Tanzania attacked Uganda in retaliation nonetheless. Dad's soldiers were not driven from

Tanzania as has been reported. They had withdrawn from the Kagera salient when Tanzania attacked Uganda.

According to another critic, "There was more to come as the Ugandan exiles seized the opportunity of the hostility that their members orchestrated between Tanzania and Uganda to implement their agenda to overthrow Idi Amin from power. The most gruesome atrocities committed by the exiles on innocent Tanzanians forced Julius Nyerere to jump on the exiles' bandwagon because the culprits made it look like the horrific atrocities were committed by Idi Amin's so-called invading army".

Stories and first hand accounts by individuals who were caught in the "crossfire" of the war between Uganda and Tanzania abound. They will be made available through the section of the series titled "Other People Speak", along with information relating to routes taken by the Liberators in Tanzania and Uganda.

An unnerving phone call to Dad about the war with Tanzania

I will never forget the time when my siblings and I were with Dad in the room as he took a call related to the hostility that was going on between Uganda and Tanzania. We were giving Dad the usual massage that day when he picked up the phone then slammed it down. He looked at me while I worked the sole of his 14-inch feet and said, "They have attacked me again...The Tanzanians. It is a big force this time".

After that momentous phone call and on our outing to Cape Town View Munyonyo, a long convoy of fancy cars brought the High Command up to the resort at "Cape Town View" in Kampala for a meeting with Dad. It was his style to have his children around him at his most trying of hours for he should have loaded us onto the Ubiquitous (Nissan Civillian) Omni Bus which used to transport the majority of his children to and from State House Entebbe. However, at this moment he kept us around.

Dad had the best Strike Force Protection Unit but having his children around him during times of war while on holiday seemed to be a comfort to him as is normal with any parent. There were rumors of a coup and the agenda from the delegation of high ranking officers was to ask him to step down.

Dad normally took us to Cape Town View Munyonyo during our school holidays and this was the last school holiday I spent with him before I joined Primary Six in 1979 at Kabale Preparatory School. It was a very tense time indeed and I realized that something was wrong because there were hordes of soldiers around whom I did not recognize - Bodyguards and Drivers of each individual Battalion and Brigade Commander. The High Command Council was trying to convince Dad to stand down and he said, "How can you ask me to do this?"

The situation worsened from then on and Dad relied on Non-Commissioned Officers and a sprinkling of Majors, Captains, others and his Crack Marines at Bugolobi, Moroto and the Uganda Air Force.

The death of the valiant Christian Lieutenant Colonel Godwin Sule

After the confrontation with the High Command at Cape Town View Munyonyo, Dad's looming defeat was becoming obvious when suspicion around a so-called Friendly Fire was determined as the cause of death of the Valiant Christian Lieutenant Colonel Godwin Sule. He was one of the contingents of Anyanya troops who served the 2nd Republic of Uganda with diligence and care. After the so-called Friendly Fire incident, the regular soldiers lost morale yet on hindsight the Tanzania People's Defence Force invaders in 1979 had suffered a resounding setback at Rakai during what Sergeant Peter Andia a Keliko (Kaliko) from Jaki County Congo would have considered a Battle Royale. Sergeant Peter Andia joined the Uganda Army in 1966.

It was therefore a mystery for the then Chief of Staff to issue a "Part One Order" requesting all Battalions to withdraw 50 miles from Rakai into the swampy plains of Lukaya away from their resounding scene of victory. Normally an army would have consolidated their positions before retreating but they didn't, which lends credibility to allegations that Dad's army had been infiltrated by the enemy. Moreover coordinates given to the Air Force Pilots were "erroneously" targeting Uganda Army positions and not Tanzania People's Defence Force positions! The people behind this were allegedly found to be Lieutenant Colonel Yorecam and others.

Isaac Maliyamungu, Yusuf Gowa (Gowan), Lieutenant Colonel Yorecam, Brigadier General Taban Lupayi, a Sudanese Christian and a Muganda head of Military Logistics were accused of being bribed and alleged to have received fake dollars as part of a plot to defeat Dad's army from "within". It was alleged that the Logistics Personnel would "erroneously" reroute mortar shells to artillery gunners while artillery shells were sent to Battle Tank Position all in an effort to stall the war efforts and eventually defeat Dad.

It was alleged that Lieutenant Colonel Yorecam was found to be giving positions of the Uganda Army troops to the Uganda Air Force leading to consistent "Friendly Fire" on Uganda Army positions. This he allegedly did while also giving coordinates of Uganda Army troops to members of the Tanzania People's Defence Force who would continue to bomb the Uganda Army Troop Formations at the battle front.

African mysticism came to the fore when every time the Uganda Army soldiers changed Battle Formation they were met immediately with a barrage of BM21 Rocket fire, which was personally manned by one Major Boris of the USSR. The bullets were raining in like a scene from a Biblical hail and brimstones until they started believing a gun the soldiers dubbed "The "Saba Saba"" had a sophisticated roving eye, not realizing it was their very own Field Commander who was directly compromising them from within. When he was discovered with the very latest coordinates and the very next battle formation coordinates while radioing them out to the Tanzania People's Defence Force, his very troops waylaid him with lethal vengeance.

According to reliable sources, Brigadier General Taban Lupayi, a Sudanese Pojulu could have been implicated in the very same scheme for he put a lot of miles between himself and the war front together with Isaac Maliyamungu, a Zairian Kakwa when the 50 miles withdrawal took effect. The rot had truly set in!

The scene was set for the Uganda Army's last stand in the marshy plains of Lukaya where the so-called friendly fire that killed Godwin Sule occurred. With only 3 T55 Soviet Battle Tanks and a 106 Jeep, the rest of the Army had withdrawn or been hit on the battle field. The incompetent withdrawal or deliberate ploy to withdraw allowed the invading Tanzania Peoples' Defence Force to position, strengthen and consolidate their gains on the war front.

Dad at the frontline waving at the Tanzania People's Defence Forces

As all this was going on, Dad did something only he could have done. He drove to the scene of Lieutenant Colonel Godwin Sule's death and actually waved at the Tanzania People's Defence Force Detachment that was fighting the Ugandan troops. The Detachment was a few meters away but instead of firing at Dad and killing him, they waved back in excitement like school children – the irony of an unnecessary war between Uganda and

Tanzania! The Tanzanian troops clearly saw and knew that it was Dad waving at them but they did not shoot him!

After that incident, Dad had stormed into Nakasero Lodge that very night, in the Elevated Kangaroo Springed 200 E series Benz, which was a factory prepared rally car, with a string of "Five O Fours" in tow and the white Communication Land Rover at the rear. The vehicles were all covered - actually caked in camouflage river mud as a precaution against reflection. That day, Dad alighted with his usual tearful earthquake laugh. He was laughing at the spectacle of not being shot at by members of the Tanzania Peoples' Defence Force. He had alighted into the welcoming arms of the Nakasero-Kabale Preparatory School contingent that was now under the care of his favourite wife Sarah Kyolaba whom he married in 1975.

We were amused the next day to hear on the News that "Suicide Sarah" as my stepmother Sarah Kyolaba was referred to, had toured the Frontline with her husband Idi Amin. We rushed to her to confirm the news only for her to deny the News Item.

"I was here the whole night. That is your father on one of his pranks. He probably went with that new Musoga bride of his".

Dad married Mama Nnabirye, a Police Officer, Soldier and Presidential Escort in 1978. The incident that involved him driving to the Frontline and waving to the Tanzania Peoples' Defence Forces occurred around the time there was the constant boom sound reverberating over Kampala in March 1979.

"Part One Order" to repatriate the soldiers' families to safety

The die was cast when Lieutenant Colonel Sule was reportedly shot from behind while making a valiant defence of the marshy plains of Lukaya. The second damning Order from the Chief of the Defence Staff Major General Yusuf Gowa (nicknamed Gowan) of the Mijale Kakwa clan near the Aringa border in West Nile was for soldiers to repatriate their families to safety. Some claim it was a directive from Dad following the Cape Town View Munyonyo showdown during which his senior officers told him to step down. After Dad refused to step down, they allegedly said things like, "Let his Strike Force and Marines do the fighting if he does not want to step down".

This "Part One Order" dealt the last nail in the Uganda Army coffin because suddenly the most amazing logistical operation swung into action for all soldiers hailing from the West Nile District in Jaki County, the Congo in Kakwa County and Southern Sudan. There was total disarray in the whole rank and file of the Uganda Army because of its homogenous composition for truly speaking the Uganda Army was a complete composition of the whole country. They seemed to melt into the western, eastern northern hinterlands just like a scene from the Second Gulf War when 200,000 strong Republican Guards simply melted away into the hinterlands as the American Army attacked Baghdad.

That time, an estimated 36,000 to 40,000 Uganda Army soldiers melted away from the battle front leaving only the bombing sorties by the Air Force to keep the Tanzania Peoples' Defence Force at bay.

Amazingly, a reconciliation took place between Abiriga 99 whom Dad had discharged from the army and Dad and he was able to swing in his Aringa factions into a last ditch effort to defend Dad's regime. The whole High Command had dissipated for they must have "signed consent" to the request to ask Dad to step down and they must have duly given him the mutiny notice at that very extended Cape Town View meeting, leading to his blanket condemnation of all officers. Dad's High Command from Lieutenant Colonel right up to General was implicated in the request for him to step down.

Dad now relied on his Crack Marines and the Air Force while the rest of the Battalions went into irreversible implosion, with pockets from Moroto, Mbale and Abiriga 99's contingent from north western Bunyoro. By this time, Dad could only rely on a sprinkling of Majors and other senior officer ranks, Captains and Non-Commissioned Officers to run the last ditch efforts to shore up his regime, which was in decline.

Dad only had the Iraqi trained Marines at his last hour although Taban Lupayi had removed most of his Sudanese contingent during the infamous 50 miles withdrawal. It looked like only the 15,000 new recruits who were passed out just when the Kagera war started in 1978 were being deployed to the war front. The rest were in disarray.

The resounding factor that keeps replaying in all strong men regimes is the high propensity to have a "Republican Guard"-like Brigade that owes allegiance to the ruler. This recurrent theme in most "Third World" countries played into the familiar process of defeat just like what happened a decade later with the DSP in Mobutu's Zaire and then the Republican Guards in Saddam Hussein's Iraq. Quite often, grudges come to the fore at the final hour of defeat and quite often the regular soldiers leave the so-called Elite to "face the music". It was recalled by many how the regulars would say, "Let his Marines and Strike Force fight his battle for they always got the best from the rest." Grudges came to the fore during that time.

The last standing command centre comprised of Major Muhammed Luka Yuma of the Strike Force Presidential Guards, Major Mzee Yosa with Operations Intelligence Services, State Research Bureau, Captain Asio with State House Signals, 3 T55 Soviet Battle Tanks Marine and 1 "one zero six" Jeep at Malire.

The rot started with the dismissals of key Aringas who owed their loyalty to the Vice President by tribal affiliation and it continued after Dad's ouster including incidents that occurred during a future "war" between the Kakwa tribe and the Aringa tribe in October 1980.

Allegations that Dad's army had been bought off

There was talk of the entire Uganda Army High Command from the Generals right down to the Majors having been bought off with fake US dollars to stall the defense efforts of the Uganda Army. Dad was aware of this and he was increasingly relying on the Junior Officers and his Crack Striking Force Bodyguards under Major Luka's Command.

Dad's last stand in 1979 was that undertaken by the valiant Lieutenant Colonel Godwin Sule of the Paratroopers School Malire who died in the "frontline" at Lukaya, fighting the combined Tanzania Peoples' Defence Forces and Ugandan guerrillas. Henceforth, the battle swung in favour of the guerrillas and the Tanzania Peoples' Defence Forces.

On March 19, 1979, following Lukaya and Lieutenant Colonel Godwin's death resulting from a so-called "Friendly Fire", Dad seemed to have been discouraged and presumed to have disappeared into a world of fantasy with those bombastic propaganda statements of his on Uganda Broadcasting Corporation (Radio Uganda). The state controlled Radio Station reported that Dad was visiting Mbarara for top-level strategic discussions with the officers of the Simba (Lion) and Chui (Leopard) Battalions.

Our rescue by a Platoon from Kabale Preparatory School

Caught up in the momentous "surge" were a bunch of pre-teenage children of the man the Liberators wanted to topple – my siblings and I!

As it turned out, Mbarara had been in enemy hands for almost a month and the two units mentioned above had ceased to exist as organized forces. Although on hind sight, the announcement somehow or other coincided with a personal mission to rescue his loved ones from Kigezi District – my siblings and I.

Dad sent a King Air Turbo Propeller Plane to pick us up after we were rescued from our Boarding School in Kigezi District by a Platoon he sent and a lengthy stay at Hotel Marguerita. I believe it was during our stay at Hotel Marguerita that Dad needed to give the impression that Mbarara was still under the control of his government and the two Uganda Army units were still in existence. He needed to maintain that façade until he had sent the Plane that transported us to safety from our lengthy stay at the Hotel Marguerite.

We always knew Dad loved and cared for us very deeply. However the length to which he went to organize a daring rescue to get my siblings and I out of harm's way from the war zone could not have been a truer testimony of that love!

In 1979, while the war between Uganda and Tanzania was heating up, Dad sent an Army Platoon to rescue my siblings and I from being cut off by forces determined to overthrow his regime. This happened while we were still studying in Boarding School in Kabale in Kigezi District.

My siblings and I were sent to the elite missionary schools such as Kabale Preparatory School in Kigezi District for the boys and St. Mary's Namagunga for the girls. Dad felt good that we could attend the elite schools to which he had once been denied access because his family was erroneously considered Sudanese and "outsiders". Because they were not considered Ugandans, Dad was denied formal education. That was why he only attempted Primary School up to Primary IV, which was the limit set by the Colonial Administration for Muslims. He sporadically combined this attempt with Garaya (School of Qur'anic Studies/Readings). This had happened from the year 1940 when he was 12 years old to the year 1944 when he was 16 years old.

Al-Qadhafi Garrison Primary School, one of the schools my siblings and I went to was close to an armory and the site of a confrontation between troops loyal to my father and the opposition in June-July 1971. Everyone was in the dormitory under big metal beds with gunfire raging outside. It was unbelievable for a small kid. Our guardian eventually came in and told us everything was fine. The people trying to attack had been forced back.

After that confrontation between Dad's forces and the opposition, we were transferred to another barracks. I suppose you could say our father had put us in danger, but he always had key people to look after his affairs. He made sure we had Guardian Angels. So when it became evident that my brothers and I would be cut off by the troops that overthrew him in 1979, Dad did everything possible to rescue us.

Sergeant Tirikwendera a Munyamulenga from Goma in my Dad's Crack Presidential Guards, ominously pestered Dad to rescue us his children. We were about to be cut off in the Kigezi District in 1979 when the Liberation Forces were making their rapid push for Masaka and Ankole District during their lightning advance towards Uganda's Capital Kampala. Dad had initially thought that we would be safe in the care of the missionaries. However, Sergeant Tirikwendera insisted that the Hima/Tutsi grapevine was giving ominous signs that "Amin's children at Kabale Preparatory School would be targeted for destruction". Eventually, Dad gave up and put Sergeant Tirikwendera in charge of a Platoon that set off in a Brilliant (convict) Orange 4X4 All Terrain Military Bus (Fiat 75) towards Kabale, passing Masaka and Ankole just before the Tanzanian Army took over the Area.

Previously we had unexpectedly started to receive Military Police Guards from Baba Rajab (Captain Rajab of the Kakwa ethnic group) every evening that guarded each and every one of the three dormitories that we resided in at Kabale Preparatory School. When the missionaries asked us to inquire why the military were being posted outside every dormitory, the soldiers simply stated that they had orders to guard the President's children.

That eventful night, Miss Samna from Mersey side who was the Resident Matron at "The Warren" dormitory where I resided woke us up deep in the night informing us to dress quickly and prepare to leave. I did not know why and was surprised that we were leaving for home just shortly after the Half Term of my 1st term PLE in P6 of February 1979. We were not required as it were to take anything and I remember eyeing my chocolate brown Haji Kadingidi Platforms, checkered beige Bell Bottoms and chocolate brown Polo neck top with longing when we were forced to leave everything behind.

I only got a very last glimpse of my beloved Miss Mary Hayward just as we climbed into the Orange Fiat 75. I was struck by the multitude of weaponry inside the All Terrain Bus and the stern attention from the Platoon sent to rescue us. They were Dad's Presidential Strike Force Guards.

To us children and to my mind in particular this was straight out of the Famous Five series. As the powerful bus set off, I even asked Sergeant

Tirikwendera why we were not heading towards Mbarara when he turned towards Kisoro having descended down Rugarama Hill and just past my classmate Ezekiel's house. He solemnly told me that part of the country had been cut off by the invading Tanzanian Army.

We trudged through Wakaraba valley towards Kisoro. Mbarara was now in enemy hands and the two Uganda Army units there had ceased to exist as an organized force in the area. We would have to head for Kisoro, pass into Rwanda, cross over into Zaire (Congo) and then back into Uganda around Lake George and Lake Edward through the Queen Elizabeth National Park in order to escape the invading Tanzanian Army. We would then go to the Hotel Marguerite where we would wait for a plane Dad was sending to fly us to Entebbe.

I remember the tremendously steep descent enroute around the Kisoro area. The soldiers later told me that we were lucky witnessing the location deep in the night because the abyss was not a sight for the faint hearted. What an amazing trek!

This will always stick in my mind's eye. We only had a Military Police backup from the Kabale Barracks who escorted us in a Military Land Rover. Just as we entered the National Park deep in the night, somehow one of the sockets to the battery power came off and the powerful bus ground to a halt right in the middle of the National Park. The Military Police tried to alight and fix the problem but they were very alarmed by the slowly advancing laughter from hyenas in the area, which seemed to be daring the soldiers to try their luck! Anyone who has ever heard the sound of a hyena's laugh will know what I am talking about. The Captain Officer in Charge then decided that we would have to rest in the car until early morning the next day.

At dawn, Sergeant Tirikwendera, probably a veteran Truck Driver alighted and simply re-plugged the battery and the powerful machine kick-started instantly. We set off on a speedy romp through the park but came to a mile long traffic jam of heavy goods trucks —trucks that had got stuck in metre deep ditches. I will always remember the initial bemused looks on the hardened Truck Driver's faces when Sergeant Tirikwendera made a detour on the side of the stranded trucks, then amazingly managed to pass the multitude of trucks to the grudgingly respectful stares of the Truck Drivers.

The drivers longingly looked on as we effortlessly trudged forwards in that brilliantly orange All Terrain Military Bus. We came out near the Kazinga Channel, a conduit that links Lake George to Lake Edward. We were able to join the tarmac road right up to Hotel Marguerita at the foothill of Mountain Rwenzori, inside Queen Elizabeth II National Park.

Dad sent a King Air Turbo Propeller Plane to pick us up after a lengthy stay at this memorable hotel that bears my mother's name. While residing at Hotel Marguerita, the Officer in Charge of Kabale Military Police Barracks one Captain Rajab Rembi, a former Uganda Cranes no 11 winger in the 1960s tentatively managed to teach a gangly flat footed laid back 12-year old how to play pool in the Bar room area. I still remember the lessons I received from Captain Rajab. I also remember the misty atmosphere one sees at the foot of Mount Rwenzori. What a beautiful sight! Dad later shocked us when he claimed that there was an attempt by the advancing Liberation Forces to shoot down the plane with Anti-Aircraft Fire as it approached the Mpigi Area.

Other than the turbulence experienced around the lakeshores as the King Air Plane approached Entebbe Airport, nothing much happened apart from my sister Asha Aate Mbabazi tagging my sweater and owning up that she had wet herself. I placed my 6-year old sister to the side and indeed my "Idi Best" ("Sunday Best") trousers were all wet. Upon arrival, I rushed to the Children's Wing to change, while she was rushed to her mother Mama Mary's. At the time, Mama Mary was the Private Secretary for Social Affairs at the President's Office.

Our last days in Uganda and Dad's impending downfall

Upon arriving in Kampala, we were tentatively placed at Buganda Road Primary School by the Chief Presidential Protocol Nasr Ondoga who was responsible for all the President's personal affairs, for the final duration of our childhood stay in our beloved country. All the children who had left Kabale (apart from Mwanga Alemi and Asha Mbabazi) went to reside with Mama Sarah Kyolaba at the present day Kampala State House Nakasero (formerly Nakasero Lodge). Mwanga Alemi went to reside with his mother at Command Post Kololo and Asha Mbabazi went to reside with her mother also in Kololo.

During this time, no one was residing at Entebbe State House and it was only used for State Functions as Entebbe was near the war front and constant infiltration from the porous "Masaka, Mpigi Coastline" rendered it unsafe to stay in. This was mostly in March 1979 and Kampala was taken in April 1979.

Dad's bombastic propaganda statements continued on radio. On March 26, 1979 the Uganda Broadcasting Corporation (Radio Uganda) announced that the President was "cut off at Entebbe." We would go so much as to affirm Dad's victory announced by the Uganda Broadcasting Corporation on March 26, 1979 when it announced that "the President was "cut off at Entebbe" but managed to repel the enemy forces with the support of loyal troops". The announcement by the Radio Station might have had some truth in it since this was the exact time Dad was negotiating with Al-Qadhafi to receive his immediate family into Tripoli and he needed the still useful Entebbe International Airport. The invading troops were still more than 70 miles away from Kampala when Dad was negotiating with Al-Qadhafi to receive us. Since vanguards of the so-called Liberation Forces had possibly already infiltrated some parts of the route to Entebbe by the time Dad was frantically trying to get us out of Uganda, he addressed the nation during which he asked "Ugandans who believe in God to pray day and night."

The Liberators intensified their efforts because they were hell bent on overthrowing Dad. On March 27, 1979, the "Liberation bombs" commonly referred to by Indigenous Ugandans as "Saba-Saba", landed on the compounds of the Republic House at Mengo and the Army Shop nearby in the evening. Meanwhile, a cabinet in waiting had been formed by The Uganda National Liberation Front (UNLF) in Moshi on March 24 and 25, 1979. This cabinet had been formed out of 22 political groups that had emerged in opposition to Dad's regime. Details about these groups and the formation of the cabinet are contained in a subsequent part of the series titled "The Liberators' Dysfunctional Alliances".

On March 28, 1979, about 9:00am, Lieutenant Colonel Pangarasio Onek, CO (Commanding Officer) of General Headquarters, Mbuya, instructed his troops to ambush any available means of communication: matatus, trucks, tractors, cars, taxis, etceteras, to take their families "home." My Avatar Yuga Juma Onziga knew there and then that it was "a game over" for Dad's regime. Dad's Army was in total disarray and it was now fighting to "save their skins."

The war ended at Lukaya when most of the soldiers and Secret Service Personnel either said "Congo na gawa" or "Sudan na gawa" and high-tailed it out of the country. Some even said let him fight this out with his favourite Air Force and Marines – a reminder of the dangers of favoring particular units in the military over others.

As Dad's Army continued to disintegrate, his bombastic propaganda statements continued on state controlled radio but by now Dad knew better. On March 28, 1979, the Uganda Broadcasting Corporation (Radio Uganda) claimed that Dad had "smashed through the Tanzanian forces and reopened the road to Entebbe" from it being closed by the Liberators. The Uganda Broadcasting Corporation (Radio Uganda) and Dad may have been living in a dream world as the world would have wished it to be but privately Dad knew better. The bluff and the bombast that had served him well for eight years were rapidly losing their effect. As a consolation, Dad was now fighting a private war to evacuate some eighty members of his family and close associates to safety in Libya. Meanwhile the District Commissioner of Kampala, Muhammad, addressed a rally in Kampala and he urged people to turn for work and business as usual, yet the rebels were actually 20 miles outside Entebbe at the time.

On March 28, 1979 at about 4:00 pm, my Avatar Yuga Juma Onziga along with his wife and a two-week old baby girl, his father and brother, fled to Arua. But, at between Kiryadongo Hospital and Karuma Falls, the car, a Toyota matatu, they rented overturned and some people were injured but none seriously. The matatu was totally written off and Juma lost his JVC radio and stereo cassette in this accident.

Fortunately, his younger brother, who was driving later from Kampala also to Arua, stopped by and conveyed his wife and child along to Arua. The rest of them transferred to a nearby lorry and arrived in Arua early in the morning of March 29. They finally converged at their clan village of Rugbuza later that afternoon. The rest is history!

The same day March 28, 1979, Tanzanian long-range artillery began bombing Kampala. At about 11:20 pm, the Uganda Broadcasting Corporation broadcasted a news flash saying the attack was close by. "Tonight ... is the first time when the Tanzanian aggressors with mercenaries and traitors, using long-range artillery, have bombarded Kampala..." a newscaster announced. This admission of truth by the Uganda Broadcasting Corporation made Ugandans realize how close Dad's fall was.

At that time the truth about Dad's impending downfall remained concealed by the Kampala authorities. However, BBC World Service regularly intercepted Radio Uganda broadcasts from their monitoring station at Caversham Park in England. Ugandans who were brave and bold enough to follow the events at the risk of being discovered by the notorious State Research Bureau intelligence agents continued to quietly keep track of

BBC broadcasts and the truth about Dad's impending defeat. They had begun to do so early in the war.

I will never forget the last days of our stay in Uganda due to the constant boom sound made by the "Saba-Saba BM21", the Artillery and BM 21 rocket shellfire into the Capital Kampala by the Liberators. Having been picked up from Dad's residence in Nakasero where we were residing at the time, we were all gathered at Command Post, another residence of Dad's. Then we set off in a convoy towards Munyonyo (Cape Town View) and used the Garuga detour towards Entebbe, coming out near Kajansi since some Liberation troops had already cut off and probably laid an ambush on the Main Road probably around the Lubowa Estates Area. We arrived at the old colonial residences (State House Entebbe), to await the planned flight to Tripoli, Libya.

Mama Sara Kyolaba had preferred to stay at Nakasero Lodge in Kampala even though she and Dad's wife Mama Madina previously jointly shifted to State House Entebbe, which has a better defense position following attempts to raid the Kampala residences by insurgents. In 1978, Mama Madina had left to go to Iraq together with Mama Nnabirye the Presidential Bodyguard Dad married during the same year 1978. Mama Nnabirye was in residence at the Cape Town View Resort before leaving to go to Iraq with Mama Madina.

Mama Madina had a detached retina while the expectant bride Mama Nnabirye went for precautionary tests. After the fall of Dad's government, the two women ended up first in Central Africa then in Paris, France after the fall of Bokassa, President of the Central African Republic and Dad's friend, also in 1979. My sister Zamzam Mama Nnabirye's daughter was born in Bangui the capital of the Central African Republic on the night of the Military Coup against Bokassa. Then she and Mama Madina left together for Mobutu's Kinshasa in 1979 via Paris, France where Catherine Bokassa had taken refuge.

The day my family fled to Libya in a Cargo Plane

The day my family fled to Libya we could hear the artillery shells in the distance getting closer. It was amazing and there was a sense of disbelief. This huge convoy set out from Kampala to Entebbe Airport. Dad was having 60 to 80 seats installed in a Cargo Plane for all of us. He was talking to Al-Qadhafi on the phone, telling him, "My children are coming". Dad sent us ahead but he wanted to stay on to make his last stand, even though he knew that the war was lost.

Apparently, a reluctant Egyptian pilot had to be commandeered and he was paid cash down in hard currency so that he could accept to fly the President's children out of the country to safety. The bombardment was only 20 miles away then. The Boeing 707 Cargo Plane had recently come in from one of its expensive cargo transport flight of coffee to the USA and he (The Pilot) was very tired. It had no seats whatsoever. So, some sixty to eighty seats were hurriedly placed in the plane to accommodate probably sixty persons who were given blankets against the cold emanating from the bare aluminum floor. I had actually been hurriedly discharged from Mulago Hospital following a sprain of my ankle and still had an itchy plaster of Paris on.

The Boeing 707 managed to take off under strange circumstances, due to the fact that artillery shellfire was now raining into the airport area. The Bodyguards were forced to place four cars around the plane and they raced down the runway as lighting for the pilot until we were airborne!

What an uncomfortable ride to safety this was, all the way to Tripoli! The plane ride to Tripoli, Libya was rough and uncomfortable. I have often reflected about what could have gone wrong with a plane that had no seats and was flown by a reluctant Egyptian pilot that had to be commandeered and paid in hard currency, before accepting to fly the President's children out of the country to safety. I have often wondered what would have happened if the Egyptian Pilot didn't honour the hefty bribe he received from Dad to fly us out of Uganda to safety but decided not to dwell on the predicament. Some say it was the fatigue that built the reluctance and no civilian pilot wants to work under a war situation, which was understandable under the circumstances.

We left behind some very prized items. I still see in my mind's eye an ornate golden Mantle Clock left in my Dad's state bedroom that was given to Dad by Tito of Yugoslavia on one of his last state visits to the Balkans. That visit holds a lot of meaning to me since Dad had promised me that if my grades improved he would take me on his next visit abroad. My grades did improve but my brother Lumumba was chosen on that particular trip and I remember my kid brother feeding a giraffe in the Belgrade Zoo on a photo shoot with the World War II hero. I remember asking my stepmother Mama Sarah if she had remembered to bring the Mantle Clock and she regretted that alas it had stayed in State House Entebbe.

The time Dad's Presidential Guards waylaid him to get him out

Mzee Yosa and Sergeant 'Bhuga played an exemplary role in getting Dad out of harm's way. For all the allegations of cowardice and other characterizations leveled against Dad over the years by his foes, at the 11th hour, Dad proved all these allegations and characterizations wrong. Here was a man true to character of the old colonial Kings African Rifles, who against the advice of his officers and Crack Presidential Guards had decided to remain in Kampala to await his fate after having ensured that his loved ones had been evacuated. "A Captain does not abandon his ship" scenario was played out to devastating effect on April 6, 1979 when Dad made an announcement on radio that he would stay in Uganda.

Dad made a final broadcast in Kampala on Uganda Broadcasting Corporation. During this broadcast he called Ugandans not to be afraid of the "cowardly enemy bombardment with a long range Artillery", adding that "the enemy has only seized part of South Buganda, together with a little part of Ankole." Dad insisted, "I will stay here except when I leave Kampala for another place in Uganda". This announcement by Dad prompted Senior Army Officers Mzee Yosa, Sergeant 'Bhuga from the Gimara Kakwa clan, Captain Asio of the Nyooke Kakwa clan and several hefty Presidential Guards to waylay their Commander-in-Chief and restrain him. They actually immobilized him in the process with straps and placed him in his factory prepared 200 series Mercedes Benz copue Rally car. On April 11, 1979 when his government was overthrown, Dad was still at Munyonyo in the vicinity of Kampala. He wanted to die in battle like a true soldier but several of his Presidential Guards would not let him. Then the convoy of Expensive Flagship Mercedes Benz 240 SEL 6.4s set off in tow for Jinja just as Kampala was overwhelmed by the Liberators. Major Mzee Yosa and Sergeant 'Bhuga and Captain Asio played an exemplary role in getting Dad out of harm's way.

Dad's last emotional speech

At Jinja, Dad made an emotional speech to Ugandans in general and the Basoga in particular as he was fleeing to safety in a convoy headed for Arua and Ko'boko in Northern Uganda. He had stopped over in Jinja, Busoga when he addressed Ugandans through an assembled crowd of Basoga. He actually spent one week in Jinja while the Uganda National

Liberation Front, the exiled group that overthrew his government through Tanzania consolidated their hold on Kampala.

While Dad was still at Jinja, he announced that this was where he would stand and die. He made the Ad-hoc speech in front of the Basoga reminding them and his country men of all the goodness he had tried to do for his fellow native Africans and yet "all the thanks he gets for it is them turning against him". He made an impassioned reminder to them to recall how they would even curiously heft up several flocks of livestock at will to where they resided without anyone disturbing their peace. Some of the people would even heft their livestock up to their high-rise apartments and no one would stop them. "You want me to go but one day you will lament that maybe I was good for the country after all." "You will then look for me but you will not find me". "People will cry after me but they will not find me" Dad continued, amidst the initial murmurs of "Agende Kajam-biya".

Ironically, Dad's address to Ugandans through an assembled crowd of Basoga is the same speech Ugandans lament over decades later after witnessing years of grinding poverty and seeing the truth come to pass in that singular farewell. According to him, he spent the one week post April 11, 1979 the day of his total defeat and overthrow with Jumba Masagazi between Jinja and the Malaba-Busia Border trying to release the fuel his regime had paid for but they claimed that a new government was in place.

On Wednesday April 11, 1979 at 7:00 am, deposed Dad advised his troops on Radio Deutsche Welle in the Federal Republic of West Germany:

"Mimi badu Rahisi ya Uganda. Usi tupa bunduki yaku. Kufa na bunduki yaku" ("I am still the President of Uganda. Don't throw away your gun. Die with your gun"). That was the first time many people (including my Avatar Juma) heard him speak after his final broadcast in Kampala.

The fall of Kampala, a cabinet in waiting and celebrations

On Wednesday, April 11, 1979, the BBC World Service announced the fall of Kampala to the Tanzanian forces commanded by Colonel Benjamin Msuya. BBC correspondent John Osman and BBC stringer Charles Harrison had kept the world abreast with the rapidly changing military situation in Uganda. Late on April 10, 1979, unconfirmed reports had said the Tanzanian forces were already in Kampala. John Osman the BBC Correspondent had interviewed Dad in February 1977 on the circumstances of the deaths of Anglican Archbishop Janan Luwum and two cabinet ministers Lieutenant Colonel Wilson Erinayo Oryema and Charles Oboth-Ofumbi. So he had closely followed events that unfolded in Uganda that preceded Dad's "speedy" fall from the "highest position in the land" and he was familiar with Uganda's politics. However, Radio Uganda was silent on the news. Instead the home service on medium wave and the external service on short wave frequencies were both playing light music between transmission intervals.

Then at about 3:56 pm on April 11, 1979, transmission on Uganda Broadcasting Corporation (Radio Uganda) was interrupted. After a few moments of silence, the heavy Luo-accented voice of a man came on air. He introduced himself as Lieutenant Colonel David Oyite-Ojok. In a broadcast that was not very clear, the words "...Idi Amin is no longer in power..." filtered through. At 4:20 pm that afternoon, Lieutenant Colonel Oyite-Ojok's announcement was repeated on the home service of Radio Uganda. This was the historic message broadcast on that fateful day by David Oyite-Ojok:

"Fellow countrymen, I am Lieutenant Colonel David Oyite-Ojok. On behalf of the Uganda National Liberation Forces, I bring you good news. The Ugandan Liberation Forces have captured the Uganda...capital of Kampala today Wednesday, 11 April 1979...Idi Amin is no longer in power..."

However, something odd happened at 5:00 pm when the external frequency of Uganda Broadcasting Corporation (Radio Uganda) came on air on short wave, out of the blue, playing light music. Those old enough to remember would know that the external service of Radio Uganda broadcasted from the Dakabela relay station in Soroti, 208 km east of Kampala. Then it went off air as abruptly as it had come on.

"What was going on?" asked nervous Ugandans. There was silence for more than four hours, which only heightened the tension in Kampala. Then at 8:00 pm, the state owned radio in Dar-es-Salaam, Tanzania announced in Kiswahili that it was now going to link up with Radio Uganda in Kampala for a special message. Then in English, came the announcement, "This is Radio Uganda. Stand by for an address to the nation by Mr. Yusuf K. Lule, Chairman of the Executive Committee of the Uganda National Liberation Front." During that broadcast, it was formally announced that Yusuf Lule had become the new president of the Republic of Uganda. A provisional government was announced and Ugandans were told that elections would be held "as soon as possible."

Significantly, Uganda's radio station had called itself "Radio Uganda" rather than "Uganda Broadcasting Corporation" as it was known in Dad's era. As the then BBC Nairobi Editor for monitoring, Tom Heaton recalls, "This gave us a clue as to what to watch out for on the Soroti external frequency." At 10:00 O'clock the same night, the home service of Radio Uganda closed down but 35 minutes later, the external service short wave frequency broadcasting from Soroti suddenly announced, "Dear listeners, this is the external service of Uganda Broadcasting Corporation..."

At 10:41 pm, there came another segment of broadcasting. There were two voices - one male and unknown, the other, a low soft Baritone bass familiar to Ugandans, the international community and especially weary diplomats for eight long years. That voice was Dad's and the broadcast segment went like this: Voice one: "Hello!" Voice two: "Are you ready?" Voice one: "Yes, we are ready, please, Your Excellency." Then voice two again: "I, President Idi Amin Dada of the Republic of Uganda, I would like to denounce the announcement made by Lieutenant Colonel Oyite-Ojok, the so-called Chief of Staff, that my government has been overthrown and they have formed their rebellion government in Uganda…"

It was now clear that Dad was in Soroti, broadcasting on his sophisticated electronic equipment that he had frequently used on his upcountry tours. Dad gave a second version of his speech from Soroti in Kiswahili but it was the largely ineffective defiance of a desperate leader, now deposed.

Unbeknown to most Ugandans, there were three individuals who had particular vested interests in events that were unfolding in Uganda at the time Dad was overthrown. These three people followed broadcasts on Radio Uganda with intense interest. Listening to Radio Uganda from Jinja but utilizing his wireless communication facility was Dad, the 51-year old now deposed President of Uganda while the 54-year old former President of Uganda Apollo Milton Obote was also intently listening in Dar-es-Salaam, to developments in Kampala. This was happening as Uganda's new Minister of State for Defence, 35-year old Yoweri Kaguta Museveni was listening to developments live on Radio Uganda in Kampala as he actively helped to secure the captured city Kampala, in dark green battle fatigue.

The first scene of Rembi's Mystical Legacy on January 25, 1971 to April 11, 1979 was finished. The second scene was 13 months away and it would happen in Bushenyi on May 27, 1980 when Apollo Milton Obote alighted and Pope-like kissed mother Earth as he stepped on Ugandan soil again. The third scene was to wait for February 6, 1981 at Kabamba Barracks. It was to strike Liberation Politics when a disgruntled politician cum

Freedom Fighter Yoweri Kaguta Museveni, along with an overwhelmingly Tutsi fighting force decided that the barrel of the gun was the only option for the ultimate route to power. Whether he should have given the chair to the rightful winner of Uganda's first elections after Dad was deposed, Democratic Party boss Semogerere was besides the point in the "Roots of Treason". The "Roots of Treason" is what I have titled my explanation of the "Domino Effect" and the anarchy that occurred when the power vacuum enveloped Uganda after Dad's fall from grace which I outline in my book titled "Rembi's Mystical Legacy."

On April 11, 1979, Dad was toppled and there was a Cabinet in waiting ready to take over the Uganda Government. However, President Yusuf K. Lule ignored the list compiled by Apollo Milton Obote at Julius Nyerere's request and hastily named a cabinet of his own, which would lead to his speedy downfall and set off a multitude of coups that characterized an unprecedented dysfunction in Ugandan Politics.

On the day Dad was toppled, there were "celebrations", "celebrations" and more "celebrations" reminiscent of the ones that occurred when he took over power from Apollo Milton Obote in 1971. There were also rampant killings of people labeled as Dad's henchmen - the sometimes-unfair reference to anybody associated to Dad by tribe, religion and region of origin, including people who did not benefit from his rule in Uganda. These scenes replayed themselves over and over again.

On Wednesday, April 11, 1979 when his government was overthrown, Dad was still at Munyonyo in the vicinity of Kampala. He wanted to die in battle, like a true Soldier but several of his Presidential Guards would not let him.

Dad running the gauntlet on the way to safety

On April 22, 1979, when Dad passed through Lira and Gulu in Northern Uganda, he was still intended on hanging on to power. However it was only a distant dream at this time. Nonetheless, he continued his feeble attempts to hang onto power.

On April 13, 1979, while still broadcasting from the relay station in Soroti in Teso District and later still, on the Gilgili Radio Station at Arua probably on a recorded tape, Dad was still telling Ugandans that he was their President. However, deep down, he knew that he had been done in.

One of Dad's associates and entourage Mzee (Elder) Kivumbi was able to give a blow by blow account of their movements between April 10, 1979 and April 23, 1979 when they arrived in Arua. According to reports, there were incidents of them running the gauntlet between heavy fighting in Teso, trees being cut onto the roads in Lan'go land to block Dad's convoy from passing through and an incident in Gulu. The so-called Luo Militias had risen up, realizing that the Nation had changed hands but Dad passed through all hostile territory without being hurt and experiencing some of the fiction included in the book and film about him titled "Rise and Fall of Idi Amin".

A harrowing incident which showed both Dad's bravery and ability to calm agitated soldiers happened in Gulu when an artillery gunman scouted the fast moving Presidential Convoy and leveled his artillery towards the oncoming convoy then he gave the conventional Holuko - HALT! Then the soldier started to harangue his Commander in Chief.

"All the officers have left. We are only soldiers and NCOs. Now you Affende are leaving? Better we die here and now rather than leave you to pass" [sic].

According to Dad, in a hushed tone, he got out of the E 200 Series Merc Coupe and strode towards the 3,000 plus remnants of his Fighting Force and pointed at the daring soldier in reply.

"Here is a soldier. If I had twenty or more like him, we could not be defeated".

This short speech made the soldier hang his head, with tears in his eyes, having realized that he had confronted the Commander in Chief, but the speech had also turned the tide into sympathy from a hostile 3,000 strong battle weary amalgamation of the last Fighting Force.

"Where are the Field Commanders?" Dad asked the soldiers.

"They all headed for Arua" they answered.

"Soldiers, let me go and try and convince them to return to the battle field" interjected Dad.

"We also need reinforcements from Libya and Gulu and Arua Airfield are still in our hands. We will check whether Nakasongola is still in our hands. Kenya has blocked our fuel supply. The only way through is through the Sudan and Libya".

All was lost when Dad got to Arua, for he met with a crescendo of gunfire from soldiers shooting aimlessly. He met with senior officers who sought his audience one by one. He was saddened to hear of the death of

Governor Odong of the Chope who was apparently killed by friendly fire - another mystery like that of Godwin Sule in Lukaya.

According to reliable sources, a significant thing happened. Dad finally sought audience with his Minister of Education to whom he handed over the Instruments of Power and asked him to become the President of Uganda. Therefore for all intents and purposes, Brigadier Barnabas Kili was the Interim President of Uganda after Dad was overthrown in 1979 before he handed over the Instruments of Power to the Tanzania Peoples' Defence Force as a sign of the country having been taken over. It seems Dad kept the Marines Colours and the Army Colours but handed over the Police and the Country's Colours.

Refugees

After Dad's overthrow, the mass exodus of Ugandan Refugees into neighbouring Congo and Sudan began. Between April 4 and 5, 1979, the guerrillas took over the reins of Dad's regime and Yusuf Lule was installed as the new President of Uganda. That evening, Juma's cousin Nasur 'Baseke son of Haruna Fere of the Lurujo clan and Juma, as well as his mother Jumia, attended the funeral of the late Murjani Abukaya of the Ginyako Kakwa clan. Suddenly, Juma overheard Major Amimi of Bombo saying that he had never heard the guns that the guerillas were using before in his entire military life. What a pity!!

Here was a man who was supposedly a Major and a veteran at that!!! Juma realized straight away that Dad's Uganda was now history. He also saw Mukungu (or block-chief) Sururu Amurumu of Lurujo taking his cattle and properties in the middle of the night to hurry to the Zaire (Congo) border.

With Nasur and Juma having retired home during the night, he heard his mother scream that the guerrillas were now at Pakwach on the way to Arua. All his attempts to convince her otherwise failed. So, in the middle of the night she mobilized Juma's wife and child and his brother's wives to leave for Zaire (Congo), which they did.

A special Libyan C-130 Hercules Plane and Dad's outbound journey

After Dad arrived in Arua, he continued his feeble broadcasts on the Gilgili Radio Station at Arua. On April 23, 1979, he was still in Arua when a Libyan C-130 Hercules landed at Arua Airstrip right next to his Tanganyika Residence to pick him and several of his associates for the plane trip to

Libya. That fateful day, Dad embarked on the outbound journey into exile. He and his entourage left Arua for Libya in a special plane that flew him to Tripoli, Libya where he was reunited with us.

The Russian Embassy had approached him with an ultimatum that if he signed a Pact with the USSR, they would land 25,000 Cubans to restore his regime. The price was Communism. Whether it was beside the point or not, Dad's answer was poignant, for unlike a drowning man who grasps at straws to survive, he told the Soviets "I will not sell a single inch of Ugandan soil just to remain in power. It is my officers who have failed us".

Mzee Doka Bai our Ayivu Elder (Opi) and neighbour in Arua was the last person Dad talked to before he was driven to the awaiting C130 Hercules on his way to Libya. He remembers watching just off our water tank as the plane ascended into the skies.

Dad had told him in passing "I am going to discuss with the Russians in Libya my return. However, if they insist on being the Communist overloads like in Ethiopia then I will not agree to sign, but let the Uganda High Command officers know that they are the ones who failed this country".

"Goodbye my brother" Doka Bai had uttered as the C130 Hercules carrying Dad disappeared into the skies on its way to Libya.

After Dad's departure to go to Libya, there was a lot of aimless gunfire in Arua that night.

On April 23, 1979, Dad had passed by Mzee Doka Bai's house, which is just opposite his water tank on his way to board the C130 plane. He had stopped on a final courtesy call on his neighbour and fellow child of the Okapi for Mzee Doka's mother's maternal uncles were Okapi from Ole'ba in Maracha District.

His friend, brother and neighbour (Dad) had intimated to him, "I am going to get some more reinforcement from Libya but if the Soviets insist that they are in control then I will never allow a single inch of Uganda soil to be under their control. Let it be (wacha na keti basi)".

Dad then put his hands in his pockets and came out with whatever was there but thoughtfully in foreign currency for even he was aware that his 2nd Republic notes were losing value rapidly. He then handed over the dollars to his friend, cousin-brother and neighbour who used to join him in training when he was still the East African Light Weight Champion.

On one of Dad's Annual Leave saunters around Tanganyika Village in Arua, the two were responsible for courting and finally getting Mama Ingi one of Dad's very first concubines in trouble in 1952 when my sister Amina Ingi was born.

Mzee Doka remembered standing, watching towards the northern direction as the C130 took up speed and graciously ascended into the sky with resounding bullets flying around in the Jiako area as soldiers kept firing at anything in total disregard for safety or reason as they expended ammunition. It was as though Dad was being given a 21-gun salute for even one of Doka Bai's brothers shot at some ripe mangoes, setting off a resounding rebuke from his elder brother.

"Why do you have to shoot at the mangoes using that thing? Behave yourself...."

Over the years, Mzee Doka recalled the money his cousin-brother Dad gave him so well for he used it to relocate his family to the Congo (Zaire). He also recounted this story to me when I brought him some money sent by thoughtful relatives of the Al-Amin Family who knew the significance of Mzee Doka Bai to Dad as a neighbour and a relative on his mother's maternal Okapi Lugbara Ethnic group side.

Doka Bai's mother is of the Okapi of Ole'ba, Maracha District. As a Kasanvu (coerced labourer), Mzee Doka of the Ayivu used to get 70 shillings as a Uganda British American Tobacco (BAT) Company Lorry Driver per month. When he joined Grandpa's aunt Asungha's husband's Arua Bus Syndicate Company as a Driver, they paid him 120 shillings per month.

This was in the late forties and mid fifties. The coerced labourers were paid much less. We have to put it in context. They started the Kasanvu scheme around 1919. Therefore 70 cents fit the bill I suppose.

Dad would always send supplies and place them in the hands of Mzee Doka Bai as the Family Quarter Master General, during the Duas, while most errands in the 1960s were the responsibility of the late Shaban of the Lurujo Kakwa clan. Upon his sudden demise, Shaban was later replaced by Alias of the Drimu Kakwa clan. All the above responsibility was taken up by Mzee Sergeant Hussein Diliga post 1979.

Hussein Diliga was the very person who came to pick Joseph and me at Aunt Akisu's homestead in Kayunga, Bugerere when she died in 1970. He was the very person who spied my brother Taban Idoru under the Military Bus seat and took some 20 minutes trying to extricate him from under the seats when he insisted that he wanted to go to Arua with the Funeral Procession of our aunt Akisu. The ultimate errand boy became a Foster Father of sorts replacing Sergeant John Katabarwa.

I don't believe Ugandans and Dad's detractors know that Dad boarded the Hercules plane to Libya penniless but the two countries Libya and Saudi Arabia were generous to him. I was a witness to the amounts he gained from them.

Dad arrived in Tripoli via Benghazi on April 23, 1979 and begun his long life in exile!

An orgy of destruction by the invading forces

Many of our residences were destroyed after Dad's government was overthrown. As we followed events that unfolded in Uganda during our life in exile, we vividly remember seeing a photograph of one of our residences in Kampala with visible signs of unnecessary destruction. The stone staircase to the kitchen was where Samson, son of Maliyamungu liked to do his Chinese back flips. It was also the scene of my first confrontation with my sister Kidde in 1973, over her Soviet made Bike, which I write about in a previous section.

The Ivy plants on the wall were always beautiful to watch. The curved room was where I used to sleep and it was also the scene of Mama Kay and Aunt Penina dancing on New Year's Day 1974. This they did while we jumped up and down on the bed for they woke us up at the "midnight hour" by switching on the gramophone, playing black and white "Let's Get Together." The B side had "Listen to Your Leaders, Listen", by Sonko, a local Artist. My brother Lumumba used to wing his way down the circular drive in his brand new Soviet made Bike. In the picture we saw in exile, the grassy island was strewn with whatever family albums the Uganda National Liberation Army could shred - sad indeed!

Our first days in Libya

In Libya, we were initially placed in a plush residence in downtown Tripoli, which we christened "Palace". The residence had ornate Mediterranean grapevines in the garden and we would spend endless days claiming cars as they crisscrossed a junction right in front of the "Palace" window. "Yangu Eeh Yangu!!!" ("Mine Eeh Mine!!!"), we would scream as the cars sped past the junction. We were then transferred to a Beach Resort called Madina Sahiyah awaiting Dad's arrival.

After Dad was reunited with my siblings and I and the rest of our immediate family, we were all relocated to a government-owned Hotel in Homs, towards the Tunisian border. We were transferred there along with Dad's entourage, which included Ministers, Diplomats, Officers of the Armed Forces and their families.

I recall that Dad arrived in Benghazi on April 23, 1979 from our Arua Tanganyika Aerodrome aboard the C130 Hercules Transporter that Al-Qadhafi sent to pick him up after his government was overthrown. We had a tearful reunion with Dad on April 24, 1979 in Tripoli, Libya.

After we were reunited with Dad, we spent time exploring desert oasis and the famous Roman Coliseum in Homs.

Immediately following our arrival in Libya, Al-Qadhafi in his characteristic generous nature offered to send us all of Dad's children to Malta, which had the second nearest good English schools. Egypt was nearest, but Libya's neighbour was just about to sign a Friendship Treaty with Israel and I guess it had fallen out with its Arab colleagues. By the time Dad arrived on April 23, 1979 after the fall of his government on April 11, 1979, I guess the plan had been sidelined.

An indecent pass by a Libyan Bodyguard and a physical fight

I will never forget the physical fight I started between the D12 ("The Dirty Dozen") as Dad referred to 11 of my brothers and me and a youthful Libyan Bodyguard who made an apparent indecent pass at one of my brothers. The Bodyguard made a pass at my famous brother Moses Kenyi - the one who was allegedly sacrificed and eaten by Dad in 1974! I, the firebrand Tshombe could not stand that so I got into hot water again. I was going to have none of the Libyan Bodyguard's nonsense so I alerted the rest of the D12 ("The Dirty Dozen"). "The Dirty Dozen" included me and my brothers Muhammad Luyimbazi, Hassan Ruba Ali, Yusuf Akisu, Khamis Machomingi, Hussien Juruga Lumumba, Moses Kenyi, Sulieman Geriga, Adam Ma'dira, Issa Aliga, Mao Muzzamil and Abdul Nasser Alemi Mwanga.

I was first on the scene and instinctively grabbed at the Bodyguard's lengthy hair, demanding to know what he was trying to do. The Bodyguard jokingly tried to get away but the whole bunch of the D12 was on to him and we all started beating the hell out of him. As always, I led the fray and the rest of "The Dirty Dozen" joined me. Our very own Ugandan Bodyguards were the ones who actually stopped us and rescued the Libyan Bodyguard.

Unbeknownst to us, the Libyan Bodyguard had apparently run upstairs to the second floor, which housed their quarters, to get his AK-47. He had the intention of mowing down President Amin's children but he was restrained and quickly transferred back to the Barracks away from the Hotel complex where we continued to reside.

I still have a framed reprint of a Polaroid snapshot of "The Dirty Dozen" on top of my Pentium Processor and I smile every time I look at the picture as I remember the numerous times we got into trouble. Dad used to laugh about our capacity to get in and out of trouble, as he "taunted" and fondly referred to us as the D12. Nothing came close to the fight involving the Libyan Bodyguard and any mention of that "naughty brawl" always brought about one of Dad's tearful earthquake laughs.

The West Nile region of Uganda after Dad

Additional information will be made available in sections of subsequent parts of the series, Idi Amin: Hero or Villain? His Son Jaffar Amin and Other People Speak including personal accounts by individuals who were caught in the crossfire between Dad's Army and the combined forces that overthrew his government. However, immediately following Dad's overthrow the West Nile region of Uganda teemed with thousands of unruly, leaderless and demoralized former Uganda Army soldiers.

The Kakwa population in Ko'buko (Ko'boko) plus that of the other ethnic groups in the West Nile District were increasingly fleeing to either Zaire (Congo) or to the Sudan. It was a spectacular and yet frightening sight to behold - people moving with their goats, granaries, sheep, chicken, cattle, dogs, children, the aged and pregnant mothers and facing only one direction - the Uganda-Zaire (Congo)-Sudan border. Everyone knew they needed to walk across one of the two borders into either Zaire (Congo) or the Sudan, for safety. Dad's army, the disbanded Uganda Army (UA) fired aimlessly at nothing, some just to shoot down a ripe mango fruit. Many fired into the darkness scaring away people who were out to gather kon'ga (flying edible white ants).

Although conditions of living of Kakwa ti Arua, a term used to refer to people from the Kakwa tribe that had settled in Arua have always been obviously harsh, they still believed that they were living a "better" life than their rural Kakwa counterparts in Ko'boko. Living conditions of Kakwa ti Arua were characterized by constant food and accommodation shortages for example. However, they still believed that they were better off. It is this self-conceitedness, utopia, paranoia and myopia that has consistently and foolishly tended to drive them to look down upon their distant relatives in Ko'boko. However, as if to remind them that they were refugees and foreigners in Arua after all, many of these Kakwa ti Arua were also forced to vacate West Nile's capital in 1979, after the so-called Liberation of Uganda, by the invading Tanzanian and UNLA (Uganda National Liberation Army) Forces.

In doing so, the Arua Kakwas lost most of their possessions in the district's capital. Even worse, they became worse off refugees than the rural Kakwas in Ko'boko who were already used to being self-reliant in food and accommodation, having faced decades of dire social and economic problems before - throughout much of their daily lives.

An even worse situation was faced by those Kakwa people who described themselves as ngutu ti lojo - meaning the "overseas people" or Kakwa ti lojo, a term used to refer to people from the Kakwa tribe that had settled in Eastern, Southern and Western Uganda. The word ngutu means "person" and lojo (lozo) means "across a river or lake" or simply "overseas" – in this case the River Nile. Hence, these people sometimes also call themselves Kakwa-ti-lojo (or "the overseas Kakwa"). The term generally designates the Ugandan towns and other areas of "economic vibrancy", such as Bugerere (Kayunga), Soroti, Mbale, Gulu, Moyo, Kakira, Kawolo (Lugazi), Kigumba, Kampala, Jinja, Hoima, Kakoge, Masindi, Namasali and Namasagali.

These places had become the chief centres of Kasanvu (cheap labourers/coerced labourers) drawn largely from the tribes of Northern

Uganda that include the Kakwa people. This southward migration peaked soon after World War I when Uganda's present territorial borders were finally demarcated. This migration further ushered in wave after wave of adult Kakwa males who had to work in Uganda's sugarcane, banana and coffee plantations in order to receive financial payments to pay for the newly-introduced poll tax.

Meanwhile, Kakwa ti Congo a term used to refer to people from the Kakwa tribe in the Congo, migrated to Kinshasa, Kisangani, Wacha and Bunia also as labourers or rarely during colonial times, to enlist as soldiers in the notorious Belgian Army or Force Publique. This Belgian Army was then commonly known as the Tukutuku during the colonization of Sub-Saharan Africa.

A similar migration pattern developed among Kakwa ti Sudan, a term used to refer to people from the Kakwa tribe in the Sudan who are now found in Juba, Khartoum and Port Sudan - mainly voluntarily compared to either Uganda or the Congo.

Uganda immediately following Dad's ouster

Upon Dad's arrival in Libya, he was forcefully silenced and under permanent guard, along with his entourage. However, while we lived in exile, we regularly followed events unfolding in Uganda with interest.

More in depth reading is required for a proper understanding of what transpired in Uganda after Dad was overthrown. Consequently, additional information will be made available in sections of subsequent parts of the series including a section titled "Uganda after Idi Amin". However, below is a very sketchy outline of selected events that are reported to have occurred between 1979 and 1986, for purposes of only providing context to events that unfolded after Dad's government was overthrown and as a prelude to "fuller" information and a "fuller" discussion. These events had unfolded as we settled down in exile.

We apologize for inadvertent errors, misrepresentations and inaccuracies. However, as the series unfolds, we will make any corrections and add information as Kakwa Temezi (Revered Elders) would in an Adiyo Narration Process.

According to various reports, immediately following Dad's overthrow, Uganda was characterized by a multitude of overthrows, coups, trickery, and political and military dysfunction. Following is a brief sketch of a few important events.

On April 13, 1979, Yusuf Lule was sworn in as President of Uganda, and the Baganda rejoiced, as they saw Lule's Presidency as paving the way for the return of the Kabakaship/the Kingdom of Buganda.

On June 13, 1979, Lule was voted out of office by the NCC (National Consultative Council), which was a temporary Parliament and Godfrey Binaisa took over as President of Uganda.

On June 20, 1979, Godfrey Binaisa was sworn in as President of Uganda replacing Yusuf Lule. Binaisa beat two other candidates for the presidency, namely Edward Rugumayo, one of the Cabinet Ministers that defected during Dad's rule and Paul Mwanga.

Binaisa appointed 10 UPC (Uganda Peoples Congress) Party members to his cabinet of 30 and he restored Mwanga and Museveni, the latter as Minister of State for Defence. He expanded the NCC to 127 members and initiated UNLF (Uganda National Liberation Front) organizations at the grassroots level following Tanzania's manyumba kumi (ten-house cell) system.

Meanwhile, Lule was confined to a house arrest in Dar es Salaam.

Demonstrations occurred against Binaisa and his new government in Kampala and elsewhere in Buganda but Defence Minister Yoweri Museveni who became Uganda's President in 1986 forcefully dispersed the demonstrators.

Binaisa's main challenge was the uncontrolled growth in the size of the UNLA (Uganda National Liberation Army) with each of Museveni, Mwanga and Tito Okello swelling the ranks of the UNLA with their own loyal armies.

Rapid promotions of Acholi, Lan'gi and Banyankole occurred in the UNLA (Uganda National Liberation Army). This way the army ceased to be tightly controlled but instead became an armed rabble with each component part inadequately controlled and owing loyalties to different political leaders, while being prepared to use their arms to loot or to take reprisals against anyone they or their sponsors deemed their enemies.

In 1979, The UNLA (Uganda National Liberation Army) was in disarray as it swelled uncontrollably and Obote set to organize militias in Soroti, Kitgum, Kumi and Apach, in total, nearly 24,000 soldiers!

By 1979, Obote's Kikosi Ma'lum (Special Forces) claimed to have 600 men - mostly Acholis and Lan'gi's.

Museveni enlisted 8,000 Tutsis including the late Rwigema and Kagame and Mugisha Muntu and Banyankoles like Besigye and Otafire a.k.a 'Mavi ya kuku fame' to FRONASA (Front for National Salvation).

Some Ugandans prayed that the bloodiest chapter in their history ended with Dad's departure but remember what the word "Lemi" means in Kakwa?

Family members caught in the crossfire

After Dad was overthrown, many of my family members were caught in the crossfire. From January to February 1980 many people labeled as Dad's henchman were still being targeted, including Awa (Aunt) Yungi. The so-called Liberation War found Awa Yungi the daughter of a renowned Qiyadah in the Muslim Sunni sect of the Lurujo Kakwa clan in Kampala. The Muslim Sunni sect was implicated as the leadership of the army at war.

Awa Yungi was the owner of the famous "Blue Room", a concoction of buildings overlooking Nakivubo War Memorial Stadium. So many people knew her. Her father held an esteemed position as Bearer of the Liwa, which was the Muslim flag. It is usually hoisted on a spear and accompanies the army whenever it went out to meet the enemy. Hence, it meant a secondary command in times of war. Awa Yungi's father had symbolically held an esteemed position and seat right next to Prince Badr Kakungulu at Kibuli.

Whether it was through close historical relations to Badr Kakungulu or not, this old lady was spared the wrath of the Bantu who had gone on a rampage, destroying everything in sight that reminded them of Dad and his legacy. Awa Yungi's father had left her a large piece of land and housing which was wilted down to a confined shack over the years - by the turn of the 21st century.

However in 1980, to the consternation of those seeking revenge, Binaisa arranged a bus with full escorts to accompany those hailing from West Nile who wished to return to their place of birth. Awa Yungi joined this trek back home.

By 12:00 or 12:30, the convoy embarked on the journey home to Ko'boko. This was by road instead of the usual short trip by air, which she used to have the prestigious freedom to use in the past. That time she used to land at the aerodrome - almost at Dad's doorstep, because the aerodrome was next to Dad's house at Tanganyika Village in Arua.

The convoy headed for the straight tarmac road towards Kiryadongo, setting eyes on the Karuma Falls and droves of UNLF (Uganda National Liberation Front) convoys and detached roadblocks along the way. Indeed, Awa Yungi passed through the now infamous Joseph Kony's Para National

Park route where numerous ambushes were attributed to Joseph Kony of the Lord's Resistance Army between 1986 and 2003. Joseph Kony is the head of the Lord's Resistance Army, which is currently inflicting atrocities against his own people the Acholi in Northern Uganda.

Enroute to its destination, Awa Yungi's convoy was constantly stopped by irate soldiers who were stupefied as to the reason why Binaisa was "letting the enemy go". Particular venom came from the FRONASA (Front for National Salvation) factions and the Acholi who wished to wreak revenge on these so called "Nubians" and "Anyanya". They would come up the steps in a quarrelsome and lethal mood since they would have known of the convoy's approach, until the head of the convoy would brashly show them the directive from the President and remind them to respect the order.

Interestingly the convoy crossed the Pakwach Bridge without incident, apart from hostile stares from UNLF (Uganda National Liberation Front) and FRONASA (Front for National Salvation) soldiers. They had a further 150 + km to go to get to Arua and they took the Nebbi-Arua route.

Towards Bondo Barracks where they alighted, the head of the convoy took particular care of Awa Yungi and her niece and nephew who had accompanied her from Kampala. He kindly placed them in the CO's (Commanding Officer's) quarters for the night since he did not trust the large presence of a contingent of FRONASA (Front for National Salvation) Hima/Tutsi soldiers who were openly advocating for the annihilation of everybody on the bus.

Awa Yungi was relieved to be woken in the morning and requested to board the bus for the final section of the road into Arua town proper. The convoy arrived to thunderous Takbir amongst a staunchly Muslim gathering who frowned on wailing although it did not stop some from doing so. Intermittent ululation amongst the slowly gathering crowd on a mission accomplished of getting home erupted. However Awa Yungi only felt respite when she crossed the border into Zaire (Congo).

She has always felt a sense of immense gratitude to Mzee Bin Issa as we fondly call Binaisa. Indeed there were dubious mutterings amongst the Bantu that he (Binaisa) must be a Munubi (Nubian) as they are fond of calling us people with Triage Cultural Heritages.

Violence, lawlessness and political dysfunction in Uganda after Dad

As we continued to watch events in Uganda at a distance, there was violence and lawlessness everywhere and more political and military dysfunction.

In February 1980, Binaisa took a bold step, which would lead to his downfall. He relieved Mwanga from office as Minister of the Interior because Mwanga had banned three local Newspapers. Julius Nyerere called for Mwanga's reinstatement.

In March 1980, Nyerere summoned Binaisa to Dar es Salaam to tell him of his dissatisfaction with the factionalism and corruption occurring in Uganda. Meanwhile, there was an abundance of soldiers and guns and the UNLF (Uganda National Liberation Front) decided that in December of that year, elections should be contested on a non-party basis under a "UNLF Umbrella". That meant any legally qualified Ugandan would be permitted to stand, but as an individual, rather than as a Representative of a Party. The UPC (Uganda People's Congress) Party and the DP (Democratic Party) were opposed to this arrangement.

In April 1980, Obote announced his intention to return to Uganda and compete in the elections as soon as they were announced.

On May 1, 1980 (Labour Day), UNLA (Uganda National Liberation Army) Chief of Staff, Oyite-Ojok, initiated a "Search and Impound Operation" in Kampala. 72 people, many of them journalists were illegally detained. Binaisa responded by sacking Oyite-Ojok for "insubordination and disobedience" and appointed him Ambassador to Algeria.

On May 10, 1980, the Military Commission (one of the three bodies that made up the temporary parliament the NCC (National Consultative Council) and headed by the pro-Obote Muganda, Paul Mwanga, included in its ranks Yoweri Museveni as Vice President. Oyite-Ojok and Tito Okello ordered the UNLA (Uganda National Liberation Army) to take control of the radio station and post office and place Binaisa under house arrest at State House, Entebbe, to be guarded by Tanzanian troops. At this time, Tanzania still had 20,000 troops in Uganda. Neither Nyerere nor Obote responded to Binaisa's plea for help.

On May 12, 1980, the UNLA (Uganda National Liberation Army) finalized its takeover and announced it on Radio Uganda. The Military Commission had taken over all Presidential Powers. This was an action of the Military Commission and not the Army. Mwanga declared that "The assumption of power ... shall not be questioned in any court of law and that the suspension of Political Parties (by Binaisa) is hereby lifted."

In 1980, Binaisa was overthrown. His immediate downfall was his relations with Mwanga and his bold attempt to dismiss Lieutenant Colonel Oyite-Ojok. He gave the reason of this dismissal as, to "improve relations between the public and the armed forces (Uganda National Liberation Army)", which had taken over the security duties in Kampala from the Tanzanian Defence Forces in March 1980.

Binaisa asked Oyite-Ojok to become Ambassador to Algeria or surrender but Oyite-Ojok refused to accept both offers. Mwanga came to Oyite-Ojok's defence and signed a statement accusing Binaisa of "betraying the Ugandans and the Tanzanians who had died in the fight to overthrow Idi Amin." He claimed that the Military Commission had taken charge of the country and it was committed to holding elections in which political parties would be free to sponsor candidates.

After Binaisa was overthrown, Mwanga became leader of the Military Commission, paving way for "elections."

Zed Maruru, William Omaria, Tito Okello and Oyite-Ojok were the other members of the Military Commission. While this coup took place, many of the leading political rivals were outside the country - Dan Nabudere, a Mugisu was in Yugoslavia attending Tito's funeral while Museveni and Edward Rugumayo were in Dar es Salaam. Nyerere, Moi and Nimeiry held a meeting at Arusha to discuss what had taken place in Uganda.

On May 27, 1980, Obote returned to Uganda. Anticipating that Obote would soon be campaigning for elections, Yoweri Kaguta Museveni immediately launched his own party which "must resist any attempt by a dictatorship to seize power by military force." "What a hypocritical move this surely was by Museveni!" many Ugandans "whispered" and have "whispered" over the years.

Obote entered Ugandan soil at Bushenyi for the first time since 1971. He campaigned to become President again sooner rather than later.

Obote made a "triumphant" return from exile in Tanzania and addressed a rally at Bushenyi, in Ankole District. During the rally, Obote referred to Okello and Ojok as "my commanders" and he challenged Museveni and many others who claimed to have fought Amin to "produce his own commanders".

On June 14, 1980, 4,000 people attended a rally at Kampala in which Yoweri Museveni launched his UPM (Uganda Patriotic Movement).

On June 17, 1980, the Baganda hoped that Yusuf Lule would return on this day. So they lined up between Entebbe and Kampala to welcome their son but Mwanga another Muganda prevented Lule from ever stepping on Uganda soil unless he (Lule) withdrew some of the accusations he made against the Military Commission after being ousted from the Presidency.

In June 1980, the UNLF (Uganda National Liberation Front) as formed at the Moshi Conference of March 23-26, 1979 was effectively dead following Obote's arrival to Uganda. A joint meeting with the Military Commission and the four political parties, namely, UPC (Uganda People's Congress) Party, DP (Democratic Party), CP (Conservative Party) and UPM (Uganda Patriotic Movement) agreed to ban the establishment of any new parties until after the elections.

During this period, Mwanga threatened that anyone campaigning as an Independent would be dealt with firmly. He warned candidates who defected from the UPC (Uganda People's Congress) to the DP (Democratic Party) to know how to behave "or else we shall teach them a lesson they will never forget".

It was only at this time that Ugandans awoke to the realization that Mwanga was simply preparing the UPC (Uganda People's Congress) Party and Obote for power!

In August 1980, violence and lawlessness continued unabated in and around Uganda's capital Kampala. For instance Leonard Mugwanya a DP (Democratic Party) Politician and son of one of the Party's founders was shot dead by men in uniform. All fingers pointed to Mwanga and his UNLA (Uganda National Liberation Army) henchmen.

Then Obote made a bold move to reclaim the Presidency. He campaigned at Ko'boko but there was a close call!

On August 28, 1980, Obote came to Ko'buko (Ko'boko) and addressed a sparsely attended rally and later an assassination attempt was made against him and his party, at Lo'bijo near the Nyai Trading Centre in Ko'buko (Ko'boko) County.

On October 8, 1980 there was a daring strike, invasion and revenge by the West Nile Boys and Dad's so-called henchmen - the sometimes unfair reference to anybody associated to Dad by tribe, religion and region of origin including people who did not benefit from his rule in Uganda.

After resettling their families in either Zaire (Congo) or the Sudan, Dad's so-called henchmen staged a series of daring strikes against "The Ogwals" (Obote's men). The casualties were many in and around Ko'buko (Ko'boko) and up to Bondo, Moyo, Yumbe and Adjumani.

In October 1980, these former units of Dad's Uganda Army crossed the international borders from the Congo and the Sudan and took over parts of Arua and much of the West Nile District. The UNLA (Uganda National Liberation Army) and the Tanzanian troops took this opportunity to take reprisals against the civilian population whom they accused of siding with the "rebels."

From October 25, 1980 to November 2, 1980, the Military Commission sent a "Fact Finding Mission" to the West Nile District and reported: "Things in West Nile are very bad." Testimonies from victims and reports arising from the "Fact Finding Mission" will be explored in subsequent sections of the series.

Relocating to the Kingdom of Saudi Arabia

While we lived in Libya, a rift developed between Dad and Al-Qadhafi following Al-Qadhafi's close association with Julius Nyerere while trying to gain the OAU (Organization of African Unity) seat that year 1979. Dad viewed Al-Qadhafi's close association with Julius Nyerere as betrayal. So, in characteristic defiance, he dramatically insisted on walking all the way to Makkah (Mecca) if Al-Qadhafi did not offer him safe passage to the Kingdom of Saudi Arabia.

When Dad felt a year's stay in Libya was long enough for him, he actually walked a distance of almost 5,000+ metres before he was convinced by Ugandan Diplomats, Ministers and his Personal Bodyguards to gracefully return to the hotel complex in the official car. The car had trailed the former Head of State along the whole way. This was the same hotel complex where our family and Dad's entourage had been accommodated from the time Dad landed in Libya after his government was overthrown in Uganda. The Great Libyan Leader finally relented and placed Dad, our family and an entourage of over 80 people on a flight to the Kingdom of Saudi Arabia. So, in 1980 we relocated to Jeddah, Saudi Arabia.

It would be thirty years later in the year 2009 that Al-Qadhafi would finally be elected Chairman of the African Union, which replaced the OAU (Organization of African Unity).

In Jeddah we were first placed at "The Sands" Jeddah. However because of the extensive costs involved in housing an entourage of over 80 people, the Former President's immediate family was allocated a Villa in Makarona, while some of his Ministers and Bodyguards were placed in a Flat complex. This was the same Flat complex that was used as a "ground zero" location to "dupe" the BBC (British Broadcasting Corporation) contingent of Journalist Brian Baron and Muhammed Amin when Dad gave his first Television Interview after the 1979 war.

It is the Building the BBC (British Broadcasting Corporation) contingent of Journalist Brian Baron claimed was Dad's residence in their Article on the first Television Interview Dad gave after the 1979 war. However, we referred to the building as Ujamaa Village.

After residing at "The Sands" Jeddah for a period, some of Dad's Ministers were eventually housed at this location. It was where some of the Bodyguards and Former Ministers Ismail Sebbi and Juma Bashir used to reside before they too were given bungalows in the old quarters in Old Jeddah.

Continuing events in Uganda as we settled in Saudi Arabia

Events continued to unfold in Uganda dramatically as we settled in Saudi Arabia after relocating from Libya. In December 1980, Mwanga dismissed the Chief Justice William Wambuzi who had stated, "There have been no constitutional grounds for dismissing Lule by the Military Commission."

Mwanga then dissolved the Military Commission to prepare for the General Elections.

All 4 Political Parties: UPC (Uganda People's Congress), DP (Democratic Party), UPM (Uganda Patriotic Movement) and CP (Conservative Party), agreed to the appointment of a nine-man Commonwealth Monitoring Team under the Chairmanship of Ebenezer Debra, who had recently been Ghanaian High Commissioner in London. The other members were from Australia, Barbados, Botswana, Canada, Cyprus, India, Sierra Leone and the United Kingdom.

Together with 59 Assistants, they formed the Commonwealth Observer Group (COG).

On December 10, 1980, National Elections were held in Uganda amidst violence and lawlessness and under the auspices of Mwanga and the Military Commission.

Following the "Elections" however, the COG reported on the Elections as being "free and fair".

Nevertheless, there followed more violence, lawlessness, political and military dysfunction and allegations of unfair and rigged elections in Uganda.

The largely Protestant UPC (Uganda Peoples' Congress) showed strong gains in the Nilotic Northern districts of Lan'go and Acholi and parts of Teso, Bugisu, other parts of Eastern Uganda and in Basin.

The Catholic-dominated DP (Democratic Party) and Paul Semogerere had support in the Bantu South, Western Uganda and in the West Nile.

The Pro-Monarchist CP (Conservative Party), really a modern version of the 1960s Kabaka Yekka (the Kabaka Alone), found strongest support in certain areas of Buganda. It was headed by Joshua Mayanja-Nkangi.

The UPM (Uganda Patriotic Movement) headed by Yoweri Museveni attracted little support in parts of Buganda and Western Uganda.

In the West Nile and Ma'di Districts, Mwanga took advantage of the troubles in the region to suspend elections and declare the UPC (Uganda People's Congress) "unopposed" because the UPC was the only Party to present candidates in accordance with the "regulations."

Officially, the UNLA (Uganda National Liberation Army) was still the Military Commission's Army but its members owed their loyalty to their sponsors rather than to the government. That time, up to 30,000 people died in the West Nile and Ma'di districts.

Ko'buko (Ko'boko), Yumbe and parts of the Ma'di District became "No Man's Lands".

The UNLA (Uganda National Liberation Army) was on the rampage in the West Nile region of Uganda.

At 5:00 pm, one hour before the official closure of the polls, the Electoral Commission (EC) declared that because of the late start in many districts, the polls would be counted the following day, up to 2:00 pm.

At the time of the 1980 "Elections" in Uganda, there were still 10,000 Tanzanian troops in Uganda.

On December 11, 1980, the DP (Democratic Party) claimed election victory and preemptive celebrations began in Kampala. The BBC and the VOC announced the results worldwide.

Mwanga and the largely Luo UNLA (Uganda National Liberation Army) issued a retrospective proclamation - Mwanga personally on the powers of the Election Commission. Henceforth, all returns had to be submitted to him for a decision as to whether a poll had been "free and fair".

Mwanga said his decision was final, and could not be challenged in a Court of Law. He stated that anyone who illegally announces election results "would be liable to five years in prison or a 500,000 Shillings fine".

Vincent Ssekono, after clearance by the Military Commission and Mwanga, announced the Election Results as follows:

UPC (Uganda People's Congress) - 72 seats

DP (Democratic Party) - 51 seats

UPM (Uganda Patriotic Movement) - 1 seat

The Commonwealth Observer Group (COG) reported that the Elections had been "free and fair" under the circumstances.

Obote became President of Uganda for the second time in Elections that were allegedly "rigged."

During the evening of December 11, 1980, the UNLA (Uganda National Liberation Army) coordinated a two-hour burst of fire that greeted the result of the "UPC victory", and gave warning to anyone who might have attempted to dispute the results.

So, Apollo Milton Obote attempted to return to power but he ended up being deposed again in 1985.

On December 12, 1980, he appointed Mwanga as Vice President and Minister of Defence. He announced a cabinet in which 42 out of 50 posts went to Protestants.

In 1981 the UNLA (Uganda National Liberation Army) disturbed the Origa market inside Zaire (Congo), killing four people and looting hundreds of bicycles. The Kamanyola, the Congo National Army burnt the Refugee houses at Apitiku and Mazaka in Collectivite des Kakwa or the Kakwa of the Congo areas. The Azi'da (Adjutant) of Gombe ordered all Refugees "to either go back to Uganda or go to the refugee camps inside the country Zaire (Congo) within ten days."

In February 1981, Obote tried to remove all his troops from the Capital Kampala and placed the duty of maintaining "Law and Order" in the hands of the Police.

Angered by this move, the soldiers went on rampage. They raided Rubaga Cathedral and worshipping catholics at the mission. Also, a new movement called Uganda Peoples Movement, composed largely of Baganda catholics and led by Andrew Kayiira, staged a series of attacks against Police Stations in the capital, Kampala.

Andrew Kayiira, formerly a Prisons Officer had been on a training mission in the USA in 1971 when Dad took over power from Obote. Lule had made him Minister of Internal Affairs. After his crushing defeat in 1982, Kayira again ran into exile and then returned to Uganda in 1985.

The Resistance Movement by Yoweri Museveni and more violence

In February 1981 Yoweri Museveni "ran" to the Luwero Triangle and mobilized his "Resistance Movement" there, claiming that the December 1980 National Elections had been rigged.

Meanwhile there continued to be sabotage, fighting and killing everywhere.

In 1981, various Rebel Groups made a number of forays in the vicinity of Kampala.

From March 1981 onwards, sabotages by various Rebel Groups against the Obote regime increased. For example, a military convoy was ambushed seven miles north of the capital and a number of UNLA (Uganda National Liberation Army) soldiers were killed. A few days later, rebels damaged the main electricity line from the Owen Falls Dam, plunging much of Western Uganda into total darkness. Another time, the Bugolobi Broadcasting Station was attacked. Even the UPC (Uganda People's Congress) Headquarters in the city of Kampala was attacked.

In April 1981, a Warehouse belonging to the Coffee Marketing Board (CMB) was set on fire. Three shops in Kampala, one of them belonging to Lieutenant Colonel Basilio Okello, Commander of the Kampala Garrison was damaged by explosions.

At Kakiri, 18 miles north of Kampala, an Army post was attacked.

A police station was attacked at Rubaga and the main water tower at Makerere University was put out of action by rebel gunfire.

Obote begged Nyerere not to withdraw his 10,000 Tanzanian troops from Uganda because of the insecurity prevailing in Uganda.

The Ugandan Ambassador to India, Shafiq Arain, presented a request to the British to train the UNLA (Uganda National Liberation Army) in Uganda.

An attack occurred on Mukono, where several civilians were killed by "uniformed men".

In May 1981, Prime Minister Erifasi Otema Alimadi announced that the government had the power to crush the rebels and it would do so.

Obote continued to try to hang onto power as the sabotage, fighting and killing continued everywhere. Then he released a substantial number of Dad's former soldiers.

On May 27, 1981, Obote announced the release of more than 3,000 detainees, most of whom were Dad's former soldiers.

Musa Hussein of the Bori Kakwa clan who now resides in Kibera slums in Nairobi was one of the captives who were released that day. He was a trained Special Branch Police Officer, who was later promoted to District Commissioner of Kitgum during Dad's rule and he was well liked and respected by the Acholi. Then in a strange medley, he was publicly fired from the post from instigations and accusations laid by Gowa who seemed to have a personal grudge with Musa Hussein. However, he was "demoted upwards" and became Dad's Protocol Officer in the Office of the President and "in charge of all procurements from abroad for the President's Family". It was a very powerful position indeed for he had the glamorous task of Jet Setting around the world on Personal Errands for his fellow Kakwa who so happened to be the Head of State. His errands included buying the +40 children clothes, Dad's favourite shooting sticks, Scottish Hunting Shotguns, "Church" Shoes, Van Hussein Valentinos or shirts, Omega watches from Dubai and etceteras.

Oh how we reminisce whenever he makes an inconsistent appearance in Kawempe or Bombo where his father has a property on the way to the Barracks' Main Gate and the actual Bombo Town Council! He was the very person who stopped the rot when some insurgents tried to take over the King George IV Military Garrison in July 1971.

He coordinated an attack with Captain Sulieman Bai of the Baluchistan Muslim Community of Arua who would later be promoted to Colonel, by driving a Police Bedford 3-Tonner upwards towards the Quarter Guard with a number of Military in the back of the truck laying low. As soon as they were near enough, they were able to disable the MMG man who had lodged himself in the roof tiles of the Old Colonial Quarter Guard. Apparently the trajectory of the MMG could not be lowered below a certain point that is why Musa Hussein was able to evade the lethal firing line by quickly driving below and beyond the firing range.

I told Musa Hussein that I was in the vicinity during that whole fracas as were a number of those under the care of Sergeant John Katabarwa. For all I remember is that consistent rapid fire from that intrepid rebel and it seemed his bullets would spray in an arc which dangerously came close to the school dormitories and arched outwards towards the Police Station which was further down the hill. The School dormitories were some 400 yards from the Quarter main gates of King George IV 1st Battalion Garrison Jinja.

On June 24, 1981, some 60 civilians were killed and 100 wounded at the Verona Fathers Mission of Ombaci, just outside Arua in Northern Uganda. Meanwhile business continued as usual.

The UK (United Kingdom) pledged £10 million to Uganda and so did India under Mrs. Indira Ghandi.

Obote, who was his own Finance Minster, accepted IMF (International Monetary Fund) conditions of restoring the health of the Ugandan economy. The immediate result was a drop of the Ugandan currency by 10% of its former exchange value. This was disaster for many people.

In August 1981, the village of Matuga to the north of Kampala and near the military barracks of Bombo was the scene of raids where four UNLA (Uganda National Liberation Army) soldiers were killed.

A month later, a government military tank was destroyed and not far away, a bus was destroyed. Civilians, mainly Baganda, left the villages and sought refuge in the bushes.

A Police Station was attacked at Mukono and five policemen were killed.

A landmine exploded on the road five miles out of Kampala and 25 civilians were killed.

Elsewhere in Karamoja District, the Karamojong attacked Aid workers.

In August 1981, the UNLA (Uganda National Liberation Army) fought back by killing up to 300 and probably hundreds of civilians at the Ombaci Mission. This is the now famous Ombaci Massacre in the West Nile District. Although in an unprecedented blunder in the 1990s, the newly installed Kabaka Mutebi would announce condolences to the Acholi Peoples in response to their suffering during the Ombaci Massacre! This to those in the know is the perennial lumping together of all peoples from north of the Karuma Falls by our diminutive erstwhile southern neighbours!

In October 1981, Obote did not attend the Commonwealth Meeting at Melbourne, Australia but instead he sent the Prime Minister Otema Alimadi.

Infighting between the Kakwa and Aringa and more violence

In December 1981, there was infighting between the Kakwa and Aringa, while there continued to be more sabotage, fighting and killing everywhere.

What a nasty incident! Aringas fighting Kakwas in broad afternoon across at Ora'ba - 7 Aringas lay dead and one innocent Kakwa civilian boy from Midia was killed.

For months, the suspicion and hatred between the Aringa and the Kakwa intensified, sometimes spilling over into Kaya and the Refugee Camps and Settlements.

The Aringa-dominated Uganda National Rescue Front (UNRF) founded by the exiled Moses Ali and commanded by Aringa tribesman Major Amin Onzi was strengthened after "mysterious" arms presumably from Libya had been dropped into the Aringa Airstrip near Yumbe.

The animosity between the Aringa and the Kakwa became too much for comfort for the Kakwa who abandoned the frontlines against both the Aringa and "The Ogwals" or UNLA (Uganda National Liberation Army). But they quietly regrouped and "defended" the Kakwa at the camp of Toligamago just outside the Uganda-Congo (Zaire)-Sudan border near Mount Ati.

Meanwhile, Masamba, the notorious Kamanyola Azi'da (or Adjutant) at Godiya-Gombe continued his terrorizing of the Kakwa and other refugee populations inside Zaire (Congo), especially accusing them of being ribels (or rebels).

In 1982, looking back at 1981, the DP (Democratic Party) Leader Semogerere remarked sourly that more innocent people had been killed in Uganda in 1981 than in any year he could remember since Independence.

In January 1982, George Bamutariki, a prominent member of the DP (Democratic Party) and S.Z. Okao, General Manager of the Uganda Housing and Construction Corporation were shot dead in Kampala and six persons injured.

In February 1982, 300 rebels attacked an Army Barracks from Rubaga Hill, just outside the capital, in a bid to overthrow the government. Semogerere claimed that the soldiers entered the cathedral and that 2,000 people had been arrested in the aftermath of the rebel attack, due to the overreaction of the security forces. Obote apologized to Cardinal, Nsubuga.

Trouble in the Sudan and more violence in Uganda

Meanwhile there was trouble brewing in the Sudan and it spilled over to Uganda.

In 1982, President Jaffar Al-Numeiry of the Sudan instituted his famous or infamous re-division popularly known as Kokora of the Southern Sudan. This abrogated the 1972 Addis Ababa Accord. Most Equatorians were happy with the new arrangements but the Dinka and the Nuer tribesmen were angered. As a result, they regrouped in Ethiopia to form the Sudan Peoples' Liberation Army (SPLA) led by the Dinka, John Garang.

The struggle to free the South continued to bleed the Equatoria Province of the Sudan, sending millions of people in and around the Yei River District to Ko'buko (Ko'boko) and into the Collectivite des Kakwa (or the Kakwa of Zaire (Congo)).

The Equatorians were divided into those "Pro-Kokora" (Pro-Redivision) and those "Anti-Kokora" (Anti-Redivision).

Among the most prominent of the Pro-Kokora were Eliaba Surur, the Veteran Pojulu Politician from Lanya, Engineer Sarafino Wani Swaka, a Veteran Bari, Oliver Batali from the Yei River District, Suzan Ayaba, a Kakwa from the Yei River District, Morris Lawiya, a Kakwa from the Yei River District, Ajo Dedi, a Kakwa from the Yei River District, Taban Lo Liyong, Writer and Professor at Juba University who hailed from the Kuku tribe and Engineer Joseph Tambura, from the Zande tribe.

The anti-Kokora Equatorians included Barnaba Drumo, a Kuku, Joseph Oduho, a Latuko and Lubari Ramba, a Kakwa from the Yei River District.

In April 1982, Amnesty International reported widespread torture and killings and the murder of people held in prisons. The Times expressed in an editorial, "It is now clear that Dr. Obote, mainly because of his past, is not capable of unifying the nation and governing by consent, yet it is not at all certain that anyone else could do better."

Meanwhile, Lule drew world attention to "the deteriorating human rights in my unhappy country."

In 1982, Yoweri Museveni intensified his guerrilla warfare. He visited Libya to request for military assistance to boost his guerrillas.

Dad's marriage to Sawuya Nnasali Kigundu in Saudi Arabia

In 1983, Dad married Sawuya Nnasali Kigundu in Saudi Arabia and it would be his last official marriage. To date he had married officially as follows:

1st - Sarah Mutesi Kibedi married in 1966
2nd - Kaysiya Adroa married in 1967
3rd - Nora Enin Aloba married in 1972
4th - Madina Nnajjemba married in 1972
5th - Sarah Kyolaba married in 1975
6th - Mama Nnabirye Zamzam married in 1978

Dad had learnt his lesson for all three of his first women reverted to Christianity. So after the divorce he issued the first three official wives in 1974, he went on to marry only Muslims.

Mama Madina and Dad were estranged from the time in 1978 when he married Mama Nnabirye Zamzam, his former Presidential Bodyguard. Ironically the two rivals travelled together to Baghdad, Iraq in late 1978 and they were together in Central Africa, Paris, France and finally Zaire (Congo) after Dad's fall. Madina left for Cairo shortly before the fall of Mobutu Sese

Seko and then finally returned to Uganda under an agreement with the NRM (National Resistance Movement) Government of Yoweri Museveni.

The demise of Oyite-Ojok, more violence, killings and kidnappings

On December 23, 1983, Oyite-Ojok died in a plane crash. Upon his death, Acholi-Lan'gi rivalry intensified in the UNLA (Uganda National Liberation Army).

The notion that "all Aringas are thieves" became prevalent in the Refugee Camps and Settlements as more and more Aringas were caught red-handed stealing everything from cattle to goats and money from among the refugees and the Sudanese population. The Aringas also filled most of the Prison and Detention Centres of Yei and Kaya on account of these criminal activities.

Meanwhile there were more kidnappings, more killings and insecurity.

On January 13, 1984, "The Ogwals" (Uganda National Liberation Army) crossed into Godiya-Gombe in Zaire (Congo) and kidnapped 13 men.

On January 17, 1984, "The Ogwals" (Uganda National Liberation Army) entered an area called Ojiga in Moroto District of the Southern Sudan.

More refugees crossed into Panyume, Waimba, Kimba and Mondi-kolo, all inside the Sudan.

On November 15, 1984, The UNLA (Uganda National Liberation Army) crossed into Araba Miju, inside the Sudan and just across from Kaya town, killing three refugees and abducting four others whose whereabouts are not known till now.

On November 20, 1984, many Ugandan Refugees were rounded up at Kaya and Bazi then sent to the newly opened Goli Refugee Camp near the Kakwa-Muru border.

On November 21, 1984, Kaya was plagued with insecurity as the UNLA (Uganda National Liberation Army) conspired with the Sudanese Arab merchants and soldiers stationed at the town against the Ugandan refugees.

Obote overthrown a second time and reconciliatory gestures

In 1985, Obote was overthrown a second time and there was an attempt at Reconciliation - a contradiction in post Amin Ugandan Politics!

On May 25, 1985, General Tito Okello, an Acholi from Namukora in Kitgum and a group of Obote's own military juntas deposed Obote, the Lan'gi. Tito Okello Lutwa became the new President of Uganda.

The Former Uganda Army (FUNYA) including Dad's faction joined Tito Okello Lutwa. In fact, one of my maternal uncles Wilson Toko became the de facto Vice President under Tito Okello's regime. The Northerners seemed to recognize that their decades old and stupid inter tribal feuds had brought them to nothing but animosity towards each other. I must say what a contradiction!

This was Acholi (Luos) and Kakwa (Nilo Hamites) suddenly becoming staunch allies while the Acholi tried to annihilate the other Nilo Hamitic Lan'gis!!!

What a contradiction in post-Dad Ugandan Politics!

Meanwhile, Obote fled Uganda in a helicopter into Kenya where he was temporarily given asylum by Kenya's Minister of Foreign Affairs. Obote then proceeded to Zambia for the second time as a Refugee.

Between 1981 and 1984, 100,000-200,000 people are said to have been killed during Obote's regime in his second term as President!

There were more reconciliatory gestures among "staunch tribal enemies."

A mystical gathering and reconciliation ceremony

A poignantly Mystical Gathering and Reconciliation Ceremony was called up by the father of the Late Brigadier General Pierino Yere Okoya who invited all tribes from the West Nile region of Uganda. The tribes of the West Nile together with our so-called "bitter enemies" the Acholis, converged on a sacred Acholi riverside gathering, where a ram was slaughtered. Then Okoya's father gracefully stood up and solemnly declared to the dignitaries that "Amin did not kill my son. The blame lies "elsewhere.""

Two spears were brought forth and their sharp ends were ceremonially bent backwards and Okoya's father declared that, "Amin is Okoya's friend!" "Whom shall ever amongst the Acholi fight with the people from the West Nile and they meet in battle, then may the bullet from the West

Nile strike us first. Let the vengeance between these two cultures stop forthwith I declare!"

The slaughtered ram was then sliced into tiny nuggets and eaten raw with hot spices by the whole gathering in line with the Reconciliation of two bitter rivals.

One bent spear remained with the Acholis and the other was taken by the people of West Nile back to Arua where it is kept at the Municipal Council as a reminder of the Peace Covenant between the Acholi and the People of West Nile.

"Negotiations" and a military coup by Yoweri Museveni

In July 1985, "negotiations" occurred between Yoweri Museveni and Tito Okello Lutwa in Nairobi.

This was the scene of a devastating incident when my uncle Gard Wilson Toko crossed the room and gave Yoweri Museveni a resounding slap, accusing him of being a foreigner who was causing havoc in Uganda. Quiet whispers to this day claim that Museveni never forgave him for the affront.

Museveni subsequently overthrew the Government of Tito Okello Lutwa and became President of Uganda on January 26, 1986. Okello fled to Tanzania as a refugee.

Meanwhile, Museveni enlisted the support of Moses Ali and the Aringa. However Brigadier Moses Ali was not to receive his highly cherished position of Vice President as per the agreement made in front of Al-Qadhafi in Tripoli because the alliance turned out to be a short-lived "marriage of convenience". This is because on April 7, 1990, on the political front, Moses Ali was arrested by the NRM (National Resistance Movement) and jailed at the Luzira Prison, along with Haji Moses Rajab and Yasin Amisi the latter both Aringas.

He was charged with three counts: (1) Treason (2) Terrorism and (3) The illegal possession of firearms.

The "Northern Dynasty" was effectively written off. Now, Welcome to the "Bantu Dynasty" or is it "Hima/Tutsi Dynasty!"

Apparently, Kenya's President Moi was so incensed by being duped that he was ready to send in the troops like Nyerere did in 1979 but he was stopped by the efforts of the likes of Honourable Anthony Butele who has served consistently in all the regimes.

More trouble in the Sudan

On May 25, 1986, Nimeiry was overthrown while on a tour of the USA and he settled in Egypt as a refugee. Many people attribute his overthrow to actions he took that reneged on the Addis Ababa Agreement, also known as the Addis Ababa Accord. It was a series of compromises made in 1972, which were aimed at appeasing the leaders of the insurgency in Southern Sudan, after the First Sudanese Civil War proved costly to the government in the North. At the time of the Addis Ababa Agreement, Semi-Autonomy was granted to Southern Sudan. There followed a decade of relative peace until 1983 when the Addis Ababa Agreement was cut off by Nimeiry when he imposed Shari'a Law throughout the country.

The First Sudanese Civil War, also known as Anyanya Rebellion or Anyanya I, was a conflict from 1955 to 1972 between the northern part of Sudan and a south that demanded more regional autonomy. Half a million people died over the 17 years of war, which may be divided into three stages: (1) Initial guerrilla war (2) Anyanya and (3) South Sudan Liberation Movement. However, the agreement that ended the fighting in 1972 failed to completely dispel the tensions that had originally caused the civil war, leading to a re-igniting of the north-south conflict during the Second Sudanese Civil War or Anyanya II (1983-2005). The period between 1955 and 2005 is thus sometimes considered to be a single conflict with an eleven-year cease-fire that separates two violent phases.

Dad as a devout Muslim and our Commando Training

Much to his credit, once Dad fell silent on the world stage by say 1981, he refocused his energy into understanding further his own religion Islam. For most of the 24 years he lived in exile until his death on August 16, 2003, Dad studied Islam in further depth and he was devoted to and strictly followed the teachings of Islam. During the time several of my siblings and I lived in exile with him, he encouraged us to also devote ourselves to and strictly follow the teachings of Islam.

When we lived in exile, Dad continued demonstrating his unwavering support for Arab People and the Ummah (Community of Muslim Believers). He maintained his close links with the Palestine Liberation Organization (PLO). In fact, he enrolled us the D12 ("Dirty Dozen") as he referred to 11 of my siblings and me, for the Kids' League Commandos Fidayins at the PLO Embassy in Jeddah. The Commando Training through the PLO Embassy in Jeddah was in line with Dad's demand that we understand all forms of combat. In the Commando Training, my favourite move was the Ammam Yakt Tidi. Basically, it is a front mid air flip where one lands with the shoulder blade and feet, while the pelvis is thrust away from the ground!

One eventful day, my cousin Joseph (Yusuf) Akisu brought along his camera and he was taking pictures of us making frontal rolls through a burning metal hoop wrapped with gunny bags and bathed in kerosene when something terrible and scary happened! I had made an initial jump and Yusuf confirmed that it was good but I insisted and wanted to make a second one to bug my younger siblings. They yelled in complaint but I was on a roll. I wanted to show them that I did not fear the fire so I went headlong through the hoop. Unluckily, I kept my legs outstretched too long and I had not knotted them as I executed the somersault. I hit the whole edifice and it came down on me!

I was lucky that our Yemeni Instructor was at hand and he pulled the burning hoop off me. I came out of the fire like a bat out of hell with an instinctive dash towards the sandpit.

All I remember was my brothers' laughter for surely it was hilarious. I rolled in the sand for what it was worth, rubbing sand all over to douse the fire. I still remember my badly singed maroon Adidas Track-suit.

I suffered second degree burns on my arms and legs. My legacy is a panther like mosaic on my left hand. Somehow after this incident, Dad never let us get back to the Commando Training Camp again. I kept bugging him about it but he let it pass.

Our Boxing and Kung Fu Training

When we lived in exile with Dad, my siblings and I also took up both Boxing and Kung Fu under the stern instructions of a one eyed Palestinian. I recall a time he had a particularly painful way of lumbering up us novices. We would sit cross-legged, then place the soles of our feet together then he would come round behind the novice and forcefully press outwards on each knee, exerting excruciating pain to the pubic tendons. This was supposed to make us flexible, long before I became obsessed with ways Jean Claude Van Damme would make famous in the late eighties. Anyway, at that particular moment, the exercise was particularly painful and hilarious at the same time.

As we sat in a row, the Instructor would enact the punishment as I chose to call it and I, Tshombe would let off a restrained giggle. The one eyed Palestinian Instructor would give me a nasty sidelong glance and inquire, "Why are you laughing? Hmm?"

Sorry sir, I would reply.

I kept up this charade until it came to my turn. The Instructor must have relished the effort when I let off a painful scream and the kids around me were giggling away at my suffering. I must say he reminded us a lot of the famous Bruce Lee. Just to impress us, he would let loose some amazing round the house kicks at the heavy leather bags. I was always overwhelmed by his abilities and always looked back with longing and lament about how my injury at the Commando Training Camp where I suffered second degree burns on my arms and legs stopped us from participating further.

Dad noticed my potential in the Boxing Ring early on and he would sometimes come and show me some moves in the Ring. One particularly devastating move of his was to ask me to stand motionless while he let loose on some particularly close shadow boxing, dead straight at my face. I kept praying to Allah that Dad still had the steady hand, which he proved to have in spite of that omnipotent potbelly.

A Typical day at our household in Saudi Arabia

On a typical day at our household in Saudi Arabia, we had morning prayers at 5:30am. Then at 7:00am, Dad dropped our young siblings Faisal and Khadija at the Expatriates' School, in the family's Caprice Station Wagon. Then he passed by the Safeway to buy groceries. After that, he would begin his extensive phone calls to "dependents" cum political opportunists who kept the flame of his "anticipated return" alive and the phone ringing off the hook in his skeptical ear. They had forgotten that he had told anyone who would hear and understand in Jinja that fateful day on April 12, 1979, "You do not want me now. It's okay. But, But one day you will remember me and you will search for me but you will never find me and you will cry for me Awon'go".

After the phone calls to his "dependents" cum political opportunists, Dad would have lunch at his favourite Pakistani Restaurant and then he would drive off towards the Cornishe for a dip in the sea, having collected our young siblings from school. He would then check on friends like Abdul Rahman, a member of a group they referred to as Arua Boyz or Sheikh Abu Alama and Sheikh Sharif Idris at his Old Jeddah Residence.

Dad had lots of associates with him in Jeddah. Sometimes I would act as their Chauffeur, driving them around Jeddah and neighbouring cities.

Magrib Prayers at 19:00 would find us back home with bags full of groceries for the sagging Freezer and the Frost Free Fridge for the delicate stuff.

Any hint of a malady amongst the kids and Dad would ship the lot of you to King Fahad Military Hospital for an extensive series of check ups. We often joked that Dad spent most of the +26,000 $ US allowance he received from the Saudi Royal Family on medical bills and our education than say on buying the next "Suburban SUV" or even a "Merc" for that matter. He seemed to have made a vow not to look in the direction of that most sought after mode of transportation for it might have reminded him of the past.

Fridays would find us in a long convoy for the Holy City of Makkah Al Mukaramah for Juma Prayers (Friday Prayers) and back to our Al Safa Residence by 19:00 for Magrib Prayers.

Our Spiritual experiences in Saudi Arabia, the Holy Land of Islam

We had a lot of spiritual experiences in Saudi Arabia, the Holy Land of Islam, including entering the Inner Most Sanctuary of the Holy Kaaba. My most spiritual experience took place one eventful day when Dad took us to Makkah on the date when the Governor of Makkah would be doing the annual cleansing of the Holy Site.

As we circulated, which always feels like we are in a Ja'far ("Stream") of people, the Inherent Keeper of the keys to the Kaaba recognized Dad and joyfully grabbed his hand leading him towards the Golden Door up a flight of stairs. Dad instinctively told us to stay close to him as we were given the privilege to enter the Inner Most Sanctuary of the Holy Kaaba. The Keeper of the keys instructed all the boys to pray two Rakkats at each of the four walls of the Kaaba. What struck me was the fact that at every wall and at that particular moment in time, we were facing millions of Muslims from every point of the globe who were praying towards this very centre of the Muslim Universe!

Our Islamic teaching claims that the Kaaba in Makkah is parallel to a similar Kaaba Twaffed in Heaven and that if one were to head straight up from this point, they would actually head up the mythical staircase to heaven.

We were then given the privilege to clean the inside of the Kaaba, which we did with relish and spiritual faith after which we went a final stretch of stairs up to the very top of the Kaaba where brass rings hold the Woven Black Silk Shroud.

The whole family never stopped talking about this event. Whenever I re-tell this story to Learned Imams and Sheikhs in Africa, they always tell me how lucky I was to have had this chance to enter the Inner Sanctuary of the Holy Kaaba.

The significance of the Keeper of the key to the Kaaba recognizing Dad was not lost to me. They had last met in 1972 when Dad came for his initial Haj in the company of the Late King Faisal Bin Abdul Aziz Al-Saud. On that momentous day, as soon as they walked into the Sacred Sanctuary, it started to rain. Shocked, King Faisal Bin Abdul Aziz Al-Saud looked across at his VIP visitor and said, "You must be a special visitor. This last happened centuries ago." Dad had smiled back knowingly because he knew about the renowned rain making skills of his Adibu/Bura Kakwa clan.

Here was Al-Amin being praised for his service to Islam by a descendant of a particular sect appointed by the original Al-Amin (The Prophet

Peace Be Upon Him) following the future prophet's just decision in solving a wrangle amongst the Quraish tribe. The tribes were undecided on who was supposed to place the Holy Black Stone on the newly reconstructed Kaaba.

Another highly enlightening experience was Dad's annual ritual of breaking fast at the Haram Alsharif in Makkah from the start to the finish of the Holy Month of Ramadhan. We would set off in a long convoy with him in the metallic blue "Vogue Range Rover" or the white Caprice Classic Chevrolet Estate, while we took the rear in either the burgundy Fleetwood Cadillac or the cream 505 Peugeot Estate. We normally set off right after Asir Prayers and would arrive just before the Magrib Prayers and take up vigil until the announcement to break fast, which we did with dates and fresh fruit juice.

We would then pray in congregation with fellow Muslims, the Magrib Prayers. Then we would go out for a proper supper before returning for the extended Prayer Vigil "Taraweh Prayer" after the Ishah Prayers. We would return to Jeddah before the Morning Prayer and in time to take Suhur/Dako. This ritual would be performed daily for either the 29 or 30 days in the month of Ramadhan.

Dad's immense curiosity was infectious and we would go on extended tours of the Holy Land of Islam and Holy Sites. We almost made it to the top of the famous mountain, which marked the beginning of the Hijrah where Muhammad and Abu Bakr Al Saddiq took refuge from the search by fellow Quraish. Jebel Noor has always been a photo shoot opportunity whenever members of our family came into town. We learnt about and visited Arafat, the site of the final sermon.

Our trips to the mall and the Safeway Shopping Centre

In Saudi Arabia, Dad loved to shop. So we made a lot of trips to the mall, especially the Safeway. He would go down to the Safeway, which was his favourite and all of us the kids would grab a shopping trolley and pile them high with goods. The Lebanese Security Guards would stare at us in disbelief!

Since most shopping malls open in the evening in Saudi Arabia, it was always a nice surprise for shoppers to see this "giant" with hordes of children strolling around the malls. Most were brave enough to approach him to say "How do you do Sir?" They did this with genuine love and interest in a man from whom they saw a rare bravery and camaraderie during the only time in modern time that the Arabs and some Africans tried to show Independence against Perennial Caucasian Hegemony.

Our trips for Pizza and Kentucky Fried Chicken

In Jeddah, Saudi Arabia, Dad loved taking us out as a family to fast food restaurants. He loved to take us out for Pizza and Kentucky Fried Chicken. He was fond of Pizza and he loved meat but his favourite was Kentucky Fried Chicken.

My conversations with Dad, heated arguments and the will to write

Between 1980 and 1984 I used to have to read a lot of Books, Newspapers, Magazines like the East African, DRUM, Newsweek, TIMES, The African and many others to Dad whenever there was an article written about him. Then I would explain every chapter and we would go into heated arguments based on my childish premise that what was written was true. Unfortunately that is the view of many people who have ever read anything to do with Dad.

While in exile, Dad took stock of his life. As difficult as exile was, it afforded him the opportunity to take stock of his life, but I do not believe that he would express remorse or regret. He would put it this way, "The people will appreciate what I was trying to do for the Indigenous African."

He was not defensive but he was simply saying, "God will be my Judge."

After a heated argument with Dad about allegations contained in a Book, Newspaper or Magazine I read to him, I'd ask him what happened. He'd look at me and say:

"People fought me, I fought them back but I never killed innocent people" and then say again, "God will be the one to judge me".

My will to write something in response to films that have been made about Dad and the books and "zillions" of articles that have been written about Dad is because Dad provided a lot of explanations to my probing and "annoying" questions to him. A lot of his painstaking explanations to me as a son at the time of our heated arguments are slowly being corroborated by unexpected foes. Many of these people have never had any love lost between "us and them". However, they have come forward without anyone asking them to and made statements that corroborate things Dad shared with me in Saudi Arabia, especially amongst our supposed bitterest foe the Luo.

When we lived in Saudi Arabia, I asked Dad very tough questions and challenged him about allegations contained in numerous articles, books and films. We talked about incidents of sabotage that caught the world's attention. We especially talked about self-confessed revelations that are still ironically being blamed on Dad wholesale.

Whenever a new self-confessed revelation came from saboteurs and subversive elements that Dad insisted were operating in and out of Uganda during his rule, to tarnish his reputation, he was fond of remarking that what the world was being told about him was "Parapaganda" (Propaganda). In response to the incidents that were and continue to be unfairly blamed on him, Dad always retorted, "That was their Propaganda against Muslims and Kakwas in general." But by Jove, he was not going to stand by idly while others from the very word go in 1971 took up arms and started a protracted campaign against his regime, he always asserted. He said he fought them the best and only way he could and knew how!

As I suggested before, an Independent Truth and Reconciliation Commission is the place to arrive at the actual truth about what really happened during Dad's rule in Uganda.

Dad regularly recounted the assassination attempts made on his life, especially the one that occurred in 1976, which I call "The Day of the Jakal". His version of events surrounding the assassination attempt that day was outlined in Ugandan Newspapers all over the country the following day. The Newspapers at the time show my father standing over the dead body of the Late Musa with a swollen face from the effect of the imbedded shrapnel in his head. Musa's mother, the whole Swahili community in Arua and the Archives recited and recite the events word for word.

I remember Dad talking of how the unclipped shrapnel grenade landed with a thump on his back before it lobbed to the side exploding and fatally injuring Musa his Half-Caste driver. According to Dad, apparently the one who hurled the deadly weapon had not waited long enough, having unhinged the lever before they lobbed the grenade. Dad survived that incident and drove the Jeep all the way from Mukwano Road, Nsambia to Mulago Hospital, wobbling all the way to safety. When Dad came home with the Newspaper showing the injured and dying Musa, we were very saddened and scared.

Dad vividly recalled the incident and went on to explain the technicality of the shrapnel grenade. He claimed that whoever threw the grenade did not wait long enough after releasing the lever because it normally takes some 10-15 seconds for shrapnel grenades to explode. Dad said he distinctly felt the thud when the grenade hit him on the back but it bounced to the right hand side of the Renegade JEEP.

The explosion was absorbed by the impact on the ground and the rear right tire and unluckily, Musa, one of his drivers took shrapnel inside his skull, while in the co-driver's seat inside the Renegade JEEP. Dad said he instinctively grabbed the slumping body of his fallen Aide and pulled him back into the Drop Top. Then he adjusted the hand less Larynx Motorola Communicator and continued to drive towards Mulago Hospital with the injured co-driver while he ordered for reinforcements to cordon off the whole Nsambia Barracks.

During our life in exile, I was very inquisitive and very bold in poking, prying, prodding and asking Dad very tough questions to which he provided never before heard and published answers. I include many of his answers in my projects but encourage others to speak about what they knew and know.

In asking Dad the tough questions, I wanted to get to the root of what happened during his rule in Uganda and why he was being called some of the worst names in human history, including being referred to as Devil Incarnate and I did get some answers. However, I again encourage others to speak about what they knew and know.

The opportunity to interact with my Dad always came my way because I was in a unique position. Between the eldest sons Taban Idoru Amin and Ali Nyabira Amin, there were hordes of sisters - 5 in number namely Amina Ingi, Aaliya (Aliya), Maimuna Adili, Farida Akulu Dawa and Bebi Anite. Then I Remo came along and by the time we got to Libya after Dad's government was overthrown, I was 12 years old and I spent my awakening period between the ages of 13 and 18 with Dad. For he did an unexpected thing by sending the youngsters born between 1967 and 1978 to reside in Kisangani, Zaire (Congo) with his elder brother Ramadhan Dudu Moro Amin Dada, during the dispersal of the D12 ("Dirty Dozen") in 1982. My uncle Moro is Dad's brother who accompanied Grandpa the day Dad was born in 1928. He was 9 years old at the time.

The rest went to reside with his Foster brother Muhammed Luka son of Stephan Yuma in Nairobi and Mombasa and the wild bunch ended up with Idoru Taban in Kinshasa.

The elder sons were either still training in Akba Military Airbase on the outskirts of Tripoli with Al-Qadhafi's equivalent of the Foreign Legion as a Fighter Pilot in the case of Flight Lieutenant Taban Idoru Amin or as Head of Delegation to the Magrib States of Morocco and United Arab Emirates in the case of Ali Nyabira Amin.

I was therefore Dad's proverbial errand boy, cook, housekeeper, banker, driver, Bodyguard and etceteras, by default. He had sent all the lot including maids and Bodyguards either back to Uganda or to Kenya, the Congo and the Sudan and he kept to the bare minimum those amongst his very own progeny he felt he could trust. Dad claimed and always said that the best defense could only come from the family inner circle, namely his children.

Why I was kept closely around him against the odds perplexes me and the rest of the Al-Amin Family to this day. It is the subject of vitriol I continue to get from those amongst the family who persist in believing that I am not Idi Amin Dada's son but the son of Major Luka Yuma who alas was 10 years old when I was born. So probably he was only eight and a half when I was conceived but living and interacting with Dad one-on-one gave me the once in a life time free opportunity to intimately get to know my father. I was able to talk with him, argue with him and debate family and political issues with him.

I was also a witness to the love affair between him and his Beloved last wife Nightie Nnasali Sawuya Kigundu. Having been the witness at the Nikkah (Wedding) together with my younger brother Geriga Sulieman, Dad's last wife learnt to trust and rely on me to get to understand her man. Therefore, whenever publications or newsreels came through that constantly focused on his legacy, Arusu (newly wedded wife) as we initially called her would bring them to me as an urgent assignment from Dad.

I turned into his very own "PS Balinda" his favourite Permanent Secretary during his reign in the 1970s. Alas I ran the gauntlet of having to read the bloody books and explain or interpret every detail to him. It also gave me the opportunity to clarify a few issues that came out in books like A State of Blood by Henry Kyemba and The Rise and Fall of Idi Amin by Cameron.

I must say I had the unique advantage of asking questions like a son straight to the point. I was saying it like it is and getting candid answers back from a parent who was off his guard so to speak or felt a need to answer questions laid on by his own son and not another "Brian Baron like" Journalist. Brian Baron is a journalist who interviewed Dad in Saudi Arabia and his interview will be a great addition to background information for the section of the series titled "Other People Speak".

When I asked Dad questions about his legacy, I was between the ages of 13 and 18 – the stage when teens ask the most revealing of questions.

My resumption of education in Saudi Arabia and life in England

During the Eighties, I lived in the UK, studying for "O" and "A" Levels in London and Leicester. I was discreet about my identity, went about incognito while in Britain and didn't go out of my way to make it known that I was Idi Amin's son. In all correspondence to me in England, Dad used the Palestinian Pet Name "Abu Faisal Wangita" ("Father of Faisal Wangita").

The turmoil of the late 1970s and early 1980s that occurred throughout my native country Uganda disrupted and derailed my education. During the entire period, I never once set foot inside a classroom.

In Africa, a successful revolution implies that those considered part of the "ruling regime" at any particular time have to flee into exile for fear of being killed. My father's excesses had finally caught up with him and he was overthrown on April 11, 1979. My family finally took refuge in Saudi Arabia, the Holy Land of Islam in 1980, via Tripoli in 1979, under a pre-agreement laid out between Dad and the Late Malik Faisal Ibn Abdul Aziz Al Saud Allah Yar Hamu in 1972.

By 1982, three years had passed since my last class (Primary VI or P.6. in 1979). Our general delusion was that we would be back in State House soon so any plans for life in exile were never on the agenda!

My resumption of school life was rusty, to say the least. At age sixteen, I was considered much too old for my previous class. So I was placed in Grade 8 (American System) at Manarat International in Jeddah. This is essentially an English language school that catered for children of Expatriates employed in the Kingdom of Saudi Arabia. At the time, my physical stamina was in overdrive and my love for sports was equally relentless.

Some American friends whom I hung out with introduced me to basketball although way back home in Uganda, Dad was pretty enthusiastic about the game and the whole family got caught in its magic. He once brought a celluloid action film of the Harlem Globetrotters and it was a memorable occasion at our home.

I will never forget Carly's antic like dribbling right down to the floor and dunking right after such antics. Superb! Somehow, I still hold the likes of Bilal, a half-American half-Palestinian friend responsible for the faint Anglo-American accent I have acquired. I took to the game like Daffy Duck to water! I eventually ended up with the nametag of Dr. J., at the time a kind of forerunner of the awesome Michael Jordan. I guess this came about because of my preference for those lazy long distance floater dunks that Julius Erving was famous for.

Athletics comes easy to me and I feel I could have excelled in say the Decathlon. Daley Thompson is my hero and we actually share the same height 6'1", or say the 800-meter race since I could manage a decent 21 seconds in the 200 meters. This would work out well in the longer distance since on average the 800-meter race is won by the final 50-meter kick.

I truly enjoyed my resumption of education in Saudi Arabia going right up to High School Grade 10 in 1984. Dad then sent me to the United Kingdom, arriving in the autumn (fall) of 1984, a naive 18-year old. I first took up tuition at Marsden Tutors overlooking the Queens Tennis Club! But I actually studied at Collingham Tutors located between Earl's Court and Gloucester Road Tube Stations in Central London.

Meeting my Israeli friend Nicola and the enchanting Zain Ahmes

While studying in England, I met an extremely beautiful Israeli friend called Nicola and the enchanting Zain Ahmes Alsharaf a quadruple national with a half Saudi, half Malay mother and Half Egyptian, half Turkish father. They had a residence at either Grovner Square or Belgravier Square. On the very day I reported at this Collingham Tutorial, Nicola was sitting on the middle landing of a flight of mahogany stairs facing the entrance to the Tutorial and it was from her that I inquired where the Registry Office was.

Ours was a truly plutonic affair but unsure of where I stood with the Kibbutz girl, I once let it go off the boil and she once came storming into the school library and asked to talk to me outside. When we got outside, she accused me of ignoring her. I denied it but went on to say that I did not know where I stood with her. I remember how uncomfortable she felt when she introduced me to her dance class at a posh gymnasium cum sports club. I gave up the ghost right there and then but had already once let slip to Dad about Nicola and strangely enough he encouraged me to go the whole hog not realizing that I was still a virgin and did not know what to do.

On hindsight, I cannot believe that I was daring enough to speak my inner most desires to my father. Nonetheless, his ear was always open to me at that critical time in my life. Zain on the other hand was that unattainable sophistication, whose caliber I felt I would never live up to. Her interest in me was direct but I always misinterpreted it as jesting or simply taking the wog for a ride kind of game students are fond of doing to African newcomers.

I once confronted her in front of a bunch of friends in the basement coffee room when I dramatically stated, "Zain, what do you see in me humm?" She was deeply embarrassed but somehow stood her ground which gave me the courage to tell her in front of everyone that I felt very lucky that she was showing the slightest sign of affection towards me, even if it was just for friendship, I appreciated it. She was comforted by these words since everyone could see I was sincere about it. After that, she would drive me from one location in Gloucester Road to the other location around Earl's Court in her BMW.

The infatuated lovely redhead from South Africa

Interestingly, a lovely Redhead from South Africa openly declared her love for me and wanted to have a child with me! I have managed to forget her name but I still remember that cute freckle infested face in the very same coffee room and I told her off that her Apartheid parents would not tolerate such waywardness. She, I must say was relentless and she was fond of making sketches of me, for her art class or simple doodling, which I found amusing.

Reflections on my love for music and a couple of favourite musicians

Music in general will always be the love of my life and totally held sway over me from 1982 onwards. To my mind, Teddy Riley's New Jack Swing Beat defines my musical taste. Steve Huey precisely wrote a Bio, which dove-tailed in perfectly with what I would have liked to say about my man Teddy Riley. He set up this seminal R & B trio GUY and was the first group to sport the New Jack Swing sound. Essentially traditional soul vocals melded to hip-hop beats, "Rap Rhythms and Hyped Melodies I might add" with credit for the genre's invention going to founder, multi-instrumentalist, and super producer "TR" Teddy Riley.

Riley formed his first band, Wreckx-N-Effect, while still a teenager, with brothers Markell Riley and Brandon Mitchell. Guy followed a few years later in 1987. Its first incarnation featured vocalists Aaron Hall and Timmy Gatling. Their self-titled debut album was an instant smash, producing the RandB hits "I Like," "Groove Me," "Spend the Night" and "Teddy's

Jam". Meanwhile, Riley found himself in strong demand as a Songwriter and Producer.

In 1988, Riley produced Bobby Brown's "Don't Be Cruel", the album that helped New Jack Swing cross over into the pop mainstream. Riley has also worked with Kool Moe Dee, Michael Jackson (Dangerous), Stevie Wonder, Keith Sweat, Jane Child, and SWV, among others. In between albums, Guy contributed songs to the soundtracks of "Do the Right Thing" and "New Jack City".

Alas by 1989, Guy was in turmoil. Riley's brother Brandon Mitchell was killed in a shooting and the group became involved in an acrimonious split with Manager Gene Griffin over money. 1990s "The Future" featured Hall's brother Albert Damion Hall in place of Gatling and spawned RandB hits in "Let's Chill," "Do Me Right," "D-O-G Me Out" and "Long Gone." However, by the time Riley and Guy finally started to attract media attention for their innovative and influential work, the trio had broken up. Riley concentrated on his Production and Songwriting career for several years before forming the band Blackstreet with vocalists Chauncey "Black" Hannibal, Dave Hollister, and Levi Little.

The quartet released a self-titled debut in 1994. Aaron Hall released his solo debut, "The Truth", in 1993. Brother Damion Hall followed in 1994 with "Straight to the Point". Guy reunited in 1999, issuing "Guy III" early the following year.

Also George Clinton's Funk is where the sound emanates the mastermind of the Parliament or Funkadelic collective during the 1970s. George Clinton broke up both bands by 1981 and began recording solo albums, occasionally performing live with his former band mates as the P. Funk All-Stars. Born in Kannapolis, North Carolina on July 22, 1941, Clinton became interested in doo wop while living in New Jersey during the early 1950s. He formed the Parliaments in 1955, based out of a barbershop backroom where he straightened hair [CONK].

The group had a small R & B hit during 1967, but Clinton began to mastermind the Parliament's activities two years later. Recording both as Parliament and Funkadelic, the group revolutionized R & B during the 1970s, twisting soul music into funk by adding influences from several late 1960s acid heroes: Jimi Hendrix, Frank Zappa, and Sly Stone. The Parliament/Funkadelic machine ruled black music during the 1970s, capturing over 40 R & B hit singles (including three number ones) and recording three Platinum Albums. By 1980, George Clinton began to be weighed down by legal difficulties arising from Polygram's acquisition of Parliament's label,

Casablanca. Jettisoning both the Parliament and Funkadelic names (but not the musicians), Clinton signed to Capitol in 1982 both as a solo act and as the P. Funk All-Stars. His first solo album, 1982's Computer Games, contained the Top 20 R & B hit "Loopzilla." Several months later the title track from Clinton's Atomic Dog EP hit #1 on the R & B charts.

It stayed at the top spot for four weeks, but only managed #101 on the pop charts. Clinton stayed on Capitol for three more years, releasing three studio albums and frequently charting singles -- "Nubian Nut," "Last Dance," "Do Fries Go with That Shake" -- in the R & B Top 30. During much of the three-year period from 1986 to 1989, Clinton became em-broiled in legal difficulties (resulting from the myriad royalty problem latent during the 1970s recordings of over 40 musicians for four labels under three names).

Also problematic during the latter half of the 1980s was Clinton's disintegrating reputation as a true forefather of rock. By the end of the decade however, a generation of Rappers reared on P-Funk were beginning to name-check him. In 1989, Clinton signed a contract with Prince's Paisley Park label and released his fifth solo studio album "The Cinderella Theory". After one more LP for Paisley Park (Hey Man, Smell My Finger), Clinton signed with Sony 550.

His first release, 1996's T.A.P.O.A.F.O.M. ("the awesome power of a fully operational mothership"), reunited the funk pioneer with several of his Parliament/Funkadelic comrades from the 1970s. Clinton's Greatest Funkin' Hits (1996) teamed old P-Funk hits with new-school Rappers such as Digital Underground, Ice Cube and Q-Tip. John Bush's Bio above captures the music genre I hold so dear to my life.

Bone More of Cuba is another forgotten soul whose style Cuban Son Music gives me a funny feeling as though I might have lived in that era in another life? I cannot help but feel a strange sense of exhilarating "DÉJÀ VU" whenever Cuban Son Music is played. I might be the only person on Allah's earth who seems to be connected to the Universal Heartbeat. I always find myself dancing to any sound without being taught. Honestly I seem to know what to do and my enthusiasm and zest for music has always been the heart of a party. It was sweet to see the same characteristic in my then two-year old daughter in 2001. "Let the Music Play!"

The distractions and tempo of London's Cosmopolitan fast life

I took "O" Level (Ordinary Secondary School Level) exams in June of 1985 in the subjects of English, Mathematics, Biology, Chemistry and Physics. I managed a British C grade pass in English, but failed the rest. I guess, for the impressionable teenager that I was then, the distractions and tempo of London's Cosmopolitan fast life were consuming too much of my time and money.

I had picked up an obsession for ice-skating and had become adept at illegal speed skating on the inadequate ice rink at Queens Way although the better facility was at Richmond South London. No new film release passed me by and I practically went through the London Club Scene guidebook sampling specialty nights Wednesdays through to holy Sunday. Piccadilly Circus became a rendezvous point in the midst of those flashy neon lights, heavy traffic and drizzly weather.

My very first love ever was with an exiled 29-year old Iranian lady by the name of Shah'llah from near the Russian Border (actually Kirghistan/Iran border- back then the USSR was Russia to the odd layman). I was fond of taking an early supper at Wimpy and she was one of the Attendants there. Being a regular, she would serve me and would sit at the counter. One day, just as I was finishing my dinner, I looked up and found her staring at me and I smiled.

Interestingly, she surged from her seat and headed towards me and frankly told me, "That is the first time you have ever smiled! I used to tell my friend that you never smile". Taken aback I nonetheless managed to keep the conversation going, claiming looks can be deceptive and that it did not necessarily mean that I was as grumpy as I looked.

I left the fast food restaurant and was browsing at WH Smith Bookshop right next door to Wimpy when I looked up. There she was right next to me with a wonderful smile on her face when our eyes met in the window reflection. I turned around and enquired if she had finished work, which she confirmed. "Yes!" I then enquired whether she was from Egypt and she said, "Nooo! That is what most people especially Arabs think". She then proceeded to tell me that she was from Iran and a Persian at that.

We started to stroll towards where I was renting a bed-sit. Her apartment was along the same way and she cautiously invited me up for dinner. I reminded her that I had just had supper at Her Wimpy. "Nah, that wasn't food. You should come up and taste authentic Iranian cooking." I was much obliged and followed her petit frame up a flight of stairs to the third floor where we entered a plushy furnished lounge.

Hers was the story of middle class Iranians too used to the "Peacock Throne Rule" of the Shah and who could not handle the stringent Shia Fundamentalism of Ayatollah Khomeini, which forced droves of them out of their beloved country in the 1979 Islamic Revolution. She asked me to feel comfortable while she freshened up. One thing led to another. She even taught me how to play poker, which I eventually managed to forget how to play over time and I taught her how to play good old Matatu [Karata].

I tasted some of her sumptuous cooking and just like that Kool and the Gang song I did see the light. I always reminisce and feel the comforting surroundings did the trick. I was such a natural that I would have failed to convince her that it was my very first time ever that day. Talk about that New Jack Swing adage "one minute man? No way Jose" I honoured my Dada heritage that day!

Following my very first encounter with her, I would make a Beeline to her apartment whenever I came from school. However, I childishly broke off the affair when my sisters Aaliyah (Alia), Akulu, Akujo, Atta, Araba and Sakina came from Nairobi to study in the UK. Love was such a new thing for me that I foolishly had it at the back of my mind that if my sisters ever found out this "Mario like Liaison", they would report me to Dad. My sisters have always been the "Nja ku lopa wo wa Tata" types. They would relish the prospect of snitching on Prim and Proper Tshombe. It was around the same time that Dad insisted that I seek a suitable Boarding School.

Meeting Lucas Mboya

Gabbitas Truman Thring, a Consultative Organization helped me find a Residential Service that catered for adult students. My choice was Irwin Academy (Now Irwin College) on 164 London Road in Leicester, England - a stone's throw across the park from the University of Leicester. I joined Irwin Academy in the autumn (fall) of 1985. At this Institution I took the subjects of Mathematics and Biology and changed the other two options to Economics and Business Studies at "O" Level. The former Principal Mr. Williams or the present Administration at the renamed Irwin College can provide additional information or an evaluation of my stay at this memorable institution.

At this institution, I had the fateful friendship of the son of one of Africa's most brilliant Trade Unionists cum Politician, Mr. Thomas Mboya of Kenya. Lucas Mboya a 6'2" chap was a friend in need and he was a friend indeed. Unfortunately for me at the time my whole stay in England was incognito, but somehow word did get around that I was son of so and so.

I still have this sneaky feeling that my Principal who was rumoured to be a member in the highly respected Free-Masons might have known right from the very beginning that, I was the son of Idi Amin Dada. What I then realized was that these Residential Colleges under Gabitas Truman and Thring specialized in catering for well to do so-called "Third World" students who most often were children of renowned politicians.

We got along like a house on fire! It was an Adhoc amalgamation of Africa's elite/advantaged. Following my acrimonious move from London, Dad curtailed my pocket money down to the bare minimum, realizing that it was my propensity to spend that was distracting me from my studies. However Lucas Mboya seemed to sense my discomfort and he was in the habit of insisting that as a team we would move out together to clubs and the like at his expense. Being the live wire that we then were, we would rave till "Da break ah break" of dawn. Our main interest was Music! Music! Music! then the ladies and booze - apple cider in particular for my part. It was a well-replayed joke that I was always first on the dance floor and the last to leave! My obsession for Navy Blazer Jackets, tanned flannels, Italian Silk Ties and Allen Edmonds Brogues earned me the title "Renaissance Man". Lucas used to call my taste in shoes "grandfather shoes". I could not for my life convince the others of the soundness of slipping your feet into the expensive leather from renowned shoemakers like "Church" and "Allen Edmonds".

My "dance related" injury and reconciliation with Mama Mariam

A particularly heartfelt event or call it reconciliation, took place between me and Dad's former senior wife Mama Mariam Mutesi Kibedi in 1986. A "dance related" incident precipitated this poignant event.

I had gone out dancing the night away at Maximus Disco right next to the Famous Legend Disco frequented by American tourists and was in full swing doing my thing on the cramped dance floor at Maximus when I felt a bullet shot sound run through my frame! I turned round to see what had hit me to no avail. I took a step with my right foot only to feel excruciating pain around my ankle and Achilles tendon. I quickly learned that the only way to move was to use the heel and avoid touching down with my toe tip.

I felt down around what used to be tight and springy, only to feel fleshy skin and not the usual tight bounce and then I realized something serious had happened to me. This was on a Friday night and I had come to London for holidays from Leicester. I hobbled down to the Piccadilly Circus Tube Station on a ride back towards Gloucester Road Tube Station.

A very touching event happened when an old lady entered the Tube Train and could not find a secure place to hold on to and bravely or felt safe enough to hold on to me elbow through elbow. Not realizing the state in which I was in, I felt comforted since my mind was in turmoil at what might have happened to me.

I hobbled off the Tube saying goodbye to the old lady at Gloucester Road Tube Station and headed to a posh apartment Dad had rented for the family a short distance away from Hyde Park. I remember Akujo Kulthum was in the lounge when I entered and she noticed my limp. I told her I had injured my Achilles tendon but hoped it would heal. She was alarmed at no evidence of the tendon to the touch and told me to go and see a doctor. I thought I had sprained my foot and it might get better after a hot shower. Alas it never did but got worse the longer I stayed. Amazingly I stayed with it until Sunday when I was obliged to go to the local General Practitioner in the Area who referred me to I think St. Thomas Hospital. I am not certain but it had one of those saintly names to it.

The doctor confirmed it was what he termed a Ruptured Achilles Tendon that would need immediate surgery. To him it was also a rare chance to do such an operation. Luckily because of the gravity of the situation, the doctor told me that the tendon was in danger of shriveling up thus becoming useless. I must have jumped a whole pile on the NHS (National Health Services) waiting list.

He asked me how it happened and when I mentioned dancing he was really amused. He told me it usually happened to Badminton Players due to the short and sharp movements involved in the game. I remember the anesthetist telling me to count up to ten when they put the mask on my face. I never got to ten and woke up in a ward. My saving grace was listening to Capital Radio (London) on a piped music contraption on the bedpost.

I absolutely loathed the hospital environment and the nurses noticed. Obviously in pain I would shun painkillers trying to brave it out. Even a saintly Chinese Matron asked me when I was being discharged and why I hated the hospital staff so much and I truthfully told her it was not the people. I simply was very scared of the hospital environment.

My second saving grace during the hospital ordeal was a daily visit from my supposed enemy Mama Mariam. According to those in the know of our past history and what my mother had told me about the past, I was surprised by Mama Mariam's visits to me at the hospital but appreciated them. I felt that every time she came to see me with flowers and a get well card, she couldn't help thinking about the past. However, I accepted the fact that Mama Mariam was coming to terms with what my birth had done to her marriage to Dad and she must have felt the need to care for someone who was the son of her distant cousin – my mother.

I felt very touched and from that day onwards we have been very close, much to the chagrin of my own mother who does not trust her. As far as my mother is concerned, she would have thrown Mama Mariam as far away from us as possible if she had the strength. This is because of the accusation she levied on mum after she became pregnant with me and the ensuing Deadly "Paternity Test" Grandma subjected me to, which could have cost me my life. I am fond of reminding mum that it was her who had wronged her cousin and not the other way round since Mama Sarah Mutesi Kibedi was the rightful wife.

Interestingly, Mama Mariam was the only person who visited my lonely world at that critical moment, which speaks volumes. Even Dad's new wife Mama Petit (Arusu/newly wedded wife) who was in the country to place my siblings Faisal Wangita and Emira Hawa Amin in a Boarding School way up in Bedford did not feel a need to come and see me in hospital. Apart from those thrillingly unexpected visits from our mother "Mama Maliyamu" as the Bantu are fond of calling her, this I believe was a true reconciliation between what I represent to her and about our past.

I spent nine painful months in another plaster of Paris and was totally disoriented from my exams and failed miserably for the second time. I only managed to pass all of them in the summer and fall exams of 1987. I then enrolled for two options in Advanced School Certificate Level - Economics and Business studies. I passed my Business Studies with an E Grade (British) the least I could do under the circumstances.

We next met with Mama Mariam when she made a memorable trip to Uganda at the beginning of the millennium and it came out in the papers as her first trip back home. I recount what transpired then in a subsequent section.

A visit in Saudi Arabia from our uncle Ramadhan Dudu Moro

I have fond memories of our uncle Baba Ramadhan Dudu Moro Amin Dada. Memorably in 1987 while on a school break, I was given the task of being an Honourary Mutawaf (Guide) for him, with the responsibility of guiding him through a complete Ummrah.

That time, we set off for Makkah as a group comprising the whole family. Then Dad bought tickets on the Domestic Saudia Flight to Madinah - just the two of us. We arrived to a fully packed Harram Al-Shari.

I was able to show my uncle Ramadhan Dudu Moro Amin Dada the Holy Site at the Mimbar where it is recommended to pray two Rakkats since it was highly valued as a site where Arch Angel Jibril would often descend from Heaven to convey the message from Allah. We then joined a long line towards the viewing portal of the graves of Umar, Abu Bakr and Muhammad (Peace Be Upon Him).

From there, we moved onto a marbled wall where we also prayed two Rakkats since it was also a location where quite often the Arch Angel Jibril would also descend with a message from Allah sub hanah wat Allah. We then moved onto the very first Masjid Al Kubah. From there, we went and visited the battlefield of Uhhud, the burial site of Hammzah Alayhi Sallam.

I showed our uncle the point on the mountain side where at the point of defeat when Khalid Ibn Walid's brilliant military tactics almost cost the Holy Prophet his life, droves of Angels came winging down to earth at that very spot to defend the Holy Prophet. He came out of the attack with a broken tooth and to this day the place is considered close to Heaven as a point of entry and exit for the Holy Angels.

We then went to other points of the steady war front where at a particular location, the Sahabahs had built mosques on the battlefield and they would always pray two Rakkats at each site. I also showed him the mosque at which the commandment came to shift direction from Masjid Al Aqsa towards Makkah and the Holy Kaaba and then went to show him the burial site of the Muhajirin in the centre of Madinah Al Munawarah.

Finally, we set off on a +200 km drive back to Jeddah inside an air-conditioned Kangaroo Spring Hilux Toyota Double Cabin Truck. Sadly, the tour had had some tragic overtone since misleading information had reached us that maybe Mariyam Arube Babirye and Hussien Minari Kato had died. My elder sister Salamssidah and the remaining wife Mama Ariye had probably panicked when sending the information, which turned out thankfully not to be true.

I remember while we were on the flight to Madinah, Baba Ramadhan Dudu Moro Amin Dada suddenly broke down in tears. All I could do was place my hand over his trying to comfort him. The mother of the twins had decided to go back to Uganda leaving the children in Kisangani at the tender age of only four months!

On his hurried way back to Zaire (Congo) on Ethiopian Airlines, I remember the two brothers sitting at the Departure Lounge in an extended heart to heart discussion. What I only found out later on our regular trips for swimming at the Cornishe with Dad was he told me that Baba Ramadhan Dudu Moro Amin Dada had requested Dad to send me to Kisangani to look after him. But Dad had declined claiming that I was still studying in the UK but that when I finished he would think about it.

I always felt touched by that request and in some way my coming to Uganda in 1990 and Baba Ramadhan Dudu Moro Amin Dada's eventful return to his homeland in the early 1990s brought us together again. At the back of his mind he has always had it that I was a very knowledgeable person as far as our religion Islam was concerned which I found amusing.

A pleasant reunion with my siblings in Jeddah, Saudi Arabia

A particularly pleasant reunion took place in 1987 in Jeddah, Saudi Arabia between remnants of the D12 ("Dirty Dozen") as Dad chose to call me and eleven of my brothers. Alas, Hassan Ruba son of the late Ali Lopuli Amin Dada had succumbed to death following a chest injury and internal bleeding in Kinshasa in the Democratic Republic of the Congo when he got involved in a gang fight in the Congo capital. Yusuf Akisu departed for the mineral and rebel infested areas of East Angola, following a stint with some Senegalese friends in Kinshasa. He never felt the need to contact the family again although his last mail showed the UNHCR (United Nations High Commissioner for Refugees) address in Luanda, Angola.

Muhammad Luyimbazi had decided to go and live deep in the interior folds of the Mbandundu Rain Forest but finally decided to come back to Uganda and now resides in Kampala. Abdul Nasser Alemi Mwanga was living a life of material comfort with his mother Mama Nnalongo Madina Amin in Kinshasa under the fatherly protection of the Late Mobutu Sese Seko Kuku Waza Banga. After Kinshasa, they were relocated to Cairo, Egypt from where they negotiated their return to Uganda. However peculiarly, Dad had sent the "Cream dela Cream", noticeably Moses Kenyi, Hussien Juruga Lumumba, Adam Ma'dira, Issa Aliga and Mao Muzzamil to live in Kisangani, while Sulieman Geriga and Khamis Machomingi resided in Nairobi, Kenya - eventually settling in Germany and London respectively.

I, flat footed floogy of all unexpected intentions, got the choicest destination of London, England in 1984 to the chagrin of all concerned! However Dad had a change of mind and pulled out the "Kisangani Boys" out of Zaire (Congo) and sent them to Lyon, France in 1987. We were able to link up come the extended summer vacation of 1987. Dad's expensive SLR EOS Canon was at hand to mark the occasion and we merrily clicked away.

After the reunion in 1987, I left for London still amazed at the transformation that had taken place amongst siblings who forever in my mind's eye I used to visualize as tiny but on that day had metamorphosed into towering giants! I in fact took up the rear in the size department at 6'1" while the majority were 6'4"+ - in fact towering over Dad himself! We do make a useful Basketball Squad indeed with reserves to spare - even siblings born post 1978-79 are considerably much taller than I am.

Running into Nation of Islam's Louis Farrakhan and his entourage

While we lived in exile in Saudi Arabia, one amazing experience we had was running into Nation of Islam's Louis Farrakhan and his entourage in Saudi Arabia in 1989. The occasion brought back memories of the time in 1975 when Dad invited "Black Empowerment Groups", including the Nation of Islam, Black Panthers, the PLO and other Arab Nationalist Groups to the OAU (Organization of African Unity) Summit in Kampala during the time he was the organization's Chairman. That time, Dad called on the Black Peoples in the American Diaspora to unite and used the occasion of the OAU Summit to implement that agenda.

The day we ran into Louis Farrakhan at the airport in Jeddah, we had escorted my kid brother Moses who was flying back to Paris where he was studying. The way it always happened was that whoever amongst us was next out after a vacation period would receive a formal Kuwerekera (Escort) from Dad and the other siblings.

So, on one of those outward movements, Dad sauntered to the nearest Soda Fountain joint to await departure while we booked in my kid brother Moses, when lo and behold the tiny frame of Louis Farrakhan loomed large with an equally large entourage. I braved myself and approached Louis Farrakhan to pay my respects and he asked where my siblings and I were from. I ventured, Busoga, saw the smiles from my siblings and quickly changed tack, realizing this was a family friend and told him the truth about being from Uganda.

When Louis Farrakhan started rubbing his chin and lamenting that he was leaving but he had wanted to meet Idi Amin again, I winked at my brother Aliga and told the great man to wait just long enough. Shortly after that, Dad approached his good friend, with that familiar great stride with the arms swinging like paddles. What amused us the most was Louis Farrakhan's son who jumped upwards like Atlanta Hawks' Spud Webb for Dad's neck, embracing the giant of a man, who gleefully enjoyed the spectacle. Dad and Louis Farrakhan were then ushered into the VIP Lounge for an extended discussion. That time, Louis Farrakhan also intimated that his daughter and her husband, the Chief of Staff of the Nation of Islam would remain and pay the family a visit.

It was an honour to do the usual run around with our guests. Donna Farrakhan preferred the Popeye Fast Food Restaurant, which had opened a Popeye Branch just off the road to Sands Hotel where we resided when we first arrived in Jeddah in 1980 while we were used to Kentucky Fried Chicken. I did not realize until later that she had just then acquired 3 Popeye Franchises in the State of Illinois. The Kentucky Fried Chicken Restaurant we frequented was located at the very turn towards Dad's favourite Safeway, which is across the road from Sands Hotel, Jeddah.

I will never forget how it tickled Leonard Muhammad, Louis Farrakhan's son-in-law and Chief of Staff, to find me listening to MC Hammer. Born Leonard Searcy in 1945, Mr. Muhammad married Donna Farrakhan, Mr. Farrakhan's daughter in 1983 and changed his name to Leonard Farrakhan Muhammad.

"You like MC Hammer?" queried the Chief of Staff.

I said I am a discerning dancer and to my mind he is the only one who could beat me in a dance competition.

"How about Michael?" Louis Farrakhan's Chief of Staff inquired.

With disgust I frowned and commented Michael can't dance. That is not Soul Dancing, but the Hammer can dance. I also like Bobby Brown but my favourite thung at the moment is the New Jack Swing thung coming from Teddy Riley, I offered in "Black American English".

Muhammad's wife Donna Farrakhan - a cross between Jada Pinket and Beyonce was the leader of the Fruits of Islam Bodyguards no less. I could not help imagining her at our Fidayin Boot Camp in the desert and even dared to ask her.

Your father told us yesterday that you are the Trainer of the Fruits of Islam. I also train and do go through training with the PLO Fidayins, I offered.

Bless her, she blushed but gave a guarded acceptance.

The whole family is light; her mother is an Amer-Indian. So, the blush was obvious. Since the revelations came from her father, I took this chance to ask her to tell her father that Muslim Inc. under Betty Shabbaz and Nation of Islam should make up, for I believe that despite all the misunderstandings, we were in this together, I intimated.

I wonder where she keeps the snapshots we took at the Inter-Continental with the Chief of Staff of the Nation of Islam.

The Nation of Islam dignitaries came to Uganda on Dad's invitation during the OAU (Organization for African Unity) Summit in Kampala in

1975. That year, Dad lined all of us his children at Nile Mansions Hotel (Serena Hotel) and went through a formal introduction of all of us.

I remembered the beautiful bride-to-be who had on the original Whoopi Goldberg beads way before Whoopi showed up on the radar screen and her future husband the bald cameraman. I remembered how she kept asking, with marked wonder, "Are these all your children?" and Dad responding "Yes".

I was at the very end of the row of about 35 children and I could see the bald headed husband to be grinning right next to her. It is funny that I eventually ended up with the very same Isaac Hayes close shaven head.

I asked the Chief of Staff about this golden couple in 1989 when we ran into Louis Farrakhan and his entourage in Jeddah, Saudi Arabia and even Dad was surprised at how I could remember that 1975 occasion. I told him that it was because the groom's "bald head" style is the one I wear today, for they actually got married either in Uganda or Morocco. They actually traversed the country filming and I pray I can get footages and snap shots of their travels. The two lovebirds kept taking photos of the whole Al-Amin brood using expensive cameras - priceless colour photos in 1975.

We got used to Technicolour way back, as per the coloured pictures Dad was fond of taking with his favourite Aluminum Polaroid Camera. That time the Satellite was up and running in Uganda and Dad brought in the earliest versions of Toshiba Colour Televisions - Sony Video decks and the works.

Dad's "low profile" visit to Mobutu in Kinshasa, Zaire (Congo)

In 1989, Dad made a "low profile" visit to Mobutu in Kinshasa, Zaire (Congo) from Saudi Arabia, which made me recall times when he hosted him and other dignitaries in Uganda during the "good old days".

There would always be much excitement when Mobutu with all his bands and the likes of Mpongo Love, pure Raz mataz and other dignitaries visited Uganda!

Dad had a very close relationship with Mobutu, which is how he visited Mobutu in 1989 with a fake Zairian Passport.

On the day Dad flew to Kinshasa, Zaire, the Ethiopian Airlines which lifted off at Jeddah Airport with a very huge Zairian passenger with an equally tall 6'4" son my brother Aliga Issa flew via Addis Ababa, Ethiopia then onwards to Kano, Nigeria where the huge man was noticed. A Western Journalist managed to get on the plane on its onwards flight to Lagos and down to Kinshasa but it took her sometime to become convinced that it was indeed Idi Amin on the plane to Kinshasa.

As the plane was in midair, the lady suddenly took up courage and asked Dad, "Idi Amin what are you doing back in Africa?"

In response to the Journalist's question, Dad looked towards my brother Aliga and asked for Bottled Water. Then he turned towards the Reporter and said, "You see this" pointing to the bottled water, "I missed the taste of pure African water".

Flabbergasted, the Reporter asked no more.

Dad had gone to Kinshasa to visit his older brother Ramadhan Dudu Moro Amin Dada and to collect the 8 Instruments of Power that had ended up in Zaire (Congo) after his government was overthrown in 1979.

That time, Mobutu hired a French Falcon 2000 Lear Jet to fly Dad back to Saudi Arabia. Contrary to false reports that Mobutu booted Dad out of Zaire, he actually welcomed Dad, then paid for a luxury plane for the return trip to Jeddah. However, he did retrieve the fake passport Dad used as a Zairian National, a souvenir as the last Nationality Dad ever held apart from the Ugandan Red Diplomatic Passport as Head of State, which sits in his High Gloss Burgundy briefcase in Jeddah. It is a priceless souvenir of his Globetrotting self proclaimed Spokesperson of the so-called "Third World" days, which occurred during the heydays of the OPEC (Organisation of Petroleum Exporting Countries) Cartel between 1972 and1979 when he toured the OIC (Organisation of Islamic Conference) countries. He was unhindered then and on a Personal Crusade to right the wrongs he felt Imperialism had wrought on the so-called Third World Countries. According to Dad, others like Julius Nyerere felt he did not deserve that role and the likes of Jomo Kenyatta only saw an upstart who reminded him of himself.

While on this trip to Kinshasa, Dad was his usual pleasant self and he even offered to assist an American fellow passenger. A source offers:

"In Kinshasa, Zaire when having difficulties boarding a flight to Goma, Andy was surprised to get help from Idi Amin. When Andy thanked him, Mr. Amin replied, "No problem. Just call me Idi"."

That is a side of Dad that most media houses haven't bothered to highlight in their preoccupation and resolve to continue riding the wagon that has only painted Dad as evil - the continuing slander after his ugly "divorce" from Israel and Britain as the critics suggest!

What amused my brother Aliga Issa Amin was Dad's ready hand on his machine pistol given to him by PLO's Yasser Arafat in the 1970s, as he kept his eyes on the Radar Tracker Consol. It shows the Executive Passengers the exact location the plane is at, for it never left his eyes, which were trained on the route, as the Falcon flew out of Ngili over Kisangani, Southern Sudan and Khartoum. Dad only began to relax as they were above the Red Sea although it would only take a simple maneuver to head towards the direction of Tabuk and into Israel for that matter. The familiar approach to Jeddah is very similar to the approach to Los Angeles Airport (on a flight from say Barack Obama's Hawaii) of a long distance flight from Tokyo.

In September 2009, 30 years to the time I was last in Libya, it tickled me to see that similar radar trackers had become commercialized with Radar Consols on every back seat rest in the ultra modern Boeing 777 that flew us on an Emirates Flight. The Flight originated in Entebbe and travelled via Addis-Ababa with a compulsory transitory stop over in Dubai. Then we made a connection flight to our final destination Tripoli to celebrate the 1st September Arab Libyan Jamahiriya and attend the Second Forum of Cultural Leaders of Africa between September 4, 2009 and September 13, 2009 when I returned to Uganda via Dubai.

After Dad got back home to Jeddah, he called every child to say he was okay. You should have seen us at the Hyde Park Apartment shedding tears of joy for the Press was up in arms wanting him to be arrested in Kinshasa.

"Tshombe I am ok", Dad said in a telephone call to me.

I remember the last wiring of 1,000 pounds to every child around the globe on his way out when he told us that he was not coming back to Saudi Arabia. That really shocked the whole family.

The release of Nelson Mandela from prison and praises to him by dad

Another notable event that occurred when we lived in Jeddah, Saudi Arabia was the release of Nelson Mandela from prison. We were glued to the Television as events unfolded in South Africa and around the world in relation to the release of Madiba. Dad could not heap enough praises on one of Africa's greatest men. He was ecstatic as Mandela walked out of the notorious Prison at Roben Island and Apartheid ended at last!

As President of Uganda and Chairman of the OAU (Organization for African Unity) in 1975, Dad had galvanized the Frontline States against South Africa and facilitated the building of an African United Armed Corps which was placed in Tanzania after the 1975 OAU Summit in Kampala. He had been consistent in uttering bombastic statements about liberating South Africa by force!

Following his release, Mandela shocked everybody by thanking Dad for his great contribution to the fight against Apartheid but his appreciation was from the heart!

A reflection on Dad's rule in Uganda

While we lived in exile in Saudi Arabia, I reflected a great deal on Dad's rule in Uganda and we had lots of conversations at the dinner table about Dad's love for things British. Dad was an Anglophone at heart and I also reflected about that as we shared father- son conversations.

Severely limited in so many intellectual spheres and often ridiculed for his limited knowledge of English, Dad's astonishing ability to lead a country was due to his extraordinary fluency in at least a dozen African languages. His memory for words, people and places never ceased to amaze his former Commanding Officer Major Iain Grahame.

Dad was certainly an outstanding soldier, within the context of that colonial period and yet his qualities of leadership and loyalty, brute force and bravery served merely to accentuate the very fragile thread on which the future of Uganda then hung. Dad's mixed background gave him an adequate understanding of Kakwa and Luganda having been raised in Buganda. From the Army, he learnt Swahili which is the language of Command, as well as adequate English, Lugbara, Ma'di, Luo and Creole Arabic or Kinubi.

Dad as an Anglophone at heart

Without a doubt, Dad was an Anglophone at heart. He was a real Anglophile and he had a love-hate relationship with Britain. He wanted to be a loyal servant, despite his mannerisms. Don't forget that he took power with the help of the British. I am an example of what he wanted because he sent me to England for my education when we went into exile.

When Dad felt rejected by the British Government, he focused on Scotland. A lot of the colonial and Army officers early in Dad's career were Scottish. They were the backbone of the British Empire. He even offered to help them win secession from the United Kingdom hence the fictional movie title "The Last King of Scotland".

When we lived in exile, Dad continued to love and play Scottish music. He spent a lot of time playing the Accordion. He played mainly Scottish military music as he was in a Highlanders band in the Fifties.

Dad's unusual exercise "sprinting" after a speeding car

Dad and I had a lot of one-on-one time in the 1980s. I will never forget the unusual but favourite exercise Dad continued from his 1950s hey days, at his favourite Play Exercise Ground at the Cornishe in Jeddah, Saudi Arabia.

Dad's favourite Play Exercise Ground at the Cornishe in Jeddah was near a small estuary Inlet from the Red Sea, with that familiar dilapidated Yacht seemingly abandoned, and anchored indefinitely in the shallow waters. We would leave the likes of Mama Iman (Mama Petit) and the young ones, pre-Iman, Leila and Rajab gang of three. Faisal Wangita and Khadija Abiriya were still the youngest then.

We still had the white Chevrolet Camaro 1980s coupe (the avid competitor to the Famous Burt Reynold's/Smokie Series Pontiac Transam).

Dad and I would drive along a straight stretch of the road along the Cornishe in Jeddah. Then he would get out of the car and start jogging behind the car. Then he would instruct me to steadily increase the speed of this loud American Sports Car, while he steadily kept pace with me.

Dad kept urging me to increase the speed while he gave chase!!!

I could not believe my eyes. This was indeed something to behold, man! This enormous 150-200 kgs garth of a man giving chase! - Actually sprinting.

Images of the 200-100 yards KAR Champion in the Fifties flashed through my Athletics Trained Sprinter's mind as I saw his knees steadily rising towards his solar plexus, in a Rhythmic Metronome action typical of natural sprinters. Then at say 200 metres, the illusion was broken when he suddenly stopped and bent low, exasperated and breathing heavily!

Alarmed at what I saw from the rear side view I braked the Camaro, screeching with that familiar "Over Stir" that often swings most American cars perilously towards the embankment. I parked the sports car, got out and rushed back to Dad, concerned. He shrugged me off and said he was okay, just getting back his breath. Incredibly he asked for "maratena - a second round!" which we did! Then we drove back to the seashore, where he went in for his daily dip in the Red Sea, at his favourite spot, near the very same dilapidated yacht. Hmmm!?!?!?

Dad's encounter with a shark while swimming in the Red Sea

My brother Aliga could not stop laughing as he recounted an encounter Dad had with a shark in the Red Sea. "Shark", "shark", "shark" we always teased when we recounted stories about Dad's weekly dips in the Red Sea in Saudi Arabia and an encounter with a shark.

Apparently, one day, Dad headed out as usual in the same location, swimming out gently towards the same dilapidated yacht that sat in the middle of the estuary and moved past it heading out to sea. My brother Aliga was still lounging on the sand when he suddenly glimpsed Dad heading back to shore with strong strokes, in total urgency to get to the shore. He did get to the shore, lumbering out of the water with his hand pointing backwards while he shrieked shark! shark! Ha ha ha ha, we did laugh - Aliga, Geriga and me at Dad's capacity to get in and out of trouble.

It brought back memories of the times Dad told us about how he defied the warnings of locals in Somalia and jumped into a crocodile infested river for a swim. In 1949, Dad's Kings African Rifles (KAR) 4th Battalion went to Somalia and stayed there until 1950 and one particularly horrifying incident happened to Dad in Somalia.

While taking a dip in a river, a marauding crocodile grabbed him around the ankle line and dragged him for some distance. Dad had been warned by the locals (Somalis) not to swim in the crocodile infested river but he did not heed their warning and jumped in. How he survived nobody knows but somehow he got away!

Cherished memories about our father

My siblings and I have a lot of standing jokes about Dad's continuing "mischief" in exile and capacity to get in and out of trouble. We would always laugh hard at the many stories we shared. We shared cherished and precious memories, traded jokes about Dad and laughed incessantly.

On cherished memories about our father, my sister Halima Atta contributes:

"Good memories like they say are more precious than any commodity or monetary value. One such memory sticks to mind. Dad as usual woke us up early (Me, Fatuma, Araba, Khadija, Faisal) in preparation for our journey to Mecca that Friday. We set off along with Ma Petite in the blue Range Rover, which was always tilted heavily towards Dad's side - ha ha ha.

Anyway, so we got to Mecca, prayed, had lunch and then we all got in the car to head back to Jeddah. Dad tried in vain to start the engine but the car would not start. The Dantatas whom we often saw at Mecca on a Friday approached us and their driver asked if we wanted a lift back. Dad refused but instead he spoke to the escorts who arranged for a mechanic. He packed his wife along with Khadija and Faisal in a taxi. He then spotted a yemenia tiny Pick up, Open-Air datsun - you know the type. He asked the man how much it would cost us to get to Jeddah, which was small change. Dad then instructed me, Fatuma and Araba to get in the Pick up Truck with him for the long drive back to Jeddah. Many people standing around were flabbergasted that a former Head of State was getting into a small, dirty truck driven by some Arab nomad but that's our Mzee (old man) for you! I will never forget how the wind blew in our faces and we could not stop laughing and feeling embarrassed. Mzee didn't have a care in the world as usual. That is one journey I will never forget in my life and I look back at it fondly. I also remember the look on the Pick-up driver's face after Dad thanked him for the ride and gave him some money with baksheesh (tip). He felt humbled and honoured."

My siblings and I still laugh about funny encounters we had growing up as Idi Amin's children. It was the same way Ugandans used to laugh as they had funny encounters with their "wayward" President and mimicked the way he talked and walked. We have a myriad of standing jokes about Dad like the time my brother Ali nicknamed him Bahrain and my sister Halima shared the funny incident regarding being stuck in the middle of nowhere while we lived in exile in Saudi Arabia. It had occurred during a trip the family took to Mecca for Juma (Friday) Prayers.

Regarding the "Bahrain" nickname, Dad would head furiously for the Communication Services Centre in Jeddah and call the Bahrain BBC Bureau, vehemently explaining the issue of the Expropriated Property relating to the Asians he ordered out of Uganda in 1972. He insisted that the Asians had been fully compensated for the Properties they left behind even though no one paid any attention to his honest explanations and protests regarding how unfair he was treated and perceived in the Asian saga. Then he would gather us around to listen to the Focus On Africa news at 19:00 East African Time with that "Qwilili Qwilli" signature tune. "Oooogh! Amonye (father) is at it again" we would laugh, until it became a standing joke amongst the inner circle of siblings and my brother Ali Nyabira Kirunda code named Dad Bahrain.

Malcolm X (Malik El Shabbaz) and drawing parallels to Dad

I have regularly reflected on Malcolm X (Malik El Shabbaz) and drawn Parallels to Dad. To my mind, The Pillar of a role model second only to the Holy Messenger in Islam Muhammad Ibn Abd Allah Peace Be upon Him, will always be the late Malik El Shabbaz (a.k.a Malcolm X Little). Dad, in many ways, instilled in me the very same virtues possessed by Malcolm X. Here was a man who had the wherewithal, the attitude, the spiritual belief and the courage plus the privilege to reaffirm our heritage and fulfill "Rembi's Mystical Legacy" in being both a Kakwa and a Muslim by any means necessary! I surely believe and solemnly swear that, I, Jaffar, will never suffer from an inferiority complex because my heritage has an absolutely solid and recorded history of affirmative action and that out and out stance of the Black Panthers that I have personally identified and taken as both my heritage and destiny.

Dad's underlining gift to Ugandans is our lack of an inferiority complex. We completely shed that colonial mentality for good, picked ourselves up and counted ourselves amongst self-determinants of the world.

Lamenting about being a refugee and a farewell to Dad

While living in exile, I lamented about being a refugee in a foreign land. Dad was given a monthly allowance that funded an opulent lifestyle but life in exile was still hard. When we left Uganda after Dad was overthrown in 1979, we fell from the highest of the high, from a position of extravagance and power, to the lowest of the low and it has been very difficult. We had come from absolute power to almost nothing. Dad felt like the man who was once a Corporate Executive in New York but was now retired in Florida and had only the fishing to look forward to.

Although Al-Qadhafi was the most generous person I have ever known, Dad eventually felt betrayed by his socialist agenda, when he sought the votes of African leaders to become the next OAU (Organization for African Unity) Chairman in 1979. These African leaders included my father's Nemesis Julius Nyerere so Dad felt he could not trust Al-Qadhafi anymore. Instead, Dad began to talk about going to Saudi Arabia since he had taken up a Saudi offer of refuge when he decided to become a staunch supporter of the Arab and Islamic struggle in 1972.

We lived in luxury but it was still not home. I was with Dad in Libya and Saudi Arabia and remember the luxury well.

In Saudi Arabia, there was marble everywhere in our 15-room house but it was still not home. Dad was paid $30,000.00 a month by the Saudis. He had more than 30 of us with him and he would regularly tell us, "You have to liberate Uganda with the Fedayeen (Islamic soldiers)."

The 1991 First Gulf War referred to as "Desert Storm" found me in Saudi Arabia. I was saddened by events that unfolded in relation to another interruption to my schooling and have recollections of the war which forced me to return to Uganda.

I initially got an admission to Schillar International University in London for the 1989 -1990 Semester but Dad was adamant that American Universities were not accredited. I feel his strong alignment towards all things British curtailed my chances at this initial critical point in furthering my education. I later came to realize that the Saudis would not allow me to study at a Jewish sounding school of higher education. Pity me! Then the University of Cincinnati in Ohio, USA offered me a tentative admission for the fall semester 1990/91 enrolment in its college of Arts with the eventual possibility of a transfer to the Marketing Degree in my sophomore year provided my freshman grades were tolerable. But as fate would have it, the Persian War Crisis erupted in 1989-1990 and doomed any chances of obtaining the necessary funding.

We as a family are totally beholden to the Saudi Royal Family for our wellbeing and sustenance, to this very day. We had expected charitable offerings from them to sponsor me but at the time they were rightly preoccupied with the spectre of being invaded by Saddam Hussein's Iraq. Unable to find the means to finance my higher education, I therefore returned to my native Uganda.

I will always remember coming of age at 23 years, the last "face to face" encounters with Dad and the farewell that would prompt me to research Dad's story and investigate my own roots.

Dad had said to me in 1989, just when the Iraqi Army was threatening to march right up to Riyadh, "When will you get to know your country Uganda?" "It will be alright." "Do not forget to write to me always."

An air of uncertainty encompassed the Holy Land of Saudi Arabia and Kuwait was already under Iraqi hegemony at the time. So, Dad decided that it would be best if I returned to Uganda.

This series of books is my letter to Amonye (Father).

Come to think of it, my return to Uganda, which I now refer to as "The return of Idi Amin's Prodigal Son" on October 1, 1990, was a Blessing in disguise.

The day I set foot back in Uganda and events that followed my arrival

The day I set foot back in Uganda, the country of my birth on October 1, 1990 I continued reflecting about my last "face to face" encounter with Dad. My exile ended in 1990 when I returned to Uganda but many of my siblings have chosen to live abroad, often preferring to stay silent about Dad's legacy and name. Living in exile was hard and it had a great impact on my life. For example, I have taken a culture on board that is more English than Ugandan. I cannot even speak Kakwa, my father's tongue leave alone that of my mother's Mulamoji Bantu ethnic group but I am trying to learn it now. Moreover my keen interest in my genealogy and anthropological roots has given me the basic rudiments of the language.

On October 1, 1990, at age 23 years old, I set foot back in the country of my birth Uganda for the first time after a decade long hiatus in exile. I have somehow managed to find a life with which to live out my cherished hopes and aspirations from quite unexpected circumstances within the realm of relative urban peace, unity and modernization which has been the surprising definition of President Yoweri Museveni's regime.

Imagine October 1, 1990, just as the late Rwigema was crossing the Ugandan border into Rwanda, a bitter 23-year old man was crossing into Uganda from Kenya on the Mawingo Bus from Nairobi, following my acrimonious schism with Dad. Bitter in the sense that I felt given a chance, I would be able to join the fall semester at Cincinnati University in Ohio, USA. I had felt that if only Dad would put in his funds for the first semester, then hopefully if the Persian Gulf Crisis stabilized, the Al Saud Royal Family would be able to continue with the funding of my education.

Dad would have none of it since at the time, he was listening more to the Northern Arab Clique - the likes of his good friend Mazin - Palestinian factions who had dubious leanings or coffee side table bets towards Saddam Hussein winning the standoff on the eve of "Desert Storm". This Northern Alliance so to speak would later be discredited and their hopes and aspirations would be put into indefinite limbo when the likes of Palestine Liberation Organization's Yasser Arafat and even the trustworthy Late King Hussein of Jordan were found not to fully support the coalition against Saddam Hussein.

Anyway, alas, at the time, Dad saw the worst case scenario and he was inclined to count his eggs before the chickens hatched. Considering my lackluster showing over the years and laissez faire attitude to life in general and overall, he looked me dead straight in the eyes and told me in front of the family, "No child of mine have I spent so much on and gained so little. What I paid for you per term in Great Britain over the years was the equivalent of four of your brothers in France! Honestly what I have done for you is enough".

Dad considered the prospect of spending almost 15,000 US dollars per semester at the University of Cincinnati for the Business Administration Degree a waste of money. Interestingly all three of us had taken the same degree courses in Business Administration but considering the rampant insecurity in Saudi Arabia that time, Dad felt my brothers Moses Kenyi and Lumumba Juruga Hussien stood the better chance of succeeding, considering their excellent performance over the years. Dad felt that my two brothers would continue forward but I would have to stop right there and be content with what I had achieved so far. Alas his decision was final. So he bought me a one way ticket to Nairobi, Kenya on Saudia Airlines and gave me seven hundred and thirty five US dollars while my brothers set off to go back to France with their future assured on a whim.

As a parting shot and resigned to my fate and conscious of my past misdeeds, I placed Dad's hand on my forehead and then kissed it in a respectful Islamic (Nubian) farewell. I must say he was taken aback since he had anticipated my usual temper tantrums, which never materialized. I simply requested to get my Original "O" Level and "A" Level Certificates that I had placed in the safe hands of our beloved stepmother Mama Iman Chumaru, Dad's last wife and departed for Africa.

On hindsight my choice of Marketing as a career prospect had been out of a desire to help fulfill in a modest way the difference in need for skilled labour in our newly emerging market economy in our country. I had intended to major in Marketing at Cincinnati University in Ohio, USA.

Deep down, I still feel that Dad had misplaced sentiments and was falling into the very same power play adage that had been leveled against him by real foes in the past. His real foes had leveled that he despised education and felt threatened by anyone he felt might show signs of independent thought.

I was always baffled with his ranting behaviour at the dinner table whenever he would bombastically state, "Some of you think you know more. I would rather live with the ignorant rather than those who think they know more." Dad would always be ambiguous when making this statement and it would disorientate me for days to come.

Anyway, back on Terra- Firma, on October 1, 1990, my first stop was at my brother Ali Nyabira Kirunda's home in Mbiko Mukono District where I resided for the duration of that "Turkey Shoot" (Gulf War) as I prefer to call it. The NATO alliance was basically unloading stockpiles of ammunition that had been around for most of forty years during the Cold War Era! This to me was nothing more than Target Practice for NATO, using live bullets and opponents.

As I settled down at my brother Ali Nyabira Kirunda's home, I couldn't help reflecting on my Avatars to date – people who had made a big difference in my life and made me who I had become at the ripe age of 23. My biological mother Nakoli was my very first Avatar from 1967 to 1968 followed by Grandma Aisha Chumaru Aate from 1968 to 1969 and then Aunt Akisu from 1969 to 1970. My cousins Alias and Atiki were my Avatars from 1970 to 1972 followed by my Foster Parents Mama Joyce and Sergeant Katabarwa from 1971 to 1972 and Grandpa Sosteni in 1972. Mama Kay was my Avatar from 1973 to 1974 followed by Miss Hayward from 1974 to 1979, Nnalongo Madina from 1974 to 1975 and Mama Sarah Kyolaba from 1975 to 1979.

A number of events unfolded after I returned to Uganda. For example, in October 1991, Haji Moses Rajab died in his cell at the Luzira Prison. On June 5, 1992, Moses Ali and Amisi were acquitted after languishing for 26 months in Luzira Prison!

The time I was totally isolated from family members

By 1992, I decided to leave my brother's homestead when I felt I was becoming a burden on him and a monya tiyo (stranger in the house) and headed for Kampala where I thought I might find a job.

The year 1992 shall always remain a Nadir year for me. I was totally isolated from family members who felt threatened by my presence, following Dad's edit/Fatwa to all and sundry not to associate with me Tshombe. Totally ostracized and in a hostile environment where I could not speak a word of Luganda, I managed to find comfort at the family of Ismail Bure a Kakwa and brother to Mzee Yosa who lived in Najanankumbi before relocating to Yusuf Yongole's home in Bulumaji. Ironically, Ismail Bure was thankful to help Idi Amin's son especially because of the helpful deed Dad had apparently rendered to his family.

Taking refuge with my maternal family and a reflection on my mother

Between 1990 and 1993, I sought refuge with the other side of my family, which I last got to know or live with in 1969. Getting to know children who shared the same womb with me was a miracle in a sense since I could openly show affection for someone who was truly my own flesh and blood.

In 1968, mum had met and fallen in love with a "Beau" from Kamuli District who formally approached Mzee Eryakesi Bulima my maternal grandfather. He had actually prepared the traditional Kwanjula ceremony since the couple were expecting Richard who was well on the way, only for their plans to be thwarted when well meaning friends warned the bridegroom that mum was actually the Army Commander's woman and had borne him a son. Richard the second born was well on the way but alas the marriage was sidelined. The father of Robert and his Twin brother E'Ngo's father also got cold feet and unfortunately so did the late Josephine's father and Deo Waiswa's too!

Dad's shadow was all pervasive and overwhelming and mum's only peace and recompense came about when Dad was overthrown in 1979 and she met Gershom (Tata Suzanne), a gentle Muhururo from Rukingiri who has finally settled the troubled waters that have been the legacy of my mother's earlier life. Steadfastly, Suzanne Komuhanje, Kenneth, Wendy Nahurira, Lazarus, Joshua, David were born and eventually our darling youngest sister Lillian Tashobya blessed us with her presence.

I was happy to be reunited with part of an amazing line up of thirteen bouncing offspring over a period stretching from 1967 to 1993. At the height of the culture clash following my return, I found myself embraced in a lot of love and warmth after having returned to my motherland. I discovered this maternal side of my family tree truly shows love and affection without any form, formality or sibling rivalry. They kept confusing me for an uncle of sorts since I bear a striking resemblance to mum. I took that in stride and did not mind being regarded as an uncle instead of a brother, as long as I could get to know them better. The contrast in skin colour is also of interest to me.

I am unashamedly "Jet Black" while Suzanne, Kenneth, Lazarus, Joshua, David and Lillian have this "Caramel Tone" to their skin yet the majority of us share the same facial features like our mother - hmmm. Interesting, Wendy (quiet Wendy) is the exception. She is mother's clone so to speak.

We had a lot of catching up to do - my mother and me. So, we would sit and reminisce for hours on end. I liked to come in early and she would cook breakfast for me. I would stay for lunch and then I would have to forcefully pull myself away come evening and head back to Bulumaji.

Deep down in me, misplaced sentiments had previously made me unconsciously always blame mum for "leaving me". Psychologists claim this is a normal reaction when a separation takes place between mother and child but I took my vendetta to the extreme. At age three, somehow mum says she actually caught a first glimpse of this distinct character of mine when she weaned me off breast milk. Apparently, I cried on and off for three days then amazingly started to ignore her with determined fortitude and a comical independence.

I remember when Dad was opening the Kibimba Rice Scheme set up by the Peoples Republic of China in the then Busoga District in the 1970s, I went along with Dad since he had a habit or Public Relations strategy of always taking along a son or daughter whose mother hails from the particular region in which a state function was taking place.

Dad later tried to unite me with my mother but I rejected her. He had sent me to live with our Foster Parent Sergeant John Katabarwa at Jinja again, during school holidays from Kabale Preparatory School but I put up a storm whenever mum came visiting and locked myself in my room.

Another time Dad set up a meeting at "Cape Town View", our home at Gaba/Munyonyo. With brazen contempt, I walked into the Lounge, greeted the guests - mum included, and walked out. I headed out for Dad's Lounge (Madhvani's actually) and watched the tide lap up under the pier.

I was harshly rebuked by Mama Sarah Kyolaba about my behaviour but surprisingly, throughout these attempts at unification with my mother, Dad never once let on in reaction or confrontation to what I was doing. I guess deep down, he must have felt that a gradual acclimatization was the best policy to use in my case.

Reality hit home when RSM (Regimental Staff Sergeant) Kapere, our driver, a Ma'di by tribe, in 1977/1978, with great care and affection first jokingly, then with deep emotion, asked, "Tshombe, how can you reject your mother?"

I was at a loss for words and even tried my best to tell him that I loved my mother. I must say he was heartened by my words and somehow, the words got to Dad.

While listening to stories about Dad and making inquiries about my legitimacy in the Dada family, our aunt Araba Deiyah told me a revealing point. She said that in the early years of my life, she was instructed by her younger brother Dad to take the atonement bride price to my grandfather Mzee Eryakesi Bulima in Kaliro, which she did. According to her, at the time she took the atonement bride price to my grandfather she was escorted by Baba Diliga and the driver who took them there was the very RSM (Regimental Staff Sergeant) Kapere who asked me the question about rejecting my mother.

At the time our aunt Araba Deiyah made the revelation about the atonement bride price that my maternal grandfather received, I was complaining to her that the problems I was experiencing with my siblings are because I am illegitimate. I was referring to the sibling rivalry that characterizes most large African families.

However, Aunt Araba Deiyah countered unexpectedly for she was the renowned type in the Al-Amin family to dig in her younger brother's illegitimate status from what she heard from her mother Mariam Poya. She went on to enlighten me that she was a witness to the cultural atonement and house cleaning ceremony that took place after my birth so as far as she was concerned I was legitimate in the eyes of culture. We had this interesting talk during the one year July 2007-July 2008 that I spent with her in Arua after the demise of my very last Paternal "father" Amule Kivumbi Amin in July 2007. It was a very revealing time because she and my other aunts told me a lot of "priceless" stories about Dad and the Dada family and I was a very willing and very attentive listener.

I remember there was an Annual Trade Show taking place in Jinja in either 1977 or 1978 and the whole family minus Mama Sarah Kyolaba and Mama Madina were gathered at Madhvani's ultra Luxurious Lodge (Jinja Lodge). The gathering actually turned out to be Dad's Nikkah (marriage, wedding) to Mama Khasfa Zamzam Nabirye, one of his Crack Female Commando "Kamanyola" Bodyguards - much in the mould of Muamar Al-Qadhafi's Famous Virgin Female Bodyguards. This was actually Dad's final marriage while he was still the Head of State. The next and last marriage would be to Mama Iman Chumaru in Saudi Arabia.

On that momentous day, I apprehensively set off with RSM (Regimental Staff Sergeant) Kapere for my mother's homestead. At the time, she was residing with Julius Zziwa's mother, an aunt of mine, at the Railway Junction on the road to Bugembe. I still remember that I actually looked back apprehensively when RSM (Regimental Staff Sergeant) Kapere set off back to Jinja Lodge saying he would return later.

My brothers Khamis Machomingi, Joseph Akisu and others had accompanied me to my mum's and it was heartening when mum remembered Joseph. She had met him during the time I lived with Aunt Akisu in Kayunga, Bugerere as a toddler. After Aunt Akisu's demise, I and several of my siblings had been sent to live with our Foster Parent Sergeant John Katabarwa before being sent together with Sukeji and Machomingi to Mbarara where we got caught up in the 1972 "Mutukula Invasion".

I often look back to the period between 1977 and 1978 and smile thinking how the whole gang of maternal uncles and aunts kept picking on the way I spoke. I guess schooling around Caucasian English Missionaries and my understandably particular attachment to one outstanding matriarch figure like Miss Hayward must have rubbed off a bit of their particular speech pattern (accent).

Mum and the rest kept repeating my attempts at answers while making comical jerks of the head and squealing like two naughty little girls (Mum and Aunt Owa Railway, a Schoolteacher). Uncle Patrick Aggrey, who hailed from the Royal Baise Ngobi of my grandmother Marie Celeste, a choir teacher at Kaliro Teacher Training College had also come to see the Prodigal Son.

When I realized they were teasing me, I kept a silly grin on my face which must have amused them even more. I also kept giving shy sidelong gazes at my mum probably sizing her for the very first time.

I kept telling her that I was too young to know any better when I did all those things. She cheekily told me off, "I am your mother whether you like it or not. I might not look or dress in fancy clothes like your stepmothers who you seem to have taken a liking to but I am your mother!"

I must say I was totally embarrassed and I went on and on saying "I am sorry". I got a hug for all my childish shenanigans. I went on to tell mum that I was preparing for my PLE (Primary Leaving Examination) P.6 but would tell Dad that I wish to come and stay with her every holiday in Jinja and felt that I was in a better position to explain and express myself. What a day that was!

Alas the invasion from Tanzania split us up and I only met up with mum briefly in September 1986 at the manly age of 19 years just when Yoweri Museveni took over the country. Then memorably in 1989 when Dad sent me to test the waters during the time my brother Ali Nyabira

Kirunda was jailed for subversive activity and finally in 1990 when I came back to Uganda for good.

My life with Yusuf Yongole in Bulumaji

On a chance meeting with my stepfather Major Muhammad Luka Youm's wife Fiona Gossens, a Belgian National, she was able to talk to Yusuf Yongole, younger brother to Dr. Omari Haruna Kokole who invited me to his homestead in Bulumaji. I arrived at Bulumaji on January 8, 1993, where to my surprise, Yusuf was in fact married to my niece Fatima the daughter of a cousin of mine called Apayi, the daughter of Baba Juma, son of Rajab Yangu, the brother of Grandpa Amin Dada Nyabira.

I was to discover that the House of Ferre (Dr. Omari Kokole's Father) was extremely close to my grandmother and they were very familiar with my stay at Grandma's as a toddler at Kidusu-Bundo just off the Old Jinja Road, where they had a homestead also.

Coming back to the place where I spent some of my childhood afforded me the opportunity to reminisce about the time I lived with Grandma and Aunt Akisu.

It was extremely heartening when an old lady who I had known for ages in the area whence I used to live with my brother Ali Nyabira Kirunda Amin in Mbiko came up to me, laid down her bunch of sugar cane and asked me if I was Sombe? This old lady would always move around selling sugar cane and she seemed to know most people.

I smiled at the way she pronounced my name Tshombe but answered in the affirmative. Yes, I am Tshombe.

"Yes, Yes, Yes!" she exclaimed before adding, "I remember you when you were still a baby. If you ask around you will know that I was left to guard your grandmother's homestead when her body was flown by the Israelites to Arua for burial at the Arua Mosque [Masjid Noor]."

I must say I was fascinated by someone who could recognize a 25 year old man she had last seen as a toddler - considering I was only three years old the last time she set eyes on me. She was also familiar with the time I was then taken to Aunt Akisu in Bugerere to stay with her after the demise of Grandmother Aisha Aate.

In the same vein, an old man who to that very day drove a Tractor for the Metha Sugar Plantation also put up the courage once and approached me with a bemused smile on his face saying, "Are you Sombe?" Having gotten used to the fact that I had mysteriously returned to the very place of my childhood and knowing the high chances of meeting people from a time I was too young to know any better, I answered, Yes. Then he went on to explain that his homestead is opposite Grandma Aisha Aate's at Kidusu-Bundo in Buyukwe and that I was their constant companion as a toddler. He said he was surprised that I could not speak Kakwa since he was certain that I used to speak it when I was a toddler. I doubted that claim but he insisted that it was the only language Grandma Aate ever used when she was apparently talking to me, in an effort to get me to speak my father's tongue.

After Grandma's demise, I was placed at Aunt Akisu's home in Kayunga, Bugerere. She had felt that it was her right to be Grandma's heir and to take over Grandma's role and position as shaman. However, fate would not be kind to her for she was to die shortly after the death of Grandma Aisha. While speculation ran rampant that Aunt Akisu died because she had usurped her junior mother's "Yakanye" powers and responsibility as shaman without the consent of the Okapi clan, Dad was forced to place me in the care of Sergeant John Katabarwa at Al-Qadhafi Garrison. The Coup D'etat in 1971 found me at this particular barracks. I do remember the unbelievable noise when the Armourer at the Quarter Guard was attacked. All the children were quaking under the bunco spring beds during the whole attack.

Attempting to walk in Dad's sporting footsteps especially boxing

As I was re-establishing my roots back in Uganda, I attempted to walk in Dad's sporting footsteps, especially boxing. However I was unsuccessful at Boxing as a career and failed miserably.

It was interesting that decades after Dad had earned accolades as an Athlete, I followed his footsteps to the same Boxing Arena at Al-Qadhafi Garrison and joined the soldiers in training camp as a novice civilian in training. I felt my life was going nowhere. I was depressed since my date with Cincinnati University in Ohio, USA had passed and I felt so much that I had no future and might as well utilize the one thing I had in plenty - pent up aggression and natural strength I must have inherited from Dad.

I had in mind an advice he once gave me while I was driving him back from our weekend outing swimming at the Corniche in Jeddah in 1989-90 on the eve of the Gulf Crisis (Gulf War). He told me, "Tshombe, considering your 6' 1" height and your weight, you could make a good Middle Weight Boxer and you can actually go very far." At the time, I was totally enthralled with my prospect of joining College in Cincinnati, Ohio in the USA and his suggestion was the furthest thing on my mind. To my mind, I never relished the regimen I would have to go through to reduce my weight from its normal 90 kgs - 95 kgs category, down to around 75 kgs! I loved my Kentucky Fried Chicken and was not about to change my diet to please my Dad's off hand aspirations.

Anyway, at that point in time, when I found myself at a dead end, boxing seemed the quickest way to success and I duly joined the NRA (National Resistance Army) Military Boxing Club under the Coach, Sergeant Musa Kent. I only later found out that his wife was actually my very own Mualim Hussein's niece!

Offhand, Musa had asked me what tribe I was and I told him I was a Kakwa and the wife had tested my ability to speak my father tongue, which I failed miserably to the amusement of all. I explained the nature of my heritage and why I could not speak the tongue, which they accepted willingly.

I will never forget the hilarious events that ensued during my attempts at emulating the likes of Dad, Evander Holyfield, Sumbu Kalambe, Marvin Hagler, The Hitman Herns and GOAT a.k.a "We be floatin' like a butterfly. We be stingin' like a B," Muhammad Ali.

In boxing, there is a useful tool used by the coaches to test the ferocity, strength and accuracy of the trainee's punching ability. This is a padded leather pad worn and intricately positioned with furious motion by the coach with one requirement that the boxer persistently punch at the pad. This particular day, one of our top flight boxers under "The Bombers" (Our National Boxing Squad) Sergeant Lubwama a.k.a. "African Express" was taking me through the motions using this pad. I must say I was getting the feel of it although he kept noticing a weaker punch action from my lead right which he insisted I strengthen. However, as the relentless punch action continued, I felt a distant rumble in my gut and tell tale leaks of affluence at my back end! I shot out Affende I request to go to the toilet Sir! His reply was, "Hit the pad man. Cut out with your cowardice man". Relentlessly, I kept on the furious punch action but my backside had other ideas!

Affende, I shouted I request to urgently go to the toilet sir! He stopped the session, looked in my eyes and realized my plea was genuine. "Okay. Go!" I was out of the gym with a roar of soldiers laughing at the spectacle. I hit the john with instinctive haste and let loose with a barrage of unthinkable bog. What a relief!

A stern face met me at the gym when I returned and the advice was, "Never eat heavily in the morning before training you hear me?" Yes Affende, I replied.

What became clear to everybody were my amazing speed and agility plus enormous reserves of energy and punching power. I could actually manage the punch actions and nimble footsteps of a Welterweight, from years of dancing in clubs and rave parties across England, without feeling the strain or exhaustion, which impressed everyone. Since I was scheduled to be their new signing as a Super Heavy Weight (95 kgs +), my Achilles heel was my fear of taking a punch.

I am basically a coward at heart. Deep down, my basic instinct is flight whenever confronted by danger although I am decidedly a courageous fighter when cornered and feel I have no way out. Moreover, the little education in me had calculated that for every punch I took I was possibly irreparably damaging the "Gray Matter" in my brain cells. Images of GOAT a.k.a. Muhammad Ali and the general "Punch Drunk" nature of boxers around heightened this feeling of dread every time a soldier's punch caught me.

My coach could not believe that with all the natural ability I had, cowardice could be my shortfall. I had got into the habit of dropping like a sack of potatoes every time I felt the knocks I was receiving were incessant. The coach was not amused and told me so.

"Jaffar, you are faking KOs and I do not like it. You are becoming a spectacle. Every time you get in the ring, your colleagues are saying Bozo is on and they gather around to watch the spectacle. Jaffar, you should see the shudder and awe from the soldiers every time you throw a good punch. You have a lot of natural strength. Build up your confidence and use your jab and right hand leads. That in itself will give your opponents the fear and respect to keep at bay. You should go home and think about this very hard Jaffar and ask yourself whether boxing is what you want to do in life."

I did go and never returned. This honourable man had told me the truth about myself and for his honourable ability to train, I did not wish and want to continue to be a spectacle. I have always believed that with sports you are born with the talent and you cannot be trained. I felt by the time I learned the rudiments of boxing I would be a battered soul both physically and mentally. I remember going to Aunt (Awa) Asia who lives in Mbiko for lunch on my way back to Bulumaji, with a horrendous headache from all those punches and telling her my decision.

Awa Asia, I have given up on chasing my Dad's footsteps in boxing, I said.

She blew up with an overwhelming chesty laugh.

"I told you so! I told you so! Men from your father's age were built differently. Hardened by life. You have been brought up in a life of luxury. There is no way your body could have taken the kind of punches those men absorbed. I remember I used to bake 2 kilos of Ugali for your father during his boxing training!"

With painful resignation, I accepted her words of experienced wisdom and headed back to Mzee Ferre's residence in Bulumaji on the junction towards Nyenga and Kidusu where I was residing with Yusuf and his mother Maryam Ferre.

Reuniting with my paternal uncle Baba Ramadhan Dudu Moro

Just as I was losing hope on a particular eventful occasion, Yusuf Haruna Yongole Ferre came to inform me that my paternal uncle Baba Ramadhan Dudu Moro Amin had returned from Zaire (Congo). He told me that he was residing at Mzee Sebbi Issa 'Dimba's homestead in Kulumba Zone in Kawempe Mbogo Division. He felt it right that we make a formal visit.

I felt so isolated and was rightly apprehensive about meeting up with my family again. However, I was heartened to know that the head of our Adibu Likamero Kakwa clan had finally put up the courage to return to his country of birth under an agreement with the government of Yoweri Museveni.

We set off for Kampala and drove to Kawempe with Yusuf Yongole and Muhammad Lugala who was a clan member of the Leiko Kakwa clan on Mzee Issa 'Dimba's side. At the meeting, I met my uncle Baba Ramadhan Dudu Moro Amin, Mzee Walala of the Morodu, Mzee Sebbi Issa 'Dimba, Mzee Khamis Issa 'Dimba, Mzee Juma Kuri, Mzee Abdul Majid Khamis Walala, Mzee Ibrahim and a host of very important elders in my community. As one of the first Kakwa recruits to join the Kings African Rifles, Juma Kuri, a renowned Piza/Godiya Warrior was instrumental in Dad's initial passage into the rank and file of the Kings African Rifles warrior life. Here was a home coming fit for the Elder clan member of my immediate family.

Poignantly it was around the same period during which Tito Okello returned from exile during Yoweri Museveni's magnanimous rule in the

1990s. That time, the aging former ruler, strangely without being prompted or any need to support a sworn enemy like Dad, claimed he knew who killed Okoya and that it was not Dad after all.

This remark caused quite a stir in the Luo community who through bitter tribulations had willingly learnt to instinctively blame all their problems on Dad. In fact, Dad once painfully complained and pleaded that he did not kill Okoya stating, "Okoya was my Friend!"

As I continued settling back in Uganda, events continued unfolding in Uganda and the neighbouring countries.

On August 11, 1993, the SPLA (Sudan People's Liberation Army) were pushed out of Morobu, Yei, Bazi and other areas they claimed to have held for 10 years. Nearly 100,000 Refugees were registered in Ko'buko (Ko'boko), Uganda.

In October 1993, Cote Adams of the local Global News TV, in Toronto, Canada, reported from Ko'buko (Ko'boko) about the "forgotten war" which had resulted in the pushing into Ko'buko (Ko'boko) of thousands of Refugees from across the Sudanese border.

On January 10, 1994, the most famous, patriotic and respected son of the Kakwa of Ko'buko (Ko'boko) after Dad, Colonel Elly Aseni, son of Siwu of the Godiya Kakwa clan died. What a great loss to the Kakwa!

Elly Aseni was Uganda's Ambassador to Moscow (USSR) when Dad fell in 1979. He had been appointed to that post as a "consolation" for the attempted coup against Dad by him, General Lumago and the Late Charles Arube in early 1974.

Ugandans going to the polls in 1994

On March 28, 1994, the people of Uganda went to the polls and elected delegates to the Constituent Assembly (CA). These delegates debated, promulgated and enacted the Draft Constitution.

In March 1994, the Kakwa people of Ko'buko (Ko'boko) elected the following local Members of Parliament (MPS):

Haruna 'Data Sebi, a Muslim and formerly a Secondary School teacher at Ko'buko (Ko'boko) Secondary School from the Midia Kakwa clan.

Francis Ayume, a Protestant and Solicitor General for Uganda during Dad's regime from the Leiko Kakwa clan.

Alex Lobida, a Protestant and Veteran UPC (Uganda Peoples Congress) Politician and former Deputy Minister of Labour in the 1st Republic of Uganda (Obote I) from the Leiko clan.

Benjamin Moro, a Catholic and former Education Officer in North Nile District from the Ludara clan.

Congratulations were in order to Haruna Sebi 'Data for his landslide victory!

Looking for a job as Idi Amin's son and a credit to Yoweri Museveni

I still vividly recall the time I was looking for a job and the hurdles I anticipated facing as Idi Amin's son. I half expected to be lynched by the populace for daring to step back on Ugandan soil, yet, when I first stepped back and a person got to know who I was, you cannot believe the warmth of the reception even from the most unexpected of quarters.

I eventually landed a lucrative job at DHL and was pleasantly surprised by the rapid promotions I got despite being Idi Amin's son and my superiors knowing that I was Idi Amin's son. I give credit for the relative ease with which I got this job and the relative safety I have enjoyed in Uganda to President Yoweri Museveni and my fellow Ugandans.

I give credit and tribute to President Yoweri Museveni for managing to maintain peace in Uganda. Surely in most observers' opinion, without the relative peace brought about by Yoweri Museveni in 1986, the bitter cycle of violence and Tit for Tat retribution in our country Uganda would be with us to this very day. We as a nation are slowly but surely moving away from our perennial short term forecast on all things essential to our daily lives towards a longer term sense of planning and have literally come home to stay.

My experience in Uganda has shown me and I believe my family that we can come back to Uganda and succeed in life through our renowned honest struggle and a forthright view of our society at large. It has shown me that we can succeed regardless of the continuing open animosity directed towards our ethnicity and sect as Kakwa and Muslims.

I must say I have never been victimized by Yoweri Museveni's government and I feel reassured that there is sufficient respect for the rule of law, which lends well to the future of the country as well. I pray daily that this relatively peaceful co-existence amongst the multitude of Tribes and Sects thrown together by the colonial powers remains the way it is for the rest of this fledgling "democracy". I put the word democracy in quotes because I am aware of opinions in the public domain by people who grudgingly give credit where it is due while accusing Museveni of different things, including undermining democracy.

Some accuse him of having the task of keeping a bunch of YES PERSONS at bay who "run about town" making things difficult for those developmentally-minded Ugandans who want to serve the people at the grassroots level. However, like I intimated above, our family has never been victimized by Yoweri Museveni's government on account of our father Idi Amin, which is a credit and tribute due to Yoweri Museveni.

However, despite the relative peace that has existed in most parts of Uganda since Museveni took over power in a Military Coup in January 1986, there has been continuing victimization of the Kakwa tribe and pockets of Muslims, long after Dad's rule in Uganda.

Believe you me the number of disillusioned souls amongst my community is disheartening. I always assert that as the youth, we should stand up and make an example to our community. Despite the minimal education we have and all the odds stacked against us Muslims/Kakwas, we must at least try and achieve some hope in life well within the boundaries of our beloved country Uganda. I would dearly love to be an example to my Muslim/Kakwa community that as returnees from exile, we can achieve great things within our beloved motherland Uganda, throughout Africa and in the global community.

I wish to consolidate my achievement over the past several years and begin contributing substantially to my country Uganda, my continent Africa and the global community. The lines of profession I have been at since I returned to Uganda, along with my social activism have prepared me well for my aspirations.

I wish to demonstrate that a lot can be achieved through hard work instead of the perennial wait for a saviour (Dad) who alas never returned mentality – the same mentality that has plagued the African continent for decades now.

Rembi! Rembi! Rembi! (War Cry)

_____ to the job I held at DHL, I got a second parallel career
_____ have held this job since 1994 and still "voice-
_____ dio and Television Channels, along with
_____ mainly for advertisement purposes, Docu-
_____ and bite sweepers for radio stations. I also
_____ Ceremony) work at functions across the city

My acquired Anglo-American accent, which I picked up during our extended stay in exile, has surprisingly been to my advantage and not a hindrance as I might have initially thought. I love music and dancing and I am keen on athletics (decathlon) and Basketball, both of which have given me access to a large social network.

Celebrity status is also a surprising bit that I have achieved on merit. For despite the fact that the media could lash into me for every small mistake I have made - like trying to run a whole night club in competition with the established clubs like Ange Noir and Silk Royale, I was given an unwritten goodwill from everyone I came across.

This I must say stems from my number one rule to always keep sincerity as the centre piece of my approach to all I meet whether journalists or Secret Service Agents trying to gauge my intended agenda in life. Some honestly come back to me and tell me "Jaffar Amin, you do not know your potential….."

I always reply, unfortunately I do know my potential but do realize the country has had enough of the overwhelming figure of Idi Amin. It would be hard for the older generation to stomach a Mark II who was educated but still carried the very self-assured stance of the Great man.

I do know who I am, where I have come from, what I am worth and where I want to go but I believe we should be tolerant of everybody's culture and religion. That is why I place all my hope on the 60 percent population below the age of 29 years. They are the future.

Reuniting with Mama Mariam in Uganda

While I was working at DHL Express, Dad's former official first wife, my stepmother Mama Mariam visited Uganda. She made a memorable trip to Uganda at the beginning of the Millennium and it came out in the papers as her first trip back home after having fled the country in 1974. I was at hand to drive her around in my old red Jalopy 4 litre Petrol, gas guzzler 4Runner and never forgot the time I spent at a London Hospital following a ruptured Achilles tendon which I sustained while dancing at a London Night Club.

During my hospital ordeal, my stepmother Mama Mariam was ly visitor. Considering what my birth had done to her marriage to had been pleasantly surprised by her daily visits to me at the ho next met when she made the memorable trip to Uganda at the the millennium.

As Services Manager at DHL Express at the time, I had security access right up to the tarmac and onto the plane when we did the formal Kuwerekera (Escort) to the Airport Terminal on her way back to Great Britain. So I was able to help her in her disabled state right onto the plane, for she never recovered from a nasty car accident that she was in, in 1974.

Bless her. She would smile all the way as we carried her up the stairs onto the Emirates Flight she took back to London. I kept telling anyone who was around and meant it. This is my mother. Look after her you hear me? I asserted, while giving the Air Stewardess that renowned "Idi Amin frown" I give whenever I want to get someone's attention.

This to me was a blessed reunion. We had met several times at her brother Wanume Kibedi's Sir Apollo Kaggwa House and at her younger sister's home in Ntinda - the younger late sister being a qualified medical doctor and Wanume Kibedi a practicing lawyer in the UK.

That time, I went with my brother Lumumba Juruga Amin who was then a Production Manager at Capital Radio Uganda and my whole Remo Amin family including my children Remo Jr. and Aate Sauda. We went to meet their grandmother "Mama Maliyamu" at Wanume Kibedi's house just off Sir Apollo Kaggwa Road, Kampala.

I pray she has kept those New Millennium group pictures from that momentous return to Uganda.

As I continued to enjoy the relative peace that has existed in most parts of Uganda since Yoweri Museveni became the President in 1986, I followed developments in Uganda with interest. I also reflected on the war that has continued to ravage the Acholi people of Northern Uganda. In particular, I reflected on how Wananchi (fellow citizens) can come together to end that brutal war and unite around an agenda for Peace, Truth and Reconciliation for the whole country.

For over two decades now, a war has been raging on in Northern Uganda between the government of Uganda and a rebel group known as the Lord's Resistance Army (LRA). This war has devastated Northern Uganda in general and the Acholi tribe of Uganda in particular. Information is available through various sources.

On October 8, 1995, Uganda's new Constitution came into force. However, five months after this achievement, on March 12, 1996, the Lord's Resistance Army (LRA) attacked a 17-vehicle convoy along the Karuma-Pakwach Road. Over 130 West Nileans were killed.

Between May and June 1996 Yoweri Museveni allowed elections to take place in Uganda but under a cloud of insecurity in the North and rampant suspicions and allegations of irregularities.

The first time I set eyes on Lady Issa

The first time I set eyes on Lady Issa as I fondly still call her, I knew she was "the one". I had initially noticed her when Dad's brother my uncle Baba Ramadhan Dudu Moro was residing at their home in Kawempe Mbogo upon his return from exile. When Zaitun brought us some tea and food and Baba Ramadhan Dudu Moro remarked that she took after her grandfather Mzee Issa 'Dimba of the Leiko Yatwa Kakwa clan who was of gigantic proportions, my eyes fell on her and I was indeed struck by her size. She was six feet tall, yet her structure was well proportioned. I guess beauty is always in the eyes of the beholder, but in my heart of hearts I knew I had met my better half and the love of my life!

I distinctly remember going back once to Bulumaji and then finding time to visit my mother Nakoli in Jinja town with my first tentative news about having met my future wife:

Mum, I think I have met the woman I want to marry, I blurted out. She is still in Senior Five but I can wait. She does not know my thought or my feelings towards her but I feel I should tell you.

I promised to get a snapshot of Zaitun the next time I visited her home so that my mother could make an opinion of Lady Issa and I did just that. Mum was ecstatic with my choice.

Zaitun Tiko Sebbi Issa 'Dimba is the daughter of Mzee (Elder) Mustafa Sebbi, Kakwas of the Leiko Yatwa clan. Historically Grandma Aate was brought up under the care of Mzee 'Dimba's family during her childhood. A giant Leiko renowned for his height was a close stepbrother to Grandma Aate of the Okapi clan. They are related because the Leiko-Kozoru [variant Kojoru sic] and the Leiko-Origa are brothers with Leiko-Yatwa and Leiko-Buran'ga.

A marriage proposal to Lady Issa and memorable St. Valentine's Day

I vouched for the proper Islamic way of proposing to a girl, so I went through Lady Issa's father to ask for her hand in marriage. However, when I tentatively wrote to Mzee 'Dimba with my proposal to marry Lady Issa, the issue of how close the family was cropped up. My proposal was not given to Lady Issa initially. So, I took matters in my own hands and enlisted the assistance of a number of relatives. I first asked Mama Ariye the junior wife of my uncle Baba Ramadhan Dudu Moro to call Zaitun for a heart to heart meeting and she obliged. For that first meeting, Zaitun was interviewed in the presence of two of my close matriarch family members, including the junior wife of a prominent Karimojong business tycoon Mzee Kodet who operated businesses during the late seventies and throughout the eighties. The second relative was Sakina Bint Mzee Ayub of Bujumbura, a first cousin to Mama Ariye.

Shocked at the marriage proposal in light of the assumption that we were cousins, Lady Issa was adamant that the only way she would consider my marriage proposal would be for me to approach her father since she would not be in a position to make that decision. At that time, Lady Issa also felt it right to inform me that she was in a relationship with another young Beau called Kassim.

I had gained the impetus having got wind of my rival when she sent a request line through my brother Lumumba who at the time was then a very popular presenter on Sanyu FM Radio. Fate had been on my side because Zaitun had given me the note in confidence, asking me to convey it to my brother who was to read it on Air. I broke her confidence by reading the note before I gave it to my younger brother, in effect getting wind of Kassim and her affection for him. Call me snoopy but I needed to know!

The heart to heart meeting organized by Mama Ariye the junior wife of my paternal uncle Baba Ramadhan Dudu Moro gave me the courage to approach him and Baba Moshe. I regard Baba Ramadhan Dudu Moro as a stepfather because the majority of Africans consider their father's brother as a stepfather. Only the uncles on the maternal side are referred to as uncle in the Western sense of the word. Baba Ramadhan Dudu Moro and Baba Moshe felt honoured that amongst Dad's children, I had found it right to approach them first with the issue of marriage to my beautiful Lady Issa.

Baba Ramadhan Dudu Moro confirmed that his mother, Grandma Aisha Aate was only brought up in the family of Mzee Issa 'Dimba and thus the question of blood ties was not so grave. However, he felt that Baba Moshe would be the right person to initiate a formal approach to Mzee 'Dimba with my marriage proposal. This peculiarly crablike approach is all pervasive in the Kakwa culture.

Baba Ramadhan Dudu Moro claimed that even if Dad was around, he would not be the person to actually approach Zaitun's Leiko Yatwa clan.

Therefore, it was fitting that Baba Moshe would also write to Mzee Khamis 'Dimba and not Mzee Mustafa Sebbi.

The reply to my marriage proposal was long in coming since they had to consult with Elders in Leiko Yatwa on the issue of the close blood-line. Amazingly, the reply came on February 7, 1996, but mysteriously Baba Moshe decided to inform me on February 14, 1996 (Valentine's Day!) which made that day a memorable St. Valentine's Day. To me, this was a good omen and I have always cherished Valentine's Day from this day forth since it now has a tangible meaning to me. It was also around the same date (February 15, 1996) that I was sent my acceptance to Broome Community College in New York, for the fall of the 1996 Semester in the Business Administration Curriculum!

My Admission to Broome Community College in New York

I was expected at Broome Community College in Binghamton, New York by August 14, 1996, to participate in an International Student Orientation Program. I actually received the confirmation letter on March 5, 1996 and went ahead and informed my Services Manager of my intentions to join the fall Semester that year but was surprised and confused when he promptly went ahead and promoted me to the position of Air Operations Supervisor. This he did despite his knowledge of my intention to leave DHL, where I had worked since December 1, 1994, my very first job ever since I returned to Uganda from Saudi Arabia.

What a gambit that was, because the dilemma I found myself in was only resolved when I sent a most poignant e-mail to my sponsor Dr. Kokole on August 12, 1996 with the following resolution:

Dear Brother,

Assalam Alaykum!

This is indeed a difficult letter for me. Love is truly a strange animal. The fear of losing Zaitun to a rival is forcing me to re-arrange my plans. Secondly the expiry date of my Passport is way below the six months required by the US Embassy rulebook. To add to my indecision they have promoted me over to Air Ops Supervisor DHL Uganda. Despite advance notice on my part of my intentions to come 14th August to join BCC, you can imagine the state of turmoil I am in at the moment.

Herein lies my dilemma. An abundance of good fortune and I am at a loss as to what to choose. The pure love of a woman, a secure job or the prospect of fulfilling my innermost desire for a College Degree. Let me explain. If I were to join Broome College by the 14th, it would entail postponing the wedding plans since I applied as a single. Furthermore, my Passport issued on 20.08.1991, expires on19.08.1996 since the Application for Non-immigrant Visas states: "Submit Your Passport with the completed Application Form; Your Passport should Be Valid for at least 6 months longer than your intended period of stay in the USA".

As far as the Wedding is concerned, we went together for the all-important HIV I and II Test and we both came out negative! Alhamdulillah! I had actually been approached with a Cultural Bride Price that was truly hefty to say the least.

Furthermore, the direction of cultural instead of religious Nikkah, which to me is acceptable, left me uneasy since I was not conversant with the rules of procedure. At least now, I know where I stand and actually the ball is in my court now since they (Leiko Yatwa Clan) have agreed to the religious line which is much simpler. Baba Mustafa Sebbi actually sent me a messenger so to speak. I am quite confident.

I have been out there in the wilderness. My mind in turmoil and the only recompense is to concentrate on the job at hand. Please understand my point of view. That having gained so much I am timid to tempt fate. It is also a question of Independence/Dependence. I gained the former. It seems I am hanging on to it for dear life.

I do realise I am foregoing a once and for all chance at Higher Education. Nonetheless, it is not too late to try later on. There were too many important issues that came at the same time. I had to make a choice. But to tell you the truth I have always been ruled by my heart. I am instinctive by nature.

Hey Thanxx! for the political Bible/Qur-an?

Sincerely yours

TJ.Remo

12th August 1996.

In response, Dr. Omari H. Kokole (and I pay tribute to him) called me on the 14th to inform me that he agreed and understood my e-mail. However, what I did not realize at the time was that the phone call was his farewell call to me because sadly, he died five days later on August 19, 1996. What shocked me the most was that if I had enrolled by the 14th I would have been present when he died in New York State.

Dr. Kokole believed in me like no other. He would forever be the benchmark with which I judge my achievements in life. He would forever be the surrogate father figure I had taken up following my painful schism with my father. Dr. Kokole was the one I would turn to, much in the same way I used to turn to Dad for advice and help.

Dr. Kokole of the Lurujo Kakwa clan had made a personal obligation to carry on forward where Dad felt he had gone far enough in my education. Yongole his younger brother once told me that considering the close-knit history of the house of Ferre [Pere] and Dada, Dr. Kokole might have felt a just obligation to help one of his own. Yongole even told me that Dr. Kokole felt let down when I sent him that e-mail showing my intention not to take up the offer for Higher Education. That time, I pointedly told Yongole that for all that we know Allah's hand was guiding my decision not to go to the USA since on hindsight the tragedy of Dr. Kokole's unexpected heart attack would have met me in the USA. Also, considering the loss of my singular sponsor, the American system would probably never have looked kindly to an International Student especially from Africa who had lost a key sponsor.

The day of our Nikkah (Wedding)

I couldn't contain my excitement on the day of our Nikkah (Wedding) on December 21, 1996. On that very fateful day, I went hurriedly to my tailor for the two Black Spencer Suits I had ordered. I could not believe my eyes when I arrived and he had not finished fitting the attire. My worst nightmare had come to haunt me at the 11th hour because the Nikkah was scheduled for 1500Hrs and I was stuck in a tailor's shop in liaison between two unreliable tailors who were fixing brass buttons and the like.

I was out of there by three thirty driving like a mad man towards Kazo Bwaise where my wedding party was waiting for me the groom and will never forget the look of incredulity on the face of the leader of my delegation Mualim Hussein Aligo when I arrived late. He only managed to mumble, "We have already sent a vanguard who will inform the other side that we would be late in order to avoid the fine."

I barked for my younger brother Lumumba to be called and rushed to my living quarters to change. Since I felt the only way to restore confidence in that Imam was to look the part, by the time we came down the steps I could see the effect the Black Officer-like Spencer suits had on a generation brought up in the Kings African Rifles era. My Imam Mualim, Aligo tried in vain to find out if I had the Makhari but I brushed the question aside reminding him that we were already late and ought to get moving.

What struck me first was the multitude of people at the Nikkah function. Literally the whole Kakwa/Nubian community was there. Word had got around that one of Amonye's (Idi Amin's) sons was tying the knot with a fellow Kakwa girl. I only restored my confidence when Kassim, one of Dad's former bodyguards opened the car door for me and led me and my younger brother, who was my Wazir (Best Man) to the tented canopy where the function was to begin.

As I took off my shoes in the customary Islamic requirement and stood up to my full height in the tented canopy, I uttered the Muslim greeting "Assalam Alaykum" and was heartened to feel the warmth of the response from the congregation "Alaykum Muslim war Rahmat ul Allah wa Barrakatu". This indeed was a congregation wherein at last I was indeed finally able to sanctify my love for Lady Issa. What I cherished the most that day was the fact that the Speaker of the Kingdom of Buganda Sheikh Islam Ali Kulumba was the officiating Imam who would bear witness of the sanctification (Nikkah).

He rose up and gave a Sermon (Khutba) to the congregation. Lady Issa's side gave a brief review of her life and my side gave theirs. Words of advice were bestowed on us before a formal request was asked for the Makhari, which she had requested in the amount of 50,000 /=. I took this amount out of my inside pocket and handed it over to Mzee Diliga who took the Makhari to the bride.

Sheikh Islam Ali Kulumba then solemnly requested for the presence of the Father of the Bride who was giving away his daughter. Mzee Khamis 'Dimba came forward representing his younger brother at the function. I was requested to move to the middle of the room and we held hands with Mzee 'Dimba. Sheikh Islam Ali Kulumba then placed a handkerchief over our intertwined hands and requested the consent from the father. He also requested my adherence to the sanctification, which was repeated three times. Sheikh Kulumba then formally sanctified our marriage with a duwa and declared Remo and Tiko man and wife in the eyes of Allah and in the presence of the whole congregation.

I will never forget the moment I was asked to stand and greet the dignitaries. By the time I came full circle and approached Baba Yusuf of the Leiko clan, I had fully blown tears washing down my cheeks and I was only stopped with murmurs from the congregation that men do not cry. Honestly, these were tears of joy! The elation in my heart was indescribable. The formal marriage certificate was signed by myself and then sent to the bride who also signed our fate for better or for worse.

When we returned to Baba Ramadhan Dudu Moro's home with the bride, I heard that three Doluka Bands were playing music and dancing. These three bands represented the Kakwa/Nubian community at the after party and over 1,000 guests "invited themselves" to a function that clearly held more meaning as a galvanizing force amongst my community who needed something to cheer up about. I will forever cherish the wholesome merry making and genuine love shown to me and what I represented for my Kakwa/Muslim community.

Our first born son

Mysteries never seem to end. In October 1997, I was highly expecting my first born with my wife Lady Issa. I recall that on that fateful date October 27, 1997, I had a Voice Over Session at Sanyu Television and the Radio Sanyu dark blue shuttle van had picked me up from my place of work in order to drop me at the Television Station. We went along with some technicians on the short trip to Naguru. With me was a half Canadian, half Muganda technician friend called Sanyu on the trip and offhand I told her that I was actually celebrating my birthday but would dearly wish it that the child Lady Issa and I were expecting would be born on the same date!

That time, Lady Issa had gone to live with her uncle the late Francis Ayume at his residence in Nakasero. Ayume, a Leiko clan member was the Speaker of the Uganda Parliament at the time and he was subsequently appointed the Attorney General of Uganda for the period 2001 - 2006 before his untimely death.

Lady Issa intimately recalled the Sunday before Remo Junior was born when I called up the Speaker's residence asking to speak with my wife. Impatient as usual, I asked her when the baby was due, intimating why it was not here by now. Lady Issa rudely answered back with a question…. On hindsight, she was deeply in pain and must have heard the same question over and over. I placed back the phone receiver thoroughly rebuked and promising never to call again. Her ceremonial mother, the wife of the Speaker, a Half Masai and Half Somali noticed Lady Issa's discomfort but insisted that she go out for her daily afternoon stroll. So she set out with Ndagire the granddaughter to Mrs. Ayume. They made for Wandegeya on the winding road that circles Nakasero hill anti clock wise, passing in front of the Indian Embassy/Residence and even went right round and up to Christ the King Church, a stone's throw from State House Nakasero. Unbeknownst to the unborn child and expectant mother, these were my childhood haunts and it was actually where we used to reside when Dad was President of Uganda.

Lady Issa rested on the grounds of the church, feeling out of breath. Then they set off down Akii Bua Road named by Dad after Uganda's famous Olympic hero, John Akii Bua. Then they passed in front of the Nakasero Blood Bank and back to the Speaker's Residence. At the gate, a Munyankole Police Officer asked the very same question I asked and she replied in a foul mood, to which he, taken aback replied "Aren't we rude today?" Lady Issa lamented and tried to apologize to the Police Officer who answered, "It is alright, since it must be tiresome waiting for the child." Lady Issa spent Sunday night trudging up and down at the back of the Staff Quarter, to the chagrin of the soldiers in the next residence who commented to her in the morning "You spent the night on guard duty or what?" Then noticing that she was heavy with child, they understood.

Mrs. Ayume came to Lady Issa and her cousin Akulia Ayume said she had not slept for the whole night. Mrs. Ayume asked if she felt it was time and she answered in the affirmative. The Speaker's Official Vehicle was out but a friend had come to see the Ayumes and was much obliged to drive across the valley to Mulago Hospital. He commented that it would be a blessed boy, being as it was his first time to take an expectant mother to hospital.

They arrived at the Maternity Ward and Lady Issa was checked to ensure that all was well then the waiting started. What a vigil it turned out to be! Strangely, although in pain, she managed to hide it as per Kakwa tradition of showing courage under adversity. She fell into bouts of masked gleeful laughter watching fellow expectant mothers going through the pain. One particularly hilarious one was a giant Policewoman who decided to start marching up and down the ward - "left", "right", "left" "right" "about turn" "left!" This scene thoroughly brought a smile and masked giggles to my wife. Unbeknownst to her, one of the Matrons was watching her and she approached her.

"You take pleasure out of watching your colleagues in pain?"

"Noo!" Lady Issa blurted.

"Is this your first pregnancy?" the matron continued.

"Yes".

"Aren't you feeling the pain?"

"I am but what to do?" offered Lady Issa before continuing, "Whether I want to or not it will continue to hurt, I just have to bear it."

"Where are you from? Ankole?"

"No, I am from West Nile".

"West Nile!?"

"I am from Ko'boko."

"You look like a Muhima".

"No I am a Kakwa."

"What do you find amusing?" the matron insisted.

"The giant Policewoman particularly amused me and my neighbour here who claims to be on her eighth pregnancy and was insisting to submit to sterilization after this one, claiming eight was enough. I asked why she felt eight was enough and she claimed not so much the feeding but the education which was the problem since school fees has become unbearable these days. Hopefully the older ones would have finished university and would help the younger ones come through."

At around 10:30 pm, the labour pains became unbearable and Lady Issa informed the Matron. Remo Junior was born as the hour approached midnight - sufficient enough to be born on that magical date October 27, 1997 – my Birthday! Lady Issa became the talk of the ward because of her strength under adversity. Alas! She could not escape the Leiko tradition of Female Warriors of old, of showing grace under pressure.

Mama Remo (Lady Issa) insisted that I should be called but Mrs. Ayume said, "He must be busy. Let's wait and we will call him in due time" she insisted. On hindsight I had grown tired of bugging my wife about when the baby was due and had vowed that previous Sunday night never to call again. However, out of frustration, I put up the courage on Wednesday and called Mrs. Ayume who joyfully announced that Lady Issa had given birth!

What child? I asked.

"A 4.0 kgs boy", she exclaimed.

What! What! I blurted. When?

"On 27th October 1997", she replied.

I remember the initial jealous rage that washed over me that they did not call me on the date but had to let two days pass by from that blissful date. Almost out of fear and a sense of having lost control of my son's destiny, I declared the son's names "Tshombe Jaffar Remo Jr." I made sure Mrs. Ayume wrote my exceedingly difficult names down and made sure she repeated them to me! I jumped from my desk and rushed to my Services Manager Apollo Spencer Kamugisha's with the good news.

A Son! A Son! A Son! I exclaimed.

Mrs. Ayume discharged her ceremonial daughter and then insisted on passing by my office with the baby. Upon their arrival, I went exclaiming to the parked Landcruiser while commenting that Pat my colleague should come and see my son.

The first comment was from Mrs. Ayume who said, "Come and see the size of his feet. This one will be a tall fellow."

Indeed rosy Patagonia feet knee jacked away and Remo's eyes flickered open with annoyance, at the feel and the cold breeze that wafted through. Mrs. Ayume insisted I come to the house after work to see the child. I confirmed I would and would make a Beeline to the residence every time after work before I went back home.

Our daughter

By 1999, my beautiful daughter was almost never born. Lady Issa and I as a couple were going through a rough patch in our marriage because we were not seeing eye-to-eye on every aspect of our life. Alas the honeymoon had finally come to an end. One particular incident led to a prolonged period when we were not talking to each other and as is inevitable, we finally made up but it was short-lived because after a brief "hiatus", we reverted back to the turbulence, which is characteristic of two strong-willed people. However, all is well that ends well because on September 23, 1999, at 11:00 pm, at 3.0 kgs, Iya Aate Mangarita Sauda was born. I named her after my mother and paternal grandmother. "Iya" means "my mother" in the Lugbara language and she was born on the National day of the Kingdom of Saudi Arabia (Black Arabia) - i.e. "My mother Mangarita the Black one".

Our son Alemi was born on January 30, 2004 at 11:45 pm, weighing a hefty 4.4 kgs! We were blessed with the twins Al-Hassan and Al-Husayn on the most misunderstood date on the Christian Calendar 06.06.2006 (666) at 4:00 pm and the second twin at 4:30 pm, weighing in at 2.2 kgs and 3.2 kgs respectively but a blessing nevertheless, to the Dada clan.

It is heartening to witness the likeness in my small family. Junior is the spitting image of his mother Mama Remo while Iya is the apple of my eye. Blessed she is because she came to us at the very period when I achieved the pinnacle of a native's successful aspirations in a multinational company. I was appointed the Services Station Manager and I mystically believe and owe it to that energetic bundle of joy. Idi Amin is the spitting image of his illustrious grandfather, my Dad. Baba the elder Fraternal Twin is the spitting image of his grandmother Nakoli my mother and Dada is the

spitting image of Ramadhan Dudu Moro our Late Kayo (Elder) of the
Adibu Nyikamero (Likamero) clan.

A heartfelt thank you to Lady Issa

Words cannot express how thankful I am to Lady Issa but I want
to convey a heartfelt thank you to her and say, Thanks to Nnalongo Tiko
(Lady Issa) my lovely Ayike (Beloved, Favoured One). Thank you for
loving me just for the moment and bearing for me five beautiful children,
Tshombe Jaffar Remo II, Iya Sauda Aate II, Idi Al-Amin Alemi II, the
twins Muhammed Al-Hassan Baba II and Ahmed Al-Husayn Dada IV.

I gained the Honourary title Ssalongo as the first progeny of Idi
Amin Dada to get twins when Nnalongo Tiko (Lady Issa) blessed us with
twins Al-Hassan Muhammed Baba and Al-Husayn Ahmed Dada. This
happened on the most misunderstood date on the Judeo-Christian
calendar 06.06.06 at 04H00 and the second twin at 04H30. The twins
weighed in at 2.2 kgs and 3.2 kgs respectively - a blessing indeed to our
Dada Clan.

My physiological bearing, general interests and Kakwa language

Although I inherited the physiological bearing of my father's renowned stature, I do bear a striking facial resemblance to my dear and beloved mother Mangarita. At 6'1" in height and on average 90+ kilograms in weight, I am considered an XL in my society but well below Dad's 6'4" and XXXL 120-150+ kilograms physiology.

Concerning my general interests in life, I would say that I am philosophical and in a sense even religious. I tend to be thoughtful, understanding and analytical. I also love to observe and study human nature and behaviour. Psychology and Anthropology are subjects that enthrall me.

Although Kakwa is my native tongue, it was rarely used within our ethnically mixed household. Rather what is considered Pidgin Swahili Ki-coloni (Creole-Swahili) was and continues to be my family's Lingua franca. However a Creole-Arabic called Nubi (often mistakenly referred to as "Nubian") comes a close second to Swahili in the community I grew up in. Lingala has however taken up a large chunk of the language spoken by my family members who had the pleasure of residing in the Congo during our long stay in exile.

I was introduced to the English language when I was finally brought into my Dad's household at Nakasero Lodge under the just motherhood of the late Mama Kay. I joined Elementary School in 1973 at the tender age of 6. The school in question was Nakasero Primary School in Kampala.

The following year, Mama Kay sent some of my siblings (Hussien Juruga Lumumba, Sofia Sukeji, Khamis Machomingi) and I to a Preparatory School in the most temperate zone in my country, Kigezi District. This district was and continues to be popularly known and called the Switzerland of Africa. Kabale Preparatory School (KPS) was run by Protestant Missionaries from England.

My other siblings (Sulieman Geriga, Muhammad Luyimbazi, Mariam Aaliyah, Maimuna, Issa Aliga, Adam Ma'dira, Mao Muzzamil, Abdul Nasser Mwanga, Moses Amin Kenyi and Asha Mbabazi Al-Amin) later joined us at Kabale Preparatory School between 1974 and 1979.

My triad cultural heritage

A photograph taken at the reception that followed my marriage to Lady Issa on December 21, 1996 best illustrates my triad cultural heritage - a Nubian, a Kakwa and an Anglo-Saxon at heart all at the same time.

In the photograph, my wife Zaitun (Lady Issa) is wearing colourful Nubian attire while Mualim Hussein Aligo of the Muredu Kakwa clan and the leader of my wedding delegation is wearing traditional Islamic/Muslim Garb. He looks on in the background as my brother Lumumba Juruga and I wearing Tuxedos, admire the bride.

The images of Lady Issa in the colourful Nubian attire and Mualim Hussein Aligo in the traditional Islamic/Muslim Garb represent the Nubian influence and Islam's benign presence in our family. In the photograph, images of the Bashful Bride Zaitun (Lady Issa) and Joyce Adrili the Matron donning a blue attire and attending to the beautiful bride also represent our Orientalist Nubian Triad requirement for the Lady to maintain that feminine etiquette.

My brother Lumumba Juruga and I represent our British Kings African Rifles oriented heritage. However, despite this Nubian influence and Islam's benign presence in our family, our Kakwa roots were always strong and prevalent. The photograph was taken at our After Party on December 21, 1996.

Notwithstanding the influences of the "Nubian culture", Islam and Kakwa culture, we were also exposed to "Anglo-Saxon culture", through Uganda's British colonial history and Dad's "obsession" with everything British. In the photograph, the images of my brother Lumumba Juruga and I represent our British oriented heritage.

Zaitun's colourful Nubian attire is a glaring contrast to the white Wedding dress she wore during the ceremonies and festivities that were part of the Nikkah (Wedding) - another image that represents our British oriented Triad Cultural Heritage.

Islam's benign presence in our family

I will provide additional information on the Nubians of Uganda in a subsequent section of the series which along with sections on Grandpa's conversion to Islam and Dad's childhood provide information about the Nubian influence and Islam's benign presence in our family and how my family acquired the Nubian components of our Triad

Cultural Heritage. The cultural heritages of Nubian, Kakwa and Anglo-Saxon at heart will be evident throughout the series.

You will recall that Grandpa was converted to Islam by a fellow Kakwa with the title Sultan Ali Kenyi of the Drimu Kakwa clan of Ko'buko (Ko'boko) and my family has had a strong Muslim background ever since. You will also recall that the day Dad was born in 1928, my Grandpa Amin Dada Nyabira Temeresu (Tomuresu) had set off for Eid Al-Adha Prayers amongst the Nubian Muslim Settlement on Kibuli Hill, a suburb of the Ugandan city of Kampala. Dad's brother, my uncle Ramadhan Dudu Moro, who was 9 years old at the time accompanied Grandpa on this day in 1928 that fell on the religious festival Eid Al-Adha which is celebrated by Muslims worldwide. You will further recall that after my grandparents divorced over false allegations that King Daudi Chwa fathered Dad and not Grandpa, Grandma left with Dad to live with her relatives who had retired from the Kings African Rifles and were living in Bombo, Semuto-Luwero, on the outskirts of Kampala.

As I recounted in a previous section, by the time several of my extended family members were discharged from the Kings African Rifles and "settled" as peasants and indentured labourers, the bulk of my family had fully embraced Islam and fully amalgamated with the "Nubi (Nubian) tribe" of Uganda. Many of them had also fully assimilated into the Baganda (Ganda) tribe of Uganda which is how my family became "entangled" with gossiping Ganda and Nubians and caused Dad to be subjected to the Deadly "Paternity Test" on account of Grandma's close relationship with the Ganda Royal Family.

As you also recall, Dad and Grandma lived at Semuto-Luwero for 4 years, from 1937 to 1940 when Dad was between the ages of 9 and 12 years old. During their stay at Semuto-Luwero, Dad studied at the Al-Qadriyah Darasah Bombo (Al-Qadriyah Khanqa, Masgid Noor Bombo), Uganda. He attempted Primary School while at Bombo, sporadically combining this with Garaya [Qur'an Studies].

I have images of the youthful Dad chanting the fantastic voyage of the Holy Prophet's Mihraj (tour to heaven) to a transfixed audience filled to capacity with dignitaries from around the world on an annual Mawlid Ziyarah to Masgid Noor Futuwah in Bombo in the 1930s and 1940s.

By then, Dad was reputed to have attained the level of an adept and he was aware and cultivated a sense of Alam Al Mithal, the mystical world of pure images. Some even claim that Dad's intuition was legendary. He was a renowned seer to some for his eerie ability - a certain ability to foretell future events with amazing accuracy. It was a mystical trait cultivated from his strong association with the Al Qadriyah Order and from having inherited the same ability from his Okapi/Bura mother. Grandma Aisha Chumaru Aate was by far the most revered and powerful member of the "Yakanye Allah Water Movement" at the Fourth Battalion Jinja under the Kings African Rifles. I provide snippets of the "Allah Water Movement" also in a subsequent section of the series.

The Fourth Battalion Jinja under the Kings African Rifles was later converted to the 1st Battalion Jinja under the Uganda Rifles and finally my Dad as Head of State renamed the barracks Al-Qadhafi Garrison. The renaming of the barracks Al-Qadhafi Garrison followed Dad and Al-Qadhafi's Bilateral Joint Declaration on February 14, 1972 between the Great People's Jamahiriya of Libya and the 2nd Republic of Uganda. I write about this Declaration in a previous section of this "Introductory Edition".

From the time Grandpa Amin Dada Nyabira Temeresu (Tomuresu) converted from Catholicism to Islam during the first decade of the 20th Century, the Muslim religion has deeply permeated my immediate family, leading to Dad's strong affiliations with the Muslim Ummah. A case in point was when Dad curtailed his equally strong relationship with Israel in favour of the Muslim Ummah, personified by Muamar Al-Qadhafi of Libya and the Late King Faisal Bin Abdul Aziz Al-Saud of Saudi Arabia, during Dad's rule in Uganda.

The search for my roots and culture was what prompted a passion and hunger in me to begin investigating the various "threads" comprising my "Triad Cultural Heritage". It is also what has encouraged me to uncover Dad's story layer by layer and led me to partner with various individuals interested in Dad's conflicted legacy of hero and villain at the same time. A number of book projects I have embarked on provide the background information for the current project.

I have also embarked on an agenda for Peace, Truth and Reconciliation as outlined in various documents under the Al-Amin Foundation.

Dad's Gulomo Funeral Ceremony

Between August 16, 2003 and August 23, 2003, I attended various ceremonies organized to honour Dad upon his demise. These included his own Gulomo Funeral Ceremony (Kakwa tribal ceremony honouring and telling the story of the dead) when the whole of the Kakwa community fell into despair and mourned the loss of their Bull Elephant Awon'go, son of Aate. A Gulomo Funeral Ceremony is a ceremony organized to tell the story of the dead in Adiyo narration style and format (oral historical narrative account of history, events of the past).

Telling Adiyo is an age old practice of narrations which include telling the story of the Kakwa tribe. The narrations are usually done during weddings, funerals and on special occasions called gbadru where mature bulls are slaughtered for each clan member and the n'gerin'gizi (nephews) to enjoy.

The narration is usually also done by the clan leader who is flanked by a Council of Elders. The latter follow the narration attentively and they may jump in to make any corrections or to fill in a forgotten issue.

The narrator always holds in his right hand a special stick of honour called Aruweta (plural Aruwezi). The Aruweta is a stick roughly the size of the narrator and about 5 centimetres in diameter. Its colour is shiny brown to black - the intensity of this colour being especially increased due to its age. The stick is passed from generation to generation and kept in very sacred places. Every Kakwa clan has its Elders and every one of them knows their ethno history, for this has been passed on to them through their parents, grandparents and other Elders.

For our Adibu Nyikamero (Likamero) Kakwa clan, Aruweta is our ancestor Temeresu's (Tomuresu's) spear which is usually speared into the sacred ground at the very beginning of the Adiyo recital, while the recitalist holds onto another ancestor Dada's Bow and Arrows throughout the recital. The Aruweta is not dropped at all, especially during the Adiyo narration process.

An interesting feature of the Adiyo narration ritual is the insertion of a song or songs which not only appropriately emphasize, consolidate or authenticate the point in question but they also give "colour" to the whole story, much in similar tradition to the famous Gruerios of West Africa. Another interesting feature is that all the events of the past are reduced to kaze (yesterday).

Additional details about Dad's Gulomo Funeral Ceremony will be provided as the series, Idi Amin: Hero or Villain? His Son Jaffar Amin and Other People Speak, unfolds. However, suffice it to state here that some key themes emerged during the ceremony. For example, an Elder Awon'go of the Godiya Kelipi Kakwa clan went back to the time my grandfather was a child and narrated aspects of his life before telling aspects of Dad's story as I recount in this series. Elders from the Rikazu Kakwa clan and Okapi Lugbara clans told Grandma's story.

A Son's Eulogy

Assalam Alykum Wa Rahmat Ul Allah Wa Barakatu

On behalf of the Kakwa and Muslim Ummah, I wish to convey our gratitude to the Al Saud Royal Family for the hospitality bestowed on the Dada family through the past 26 years.

We are grateful for the honour bestowed on father when he was buried in the Kingdom of Saudi Arabia.

To our father's credit, once he fell silent on the world stage for most of 24 years, he refocused his energy into understanding further his religion, Islam.

He donated Sadakat Al-Jariah towards Islamic causes. We would go on tours of the holy sites in the Kingdom of Saudi Arabia, like Jebel Noor.

We also climbed the mountain, which marked the beginning of the Hijrah.

We visited distant places like Badr, the site of the 1st battle.

We also went on extended tours of Madinah.

We visited Mount Arafat, the site of the final sermon and the surrounding areas of Mina and Muzdalifah.

Another highly enlightening experience which I had the privilege to witness and to which everyone of the 1.5 billion Muslims world wide seek repentance as an obligation annually, was our father's ritual of breaking fast at the Haram Alsharif in Makkah from the start to the finish of our holy month of Ramadhan.

This ritual would be performed daily for either the 29 or 30 days in the holy month of Ramadhan. His level of dedication was that high! Our father embraced his Islamic religion totally.

I wish to emphasize key issues that were discussed but over-looked by key detractors over the years or what I term preconceived objectives. I would also like to correct that my father was more determined than angry. This fueled his focused determination to effect change by any means necessary:

1. The subversive elements in exile favoured what they termed a protracted people's struggle, involving acts of sabotage and political assassinations, at grassroots around the country, between 1971 and 1979. Others favoured engaging the Uganda Army in a sudden invasion like the one that took place in 1972, hoping that the disgruntled Ugandan population would rise up against the 2nd Republic, but they had failed to understand that Idi Amin's humble upbringing and crowd-pleasing style resonated with the teeming masses. This style stemmed from his gift of speech. He had the astonishing ability to lead a Nation due to his extraordinary fluency in at least a dozen indigenous African languages. His memory for words, for people and places never ceased to amaze his former KAR-CO Major Iain Grahame. He spoke directly to the people in a language they understood. The essence of good communication in today's ICT generation is the ability to get your message across. This factor is quite often ignored by his detractors, but it is the most indelible testament as to why he continues to resonate with the majority of the now revived underclass (common man) under this structurally adjusted society in the 21st century.

2. His militant stance as the de facto spokesman for the Non-Aligned "Third World" countries did more to quicken his fall from grace than the grave and protracted efforts of the subversives.

3. The Western world powers also resented his keen interest in the (still ongoing) Arab - Israeli nationalist conflict.

4. His keen interest in the twin problems of Caucasian supremacists in Southern Africa and the dire plight of African Americans rubbed the Western powers that be the wrong way, with his open and wholehearted support to various movements like the Nation of Islam, Black Panthers, SWAPO, ANC, ZANU and the PLO, both spiritually and financially. So much so that as OAU Chairman at the time, he commanded centre stage when he dramatically held fort at the UN Assembly, New York (USA) in 1975 and successfully managed to effect a UN Resolution likening Zionism to Racism and Apartheid. This was the watershed for the world powers when they finally realized that they were not dealing with a rustic buffoon but a man on a mission to effect genuine change - someone who was

determined and seemingly intent on upsetting the political landscape and in turn set up his own agenda.

5. To date, some still persist on feigning disbelief and perplexed mutterings of frustration, claiming Idi Amin Dada did not realize or understand what he had got himself into or the significance of the high political stakes he was playing at. However I believe and he did intimate in some way to me that he was supremely aware of the situation based on our very own Islamic ideology which focuses on a global perspective vis-à-vis our dichotomous arena of Dar el Harb and Dar el Salam. This unique perspective still holds strong amongst the now largest religion in the world with the Muslim Ummah now standing an impressive 1.5 billion and still the fastest growing religion in the world.

6. That historic UN resolution stood the test of time from 1975 to 1991 when it was finally overturned by an even shrewder Caucasian supremacists' advocate President Bush Sr. when he encapsulated his "New World Order" on the eve of "Desert Storm".

Al marhum (The Late) was considered a true brother by the Al Saudi Family and Muslims in general and the most positive opinion of him was that he was a courageous Muslim under the circumstances. That is why he was honoured with the highest Islamic accolade when funeral prayers were offered in his name at our three holiest sites of Jerusalem, Madinah and Makkah the day he passed away on 16th August 2003. Allah Yar Hamu Fil Janat In Sha Allah.

Amonye (Father) in many ways instilled in me the very same virtues of independence, racial pride, love of culture, a pro Islamic and indelible Afrocentric point of view.

Here was a man who had the wherewithal, the attitude, the spiritual belief and the courage plus the privilege and means (OPEC Cartel Support) to reaffirm our heritage and fulfill our Rembi's Mystical Legacy by any means necessary!

I surely believe and solemnly swear that I, Ssalongo Jaffar, will never suffer from an inferiority complex because my heritage has an absolutely solid and recorded history of affirmative action and that out and out stance of the Black Panthers that I have personally identified and taken as both my heritage and destiny.

Amonye's (Father's) underlining gift to Ugandans is our lack of an inferiority complex.

We completely shed that colonial mentality for good, picked ourselves up and counted ourselves amongst self-determinants of the world.

It is a shame that we are now back to square one, laden with the very same issues that plagued our fore fathers.

Al Hammadulillah he was given the honour and distinction of simultaneous salat al janazah/Funeral Prayers in Makkah Al Mukaramah, Madinah Al Munawarah and Masgid Al-Aqsa on 16th August 2003.

Sorrow does follow the loss of loved ones but in Islam we are enjoined to say:

Ina Lillahi wa inah illayhi Raji-un.

Ssalongo Jaffar Idi Amin

An Admirer's Eulogy

My Idi Amin Dada - Recollections and a Tribute to Idi Amin Dada

I was born on May 5, 1957 in Mbarara Hospital in Ankole in Western Uganda. I spent the first 12 years of my life in Ankole and I spoke the Runyankole language fluently so was my Luganda language. I'm a proper product of mixed marriages and I grew up in the full view of tribalism at its highest. I can't even imagine what both my parents mainly my mother went through before and during their relationship. It must have been so difficult for both of them but I believe their love for each other and their three girls kept them going strong until they fell apart as all failed relationships do.

In 1969 my father was transferred to Masindi, Bunyoro. I with my two sisters was left behind to finish our year for that school term. In Masindi I was admitted at a Catholic Girls School. It was to be my best school ever. I then went to Jinja in Busoga to live with my aunt who had come to Mbarara in 1967 to see my father and asked my father if she could have me. She claimed that my father was not strict enough because the day she came to visit, we came home late and to her that was not good enough. My father was not strong too.

In 1970 I went for my Primary Seven education - this time in Jinja Barracks Primary School. I was received by my aunt - a sister to my father. Like my father's home, my aunt's home was also a very welcoming home, full of all sorts of people - different tribes and classes. I didn't feel the difference because both families were the same. The only problem was the new language I had to adopt. In my new home the spoken language was Swahili and I couldn't speak a word. I was young so it didn't take me long and I was very good with other languages. This made me popular as I was in the Jinja Army Barracks School where all tribes were represented and the languages spoken were as many.

One day, I was home with my young cousins and nieces when I received a telephone call asking for my aunt's husband. I was asked to make tea for this gentleman who called the house and said that he was coming home immediately. It was Idi Amin. I prepared the tea, eggs and bread - ready on a tray and waited for who was coming.

Then a convoy of Army Escorts all dressed in very beautiful Army Service Uniforms with motorcycles appeared and a line of them pulled outside the house for me to receive them. This huge tall man came out and I ran as usual and welcomed him. He asked me with a smile, "Is my tea ready?" He was very kind to me and treated me very well in that small time - with a lot of care like his child. I replied "Yes, it is ready sir". He then asked me where the toilet was. I showed him around. He looked like he knew the place well enough to feel comfortable and at home.

When he came out, he said he couldn't take the tea; that he was late and he will take the tea later when he comes back from Magamaga Barracks where the function was held. There were some official functions. I can't remember what it was but it seemed very important according to what he was wearing and his Army Convoy. This was my first eye to eye encounter with the man General Idi Amin Dada. I still adore him today! I had heard about him in stories that I didn't understand well as a child but here he was with me in a house without anyone there apart from my young relatives - wonderful!

I'm not sure how long it was after our Magamaga encounter but on January 25, 1971, the government of Dr. Apollo Milton Obote was over and General Idi Amin Dada took over power and people mainly from the central part of Uganda in Kampala were celebrating. At this time we were in Jinja. So apart from watching television at home, I didn't know much going on outside my new adopted home.

We woke up and went to school as usual which was an Army and Police School without knowing what had happened. The previous night I had received a telephone call for my aunt's husband from someone who called himself Dominiko. It didn't sound normal to receive a call of that nature by someone called Dominiko and I had not heard about that name. It was after we went to school that we found out that we were actually not going to have classes as normal and we were sent home.

Some of my friends didn't come back after school and we later knew what had happened in Uganda. We had a new President called Major

General Idi Amin Dada. It was a new government and new everything at home and new speeches and to me everything was new. Previously at my father's home, there was no television, so having a television was new and the news on television were more interesting than my radio news with my father. I used to listen to the news with my father and Civics was one of my best subjects at school which made me know what was going on around me and mainly in the news. No one in my class could beat me in the Civics subject.

The Amin family and my aunt's family in Jinja were close and we the children played together. We visited each other a lot and my aunt was very good friends with Amin's wives. I didn't know who was her best friend among them. All I knew was that they were all friends with her. With my aunt, we often visited the Amin family at Command Post in Kololo. At this time, Amin had 4 wives who lived together – Mama Mariam (Sarah Mutesi Kibedi), Kay, Norah and Madina.

I still remember the time Mama Mariam and Amin had to go for their State Visits to Israel and Great Britain in July 1971. I remember the time very well because they had brought a village girl to go and work for the Amin family as a house girl, only a few days later to see her boarding a plane to England. We were all so surprised and it has always been one of my lines of hope, whenever I remember seeing that poor girl coming to do her house girl work and ending up boarding a plane to London.

My father had two wives and my aunt's husband had two official wives. This was so normal in our Ugandan society and there was no complaining. We and our mothers were added on each other without any complaint in many cultures and tribes in Uganda.

I did my Primary Leaving Examinations in Jinja and passed well. I joined the PMM Senior Secondary School. That was where I was studying when Idi Amin ordered all foreigners in Uganda to register their Nationalities. PMM was predominantly Asian. You had to have very good grades to get in the school. Students were registering their names. My surprise was that they were all British Nationals. That was what they wrote down.

I had many Indian friends and when we were asked which second language to study, I chose the Gujarati language after English. We had English, French and Gujarati as a Second Language. After the registration nationwide, President Amin welcomed all those Ugandans to stay home because indeed Uganda was their home. He said those who were not Ugandan citizens or didn't hold Uganda Passports should leave Uganda and he gave the foreigners 90 days to leave.

Before Amin married Madina, while staying with my aunt, rumour was passing that Amin had a new girlfriend. After sometime, Amin came home with a very beautiful woman called Madina Nnajjemba. They married in 1972.

One day, everyone was home and my aunt and her husband were entertaining the visitors. I was called to make coffee, which I did.

When Idi was having the coffee I had made, he asked, "Who made this beautiful coffee?"

He was told "our child Nakalanzi." I was then called out loud, "Nakalanzi", I replied, "Nam!" in the respectful traditional Nubian way.

I ran to the sitting room and knelt down as I always did while talking to the Elders.

Amin looked and was very impressed by my age and the coffee I had made. He then asked me to go and teach Madina how to make coffee. I was so happy to have been appreciated and to be asked to go to Command Post to teach Madina how to make coffee. At this time she was living at the Command Post in Kololo and the other wives were at State House Entebbe and State House Nakasero. We still visited both places and were a bit of regulars.

I was then asked by my aunt to go and teach Madina to make the coffee.

The day I went to Command Post, my aunt took me to the Taxi Park and I headed to Kampala. In the Taxi Park, came a very beautiful black car which pulled over and I was off to Command Post at Kololo. I was met by Madina. She was so kind and asked me how my aunt was and she took me around her new home. Madina took me to her bedroom, which was huge and beautiful. She showed me her dresses. She told me, "That one cost 100 shillings". It was too much at the time. She then gave me a green chiffon dress, round skirt and I adored the dress. It was so beautiful. I suppose that was the beginning of my elegant style. I still love to feel elegant to this day. Thanks to my early life of elegant lifestyles.

Meantime I was given a very good meal with all sorts of food. It was very nice but I was full of happiness and couldn't eat well as a result. I only regretted after I started feeling hungry when I was going home.

By the time of giving Asian businesses and properties to Black Ugandans, I was living with my brother, a soldier in the Uganda Army. At the time we lived in that famous Malire Barracks (Lubili) in a Kampala suburb. I'm a Barracks or Army girl! Today my brother is popular by his nickname.

I remember my brother getting forms for the "Mafuta Miingi" Asian properties as it was known then. Unfortunately for him he couldn't get involved because he was in the Army and no Army serving man was allowed to get the share of Asian properties. It was strictly Ugandan civilians and no more. No favours were made to the Army.

Ugandans were in the streets lining up for shops and businesses. I was young and I didn't know much about the business and the politics involved but I remember how General Idi Amin told us how the Black Ugandans were not treated well in their own country. He constantly told us about the Imperialists and Zionists, which many of the Ugandan community including me didn't understand well at the time. Songs were sung about the previous government of Dr. Apollo Milton Obote and the Asian domination of our economy. The messages in those songs still ring in my head, like the Sebaduka song named "Abayindi abanyunyunsi!" ("Indians have left!").

Other Eulogies

Other Eulogies will be made available as the series, Idi Amin: Hero or Villain? His Son Jaffar Amin and Other People Speak unfolds.

Several of my siblings were with Dad at his deathbed, including Lumumba Juruga, Aliga Alemi, Mwanga Abdul Nasser, Mao Ari'dhi, Kato Moga and Rajab Yan'gu.

Because of the seriousness of the allegations made against Dad, I strongly believe that it is critical for living witnesses to come forward. It is important for them to come forward with the names of all individuals they or other people know or knew who were allegedly murdered by Dad or ordered to be murdered by him during his rule. This will shed light onto deliberate attempts to "hide behind" generalities without providing specifics required in a proper Court of Law and not the "kangaroo courts" that have presided over Dad's "trial" to date. Saying that Dad murdered "countless" individuals and so-called hundreds and thousands of people without providing the specifics is nonsense and many people agree!

Throughout the series, Idi Amin: Hero or Villain? His Son Jaffar Amin and Other People Speak, there will be opportunities for other people to speak about the issue of Dad allegedly murdering or ordering the murder of so-called hundreds and thousands of people in Uganda during his rule. Their reflections will be recommended for the section of the series titled "Other People Speak". However, an Article by Vali Jamal an original Ugandan Asian expelled from Uganda by Dad in 1972 titled, "Rethinking Amin: An Asian's perspective", speaks to the false allegations relating to Dad murdering so-called hundreds and thousands of people in Uganda during his rule.

Vali Jamal wrote the Article in response to discussions surrounding the 30th Anniversary of Dad's overthrow on April 11, 1979 and the Article appeared in a Ugandan Newspaper, Sunday Monitor on-line on Sunday, April 26, 2009. Vali Jamal is also writing a major book on the 1972 Asian expulsion from Uganda in the words of the expellees. The book, which includes Vali Jamal's experience and the experiences of other Asians expelled from Uganda by Dad in 1972 and ones who chose to stay is recommended for the section of the series titled "Other People Speak", along with additional articles by him and others.

I very much appreciate the objective, fair, truthful, responsible and ethical manner in which Vali Jamal approaches his writings. He could have easily "slandered" Dad like others have done, as an individual who was "victimized" during his rule but he chooses not to. I laud Vali Jamal for choosing not to blindly accept "everything" said, written and depicted about Dad as the "gospel truth" but undertaking his own independent research and offering objective opinions instead. As a "victim", Vali Jamal has no reason to defend Dad at all but his efforts to speak and write only the truth are a testimony to his integrity!

The Fictionalized Novel and Hit Movie "The Last King of Scotland"

"The Last King of Scotland" is a fictionalized version of Dad's rule in Uganda from January 25, 1971 to April 11, 1979. A hit movie by the same name was seen in movie theatres around the world beginning in 2006. I watched a DVD of the movie, which stars African American Forest Whitaker as Dad and James McAvoy as his Scottish adviser Nicholas Garrigan. Forest Whitaker won a well-deserved Oscar for his role as Dad and I have great admiration for his impeccable acting skills. I also have great admiration for Mr. Whitaker's objectivity while undertaking some of the limited research "allowed" by the directors of the hit movie which in my opinion was "encouraged" to lend credibility to their presenting the fictional hit movie as fact.

I am pleased to know that Forest Whitaker actually took time to visit our homestead in the place in Arua, Uganda christened Tanganyika Village after my Grandpa and others were allotted plots there upon returning from tours of duty in the Second World War in Tanganyika. As members of the Kings African Rifles, my Grandpa and the other surviving soldiers were allotted these plots as a reward for fighting alongside British Soldiers during the Second World War.

During his visit to our homestead in Arua, Mr. Whitaker met with my uncle Baba Amule Kivumbi Amin and Awa (Aunt) Deiyah and even signed the Visitors' Book. Uncle Amule and Aunt Deiyah definitely offered a little insight into my father's "convoluted" story. However, that short visit alone could not provide the in-depth research necessary to understand my father's complicated legacy. Nonetheless, Mr. Whitaker was objective enough to observe and offer in an interview that Dad was no saint, but he was not the monster that has been portrayed in the West.

Here are statements made by Forest Whitaker who noted that he appreciated Dad's virulent abhorrence of European colonialism:

"Idi Amin was no saint, but he was not the monster that has been portrayed in the West."

"I'm not trying to defend Amin ... the Amin I found was not a good man, but not the monster as presented."

"When I first decided to act Amin, I had that perception of Amin as presented by the West."

"After I started researching his rule and life, what was being portrayed in the west was not his real image."

"Now, I have come to appreciate and understand why he made certain decisions at certain times. He did things like other big men who did things that helped their countries."

As Mr. Whitaker rightfully said, he was not trying to defend Dad but I appreciate the fact that he made his own observations and conclusions and stated an objective opinion. I appreciate that Mr. Whitaker's opinion was based on his own research and not on information that has been deliberately "twisted", "designed" and "crafted" to provide a lopsided picture of my father. Mr. Whitaker's attitude speaks volumes about him as a person of integrity and demonstrates the objectivity with which he approached his role as a Lead Actor who portrayed Dad in the hit movie "The Last King of Scotland".

As I have always said, our father had his faults. I do not see the period of his rule in Uganda with "rose-tinted glasses". However, we need to counter-balance history with all the truth! To avoid doing that is to rob the global community of lessons offered by my father's lifestory.

With that in mind, I am pleased to participate in this series designed to tell and uncover my father's story in its entirely, layer by layer. I have continued to listen to stories about my father as recounted by family members and associates of his who knew him outside the confines of our family home. These stories, along with ones told to me by my father himself and my own experience as Idi Amin's son, provide some of the background information for the series. As Forest Whitaker alludes to in the visitors' book he signed while visiting Arua, Uganda to speak to members of my family, the project has provided "True Insight....." into the life of a man simply known to me and my siblings as Dad.

A statement made by Mr. Whitaker to the effect that his research for the role in the film had changed his perception of Dad should provide the impetus to read, listen and watch movie accounts about my Dad with a "grain of salt". Before Mr. Whitaker undertook his own research about Dad in preparation for his role as Dad, he too perceived Dad as presented by the West. However, he quickly realized that what was being portrayed in the Western world was not Dad's real image. As I have stated in various media interviews, it is so easy to make my Dad a simple caricature but he was a complex man. Hollywood and the terribly slanted writings and films about my Dad missed his other side and I intend to capture that in many projects starting with this project.

As alluded to by Mr. Whitaker, Dad abhorred colonialism and bit the "massa" in the leg in defiance and every oppressed group knows "underdogs" don't do that without paying a heavy price. In Dad's case, the price was innocent lives and deliberate propaganda to tarnish his image through media sensationalism.

It is possible for the global community to become fully informed about my Dad so that any opinions formed by parties are based on substantiated facts and not fiction. Consequently, it is my hope that the series, Idi Amin: Hero or Villain? His Son Jaffar Amin and Other People Speak will provide a clearer picture than the deliberately misleading and sometimes ignorant "convolutions" that have characterized the telling of my father's story. It is in the interest of the global community to learn about my father's story in its entirety that is why I am participating in this series.

In "The Last King of Scotland", the fictional character Nicholas Garrigan is loosely based on the relationship between Dad and Major Bob Astles, Dad's British born right hand man. There are allegations that Dad ordered Bob Astles' death whenever he tired of his company but I remember Bob Astles well and I don't believe Dad ordered his death. They were chums. Dad and Bob Astles became friends in 1964 while Dad was serving in the Kings African Rifles. Mr. Astles was an ex-Royal Engineer in Kenya, who left the Kings African Rifles in 1952 and became an employee of the Public Works Department in Uganda. He also worked as a pilot. Actually, I think Astles was MI6, briefed to do whatever was necessary to protect British interests in Uganda.

However, in a way, I have a lot of respect for Major Astles because he stayed the course but I wish the writer of the fictional novel and filmmakers had stuck to the facts rather than the fiction that has been widely distributed as fact. They should have talked to me, more of my family members and Dad's associates about Dad in order to obtain a bit more information. Maybe then they could have made a documentary and feature film reflecting the facts rather than perpetuating the same old same old stereotypes about Dad. The film compounds many of the negative images that have been deliberately perpetuated in writings and films about my Dad.

At the time of compiling information for the "Introductory Edition" of the series Idi Amin: Hero or Villain? His Son Jaffar Amin and

Other People Speak "The Last King of Scotland" was the most recent attempt at telling Dad's story. In the next section, I offer some thoughts about the fictional novel and hit movie through a partial list of questions posed to me by Margaret Akulia that arose from the novel and depictions of Dad in the resulting hit movie. I will respond to more questions as the series unfolds.

In order to gain an in depth understanding of the views I express in my answers, I encourage readers to refer to information included in this "Introductory Edition" of the series as well as information that will be presented in subsequent parts of the series. Sections of subsequent parts of the series titled "Other People Speak", "No Holds Barred Q & A Forum" and "Questions for Discussion" will facilitate a comparison and reflection on the narrative accounts presented as fact, in the fictional novel and hit movie. The sections will also provide opportunities for others to voice opinions about my Dad including issues raised by the fictional novel and resulting hit movie. Initial thoughts expressed by various parties will be great additions to the background information for the section of the series titled "Other People Speak" along with other material relating to the debate about whether Dad was a hero or villain to the core.

A statement made by an individual who identified himself as Christopher from Houston, Texas, USA in an email directed to me provides a great place to begin. He wrote:

"Mr. Amin, I have no particular question", began Christopher before continuing, "I just wanted to tell you that I never realised LAST KING OF SCOTLAND was a work of fiction supposedly based on "true" events. It has become obvious it was marketed as to have people believe it was an entirely accurate (albeit slanted) depiction of a misunderstood man in a very unstable place in a very uneasy time. I find this to be unfortunate. I would've preferred to learn about the REAL Idi Amin."

I welcome the contribution of Giles Folden the author of "The Last King of Scotland" to the debate that will undoubtedly be an interesting exercise in "free speech". Interviews given by Mr. Giles which relate to the fictional novel and hit movie along with information presented in this series will provide ample information to begin the discourse and discussions, especially the attitudes and role of Westerners in Africa.

In this section, Jaffar Amin responds to a partial list of questions posed to him that arose from the fictional novel "The Last King of Scotland" and depictions of Idi Amin in the hit movie by the same name. In order to gain an in-depth understanding of the views expressed by Jaffar Amin in his answers, readers are encouraged to refer to information included in this "Introductory Edition" of the series as well as information that will be presented in subsequent parts of the series. Sections of subsequent parts of the series titled "Other People Speak", "No Holds Barred Q & A Forum" and "Questions for Discussion" will facilitate a comparison and reflection on the fictional narrative accounts presented as fact, in the novel and hit movie.

Here is what Jaffar Amin said in June 2008. Additional questions and responses will be made available as the series unfolds:

MA: Are there any "threads of truth" in your Dad's character in the fictional novel and hit movie "The Last King of Scotland?" If yes, what are they?

JA: Dad's intuitive response to unease like when Nicholas Garrigan, the fictional Scottish Doctor wanted to tell him something but hesitated until Dad's character looks up from his desks and asks, "Is there anything you want to tell me?" and the parenting aspect in his approach to managing the country.

MA: Can you share other incidences where your Dad demonstrated the same intuition depicted in "The Last King of Scotland?"

JA: On the fateful day in 1976 when someone attacked Dad's Jeep Renegade. He was about to enter the co-driver's seat, but then he instinctively told the late Musa, he would drive after they pass out of the new Police Recruits area. That change in sitting arrangement saved Dad's life but Marhum (Late) Musa died that day.

MA: Was your Dad driving instead of Musa when the assassination attempt was made on his life?

JA: Yes

MA: Do you have any other thoughts about what could also be perceived as a "strange" twist of fate?

JA: Dad had a distinctive 6th sense to danger.

MA: Was your Dad a Nationalist at heart?

JA: Yes

MA: What is your understanding of Nationalism as it pertains to Uganda and other African countries? What would this look like in a country like Uganda with all the "baggage" that has been "hauled" along since colonial times?

JA: Love of culture, love of our traditions and the way we dress. Knowing that true independence is the act of releasing the country from the harness and shackles of colonialism and slavery. Knowing fully well that given a chance, the indigenous peoples can take up responsibility and full ownership of our country.

MA: Can you give examples of "the parenting aspect in your Dad's approach to managing the country" and any personal experiences?

JA: Dad gave his famous telephone line 2241- 20241 to everyone and actually, he had the pioneer Cellular Telephone (20241) from Marubeni, which he drove around with in his Maserati. He was on tap to anyone who sought his help and was fond of turning up at village funeral vigils or parties uninvited. The man knew each and every nook and cranny of the country he ruled and traversed it without Escorts. He also had a Beetle VW Car Registration Number UUU 017, which he moved around with. For long distance trips, he had the Bell Helicopter with which he moved around to distant places like Kigezi and Karamoja.

MA: Can you share more incidences and examples relating to "the parenting aspect in your Dad's approach to managing the country?"

JA: He would request all the doctors to assemble at a specific time, ask them to list their names at the door, find out their needs and respond immediately. Some doctors missed out on brand new cars because they thought the ubiquitous list was "a death list". Some still lament for they had written fictitious names and could not then come up and claim their prize.

MA: Did your Dad have a Personal Physician or anyone closely resembling the fictional Doctor Garrigan?

JA: [Dr.] Brigadier-General Bogere was our family doctor.

MA: Can you share more information about [Dr.] Brigadier-General Bogere?

JA: He was a Male Nurse who somehow found favour with Dad and continued to serve the family the length and breadth of Uganda and Dad referred to him as Dr.

MA: Was your Dad a controlling man?

JA: Dad was military born and bred. His father before him also served in the Kings African Rifles. He believed in loyalty and order in the scheme of things, which is actually Islamic as well but we had our say whenever we were given audience by him.

MA: Can you expand on all the above, giving specific examples?

JA: Dad was a strict but loving father. He always reminded us of where he had come from through hardship and he did not like it when we played the spoilt brat "1st son mannerism". He was quick to clip such a tendency even in exile in Saudi Arabia where the luxury was even more pronounced.

MA: Can you share a few more examples and details relating to how your Dad's belief in loyalty and order manifested itself in his role as a President and Dad?

JA: He was out and about in the beige VW Registration Number UUU 017 when a motherly lady hailed the buggy and he stopped. She got in and asked to be dropped off at Kawempe Kiyindi zone. On their way, she started to bitterly lament the effects of the Economic War on the citizens and concluded that Idi Amin Dada was a bad man. Unbeknownst to her, she was lamenting directly to the very man incognito. "There is no sugar, no salt and the basic minimum since the Indians left", lamented the motherly lady. When they got to her homestead, her husband was at hand to welcome them in shock, knowing the famous UUU 017 buggy. He was surprised to see his wife come out of the famous buggy. She thanked the driver profusely and took her groceries out of the front boot of the buggy.

Just as the mystery man drove off, the husband asked his wife, "Do you know the man who just dropped you off?"

"No but he is a very good man".

"That was the President of the country Idi Amin Dada."

"Mama Nyaboo nfudde!" the woman slumped to the ground in shock lamenting of her impending death. She explained to her husband how she had lamented the state of affairs in the country not knowing she was talking to the very person she harangued. As a family they decided to vacate their house that very night and headed to their home village in Mubende.

Just as he got home, he called up Permanent Secretary Balinda to find out how he could help the lady acquire a business. Then a search party was sent to convey the good news only to find that the whole family had disappeared. Dad insisted they be found and when the good news was explained to the neighbours, the family was able to be located. To this day, the lady lives an affluent lifestyle but cannot for her life stop explaining the fear that went through her when she realized she had been insulting a whole

President to his face. Dad once lamented that with the Embargo, the Economic War was a harder war to win than say the success of the 1972 Mutukula invasion.

Today the famous Registration UUU 017 has turned up in the hands of the brightest prospects in the Ugandan Music Industry. Maurice Kiirya is the proud owner of the Registration UUU 017 and wherever he goes with the famous buggy the old folks ask him where he got the Field Marshall's car from. They all seem to know it from memory and in a sense it shows that they were aware of his movements, but like he said, "I do not need security, the citizens will protect me". He believed in Patriotism for what it was worth.

MA: Did your Dad have "mood swings" and "unpredictability" as depicted in "The Last King of Scotland?"

JA: Dad's so-called mood swings would occur in response to danger which was very much part of his military training. He survived over 14 assassination attempts planned by the best secret service organizations across the world. That is why they claim he had the best Intelligence Counter Espionage Service in Sub-Saharan Africa. The threats to Dad's life were real and what are labeled as "mood swings" were his intuitive responses to sense danger, protect himself and keep ever present "internal" and "external" enemies at bay and "on notice."

MA: Can you share more details and instances relating to how your Dad's so-called "mood swings" manifested themselves?

JA: I do not accept the notion of mood swings period. We tend to have a serious permanent frown on our faces. It is the mark of the man (Genetic Trait). It is funny how at the dinner table he would tell me in front of the rest, "Achana na ku chafuwa sura yako" ("Stop spoiling your face"). "You should smile sometimes." I would look up and wonder where the hell he thought I got the habit or the facial structure to frown, snarl - call it what you may. The French Director captured it very well during the making of the "French Documentary" in 1974 and got a kick out of just letting Dad stare into the camera lens without saying anything, probably knowing that Dad was indeed waiting for the next question that never came. One wonders who got the final laugh out of the film. Most of what Dad said in the 1974 film came to pass.

MA: Are you able to outline the dates, natures and details of the 14 assassination attempts on your Dad?

JA: The fact that he survived is all that matters. The protagonists are out there and they do lament "How!? How!?" We respond, Yakanye ha ha ha ha, it really does work ha ha ha.

MA: Can you explain what you mean?

JA: The war ended at Lukaya when most of the soldiers and Secret Service Personnel either said Congo na gawa or Sudan na gawa and high tailed it out of the country. Some even said let him fight this out with his favourite Air Force and Marines – a reminder of the dangers of favoring particular units in the military over others. Today the State Research boys are alive, the Uganda Army men are alive, FRONASA is in power, NASA agents sit licking their wounds from missed opportunity. Dad like most Kakwa and Nubians was fatalistic. He had a strong belief in Al-Qadar-Predestination. Some mystical beliefs based on the "Yakanye Order" that my Grandma was Priestess for still do persist. The "Order" believed that someone could not be killed by the gun once they had been cleansed with the "Yakanye Water". Dad even stood in front of his troops after the Nsambia grenade assassination attempt in 1976 and mystically announced "No bullet can harm me. You can bring a full magazine and empty it in my chest and nothing will harm me." Following an injury he sustained in the Kenyan Jungles during the Mau Mau war, Grandma Aate had told him that he would not be harmed by bullets.

MA: What are your thoughts about your Dad being labeled by some International Newspapers as a "mad man and cannibal" which the author of "The Last King of Scotland" also seemed to highlight and present as truth?

JA: The accusations and false labels sold papers. Dad is a highly marketable personality. He still is. This latest acclaim "The Last King of Scotland" is a testament. Even Moses, his favourite son is alive and well, yet even his own mother in exile believed the lies that he was sacrificed and eaten by his own father!

MA: Who is Moses' biological mother?

JA: Sarah Mutesi Kibedi of the Ba-Isemena Basoga Ethnic Group.

MA: Is Sarah Mutesi Kibedi the one also known as Mama Mariam?

JA: Yes the beautiful Golden Couple in the 1961 photograph.

MA: Are you able to expand on the above statement relating to Moses' mother Mama Mariam believing that her son was sacrificed and eaten by your Dad?

JA: For political reasons, Mama Mariam's younger brother Wanume Kibedi duped his elder sister who had put him through school right up to the elevated status of Foreign Minister no less using her husband's resources. He made her sign an Affidavit that her son had been sacrificed and eaten by his own father. To convince the family that the reports were false and the same relentless propaganda Dad was subjected to during his rule, Dad had to round up Menha Moses and his older sisters from the same womb. Then he sent a large convoy to Busembatiya where they found Moses' Funeral Vigil. You should have seen the elation on the grandparents' faces when their grandson who is a spitting image of Prince Menha arrived. Moses was then given that illustrious name Menha of the Babito Bunyoro Kitara Kingdom.

MA: Do you know why Wanume Kibedi "crafted" such a scheme?

JA: He was UPC. Most Basoga are UPC diehards and he had attained a certain level of masked contempt for a person who in his eyes got everything by sheer luck of the draw, leave alone that he was actually put through school and lodging by the very man whom he despised. You bring in the proverbial leopard cub. What do you expect? A Puss in boots? He now tries to show up his short history in power as "The Power behind the Throne".

MA: Is there anyone else who can substantiate the above?

JA: The whole of the Ba-Isemena clan and the Basoga tribe. We have no less than 7 mothers (wives and concubines of Dad) with children from that very Ethnic group in the Dada Family, including my mother:

1.   Mama Mariam
2.   Mama Kirunda
3.   Mama Tshombe
4.   Mama Kagera
5.   Mama Kenneth
6.   Mama Fatuma Nabirye
7.   Others.

MA: Did Moses' mother knowingly sign the Affidavit that her son had been sacrificed and eaten by your Dad and did she honestly believe that her son Moses had been sacrificed and eaten?

JA: No. She was coerced with the accusation that her son had been eaten. She only later confirmed the blatantly false allegations when it was too late. The damage had been done and Dad's antagonists and the hostile Media had "run with it".

MA: Who are Moses' older sisters and do they have any recollection of the above to share?

JA: Nawume, Jennifer, Aliya, Farida, Anite, Akujo and Atta.

MA: Where is Moses now?

JA: Paris, France.

The lie by Wanume Kibedi about his nephew, my brother Moses being sacrificed and eaten by Dad would persist and be used to give credence to lies that Dad was a cannibal. It would also contribute to the "slippery" path that led to Dad becoming one of the most reviled figures in history in the eyes of people who blindly went along with the biased accounts of a powerful media that began "lynching" Dad when he couldn't be "controlled".

MA: Is Moses willing to step forward to identify himself and provide a statement about the false allegations about your Dad?

JA: The majority of my siblings have learnt to cherish their own obscurity and wish to be left alone.

MA: Does Moses Support the project we have embarked on? Would he be open to the idea of giving interviews and making appearances on talk shows?

JA: I would encourage Moses, Mwanga and the rest of my siblings to give interviews to and make appearances on talk shows run by objective interviewers and sincerely answer their questions. Wherever Jaffar has got to with his Charger, the way should have opened for a chance at understanding by that time.

My siblings all think I am treading where angels fear to tread. Some give tacit support but the rest are quiet. I always respond that considering the benefit of doubt that I have received from the leading world media houses like CNN, BBC, AP, I must be on the right track. Sincerity and integrity are the hallmarks I wish to place in this project. Short of that, I feel I would have done my father's remark in July 2003 an injustice when he said "Tshombe mimi na sikiya we na sanya Wenzako, hi ni muzuri, Chunga Wenzako" ("Tshombe I hear you are gathering your siblings, this is good, look after your siblings").

That also means taking the lead like Ja'far Ibn Abi Talib my Charger has taken off - like some scene from the "Kingdom of God", Lance Held Up Front and the Al-Amin Foundation Banner flapping in the breeze. I am making a headlong dash into the fray - deep into hostile territory with one burning issue and belief that the truth shall hold clear from deceit, come what may.

MA: What are your thoughts about your Dad being accused of having erratic behavior, including paranoia, random outbursts, etc.?

JA: Dad was a calm and collected person. His speech was slow and measured. The "Western World" has always tried to show Africans as erratic and loud. It is a racist label and supposed to measure up to their Hollywood portrayal of People of Colour. We are supposed to come across as less intelligent and erratic when nothing could be further from the truth. Even Hitler a Caucasian was known to be a ranting and raving personality in his speeches, but Dad was calm and collected and unfairly compared to Hitler and labeled as erratic, paranoid and predisposed to random outbursts because they couldn't "control" him with their hidden agendas. Dad actually showed anger through silence, very much our Kakwa way. We have a saying, "Be very concerned when a Kakwa laughs. He just might be angry."

MA: The names "Campbell" and "Mackenzie" are fictitious names given to fictitious children the author of "The Last King of Scotland" decided to assign to Kay. What do Kay's real children think about the movie and story line about their mother?

JA: Dad was always inclined to give his children African names and the names of African leaders, along "Islamic" (Arabic) names than the presumed names from Scottish clans. My stepmother Kay had three male sons Lumumba, Adam, Mao and one daughter Kidde and we do not suffer from Epilepsy in our family.

MA: Would any of Kay's children be willing to step forward to provide a statement in opposition to the way they and their mother was portrayed in "The Last King of Scotland?"

JA: Again, the majority of my siblings have learnt to cherish their own obscurity and they wish to be left alone.

MA: Do Kay's biological children support the project we have embarked on? Would they be open to the idea of giving interviews and making appearances on talk shows?

JA: Again, the majority of my siblings have learnt to cherish their own obscurity and they wish to be left alone.

MA: What do they think about the depiction of their mother's character in the movie?

JA: The portrayal of their mother as someone of loose morals goes contrary to the image of who Mama Kay was in real life. She was the daughter of a clergyman Archdeacon Adroa and a highly educated person. My siblings and I take offense at the way my stepmother Kay was slandered and her memory defiled in "The Last King of Scotland".

MA: Are there any "threads of truth" to the story line relating to Kay sleeping with Doctor Nicholas Garrigan? If so, what are they?

JA: None whatsoever. The story line and related image lends well with the "Settler" mentality fantasy of "bedding" the wife of the most powerful man in the land. Incidentally the Settlers' worst fear as that of "the Slave Master" was for the "field slaves" to "bed" either their wives or daughters. It was an absolute nightmare to them.

MA: In the movie, your Dad is described as crazy. Do you have any thoughts about that?

JA: He did the unthinkable when he stopped listening to the Brits and "taunted" especially the Royal Family through his "wayward jests". He also did the unthinkable when he "tossed out" the "Caste System" practicing Indians, the Americans and the most sacred of them all the Israelites, despite Grandma always referring to them as God's chosen people!!!! Of course they would call him mad but to him he was giving back to Ugandans what belonged to Indigenous Ugandans.

MA: Did the British "create" Idi Amin as some cynics suggest?

JA: He served them directly for 17 years. When they supported the coup against Apollo Milton Obote, they thought he could be controlled but discovered the hard way that he couldn't. He had other ideas. He believed in his destiny. People are now waking up to the reality that his religion Islam has always had a Global Perspective and is now considered the enemy, following the demise of the Soviets. It has always been a clash of civilizations. Some still insist that he had no ideology. However, he used to say, "like our "Adibu Bull Elephant", we walk in the middle of the road. We neither pander to the East nor to the West but we take what is good from either." So he had an ideology, contrary to claims that he didn't have one. He was Non-Aligned by design!

MA: Was it fair to depict your Dad the way they did in "The Last King of Scotland" and other films, without providing any background and historical information relating to:

a) How he was "molded"?

JA: No. Colonialism made an indelible mark on all indigenous Africans including my father who served the Brits.

b) How and why he ended up becoming President of Uganda through a Military Coup?

JA: Because of a brilliant track record in the KAR he was their 1st choice when it came to taking power.

c) Why he acted the way he did?

JA: Since he had lived the era and actually rose from an Indentured Labourer to the Head of State, he felt that this "Rags to Riches Story" could be the benchmark with which he would effect change in the segregated atmosphere following "Independence" (Uhuru 1962). Coming to power in

1971 gave him this once and for all chance to effect genuine change, which he achieved in his lifetime.

d) The circumstances surrounding his regime, such as allegations of being sabotaged and maligned and others allegedly committing murders that were blamed on him, as part of the sabotage and propaganda to deliberately "soil" his reputation?

JA: The books written about Dad and films made about him are exaggerations at best. The questionable killings attributed to him, plus the so-called Liberators coming to a gathering and shocking the multitude with statements that they were working with the Archbishop to smuggle weapons into the country speak for themselves. Their admission that they killed key political personalities and figures in order to tarnish Dad's name has been recorded. It is in the public domain, despite the large number of illiterate populace who are not aware of the existence of these records.

MA: Is it possible for anyone to gather and present/share information relating to the Liberators "setting up" Archbishop Luwum and "bragging" about murdering prominent Ugandans in Uganda?

JA: Most Papers in the 1980s carried these pronouncements and can be located, yes.

MA: Do you have any thoughts and comments about the State Research Bureau instituted during your Dad's rule and their activities related to "State Security" including torture chambers, murders and "disappearances"?

JA: I prefer a Truth and Reconciliation Commission to tackle that issue. Most of the protagonists are alive and well on both sides of the equation. So, they can provide factual and truthful information.

MA: Do you have any thoughts about the following statements expressed in articles that are in the public domain?

"August 17, 2003 - End of bad chapter, say Uganda Indians
By Kennedy Lule"

"No curse - Nadduli Luweero LC-V Chairman, Haji Abdul Nadduli said that those condemning Amin, after his death, have committed an abominable act."

"Nadduli said some of the people allegedly killed by Amin's notorious State Research Bureau, died at the hands of Ugandans who used to destabilise the country - from Tanzania."

"He said people like Akena Adoko, the head of General Service Unit under Obote I, confessed to sabotaging Amin's regime, from Tanzania."

JA: This is the fountainhead of the Elite I keep stressing took up arms and fought Dad. However these were Secret Service Agents from the GSU (General Service Unit) and they fought covert wars using Franz Fanon's tactics and Maoist terror tactics that cynically state "Move amongst the people like fish in the water". It caused untold damage. Obote even stated it clearly seemingly in exoneration that the victims of Idi Amin's rule were the Elite and the Politicians yet other regimes target the masses. I tried to highlight this in my Eulogy to my late Father.

MA: Were there innocent victims? If yes, what are your thoughts about that? Did your Dad personally carry out some executions? Were people executed under your Dad's orders? Can you describe some of the characteristics possessed by members of the State Research Bureau?

JA: I prefer a Truth and Reconciliation Commission to tackle those issues. Most of the protagonists are alive and well on both sides of the equation. So, they can provide factual and truthful information.

MA: What are your thoughts about the description of your Dad as a contradictory, murderous, playful, brutal and sentimental character?

JA: Due to books like A State of Blood, images of the man did not add up to the accusations thrown at him. Therefore he always came across as very attractive and genuinely warm yet to the Intellectuals and the Elite he represented the underclass usurping their God-given privileges despite the fact that he had been in an Elite status for much longer than some of them had ever been. But he came from "the wrong" religion Islam and "the wrong" part of Uganda namely West Nile and Northern Uganda.

MA: What are your thoughts about the "convincing" nature of "The Last King of Scotland" (LKS) and the following remarks by someone who gave acclaim for "The Last King of Scotland?"

LKS: "The characterization of Amin is highly convincing, the childish grossness and wonky charm far too much like the real thing for comfort. He is a vividly present personality, weak when tempted, forceful when thwarted, massively ignorant but with a fatal gleam of intelligence...An imposing debut."

a) Why do you think someone would make the foregoing remarks?

JA: The Caucasian mindset is deeply rooted in the Darwin class and caste ladder aspect of viewing different cultures. They find it hard to accept or take in instances of brilliance from the Indigenous "Afrikan". We still have that mindset deep into the 21st century. Look at Obama. Alas the 60% over 65 year olds of the over 250 million Americans will vote the Republicans represented by John McCain back into power if ever Obama does the impossible and runs for President of the United States by beating Hillary Clinton to the podium. Dad predicted and even asked the Black Americans to run for Secretary of State in the 1974 French Documentary and this came to pass with the appointments of Colin Powell and Condoleezza Rice to the position. In that 1974 French Documentary and other assertions, Dad also asked the Black Americans to run for President and I believe this will also come to pass.

PS: The Above remarks were made by Jaffar Amin in June 2008 in the middle of the US Presidential Elections for the 44th President of the United States of America.

MA: Do you have any more thoughts about the fact that "The Last King of Scotland" is being presented and passed as truth and not fiction? What about the following remarks:

LKS: "Foden's Idi is a startlingly interesting creation. He has the measure of the despot's "wicked brilliance"".

JA: A State of Blood is still the benchmark used for judging my father's character. All writers subconsciously use extracts and opinions from that horrible book including Foden. The book is full of false information presented and blindly accepted as truth.

MA: Cynics have accused Henry Kyemba of deliberately "crafting" A State of Blood. Why do you think he wrote it? What did he stand to "benefit" if any?

JA: He was Obote's Permanent Secretary in the 60s before being promoted to Minister in Dad's regime between 1971 and 1977 when he allegedly ran off with between 1-36 million dollars. I was corrected by someone in the know that it was actually 36 million dollars of funds meant to buy medicine since the Brits insisted that all transactions should be done in cash over the barrel. Kyemba's angle seems to be a parochial contempt for Nilotics by my "maternal uncles" the Bantu. The very same sentiments come out very clearly in a book by Kirunda Kivejinja, who despised the notion that an illiterate and "dark skinned" Northerner could seemingly hold office for almost nine years. It was a miracle. A State of Blood is a book that is written by Henry Kyemba, a man who served as Principal Private Secretary to Milton Obote and as a Minister in Dad's government.

MA: What are your thoughts about what fictional works such as "The Last King of Scotland" do to efforts by Ugandans to uncover the truth about what happened in Uganda during your Dad's rule and heal from the political instability and additional killings that have occurred since your Dad was overthrown?

JA: They undermine these efforts.

MA: Are the eyewitness statements the author gives credence to in his Acknowledgements authentic and credible? For example Mohamed Amin (deceased), Major Iain Grahame, Bishop Festo Kivengere (deceased), Henry Kyemba, Ali Mazrui, Yoweri Museveni?

JA: Let the intellectuals like Al-Amin Mazrui and other more credible people fight for a Truth and Reconciliation Commission. The present leaders were political foe and the likes of Henry Kyemba were typical Parochial Stooges who were used for other people's gains. Anyone who was and is a foe of Dad's should not be intimately involved in uncovering the truth about Dad or presenting evidence against Dad. It defeats the purpose of a proper Truth and Reconciliation Commission and makes such an effort a laughable "kangaroo court".

MA: Can you elaborate on all of the above?

JA: If you made a roll call, you will find that with the exception of a few, none of the so-called credible witnesses have ever gained from their vociferous praise singing or mud slinging. Apart from Ali Mazrui who still holds high ground for his angle of approach, most of the other so-called credible witnesses could only pass the lousy standards of the laughable "kangaroo court" that characterized so-called Truth and Reconciliation Commissions conducted by Dad's foe and other people with hidden agendas. Mazrui did not expend 80% of his time like the rest trying to show or explain how much they loathed Idi Amin Dada but offered objective and honest opinions about Dad.

MA: Do you have any thoughts about the credibility of information offered to the author of "The Last King of Scotland" by deceased sources such as Mohamed Amin and Bishop Festo Kivengere? What about information offered by Iain Grahame?

JA: Save for Iain Grahame who was with Dad as a Superior in the Armed Corps for 17 years and was simply writing his own Memoirs, the rest were blowing their own trumpets or dancing to the tune of the media sensationalism designed to destroy Dad. Grahame's Memoirs dovetailed in perfectly with the lifestory of the most amazing and most talked about Indigenous African - Dad. People like Kivengere were tinged by the sectarian bug that started way back during the crusades in the 1200s.

MA: What was it like growing up in a household with so many mothers? Did they fight like "cats" and "dogs?" What were some of these fights about?

JA: Muslims accept controlled polygamy – a maximum of 4 wives. Africans do not practice controlled polygamy. Out of respect for my family's privacy, I would like to say that our numbers speak for themselves. Sibling Rivalry comes naturally. However, we have learnt to live together. Dad was the glue that kept us together.

MA: What was it like growing up with siblings from various mothers? Can you share some stories?

JA: I repeat, out of respect for my family's privacy I would like to say that our numbers speak for themselves. Sibling Rivalry comes naturally. However, we have learnt to live together. Dad was the glue that kept us together.

MA: What are your thoughts and personal beliefs about polygamy? Does your wife Zaitun have reasons to worry that you might follow in your father's footsteps?

JA: The Quran states marry two, three or four as long as you can love and provide for all, but, but if you are not able, then marry one. Most read only half of the iya, paragraph and forget the caution at the end. I am comfortable with one and it is what I can manage. Interestingly King Faisal had only one wife. He was following the Holy book to the letter.

MA: Do you have any thoughts about allegations that your Dad murdered actual and perceived opponents and anyone with a dissenting voice at will during his rule in Uganda?

JA: Most of these allegations should be brought before the proposed Truth and Reconciliation Commission. However and strangely so, even after Dad was ousted from power, no single person has ever stepped up to a court of law or Police Station in Uganda to lay personal charges or witness against Dad. No one has brought charges before an international court even posthumously, which is very strange for a man alleged to have killed hundreds of thousands of people.

MA: Why do you think no single person has ever stepped up to a court of law or Police Station in Uganda to lay personal charges or witness against your Dad and no one has brought charges before an international court even posthumously, despite the fact that your Dad is alleged to have killed hundreds of thousands of people?

JA: It beats my understanding. You half expect to be lynched by the populace for daring to step back on Ugandan soil, yet, when I first stepped back, and a person got to know who I was, you cannot believe the warmth of the reception even from the most unexpected of quarters. I will keep asking that question, for unlike the French Law which brands one guilty until proven innocent, our law brands one innocent until you are proven guilty. My father's judgment has been done wholly by a hostile and many times improperly informed "world media" and vested interests amongst the world powers who did not want to see such Indigenous Militancy and Nationalism in full flow. Here is someone at the Honourary Rank of Affende in 1959, who dared to march into the real Officers' Mess at 1st Battalion Jinja from the Sergeants' Mess having got tired of moving with a rank that did not hold water. He moved up to the "Whites Only" Officers' Mess and ordered a drink. When the Bartender told him off and rudely asked him to go to the Sergeants' Mess, he grabbed the White Bartender and pulled him straight over the counter. He then let rip with a resounding right on the Englishman's chin, to the hushed silence of the whole room full of shocked White officers.

The segregative rule was changed and Dad was even invited to join the exclusive Jinja Rugby Club. So there you have it - "Proactive Action" from Africa's most maligned Activist. He always said, "Action speaks louder than words".

Dad's stature soared the next year 1960-1961 when he beat the Cattle Rustlers, even gaining the respect of the Karamojong. This action prompted Sir Crawford to promote Dad to the unheard of rank of Lieutenant in 1961 - one of the very 1st African to attain the rank and his residence was shifted from Nalufenya in Jinja to Acacia Avenue, Kololo in Kampala.

MA: Do you have any recollections of the day an attempt was made on your Dad's life? If so, what are those recollections?

JA: I remember Dad talking of how the unclipped shrapnel grenade landed with a thump on his back before it lobbed to the side exploding and fatally injuring Musa his Half-Caste driver. According to Dad, apparently the one who hurled the deadly weapon had not waited long enough, having unhinged the lever before they lobbed the grenade. Dad survived that incident. He drove the Jeep all the way from Mukwano road, Nsambia to Mulago, wobbling all the way to safety.

MA: Was your Dad equipped to be President of Uganda?

JA: Dad was very familiar with the old style Colonial Administration System that had successfully carried the day for over 60 years for the Brits. All that Obote Dad's predecessor did was tinker with a smooth system during his tenure. Dad simply turned the whole system into a boot camp, with martial law. Remember he had served as a loyal soldier from 1946 to 1962 then in High Command from 1962 to 1971. He was familiar with administration - military no less.

MA: Can you elaborate on the above and give specific examples?

JA: Chain of Command worked well for the Colonial Brits. Grassroots village chief and sub-county chief reported to the District Councilors who reported to the District Commissioner, who reported to the Governor. Dad was a product of that form of Administration and he was no stranger to it for it had worked for the Brits between 1900 and 1962 - Part 1 Order no less.

Dad simply militarized these posts. Today we have similar positions in Uganda - LCI, LCII, LCIII, Municipal, Councilors, LCV, and Resident Commissioners. The only lapse was suspending the Judiciary and the Legislators, which left him with a soft under belly by all and sundry who frown on the notion of a Military Tribunal and simply an Executive Military Council.

MA: Do you have any thoughts about your Dad asking Asians to leave Uganda within 90 days in 1972?

JA: Dad was adamant that he compensated the Asians to the tune of 1 Billion US dollars. He had put his money where his mouth was and when we were living in Saudi Arabia, he was not amused when Obote and Museveni returned the Expropriated Property which he felt rightfully belonged to Indigenous Africans and Asians had been compensated for.

MA: Do you have any thoughts about allegations that Asians who returned to Uganda decades after their expulsion by your Dad have benefited twice for their confiscated properties, leading to loss of billions of shillings in taxpayer money as outlined in an article published on Uganda's Sunday Monitor on Sunday, February 24, 2008?

JA: It exonerates my plea for the country to talk about this grave injustice when Phoebe of the Sunday Monitor gave me an exclusive whole page Interview, for they were compensated, one billion, not one million but 1,000,000,000 $ US dollars. The 1 million was only to the Indian Sub Continent, not forgetting that America, Canada, Britain, Australia, Bangladesh, Pakistan, etceteras were also compensated as per the concerns of the United Nations who worked tirelessly to ensure that the victims were compensated. Why do you think Dad was not questioned about this issue as Chairman of the OAU when he addressed the United Nations Assembly in 1975? He was clean.

It just hurt that this man seemed to second-guess all the moves thrown at him, by doing the impossible - paying a whole one billion dollars! This today would be as much as 4-7 billion dollars in worth to Uganda if the present Government of Uganda had the guts to demand back what was paid to Asians twice, some of who continue to cry "crocodile tears". It was the only issue Dad used to persistently take issue of - short of crying his innocence, which he felt was and ought to be left to Allah to be the Judge.

I still remember that time when Dad would head furiously for the Communication Services Centre in Jeddah and call the Bahrain BBC Bureau, vehemently explaining the issue of the Expropriated Property. Then he would gather us around to listen to the Focus On Africa news at 19:00 East African Time, until it became a standing joke amongst the inner circle of siblings and Ali Nyabira Kirunda code-named him Bahrain.

Moreover, the above issue was first discussed when Phoebe of the Sunday Monitor first gave me a Q & A Full Transcript Interview. It pleases me to see that someone was listening and is delving into the murky world of subterfuge, which persists amongst the intelligentsia and many vengeful British Asians who used to live in Uganda. Out of the 50,000 who were expelled, only 2,000 have ever returned to Uganda, following the invitations to return in the 1980s by Yoweri Museveni. Why? They were paid..........

MA: Do you have any thoughts about the hostage crisis of Flight 139 – the hijacking of the plane by Palestinian Commandos that your Dad allegedly "allowed" to land at Entebbe Airport? In addition to this actual event that happened, what other actual events were depicted in "The Last King of Scotland?"

JA: Dad felt this was his chance to gain the spotlight on the world stage as a Peacemaker. Alas the world saw him as someone perilously pandering to the whims of Terrorists. He lost 27 soldiers including the seven hostage takers. Why did the Israelites not go after him if he was responsible for the very sad death of Dora Bloch, the unwitting victim of that sad event? Dad was not responsible for Dora Bloch's death. Someone else committed the unconscionable and reprehensible murder.

MA: Who was responsible for "painting" your Dad as someone perilously pandering to the whims of Terrorists and what was the reason/motivation behind the "painting"?

JA: The 1974 French Documentary "General Idi Amin Dada: A Self Portrait" brought out a lot of issues. The Documentary was meant to explain Dad's views to the world. What comes across very strongly is his strong Anti-Zionist Stance. Thus the dye had been cast prophetically with hostages taking over an Airline he had jokingly suggested on silver screen two years earlier.

MA: Are there any "threads of truth" in any of the story lines in the hit movie "The Last King of Scotland?" If yes, what are they? Did you witness any events depicted in "The Last King of Scotland" if any?" What if any, is completely "off the wall" about some of the story lines?

JA: Pure Hollywood. Completely off the wall, hook, line and sinker - Entertainment per excellence.

MA: Do you have any thoughts about the story line relating to the fictional practice done in your Dad's village that involves hanging a man by his skin to purge him of evil? According to the story line, your Dad told Nicolas that "every time the man screams, a bit of evil is released?" What do you think about such a bizarre story line?

JA: Pure Hollywood. Completely off the wall, hook, line and sinker - Entertainment per excellence. This story line is not even in the fictitious novel. I guess anything goes with Dad.

MA: Do you have any thoughts about your Dad's relationship with Israel?

JA: I still remember how Grandma Aisha Aate adored the people of Israel. She called them God's chosen people. I also have fond thoughts about our Jewish twin brothers born in 1971 and still strongly believe that Dad secretly lamented the split between himself and the Israelis. I still often wonder where my Jewish twin brothers are and imagine them being very successful soldiers because of the fact that their mother is related to Moshe Dayan. Having an exemplary soldier like Dad for a father would definitely contribute to their success as soldiers.

MA: Would you and your siblings be open to the idea of trying to locate and meet your Jewish twin brothers by an Israeli mother? Did your Dad ever meet or communicate with them? Do you know their names? Do you know their mother's name?

JA: Of course! We would definitely be open to the idea of meeting our Israeli brothers. Mind you they used to write letters every birthday from 1972 (they were born in 1971) - pictures in time with cherub twins smiling to the camera, which their mother dutifully sent to their father Idi Amin. By say 1974 they would have started to scribble a note or two just as we were doing the same at Kabale Preparatory School in Kigezi Province. The last word about them came from an Israeli Expatriate in 2008 who claimed that one twin joined his mother's profession as a Major in the Israeli Secret Service Mossad while his twin is also a Major in the Israeli Air Force. It would be touching to invite them to Mount Liru, the true place where Moshe disappeared.

MA: What was your grandmother's point of reference in adoring the people of Israel and referring to them as God's chosen people?

JA: Most Indigenous Africans have never woken up from Soyinka's Colonial Prayer. Whatever is in the Holy Bible is strictly adhered to, for example the Bible book of Joshua. Grandma was also a Christian before she converted to Islam like Grandpa, but some ideas never leave your mindset.

MA: Do you have any thoughts about allegations that your Dad was responsible for between 300,000 – 500,000 deaths in Uganda?

JA: Most of these allegations should be brought before a Truth and Reconciliation Commission. However and strangely so, even after Dad was ousted from power, no single person has ever stepped up to a court of law or Police Station in Uganda to lay personal charges or witness against him. No one has brought charges before an international court even posthumously, which is very strange for a man alleged to have killed hundreds of thousands of people.

MA: Who was responsible for the killings in Uganda during your Dad's rule?

JA: Most of these allegations should be brought before a Truth and Reconciliation Commission. However and again strangely so, even after Dad was ousted from power, no single person has ever stepped up to a court of law or Police Station in Uganda to lay personal charges or witness against him. No one has brought charges before an international court even posthumously, which is very strange for a man alleged to have killed hundreds of thousands of people.

MA: Is it important for Ugandans to know the exact number and nature of killings that took place in Uganda under your Dad's regime and who actually committed these killings? Why?

JA: Absolutely yes, in order to help with the healing process. It is hard for people to go around not knowing. Psychologically it keeps generations in limbo. Look at the positive effects A Truth and Reconciliation Commission is doing in South Africa. We have Desmond Tutu to thank for that.

MA: Did your Dad have a Personal Physician or anyone closely resembling the fictional Doctor Garrigan, a medical team or nurses in attendance?

JA: [Dr.] Brigadier Bogere and Russian and Cuban Specialists.

MA: Do you have any more thoughts about the character Doctor Garrigan who was created by the author of "The Last King of Scotland?" Do you have any idea why he picked a doctor as that particular character?

JA: Doctors often have the privileged position of knowing the inner and physical you! Quite often, compromising a person is not written into their "Oath". It is the most plausible way to understand one of the most feared persons to have ever traversed this earth through the eyes of his Personal Physician, but it is also a good way of explaining away someone's guilt, for example Bob Astle's MI6 espionage past. He had promised to write a Memoir. I still wait for that to come out.

MA: What are your thoughts about the following sentences in the novel? Are there threads of truth in the sentences? Do you recall scenes resembling the ones described in the sentences?

LKS: Paragraph 2, Page 3, sentence 2:

" …On his bullying visits to the gum-booted old chiefs out there, he would drive a red Maserati manically down the dirt tracks. Walking in the evenings, under the telegraph poles where the kestrels perched…"

JA: Ours was a Metallic Champagne SM Maserati coupe. In the movie they show a maroon Citroen saloon DS model. Dad was always jovial and well liked by the under class who saw him like the way Malcolm X was viewed on his forays into Harlem's underworld. Here was a former Indentured Labourer (Kasanvu) who had become a King.

MA: What do you think about the following phrase?

LKS: Paragraph 4, Second last sentence, Page 3:

" …That was Idi's way, you see. Punish or reward. You couldn't say no."

JA: Dad had a strong sense of loyalty, but not this view that he relished punishment per se. There are plenty of incidents that speak to his camaraderie with his soldiers, like enjoying a glass of tipple or two with the lads.

MA: How would your Dad deal with people he considered disloyal?

JA: Dismissals, transfers and humiliating demotions, like that of Brigadier Moses Ali of the Bari tribe of Juba in Southern Sudan. Brigadier Ali was demoted by Dad and he became one of Dad's staunchest enemies. Dad's act of demoting Brigadier Ali made him one of Dad's worst enemies between 1974 and 2003. However, it is ironic that Brigadier Ali made an honourary Eulogy to his fallen boss on August 16, 2003 in the Uganda Parliament. It seemed they secretly made up.

MA: Do you recall any prisoners in white cotton uniforms mowing the grass at State House as referred to on page 4 Paragraph 2?

JA: Most of the workers at State House were from Nyanza Province in Kenya and Tutsis who had been there since the 50s and not prisoners.

MA: Were the workers from Nyanza Province also Naturalized Ugandans like the Tutsis?

JA: They have been here since 1926. Dad found the ones at State House there when he became President of Uganda. George Kabera the head of his Strike Force Presidential Guards who was trained by the KGB was the son of his Tutsi Cook.

MA: Do you have recollections about your Dad hosting dignitaries? Can you share some of these recollections?

JA: I have recollections of many dignitaries hosted by Dad. I will always remember the time the Nation of Islam dignitaries came to Uganda on Dad's invitation during the 1975 OAU Summit. Mobutu, with all his Afro-Jazz Bands and the likes of Mpongo Love, Orchestra Veve and Orchestra Lipua Lipua, Pure Raz Mataz impressed me a great deal! This is because like most Ugandans, I loved Congolese Music as a child and still believe that it is one of the best demonstrations of African talent. Dad couldn't get enough of it.

MA: Did your Dad suffer from gastric difficulty? What are your thoughts about that depiction in the film?

JA: Gout, our Nubian obsession with Roasted Beef….. Southern Fried Chicken, etc.

MA: Do you have any more thoughts about the way your Dad was depicted in the movie?

JA: I appreciated the fact that they brought out the softer side of my Dad, which gave me a chance to explain it further, along the same line. I feel it is what Foden wanted to do in the first place - that ironic and inexplicable fascination with the downright dangerous amongst Caucasians.

MA: Did the character Jonah Wasswa exist - i.e. the Minister of Health or anyone closely resembling him/his character?

JA: This seems to be a salute to Henry Kyemba the author of A State of Blood, but only that he ran away with between 1-36 million dollars meant for medicine for Ugandans.

MA: Are there records and people to substantiate the above?

JA: George Kabera was in the room and actually handed over the briefcase with the 1-36 million dollars to Henry. According to eye witness accounts, George Kabera and Henry Kyemba once met at a funeral in the

1990s and "you should have seen the look on Henry's face when he set eyes on Idi Amin's Former Head of the Presidential Guard", offered a source. "He looked like a drowning rat".

MA: What is Henry Kyemba doing now and how are his living circumstances?

JA: Like our family the Al-Amin family, he lives in shear obscurity.

MA: Was Wasswa the Minister of Health a purely fictional character then?

JA: Yes, although there was someone Henry Kyemba replaced when he was promoted from Permanent Secretary before he defected from Dad's cabinet.

MA: Do you have any thoughts about the following titles outlined in the novel in relation to your Dad? How did your Dad feel about these titles? Who conferred them on him? What do VC, DSO, MC stand for? When were these titles conferred and what were the surrounding circumstances?

LKS: Page 10, Paragraph 2:

His Excellency President for Life, Field Marshall, Al Hadj, Doctor Idi Amin Dada, VC, DSO, MC, Lord of All the Beasts of the Earth and Fishes of the Sea and Conqueror of the British Empire (CBE) in Africa in General and Uganda in Particular.

JA: He relished the CBE in jest to Q.E.II. Field Marshall was in homage to Montgomery. The King of Beasts is just another of those "Settler" mentality Pub jokes thrown around by Journalists who knew they could become fact in print for anything goes with "defenseless" Idi Amin. He rarely broke the silent barrier until I came along after his demise to try and correct some of the misconceptions and outright lies.

MA: Do you have additional thoughts about the following titles:

a) CBE b) Field Marshall (Please elaborate on "Homage to Montgomery") c) His Excellency President for Life (What are your own thoughts about this?) d) Al Hadj e) Doctor Idi Amin?

JA: Dad got and deserved the Distinguished Service Order (DSO) through his over 17 years in the Kings African Rifles from 1946 to 1962. After Uganda attained "Independence" from Great Britain in 1962, Dad received rapid promotions from Major in 1963 to Major General in 1968. The only self-appointments under the so-called Military Council that was instituted during Dad's regime from 1971 to 1979 were promotion to Full General in February 1971 and Field Marshall in 1975.

Dad was one of the first Indigenous Africans to receive the True not Honourary Officer Rank of Lieutenant in 1959-1960 and he was a

Captain Pre-"Independence". Moreover, as the highest ranked Indigenous African and Chief of Staff at the time Uganda attained "Independence" from Great Britain, Dad received the new flag, which was to be hoisted on Uhuru Day (Independence Day). He also received back the Union Jack, which was lowered on October 9, 1962.

Major Iain Grahame's book on Dad provides a rare and true picture of what Dad received as per British Standards. Major Iain Grahame was one of Dad's superiors during the time he served under the British Colonial Administration and he genuinely admired Dad.

MA: What are your thoughts about the scene in the novel relating to your Dad serving a platter of dudu (bee larvae, large green bush crickets, cicadas and flying ants, fried with a little oil and salt (Page 12, Last paragraph)) and Wasswa saying they are a local delicacy?

JA: Major Grahame relished our good old White ants, Termites and Nsenene (edible grasshoppers). This issue of roaches is typical of "Settler" mentality Pub Prankster in Foden who interpolates these dishes then adds a dose of the uneatable for effect.

MA: Did your Dad ever joke about or mention eating human meat?

JA: No. To my mind, "the White Man's" worst fear about "dark" "Afrika" is that we eat people. What brings them here if not to rob us in broad daylight? Dad would always say "PARAPAGANDA" ha ha ha ha ha! Propaganda.

MA: What do you think about your Dad being portrayed as a little child in many scenes?

JA: Being jovial is African. Caucasians take it up as being childish. The same sentiment is leveled at Americans by people from the old country (Europe). They are also considered naïve yet they have been given the responsibility to rule the world.

MA: What are your thoughts about the morals of presenting the fictional novel "The Last King of Scotland" as if it was fact and convincingly so? For example, the author presents it as an actual Journal by the fictional Nicolas Garrigan who arrived in Uganda on January 24, 1971. Garrigan supposedly arrived one day before your Dad took over power from Apollo Milton Obote but relies on material from Newspapers and Broadcasts around the world to bring the story to life while convincingly presenting it as fact and an "actual" Journal.

JA: "They" own the Media. "They" can very well do what they want.

MA: Can you describe the scene as you remember it the day your Dad took over power from Apollo Milton Obote?

JA: Jubilation, hero worship, ecstatic merry making amongst the Baganda and the people of West Nile. They could not believe this upstart winning, just like France beating Brazil at the Paris World Cup. After that win, we came out in droves around Nsambia screaming our heads off in the 1990s. The 1971 take over by my Dad occurred when I was five years old. I was with Joyce and Sergeant John Katabarwa my Tutsi Guardian at King George Military Barracks in Jinja. This Barracks was later renamed Al-Qadhafi Garrison by my Dad at the height of his support for the Arab People.

MA: Is the following an accurate account of what was said on Radio Uganda the day your Dad took over power from Apollo Milton Obote?

LKS: Page 33:

"The Uganda Armed Forces have this day decided to take over power from Obote and hand it to our fellow soldier Major-General Idi Amin Dada…"

JA: The accurate account is included in the section of the series relating to Dad's first year as President of Uganda, as well as information that will be included in the section titled "Other People Speak".

MA: What are your thoughts about statements made on Page 90 to the effect:

LKS: "…When I went back to Kampala, I saw all those Anyanya and Kakwa thugs Amin has brought down from the north to put into the police and the army…Those people are not like us. Even their bodies are different. They are bonty and look angry all the time. No wonder they cut so many people…".

JA: Dad used his 20,000 strong tribes mates from Sudan who could not go back to Sudan following his agreement with Jaffar Al Numeri in 1972. He absorbed them into the Uganda Army instead.

MA: Can you share more information and details about the agreement between your Dad and Jaffar Al Numeri?

JA: By 1972 Al-Qadhafi brokered a Peace Deal with Al-Numeri. Dad met with the Sudanese leader over some bridge in Southern Sudan. The Anyanya chose to stay. So Dad absorbed most of them into the Uganda Army and actually sent most of them for extensive military courses abroad. This boosted his army to a resounding 45,000 strong by 1979.

MA: Do you have any thoughts about the statement "They are bonty and look angry all the time. No wonder they cut so many people. Even they have brought some here to the barracks"?

JA: Parochial insults and abuse from my erstwhile maternal uncles the Bantu. My mother is a Musoga.

MA: What are your thoughts about statements made by the fictitious Idi Amin on Page 96 to the effect:

LKS: "...Now, let me say this. I have been receiving some complaints about the state of affairs in Uganda. Wananchi have been complaining about searches and seizures. Well, let me tell you, anything that is done in my name, it is the right thing..."

JA: Foden here tries to show a sense of Buffoonery "they" keep throwing around about Dad.

MA: Are there any threads of truth in the above statements?

JA: My words against theirs - take it or leave it. Soon after "The Last King of Scotland" came out, "they" "invited" me to Media Interviews and kept saying, "Jaffar Amin has broken the silence...". I said in the CNN and CTV Interview that I would spend the rest of my life trying to explain Dad's Legacy.

MA: Was your Dad charismatic? Please explain and give examples.

JA: Africans are mystical and we tend to lean towards charisma rather than proven Managerial Skills.

MA: What are your thoughts about statements made on Page 106 to the effect:

LKS: "A lot of noise at the barracks one night, shooting and then a loud explosion. I could see the flames below. The next morning we heard from Waziri that a detachment from the north had killed all the Langi and Acholi soldiers....I saw the lorries taking the bodies myself, even an arm sticking out from under the tail-gate...".

JA: Jinja Barracks was attacked in July 1971. I was at the Boarding School with Sergeant John Katabarwa, a Tutsi, when it happened. It was terrible. The same thing happened when we were transferred to Simba Barracks with Colonel Fadhul and my father's uncle, Major Sosteni, Chief MTO of the Uganda Army, when the 1972 invasion took place.

MA: Do you have any more thoughts about the above? Who were John Katabarwa, Colonel Fadhul and Major Sosteni?

JA: Sergeant John Katabarwa and Mama Joyce were my Foster Parents for he did his master's bidding of looking after his illegitimate children who could not step into the Acacia Avenue and Command Post residence during the Pre 1971 years. So we were left in the hands of his key Lieutenants. We were brought from Mbarara to join Mama Kay at Nakasero Lodge in 1973 when Dad came back from a tour of the Soviet Union.

Brigadier General Ali Fadhul was the Commanding Officer of the Barracks in Mbarara and he was jailed in 1986. Uncle Sosteni was actually the one who drove the Kabaka all the way from Bulange right up to the Rwanda Border in 1966 during the "Mengo Crisis".

MA: What are your thoughts about the circumstances surrounding the two Americans' deaths? How did they meet their deaths? In the novel it is said, "The Americans argued with a fictional Major Mabuse"? How close is that statement to the truth? Did "Major Mabuse" kill the Americans? If not, what is the truth? Were they Journalists?

JA: This tragic loss should be investigated in a Truth and Reconciliation Commission.

MA: What are your thoughts about statements made on Page 113 to the effect:

LKS: "...You mean you haven't heard?..." "The Obote guerrillas came over today. They drove in with lorries. About a thousand. They attacked the barracks with a mortar but it landed here."

JA: Some three thousand invaders came in from Tanzania. Dad said they were actually singing with a thought that the populace would turn against the 2nd Republic. According to Dad, they were crushed.

MA: What are your thoughts about statements made on Page 116 to the effect:

LKS: "...Meanwhile, strange items of news were reaching us about Amin. The World Service reported, in its usual po-faced way, that he had sent a message to the Queen, with copies to the UN Secretary-General Doctor Kurt Waldheim, Soviet Premier Brezhnev and Mao Tse-Tung: 'Unless the Scots achieve their independence peacefully,' it read, 'they will take up arms and fight the English until they regain their freedom. Many of the Scottish people already consider me last King of the Scots. I am the first man to ask the British government to end their oppression of Scotland. If the Scots want me to be their King, I will."

JA: He was simply playing pranks especially on the touchy issue of the secession of Scotland and Northern Ireland from England, most of it Bob's private jokes.

MA: Was Bob Scottish?

JA: An Englishman I think.

MA: Is there truth to the above statements? Can you share some examples and details?

JA: There is a very detailed write up written by renowned Researcher Fred Guweddeko on tap online in the Public Arena if you search.

MA: What are your thoughts about statements made on Page 117 to the effect:

LKS: "… There was worse in store for me, and much worse for the Asians. One day in town, I was shocked to see a group of them surrounded by soldiers. They were scratching their faces with broken bottles. Amin had said in a speech that the idea of the Economic War had come to him in a dream…"

MA: Is there truth to the above statements? Can you share some examples and details?

JA: According to Dad, the Asians left peacefully. The exercise was supervised by the UN, but they were indeed restricted from taking out any money apart from a limited amount.

MA: What were the circumstances surrounding the expulsion of the Israelis from Uganda? On Page 119, there is a statement to the effect, "Amin says all Israeli personnel to leave within three days." Is there truth to the above statements? Can you share some examples and details?

JA: Dad's new relationship with the Arabs.

MA: Did your Dad call himself "The Last King of Scotland" on radio as suggested on page 120?

JA: No, but he offered to help the Scottish Separatists achieve Independence from England.

MA: Can you elaborate on the above?

JA: To date, Scots have and still feel bitter being under English hegemony. Some equivalent of the IRA turned up in Uganda seeking assistance to fight the English.

MA: When was this?

JA: There is an article which relays Dad's thoughts on the issue that came out in 1974 and was reissued by our renowned Researcher Fred Guweddeko in the local papers after my Dad's demise in 2003.

MA: How did your Dad treat his soldiers and what are your thoughts about a statement on page 121 to the effect, "He barked in Swahili at one of the soldiers. The man went over to the car. Idi – Amin, I should say – followed him slowly, and I followed Amin. Leaning into the boot, the soldier emerged with a bottle of Napoleon and a stack of steel tumblers. We watched as the man balanced two of the tumblers on the dented bonnet and filled them to the top with brandy. I noticed his hand was trembling as he poured – he was terrified?"

JA: Dad was very much a good Field Officer and he resonated strength and encouragement. He came across like a Father figure and not the menacing Commander in Chief portrayed in "The Last King of Scotland". He regarded the soldiers as his comrades.

MA: Were soldiers terrified of your Dad?

JA: Nooo!

MA: Where might have the author of the novel come up with all the scenes in both the novel and the feature film? Were there scenes that imitated some truth? If yes, which ones?

JA: When Dad had his back to the settee and was talking to Nicolas Garrigan about what he intends to do and his past.

MA: Are you able to clarify exactly when and where your Dad was born? Many reports claim that he was born in Ko'boko. Is there truth to that? If not, where was he born and when exactly?

JA: Dad (1928-2003) was born at Shimoni Hill Police Barracks in Nakasero-Kampala, Uganda to Aisha Aate Chumaru (1903-1969), the second wife to Mzee Amin Dada Tomuresu (1889-1976) of the Adibu Likamero Kakwa Clan. Here are the details of his birth:

Islamic Calendar 1346 Dhul-Hijja 10th Weekday Yawm Al-'Arb'a' at 04:00

Gregorian Calendar 1928 May 30th Wednesday at 04:00

Julian Calendar 1928 May 17 Wednesday 04:00

My good friend renowned Researcher Mr. Fred Guweddeko quoted the Ethiopian Julian Calendar date in his article instead of the Gregorian Calendar date used by most historians.

We Muslims are very clear on the fact that Dad was born in 1928, while Mzee Amin Dada accompanied by a 9 year old Ramadhan Dudu Moro set off for Eid Al-Ad'ha Prayers amongst the Nubian Muslim shanty Settlement on Kibuli Hill. On that day, a mystical hailstorm shower engulfed the Ugandan Capital and as an expert Cultural Midwife, Aisha Aate Chumaru of the Okapi-Bura Lugbara clan who was a renowned Holistic Medicine Expert performed a self-delivery. She told one Mangarita Nakoli that Awon'go landed onto a pile of hailstones setting off a resounding scream and crying excessively, that is why she gave him that name initially but the name came to mean backbited or false rumours too. However the Leiko-Kozoru Kakwa clan (Her Maternal Uncles) gave him the name Alemi (A Just Cause, Justice) because of the disputed issue about his paternity. Mzee Amin Dada Tomuresu (1889-1976) gave him the name Idi.

MA: Were your Dad's parents married/living together when he was born at the Shimoni Hill Police Barracks while your Grandpa was serving as a Police Officer?

JA: Yes

MA: Do you have any thoughts about the fact that the novel doesn't "jive" with the film in many cases and scenes?

JA: It always happens in the cutting room and the Director's mindset.

MA: What are your thoughts about the following passage on page 131 about Kakwa territory and practices?

LKS: "….I recently found an excellent book in the Fort William Library, by a Mr. George Ivan Smith. He says: "It is a barren region where stones are set on the hills to attract the rain. The wise men of the tribe, faced with questions of life and death, human hope or fear, sought answers by tying a long string to a chicken, attaching the string to a stake, then beheading the chicken…"

JA: There is a saying that Africans have no history. Would you believe the nerve of bigoted Caucasians to say that with a straight face?

Major Stingard does justice to all the tribes in the former Lado Enclave in his posthumous 1920s book yet everyone avoids or ignores his work, even though it describes the Kakwa in detail.

MA: What are your thoughts about the following passage on page 132?

LKS: "But back to the mother: a Lugbara (another of the Nilotic tribes) impregnated by a Kakwa man, she is that rare thing, a slave with power. For even as she is heaving in her labour to expel her twelve-pound burden into the sweating night, she is by many accounts held to be a witch…"

JA: Grandma was no Hooker/Harlot call it what you may. After Grandpa Amin Dada, there was only Mzee Ibrahim a Muganda in the Kings African Rifles.

MA: Can you share additional information about the above?

JA: After the break up with Mzee Amin Dada she lived with Mzee Ibrahim in Kawolo and then moved onward to Bundo-Kidusu just off the Old Jinja Road in Buyukwe County, Mukono District.

MA: What are your thoughts about the following passage on page 133?

LKS: "The father, he is unknown, most people believe he was a soldier- a trooper, with trooper's ways…. So the father disappears, as fathers do, and the mother plies her wares in Jinja – King's African Rifles town, town of factories and godowns, town…"

JA: Dad's father retired and worked at the DC's office in Arua after leaving the Police Service. Dad was at his father's homestead while attending Primary One to Primary Four at the Muhammadian Primary School (Arua Muslim School) together with Old Boys like Mzee Kiiza who was his lifetime friend and resided in Arua.

MA: Can you shade light on the circumstances of your Dad's birth?

JA: Dad (1928-2003) was born at Shimoni Hill Police Barracks in Nakasero-Kampala, Uganda to Aisha Aate Chumaru (1903-1969), the second wife to Mzee Amin Dada Tomuresu (Temeresu) (1889-1976) of the Adibu Likamero Kakwa Clan. Here are the details of his birth:

Islamic Calendar 1346 Dhul-Hijja 10th Weekday Yawm Al-'Arb'a' at 04:00

Gregorian Calendar 1928 May 30th Wednesday at 04:00

Julian Calendar 1928 May 17 Wednesday 04:00

My good friend renowned Researcher Mr. Fred Guweddeko quoted the Ethiopian Julian Calendar date in his article instead of the Gregorian Calendar date used by most historians.

We Muslims are very clear on the fact that Dad was born in 1928, while Mzee Amin Dada accompanied by a 9 year old Ramadhan Dudu Moro set off for Eid Al-Ad'ha Prayers amongst the Nubian Muslim Settlement on Kibuli Hill. On that day, a mystical hailstorm shower engulfed the Ugandan Capital and as an expert Cultural Midwife, Aisha Aate Chumaru of the Okapi-Bura Lugbara clan who was a renowned Holistic Medicine Expert performed a self-delivery. She told one Mangarita Nakoli that Awon'go landed onto a pile of hailstones setting off a resounding scream and crying excessively, that is why she gave him that name initially but the name also meant gossiped about, talked about or backbited. However the Leiko-Kozoru Kakwa clan (Her Maternal Uncles) gave him the name Alemi (A Just Cause, Justice) because of the disputed issue about his paternity. Mzee Amin Dada Tomuresu (1889-1976) gave him the name Idi.

The relationship between Grandpa and Grandma was strained when Grandpa thought Dad was the son of Kabaka Chwa.

MA: At what point in your Dad's life did your grandparents split? How old was he?

JA: 4 Years old.

MA: Were your grandparents married?

JA: Culturally Yes. The last Bride Price installment was finally paid in July 1967.

MA: Can you explain the above further?

JA: Ugandan Law recognizes Cultural Marriage, Islamic Marriages, Matrimonial Christian Marriages and Registering with the Registrar of Marriages. Theirs was Cultural, where over years African families wrangle over cattle (The Bride Price).

MA: What are your thoughts about the following statements/assertions on page 135?

LKS: "…that Idi will draw on, too, bringing them down in lorries for enlistment into the army or to fill the cohorts of the Public Safety Unit and the State Research Bureau – latterly as part of his Moslemization programme. Alarmed at the prospect of an independent Uganda in which, as colonial bloodhounds, they have no place, they are only too happy to comply?"

JA: General Salim Bey a Giant Makaraka made an Agreement with Lord Lugard and they overwhelmed and colonized the whole country Uganda. By "Independence" the whole Uganda Army and Uganda Police was mainly manned by the Nubians. By January 24, 1971, the top 4 positions in the Uganda Army were manned by Nubians. We have always been the Cavalry. The Military is us. It was not an overnight thing. Try and check the Kenyan Police and Army, you will understand what I mean. Parochial hogwash from Kyemba's book A State of Blood being interpolated by Foden.

MA: Can you share more reasons why Obote was overthrown in the Military Coup that saw your Dad ascend to the position of President of Uganda?

JA: He continued to aspire to Nkrumah's dreams of a Socialist Africa and this rubbed the powers that be the wrong way. Trying to introduce Socialism, Common Man's Charter, which would have disenfranchised the very same Indians who were compensated by Dad. Ironically Obote was replaced by a man who understood the pain of the common man, even though Uganda's Elites didn't immediately recognize that and his foes wouldn't give him a chance to implement his ideas.

MA: Do you have any thoughts about the statement on page 135 (second last paragraph) "Oh Israel, who could have been Uganda. I've often wondered what would have happened, actually, if it had been so, if the Zionist homeland had been there, as was mooted…?"

JA: Crawford who was the Governor could have had a hand in that train of thought for he was a Jew. Some mystic African Evangelicals believe that eons ago, the Jews wondered right up to mount Liru in Ko'boko, ha ha ha ha. Moshe's grave is said to be in the vicinity of Taranga (Tara).

MA: Do you have more thoughts about the argument that Obote's regime was oppressive and unpopular at the time your Dad overthrew him in 1971?

JA: The Baganda never forgave Obote for humiliating their King. Some even allege that he sent a lady friend to poison the Kabaka while he lived in exile in England. The animosity persists.

To be continued in subsequent parts of the series Idi Amin: Hero or Villain? His Son Jaffar Amin and Other People Speak…

www.idiamindada.com

BY MARGARET AKULIA

We wish to emphasize that these Snippets of History are only for purposes of providing context to the Introductory Edition and the rest of the series, Idi Amin: Hero or Villain? His Son Jaffar Amin and Other People Speak. They are meant as a prelude to "fuller" information about related and connected history. Consequently, we will endeavor to expand on them, provide fuller accounts and additional information in subsequent parts of the series as it unfolds. This is because more in depth information and exploration is necessary, to gain a fuller grasp, in depth knowledge and deeper understanding of activities, events and themes highlighted in the snippets. However, we trust that you will find the information as presented in the snippets useful and helpful in beginning to understand Idi Amin's convoluted, conflicted and controversial story and legacy.

World History: The Age of Exploration

The Age of Exploration was a period between the 15th century and the 17th century when Europeans initiated travels around the world in search of new trading routes and goods such as gold, silver and spices. The main reason for the Age of Exploration was a severe shortage of gold and silver in Europe, both of which the European economy was heavily dependent on. Low domestic supplies had plunged much of Europe into a recession which necessitated finding alternative sources of gold and silver. At the time of the Age of Exploration, the Turkish Ottoman Empire controlled the Eastern Trade Routes and the Turks barred Europeans from those trade routes after Constantinople fell into their hands in 1453. This made finding alternative trade routes for European economic survival even more critical.

Portugal was first in launching the great wave of Exploration Expeditions under Prince Henry the Navigator and his main project was exploring the West Coast of Africa in search of an alternative trade route linking West Africa with the Mediterranean world. The only trade routes to the West Coast of Africa at the time were over the Sahara Desert and these routes were controlled by the Muslim states of North Africa that were rivals of Portugal and Spain. With the launching of the great wave of Exploration Expeditions under Prince Henry the Navigator, the Portuguese hoped to bypass the Islamic nations occupying the Sahara Desert and trade directly with West Africa by sea. Other European nations soon followed in the footsteps of Portugal by sending their own Explorers also in search of commodities and new trade routes.

In the process of traversing the globe in ships, which was the mode of transportation at the time, these travelers encountered peoples and lands previously unknown to Europeans. Christopher Columbus, Vasco da Gama and Ferdinand Magellan were among the most famous of these Explorers.

Christopher Columbus was born in 1451 and died on May 20, 1506. As a navigator, colonizer and explorer, he was one of the first Europeans to explore the Americas after the Vikings who were members of the Scandinavian seafaring traders, warriors and pirates who raided and colonized wide areas of Europe from the late 8th to the 11th century. The Vikings had used their famed longships to travel as far east as Constantinople and the Volga River in Russia and as far west as Newfoundland in present day Canada.

Columbus' voyages across the Atlantic Ocean to the Americas led to European awareness of the Western Hemisphere, which became known to them as the "New World". The "New World" is one of the names used for the Americas. The term originated in the 15th century and it resulted from the fact that the Americas were new to the Europeans who at the time thought the whole world consisted of only Europe, Asia and Africa.

Many credit Christopher Columbus with "discovering" the Americas but like Idi Amin, there are heated debates and dissenting views about whether he was a hero or a villain. Some people assert that, "Christopher Columbus did not discover the Americas. When he "stumbled" onto the Americas, there were people who had lived there for millennia. To credit him with discovering an already inhabited land is racist and ludicrous" they protest.

"Christopher Columbus only brought death and destruction to an already thriving and existing civilization in the Americas" others insist. "He enslaved and murdered the Native people of the Americas." "He is a villain and his legacy is parallel to that of Adolf Hitler who murdered countless Jews during the Holocaust". Still others assert that "Christopher Columbus is a hero and indeed he discovered the Americas, which has nothing to do with the fact that other people had already been to the lands or inhabited it for millennia." They assert that, "it had to do with bringing the land to the attention of the "civilized world"." "He introduced "civilization" to a "savage" people who should be grateful for the resulting access to the growing civilizations of Europe - the ideas and achievements of Aristotle, Galileo, Newton, and the thousands of thinkers, writers, and inventors who followed", they advance. "Look what Christopher Columbus' "discovery" led to" admirers assert - "The United States of America - a land flowing with milk and honey."

The anniversary of Columbus' 1492 voyage is dubbed "Columbus Day" and it is observed and celebrated as a holiday throughout the Americas and in Spain on October 12. This holiday has become and it is now deeply ingrained in North American Tradition and culture and viewed by many as a positive affair. The day is celebrated in commemoration of the fact that as Columbus and his men journeyed through the Americas, a sailor aboard the ship sighted land at 2:00am on October 12, 1492. The sighting was a welcome sight after a long perilous journey that could have cost Columbus and his men their lives. Nevertheless, there are people that are vehemently opposed to celebrating Columbus' landing in the Americas as a good thing. They are working tirelessly to abolish the holiday and celebration of "Columbus Day".

In 2003, Venezuelan President Hugo Chavez urged Native American Latin Americans not to celebrate the "Columbus Day" holiday and he blamed Columbus for leading the way in the mass genocide of the Native Americans by the Spanish. Jamaican Artist Burning Spear strongly criticized Christopher Columbus in a song titled 'A Damn Blasted Liar'. The song created a lot of controversy and opened a highly opinionated debate across the Caribbean Islands on the negative effects Christopher Columbus and his leadership had on Native peoples. Advocates for Natives of the Americas take the argument further by placing culpability for the hardships suffered by these groups during the voyages and colonization of Christopher Columbus on contemporary governments and their citizens.

However, again, because of the fact that the "Columbus Day" Tradition is now deeply ingrained in North American culture and even "enjoyed", welcomed and cherished as a much deserved day of rest with family by many, much debate hasn't been "encouraged." Instead Columbus' "heroism" has been the subject of dramatizations such as the1992 feature film 1492: Conquest of Paradise which commemorates the 500th anniversary of Columbus' landing in the Americas and depicts the Spanish colonization of the Americas and the subsequent effects on the Native Peoples. Furthermore, landmarks erected in commemoration of Columbus and replications of the three ships he used for his travels continue to pay tribute to Columbus, much to the chagrin of Native Peoples of the Americas and their allies and advocates.

The debate about Columbus rages on today, as does the debate and conflicting characterization of Idi Amin as a Hero and a Villain to the core at the same time. Having made Canada my second home and befriended individuals from the Native cultures of the Americas, I have observed first hand the horrors of Columbus' legacy on Native Canadians. I can't help musing:

The legacy of Christopher Columbus does require in depth exploration and proper "telling" as does the "dysfunctional" colonial legacy that "created" Idi Amin.

The carnage that ensued in Uganda before, during and after Idi Amin's rule cannot be viewed in isolation of the "dysfunctional" colonial legacy that "created" him because it would be too simplistic. Like the devastating legacy left by Columbus' voyages and their resulting European exploration, colonization and exploitation of the Western Hemisphere and the Native people of the Americas, the in depth exploration is necessary in order to obtain a deeper understanding of what actually happened. To miss out on the opportunity of in-depth exploration is to deprive the global community of lessons that exist in stories of colonialism around the world.

I find it surprising that the Indigenous inhabitants of the Americas continued to be referred to as "Indians" even after it was realized that Columbus had mistaken them as such. He had "stumbled" onto them and their land after a long voyage, while trying to find a sea route to India, an economic hub at the time. The least he could have done was to thank them for welcoming him and his sailors to their land after a long perilous journey that could have cost them their lives. Columbus and his men could have taken time to learn the true identity of their hosts and hostesses and stopped "feeding" the "lie" that these welcoming people were Indians!

The continuing use of terms such as Pre-Columbian to refer to the peoples and cultures of the Americas before Columbus continues to baffle advocates and hinder attempts to reverse insinuations that peoples who inhabited these lands before Columbus so-called "rescued" them were sub human.

Ligito would say, "What a bunch of ignorant bigots?" Then he would add, "How can anyone be so unintelligent and racist as to suggest that life in the Americas began with Christopher Columbus when they know that there were people who lived in these lands for millennia before Columbus invaded them?"

Notwithstanding all the insinuations resulting from Christopher Columbus' landing in the Americas, I consider the Native peoples of the Americas the rightful "owners" of the lands we "outsiders" enjoy. I appreciate the open arms with which I continue to feel welcome by the Native peoples of the land, which I experienced right from the time I first set foot on Canadian soil. Way back on the day I disembarked the plane at Vancouver International Airport and followed the other passengers into the Airport Terminal, unsure how my life was going to unfold in Canada first as a Landed Immigrant and then as a Canadian Citizen. I now cherish opportunities I get to "compare notes" and common threads my Kakwa culture shares with the cultures of the Native peoples of the Americas, including the Learning Circles I have adapted from both cultures to "teach" and provide Learning Opportunities through my "Storytelling" projects.

As a "product" of colonialism and someone living the devastating effects of the "brand" that existed in Africa and elsewhere myself, I deem it appropriate to include the snippet on Columbus for context in telling Idi Amin's story. I also deem it appropriate to encourage readers to acquaint themselves with the "brand" of colonialism that existed in the lands that became The United States of America.

How and why these lands declared themselves "Free and Independent States" from Great Britain "forever" on July 4, 1776 provides an interesting and curious comparison to former British colonies in Africa that have remained in "captivity" despite being granted so-called "Independence". How and why the lands that became the United States of America successfully wrested themselves from the firm colonial clutches of the British Empire and managed to carve a "lucrative" existence for themselves while resource rich former British colonies in Africa languish in poverty is a subject worthy of exploration.

How the lands that became the United States of America have managed to attain a "melting pot" while "former colonies" in Africa are coloured by perpetual bloodbaths instigated by "diversities" that should be celebrated instead of being maligned is a subject that requires a lot of exploration. Individuals who did not know that the United States of America was once colonized by Great Britain will undoubtedly be intrigued with discovering facts related to that piece of American history! Events leading up to the drafting and signing of "The Declaration of Independence" are a great place to start.

Opening Africa to Western Exploration and Exploitation

According to historical accounts, the age of exploration ended in the early seventeenth century but exploration continued nonetheless. By this time, European vessels that had weathered experimental new technologies and ideas growing out of the Renaissance were equipped to travel anywhere on the planet. The Renaissance (French for "rebirth"), was a cultural movement that spanned roughly the 14th through the 17th century, beginning in Italy in the late Middle Ages and later spreading to the rest of Europe. Technological advances during the Renaissance had included advances in cartography, navigation, firepower and shipbuilding with the most important development being the invention of first the carrack and then the caravel in Portugal. As illustrated by Christopher Columbus' story of mislabeling Native inhabitants of the Americas as "Indians" when he "stumbled" onto their land after a long perilous voyage, many European nations wanted to find a route to Asia through the west of Europe.

Sub-Saharan Africa was a "tough cookie to crack" for Europeans until the mid to late 19th and early 20th centuries, due to the many tropical diseases unknown to Europeans at the time, most notably Malaria and because of the then powerful Muslim Ottoman Empire in the North of Africa. The influence of the Muslim Ottoman Empire extended further south and in latter centuries, it would feature very prominently in activities related to the land that became Uganda and Idi Amin's home.

Notwithstanding the hardship encountered by European Explorers venturing into Sub-Saharan Africa, the opening of Africa to Western exploration and exploitation had already begun at the end of the 18th century. So much so that by the year 1835, Europeans had mapped most of northwestern Africa and they had their eyes set on the entire continent. David Livingstone, Serpa Pinto, Richard Burton, John Speke and James Grant were among the most famous European Explorers who mapped Africa's vast hinterland. It was after this mapping that Europe realized the vast resources of Sub-Saharan Africa and began its systematic exploitation through full-blown colonization.

Africa as the "Dark Continent" and Attitudes towards its Exploration

It is important to note that for many centuries, the Western world regarded Africa as the "Dark Continent", a term vehemently opposed by activists because of its negative connotation. Originally coined by Europeans to mean an unexplored, savage and untamed area, populated by heathens and wild animals, many people continue to use the term to describe Africa and keep the continent in the shackles of colonialism. Despite the "dangers" inherent in exploring Africa, early explorers were attracted to Africa because of the "excitement" they anticipated from "navigating hostile waters" and discovering "uncharted territory", as was the case with the African continent.

Backed by their countries, many explorers felt that it was their duty to "introduce Western civilization and Christianity to Africa" a continent they felt was largely inhabited by "savage" peoples. As a result, long after the age of exploration ended in the early seventeenth century, exploration continued in Africa and it was seen as a worthy "investment". Identifying the source of the Nile became a focal point and explorers competed to be the first to reach this landmark that would play a significant role in shaping the history of the land that would become Uganda and Idi Amin's home. A notable early explorer of the interior of Africa was David Livingstone, a British pioneer medical missionary with the London Missionary Society. Cynics have advanced that "David Livingstone's honourable agenda was exploited for dishonourable and despicable purposes when the British piggy backed on his work as a missionary to exploit countries in Africa" – another subject worthy of in-depth exploration!

Colonialism and the Colonization of Sub-Saharan Africa

There is a lot more to say about colonialism and the fact that it existed long before the colonization of African lands. However, for purposes of the series Idi Amin: Hero or Villain? His Son Jaffar Amin and Other People Speak, it is important to note that voyages such as Columbus' and others that followed occurred at a time when European powers were engulfed in national imperialism and economic competition as they sought wealth from the establishment of trade routes and overseas colonies. The ability of Explorer Ships to withstand harsh climatic conditions encouraged the exploration of Sub-Saharan Africa, which is how Europeans ended in this part of the African continent that lies south of the Sahara Desert. That was how Sub-Saharan Africa was opened to Western Exploration and Exploitation. The area includes the land that became Uganda and Idi Amin's home.

It is the "brand" of colonialism and oppression that "created" Idi Amin and others around the globe that participants in the series Idi Amin: Hero or Villain? His Son Jaffar Amin and Other People Speak are encouraged to highlight. In our opinion, the murder of innocent people in Uganda during Idi Amin's rule was directly related to the legacy of that "brand" of colonialism and oppression in the African continent in general and Uganda in particular.

The colonization of Sub-Saharan Africa forms a significant part of Idi Amin's story. As a result, we outline snippets of activities that occurred and events that unfolded during that period to continue to provide context to the series, Idi Amin: Hero or Villain? His Son Jaffar Amin and Other People Speak. We reiterate that in order not to detract from the focus of the series, snippets only of the activities and events are outlined in this Introductory Edition of the series. We have stayed away from extensive details but encourage more exploration to gain a deeper understanding and in-depth knowledge about the activities, events and themes highlighted in the snippets. Focus is on the lands that became Uganda and Idi Amin's home.

It is important to note that colonization occurred around the globe and across time, despite the fact that the term has been commonly used to refer to European overseas Empires. For example, European colonialism began in the 15th century and the Portuguese and Spanish led this form of "oppression" as they explored the Americas, along with the coasts of Africa, the Middle East, India and East Asia. However, the British Empire later grew to become the largest Empire yet seen and the lands that became Uganda became one of its colonies. It is also important to note that the Muslim Ottoman Empire which was created across the Mediterranean, North Africa and South-Eastern Europe was in existence during the time European colonization of the other parts of the world was occurring.

The colonization of Africa has a long history, the most famous phase being the "Land grabbing Scheme" that became known as "The Scramble for Africa" – "the proliferation of conflicting European claims to African territory during the New Imperialism Period". It occurred during the nineteenth century, between the 1880s and World War I in 1914. This phase in the colonization of Africa is also known as "The Race for Africa". The last fifth of the 19th century saw the transition from the so-called "informal" imperialism of control through military influence and economic dominance to that of direct rule, hence "The Scramble".

Sub-Saharan Africa was attractive to Europe for mostly economic reasons. Because of the long depression that occurred between 1873 and

1896, European markets had been dealt a cruel blow and it was necessary to offset the growing deficit by income from elsewhere. Africa offered the perfect solution with its vast resources and welcoming peoples. Britain, Germany and France were major players, along with other countries in Europe.

As Britain developed into the world's first post-industrial nation, financial services became an increasingly important sector of its economy. Capital investments in its colonies in Africa and elsewhere continued to maintain a surplus which was often reinvested in the same colonies where cheap labor, limited competition and abundant raw materials ensured maximum profit. The demand for raw materials to feed European industries was another reason for colonialism and "The Scramble for Africa". Necessary raw materials such as copper, cotton, rubber, tea and tin which European consumers had grown accustomed to and upon which European industry had grown dependent were unavailable in Europe, so the colonies provided a source for them.

Excerpts from Jaffar Amin's writings titled "Eons of Plunder" and "Ki-Koloni" provide a few details that illustrate the busyness and activities that ensued following realization by Europeans that Africa was a "gold mine" and its so-called "savage" Natives needed to be "tamed" to effectively exploit its vast resources. The exploitation included the "full-fledged" greedy "Land grabbing Scheme" that became known as "The Scramble for Africa" – "the proliferation of conflicting European claims to African territory during the New Imperialism Period, between the 1880s and World War I in 1914". The excerpts taken from Jaffar Amin's writings titled "Eons of Plunder" and "Ki-Koloni", include the busyness and activities that occurred in the land that would become Uganda and they are reproduced in a section below.

According to information taken from Wikipedia, the free encyclopedia, Cecil John Rhodes was an English-born businessman, mining magnate, and politician in South Africa. He was the founder of the Diamond Company De Beers, which today markets 40% of the world's rough diamonds and at one time marketed 90%. He was an ardent believer in colonialism and was the founder of the state of Rhodesia, which was named after him. Rhodesia, later Northern and Southern Rhodesia, eventually became Zambia and Zimbabwe respectively. He is also known today for the scholarship that bears his name. He and others felt the best way to "unify the possessions, facilitate governance, enable the military to move quickly to hot spots or conduct war, help settlement, and foster trade" would be to build the "Cape to Cairo Railway". However, Cecil John Rhodes' enterprise was not without problems as France had a rival strategy in the late 1890s, to link its colonies from the West Coast of Africa to the East Coast of Africa and the Portuguese also had claims to sovereignty in Africa.

We introduce the Snippet of History relating to Cecil John Rhodes here because he featured very prominently in creating the British Empire that in turn "created" Idi Amin, as Ligito would mouth.

Ligito never shied away from repeatedly uttering:

"The British 'created' Idi Amin. They should stop abrogating their responsibility and start pointing the fingers at their damn selves and not anyone else."

"The British deserved the rudeness they got from Idi Amin because they created him."

"It was the fault of the British that Awon'go Alemi turned out the despicable way he did".

Cecil John Rhodes was instrumental in securing Southern African states for the British Empire and as outlined above, one of his projects was for Britain to control a route linking Cape Town to Cairo. He did attain his dream somewhat because as Jaffar Amin puts it:

"Cecil John Rhodes' dream indeed traverses (albeit in the ICT sector) the so-called 'Dark Continent,' from Cape Town to Cairo in multinational conglomerate shackles firmly back in place with marketing mantras which have replaced Soyinka's eternal Colonial Prayer with 'commercials' that keep us glued to 'Entertainment' - the new 'religion.'" Jaffar has reiterated the foregoing assertion many times as he reflects on his father's legacy and attempts to break the "shackles" of the oppression known as colonialism and its new form neocolonialism.

According to information taken from Wikipedia, the free encyclopedia, Cecil John Rhodes wanted to expand the British Empire because he believed that the Anglo-Saxon race was destined to greatness. In his last will and testament, Rhodes said of the British, "I contend that we are the finest race in the world and that the more of the world we inhabit the better it is for the human race." He wanted to make the British Empire a superpower in which all of the white countries in the empire, including Canada, Australia, New Zealand, and Cape Colony, would be represented in the British Parliament. Rhodes included Americans in the Rhodes scholarships and said that he wanted to breed an American elite of philosopher-kings who would have the USA rejoin the British Empire. Rhodes also respected the Germans and admired the Kaiser, and allowed Germans to be included in the

Rhodes scholarships. He believed that eventually Great Britain, the USA and Germany together would dominate the world and ensure peace together.

The Lands that Would Become Uganda

Long before Europeans landed in Sub-Saharan Africa and colonized it, there had been trade activities and trade routes through the Sahara Desert dominated by Arabs who would feature prominently in future centuries, in the history of the lands that would become Uganda and Idi Amin's home. These trade activities became known as the Trans-Saharan Trade and increased after the Islamic conquest of North Africa during the seventeenth century. The Trans-Saharan Trade involved trade in various commodities including slaves - another story that needs proper "telling" and thorough exploration.

There were a number of activities that preceded the colonization of the lands that would become Uganda and Idi Amin's home. To illustrate these activities, we now outline snippets from notes, writings and reflections by Jaffar Amin that are adapted and taken from self-explanatory sections titled "Eons of Plunder" and "Ki-Koloni". Highlights only of activities and events are provided here for context. As we indicated previously, more exploration is required, encouraged and necessary, to gain a deeper understanding and in depth knowledge about these activities, events and themes highlighted in the snippets.

We provide snippets of events that unfolded in lands situated along the Nile and in the Kingdom of Buganda during the latter half of the 19th century, to continue to shed light on the environment that existed before Idi Amin was born which contributed to "creating" him. The snippets are extracted from the period between 1800 and 1922 and several events occur concurrently. However, for clarity, they are presented as narrative accounts under two themes, namely, 1) Snippets of historical activities around the Nile from Egypt to the Kingdom of Buganda and 2) Snippets of historical activities in the Kingdom of Buganda.

Whenever possible, events and activities are recounted in chronological order, with dates assigned to them. Additional information outlining details relating to the two themes will be provided as the series unfolds, for ease of reference and to facilitate the exploration and reading necessary, to gain a deeper understanding and in depth knowledge about events and activities highlighted in snippets.

We wish to reiterate again that we are telling Idi Amin's story in Kakwa Adiyo narration style and format, which includes other participants "jumping in to make any corrections or to state a forgotten issue". Consequently, as the series unfolds, we will make any corrections and add information as Kakwa Temezi (Revered Elders) would in an Adiyo Narration Process including inadvertent errors, misrepresentations, misappropriations, inaccuracies and infringements that may occur in the Snippets of History which we again apologize for in advance.

Following are the snippets from notes, writings and reflections by Jaffar Amin that are adapted and taken from the self-explanatory sections titled "Eons of Plunder" and "Ki-Koloni". Even though the sketchy information may not be as informing initially as the fuller accounts we will endeavor to make available in subsequent parts of the series, we trust that the information as presented in this Appendix will be helpful in understanding themes that emerge in Idi Amin's story.

Excerpts adapted and taken from "Eons of Plunder" and "Ki-Koloni" by Jaffar Amin: Historical Activities around the Nile from Egypt to the Kingdom of Buganda

The latter half of the 19th century witnessed extensive travels to the Kingdom of Buganda by Arab Slave and Ivory traders and European Explorers. While these travels were occurring, concurrent events were also unfolding in lands situated along the Nile, including the Lado Enclave, historical home of Dad's Kakwa tribe. The Lado Enclave included "chunks" of present day Southern Sudan, parts of present day Congo and parts of present day Northern Uganda. Because the Nile has been the lifeline of Egyptian civilization and culture for millennia, events unfolding in Egypt at the time profoundly impacted tribes residing in the Lado Enclave. Furthermore, there was intense interest in properly mapping the Nile, which flowed through the Kingdom of Buganda and discovering its source. As a result events occurring along the Nile and the Lado Enclave inevitably became intertwined with events occurring in the Kingdom of Buganda - considered a possible "custodian" of the source of the Nile at the time.

In 1841, Mohammed Ali, a Turkish soldier and viceroy of Egypt from 1805 to 1848, turned his attention to present day Southern Sudan which at the time included parts of the Lado Enclave, original home of Dad's Kakwa tribe. He had wrested control of Egypt from a weakening

Ottoman Empire in 1811 and established a modern state in Egypt, over which his family ruled until the Egyptian Revolution of 1952.

That year, he dispatched the Turkish Naval Captain, Salim, to Gondokoro, a trading-station on the east bank of the Nile located in the Lado Enclave, because "the area was rich in Ivory and its inhabitants the Bari were disposed to bartering it for beads." The site of Gondokoro is 750 miles south of present day Khartoum, near the modern-day city of Juba, Southern Sudan. By this time, Slave Trade in the Sudan had run for decades as the Egyptian Governor-General, Ahmad Pasha Abu Widan, conquered the Sudanese centres of Kasala and Sawakin. The Turks, Arabs of the north and the European Explorers all engaged in slave trading at this time.

In 1843 Muhammad Ahmad, later known as the Mahdi was born in the province of Dongola in the Sudan. Well educated, he saw a vision in which Allah appointed him as the new Prophet or "Promised One" who would free the Sudanese from the corrupt and materialistic Egyptian rule.

In 1845, the Welsh Mining Engineer, John Petherick, explored rivers Jur, Yah and Rol in the Sudan, as he "studied" trades in Ivory and Slaves. John Petherick became the first White man to reach the Azande, Mundu and the Makaraka territories of present day Sudan, including the Kakwa Territory then controlled by the Makaraka and located in the Lado Enclave.

In 1856 Khartoum was teeming with slaves of all tribes of the present day Southern Sudan including the Lado Enclave. Annual slave exports from this part of the Sudan were between 2,000 and 15,000!

In the year 1860, the Maltese de Brono, combined Ivory Trade with Slave Trade in present day Southern Sudan and the Italian Giovani Miami, became the first European to visit what became the West Nile District of Uganda which was then part of the Lado Enclave.

The Slave Trade continued unabated and in the 1860s Jaliyin Danaqala, a Syrian merchant was protected by the Egyptian Administrators and he established slave trading posts or zeribas fortified with a palisade fence for himself and his bazingir (Arab slave soldiers).

In 1863, Isma'il Pasha became Khedive of Egypt until he was removed at the command of the British in 1879. While he was Khedive of Egypt, Isma'il greatly modernized Egypt and became westernized, as summarized by a statement he made in 1879:

"My country is no longer in Africa; we are now part of Europe. It is therefore natural for us to abandon our former ways and to adopt a new system adapted to our social conditions."

The Westernized Isma'il ruled Egypt for Turkey in the 1860s. At the same time, he was worried about the growing British influence in the Mediterranean Sea. Isma'il also wanted the British to be on his side and to increase the size of Egyptian territory. As well, he was determined "to put an end" to the Slave Trade in the Sudan.

In 1865 a) Khedive Isma'il established a Police Patrol on the Upper Nile at Fashoda due to pressure from Britain to suppress the Slave Trade. b) Sir Samuel Baker was sent to explore the source of the Nile and to end Slave Trade as well as to expand Egyptian dominions in present day Southern Sudan.

In 1869, Khedive Isma'il made the British Explorer Samuel Baker to be Governor General of the Equatorial Nile Basin. Baker had written a best selling book about his African travels titled "The Albert Nyanza", which had aroused British public opinion against the horrors of the Nile Slave Trade. Slavery had been abolished in Great Britain in 1833.

At this time, most Europeans viewed the Nile Slave Trade as proof of the barbarisms of both the Africans and the Arabs. Christianity they believed (conveniently ignoring that the Protestants and Catholics of the Confederate States of America were fighting to keep slaves in the 1860s) would never allow such a practice. Khedive Isma'il ordered Baker "to subdue to our authority the countries situated to the south of Gondokoro, to suppress the Slave Trade, to introduce a system of regular commerce and to open to navigation the Great Lakes of the Equator."

In the 1870s, Christians in England and elsewhere in Europe and the United States were absolutely convinced that the best thing for the people in all parts of the world was to be brought into the Christian Church. Non-Christians, including the followers of Mohammed (the Muslims), were considered to be heathens, damned to hell for eternity unless a missionary reached them before they died and converted into Christianity.

In 1872, Samuel Baker reached Gondokoro and managed to expel the great Arab Slave Trader in that area, Abu Sand. Next, Baker entered the Acholi area. Unlike Mutesa I, King of the Baganda, the Acholis had had no friendship with the Arab Traders and they were pleased with the Englishman Baker's work.

In 1873, Khedive Isma'il appointed Charles Gordon a British, as Governor of the Equatoria Province or Khatt al-Istiwa of which Dad's Kakwa tribe was a part. He served until 1876.

In 1874, Charles Gordon the British Governor appointed by Khedive Isma'il founded Jebel Lado (Juba) and became Governor of the Equatoria.

In 1876 a) Emin Pasha, became the Chief Physician of the Equatoria Province. b) Leopold II founded L'Association Internationale pour L'exploration et la Civilization de L'Afrique Centrale which two years later, became the Le Commite' D'etudes du haut Congo and later still, the Independent State of the Congo. c) W. Junker, the Russian-born German Explorer and Scientist arrived at Jebel Lado (now called Juba). d) The Anglo-Egyptian Slave Trade Convention was signed and Gordon's top priority became stamping out the Slave Trade in the present day Southern Sudan. e) Junker proceeded to Makaraka located in the present day Yei River District of the Equatoria Region of present day Southern Sudan then part of the Lado Enclave. He reached the Kibi (or Nzoro River) which he determined was the source of the River Welle. Note that the Kibi River is actually the source of the mighty Congo River, one of Africa's largest rivers found in the Congo and its source is Kakwa County, Collectivite des Kakwa (or the Kakwa of the Congo) area. f) Junker, coming from the northwest got to within twenty miles of the present site of Arua Station in West Nile, formerly located in the Lado Enclave. He later capitalized on this opportunity to name some of the hills in Maracha, Terego and Kakwa territories. Junker named the Legendary Kakwa Mountain Liru, Gessi and the Lugbara Mountain Wati, Baker. g) Gordon became the Governor General of the Sudan. h) Stanley and King Leopold II founded the International Congo Association, a purely private enterprise. The Belgian Government and people had nothing to do with it. At this time too, all of Africa, from the coast, was considered terra ullis, that is, "without government and claimed by nobody."

In 1878 a) Gordon harshly dealt with the Slave Traders and later paid for this action with his life. b) The same year, Emin Pasha became Governor of the Equatoria Province.

In 1879, Khedive Isma'il was deposed and Gordon left for Khartoum. Ranf Pash succeeded Gordon as Governor and he faced tremendous problems from the Slave Dealers.

In 1880 a) Gordon impressed on King Leopold II of Belgium and of the Congo Free State (CFS) to stamp out Slave Trade at its source (the Bahr-el Ghazal) but Leopold had his own hidden agenda in this Province. b) Emin Pasha visited the areas of Latuko, Makaraka and Acholi. c) German maps of the world began to include the land that is now Uganda in the East African territory that they claimed for the German Empire.

On June 29, 1881, the Mahdi, whose full names are Mohammed Ahmad Ibn Al-Sayid Abdallah, rose on the Island of Aba on the Blue Nile and proclaimed himself "Prophet" vowing to drive away the British and their Egyptian puppets and to Islamize the Sudan.

In 1883 a) the Mahdi and his Sudanese army, whose troops are called Dervishes, enjoyed several outstanding military successes. Finally, in November 1883, they completely massacred Egyptian troops under the British General Hicks. When Britain heard of this defeat, it pressurized Egypt to withdraw its troops and officials from the Sudan, including General Gordon. b) Upon rescuing Pasha, King Leopold II of Belgium offered Stanley to govern the Equatoria Province as a Congolese Province but Stanley declined.

Excerpts adapted and taken from "Eons of Plunder" and "Ki-Koloni" by Jaffar Amin: Historical Activities in the Kingdom of Buganda

In 1840, Zanzibari traders reached the shores of what would become Lake Victoria. They were seeking ivory and slaves and in return, these traders left the Baganda people with guns, beads, Islam - a new religion and the cotton cloth which led to a drastic transformation from the traditional bark cloth to cotton clothing amongst the Baganda.

In 1849, a Baluchi soldier named Isa Bin Hussein fled from his creditors in Zanzibar and entered Buganda a year later in 1850. A number of Arabs and Swahilis also arrived in Buganda during the same time. During the same year 1850, Suna, the King of Buganda at the time presented Isa Bin Hussein with three hundred Baganda concubines.

In 1852 a) Isa Bin Hussein invited Arab traders living in the land that became Tanganyika to Buganda. b) A typical Zanzibari caravan made the slow, dangerous trek from the East to what became Lake Victoria. The exhibition was led by Sheikh Snay Bin Amir, an Arab. Upon arrival, Sheikh Snay Bin Amir Al-Haris tried to convert King Suna to Islam and left a written record of his translations with the Kabaka of Buganda when he returned to the land that became Tanganyika. He wanted slaves and traded with the Kabaka who was all too willing to sell his enemies to the Arab. The price for an adult male was 2 muskets and for a female, it was 100 bullets!

Note: The Arabs eventually spread their influence at clan level and the new Kabaka Mutesa I who succeeded King Suna urged all his subjects to convert to Islam during the mid-19th century.

In January 1862, the English Explorer John Speke reached Buganda where he met Mutesa I, the King of Buganda. This was a second trip for Speke, with the first trip occurring in the late 1850s. At the time, Speke had travelled to Buganda from the Indian Ocean to Lake Tanganyika and then to Lake Victoria. He was the first British Explorer to reach Buganda.

The Royal Geographical Society paid for Speke's return journey to Africa. He left England in 1860 for the second journey and journeyed through other lands before arriving in Buganda in January 1862. While on this second trip, Speke "discovered" the source of the Nile.

On his visit to Mutesa I, John Speke was struck with the high standard of the Baganda. However, he was also appalled by what he saw - the savagery and cruelty and contempt for human life within the Lubiri, the Kabaka's Palace. The Kabaka was considered both god and king, with divine powers to massacre or maim his subjects at will. The precincts of his court were constantly stained with human blood and executions were carried out for the most trivial of offences.

Speke found that Mutesa's palace was well established with several officials as follows:

1) The dowager queen or Namasole 2) The queen sister or Lubaga and 3) The Prime Minister or Katikiro. There was also a Chief Field Marshall or Mujasi to lead the Army and the Gabunga served as the lord high. The Makujunga was the lord high executioner.

The chiefs belonged to a Council or Parliament called the Lukiko, which voted for a new Kabaka from among the old Kabaka's sons. By putting all the losers to death, the new Kabaka ensured no royal brother could challenge his authority. In addition to killing his brothers when he ascended to the throne, Mutesa ordered that hundreds of slaves should be put to death as a way of celebrating his power.

Revisiting Speke's Story - Information taken from Wikipedia, the Free Encyclopedia

John Hanning Speke (May 4, 1827 – September 15, 1864) was an officer in the British Indian Army, who made three voyages of exploration to Africa. In 1856, Speke and Burton a fellow Explorer made a voyage to East

Africa to find the Great Lakes which were rumoured to exist in the center of the continent. Both men clearly hoped that their expedition would locate the source of the Nile. The journey was extremely strenuous and both men fell ill from a variety of tropical diseases. Speke suffered severely when he became temporarily deaf after a beetle crawled into his ear and he had to remove it with a knife. He also later went temporarily blind.

After an arduous journey, the two men became the first Europeans to discover Lake Tanganyika (although Speke was still blind at this point and could not properly see the lake). They heard of a second lake in the area, but Burton was too sick to make the voyage. So Speke thus went alone, and found the lake, which he christened Lake Victoria. It was this lake which eventually proved to be the source of the River Nile. However, much of the expedition's survey equipment had been lost at this point and thus vital questions about the height and extent of the lake could not be answered.

Speke returned to England before Burton, and made their voyage famous in a speech to the Royal Geographical Society where he claimed to have discovered the source of the Nile. Burton was angered by his actions believing that they violated an agreement that the two men would speak to the society together. A further rift was caused when Speke was chosen to lead the subsequent expedition without Burton. Together with James Augustus Grant, Speke left from Zanzibar in October 1860.

When they reached present day Uganda, Grant travelled north and Speke continued his journey towards the West. Speke reached Lake Victoria on July 28 1862 and then travelled on the Westside around Lake Victoria without actually seeing much of it, but on the north side of the lake Speke found the Nile flowing out of it and discovered the Ripon Falls. Speke then sailed down the Nile and he was reunited with Grant. Next he travelled to Gondokoro in southern Sudan, where he met Samuel Baker and his wife, continuing to Khartoum, from which he sent a celebrated telegram to London: "The Nile is settled."

Speke's voyage did not resolve the issue, however. Burton claimed that because Speke had not followed the Nile from the place it flowed out of Lake Victoria to Gondokoro, he could not be sure they were the same river. A debate was planned between the two before the Royal Geographical Society on September 16, 1864, but Speke died just one day before from a self-inflicted gunshot wound. It remains uncertain whether the shot was an accident or suicide. Speke was buried in Dowlish Wake, Somerset the ancestral home of the Speke family.

The film Mountains of the Moon (1990) (starring Scottish actor Iain Glen as Speke) related the story of the Burton-Speke controversy. The film hints at a sexual intimacy between Burton and Speke. It also vaguely portrays Speke as a closeted homosexual. This was based on the William Harrison novel Burton and Speke. Mount Speke in the Ruwenzori Range, Uganda was named in honour of John Speke, as an early European explorer of this region.

Revisiting Grant's Story - Information taken from Wikipedia, the Free Encyclopedia

James Augustus Grant (April 11, 1827 – February 11, 1892) was a Scottish Explorer of Eastern Equatorial Africa. Grant was born at Nairn in the Scottish Highlands, where his father was the Parish Minister, and educated at the grammar school and Marischal College, Aberdeen. In 1846 he joined the Indian army. He saw active service in the Sikh War (1848—49), served throughout the Indian Mutiny of 1857, and was wounded in the operations for the relief of Lucknow. He returned to England in 1858, and in 1860 joined John Hanning Speke in the memorable expedition, which solved the problem of the Nile sources. The expedition left Zanzibar in October 1860 and reached Gondokoro, where the travelers were again in touch with what they regarded civilization, in February 1863. Speke was the leader, but Grant carried out several investigations independently and made valuable botanical collections. He acted throughout in absolute loyalty to his comrade.

In 1864 he published, as supplementary to Speke's account of their journey, "A Walk across Africa", in which he dealt particularly with "the ordinary life and pursuits, the habits and feelings of the natives" and the economic value of the countries traversed. In 1864 he was awarded the patron's medal of the Royal Geographical Society, and in 1866 given the Companionship of the Bath in recognition of his services in the expedition.

Grant served in the intelligence department of the Abyssinian expedition of 1868; for this he was made C.S.I and received the Abyssinian medal. At the close of the war he retired from the army with the rank of Lieutenant Colonel. Grant had married in 1865, and he now settled down at Nairn, where he died in 1892. He made contributions to the journals of various learned societies, the most notable being the "Botany of the Speke and Grant Expedition" in vol. xxix. of the Transactions of the Linnaean Society.

A Record of Grant's Illness in Africa (John Hayman MD) - Information taken from Wikipedia, the Free Encyclopedia

In his book, A Walk across Africa, Grant gives the following description of his illness, which broke out when they reached the native kingdom of Karague, on the western side of Lake Victoria in December 1861.

(Page 151): "The following account of my own ailments I give, not with a wish to parade them, but in order to convey information:- Having had fevers twice a month, in December my usual complaint assumed a new form. The right leg, from above the knee, became deformed with inflammation, and remained for a month in this unaccountable state, giving intense pain, which was relieved temporarily by a deep incision and copious discharge. For three months abscesses formed, and other incisions were made; my strength was prostrated; the knee stiff and alarmingly bent, and walking was impracticable. Many cures were attempted by the natives, who all sympathized with me in my sufferings, which they saw were scarcely endurable; but I had great faith - was all along cheerful and happy, except at the crises of this helpless state, when I felt it would have been preferable to be nearer home. The disease ran its course, and daily, to bring out the accumulated discharge, I stripped my leg like a leech. Bombay (an interpreter) had heard of a poultice made of cow-dung, salt, and mud from the lake; this was placed on hot, but merely produced the effect of a tight bandage. Baraka (another interpreter) was certain a serpent had spat upon my leg- "it could not have been a bite". Dr. M'nanagee, the sultan's brother, knew the disease perfectly; he could send me a cure for it - and a mild gentle peasant of the Wanyambo race came with his wife, a young pleasing like person, to attend me. With the soft touch of a woman he examined the limb, made cuts over the skin with a penknife, ordered all lookers-on outside the hut, when his wife produced a scroll of plantain-leaf, in which was a black paste. This was moistened from the mouth and rubbed into the bleeding cuts, making them smart; afterwards a small piece of lava was dangled against my leg and tied as a charm round the ankle......

These cures had no apparent effect, but the disease did improve. By the fifth month the complaint had exhausted itself; at last I was able to be out of the hut inhaling the sweet air, and once more permitted to behold the works of God's creation in the beautiful lake and hills below me.

(Page 187): By the end of March 1862 there were some hopes of my leaving Karague to join Speke in Uganda. The king had sent an officer and forty of his men to convey me up to the kingdom I so long wished to see. .... Being unable to walk, I was placed in a wicker stretcher (April 14, 1862), and trotted off on the heads of four Waganda (tribesmen of the area).

(Pages 189-90): On our journey, the stretcher was changed from head to the shoulder of the Waganda, who went at the rate of six miles an hour, jostling and paining my limb unmercifully. The coach and four, as I may term it, was put down every mile, or less, that the bearers might rest, laugh, joke, ... One great difficulty was to make them carry the conveyance so that the country in front could be seen in travelling; this they, for some reason, refused to do, and persisted in carrying me head first, instead of feet (fig 1-10).

(Page 210): The stretcher which had carried me part of the way from Karague had been discarded, as the Waganda saw my only ailment was lameness and a stiff knee joint.

(Page 246-7): (July 1862). Speke asked me whether I was able to make a flying march of it with him, while the baggage might be sent on towards Unyoro. At that time I was positively unable to walk twenty miles a day, especially miles of Uganda marching, through bogs and over rough ground. I therefore yielded reluctantly to the necessity of our parting; and I am anxious to be explicit on this point, as some have hastily inferred that my companion did not wish me to share in the gratification of seeing the river. Nothing could be more contrary to the fact. My state of health alone prevented me from accompanying Speke to set at rest for geographers the latitude of the interesting locality, as to which we were perfectly satisfied from native reports.

Grant's illness prevented him from being with Speke when Speke became the first white man to see the outpouring of the White Nile from Lake Victoria. However, as small compensation, his may be the first recorded case and first description of Mycobacterium ulcerans infection (Buruli ulcer). The print in his book shows Grant being carried on a wicker stretcher, leaving Karague. Reasons for regarding the illness as Mycobacterium ulcerans infection are:-

1.   The explorers passed through an area where the disease is known to occur.

2.   They passed through this area at a time just after the present maximal seasonal incidence of the disease.

3.   The history of the lesion, with a prodromal fever, swelling, followed by ulceration and a copious discharge would seem typical of the oedematous form of the disease, as occurs in the Congo.

4.   The disease was recognized by the local inhabitants who had a treatment for it, similar to the traditional remedies which may still be in use (Lunn H.F., personal communication).

5.   The history of the disease, with gradual healing after 6 months leaving residual scarring and contractures is characteristic of the more severe form of the illness.

Upon his return from Buganda, Speke reported that:

"The Nile began in Lake Victoria and the Baganda provided the perfect setting for the Protestant Missionaries from Great Britain to expand Christianity into the heart of Africa."

The two British men Speke and Grant reported that Buganda was filled with riches and fertility. What followed was a massive interest in the Eastern and Central Region.

The rest is now history!

In 1867, the Kabaka Mutesa I observed the Islamic ritual of fasting, following which Muslim influence was firmly established in Buganda until 1876.

In 1874, Samuel Baker's term as Governor General of the Equatorial Nile Basin ended after 4 years, and on paper, he claimed the Kingdom of Bunyoro in present day Uganda for Khedive Isma'il of Egypt who appointed him to the position. But the prospect of either a strong Bunyoro or a Bunyoro ruled by Egyptians posed grave threats to the independence of Buganda. Meanwhile, Mutesa I continued to fear the growing influence of the Zanzibari traders in his kingdom.

During the same year, the American, Chaille Long, arrived to the Kabaka's Palace as Emissary for Gordon and he witnessed that Mutesa I had slaughtered 30 men in his house.

In 1875 a) Linant De Bellefonds (a Belgian) was sent by Gordon to the Kabaka to survey the area to the south of the Sudan with a view to a possible annexation by Egypt. However, the Bari people killed De Bellefonds on his return to the Sudan and Gordon dealt on a wholesale slaughter of the Bari in the area to avenge his fellow white man's death. b) In the same year 1875, another English Explorer Henry Morton Stanley arrived in Buganda on a journey funded by The New York Herald and The New York Daily Telegraph. He met Mutesa I, and wrote on the King's behalf to The London Daily Telegraph, appealing for missionaries to come to Buganda.

Stanley wrote:

"Until I arrived at Mutesa's Court, the King delights in the idea that he was a follower of Islam; but by one conversion I flatter myself that I alone tumbled the newly raised religious fabric to the ground, and, if it were only followed by the arrival of a Christian mission here, the conversion of Mutesa and his Court to Christianity would, I think, be complete."

The sacred animist stipulation that the Kabaka could not spill his blood was most probably the one snag that the likes of Sheikh Snay Bin Amir Al Haris met when trying in vain to convert His Majesty Kabaka Mutesa I to Islam. Thus the issue of circumcision was out of the question. Mutesa I took this opportunity to equate the white person with supernatural powers that would neutralize the Egyptian threat from the Sudan and from King Kamurasi of Bunyoro to the Northwest. He agreed to welcome Christian missionaries to Buganda. His government enlisted new supporters who would help him ward off Egyptian invaders and help him control the growing influence of Islam.

Stanley's open letter was published in the London Newspaper, The Daily Telegraph of November 15, 1875. The letter asked for missionaries to serve in Buganda and explained that the Kabaka wanted Christians to come and save his people. An anonymous Philanthropist was so moved by the letter that he sent 5,000 Pounds Sterling to the Church Missionary Society (CMS) to aid in sending missionaries to Buganda.

In 1876, the British, Alexander Mackay (an Engineer before becoming a missionary), George Smith and C.T. Wilson accepted the funding from the Church Missionary Society (CMS) and brought Christianity to Buganda. Their work was dangerous. For example, Smith was murdered one year after arrival in Uganda. The new religion however, would prove to be equally as dangerous to Uganda as to the missionaries. It should be noted that during the same year 1876, the Anglicans landed at Zanzibar.

In 1877, Members of the British Protestant Church Missionary Society (CMS) arrived in Buganda followed by Representatives of the French Roman Catholic White Fathers in 1879. Four Anglicans of the Church Missionary Society (CMS) (Protestants) arrived in Buganda from Zanzibar. The White Fathers (Roman Catholics mainly from France) also arrived in Buganda two years later.

By the year 1879, a determined nucleus of Anglican missionaries was established in Mutesa's court. The missionaries immediately began to claim the first converts to Christianity. It was the same year 1879, that Representatives of the Church of Rome were sent to Buganda by Monsieur Lavingerie, the French Bishop of Algiers who founded the White Fathers Mission.

The group of Roman Catholic missionaries from France, the White Fathers then established a mission in Buganda. The leader of this group,

Father Lourdel, immediately tried to convince the Kabaka that his missionaries represented the true Christian religion but Alexander Mackay, who lasted the longest in Buganda, told the Kabaka not to allow the Roman Catholics to stay in Buganda. Mackay noted, "I ... distinctly told the King that we could not remain if the White Fathers were allowed to settle in the place."

Both the Church Missionary Society (CMS) and the White Fathers embarked on heated evangelization of the Baganda, including the Kabaka himself and his court.

In 1883, the banasura or mercenary guards of King Kamurasi of the Kingdom of Bunyoro were recruited from the deserters of the old Egyptian troops (defeated by the Mahdi in the Sudan), runaway slaves and riotous youths from the neighbouring states. The banasura were composed largely of the Baganda, Ma'di, Bari, Acholi, Shooli, Alur, Lan'go and Bongo. They supported the crown army of Bunyoro by terrorizing its subjects and forming combatants.

In 1884 a) The Berlin Conference was held and its outcome, the General Act of the Berlin Conference, is often seen as the formalization of "The Scramble for Africa". The conference regulated European colonization and trade in Africa during the New Imperialism period, and it coincided with Germany's sudden emergence as an Imperial Power. It was called for by Portugal and organized by Otto von Bismarck, the first Chancellor of Germany. Despite being an attempt to mediate Imperial Competition between Britain, France and Germany, the conference failed to establish definitively the competing powers' claims. b) The Society for German Colonization, a private organization had one of its goals as the inclusion of Uganda in a worldwide German Empire.

Beginning in 1884 and lasting until 1888, a series of revolts developed throughout the Southern Sudan. The Mahdists under Karam Allah (also known as Karamala) defeated Lipton Gessi's successor. The Equatoria, Hat el-Estiva, reached its "maximum development" under Emin consisting of the following districts:

I) Rol district (made up of Rol, Ayak, Ghaba Shambe, Bufe, Lessi, Rumbek and Gok) II) Lado (Juba) and III) Makaraka (including the Kakwa).

In 1884, Mutesa I died and his 17-year old son Mwanga succeeded him. He reigned from 1884 to 1888 and then from 1889 to 1897.

Between 1884 and 1885, The Imperial British East African Company (IBEAC) was formed, following the Berlin Conference. The Imperial British East Africa Company (IBEAC) was "a commercial association founded to develop African trade in the areas controlled by the British colonial power". The company was incorporated in London on April 18, 1888 and granted a Royal Charter by Queen Victoria on September 6, 1888.

The Imperial British East Africa Company (IBEAC) was granted Royal Status by the Colonial Office to open East Africa to "legitimate trade." The Church Missionary Society (CMS) and other "anti slavery" merchants of the United Kingdom founded The Imperial British East Africa Company (IBEAC).

The Church Missionary Society (CMS) established an Anglican Mission in Buganda with The Imperial British East Africa Company (IBEAC) as an important ally. For instance, Thomas Fowell Buxton, Vice President and Treasurer of the Church Missionary Society (CMS) served as a Director of The Imperial British East Africa Company (IBEAC). The Church Missionary Society (CMS) participated in lifting the financial burden out of the Colonial Government by contributing £16,500.

From November 1884 to February 1885, The Berlin Conference authorized Leopold not to stretch himself beyond the Congo Basin.

During Mwanga's rule from 1884 until 1888 and from 1889 until 1897, the hitherto smouldering religious tensions bursted into full flame. Religious wars became rampant in Buganda. Religious wars, particularly between Roman Catholics who enjoyed Mwanga's support and the Protestants, plagued the Kingdom of Buganda and The Imperial British East Africa Company (IBEAC). The internal strife proved to be more than a private company could handle. The Imperial British East Africa Company (IBEAC) was on the verge of withdrawing.

To lose control of this territory was unacceptable to the British government. So, the British stepped in and eventually declared the Uganda Protectorate. Although this declaration applied solely to Buganda, plans for the extension of the British power into other areas were already laid down. The British successfully extended their control over the Kingdoms of Bunyoro, Toro and Ankole.

To the colonialists, the Natives symbolized heathen Africans, incapable of dealing with the white men or dealing the lessons of a modern industrialized society. At best, the Natives appeared as handsome, exotic creatures whose tribal dances and ceremonies were wonderful occasions for intrepid tourists and whose stern, decorative faces made great photographs for the National Geographic.

In 1885 a) Mwanga had three Christian court pages put to death. b) In October 1885, on hearing that an Anglican Bishop James Hannington was about to enter Buganda, Mwanga had the white man murdered at Jinja. On his way to Buganda, Bishop Hannington was executed at Fort Luba in Busoga on the orders of Mwanga. c) Omar Saleh attacked the Mahdists in the Sudan but Gordon fell to the Mahdists and with him, Khartoum. d) The Mahdi was killed and buried at Omdurman. Karam Allah succeeded the Mahdi as the new "messiah" and vowed to continue fighting the holy war. e) The Congo Free State (CFS) took over the place of the International Congo Association.

In 1886 a) Alfred Tucker reached Buganda from Britain. He later became the first Bishop of Uganda. b) In May 1886, the worst massacre in Buganda occurred as Mwanga ordered the burial, alive, of 30 young Christian converts who refused to give up their new Christian religion. c) Mwanga eventually became the first Kabaka to be expelled from his throne.

In 1887 a) Leopold drove to the Nile in the guise of the Emin Pasha Relief Expedition through Stanley who was on the King's payroll throughout the Expedition. b) Beginning in 1887 until 1890, Belgian and other European Explorers opened up most of the mysteries of the Nile-Congo Divide - that is, areas in the vicinity of the Uganda, Congo and Sudan borders.

In 1888, Fadhil Al Mullah (Fodumula) rebelled against Emin Pasha and refused to accompany the ex-Governor and Stanley to Zanzibar in May 1889. About 1000 armed Sudanese together with their dependents (civilians) were left in the Equatoria Province. The rebels split into I) those led by Fadhil Al Mullah a 6 feet 4 inches tall Lugbara, who stayed at Wadelai along the Nile, near Rhino Camp and II) others led by Selim Bey a Giant Makaraka who retreated to Kavallis on Lake Albert. The two Muslim Army Officers refused to join the Mahdi. They also refused to convert the "Pagan" tribes of the Equatoria into Islam.

Between 1888 and 1893 The Imperial British East African Company (IBEAC) provided administration in the land that would become Uganda.

In 1889 a) The Pagan Baganda rebelled against the Muslims. b) Mwanga and a group of Christian exiles recaptured the throne. So, he was reinstated but Christianity now took on a deeper and stronger root in Buganda soil. Kalema fled to Bunyoro. For a while, Mwanga was in full control of Buganda. c) Emin Pasha reluctantly left for Zanzibar with Stanley accompanied by thousands of "loyal" troops and civilian porters. These porters were made up of nearly all the tribes of the Southern Sudan, Northern Uganda and North Eastern Congo. d) In May 1889, Mwanga lost power and Buganda as well as the surrounding Kingdoms, came under the powerful British Empire.

In 1890 a) A Convention between Congo Free State (CFS) and Belgium to annex the Congo was held. b) The Imperial British East Africa Company (IBEAC) assumed responsibility in Buganda on behalf of the British Government by enlisting 300 Sudanese troops in Cairo who formed part of the loyal troops in the evacuation of Emin Pasha and some levis (name for the Swahili porters) from Zanzibar. c) The Mackinnon Treaty dubbed a diplomatic coup for an advance to the Nile between the Congo Free State (CFS) and The Imperial British East Africa Company (IBEAC) was signed. By this treaty The Imperial British East Africa Company (IBEAC) agreed not to take political action on the left bank of the Nile as far as Lado (now Juba) and recognized the sovereign rights of the Congo Free State (CFS) in the area. In return the Congo Free State (CFS) ceded to The Imperial British East Africa Company (IBEAC) a corridor extending from Lake Albert to the northern end of Lake Tanganyika. d) The Belgian Captain Van Kerckhoven was secretly dispatched to the Congo Free State (CFS) to prepare to secure the Nile Valley. He decided to lead an expedition through the present Terego and Maracha areas of Uganda that would confront the Mahdists.

In July 1890, the British and the Germans arrived at a decision to partition territory in East Africa into spheres of influence for the two countries. The British received the land that became Uganda and the Germans, Tanganyika. All this was accomplished with minimal or no conversations with Mwanga, the King of Buganda and almost no negotiation with other tribes and kingdoms that were incorporated into the kingdom.

By the end of 1890, to administer the Uganda area, the British government initially granted a charter to the Imperial British East African Company (IBEAC). This private organization was empowered by the king of England to govern the area between present day Kenya and Lake Victoria.

Captain Frederick Lugard met with Mwanga on behalf of The Imperial British East Africa Company (IBEAC) and explained to him the relationship between the company and Buganda. On behalf of the company, Lugard promised to protect Buganda against her enemies. In return, Mwanga was to allow all missionaries to teach in his country and to promise that he would make no trade agreements with other nations without the company's consent.

George William was appointed by Great Britain to regulate the government of Buganda, while the United Kingdom, officially a Protestant nation, made a Muganda Protestant, Apollo Kagwa, hold the important post of Katikiro or Prime Minister.

On December 26, 1890 (Boxing Day), Kabaka Mwanga signed the historic treaty with Lugard. This Treaty called for British "protection" of Buganda.

In 1891 a) The Mahdists were in control of most of the Lado Enclave. b) The Congo Free State (CFS) advanced to Northeast Congo's Welle (Uwele) Valley and the Kakwa territory, enroute to what was to become the Lado Enclave. c) Lugard recruited nearly 2,085 of Selim Bey's forces (and 6,000 dependents) to join The Imperial British East Africa Company (IBEAC) cause. The new Sudanese or Nubian Army was deployed to man a string of forts throughout Western and Southern Uganda and to defend Buganda against its chief rival Bunyoro. d) The Belgian Captain Miltz joined the Van Kerckhoven Expedition as Deputy Commander.

In 1892 a) Van Kerckhoven was accidentally killed by his own gun bearer at Mount Wati and Miltz took over the overall command of the Expedition. The new commander was determined to push on to the Nile with the hope of enlisting the soldiers of the former Egyptian Administration, now under the command of the rebel leader Fadhil Al Mullah, a 6 feet 4 inches tall Lugbara from Terego, to serve the Congo Free State (CFS). b) Miltz marched to the Nile but did not reach the river. Miltz and his party encamped at Arave in the present Terego area. He sent errands to locate Fadhil Al Mullah. Miltz encamped at River Kibi where the ruling Keliko (Kaliko) Chief Lahmin assured the Belgian Commander of the "loyalty" of the Kaliko (Keliko) and the Kakwa to the Congo Free State (CFS). c) Miltz sent another party to Fadhil Al Mullah the 6 feet 4 inches tall Lugbara with a letter addressed to the Muslim Commander:

"That Leopold II, by the rights vested in him by the Congress in Berlin, had the authority to extend his rule throughout the Congo and to stretch it further and that, after learning that Fadhil Al Mullah and his men had been abandoned by the Egyptian Government and without essential supplies..."

King Leopold was willing to take the Equatoria into the employ of the Congo Free State (CFS). During the march northwestwards to meet Miltz at Kibi, the Lugbara (Terego or Maracha) attacked Fadhil Al Mullah, a fellow Lugbara from Terego but who was considered a Nubian and he lost 60 of his men. The remaining forces retreated to Bora.

In 1893, the Union Jack was raised over Kampala, as Mwanga was obliged to accept British "Protection."

In 1893, King Leopold's Force Publique (known by the Kakwa as Tukutuku) appeared in the Southern Sudan. The transition from The Imperial British East Africa Company (IBEAC) to direct British rule in Uganda culminated in a massive Buganda-British invasion of Bunyoro. An agreement was signed between the Congo Free State (CFS) and Great Britain to establish territorial rights and boundaries between Uganda and Congo.

From 1893 to 1894 the New Protectorate Nubian forces backed by Ganda spearmen campaigned vigorously on behalf of the British, to acquire more territory, especially from Bunyoro.

Note: Nubian troops were introduced into the land that would become Uganda and other parts of Africa. They and their descendants would eventually become Naturalized Ugandans with full citizenship rights. They would also form the bulk of Uganda's "Armed Forces" – a trend that continued throughout the history of the land that would become Uganda and to-date. Another contingent of the Nubian troops was transferred eastward to present day Kenya and they would also form the bulk of Kenya's "Armed Forces", becoming Naturalized Kenyans as well.

From 1893 to 1895 Colonel Colville led a column of British soldiers and the Nubian troops while Semei Kakungulu led a force of 14,000 Baganda irregulars against Kabarega of Bunyoro.

In 1894, Lord Lugard reinforced the Sudanese backbone of the Buganda Army through additional troops from the Sudan. These troops later formed the Uganda Rifles (UR).

The West Nile was leased to King Leopold II for his lifetime and the Franco-Congolese Agreement resulted in the creation of the Lado Enclave.

On August 14, 1894, Her Majesty Queen Victoria's Government announced in both Houses of the British Parliament its intention to assume a Protectorate over Uganda. So, Uganda became a Protectorate of Britain. It continued to use the Nubian troops of Salim Bey, the renowned giant Makaraka and Fadhil Al Mullah, the 6 feet 4 inches Lugbara, whose forces were allowed to consolidate – amounting to a force of 600 regulars formed and 300 reservists all trained by the above forces and the English.

In 1895 the Nubians or Sudanese formed the core of the Uganda Rifles (UR). Another large contingent of these troops was transferred eastward to form the Third Battalion of the Kings African Rifles (KAR) in Kenya.

In 1897 a) Mwanga, unhappy with the "new arrangements" rebelled against the British authorities as he tried unsuccessful guerrilla tactics against the British. b) Kabaka Mwanga associated with the Baganda Muslims and rebelled against British rule. He launched guerrilla activities against the British but the Bakungu chiefs led by the Regency of Apollo Kagwa, Stanislus Mugwanya and Zakaria Kasingiri were able to continue administering Buganda in the absence of the Kabaka. c) Mwanga was officially defeated and the British installed his infant son Daudi Chwa, Kabaka. Kagwa and two other chiefs served as Regents until Daudi Chwa grew old enough to reign himself.

Daudi Chwa ruled for 42 years from 1897 to 1939 and the British educated him.

The British took this opportunity to add Ankole to the Protectorate that now had active British Administrators in Busoga, Bunyoro and Toro.

In 1897 The Uganda Rifles (UR) mutinied and the army was reorganized with the addition of Baganda, Swahili and Indian troops and a few other Ugandan troops. In addition, a contingent of 200 Sikhs and Punjab Moslems was brought from India to form the 1st Battalion of the Uganda Rifles (UR). The mutiny by 500 out of 1,600 Sudanese troops was ostensibly precipitated by dissatisfaction over pay and conditions of living such as the constant duty on distant patrols and punitive Expeditions. It was complicated by the "ambitions" of some of the Nubian members of the Kings African Rifles who realized how dependent the British were upon them. The main core of the mutineers held out under siege in their garrison near Jinja. They were not entirely dispersed and brought under control until 1901.

In 1897 the Tukutuku (the nickname for King Leopold II's forces in the Kakwa territory) defeated the Ansar (the followers of the Mahdi) which were commanded by General Arabi at the Battle of Rejaf. The Belgian King vowed to annex the West side of the Nile as a reward for his efforts, including the section of the Southern Sudan known as the Lado Enclave bordered by the Nile, 5 degrees 30' North and 30 degrees East.

In 1898, the loyal Sudanese troops were disarmed, their pay raised five-fold and a major reorganization of the armed forces planned in Uganda. General Kitchener defeated the remnants of the Mahdists in the Battle of Omdurman. Anglo-French hostilities at Fashoda reached new and more dangerous heights.

On January 19, 1899, a fresh chapter in the Sudanese history opened as the Anglo-Egyptian Condominium was formed whereby both Egypt and the British became the co-rulers of the Sudan until January 1, 1956 when the Sudan attained its independence. Lord Cromer signed this Condominium Agreement for the British Government and Boutros Pasha Ghali, the Egyptian Minister for Foreign Affairs signed it for the Egyptian Government. The Agreement formed the Constitution Charter of the Sudan.

In 1899 Emin Pasha, another Asutrian-German visited the Southern Sudan. A 1,500 "African Army" - paid much lower than the Nubians was made in Uganda. British Commissioner Harry Johnston established the Uganda Police, the main composition of this force again being the Nubians. With the initial pacification of Uganda complete, the troop strength of what was now the 4th Battalion of the Kings African Rifles was composed as follows: 671 Nubians, 185 Swahilis (mainly Baganda) and 200 Sikhs - totaling 1,075 men.

Because of the fertile soil in Uganda, the British decided to develop a cash crop that could be exported from Uganda at a profit. The development of such a cash crop depended on building a modern transportation system. The profits from the crop would have to be substantial enough to pay for the construction of the new transportation system.

By the end of the 1890s, the Uganda Railway had been built from Mombasa, a port city in the British colony of Kenya, to the eastern shore of Lake Victoria. Water transportation from Kampala across Lake Victoria to the railroad was the easier part of the problem to solve. The bigger issue was how to get the cotton to Kampala.

Between 1899 and 1900, the cost of running the Uganda Protectorate was £296,226, most of which was paid by the British government. In 1914-1915, the last year that Uganda cost the British anything, the price of its management was only £10,000. The rest of the £289,213 needed to run the Protectorate in that year was raised by taxes. One crop that had changed the economic picture in Uganda was cotton!

Between 1899 and 1904 Semei Kakungulu conquered much of Teso and Sir Harry Johnson introduced hut tax with the full agreement of the Baganda chiefs.

In 1900, the British and the Prime Minister (Katikiro) of Buganda, Apollo Kagwa, signed the Agreement of 1900 to formalize the changes in the relationship between the Kabaka and the Lukiko. This legislation set the course for Uganda's development in the 20th century. Buganda was finally established as one province within the British Protectorate. Taxation and land ownership were other features of the 1900 Agreement. The British were to be paid a hut tax by every male Ganda, although taxes would be collected by Ganda tax collectors.

The British imposed their ideas of land ownership on the Baganda. Land was parceled out to individual owners - a new concept in Buganda and one that would increase wealth and thus the importance of the major chiefs who received the best and the greatest amounts of land. Similar agreements were made with Toro in 1900 and Ankole in 1901 and with Bunyoro in the 1930s.

In 1900, the Kings African Rifles, which was really an amalgamation of the forces of British Central Africa (Nyasaland, now Malawi) and East Africa (really then Kenya, Uganda and Somaliland), was formed. The components of the Kings African Rifles were the 4th Battalion (Uganda) and the 5th (Indian/Ugandan) Battalion.

In 1902, Sir Harry Johnson became the first Governor of Colonial Uganda.

In 1902 the Southern Sudan was divided between the various foreign Christian missionaries into different "religious spheres of influence." The Northerners were allowed to trade in the South only under licence. The South was divided into three Provinces of Fashoda (which later became the Upper Nile and the town of Fashoda was renamed Kodok), Mongalla and Bahr el-Ghazal.

In 1905, the Maji Maji Rebellion broke out south of Kilosa, pinning the Pogoro and Ngido against the Germans. 1,200 people, mainly Africans died when it ended in 1906 (1907).

In 1907, Colonel Bright of Britain headed the Uganda-Congo Boundary Commission. During the same year, the Governor of the Uganda Protectorate, Hesketh Bell began the development of an ambitious transportation system to solve the problem of getting the cotton to the overseas markets. Cotton was the Protectorate's most valuable export and by 1910, cotton moved to markets on a well-built system of modern roads.

In 1910, the British established constitutional monarchies in the four traditional kingdoms within the Uganda Protectorate. At this time native Ugandans had long used cowrie shells to pay for goods and services.

This year, in 1910, the British refused to allow cowrie shells as money. This severely limited the average tribesman's ability to pay his taxes. Finally, the law allowed for the Ugandans to pay their taxes in produce. An entire village might join together to capture an elephant or hippopotamus to pay taxes.

One hippo paid the tax for one hundred huts, an elephant for one thousand huts.

The Kasanvu System of Coerced Labour

Between 1909 and 1912 the West Nile, Ma'di and Acholi regions of present day Uganda were designated as "labour reserve areas" for the British Protectorate and the Lake Victoria region plantation owners. Through this exploitative system commonly referred to as "The Kasanvu System of Coerced Labour", many communities were economically exploited as cheap labour.

In 1914, the British established a station at Arua, the Capital of the present day West Nile region of Uganda. William Weatherhead (nicknamed Anzereke'de by the "Native" population because of his short stature) became the District Commissioner (DC) and Basil Wheeler became Assistant District Commissioner.

The District Commissioner described the Lugbara as being "mild, shy, unorganized and untractable". Therefore, he had trouble persuading them to cultivate cash crops. The two white men effectively spent their time hunting elephants than actually administering the district.

The Nubian forces

As outlined in a preceding section, Lugard recruited nearly 2,085 of Selim Bey's Nubian forces and 6,000 dependents to join the Imperial British East Africa Company (IBEAC) cause. The new Nubian army was deployed to man a string of forts throughout Western and Southern Uganda and to defend the Kingdom of Buganda against its chief rival the Kingdom of Bunyoro. These Nubian troops and their descendants would eventually become Naturalized Ugandans with full citizenship rights. They would also form the bulk of the KAR (King's African Rifles) and Uganda's "Armed Forces".

The KAR (Kings African Rifles) which was an amalgamation of the forces of British Central Africa (then Nyasaland, now Malawi) and East Africa (then Kenya, Uganda and Somaliland) was formed in 1900. The KAR (Kings African Rifles) performed both military and internal security functions within the East African colonies as well as external service.

Note: The Nubian forces eventually became part of a de-tribalised community referred to as the Nubi (Nubians) which is discussed in more detail in subsequent parts of the series, along with the significant role this community played in influencing Idi Amin's lifestory and "writing" his script.

Made in the USA
Middletown, DE
01 May 2019